T

D

CONTEMPO
SLANG

IRU
YFRGELL

THE MACMILLAN
DICTIONARY OF
CONTEMPORARY
SLANG

COMPILED BY
JONATHON GREEN

MACMILLAN

FOR NICK COLE

– whose researches have transcended all bounds of dedication

First published in 1984 by Pan Books
Second, revised Edition published 1992 by Pan Books
This Third Edition published 1995 by Macmillan Reference Books
a division of Macmillan Publishers Ltd
25 Eccleston Place London SW1W 9NF
and Basingstoke

Associated companies throughout the world

ISBN 0-333-63407-1

Copyright © Jonathon Green 1984, 1992 and 1995

Photoset by Parker Typesetting Service, Leicester
Printed and bound in Great Britain by
Mackays of Chatham PLC, Chatham, Kent

Acknowledgements

No compilation of slang, ancient or modern, would be possible without the pioneering efforts of the late Eric Partridge. It would have been simple, but foolish, merely to pillage his work, and I have not done so; but in many areas, especially that of possible and likely etymologies I owe a great deal to his earlier studies. Thus I would take this opportunity of making due acknowledgement here.

On a more immediate level, I must thank many people, all of whom have made a contribution of some degree to the collection of words in this dictionary or to the progress and publication of the work as a whole. I cannot name every one, but particular thanks go to:

Don Atyeo, Rosie Boycott, Linda Brown, Kyle Cathie, Colin Clarke, Katherine Clarke, Nick Cole, Peter Davies, Karen Durbin, Leslie Gardner, Arthur Green, Gabriel Green, Lucien Green, Johann (Aka) Hashim, David Leitch, Alan Marcuson, Andrew Payne, David Rattray, Susan Ready, Harriet Thistlethwaite, Pola Wickham.

Introduction
to the Second Edition

'Slang is a poor man's poetry'
John Moore (1962)

Alongside Standard English, the ostensibly 'pure' language of formal speech and writing, of *Times* leaders and BBC erudition, stand several sub-species of language, less beloved of Eng. Lit. departments, but none the less popular and possibly even more vigorous and entertaining for that very exclusion. These include cant: the language of the underworld; jargon: the special or occupational language and the 'professional slang' of a variety of interest groups; colloquialism: informal, conversational speech, used, as it were, through the dinner but not for the after-dinner speechifying; dialects: regional usages ever more besieged by television's bland mid-atlanticisms; and finally slang. It is this last that I have attempted to codify here.

This is a revised edition of my original *Dictionary of Contemporary Slang*, published in 1984. It offers a further 1,000-odd headwords in an attempt to include the new coinages of the Eighties, and 200-plus additions to or revisions of the original material. I have also rewritten this introduction, offering, I hope instructively, some comments on the etymology and definitions of 'slang' itself.

Etymology

The etymology of the word *slang* brings one up against what is, as slang lexicographer Eric Partridge put it in his own discussion of the term, 'that prize-problem word'. Sir William Craigie, dealing with slang in the Oxford English Dictionary, took the Dictionary's usual cautious view on such matters: it was 'a word of cant origin, the ultimate source of which is not apparent'; this refusal to hazard any further guess has not been modified in any subsequent supplement up to that of 1986. Craigie compounded his rejection of possible origins with a further note: 'the date and early associations of the word make it unlikely that there is any connexion with certain Norwegian forms in *sleng-* which exhibit some approximation in sense.'

This flat declaration ran quite contrary to the views of another Oxford philologist, Walter Skeat, whose *Etymological Dictionary of the English*

Language had appeared between 1879 and 1882. Skeat attributed *slang* unequivocally to the Scandinavian languages, adding examples from the Icelandic and Swedish to the Norwegian already decried by Craigie. Listing such terms as the Norwegian *sleng*: 'a slinging, an invention, device, stratagem . . . a little addition or burthen of a song, in verse and melody'; *ettersleng* (lit. after slang) 'a burthen at the end of a verse or ballad'; *slengjenamn*: nickname; *slengjeord*: an insulting word or allusion; the Icelandic *slyngr* and *slunginn*: well-versed in, cunning; and the Swedish *slanger*; to gossip, Skeat showed himself free of any doubt 'that all the above Norwegian and Icelandic words are derivatives from "sling" is quite clear . . . I see no objection to this explanation.'

Other etymologists tended to follow Skeat. Henry Bradley who succeeded Sir James Murray as editor of the OED in 1915, and was thus a colleague of both Craigie (who would succeed him in turn in 1923) and of Skeat himself, accepted the Norwegian connection. Writing on *Slang* in 1929 he plumped for Scandinavia, as did Professors Weekley and Wyld in subsequent studies. More recently Eric Partridge, never one to let caution fetter his own deductive skills, modified the Norwegian thesis in his own etymological dictionary. Partridge sees *slang* as a dialect past participle of the verb *sling*, which has its roots in Old and Middle English and links to Old Norse, thus giving the concept of 'slung' or 'thrown' language. This conveniently encompasses the abusive side of slang, e.g. 'sling off at' and is duly bolstered by the Norwegian *slenga keften* (also cited by Skeat) lit. to sling the jaw, and thus to use slang, as well as Skeat's *slengjeord*.

Definitions

'Slang is a poor man's poetry' suggested John Moore in *You English Words* (1962) and like the poor, to whom must be attributed credit for the coinage, or at least the popularization of a major portion of its vocabulary, slang is always with us. As a linguistic phenomenon it substantially predates Christ but as a word in itself only emerges into the (printed) language in the mid-eighteenth century. The Oxford English Dictionary (1933), which eschewed the bulk of slang terminology (other than that which occurred in literature) but duly defined the term, cites as a first use William Toldervy *The History of Two Orphans* (1756): 'Thomas Throw had been upon the town, knew the slang well.' The slang in question is no more than a synonym for *cant*, or criminal jargon, and does not involve the more general sense of today.

By the turn of the century the definitions had broadened. As well as standing synonymous with cant, slang began to be used as an alternative to jargon (itself most simply definable as 'professional slang') and such luminaries as Charles Kingsley (in a letter of 1857) and George Eliot (in

Middlemarch [1872]) referred quite naturally to the 'slang' of, respectively, artists and poets. More notably the word, if not the vocabulary, had been enlisted in standard English by the mid-century and dignified by John Keble (in 1818), Thackeray (in *Vanity Fair* [1848]) and many other respectable users. In 1858 Trollope, in *Dr. Thorne*, speaks of 'fast, slang men, who were fast and slang and nothing else', a citation that points up both their language and their rakehell, buckish style.

John Camden Hotten's *Slang Dictionary* (1859) ran to five editions before its author died in 1873. It remained the best available slang dictionary for the next twenty years and Hotten's comments on slang are still pertinent. 'SLANG represents that evanescent, vulgar language, ever changing with fashion and taste, . . . spoken by persons in every grade of life, rich and poor, honest and dishonest . . . Slang is indulged in from a desire to appear familiar with life, gaiety, town-humour and with the transient nick names and street jokes of the day. . . . SLANG is the language of street humour, of fast, high and low life . . . Slang is as old as speech and the congregating together of people in cities. It is the result of crowding, and excitement, and artificial life.'

Set firmly amid respectable language by the OED, *slang* as a word remains essentially unchanged as to its definitions and in its use, even if it continues to develop as a vocabulary. The philologists and lexicographers remain generally consistent in their opinions. Since the OED laid down lexicographical law they may have replaced simple definition by more complex explanation, but they differ only in the nuances. Professor George H. McKnight, writing in 1923, explained slang as 'a form of colloquial speech created in a spirit of defiance and aiming at freshness and novelty . . . Its figures are consciously far-fetched and are intentionally drawn from the most ignoble of sources. Closely akin to profanity in its spirit, its aim is to shock.' Fowler, writing on English usage in 1926, offered his own, somewhat offbeat view: 'Slang is the diction that results from the favourite game among the young and lively of playing with words and renaming things and actions; some invent new words, or mutilate or misapply the old, for the pleasure of novelty, and others catch up such words for the pleasure of being in the fashion; many slang words and phrases perish, a few establish themselves; in either case, during probation they are accounted unfit for literary use.'

The *Encyclopedia Britannica* is consistent. Henry Bradley's article on Slang in 1929 suggests that of those factors that lead to its invention, 'the two more important seem to be the desire to secure increased vivacity and the desire to secure increased sense of intimacy in the use of language.' The American expert David W. Maurer, author of the current *Britannica* revision, states 'Slang consists basically of unconventional words or phrases that express either something new or something old in a new way.

It is flippant, irreverent, indecorous; it may be indecent or obscene. Its colourful metaphors are generally directed at respectability, and it is this succinct, sometimes witty, frequently impertinent social criticism, that gives slang its characteristic flavour. Slang then, includes not just words, but words used in a special way in a certain social context.'

While one might query that final sentence, since it applies no more exclusively to slang than to a variety of specific linguistic uses, Maurer's opinion, in common with those of various of his compatriots does underline an essential difference between British and American definitions. The English, class divisions aforethought, concentrate on slang's proletarian origins; Americans, flaunting their iconoclasm, see it as an instrument of glorious revolution. The critic H.L. Mencken, who more than anyone before him set out successfully to emphasize the substantial differences between 'American' and 'English' English, is equally positive: 'Slang originates in the efforts of ingenious individuals to make the language more pungent and picturesque – to increase the store of terse and striking words, to widen the boundaries of metaphor, and to provide a vocabulary for new shades of difference in meaning.'

Unsurprisingly, slang has gained a good deal of notice from the literary world. Setting aside the ever-increasing mass of authors who use it in their work, certain of the literati have chosen to offer their own definitions, not all of them favourable. The most celebrated, if self-consciously populist, is that offered by the American poet and biographer Carl Sandburg: 'Slang is a language that takes off its coat, spits on its hands and gets to work.' Less congratulatory (and somewhat obscure) was Victor Hugo: 'Slang is a dressing room in which language, having an evil deed to prepare, puts on a disguise.' Ambrose Bierce, from whose general *oeuvre* one might have expected better support, is equally unappreciative: 'Slang n. the grunt of the human hog (*Pignoramus intolerabilis*) with an audible memory. The speech of one who utters with his tongue what he thinks with his ear, and feels the pride of a creator in accomplishing the feat of a parrot. A means (under Providence) of setting up as a wit without a capital of sense.' Walt Whitman, whose own *Leaves of Grass* (1855) was savaged for its alleged obscenity, showed greater affection: 'Slang is the wholesome fermentation or eructation of those processes eternally active in language, by which the froth and specks are thrown up, mostly to pass away, though occasionally to settle and permanently crystallize.'

Sources and Selections

Slang is primarily a spoken, rather than a written language. Dictionaries on the contrary are printed codifications, of greater or lesser complexity. Inevitably the marriage of the two forms leads to certain difficulties. In the first place, one can rarely establish a specific 'first use' of a slang word, and I have not attempted to do so. Instead I have attempted to find some form of source for the words that I have included.

As the dictionary is intended to cover only modern, contemporary vocabulary, the bulk of the sources that I have cited are post-1945 creations; indeed I have looked as far as possible only to the last decade or so. None the less, much of this contemporary vocabulary does date back to the nineteenth century and well beyond. Thus I have included Hotten's 1859 dictionary as well as a number of older source-books, if only to underline the antiquity of many current terms. In the main, however, the accent is on the more up-to-date, and whether or not the terms so indexed come from an earlier era, the sources from which I have taken them prove irrefutably that they are still going strong. As a solo compiler I have not been able, nor have I tried, to read every available slang-laden work. Where I have been helped has been in the very wide spread of slang words in all manner of writing, both for print and for the large and small screen, and I have done my best to assimilate as much as possible. There are, as will be obvious, a number of words for which I have been unable to provide a source, although I know, from my own or overheard use, that these words are popular and prevalent. I have included them on those grounds, even bereft of a suitable source.

Jonathon Green
February 1992

Introduction
to the Third Edition

Herewith a further revision of the *Dictionary of Contemporary Slang*, comprising some 1,200 extra headwords. A proportion of these have emerged into the slang lexicon in the three years since I last updated my book; a further group are simply words and phrases that, to my embarrassment, I failed to notice for inclusion in either of the earlier editions. As to the former group, slang continues, I am delighted to say, to expand. I shall attempt to keep up with it, for all that the vocabulary, slang or otherwise, continues to march on and the lexicographer's best efforts can only put him or her within hailing distance of language's current cutting edge. As Dr Johnson noted, there is no such thing as a 'fixed' language and anyone who suggests that their dictionary puts an end to word collection and development is about as worthy of respect as a quack doctor peddling nostrums for eternal life. As to the second group, I have no doubt that my sins of omission are still far from fully confessed and that the words I've missed out remain all too many. I shall no doubt attempt again to atone for such failings when next I have the opportunity for a revision.

Jonathon Green
October 1994

Abbreviations

a.	adjective	naut.	nautical
abbrev.	abbreviation	nb	note well
acro.	acronym	N.Z.	New Zealand
adv.	adverb		
aka	also known as	obs.	obsolete
Aus.	Australian	orig.	original(ly)
backsl.	backslang	p.ppl.	past participle
		phr.	phrase
C.	century	polit.	political
Can.	Canadian	poss.	possible
cf	compare	prob.	probable
Comb.	Combination	pron.	pronunciation
cp	catch phrase		
		qv	which see
derog.	derogatory		
dial.	dialect	RAF	Royal Air Force
		rhy. sl.	rhyming slang
eg	example	Rus.	Russian
esp.	especially		
ety.	etymology	Sc.	Scottish
ex	from	S. Afr.	South African
excl.	exclamation	SE	Standard English
expl.	expletive	sfx.	suffix
euph.	euphemism	Sp.	Spanish
		sp.	spelling
fig.	figuratively	spec.	specifically
Fr.	French	syn.	synonym
fr.	from		
		UK	United Kingdom
Ger.	German	UK bl	United Kingdom black
		US	United States
ie	that is	USMC	United States Marine
Ital.	Italian		Corps
		USN	United States Navy
j.	jargon	usu.	usually
journ.	journalistic		
		v.	verb
Lat.	Latin	vbl. n.	verbal noun
lit.	literally	v.i.	verb intransitive
		v.t.	verb transitive
milit.	military		
		Yid.	Yiddish
n.	noun		

A

a n. (drug use) (abbrev.) **1.**
amphetamine; thus a-head (qv.):
amphetamine user (cf: head)
Saunders; **2.** LSD (cf. acid).

a (interj.) (Black use) yes, absolutely,
certainly! (cf: fucking A) *Major*.

A1 a. excellent, perfect, first class; fr.
the top rating of a ship at Lloyds of
London *Hotten*.

a. over t. adv. (abbr.) arse over tip or
tit.

aap n. (S. Afr. use) a dagga (cannabis)
joint (qv) (cf. zol); fr. Afrikaans *aap*:
ape or monkey.

ab n. (drug use) (abbrev.) abcess; the
result of injecting with a dirty needle,
and/or using adulterated narcotics
De Lannoy & Masterson.

abbot n. (US drug use) Nembutal, the
tradename of a barbiturate,
manufactured by Abbott Labs.

abc n. (abbrev.) **1.** Australian-born
Chinese; **2.** American-born Chinese;
3. *ace boon coon* (qv.) *Folb*.

abdabs n. usu. as 'the abdabs' **1.**
terror, nerves; **2.** delirium tremens; **3.**
rage; **4.** as 'don't come the old. . .' or
'don't give me the old. . .': don't try to
fool me.

abdicate v. see: come out.

abdicated adv. (homosexual use)
ordered out of the public lavatory
where one is looking for sex *Legman*.

Abdul, Abdullah n. a Turk, but more
generally any Middle Eastern person;
it was also used briefly, in Aus. c.1920,
to refer to Afghanis.

Abe (derog.) a Jew; fr. abbrev.
Abraham (cf: Abie Kabibble) *BvdB*.

abergavenny n. (rhyming sl.) a penny
Jones:J.

a.b.f. n. the last drink of a session (fr.
abbr. a bloody final drink).

abfab a. (orig. Aus. use) a general
term of approval: first rate, very
attractive (fr. abbr. absolutely
fabulous).

Abie Kabibble n. (derog.) a Jew (cf:

Abe) *Farrell*.

a-bomb n. (US drug use) a
combination of marijuana or hashish
with opium (cf. speedball).

abortion n. an all-purpose
denigration, either of people, objects
or enterprises.

about one's speed adv. suitable, to
one's own taste.

about right a. drunk *Dickson*.

above oneself adv. over-confident,
pushy, esp. of someone who is usually
more self-effacing; usu. as 'getting
above. . .'

Abraham Lincoln n. (US black use) a
five-dollar bill (cf. Alexander
Hamilton 1., portrait of Madison).

absobloodylutely adv. all-purpose
intensifier: very much so, without a
doubt. Similar uses are found with the
stronger 'fucking' (qv) substituted for
'bloody', while a euph. version gives
'absoballylutely'.

absorb v. to drink (cf. soak).

Abyssinia! goodbye; corruption of
'I'll be seeing you!' *Whitcomb*.

ACAB (acro.) *All* Coppers *Are
Bastards*; popular tattoo in UK, esp.
among Hells Angels, etc.

Acapulco gold n. (drug use) a well-
regarded, potent variety of marijuana;
a less potent variety is Acapulco red
(cf. Congo bush, Durban poison,
Mexican green, etc.).

acca, acker n. (Aus. use) **1.** an
academic, esp. one who trades on the
proliferation of current, if ephemeral,
intellectual fads; **2.** quotidian, jargon-
laden academic writing.

accidentally on purpose phr.
deliberately; of a supposed accident
that deliberately discomforts a disliked
target.

accommodation collar n. (US police
use) an arrest made for no reason but
to raise the officer's arrest record and
thus improve his standing in the
hierarchy *Green:2*.

AC/DC a. **1.** bisexual; **2.** (homosexual use) ambivalent as to taking an active or passive role in a relationship; both derive fr. opposite varieties of electrical current *Stanley*.

ace a. good, excellent.

ace n **1.** a detective *Algren*; **2.** (US / Can.) one dollar *Caron* (the ace = 'one' in cards); **3.** (US black use) any single pill, whether amphetamine, barbiturate or tranquiliser; **4.** (US black use) best friend (cf. ace boon coon); **5.** an outstanding person, whether through character or expertise; **6.** a form of address 'Hey, ace!'.

ace v. **1.** to defeat an opponent *Underwood*, thus 'ace out of': to beat, to defeat; **2.** (Aus. use) to stop, to cease; thus 'ace it up!': stop it! *Baker*; **3.** (US use) to achieve high marks in an examination; **4.** (US use) to understand; **5.** to do well.

ace boom boom n. see: ace boon coon *Folb*.

ace boon coon n. (US Black use) one's best and most trustworthy friend *Ice T:3*.

ace coon n. (US Black) **1.** a best friend (cf. ace boon coon); **2.** an important person.

ace coon poon n. see: ace boon coon *Folb*.

ace in the hole n. a hidden asset; fr. poker use *Price:2*.

ace of spades n. (US Black use) the pudendum; fr. supposed resemblance of the shape of pubic hair *Neaman & Silver*.

ace out v. to defeat, to take something away; fr. poker use when ace is the highest card *Fiction Illus.3*.

ace over apex phr. (US euph.) head over heels (cf: arse over tit, ass over appetite, arse over teakettle, end over appetite)

ace-deuce n. **1.** (gambling use) the number 3 in cards or in craps dice; fr. addition of ace (1) plus deuce (2) *Chandler: Notebk*; **2.** a best friend (cf. ace boon coon).

aces a. wonderful, marvellous, excellent, etc.; both of objects and persons, thus 'you're aces!' '*Hill Street Blues*', Thames TV, 1983.

aces high n. (US prison use) an inmate popular amongst his peers (cf: aces) *Neaman & Silver*.

acey-deucy a. (US use) indeterminate, neither one thing nor another.

acid n. **1.** (drug use) d-lycergic acid diethylamide-25; a powerful synthetic hallucinogen based on ergot; discovered in 1943 by Dr Albert Hofmann of Sandoz Labs, Basel, and massively popularized in 1960s by Dr Timothy Leary, Ken Kesey (and his Merry Pranksters), rock groups and the 'alternative society' *Green:1*; acid re-emerged as a nickname for another hallucinogen (albeit with a very different chemistry) MMDA, better known as E or Ecstasy (qqv), in the late 1980s. **2.** cheek *Powis*.

acid casualty n. one whose brain is deemed to have suffered from an excess of hallucinogens.

acid flashback n. the repetition of hallucinations subsequent to a trip (qv), and without the stimulus of the drug.

acid house n. a. a style of music, (plus the attendant clothes, parties and allied paraphernalia), that blends house (qv) music with the drug Ecstasy (qv), otherwise known as acid (qv). Further developments (probably shortlived) included acid ska, a mix of West Indian ska music and the music that supposedly accompanied the consumption of and was inspired by Ecstasy, the preferred combination of contemporary skinheads, whose parents liked unadorned ska *Green:3*.

acid house party n. an illegal party, often held in a large building such as a warehouse, and often outside the big cities, where thousands of young people paid for their entertainment and, allegedly, consumed acid (qv) and other illegal drugs *Green:3*.

acid rapper n. one who takes extra-large doses of LSD *Wolfe:2*.

acid rock n. a musical style allegedly influenced by and purporting to recreate the sensations of LSD and similar psychedelics; orig. in 1960s but underwent a minor revival in 1980s.

acid trip n. the experience of taking a hallucinogenic drug, esp. LSD (qv).

acidhead n. a regular user of LSD (cf: acid) *Green:1*.

ackamaracka n. 1. (UK prison use) deceit, tall stories, lies *LL*; 2. tea.

ackers n. (Br. Army use) money; fr. Egyptian *akka*: one piastre.

ackle v. to work, to function, esp. as v. tr. e.g. 'Can you ackle it': 'Can you make it work?'

acky a., excl. dirty, disgusting (cf: icky, ucky, yucky)

acorn-cracker n. (US derog.) an uncouth rural person

acquire v. to steal (cf: liberate)

a-crash of, go v. to assault.

acre, acher n. 1. (Aus. use) the buttocks; 2. testicles.

across the pavement (UK criminal use) any crime committed in the street *Powis*.

across the track a. inferior, second-rate (cf: wrong side of the tracks)

act like one's shit don't stink v. (orig. US use) to behave affectedly and in an arrogant manner; also as 'act like shit wouldn't melt in one's mouth'.

act the angora v. (Aus. use) to play the fool, synon. with the older 'play the giddy goat'.

act the hog, act the monkey phr. to play the fool (cf: act the nigger)

act the nigger v. (US Black use) to draw unnecessary attention to oneself by foolish behaviour *Folb*.

act-ass n. one who poses as cleverer than they are (cf: smart ass)

action n. 1. any form of monetary deal or the profits from that deal; 2. (gambling) the play in a gambling casino, in one of the games within that casino, or in any form of betting – track, cards, dice, etc.; 3. pleasure, enjoyment, activity; usu. sexual.

action man n. orig. armed forces use,

the term is used generally to reprove / describe anyone seen as excessively macho.

action piece n. (US Black use) 1. a pistol, a revolver, a shotgun; 2. a woman *Klein*.

active a. (UK police use) an enthusiastic and efficient officer *Laurie*.

Acton Hilton n. (BBC-TV use) the BBC TV rehearsal rooms in Acton, London; the block that contains them resembles only facetiously a chain hotel.

actor n. (US Black use) anyone out to deceive, to project a phoney image *Major*.

actual, the n. money.

actual, your n. see: yer actual.

AD acro. accidental daddy; usually used in the phrase 'AD or BC?' meaning 'Are you using birth control or am I risking becoming an accidental daddy?' *AS 60.1 (1985)*.

AD n. (drug use) *d*rug *a*ddict (reversed to avoid confusion with the law's DA, district attorney) *Major*.

ad hocer n. (skiing use) a skier who arrives at a chalet without a previous booking; fr. Lat. *ad hoc*: for this purpose/for this occasion *Barr*.

Ada from Decatur n. (gambling use) aka: *eighter from Decatur*, the point of eight in craps dice *Chandler: Notebk*.

adam n. MDMA (methylene dioxymethamphetamine (cf: acid, E. ecstasy) *J Stevens Storming Heaven (1987)*.

Adam and Eve v. (rhyming sl.) to believe *Powis*.

Adam and Eve's PJs, Adam and Eve's togs n. nudity; the terms are US and UK respectively.

addict n. (US cant) one who seemingly cannot resist the blandishments of confidence tricksters and falls for every variety of trick *Neaman & Silver*.

addled a. drunk; fr. SE *addle-pated*: stupid *Dickson*.

Admiral Browning n. human excrement (cf: Browning family).

adobe (US use) a generic derog. for a Mexican, fr. the adobe bricks used to construct poor housing; thus 'adobe dollar': a Mexican peso; 'adobe maker': a Mexican or Mexican-American.

adonis a. (US campus use) very attractive male.

Adrian, Adrian Quist adv. (Aus. use) (rhy. sl) drunk; Adrian Quist = pissed (qv).

advice n. (UK police use) a severe disciplinary reprimand *Laurie*.

aerated adv. over-excited, angry (cf: up in the air).

Af, Aff n. **1.** (S. Afr. use) (abbr.) an African (cf: kaffir, munt); **2.** (drug use) (abbr.) Afghan hashish (cf: Afghani).

Afghani n. Afghan hashish (cf: black Pak, Mexican green, red Leb, etc.).

afflicted a. drunk; the implication is of mental instability *Dickson*.

AFO abbr. all fucked out *AS 60.1 (1985)*.

African cue n. (US black use) a closely cropped Afro (qv) hair style.

African dominoes n. craps dice.

African engineering n. shoddy, second-rate workmanship.

African golf n. craps dice.

African golf ball n. (US Black use) aka: *African grape*; deprecating reference to the watermelon, a cliché Black foodstuff *Folb*.

African lager see: Nigerian lager.

African Railroad n. the San Francisco municipal bus line – which is principally used by Blacks. *Maledicta 9.*

Afro n. a Black hairstyle, esp. popular in 1960s, in which usually short crinkly black hair was allowed to grow out.

Afro set n. (US Black use) anywhere that Blacks use for talking or acting in furtherance of their own social and political betterment *Klein*.

Afs n. (S. Afr. use) derog. term for Africans, white use only *Marcuson*.

afternoon delight n. sex in the afternoon (cf: nooner).

afternoon farmer n. one who gets up late.

aggravation n. (UK police/criminal use) the difficulties that both sides of the professional law make for each other *Laurie*.

aggro n. (abbrev. aggravation); **1.** spec. violence enjoyed by skinheads, esp. at football matches, beating up Asians, etc.; **2.** any form of problems, difficulties, harassment *Newman:1.*

agony aunt n. the problem-solving (usu. female) columnists of papers and magazines to whom the lovelorn and generally wretched can write, their letters will be answered in print and/or privately; the male version, logically enough, is 'agony uncle'.

ah-ah n. (US black use) a fool.

a-head n. (drug use) one who specializes in consuming quantities of amphetamines (cf: speed freak) *Green:1.*

aid n. (UK police use) temporary detective constable; fr. 'aid to CID' *Laurie*.

AIDS for grades n. (US campus use) the course Biology 40: AIDS and Other Sexually Transmitted Diseases (cf: blabs in labs, gods for clods, shocks for jocks, etc.).

ain't holding no air (US Black use) to be unimpressive, to lack credibility; to lack the basic knowledge of taking care of oneself within the ghetto *Folb*.

ain't long enough insufficient money *Folb*.

air dance n. (US prison use) a hanging.

air guitar n. the non-existent (or at best cardboard cut-out) 'guitar' 'played' at concerts by fans of heavy metal rock bands.

air hook n. the nose.

air hose n. (US preppie (qv) use) loafers worn, as is preppie style, without socks *Bernbach*.

air one's lungs v. **1.** to swear; **2.** to argue or talk at length.

air one's paunch v. **1.** to vomit; **2.** to boast.

air out v. to go for a walk; orig. Black

but now general use *Major*.

airhead n. an idiot, a fool, someone who has nothing but air, and no brains, in his head (cf: bubblehead, bimbo) *Harpers/Queen 1/83*.

airish a. 1. affected, inclined to put on airs; 2. effeminate.

airmail n. (US use) throwing garbage out of windows instead of taking it to dustbins, loading it into disposal chutes, etc. *Selby:1*.

airs n. (US teen use) state of the art high-priced trainers; from the Nike 'Air Jordan' model that was particularly prized c.1990. (cf: felony shoes) *T 8/4/91*.

airs and graces n. (rhyming sl.) 1. faces; 2. braces; 3. horse races *Jones:J*.

airy-fairy a. insubstantial, trivial, of minimal importance.

A.K. v. 1. to curry favour with, toady to; n. 2. a toady. (fr. abbr. ass kisser). 3. an old fogey (fr. Yiddish *alter kocker*: old shit).

aka n. (cant) an alias, a false name; fr. abbrev. *also known as Neaman & Silver*.

Al Capone ride n. (US Black use) any old car, both the original Capone era models and more recent ones that lack the most up-to-date gimmicks and accessories *Folb*.

Aladdin's cave n. (UK police use) the home of a successful thief, or the place where he keeps his loot (cf: slaughter) *Laurie*.

Alan Whickers n. (rhyming sl.) knickers; fr. TV personality *Wright*.

alderman n. a paunch.

alderman's nail n. (rhyming sl.) tail *Jones:J*.

aled up a. drunk *Keyes*.

Alexander Hamilton n. 1. a ten-dollar bill (cf: Abraham Lincoln, portrait of Madison); 2. one's signature.

alf n. (Aus. use) unsophisticated, nationalistic, basic Aus. male; recently overtaken by ocker (qv) *Baker*.

alfalfa n. 1. tobacco; 2. dried spinach.

alias a. (UK Black use) dangerous, violent *Thelwell*.

alias man n. (UK criminal, esp. Black use) a cheat, a hypocrite, anyone unethical *Powis*.

alive and kicking a. phr. absolutely alert and lively; often as a response to a speaker who assumes the opposite of an (absent) person: 'No, he's still alive . . .'

alkied a. drunk *Dickson*.

alko n. see alky *Welsh:1*

alky n. (abbrev.) alcoholic *Underwood*.

all at sea a. 1. confused; fr. losing one's bearings *Goulart*; 2. drunk; fr. bobbing up and down and possibly vomiting *Dickson*.

all behind like a fat woman (cp) refers to tardiness or being slow.

all bets are off all deals are cancelled, all agreements are forgotten; in gambling use, no money can be won or lost *Higgins:2*.

all chiefs and no indians (cp, orig. milit. use) all officers and no 'other ranks'; also, for a situation where no one in a group of people wants to be anything but the boss.

all day n. (US cant) a life sentence (cf: from now on); thus 'all day from a quarter': 25 years to life (cf: phoney baloney life).

all done by mirrors (cp) any event which seems remarkable but which obviously hides tricks beneath the surface.

all dressed up and nowhere to go (cp) both a literal description and one implying anticlimax or disappointment.

all fine and dandy excellent, perfect; often in ironic use.

all get out a. phr. very much, to a great extent; usu. prefixed by *as* . . .

all hair by the nose adv. very angry, in a rage (cf. hair up one's ass, have a hair crossed).

all hot and bothered a. phr. flustered, manically nervous; sometimes through the suppression of lust.

all in a. 1. exhausted, utterly tired *Wilkinson*; 2. drunk *Dickson*.

all in but one's shoestrings, – shoelaces, – bootstraps phr. utterly exhausted.

all in one n. an orgy; 'person' or 'orifice' is unstated *Klein*.

all mops and brooms a. drunk *Dickson*.

all mouth and trousers all talk and no action; a braggart, a fake (cf: all piss and wind) *'Minder', Thames TV, 1983*.

all my eye and Betty Martin n. phr. utter, absolute nonsense *Hotten*.

all of a doodah a. phr. in a fluster, in a state, very agitated.

all of a tiswas a. phr. utterly confused, very excited; Central TV, *'Tiswas'* children's light entertainment programme 1970s.

all of a tizzy see: all of a tiswas.

all one's born days a. phr. ever, at any time at all.

all out a. see: all in.

all over bar the shouting (cp) a foregone conclusion.

all over the board a. phr. eccentric, unstable *McFadden*.

all over the place a. phr. in a great mess, utterly disorganized.

all over the place like a mad woman's shit phr. (Aus. use) confused, extremely messy; also as 'all over the place like a mad woman's knitting', 'all over the place like a mad woman's lunch-box'.

all piss and wind all talk and no action (cf: all mouth and trousers).

all points bulletin n. (US campus use) a plea for help, with work, emotions, etc.; fr. police use; cf. APB *Underwood*.

all right! excl. yes indeed! I agree! etc. *Underwood*.

all she wrote, that's phr. a general exp. of finality: that's all there is.

all that jazz phr. all that sort of thing, usu. following a list of proper nouns '. . . and all that jazz'; *Capital Radio programme title 1983*.

all the beans (bingo use) 57; fr. Heinz 57 Varieties.

all the steps (bingo use) 39; fr. *The Thirty Nine Steps* by John Buchan.

all the twos (bingo use) 22; thus *all the threes*: 33; *all the fours*: 44 etc., up to *all the nines*: 99.

all the way general term of agreement, of encouragement and support.

all tits and teeth a female who capitalizes on her physical charms – esp. her smile and (presumably) large breasts – to make up for the lack of more subtle attractions.

all to cock unsatisfactory, mixed up, useless (cf: cock).

all wet a. drunk *Dickson*.

all wind and piss a loudmouth, a braggart, all talk and no action (cf: all mouth and trousers) *Powis*.

all wool and a yard wide (US cp) excellent, dependable person; fr. clothing trade self-promotions *Burroughs:Jr*.

all-and-all n. 1. one's wife; 2. one's best suit of clothes.

alley bat n. 1. a promiscuous woman; 2. a prostitute (cf: alley rat).

alley cat v. 1. to behave in a promiscuous manner; n. 2. a promiscuous woman; 3. a prostitute; 4. an illegitimate child; 5. a street urchin.

alley rat n. (US Black use) a particularly unpleasant, villainous and impoverished person *Major*.

alley-whipped a. unpaid despite one's having done the work required; fr. the hapless worker being taken out into the alley and beaten when money is requested *Safire*.

alligator n. (US Black use) any sexually aggressive male *Folb*.

alligator (rhyming sl. later; orig. 1950s cp.) 'see ya later, alligator . . . in a while, crocodile', popularized by Bill Haley and the Comets 1956 pop hit of the same name, and by the widely publicized use of the phrase by Princess Margaret *Cole*.

alligator bait n. inedible food, esp. liver.

all-fired a. extremely, very much so; euph. for hell-fired *Chandler:LG*.

all-nighter n. 1. anything that lasts all-night, whether work or entertainment; 2. spec. an all-night concert or dance; 3. (US campus use) working all night before an examination, thus 'pull an all-nighter': to work all night.

all-originals a. (US Black use) Black people only; thus *all-originals scene*: a Blacks only party, etc. *Major*.

all-over a. generalized intensive for either best or worst.

almonds n. (rhyming sl.) almond rocks = socks *Powis*.

alphonse n. (UK criminal use) a ponce (cf: Charlie Ronce, Joe Ronce, etc.) *Powis*.

also-ran n. a useless person, a failure; fr. racing use.

alter kacker, alter kocker n. old fool, old fogey (cf: A.K.); a facetious 'bilingual' version is 'alter coyote' (fr. Yiddish alter kocker: old shit).

ambidextrous a. (euph.) bisexual; fr. SE: capable of using both hands equally well (cf: AC/DC) *Neaman & Silver*.

ambulance-chaser n. a lawyer who specializes in representing the victims of street and other accidents and to whom he offers his services, which are accepted while the victim is still too shocked to make proper and rational arrangements *Green:2*.

American culture n. sexual intercourse in the face to face 'missionary position' *SMD*.

amigo n. affectionate term of address; fr. Sp. 'friend' *'Hill Street Blues', Thames TV, 1983*.

amp n. 1. (drug use) (abbrev.) ampoule; 2. (music business) (abbrev.) amplifier.

amscray v. to leave quickly, to run off.

amster n. (Aus. use; fr. rhyming sl.) amsterdam = ram (fr. ramp, qv) = one who works outside a carnival, sideshow, strip club, etc., touting the pleasures inside and pulling in the punters (qv) *Baker*.

Amy-John n. a lesbian, often derog.; fr. Amazon *Maledicta*.

anchor, anchor and chain n. one's wife (cf: ball and chain); thus 'anchored': married.

anchors n. brakes.

and a half a. (US campus use) general intensifier (cf: and then some)

and how! general excl. of agreement or approval *Southern & Hoffenberg*.

and shit phr. (US Black use) a general abstract term, usu. thrown into the end of a sentence, similar to 'y'know'.

and then some! excl. rejoinder to the last speaker: that's not all of it, either!

and you! (jocular cp) general admonition to anyone listening after one has made a given pronouncement to a given individual *Capital Radio 1983*.

Andrew n. the Royal Navy; fr. Lieut Andrew Millar (or -er); orig. sl. for man o'war *Powis*.

Andy Cain n. (rhyming sl.) rain *Jones:J*.

Andy Gump n. 1. a conspicuously receding chin (fr. the eponymous cartoon character created by Sidney Smith in 1917; he was virtually chinless; in south-western US the banded sand snake, with its deeply countersunk jaw, is an 'Andy Gump snake'); 2. a notably prominent chin.

angel n. aka: *angelina*: a passive homosexual *Legman*.

angel dust n. (drug use) PCP, phencyclidine – a dangerous hallucinogenic based on animal (pig) tranquillizer (cf: dust) *Green:1*.

angel kisses n. freckles *Grogan*.

angel with a dirty face n. a covert, closeted (qv) homosexual *Legman*.

angle n. any plan which should benefit its maker; a gimmick *Fiction Illus.3*.

anglo n. anyone of ostensibly Anglo-Saxon appearance; in short, a white person.

animal house n. aka: *animal zoo* that fraternity house on the campus of a US college that is generally rated the least efficient, the most degenerate and overall the one to avoid; the term gained international popularity with the release of the eponymously titled film, starring John Belushi, in 1978.

ankle v. to walk; thus 'ankle express': transportation by foot; walking.

ankle from one's elbow, not know one's phr. (euph) derog. phrase implying stupidity (cf: arse from one's elbow).

ankle-biters n. children; fr. their height and alleged propensities *Humphries:2*.

anna maria n. (rhyming sl.) a fire (domestic) *Jones:J*.

annihilated adv. (Valley Girls (qv) use) extremely drunk or intoxicated by some drug *Harpers/Queen 1/83*.

anno domini n. old age and its deleterious effects, esp. of physical prowess *Sharpe:2*.

answer is a lemon, the (derog. cp) a generally negative reply to a fellow speaker; fr. *lemon* anything useless, disappointing, etc.; also the fact that the fruit, like this cp, is sour.

ante up v. to pay out money; fr. poker use *Wodehouse:PGM*.

antsy a. twitchy, nervous, fr. 'ants in one's pants' *R. Stone, 'A Flag for Sunrise', 1981*.

anxious seater n. a nervous person.

any how disorganized, messy.

any old anything, whatever; a general term of vagueness; 'any old way', 'any old job', etc.

anywhere (drug use) possessing drugs, as in *are you anywhere* (cf: holding) *Burroughs:1*.

AOK intensified form of OK (qv): absolutely perfect, completely excellent, etc. (cf: A1).

Apache n. (gay use) a man who uses cosmetics *Maledicta 9*.

apartments to let phr. unhinged, insane, crazy.

APB (US police use) (abbrev.) *all points bulletin*; general alert broadcast to all officers/vehicles; thus used generally by civilians to denote a search for a given person *McFadden*.

ape n. a thug, a hoodlum *rr*.

ape oil n. liquor.

apehangers n. high, extra-long motorcycle handlebars, favoured by outlaw riders such as the Hells Angels; riding with such equipment one's arms dangle forward like those of an ape *Thompson*.

apeshit a. berserk, mad, crazy, extremely upset *Higgins:1*.

Apple n. (abbrev.) Big Apple (qv) *Price:3*.

apple n. (US Black use) 1. the vagina; 2. any pill/capsule coloured red (cf: reds); 3. large-brimmed, oversized hat, in 1930s/40s style *Folb*; 4. a derog. term describing a Native American (Red Indian) who is 'red on the outside but white within' (cf: oreo, Uncle Tomahawk).

apple fritter n. (rhyming sl.) bitter beer *Jones:J*.

apple pie n. (rhy. sl.) the sky.

apple sauce n. 1. nonsense, balderdash; 2. flattery, insincere talk; anything easy; v. 3. to take advantage of, to flatter.

apple shine v. to toady, to curry favour (cf: apple-polisher, apple up).

apple up v. see: apple shine.

apple-knocker n. 1. spec. itinerant fruit worker; 2. rural, unsophisticated person, thus, 'apple knock' v.: to act the yokel, to behave in an unsophisticated manner, *Grogan*.

apple-polisher n. a toady, a sycophant; the apple being polished is that presented to the teacher by the class goody-goody (cf: wax up).

apples n. 1. breasts *Folb*; 2. (rhyming sl.) apples and pears = stairs *Powis*.

apples adv. (Aus.) satisfactory; fr. 'apple-pie order' or rhyming sl. apples and spice = nice *Humphries*.

apples and rice n. (rhyming sl.) nice, usu. used ironically, unlike 'apples' in Aus. use (qv) which is approving *Cole*.

apples and spice a. (Aus.) see apples.

apples from oranges, not to know phr. to be stupid (cf: how many beans make five, pancake tuesday or half-past breakfast time).

appointment, have an v. (US campus) to go out drinking (cf: go to the doctor).

april fools n. (rhyming sl.) 1. stools;

2. tools; 3. football pools *Jones:J*.

april showers n. (rhyming sl.) flowers *Jones:J*.

apron n. 1. a woman; 2. a bartender; both uses stem fr. the representative garment *Major*.

arab n. (US use) any wild or excitable looking person.

arab v. (US use) to sell or peddle on the streets.

Archer n. £2000 (fr. a sum of £2000, the disputed payment of which formed the basis of the libel case against the *Daily Star* newspaper which the popular writer Jeffrey Archer – now Lord Archer – won in 1987).

arctic a. (US campus use) (of a person) emotionally chilly, very distant.

are you prepared? (homosexual use) excl. implying amazement or shock, both approving and disapproving *Stanley*.

are you ready? see: are you prepared? *Stanley*.

are you saving it for the worms? (Can. cp) addressed to a supposed virgin, this phrase is intended to shame her into intercourse *Neaman & Silver*.

area n. (US campus use) genitals; fr. abbrev. pubic area *Underwood*.

Argie n. a slang diminutive coined by the *Sun* newspaper to describe the Argentinians during the Falklands War of May-June 1982 the *Sun* passim.

argy-bargy n. argument, confusion, confrontation; fr. argument *Keyes*.

Aristotle n. (rhyming sl.) bottle; usu. abbrev. as Arry *Franklyn*. (cf: Arris).

Arizona a. generic derog. term (cf: Arkansas); usu. found in a variety of combinations; thus 'Arizona cloudburst' n. a sandstorm; 'Arizona nightingale': a donkey or mule; 'Arizona paint job': no paint at all; 'Arizona tenor': a victim of tuberculosis who coughs deeply and often.

Arkansas, arkansaw a. generic derog. term (cf: Arizona); usu. found

in a variety of combinations; thus 'Arkansas chicken': salt pork; 'Arkansas fire extinguisher': a chamber pot; 'Arkansas lizard': a flea; 'Arkansas T-bone': bacon; 'Arkansas wedding cake': corn bread.

arkansaw v. 1. to cheat, to take advantage of; 2. to shoot in an unsportsmanlike manner, whether targetting animals or humans; 3. see: go dutch.

arm n. penis *Milner*.

armed for bear a. phr. very heavily armed; fr. hunting use *Himes:1*.

armpit n. the least appetizing, poorest, most rundown, and possibly dangerous, area of a given city or town; often as 'armpit of the universe' *Klein*.

army and navy n. (rhyming sl.) gravy *Cole*.

arnchy n. (US Black use) one who puts on airs (? fr. corruption of SE 'aren't you', e.g. 'aren't you the one', 'aren't you the big shot', etc.).

aroma n. (drug use) amyl nitrate (cf: poppers).

around the bend a. phr. crazy, insane.

around the world licking and sucking the partner's body, incl. the genitals and sometimes the anus; usu. used by prostitutes as part of possible paid services *Legman*.

arrest v. (US campus use) to accuse another of dressing unfashionably (usu. behind their back) (cf: fashion arrest).

Arris n. the buttocks, the behind; fr. rhyming sl. Aristotle = bottle = bottle and glass = arse (qv).

arrow n. a dart, used in the *arrows game*: darts *BBC-TV passim*.

arse n. 1. spec. buttocks; 2. fool, idiot; 3. (Aus. use) cheek, effrontery; 4. (Aus. use) sexual conquests, thus a woman/women *Wilkes*.

NB: for the purposes of this dictionary, the spelling *ass* (preferred in the US) has been used for many words and phrases otherwise found under *arse*.

arse about v. 1. to fool around; 2. to

waste time (cf: bugger about, fuck
about, piss about, sod about)

arse about face phr. back to front.

arse around v. to mess about, to play
the fool, waste time (cf: bugger
around, fuck around, piss around, sod
around)

arse backwards adv. out of order, to
back front (cf: ass-end-to,ass-
frontwards, assy-fussy, back-asswards,
half-assed-backwards)

arse bandit n. homosexual male.

arse from one's elbow, not know v.
to be ignorant, to be stupid; one of
many syns. all initiated by 'not
know. . .' and including 'ass from a
hole in the ground', 'chicken shit from
chicken salad', 'hawk from a
handsaw', 'shit from shinola', etc.

arse on backwards a. back to front,
confused (cf: ass- backwards, ass-end-
to, etc.)

arse over tit head over heels (cf: ass
over appetite).

arse wipe n. lavatory paper.

arseholed a. very drunk H. Page.

arseholes! excl. rubbish! nonsense!
BBC-2 TV 1983.

arsy-versy back to front (cf: arse over
tit); corruption of vice-versa.

art fag n. (US campus use) derog. one
who is overly affected, pretentious or
'arty'.

artful dodger n. (rhyming sl.) lodger;
with the implication of the lodger's
traditional interest in his landlady
Cole.

Arthur n. (rhyming sl.) bank = Arthur
Rank (cf: J. Arthur) Powis.

article nine (US criminal/drug use)
Federal legal provision that states that
anyone considered under the influence
of drugs, esp. an addict, is thus not
responsible for a given crime and will
be sent to the Federal Narcotics Farm
at Lexington, Ky. for supposed curing
Burroughs:Jr.

artillery n. beans.

artist n. an expert/devotee of a given
activity; ie: piss artist, punchout artist
(qqv), etc. (cf: bandit) Powis.

artsy-craftsy a. pretentious,

humourless, self-opinionated; often
garbed, metaphorically, in open-toed
sandals, home-woven garments and
resident in a converted mill Whitcomb.

arty n. (US milit. use) (abbrev.)
artillery Del Vecchio.

arty-farty a. pretentious, overly
intellectual/artistic, exhibiting
superficial form and little positive
content, etc. L. K. Johnson.

arvo n. (Aus. use) afternoon
Humphries:2.

as a bean (Aus. use) general
intensifier; ie: 'keen as a bean' Ready.

as easy as cake and ice cream see:
piece of cake.

as the actress said to the bishop
(cp) turning what may have been a
perfectly innocent phrase into a sexual
innuendo; thus: 'Pull it out and we'll
see how long it is.' 'As the actress
said . . .'

asafp acro. (US campus use) very
quickly indeed, immediately (fr. 'as
soon as fucking possible').

ash-spots n. 1. goose pimples; 2. (US
black use) lighter spots that appear on
one's arms and legs when one gets
cold; thus ashy: pale, ashen-faced.

asiatic a. crazy, eccentric; fr. orig. US
Navy use.

ask for the ring v. to practise anal
intercourse (cf: bit of ring) Folb.

asleep at the wheel adv. inattentive,
not concentrating on a given task.

asoc, asocial n. (US cant) a child
molestor.

—ass sfx. a person, a character (cf:
bad-ass, cool-ass)

ass n. spec. buttocks, usu. with sexual
connotation Price:2. (See note under
arse.)

ass deep phr. very deep; usu. in such
phr. as .'ass deep to a tall Indian', 'ass
deep to a tall moose'.

ass fucking n. anal intercourse
Price:2.

ass hammer n. (US campus use)
motorcycle; fr. the battering one
receives from its seat on one's own
Underwood.

ass man n. a man who finds a

woman's buttocks her most alluring feature (cf: leg man, tit man).

ass on backwards a. drunk (cf: can't find one's ass with both hands) *Dickson*.

ass over appetite head over heels (cf: arse over tit) *Algren:2*.

ass over teakettle phr. see: ass over appetite.

ass peddler n. anyone who sells their body as a prostitute, male or female *Major*.

ass up to v. to toady to, to curry favour (cf: ass-kiss, ass-lick).

assed up a. confused, mixed up (the mildest of such syns. as buggered up, fucked up, etc.).

ass-end-backwards a. (cf: ass backwards).

ass-end-to a. (cf: ass backwards).

assface n. (US campus use) derog. an unpleasant, stupid person.

ass-frontwards a. (cf: ass backwards).

asshole n. spec. anus; thus derog. description of a given subject *Price:2*.

asshole buddy n. extremely close friend *Higgins:3*.

asshole from one's elbow, not know v. see: arse from one's elbow, not know.

ass-kicker n. 1. an aggressive, domineering person, a bully *Wolfe:2*; 2. a shoe, esp. a pointed man's shoe.

ass-kiss v. see: kiss ass.

ass-kisser n. sycophant (cf: ass licker, brown-noser) *Price:2*.

ass-licker n. a sycophant (cf: ass-kisser).

ass-poots n. beans.

ass-side-before a. see: ass-backwards.

ass-sucker n. see: ass kisser.

ass-up-to-teacup adv. see: ass over teakettle.

asswipe n. 1. spec. lavatory paper; 2. derog. term of abuse *Price:1*.

ass-wiper n. see: ass-kisser.

assy-fussy a. see: ass-backwards.

at a pinch in an emergency; if really necessary.

at a rate of knots very fast; fr. naut. use.

at it 1. involved in some form of criminality *Newman:1*; 2. engaged in sexual activity (cf: on the job).

at sparrow's-fart at dawn, early in the morning; usu. *up at* . . .

at the death in the end; in conclusion *Norman:1*.

at the mark-up (UK criminal use) taking an unfairly large proportion of the loot or proceeds from a given swindle, robbery or whatever *Powis*.

at the micks causing trouble; fr. the mix, ie. mixing it (qv) *Powis*.

at the push-up (UK criminal/police use) stealing by pickpocketing amongst a large crowd *Powis*.

at the switch (UK criminal/police use) to steal property from a shop and then take it back and demand a cash refund *Powis*.

at the wash (UK police/criminal use) stealing from coats and jackets left hanging up in a washroom or public lavatory *Powis*.

Athenian n. (gay slang) a pederast *Maledicta 9*.

atlas n. (US prison use) 1. a very strong prisoner; 2. a prisoner who attempts to carry out everything unaided; both fr. the mythical Atlas who held up the earth in his hands *Klein*.

attitude n. one's whole posture towards society, its rules and one's own place amongst them *'Hill Street Blues', Thames TV, 1983*.

audi v. (US teen use) to run; from the make of fast German car T. 8/4/91.

August ham n. (US black use) a watermelon.

aunt n. euph. for menstruation; usu. in such phr. as 'Aunt Flo is visiting', 'my redheaded aunt has arrived', 'Aunt Jody's come with her suitcase', etc.

Aunt Jane n. see: Aunt Jemima *Major*.

Aunt Jemima n. (US Black use) a subservient, obsequious Black woman, the female version of Uncle

Tom (qv); an early fast-food chain, 'Aunt Jemima's Kitchen', featuring pictures of a stereotype 'Black Mammy' existed in the 1960s *Folb*.

Aunt Thomasina n. (US black use) the female equivalent of Uncle Tom.

Auntie n. 1. (UK) the British Broadcasting Corporation; orig. use by independent TV companies, but now general; 2. (Aus. use) (fr. UK origins) Australian Broadcasting Commission (ABC).

auntie n. ageing male homosexual *Jay & Young*.

Auntie Ella n. (rhyming sl.) umbrella *Jones:J*.

Auntie Nelly n. (rhyming sl.) belly *Wright*.

autograph n. (con-man use) a blank piece of paper which the victim is induced to sign and which may be used for some criminal purpose *Neaman & Silver*.

awash a. drunk *Dickson*.

away a. 1. in prison; London use: any prison outside London *Cole*; 2. (UK prison/police use) escaped, fr. gaol or police cells *Cole*.

away to fuck! interj. general dismissive phr, usu. Scots. *Welsh:1*

awesome a. (orig. Valley Girls (qv)

use) indicates tremendous approval; the term gained a whole new currency, especially among the pre-teens, with the popularity c.1990 of the Teenage Mutant Ninja Turtles, where it featured heavily *Harpers/Queen 1/83*.

A-wiper n. see: ass-wiper

AWOL (milit. use) (acro.) absent without leave *Del Vecchio*.

AWOL acro. *a*mour *w*ithout *l*ove; used by habituees of singles bars to denote their brief (strictly sexual) entanglements. *AS 60:1 (1985)*.

awright! that's good, I feel great, etc. (phonetic trans. of US pron. of 'all right' as a greeting/excl.) *McFadden*.

axe n. any musical instrument, esp. guitar; fr. Black jazz use, when instrument more likely saxophone or trumpet *Green, Book of Rock Quotes vol 1, 1977*.

axe v. to close down, to terminate, esp. of businesses, jobs *Capital Radio 1983*.

axle grease n. 1. a thick application used for one's hair *Major*; 2. semen *Klein*.

Aztec two-step / Aztec hop n. diarrhoea, often contracted on a foreign holiday (cf: Delhi belly, gippy tummy, Montezuma's revenge).

B

B n. (drug use) (abbrev.) benzedrine *Major*.

baa-lamb n. 1. anyone mild, pleasing, amicable; often used by women of malleable men *Wodehouse:passim*; 2. euph. for bastard.

B.A.B. n. a nude bathing beach (fr. acro. Bare Ass Beach).

babbler n. (Aus. use; rhyming sl.) babbling brook = cook, esp. in an institution, mining camp, farm, etc. *Wilkes*.

babbling brook n. (rhyming sl.) 1. cook (cf: babbler); 2. crook *Jones:J*.

babe n. (orig. US) 1. a woman, esp. an attractive one; 2. (used congratulatorily) a person of either sex; thus (late 20C) 'babe magnet': anything that attracts the desired person (cf: babe lair, babelicious, babylegs, babylon 2., hop on a babe, real babe).

babe lair n. an apartment used by a man for the seduction of women.

babelicious a. (of a woman) very beautiful, very sexy.

babes term of affection or simply address between either sex *Wolfe:1*.

baby n. 1. (US Black use) term of affection/general address between men and women or men and men *Himes:1*; 2. pet project, obsession, personal concern; 'it's my baby'; 3. a small- or half-sized bottle, whether of spirits or a non-alcoholic drink.

baby buster n. one who was born in the period after the baby boom that followed World War II.

baby life n. (US prison use) the maximum sentence that a prisoner must serve – 6 yrs, 4 mths – before a parole board is bound to consider his case for the first time; baby = miniature.

babyblues n. human eyes, irrespective of actual colour.

babycakes term of affection between friends *Price:3*.

baby-kisser n. (US Black use) a politician.

babylegs n. teenage girl, usually pretty and sexually alluring. *M Cropper*.

Babylon n. (UK Black/Rastafarian use) 1. spec. the police; 2. Western society; 3. any oppression or the forces that oppress the Black (Rasta) man. Babylon is opposed to Zion – the promised land of Africa, and esp. Ethiopia *Thelwell*; 4. anywhere that attractive girls are supposed to congregate or, mythically, are supposed to have their origin.

baby-pro n. (US pimp use) a prostitute under the age of legal consent *Shulman*.

babysit v. (drug use) to take care of someone either under the influence of a drug (esp. LSD) or, more often, recovering from an unpleasant, drug-induced experience *Underwood*.

baby-sitting n. (journalistic use) looking after the source of a major story, often by staying with them in a hotel, expenses paid by the newspaper, so as to stop any rival paper obtaining the subject's interview *World In Action, Granada TV, 1983*.

baby-snatching n. marrying or having an affair with someone much younger

than oneself; applies to either sex.

bachelor's baby n. (US Black use) an illegitimate child (cf: trick baby) *Klein*.

back alley n. (US Black use) the main street of an otherwise run-down or 'red-light' area; (NB it is a term of approval; back alley is another variety of the Black reversal of White values, cf: bad, wicked).

back alley deal n. (US Black use) any deal between one unsuspecting victim and the person who intends and succeeds in cheating him *Klein*.

back door man n. 1. an adulterous lover who comes in at the back door as the husband leaves by the front; 2. one who practises anal intercourse *J. Morrison, song title 1968*.

back door parole n. (US prison use) dying in prison before one's sentence is over *Chandler: Notebk.*

back eye n. the anus; thus anal intercourse *Klein*.

back forty n. an out-of-the-way, usu. barren piece of land (cf: plough the back forty).

back gate exit n. (US prison use) an inmate's death in jail (cf: back-door parole, back gate parole, pine box parole).

back in the saddle (again) a. menstruating.

back in the woods phr. unsophisticated, gauche.

back jump n. (US Black use) anal intercourse, either hetero- or homosexual *Klein*.

back number n. an irrelevant person, a 'has been', esp. of a former lover, now discarded; fr. the previous and thus 'dead' editions of newspapers.

back of beyond n. anywhere considered by the speaker as inaccessible, outside the purlieus of civilization.

back of Bourke (Aus. use) the wilds, the back of beyond, the edge of 'civilization' *Ready*.

back of the net (excl.) wonderful, perfect, fr. football commentator use to applaud a goal *Payne*.

back off (excl.) go away! stop
bothering a person *Major*.

back one's play v. to support one's
statement or back up another person.

back slice n. the anus, of a man or
woman *Klein*.

back slit see: back slice *Klein*.

back to square one v. phr. start again
at the beginning; fr. early BBC radio
soccer broadcasts when commentators
directed their audience around a
squared grid (printed in *Radio Times*),
dividing the area of a soccer pitch, as
they followed the progress of the ball.

back to the drawing board (cp) let's
start again with new plans; used when
one plan or idea has come to nothing
Manser.

back up v. to have serial sex with a
woman.

back yard n. that area of a town where
the poorer citizens live (cf: back-ah-
yard, front yard).

back-ah-yard n. (UK Black use) the
Caribbean, home *Powis*.

backchat n. cheek, impudence (cf:
back-sass, back-talk).

back-ended a. 1. back to front; 2. (of
a person) perverse, eccentric (cf:
back-end-to).

back-hander n. 1. a bribe (cf:
kickback); 2. a slap in the face.

back-jaw (US black use) v. 1. to
answer back rudely; n. 2. an insolent
reply (cf: backchat, back-sass).

backmark (US Black use)
1. undersirable characteristic; 2. spec.
an informer, esp. in prison *Klein*.

backfire v. (euph.) to fart *Neaman &
Silver*.

back-room boys n. unsung,
anonymous but vital experts,
inventors, scientists, theorists, etc.
who provide much of the muscle
behind a business, factory or other
organization.

back-sass v. see: back-jaw; thus
'back-sasser': a cheeky person.

back-seat driver n. anyone who offers
unwanted advice to the person who is
actually in charge or at least
performing the task for which the

advice is given (cf: kibitzer).

backside of nowhere n. nowhere, a
very out-of-the-way place.

back-talking n. gossip

backtrack v. (drug use) to take back
blood into a syringe, thus mixing it
with the heroin/water mixture before
re-injecting it into the vein. *Guardian
6/6/87*.

backward thinking (US Black use)
confused,muddled thinking *Klein*.

**backyard cousin, backyard
relation** n. a relation, possibly an
illegitimate child, of whom the
speaker is not proud.

backyard telephone booth n. a
privy.

bacon n. (US Black use) the good life,
material success.

bacon and eggs n. (rhyming sl.) legs
Jones:J.

bacon hole n. the mouth (cf: cakehole).

bacon sandwich n. the vagina.

bad a. good; the inference being that
the individual/object so defined is bad
in Establishment eyes and thus good in
those of any outlaw – criminal, drug,
minority – culture, esp. in Black use
(cf: vicious, mean, wicked etc.) *Seale*.

bad boy n. (US Black use) clever,
attractive black male *Folb*.

bad clothes n. (US black use) see:
bad rags.

bad count n. 1. an unfair decision; 2. a
short measure of drugs.

bad egg n. rogue, villain
Wodehouse:passim.

bad hair n. (US black use) a black
person's naturally kinky hair (cf: good
hair).

bad paper n. 1. any form of fraudulent
documents, counterfeit money or
similar written or printed frauds or
forgeries.

bad hat n. rogue, untrustworthy
person *Wodehouse:passim*.

bad in the head a. (US Black use)
eccentric, out of control; unhappy
Folb.

bad lot n. see: bad egg, bad hat
Wodehouse:passim.

bad news n. an unattractive, unpleasant person; an unpleasant situation *Underwood*.

bad nigger n. (US Black use) any Black who rejects the second-class role offered by the dominant white society (cf: bad-ass nigger) *Major*.

bad place in the road, bad spot in the road n. an out-of-the-way, unimportant place or settlement.

bad rags n. (US black use) one's best, most fashionable clothes.

bad rap n. 1. a serious criminal charge; 2. an unfair criminal charge *PT*.

bad scene n. an unpleasant situation (cf: bad news 2).

bad shape troubled or depressed state *Underwood*.

bad shit n. 1. better than average marijuana (cf: bad); 2. worse than average problems *Price:2*.

bad talk n. (US Black use) conversation or writing that considers and/or urges revolutionary attitudes and actions; such talk is 'bad' both in white eyes and as the prerogative of 'bad niggers' *Major*.

bad weave n. (US black use) see: bad rags.

bad-ass a. tough, aggressive, frightening *Price:2*.

bad-ass nigger n. (US Black use) an aggressive, tough black man who rejects the constraints and humiliation of the role the white authorities have selected for him.

baddest a. (US Black use) the very best, supreme *Folb*.

bad-mouth v. to attack verbally, to slander *Big Ass Comics 1*.

bad-rap v. see: bum-rap.

bag n. 1. a measure of narcotics, sold as *nickel bag*: $5 worth, *dime bag*: $10, etc.; 2. a contraceptive sheath *Price:2*; 3. taste, occupation, preference: 'that's my bag'; fr. jazz use 1950s; 4. old unattractive woman; fr. 19th cent. hag-bag *Wright*; 5. (US/Aus.) a suit of clothes (fr. rhy. sl. bag of fruit = suit).

bag v. 1. (drug use) to divide bulk

purchases of drugs into smaller quantities for dealing *Larner*; 2. (US Black use) to swallow semen or vaginal fluid during oral intercourse *Folb*; 3. (Aus. use) to denigrate, to criticize *Wilkes*; 4. v.t. (Valley Girls (qv) use) to hide something unpleasant from the speaker's sight (cf: bag your face!) *Harpers/Queen 1/83*; 5. to grab (cf: bags I!).

bag lady n. (abbrev.) shopping bag lady; a female derelict, usu. sleeping rough or in shelters, often an alcoholic or meths drinker, whose most cherished possessions are the numbers of (to an outsider) junk-filled shopping bags which festoon her as she walks and which never leave her side *Shulman*.

bag man n. 1. go between, one who conveys a bribe from the one who offers it to the one who accepts *San Francisco Comics no.2*; 2. a drug dealer.

bag of bones n. 1. (US Black use) marijuana cigarettes *Klein*; 2. a noticeably thin person *Algren*.

bag of coke n. sexual intercourse (fr. rhy. sl. bag of coke = poke (qv).)

bag off v. to pair off.

bag one's head v. 1. to give in, to back off, to admit defeat; thus 2. (US / Aus.) excl. go bag your head (cf: bag your face!).

bag some rays v. to sunbathe, to get a suntan.

bag that! excl. forget it!

bag your face! (Valley Girls (qv) use) general term of abuse, basically requesting a person to put their face into a rubbish bag and throw it away; general Aus. use: *go bag your head* predates this.

bag Zs v. (US preppie (qv) use) to nap, to sleep (cf: cop some Zs) *Bernbach*.

bagel bender n. (derog.) a Jew; fr. bagel, a style of doughnut-shaped roll popular among Jews *Dunne*.

bagels n. (US use) bulges of fat that accumulate around the hips and thighs, usu. used of women despite their universality amongst the overweight; fr. the shape of the popular Jewish roll (cf: love handles) *Neaman & Silver*.

baggage smasher n. (film use) a clumsy person *Chandler: Notebk.*

baggage-box, baggage-boy n. (US gay use) a homosexual prostitute who offers active sex to clients, i.e. as well as the usual passive participation in sodomy, he will play the active sodomiser and also offer fellatio.

bagged a. drunk; thus *to tie a bag on*, *to have a bag on Dickson*.

bagged v.i. arrested, caught *Higgins:1*.

bagged a. easy, simple, no problem (cf: in the bag) *Heller*

bagged out a. style-less, shabby, run-down; fr. resemblance to a bag lady (qv) *Pond*.

bagger n. a clumsy person (cf: one-bagger, two-bagger).

baggies n. 1. (drug use) plastic food bags used popularly for holding small amounts of marijuana *Green:1*; 2. (surfing use) loose-fitting 'boxer short' style of swimming trunks *Whitcomb*.

bagpipe it v. (Valley Girls (qv) use) forget it *Pond*.

bagpiping n. intercourse under the armpit, generally a homosexual practise *Rodgers*.

bags !! (UK school use) that's mine, I want to do that!; an allied formula, mainly in prep schools, is *quis*? (Lat: who) to offer an object, to which the responses are *ego*! (Lat: I) if one wishes to make a claim, or *baggy* (bags I) *no par* (no part) if one wishes to be excluded.

bahakas n. buttocks, behind *Morgan*.

Bahama Mama n. (US Black use) a fat, unattractive 'Black Mammy', supposedly typical of West Indies *Folb*.

bail v. (US teen use) to leave, to play truant; fr. 'bail out' *Pond*.

bail / bale on v. (US teen use) to oppress, to give a hard time to, to trouble.

bail up v. (Aus. use) to trap, to corner; orig. use to describe the 'stand and deliver' tactics of late 19th-C. bushrangers *Ready*.

bait n. an attractive man or woman to lure a victim into a con-game or a mugging *Klein*. (cf: fry)

bake v. (US prison use) to execute in the electric chair *Klein*.

baked a. 1. under the influence of marijuana; 2. sun-burned or very tanned.

balaclava v. to have sexual intercourse. (fr. rhy. sl. balaclava = charver, qv).

bald-tyre bandits n. (UK criminal use) traffic police *Powis*.

bale of straw n. (US Black use) a white woman, esp. a blonde *Major*.

ball n. 1. sexual intercourse *Price:2*; 2. a good time *Price:2*; 3. (rhyming sl.) ball of chalk = a walk *Powis*.

ball v. to have sexual intercourse *Price:2*.

ball and chain n. the wife *Major*.

ball and chalk n. aka: *ball of chalk* (rhyming sl.) walk *Cole*.

ball buster n. 1. spec. a nagging woman (cf: break one's balls); 2. any overbearingly unpleasant person or circumstances *Price:1*.

ball park figure a round figure for general estimation, assessment; fr. the rough estimate of fans watching a sporting event *Green:2*.

ball up n. (US use) a mess, a confusion; thus *to ball up*: to err, to blunder.

ball-breaker n. see: ball-buster.

ball-crusher n. a sexually voracious woman who exhausts her partner's virility; unlike the domineering ball-breaker or ball-buster (qqv) the ball-crusher injures rather than destroys the testicles; they have, the term implies, a chance of recovery.

baller n. (US Black use) a rich ghetto drug dealer (cf: high roller 2).

ballgame n. (US milit. use) any operation, esp. one involving contact with an enemy *Del Vecchio*.

ballhead n. (UK Black use) a white

person.

balling the jack driving a truck very fast; working very hard; any speedy activity; fr. lumberjack use *N. Cassady, 'The First Third', 1971.*

ballock, bollock v. 1. [early 20C+] to reprimand, to scold.

ballocks n. 1. excl. balls (qv)! rubbish!; 2. testicles *Norman:1.*

ballocks about, ballocks around v. to mess about, to play the fool.

ballocksed, bollixed a. ruined, messed up, thwarted.

ball of string, feel like v. (Aus.) to feel exhausted.

balloon n. saloon bar of a public house; fr. rhyming sl. balloon car = bar *Powis.*

balloon v. to try out a new idea or concept; on the same lines as 'let's run it up the flagpole and see if anyone salutes' *Higgins:5.*

balloon goes up (milit. use) the start of hostilities or of a given operation; either the onset of war or of events during that war *Pynchon.*

balloon room n. (US Black use) a place where people gather to smoke marijuana and thus get high (qv).

balloons n. conspicuously large female breasts *Klein.*

ball-park, in the right phr. approximately accurate (cf: ballpark figure).

ballroom without a parachute n. (US Black use) a disappointment, a let-down, esp. a place where one has been promised a smoke of marijuana, but which in fact offers no supply.

balls n. 1. spec. testicles; 2. by ext. fr. 1: courage, bravery; supposedly quintessential male qualities; 3. (excl.) rubbish, nonsense *Austin.*

balls out adv. at full tilt, absolutely committed, full-scale.

balls-aching nagging, complaining (cf: bellyache, ball buster).

balls-up n. a blunder, an error *Price:3.*

ballsy a. tough, masculine, courageous (cf: balls) *White.*

balltearer (Aus. use) 1. an aggressive woman (cf: ball buster) *Humphries:2;*

2. a demanding, physically or mentally exhausting task; 3. anything spectacular or notably impressive.

bally a. (euph.) bloody *Wodehouse:passim.*

ballyhoo v. to publicize to excess, often when the product cannot live up to the manufactured image; fr. carnival and fairground use.

baloney n. aka: boloney; nonsense, rubbish *Yellow Dog 22.*

bam n. 1. (drug use) amphetamine; fr. Mex. *bambita Major*; 2. a violent person.

bam v. 1. to hit.

Bama n. (US black use) generic term for the South and things Southern; thus, 'Bama chukker' (US Black use): a poor Southern rural white.

Bambi effect n. the turning in spring of a young (otherwise homosexual) man's fancy to (heterosexual) love; fr. the parting of the youthful Bambi and his erstwhile pal Thumper *Jay & Young.*

bamboozle v. to deceive, to fool, to hoax deliberately *Hotten.*

banana n. 1. (US Black use) a light-skinned Black, esp. an attractive woman *Major*; 2. (Black use) the penis (cf: tummy banana) *Klein.*

banana bender n. (Aus. use) Queenslander (cf: Bananaland) *Ready* BBC Radio 3, 1985.

banana oil n. (US use) nonsense, insincere or hypocritical talk *Neaman & Silver.*

banana peddler, banana pusher n. (US derog.) an Italian immigrant.

Bananaland n. (Aus. use) Queensland; fr. the banana crop produced there *Wilkes.*

bananas a. crazy, eccentric *Woody Allen, film title, 1971.*

bananas n. (US criminal use) a homosexual *Legman.*

band n. (US Black use) a woman *Major.*

band in the box n. (rhyming sl.) pox, venereal disease *Jones:J.*

band of hope n. (rhyming sl.) soap *Jones:J.*

band rat n. a woman who associates herself with musicians, usu. offering sex in return for proxy celebrity (cf: groupie) *Bruce:2*.

band-aid n. (US milit. use) a medic or corpsman; fr. US name for UK 'Elastoplast' *Del Vecchio*.

bander n. (Aus. use) soap (fr. pron. of rhy. sl. band of hope).

bandit n. (UK police use) a villain, a criminal, usu. with a specific speciality: *knickers bandit*: steals underwear from washing lines; *gas meter bandit*: steals from gas meters, or similarly paltry sums; *piss-hole bandit*: homosexual who solicits in public lavatories, etc. (cf: artist) *Powis*.

bang n. 1. spec. an injection of narcotics; 2. a blow; 3. a thrill *Price:2*; 4. sexual intercourse G. *Macdonald Fraser, 'Flashman & the Indians', 1983*; 5. a crowd of people (cf: shebang); 6. cannabis, esp. in the form of hashish (fr. Urdu *ghang*: Indian hemp (*Cannabis indica*); the terms appears in Eng. in mid-16C but its use (through to mid-20C) is simply as an exotic foreign word; only with the spread of the Hippie Trail of the 1960s was it incorporated, slightly mis-spelt, into popular slang; bhang itself remains a technical term, used to describe cannabis as produced and consumed in India and Pakistan).

bang v. 1. to copulate; like many sl. terms involving sex, this implies an aggression irrespective of any affection (cf: do, poke, screw, etc.); 2. to use heroin (cf: hit, slam).

bang a. extremely, very; ie: 'bang in trouble' *Performance*.

bang a hanger v. to steal a purse.

bang and biff n. syphilis. (fr. rhy. sl. bang and biff = the siff = syphilis).

bang around to make one's presence felt, with little practical result *Goulart*.

bang like a shithouse door (in a gale) v. to rate as an enthusiastic sexual performer; usu. said by men of women *Humphries*.

bang on v. to talk repetitiously and tediously *Whitcomb*.

bang on a. absolutely right, exactly so, etc. *Manser*.

bang the bishop to masturbate *Barr*.

bang to rights caught in the act *Norman:1*.

bang up v. 1. to inject a narcotic drug; 2. (UK prison use) to lock a prisoner in his/her cell *Norman:1*.

bang up (against) aka: *bung up (against)*: very close.

banged adv. shot down *rr*.

banged up a. (of people) beaten up, injured; (of objects) broken, battered esp. of a car that has notable damage to its panel-work (cf: banger).

banger n. 1. a dilapidated motor car; fr. the noisy engine, parts dropping off, etc. *Powis*; 2. a sausage; orig. naval use; 3. (US Black use) a gang member (cf: banging, gangbanging).

banging n. see: gangbanging.

bangtail n. (US Black use) a prostitute (cf: bang, tail) *Klein*.

bang-up a. first-rate, excellent *Hotten*.

banjaxed broken, ruined, smashed up; usu. Irish use *Terry Wogan, bk. title, 1980*.

banjo n. (Aus. use) a shovel; fr. shape *Wilkes*.

banjo v. (UK milit. use) to hit, to beat up *Green:2*.

bank n. 1. (US prison use) a shot of a narcotic *Chandler:Notebk*; 2. (Aus./ US Black use) money (cf: bank on).

bank on v. to take for granted; to assume as a certainty; fr. gambling use *Runyon:1*.

banker n. 1. (UK taxi-driver use) one of a series of routes that are most often requested by passengers, ie. Heathrow to the Hilton, etc.; fr. gambling use; 2. (orig. gambling use) a sure thing, something on which one can depend, a safe bet (fig. and lit.).

bankroll v. to provide financial backing for a project, legal or otherwise *Fiction Illus.3*.

bantam n. (US Black use) a young woman.

bar n. one pound sterling *LL.*

bar steward n. euph. for bastard (cf: basket).

barb wire deal n. a difficult situation.

barbecue v. (US Black use) an attractive woman, esp. one who enjoys/offers oral sex *Major.*

barbecue (stool) n. (US prison use) the electric chair.

barber v. 1. to gossip, to chatter; fr. supposed predeliction of barbers to chatter on at their captive customers *Farrell;* 2. v. (orig. Aus) to rob, to steal; thus hotel barber: a thief who specialises in robbing hotel guests (fr. a pun on SE barber, who gives his clients a trim).

barbie n. a barbecue; originally Aus. use, but widely imported into the UK.

Barbie Doll n. a super-conformist, conventionally attractive, WASP (qv) American woman; fr. the name of a blue-eyed, blonde-haired designer labelled plastic doll *H. Thompson, 'The Great Shark Hunt', 1980.*

barbs n. (drug use) (abbrev.) barbiturates *Green:1.*

Barclay's n. masturbation (cf: J. Arthur, Jodrell, Levy) (fr. rhy. sl. Barclay's Bank = wank (qv).).

Barcoo salute n. (Aus. use) a characteristics gesture in Aus. of brushing away flies from one's face; fr. river and district of Queensland *Wilkes.*

Barcoo sandwich n. (Aus.) 1. a curlew between two sheets of bark; 2. a goanna between two sheets of bark; 3. a double rum between two beers.

Barcoo spew n. (Aus.) severe vomiting brought on by drinking bad water and often accompanied by attacks of dysentery.

bare-ass a. naked *Higgins:1.*

bareback a. making love without using a contraceptive sheath *Price:2.*

barf v. (usu. US campus use) to vomit *Underwood.*

barf! (interj.) general expression of disgust (cf: barf, v.) *Underwood.*

barf city n. (US teen. use) anything particularly unpleasant (cf: barf) *Pond.*

barf me out! excl. (Valley Girls (qv) use) exclamation indicating absolute disapproval *Harpers/Queen 1/83.*

barfly n. the habitual occupier of a given bar, day in, day out *Schulberg.*

barge n. 1. a large foot (cf: canal boat); 2. a particularly large vagina; 3. (US Black use) a large car, esp. a Cadillac.

barge in v. to interrupt rudely, to push one's way in *Seale.*

bark n. (US Black use) the human skin.

barked a. bald.

barker n. (UK criminal use) a small pistol; fr. late 18th-C. 'barking iron' *Powis.*

barking spiders n. (US campus use) the audible breaking of wind.

barm pot n. an eccentric, a crazy person; like barmy (qv) the word comes from dial. and offers an image of foaming, fermenting yeast.

barmy a. insane, eccentric; fr. dial. *barm:* yeast, thus frothing like fermenting yeast *Performance.*

barn burner n. a huge and resounding success.

barn door is open, your phr. (orig. US) advice to a man or boy that his trouser fly is open; sometimes rounded off by 'and the sheep will get out' (cf: garage door is open).

Barnaby Rudge n. (rhyming sl.) judge; fr. C. Dickens character *Cole.*

barnet n. (rhyming sl.) Barnet fair = hair *Norman:2.*

barney n. (US campus use) an unsophisticated person, one who is not part of currently approved fashions or attitudes. (fr. proper name Barney Rubble: a character in the TV cartoon (and latterly the film) *The Flintstones*).

barney n. a fight *Tidy.*

Barney's brig, like a. phr. completely disorganized (cf: barney's bull).

Barney's bull n. (Aus./N.Z.) n. 1. a worthless person or thing; 2. nonsense, rubbish (cf: Barney's brig); a. 3. exhausted, tired out; phr. 4. all behind like Barney's bull: late, delayed or overweight (cf: all behind like a fat woman).

barnyard trots n. see: backdoor trots.

baron n. an influential convict within the prison; esp. one who trades in the prison currency, tobacco, thus verb: to baron (cf: daddy) *Norman:1*.

baroning selling contraband luxuries within the prison, carried out by prisoners (cf: baron) *LL*.

barrack v. (Aus. use) to support a given team or individual in a sporting context; unlike SE use, no antagonism implied, other than usual partisanship *Wilkes*.

barrack-room lawyer n. any amateur, esp. in the services or in prison, who considers himself more expert in the law, esp. Queen's Regulations or prison rules, than any professional and who will offer services, often to their detriment, to his peers *LL*.

barrel v. (Aus. use) to knock down, to hit, esp. as a result of a tackle in football *Wilkes*.

barrel, right up one's phr. (Aus.) absolutely perfect, completely to one's taste.

barrelass v. to rush headlong, to charge at *Higgins:4*.

barrelhouse 1. a brothel or cheap saloon; thus **2.** (jazz use) rough and tough unpretentious music that started off in the repertoire of the musicians who played for such saloons *Major*.

barry a. lovely, sweet.

base n. a synonym for crack (qv), although base is an abbrev. of freebase (qv) which refers not to crack, but to base cocaine.

base! (Valley Girls (qv) use) excl. of approval at another person's cruel but accurate attack on a third (absent) party *Pond*.

base v. **1.** (drug use) (abbrev.) free-base (qv); **2.** to disparage, criticize, humiliate another person *Pond*; **3.** to argue; both **2.** and **3.** presumably come from SE 'debase'.

base crazies n. the psychosis that can overtake regular consumers of crack (qv) cocaine.

basehead n. a regular consumer of crack (qv) cocaine (cf: acidhead, cokehead, crackhead, pillhead, pothead, smackhead).

basehouse n. a place where users gather to consume crack (qv) cocaine (cf: basing gallery).

bash n. **1.** sexual intercourse (cf: biff, bonk, do, drill, grind, knock (off), plank, plonk, plug, poke, pound, prod, root, screw, spread, tonk); **2.** a party; **3.** an attempt, a try, esp. as phr. 'have a bash (at)'. (fr. SE bash: a heavy blow).

bash v. **1.** to hit, to batter *Performance*; **2.** to work as a prostitute (cf: BATTER); **3.** (Aus.) to drink heavily, also 'bash it', 'give it a bash'.

bash, on the adv. **1.** drinking, usu. to excess; **2.** working as a prostitute (cf: batter).

bash the bishop v. to masturbate.

bash the bumps v. (skiing use) skiing through a crowded field of rich skiers *Barr*.

basher n. **1.** (orig. milit. use) generic for fellow, chap, person (cf: bible-basher, swede basher); **2.** a makeshift shelter; the original use was military (and the spelling 'basha'): it denoted a shelter made of bamboo and attap (a type of palm frond used for thatching) which was common in south-east Asia. More recently it can be found among the homeless denizens of London's Cardboard City (qv) or the protestors at the women's camp at Greenham Common.

basic a. unexciting, unexceptional, uneventful *Underwood*.

basinful n. an excessive amount, more than enough, usu. as phr. 'I've had a basinful of. . .'.

basing n. using crack (qv) cocaine (cf: base).

basing gallery n. a place where crack (qv) cocaine users gather to consume their drug; the precursor of a basehouse (qv).

basket n. **1.** (orig. US Black use) the stomach; thence **2.** (homosexual use) the male genitals (cf: basketeer, take one's meat out of the basket); **3.** (euph.) bastard *Humphries*.

basket case n. cripple, either mentally or physically *Price:2*.

basket lunch n. (mainly gay use) fellatio.

basket picnic n. see: basketeer *Legman*.

basketeer v. (homosexual use) to wander the streets gazing at male genitals; this can provide some men with adequate satisfaction, others may be simply sizing up the available talent for later developments *Legman*.

bass-ackwards a. see: ass-backwards.

bastard n. general term for a man, people; not esp. derog. *Humphries*.

baste v. (US Black use) to attack or ridicule someone behind their back.

basted a. drunk *Dickson*.

bat n. **1.** an unattractive woman, often old; **2.** a drunken binge, a spree, thus *go to bat Grogan*.

bat a. (US campus use) good, attractive, fr. play on *bad* (qv) *Underwood*.

bat and wicket n. (rhyming sl.) ticket *Jones:J*.

bat phone n. (UK police use) the officer's personal radio set; fr. 'Batman' comic-TV show superhero *Powis*.

bat the breeze v. to chatter, to gossip; orig. milit. use.

batchy a. silly, stupid *Sillitoe*.

bate n. (UK society use) temper; orig. prep school/public school use, thus inevitably carried into adult life *Barr*.

bath bun n. (rhyming sl) **1.** sun; **2.** son *Jones:J*.

bathouse a. mad, crazy, insane (cf: bats, bats in the belfry, batshit, batty).

bathtub scum n. (US campus use) an unpleasant person (cf: pond scum, shower scum).

bato n. (US Black use) any Mexican, Puerto Rican or other Latin person *Folb*.

bats a. crazy, insane, eccentric; abbrev. bats in the belfry (qv) *Dickson*.

bats in the belfry a. eccentric, crazy; often as verb: *to have bats . . .*

batshit a. insane, crazy, fr. batty plus apeshit (qqv) *Price:3*.

batti n. (Jamaican use) the buttocks *Thelwell*.

batting average n. (US police use) an officer's current record of arrests, upon which his promotion may depend (cf: accommodation collar) *Neaman & Silver*.

battle v. (Aus. use) to struggle for a livelihood, to work in a low-paid job; both senses imply some self-congratulation *Lawson*.

battle (and) cruiser n. (rhyming sl.) boozer = public house *Cole*.

battle-axe n. a formidable (older) woman.

batty insane, crazy, eccentric; fr. Fitzherbert Batty, a 19th-C. barrister whose certification as mad in 1839 caused much interest *Higgins:1*.

battyman n. (West Indian sl.) a homosexual, prob. fr. batti (qv) *Powis*.

B.A.V. n. (US campus use) one who has not had sexual intercourse for a long time. (fr. acro. Born Again Virgin).

bawl out v. to scold, to reprimand, to criticize; all such attacks are delivered at the top of the voice.

Bay City n. (US trucker use) San Francisco, Calif.; however, the fictitious (and massively corrupt) 'Bay City' created by Raymond Chandler is generally seen to be Oakland, Calif. *CB*.

bazongas n. the female breasts (cf: bazooms, gazongas, gazungas).

bazoo n. mouth *Farrell*.

bazooka n. **1.** the penis (cf: cannon, cock, gun, peacemaker); **2.** the buttocks; **3.** (US Black use) a especially large and potent marijuana cigarette, laced with cocaine.

bazoom n. humorous pron. of bosom.

B.B. head n. (US Black use) an unattractive female; esp. one with short nappy hair *Folb*.

B & D n. (acro.) bondage and

discipline, a sexual 'speciality' *Jay & Young*.

BDT see: backdoor trots.

B & E (police use/cant) (acro.) breaking and entering *Higgins:2*.

be a devil! take a risk!; I dare you!; usu. used facetiously to someone for whom the tiniest breach of 'normality' is a major event *Manser*.

be all v. to take an attitude, to adopt a pose; the phr. is often used with an accompanying gesture: 'He was all. . .'.

beamy a. (of a person) broad, wide, overweight; thus broad in the beam.

be brought out v. to be initiated into the homosexual life (cf: come out) *Legman*.

be down (Black pimp use) to be prepared, aware *Milner*.

be in the hot seat v. to be in a difficult, poss. embarrassing, certainly demanding position.

be missing! (excl.) go away! a phrase first used by Chicago mobster Spike O'Donnell in rejecting the overtures/ threats of Al Capone (*see 'Raymond Chandler Speaking', 1962*) *Chandler: LG*.

be my guest! (cp) help yourself, make yourself at home, etc.

be one of the knights v. (homosexual use) to have syphilis *Legman*.

be your age! excl. of contempt, based in the condemnation of one who the speaker considers is acting childishly *Baker*.

bead-puller n. derog. a Roman Catholic (cf: statue-lover).

beak n. 1. judge, magistrate *Chandler Notebk.*; 2. the nose *Wodehouse: RHJ*.

beam up v. (US teen use) to get high; from the *Star Trek* cp 'Beam me up, Scottie'. *T 8/4/91*.

bean n. the head *Farrell*.

bean v. to hit on the head *Price:2*.

bean eater n. aka: *bean choker*; (derog.) Mexican *BvdB*.

Bean Town n. (US trucker use) Boston, Mass. *CB*.

beanbag v. to have sexual intercourse

'Hill Street Blues', Thames TV, 1983.

beaner n. 1. (Valley Girls (qv) use, although general derog.): Mexican (cf: bean eater) *Harpers/Queen 1/83*; 2. something excellent.

bean-feast n. a party, a celebration, usu. with food and drink; fr. early 19th C. tradition of employers giving their workers an annual banquet.

bean-head n. a fool (cf: beef-head, cabbage-head, meathead, mutton-head).

beano n. a party, a celebration; fr. bean-feast (qv) *Wolfe:2*.

beans n. 1. (US Black use) any drug available in a pill form and swallowed as such *Klein*; 2. dollars *Price:3*.

bear n. 1. (US Black use) a particularly ugly woman *Folb*; 2. (US campus use) any difficult course (cf: gut) *Underwood*; 3. (CB use) a policeman; fr. US Forest Service's mascot 'Smokey the Bear' (cf: smokies) *CB*.

bear cat n. something excellent, first-rate.

bear in the air n. (CB use) a police helicopter *CB*.

bear tracker n. a detective.

beard n. (lesbian use) a male used as an ostensible lover or even husband, as a disguise for one's real preference *Maledicta*.

bearded clam v. the vagina *Morgan*.

bear-leader n. an expert who teaches his pupils by example; fr. nickname for the tutors of the 18th C. who ferried their aristocratic pupils around the 'Grand Tour' of Europe *J. Le Carré, 'Smiley's People', 1980*.

bear's paw n. (rhyming sl.) saw *Jones:J*.

beast n. (US Black use) 1. white person; 2. heroin *Klein*.

beast n. 1. (UK prison use) a child molester, a sexual offender (cf: nonce); 2. the police *Indep. 3/9/91*.

beastie n. (Valley Girls (qv) use) anyone considered outside the group talking, esp. if unattractive, empty-headed, etc. *Pond*.

beat a. 1. exhausted, tired out *Selby*;

2. out of funds *Higgins:3*.

beat n. (pimp use) a client who likes to be beaten, often bringing his own equipment with him *OUI 8/75*.

beat v. (US prison use) to escape.

beat a rap v. to be found not guilty in a court *Hoffman:a*.

beat a trick v. (sex industry use) to rob a client *Maledicta 9*.

beat about the bush v. to avoid a given topic, to fail deliberately to come to the point *Humphries:2*.

beat around the bush v. see: beat about the bush.

beat down (US Black use) v. **1.** to fight, n. **2.** a fight.

beat feet v. (US campus use) to leave, to depart *Underwood*.

beat for v. to take a person's money, whether it is offered or not *Burroughs:1*.

beat it v. to go away, usu. as excl: *beat it! Manser*.

beat off v. masturbate (cf: beat one's meat) *Higgins:1*.

beat one out of v. to cheat, to steal from, to defraud *Larner*.

beat one to the punch v. **1.** (US Black use) to arrive at destination sooner than another person; **2.** to appreciate or understand something faster than another person; both fr. boxing use *Klein*.

beat one's chops v. see: beat one's gums.

beat one's dummy v. to masturbate *Folb*.

beat one's gums v. to talk incessantly *Morgan*.

beat one's hog v. to masturbate *Higgins:2*.

beat one's meat v. to masturbate *Junker*.

beat out v. to overcome, to beat a rival *Algren*.

beat the hound out of v. to thrash severely

beat the rap v. to be found innocent of a charge in court *Dunne*.

beat up v. **1.** assault, attack (cf: stomp); **2.** to nag, harass *Higgins:1*.

beatbox n. see: ghetto blaster.

beat-off n. see: jerk-off (n.) *Underwood*.

beats me! general excl. of incomprehension; I just can't understand it *PT*.

beat-up a. dilapidated, run down, ageing *Price:2*.

beaut! (Aus. use) all-purpose Aus. term of approbation, can equally well be used as adj.; also as beauty! (pron. bewdy) *Humphries:2*.

beaver n. vagina, esp. in commercial pornography use *Higgins:2*.

beaver shot n. a close-up photograph or camera-angle on the female genitals; used in commercial pornography.

bebopper n. (US Black use) an inexperienced, naïve and on those grounds unpopular person; fr. the bebop jazz craze, new and sophisticated in 1940s, but archaic by 1980s *Folb*.

bed and breakfast (bingo use) 26; fr. 2/6d, at one stage the going rate for a B&B establishment *LL*.

bedbug alley, bedbug row n. the poorest area of a town.

bedhop v. to live a sexually promiscuous life *Blacker*.

Bedpan line n. (British Rail use) the electrified commuter line between Bedford and St Pancras; post 1983, though the line, on diesel power, pre-existed without this name.

bedroom eyes n. a look in the eyes that invites its subject towards seduction *Algren*.

bedstead relation n. in-laws, relations by marriage.

Beeb n. the British Broadcasting Corporation (BBC).

Beecham's pill n. (rhyming sl.) **1.** bill; **2.** still (photograph) *Jones:J*.

beef n. **1.** a complaint, a problem *Higgins*; **2.** a court case, usu. as defendant; **3.** (US Black use) penis *Folb*.

beef v. **1.** to complain; **2.** to engage in sexual intercourse *Underwood*.

beef bayonet n. the penis (cf: pork sword).

beef to the heel phr. (of a person) heavy, stocky, esp. of thick, strong legs.

beef up v. to strengthen, to improve *Caserta*.

beefcake n. a male pinup (cf: cheesecake).

beefy a. well-built, muscled, stolid *Wodehouse:AAG*.

beemal n. (butchers' back-sl.) lamb *Cole*.

been and gone and done it (cp) mocking response to a confession of some minor error or peccadillo; usu.: 'now you've . . .' *Manser*.

been there to have seduced someone *Dury, 'Laughter', 1979*.

beer belly n. a fat stomach, the result of an excess of beer-drinking *Powis*.

beer bottle beat n. (pimp use) a client who likes to be beaten by a prostitute who is wielding a beer bottle *OUI 8/75*.

beer bust n. a drinking party that concentrates on beer *Whitcomb*.

beer gut n. see: beer belly *Cole*.

beer-up n. (Aus. use) a riotous, drunken party (cf: piss-up) *Wilkes*.

bees and honey n. (rhyming sl.) money *Franklyn*.

bee's knees a. wonderful, the best, perfect (cf: cat's pyjamas).

beeswax, none of your phr. none of your business.

beetle off v. to leave, to wander off *Barr*.

beetle-crushers n. large, heavy boots, often as worn by policemen, labourers or the army *P. MacDonald, 'X v. Rex', 1933*.

beevos n. (US college use) beer; corruption of 'beverage' (cf: bevvy) *Bernbach*.

beezer n. the nose *Wodehouse:JO*.

beggar my neighbour (rhyming sl.) on the Labour = visiting the Labour Exchange/Unemployment Office to draw one's dole/unemployment benefit *Cole*.

beggar's lagging n. see: tramp's lagging *LL*.

beggar-trash n. (of people)

worthless, low-class, inferior.

begging for it a male comment on a woman who, supposedly if not actually, is inflamed with lust.

begorra! (euph.) by God! the cliché expletive of each and every stage Irishman yet created (cf: bejabers!).

behind 1. involved with, concerned about, believing in *Michaels & Ricks*; 2. (Black use) the cause of something *Milner*.

behind one's door (UK prison use) locked up in solitary confinement *Newman:3*.

behind the walls n. in prison (cf: over the wall).

beige a. (Valley Girls (qv) use) deeply tedious person *Pond*.

be-in n. (hippie use) fr. the original Human Be-in, Golden Gate Park, San Francisco 1967, a gathering of hippies for mutual admiration, smoking of cannabis and listening to music. The *-in* suffix extended around the hippie vocabulary, incl. *fuck-in*, *smoke-in*, *love-in*, etc. *Hoffman:a*.

bejabers! (euph.) by Jesus! those stage Irishmen who do not say begorra (qv) will certainly say bejabers! many manage both.

bejazus (euph.) by Jesus; often in knock the bejazus out of (qv).

belcher n. (US cant) an informer.

bell n. (US Black use) personal notoriety *Major*.

bell v. to call on the telephone *Payne*.

bell ringers n. (rhyming sl.) fingers *Wright*.

belle n. (homosexual use) a good-looking, young homosexual *Legman*.

bells n. (US Black use) (abbrev.) wedding bells; an expression of approval *Major*.

belly cheater n. see: belly robber.

belly gun n. a small gun that is most effective when fired at short range, esp. when aimed at a victim's abdomen.

belly habit n. (drug use) pains in the stomach that may accompany withdrawal from continued heroin use *Major*.

belly robber n. a cook or steward.

belly up a. drunk *Dickson*.

belly up, go v. to die; the image is of a dead fish.

belly up to v. to move straight at, to approach directly; fr. the pushing forward of one's stomach.

belly wash n. 1. a soft drink; 2. a weak or bad alcoholic drink; 3. nonsense (cf: hogwash).

bellyache v. to complain, to moan *Higgins:2*.

bellyful n. enough, if not too much, satiety; esp. in have a bellyful (qv).

below the belt underhand, unfair, illegal, cheating; fr. boxing use which declares such blows as foul.

below the mahogany a. drunk; the mahogany is the bar, beneath which the drinker has slipped *Dickson*.

belt n. a measure of spirits.

belt v. to hit *Price:2*.

belt along v. to run fast, to hurry *Tidy*.

belt it v. to drive exceptionally fast *Humphries:2*.

belt it out v. to sing loudly and enthusiastically *Hoffman:a*.

belt one's hog v. to masturbate *Dunne*.

belt out v. to knock down; to destroy *Breslin*.

belt up! (excl.) be quiet, shut up! *Manser*.

belted a. drunk *Dickson*.

belter n. an admirable, exciting, thrilling, etc. event or circumstance.

BEM n. (acro.) Bug-Eyed Monster(s); a popular category of science fiction writing and described as such by fans *'Twilight Zone' magazine: passim*.

bend one's ear v. to chatter on interminably and probably tediously *Powis*.

bend one's elbow v. to have a drink *Powis*.

bend over (for) v. to submit to; the image is of submitting to buggery, but the popular use is less specific.

bended knees n. (rhyming sl.) cheese *Wright*.

bender n. 1. a bout of riotous

drinking, often lasting several days and including random acts of excess, violence, etc. *Higgins:3*; 2. a homosexual (cf: bent).

benies n. (US campus) (abbrev.) benefits, spec. those of the GI Bill that puts US service veterans through college for free *Underwood*.

bennies n. (abbrev.) benzedrine (cf: B) *Tuff Shit Comics*.

benny n. an overcoat *Folb*.

benny n. as used by the British Army, an inhabitant of the Falkland Islands; a derogatory reference derived from a intellectually deficient rural character in the TV serial *'Crossroads'*. *Green:3*.

benny house n. a brothel which essentially caters for heterosexuals, but will obtain male prostitutes on request *Legman*.

beno fr. 'there'll be no fun': the period of menstruation and thus, traditionally, no sex *Rawson*.

bent n. a homosexual.

bent a. 1. corrupt, esp. 'bent copper': corrupt policeman *Payne*; 2. sexually eccentric, esp. homosexual.

bent as a nine bob note dishonest (of a person); stolen (of an object) *Cole*.

bent out of shape intoxicated by a drug, esp. cannabis or LSD, or extremely drunk *Goldman*.

benz n. (abbrev.) 1. benzedrine (cf: bennies, B) *Norman:2*; 2. abbrev. for Mercedes Benz.

Berdoo n. San Bernardino, Calif. *Thompson*.

berk n. (rhyming sl.) Berkeley Hunt or Berkshire Hunt = cunt (qv) = fool, incompetent *Humphries*.

Berkeley Hunt n. see: berk *Cole*.

Berkshire Hunt n. see: berk *Cole*.

berries n. (US Black use) wine *Folb*.

berries, the n. 1. the best, the superlative; 2. the ultimate, the last straw.

berry n. a dollar.

berry picker n. a rural person, a country dweller.

best bib and tucker in one's best clothes.

best-built a. women with voluptuous

figures *Higgins:1*.

bet one's boots v. to be certain, to wager everything in total confidence *Dury, 'Do It Yourself', 1979*.

bet one's bottom dollar v. bet one's boots *Wodehouse: PGM*.

bet one's kettle v. to be drunk *Dickson*.

bet your ass v. 1. to bet heavily on an apparent 'sure thing'; 2. excl.: .'you must be joking!' *Higgins:1*.

bet your life see: bet your ass; bet one's bottom dollar, etc.

betcha! fr. bet you! see: you bet!

Bethlehem steel (US Black use) a boastful description of the rigidity of one's erect penis; fr. the US steel producer *Klein*.

Betsy n. a revolver, a pistol *Runyon:1*.

better half n. the wife, usu. joking use *Manser*.

better than a poke in the eye with a blunt stick see: better than a slap in the belly with a wet fish.

better than a slap in the belly with a wet fish (cp) a situation that certainly might be worse.

betty n. 1. a chamber pot; 2. a schoolteacher.

between hell and high water caught between two extremes, neither of which is particularly palatable.

between the devil and the deep blue sea caught between two equally unappealing extremes.

between the rock and the hard place (mainly US use) see: between the devil and the deep blue sea; between hell and high water.

betwixt and between undecided, uncertain, 'neither one thing nor the other'.

bevvied a. drunk; fr. beverage *Wilkinson*.

bevvy n. alcohol, esp. beer (cf: beevos) *Wright*.

beyond the rabbit-proof fence (Aus. use) very far away, beyond 'civilization' (cf: back of Bourke) *Bickerton*.

bf (abbrev.) *bloody fool*.

B-52 n. (US milit. use) a can opener;

fr. the heavy bomber of the same name *Del Vecchio*.

B-girl (abbrev.) bar-girl: amateur prostitutes who solicit from bars *Goldman*.

bhani ghani (US Black use) a form of greeting (cf: what's happening?), poss. fr. Swahili: *abari gani* what's news? *Folb*.

bi a. (abbrev.) bisexual (cf: ambidextrous).

Bible-banger n. (US campus use) aka: *Bible beater*: a religious fanatic *Underwood*.

bible-puncher n. a religious person, usu. one who wishes to thrust their beliefs on any who will listen and many who would rather not.

biddy n. old lady, spec. Irish servant girl, fr. common Irish name *Bruce:1*.

biddy-peck v. to nag mildly.

biff v. 1. to hit; thus; 2. to kill, to murder *Goulart*.

biffy n. 1. a privy, an outdoor lavatory; 2. an indoor lavatory.

big a. (gambling use) multiples of ten thousand; high stakes used in poker games where (as in drug use) the convention talks of *nickels* ($500) and *dimes* ($1000), thus *big nickel* $5000 and *big dime* $10000 *Al Alvarez, Sunday Times, 5/6/83*.

big v. to make pregnant, thus bigged: pregnant.

big A n. (Aus. use) brush-off, rejection, dismissal; fr. abbrev. the Big Arse (cf: big E).

Big A n. (US trucker use) 1. Amarillo, Texas; 2. Atlanta, Georgia *CB*.

Big Apple n. New York City *Capital Radio, 30/9/83*.

big ass a. large, powerful, self-opinionated; fr. the supposed crushing power of such massive buttocks *Big Ass Comics, title 1969, Rip Off Press*.

big boat n. large, traditional American car, esp. station wagon *Price:3*.

big boy n. a shotgun (cf: big toter)

big bucks n. large sums of money, esp. those earned by performers or stolen by criminals *Capital Radio, 29/*

6/83.

big C n. **1.** excl. cancer; the horror disease (pace AIDS) of the 20th century which, as the supreme threat to life, cannot even be named in full without a shudder *Welsh:1*; **2.** cocaine *Shell*.

big cheese n. important person, influential figure, boss in a given situation/job *'Hill Street Blues', Thames TV, 1983*.

big cog n. an important or self-important person (cf: big wheel).

big daddy, big papa n. grandfather (cf: big mamma).

big deal! excl. what's important about that?, why bother me? *McFadden*.

big deal a. important, vital, urgent, impressive, etc. *McFadden*.

Big Deuce n. (US teen. use) Second World War *Sculatti*.

big Dick (from Boston) (gambling use) the point of ten in craps dice *Algren*.

Big Ditch n. the Atlantic Ocean.

big doings n. **1.** a party; **2.** a boaster, a braggart; a. **3.** conceited, self-opinionated, snobbish.

big E n. a brush-off, a rejection; *E* is abbrev. for elbow (qv) *Barr*.

Big Easy, the n. New Orleans *Morgan*.

big enchilada n. a phrase much the same as big shot, big cheese (qqv), momentarily very popular during the Watergate Scandal (1973/4) when the White House tapes used it variously to describe corrupt personnel *PT*.

big fish n. an important, powerful person *PT*.

big girl's blouse n. a weakling, an ineffectual person; usually found as a direct statement: 'You big girl's blouse!'; the phrase, now widespread, originated like the similarly deracinated gobsmacked (qv) in the North.

Big Green (US college use) nickname for Dartmouth College *Bernbach*.

big H (drug use) heroin *Underwood*.

big hat n. **1.** a policeman or state trooper; **2.** see: big bug; **3.** a Mexican.

big herb n. an important person.

big hit n. (Aus. use, rhyming sl.) shit = excrement *Franklyn*.

big hit n. (US prison use) a long term of imprisonment, usu. 3 years or more (cf: big time) *Klein*.

big house n. (US criminal use) prison *Wodehouse passim*.

big jobs n. (US child use) excreta *Dury, 'Laughter', 1979*.

Big John n. (US Black use) the police *Folb*.

big jump n. death.

Big Kahoona n. (surfing use) a legendary monstrous 'perfect' wave – never encountered, but continually sought out *Whitcomb*.

big league a. important, substantial, powerful; fr. sporting use *Schulberg:2*.

big legs n. a big spender *Maledicta 9*.

big mamma, big nana n. one's grandmother (cf: big daddy).

big man n. a gallon of wine.

big noise n. an important, powerful person.

big O n. orgasm *Jay & Young*.

big one n. a tall story, an exaggerated tale.

big one n. £100, $100 *Higgins:3*; but $1000 *Higgins:4*.

big razzoo n. a gesture of extreme contempt or scorn (cf: razz, raspberry) *Chandler:LG*.

Big Red n. (US college use) Cornell University *Bernbach*.

big shot n. superior person, or one who claims to be (cf: big noise) *Price:2*.

big sleep n. death; coined by Raymond Chandler as title of his book, 1939.

Big Smoke n. (Aus. use) Sydney; fr. UK use for London (cf: smoke) *Humphries:2*.

big split n. (Aus. use) the act of vomiting *Humphries:2*.

big stuff n. an important or self-important person (cf: big bug, big cog, big noise, big wheel).

Big T n. (US trucker use) Tucson, Arizona *CB*.

big ticket n. expensive, requiring a considerable financial outlay.

big time n., a. success, fame, power; fr. theatrical use: vaudeville theatres with top-line acts and thus only two shows per day, the opposite of small time (qv) *Whitcomb*.

big time n. (US prison use) a lengthy sentence, 3 years plus (cf: big bit) *Seale*.

big wheel n. an important, influential person, esp. in business (cf: big noise, etc.) *Chandler:LG*.

big wig n. a powerful, important person, often a politician or bureaucrat.

big-feeler n. an arrogant, self-important person (cf: big bug, big dude, etc.).

biggie n. anything or anyone large, important, successful, esp. used in entertainment industries (cf: gorilla) *Dickson*.

big-note artist n. (Aus. use) braggart, esp. concerning alleged sums of money he possesses *Baker*.

bike n. a promiscuous woman (cf: town bicycle) *Powis*.

biker n. a motorcycle rider, usu. a member of an outlaw motorcycle gang *San Francisco Comics 3*.

bilge n. nonsense, rubbish, piffle; fr. nautical use: bilgewater.

bilge artist n. aka: *bull artist*; a braggart, one given to boasting.

bill n. the nose.

Bill n. **1.** (abbrev.) Old Bill (qv) *Newman:1*; **2.** (abbrev.) dollar bill (cf: billies) *Price:1*; **3.** $100 *Schulberg*.

bill n. (taxi-driver use) the taxi-driver's licence *Powis*.

bill of goods false promises, a hoax, theories that are not followed up by practice *Uris*.

bill shop n. police station (cf: cop shop) *Powis*.

bill-be-damned, Billy Bedam n. comparative phr. used to indicate absoluteness, eg. 'dead as. . .', 'cold as. . .'.

billies n. (Valley Girls (qv) use) money, diminutive of bill (qv).

billy n. a policeman.

billy n. (US police use) the policeman's wooden club (cf: Mr Wood).

Billy Barlow n. a large pocket knife with folding blades (? fr. brand name).

billy of the wash-house, the n. a complainer, a dog in the manger *Welsh:1*.

Billy Whiz n. (drug use) a mixture of heroin and cocaine (cf: speedball); the term comes from the name of a character in a children's comic. *Guardian 6/6/87*.

billy-goat alley, billy-goat hill n. the poorest section of a town.

billy-jack a. (US Black use) unsophisticated, from the back woods *Klein*.

bim n. (abbrev.) bimbo (qv) *Chandler:LG*.

bimbette n. a junior or aspirant bimbo (qv).

bimbo n. a young man or woman; the bimbo gained a new currency during the 1980s when it came to describe a young girl, usually something of a gold-digger and indulged as such by rich and/or powerful older men and the media to whom they tell or sell their tales. The original '80s bimbo was a 'model', Fiona Wright, who delighted the press with revelations of her relationship with Sir Ralph Halpern, a millionaire businessman. *Jay & Young*.

Bimi n. West Indian *Price:2*.

bimps n. (US campus use, spec. U. of Arkansas) french fried potatoes *Underwood*.

bin n. **1.** pocket *Griffith*; **2.** (abbrev.) loony bin (qv).

bin (it) v. to throw away.

bind n. a problem, which 'ties one up' *Higgins:3*.

bindle n. (drug use) a small measure of narcotics, wrapped in a folded square of paper; fr. hobo use, a bindle was a bedroll which was carried folded up *De Lannoy & Masterson*.

bindle stiff n. a tramp, spec. one carrying a bedroll 'bindle'; formerly a migrant worker *Grogan*.

bing v. to hit (cf: bip, bop).

bingo n. (Can. prison use) a riot *Caron*.

binky n. the buttocks.

bins n. **1.** binoculars, eyes *Wright*; **2.** glasses, spectacles *Payne:2*; **3.** pair of trousers, fr. bin: pocket *Norman:2*.

bint n. a young girl, fr. Arabic *Powis*.

bip bam thank you ma'am see: wham bam thank you ma'am *Major*.

Bird n. Thunderbird, a motor car *Higgins:2*.

bird n. **1.** (US Black use) an experienced, tough female prostitute *Klein*; **2.** a girl; a girl-friend *Norman:1*; **3.** (rhyming sl.) bird lime = time = a prison sentence *Performance*; **4.** penis *Price:2*; **5.** (US milit. use) a helicopter *Del Vecchio*; **6.** (US campus use) an obscene gesture of dismissal, mockery; fr. flip the bird (qv) *Underwood*.

bird dog n. **1.** (US milit. use) a forward air controller, usu. in a single-engined propellor plane, directing military movements, bombing, etc.; fr. hunting use *Del Vecchio*; **2.** (US criminal use) a contact man for stock and bond thieves; fr. hunting use *AS 41 (1966)*; **3.** the buttocks.

bird dog v. (US teen. use) **1.** to steal another person's girl-friend; to break up a school or college romance *The Everley Brothers, 'Bird Dog', 1958*; **2.** to hang around in the hope of making a pickup *Morgan*.

bird dogger n. one who tries overly hard to gain acceptance or approval.

bird eater n. a finicky eater.

birdie n. an effeminate male; fr. bird (qv) *Legman*.

birdseye n. (drug use) a small amount of narcotics *De Lannoy & Masterson*.

birdsnesting n. (skiing use) skiing through trees *Barr*.

Birmingham screwdriver n. a hammer; fr. supposed oafishness of the Birmingham worker who would rather hammer in a screw than use the correct tool; despite normal racial stereotypes (and their supposed jobs)

a US usage *yiddish screwdriver* has been noted *c.1939*.

birthday suit n. the naked body; fr. the state in which one emerges from the maternal womb *Humphries*.

biscuit beggar n. derog. an American Indian.

biscuit hooks n. the hands (cf: bread hooks, lunch hooks).

biscuits and cheese n. (rhyming sl.) knees *Jones:J*.

bit n. **1.** situation, circumstance, usu. with a descriptive noun: 'the whole punk bit', etc. *McFadden*; **2.** a prison sentence – any length (cf: big bit) *Selby:1*.

bit of a lad n. a cheeky, self-possessed youth who 'fancies himself' (cf: Jack the Lad).

bit of all right n. an attractive female, usu. young.

bit of crackling n. an attractive girl.

bit of fluff n. **1.** any thing or person considered insignificant, ineffectual *Capital Radio, 1983*; **2.** an attractive, but otherwise unexceptional female *Chandler:LG*.

bit of how's yer father n. sexual intercourse; occasional use as general euph. 'swear like how's yer father' ('Cool for Cats', Squeeze) *Capital Radio 1983*.

bit of mess n. (UK criminal use) a prostitute's male lover, who is neither ponce nor client *Powis*.

bit of ring n. anal intercourse *Legman*.

bit of slap and tickle n. sexual by-play, necking.

bit of spare n. an unattached female, usu. at a party or club *Powis*.

bit of stuff n. a girl, usually attractive; stuff = material and descends fr. mid-19th C. *bit of muslin*: a young girl, prob. a prostitute.

bit of the other n. sexual intercourse *May*.

bit on the side n. an affair; a lover other than one's regular partner (married or otherwise) *Farren*.

bit previous in poor taste, uncalled for (cf: out of order).

bit swift (UK criminal/police use) the taking of unfair advantage, usu. the complaint is made by the villain against the man who arrests him *Powis*.

bit thick a. unpleasant, insufferable, distasteful *Wodehouse:MOJ*.

bitch n. 1. (homosexual use) an effeminate male, supposedly the 'passive' partner in a homosexual couple *Folb*; 2. (derog.) a woman; esp. Black pimp use *Milner*; 3. (Can. prison use) an habitual criminal *Caron*.

bitch v. to complain *Price:2*.

bitch bath n. a 'bath' in which the usual water is replaced by an application of cosmetics, masking the dirt rather than removing it.

bitch box n. (US army use) Tannoy, public address system; its announcements usually mean inconvenience or trouble for the troops (cf: bitch, v.) *Seale*.

bitch off v. (US campus use) to annoy, irritate *Underwood*.

bitch up v. to make a mess of things, to make a mistake *Sanchez*.

bitchen a. see: bitchin.

bitchin a. (excl.) wonderful, great, esp. in surfer use: subseq. adopted by Valley Girls of 1980s Calif. *Wolfe:1*.

bitchin twitchin superlative form of bitchin (qv) *Pond*.

bitch's bastard n. (UK prison use) a severe, possibly violent warder *AS 41 (1966)*.

bite n. an attempt to obtain a loan *Runyon:1*.

bite v. to worry, to annoy; usu. in 'what's biting you/him/etc.?' *Howard*.

bite one's bait v. to pause before making too precipitate a decision.

bite one's crank v. to fellate; fr. 'crank-handle'.

bite the bullet v. to suffer in silence; fr. the placing of a bullet between the teeth of wounded soldiers/sailors when undergoing surgery in pre-anaesthesia days *Dickson*.

bite the ice (Valley Girls (qv) use) excl. of dismissal, 'go to hell!' *Pond*.

bitter half n. one's wife.

blab v. 1. spec. to confess; 2. to talk; 3. to inform *Higgins:1*.

blabbermouth n. a gossip, an indiscreet talker *Dunne*.

blab-blab n. a gossip; thus blab-fest: a gathering where those involved devote themselves to talking, esp. to unashamed gossip.

blabs in labs (US campus use) course in linguistics, the 'labs' are language laboratories *Bernbach*.

black n. (abbrev.) blackmail *LL*.

black a. depressed, sullen, irritable *Sillitoe*.

Black 360° a. (US Black use) intensely and specifically Black in personality and consciousness; 360° describes a complete circle *Major*.

black and white n. US police car painted this *R. Newman, 'Jolly Coppers', 1979*.

black ankle n. a person of mixed race; usu. Black, Indian and White (cf: dominicker 2.).

black bagging n. the pudenda of black women, used collectively.

black beauties n. (drug use) strong amphetamine capsules *Green:1*.

Black Belt n. that part of a larger urban area in which the Black community lives; the black ghetto.

black bezer n. a black person's face (cf: beezer).

black bird n. (US Black use) particularly dark-skinned black person *Folb*.

black bomber n. (drug use) strong capsules of amphetamine, coloured black *Green:1*.

Black Bottom n. see: Black Belt.

black dust n. (US Black use) an extremely black-skinned person *Klein*.

black fay n. (US black use) derog. a black considered subservient to whites (cf. ofay).

black gang n. (RN use) stokers and engine-room crew; fr. days of coal-powered ships.

black gungeon n. (drug use) especially potent form of marijuana *Green:1*.

black jack n. (gay slang) a black man's penis.

black joke n. a black woman's pudendum.

Black justice n. (US Black use) Black self-determination; as opposed to white justice which Black radicals experience only as a prejudiced farce *Major*.

black Maria n. **1**: a black prostitute; **2**: a black woman's pudendum.

black meat n. a black woman's pudendum.

black moat n. (drug use) particularly potent variety of marijuana, with notably dark colouring *Green:1*.

black mouth n. a black woman's pudendum.

black on black n. (US Black use) a car with black paintwork and all-black interior upholstery and fittings *Folb*.

black pencil n. black man's penis.

black pope n. (relig. use) the head of the Jesuit order; fr. the colour of their clothes *BBC-1 TV, 1983*.

Black Power dance n. (US Black use) looting; fr. 1960s riots when militant US Blacks looted in the big city ghettoes *Major*.

black rock n. wind-dried pork, the porcine equivalent to beef jerky or biltong.

black sheep v. to take advantage of another person's temporary disability or absence to steal their job.

black taxi n. (Aus. use) an official limousine that ferries government members, etc. to and from houses, appointments and the like *Wilkes*.

Black Town n. see Black Belt.

black widow n. (drug use) black capsule containing amphetamine (cf: black bomber) *Underwood*.

black wings (Hells Angel use) performing cunnilingus on a menstruating black woman *Thompson*. (cf: brown, red wings)

black-leg n. a strike-breaker (cf: scab) *BBC-1 TV, 1984*.

blackleg n. a black man's penis.

blackmun n. the anus; in his novel *Myron* (1974) Gore Vidal responded

to a US Supreme Court decision whereby any local authority can censor any book, play, film, etc., by replacing the 'bad' or 'dirty' words by the surnames of the current Supreme Justices: thus Blackmun, 'Whizzer' White: cunt; Powell: balls; Rehnquist: cock; Father Hill (a 'warrior against smut'): tits; Burger: to fuck.

blackplate n. soul food; a pun on the US restaurant dish, the 'blue plate special'.

blacksmith's shop n. a house of prostitution run by a black madame.

bladder n. newspaper; fr. Ger. *blatt*: newspaper *Runyon:1*.

bladder of lard n. (rhyming sl.) playing card *Jones:J*.

blade n. **1**. any knife *Higgins:1*; **2**. (US Black use) a Cadillac, because it is so 'sharp' (qv) *Folb*.

blag v. (UK criminal use) to steal *Capital Radio 1983*.

blagger n. a thief *Newman:1*.

blah n. pompous, banal, verbosity *Whitcomb*.

blah v. to speak in a blah (qv) manner *Whitcomb*.

blanco n. (US Black use) white person; fr. Sp. *Jones*.

blank n. **1**. (UK prison use) a rejection, esp. of a parole application (cf: knockback) *Obs. 1981*; **2**. (drug use) any powder sold as a narcotic but which is in fact absolutely without effect *Major*.

blank v. to ignore, wipe out, reject *Price:2*.

blanket n. **1**. an overcoat; **2**. a dollar bill (fr. abbr. saddle-blanket).

blanket fever n. the desire to lie in bed rather than get up and go to work.

blanket man n. (US criminal use) an arsonist's accomplice who holds a blanket ready to douse the flames that may have started to burn the person actually setting the fire *Breslin*.

blanket party n. (US prison use) an initiation rite whereby a new prisoner is forcibly smothered in a blanket, then beaten up by his fellows *Folb*.

blanket-ass n. derog. a Native

American Indian (cf: blanket-buck).

blanket-buck n. derog. Native American Indian.

blanny v. to flatter. (cf. blarney).

blared, blare-eyed a. having staring, wild eyes.

blarney n. nonsense, charming but empty chatter; fr. Irish use for traditional 'gift of the gab', a facility which is ensured by kissing the Blarney Stone at Blarney Castle, Eire *Dunne*.

blast n. an uproarious party *Underwood*.

blast v. to smoke marijuana or hashish cigarettes *Selby:1*.

blasted a. 1. (euph.) damned *Rawson*; 2. very drunk or heavily influenced by a given drug *Bernbach*.

blathergab n. gossip, chatterer (cf: blatherskite).

blatherskite n. aka: *bletherskate* a voluble, boastful speaker *Dickens*.

blaze on v. (US Black use) to attack or knock down without warning *Folb*.

blazed a. (drug use) intoxicated by a drug.

blazing a. general intensifier, esp. in 'a blazing row': a vicious argument (cf: flaming).

bleat n. (UK prison use) a petition to the Home Secretary for reduction or repeal of one's sentence; the weak chance this has of success is underlined by the allusion to the sound of a sheep *LL*.

bleed n. (US Black use) a black person (cf: blood) *Folb*.

bleed v. 1. to sweat profusely; 2. to take advantage of.

bleed white v. to submit to excessive extortion; thus draining every drop of money/blood.

bleeder n. a person, with usu. but not invariable derog. implications *Performance*.

bleeding a. exclamatory adjective, intensifier: 'bleeding hell', etc. *Performance*.

bleeding dirt (homosexual use) aka: *the mouse* extorting money from homosexuals *Legman*.

blend v. to marry.

bless one's little cotton socks (cp) general expression of affection.

blew in v. to waste, usu. money.

blighter n. a person, usu. unfortunate or unpleasant; one who 'blights' a situation *Wodehouse:CW*.

Blighty n. England, orig. in Indian Army fr. Hindustani: *bilyati*: foreign; currently used ironically or in military/patriotic context (Falklands war reporting, etc.).

blikkeys n. fake crack (qv) which has been manufactured from flakes of soap powder.

blim n. a small piece of hashish, not really sufficient to make a full-strength three-paper joint (qv) but enough for perhaps a weak one or a single-skin effort. *M Newell*.

blimey! (excl.) denoting surprise or disbelief fr. 'God blind me!' (cf: gor blimey, Gordon Bennett).

blimp n. (necrophile use) a body in intermediate stage of decomposition, at which time the stomach is grossly distended.

blind v. to expose another's ignorance.

blind n. (homosexual use) an uncircumcised penis (cf: near-sighted) *Legman*.

blind a. 1. extremely drunk, often as phr. *blind drunk Farrell*; 2. utterly, completely, ie: *steal them blind Eagles, 'Desperado', 1975*; 3. negative intensifier: *not a blind bit of use*; *a blind word*, etc.

blind Freddy n. (Aus. use) a person of absolute and unassailable incompetence; fr. a blind beggar in the streets of Sydney in the 1920s *Baker*.

blind pig n. an unlicensed drinking house; a speakeasy *Salisbury*.

blind staggers n. extreme drunkenness *Dickson*.

blind twenty n. (bingo use) 20; thus *blind thirty*; *blind forty*, etc. up to *blind ninety*.

blinder n. a hard and exciting sporting encounter; esp. as *to play a blinder*.

blinding a. wonderful, terrific,

perfect, etc. *Cole*.

blindside v. to take by surprise; fr. football use *Higgins:5*.

blinger n. the extreme example of a given type or situation.

blinked out a. malfunctioning, out of order.

blinker n. **1.** a camera *Chandler: Notebk.*; **2.** (US criminal use) a police surveillance helicopter *Folb*.

blinking a. mild perjorative *Wright*.

blip n. a temporary hiatus.

blister n. an offensive person, usu. 'old blister' *Wodehouse:PGM*.

blitz, the n. menstruation.

blitzed a. drunk; fr. Ger. *blitzkrieg*: saturation bombing tactics (cf: bombed) *Pond*.

blob n. the score of 0 in a cricket match *S. Sassoon, 'Diaries', 1983*.

block n. **1.** (UK prison use) the punishment cells *Cole*; **2.** a ban, a rejection (cf: blank) *Norman:2*; **3.** the head; but nearly always in 'knock one's block off' (qv) *Hotten*.

block and tackle n. the male genitalia *Express Magazine 1/92*.

blockbuster n. anything enormous, gigantic; often used of a best-selling novel, film, TV series, etc.

block-buster n. **1.** orig.: the first black family to move into a formerly all-white inner city area; **2.** current: the first white family to move back into an inner city area, driving out the poor minority tenants and starting the process of gentrification.

blocked a. intoxicated on a given drug, usu. cannabis or barbiturates *Keyes*.

blocker n. a hanger-on, one who will not 'get out of the way'.

blocker n. (US criminal use) in a shoplifting team (cf: booster) the member who deliberately acts in a suspicious manner in order to divert attention from the real thief *Breslin*.

bloke n. a person, a man *Performance*.

blood excl. (US black use) a general intensifier (cf: bloody).

blood n. (Black use) (abbrev.) blood brother: term of address to fellow Black; by extn. general term of address (cf: bleed) *Price:2*.

blood and sand n. (usu. male use) menstruation.

blood claat n. (West Indian use) lit. blood cloth, used to wipe away menstrual blood, thus highly derog. description of another person; also used as adj.

blood oath! (Aus. use) expression of agreement *Ready*.

blood wagon n. (skiing use) a stretcher *Barr*.

bloodbath n. (boxing use) the (often dubious) division of a fighter's earnings; his manager is paid the actual cash and the boxer may well feel he has gained too small a share for his efforts *Heller*.

bloody n. (US preppie (qv) use) (abbrev.) bloody Mary; a drink of which the chief constituents are vodka and tomato juice *Bernbach*.

bloody a. a general negative intensifier, esp. in UK and Aus, where it is so widespread as to be termed 'the great Australian adjective'; bloody, like fucking (qv), is often inserted betw. the syllables of other words or phrases, eg: abso-bloody-lutely, not bloody likely, etc.

Bloody Mary n. a menstruating woman; used by a woman of herself, eg. 'I'm Bloody Mary today'.

bloody monthlies n. (usu. male use) menstruation.

bloody-minded a. stubborn, unrelenting, deliberately inconsiderate in pursuing one's own opinions, ideas, etc.

bloomer n. an error, a slip (cf: blooper).

blooming a. (euph.) bloody *Humphries:2*.

blooper n. an embarrassing verbal error, often delivered by a public or authority figure to his own detriment (cf: bloomer) *Rawson*.

blooterer n. scourge, persecutor *Welsh:1*.

blort n. cocaine; fr. 'blow' + 'snort' (qqv) *Safire*.

blot n. (Aus. use) the anus (cf: freckle) *Wilkes*.

blot one's copybook v. to make an error, both practical and behavioural.

blotch n. (mainly school use) blotting paper *G. Willans & R. Searle, 'The Compleet Molesworth', 1959*.

blotto a. drunk *Wright*.

blow n. 1. cocaine; 2. a snort or sniff of cocaine *Milner*.

blow v. 1. to fellate (cf: eat, go down on) *P. Roth, 'Portnoy's Complaint', 1969*; 2. to depart, to walk away *rr*; 3. to ruin, to upset, to destroy, to lose *Higgins:1*; 4. of money: to squander, to waste *Breslin*; 5. (musician use) to play music; orig. Black use, fr. blowing of various wind instruments; 6. (US Black use) to talk enthusiastically and fluently; fr. jazz use: the lyrical playing of an instrument *Seale*; 7. (Aus. use) to boast, to brag *Wilkes*; 8. to smoke marijuana, thus blow dope (qv), blow grass (qv); 9. (US prison use) to escape from prison.

blow! (excl.) go away! *Jones*.

blow a fuse v. to explode with rage; fr. the fault that occurs when a wire is overloaded with electrical current.

blow a raspberry v. to make an obscene noise with one's lips, usu. intended to imply derision; fr. rhyming sl. raspberry tart = fart (qv).

blow ass v. to walk fast, to run off *Folb*.

blow away v. 1. to shoot dead *Himes:1*; 2. to impress, to bowl over *Bernbach*.

blow Black v. (US Black use) to talk about and/or initiate Black activism, social change, revolution and any similar form of racial advancement (cf: blow great guns) *Folb*.

blow domes v. amaze, astound (cf: blow one's mind).

blow down one's ear v. aka: *blow in one's ear*: to whisper *Powis*.

blow fire v. (US Black use) to do anything well and keenly, esp. dancing, musicianship *Folb*.

blow great guns v. 1. to blow a

violent storm; 2. (by extension) to make a great fuss about something.

blow heavy v. (US Black use) to talk seriously of contextually vital matter (cf: blow Black) *Folb*.

blow in v. to arrive unexpectedly and casually; fr. image of being wafted by a chance breeze.

blow it! excl. of annoyance; euph. for a variety of 'stronger' synonyms, *fuck it, bugger it*, etc. *Manser*.

blow it out your ass! general excl. of derision, contempt or dismissal of the previous speaker's statement *Dunne*.

blow me down! excl. of surprise; fr. you could have blown/knocked me down with a feather (qv) *Manser*.

blow off n. (US teen. use) anything considered exceptionally easy *Pond*.

blow off steam v. aka: *let off steam* to release one's (pent-up) emotions, thus, to become angry or noisy and excited; fr. railway use (cf: blow one's stack).

blow one away v. (teen. use) to astound, to amaze, etc. *Pond*.

blow one out v. 1. to exhaust; 2. to shock; 3. for one of a couple to abandon the relationship *'Tucker's Luck', BBC-2 TV, 1983*.

blow one's cookies v. 1. to vomit; 'cookies' = food consumed *Junker*; 2. to fellate; 'cookies' = male genitals.

blow one's cool v. to lose control, to freak out (qv) *Hoffman:a*.

blow one's doughnuts v. (US campus use) to vomit *Bernbach*.

blow one's gasket v. see: blow one's top; fr. automobile imagery *Neaman & Silver*.

blow one's glass v. to perform fellatio on a man *Dunne*.

blow one's groceries v. (US campus use) to vomit *Bernbach*.

blow one's horn v. to break wind.

blow one's lunch v. to vomit *Junker*.

blow one's mind v. 1. spec. to become intoxicated with a given drug or drugs; 2. to surprise, to amaze *Uneeda Comix*.

blow one's nose v. to inform *Schulberg*.

blow one's own trumpet v. to boast unashamedly.

blow one's roof v. 1. (drug use) to smoke marijuana or cannabis (cf: blow); 2. to act hysterically, to act irrationally (cf: blow one's stack).

blow one's shoes v. to lose control, to lose one's composure.

blow one's stack v. to lose control, to lose one's temper; fr. railroad use (cf: blow one's top) *Schulberg*.

blow one's top v. to lose one's temper; to lose one's sanity *Runyon:1*.

blow out v. 1. to reject, to break a promise, neglect a rendezvous, etc.; 2. (UK police use) for a case, a theory, an accusation to fall through *Laurie*.

blow out of v. to leave, to depart *Gruber*.

blow out one's lamp, blow out one's light v. to murder, to kill (cf: put one's lights out).

blow past v. to deceive, to fool, to confuse *Higgins:5*.

blow smoke up one's ass v. to confuse, to tell lies *Higgins:1*.

blow some tunes v. (US Black use) to perform cunnilingus *Folb*.

blow stick n. penis *Jay & Young*.

blow the gaff v. to reveal a secret, esp. a hoax or deception *Humphries*.

blow the skin flute v. to fellate *Legman*.

blow the whistle on v. to inform against someone; the whistle summons the police *Powis*.

blow through v. (UK police use) to phone through information, fr. blower *Laurie*.

blow up v. 1. to break down, both of people (usu. athletes) animals (racehorses, greyhounds) and machinery *Wodehouse:AAG*; 2. to lose control, to lose patience, to become enraged *rr*.

blow your copper v. (US prison use) to lose good conduct credits *Chandler: Notebk*.

blow Z's v. to snore.

blowed (euph.) damned; usu. as in I'll be blowed! (qv) *Rawson*.

blower n. 1. telephone; fr. earlier 'speaking tubes' down which one had to blow to alert the other person *Caron*; 2. (bookmaker use) the betting shop public address system that broadcasts races, odds and results; 3. a shotgun (cf: blowpipe).

blowfly n. see: blowhard.

blowhard n. a boaster; a loud and egocentric talker *White*.

blow-job n. fellatio (cf: head) *Price:2*.

blown out a. shocked, exhausted, overcome *Price:2*.

blown up a. drunk

blowout n. a binge of eating, drinking and debauchery *Uris*.

blowpipe n. a rifle (cf: blower 3.).

blowser n. a glue sniffer; thus blowsing: glue sniffing.

blow-up n. a quarrel, an argument.

blub v. to cry, to burst into tears; usu. juv. use *BBC Radio 3, 1983*.

bludge v. (Aus. use) to impose on, to scrounge *Humphries*.

bludger n. (Aus. use) orig. a pimp; latterly a scrounger, a beggar, one who leeches on others for his subsistence *Ready*.

blue n. 1. (US Black use) a dark-complexioned black person (cf: blueskin: a half-caste, 18/19th C.) *Klein*; 2. (Aus. use) a brawl, a quarrel; 3. (Aus. use) a blunder, a mistake *Wilkes*.

blue a. 1. pornographic; thus *blue movie*, etc. *Higgins:5*; 2. depressed, unhappy, dissatisfied.

blue and white n. US police car, painted in those colours (as in New York) (cf: black and white).

blue angel n. (drug use) amytal barbiturate, which is packaged in blue capsules *Green:1*.

blue around the gills a. feeling and looking sick, esp. from an excess of alcohol *Dickson*.

blue balls a feeling of intense sexual frustration *Higgins:1*.

blue chips n. cast-iron, undeniable facts; fr. Stock Exchange use: ultimately dependable securities *PT*.

blue dangers n. (US criminal use) marked police cars (when painted blue, as in New York), blue uniformed police *Shulman*.

blue feature n. (US milit. use) any indication of water, coloured blue, on a map *Del Vecchio*.

blue funk n. abject terror, utter cowardice.

blue goose v. (US black use) to engage in sexual affairs.

blue lights n. (US bl.) motorcar police *Ice T:2*.

blue meanies n. (hippie use) the establishment in general and the police (who wear blue) in particular; a short-lived perjorative, stemming fr. *Yellow Submarine*, an animated film featuring The Beatles (1968) in which the 'baddies' were so named.

blue noses n. a puritan, a killjoy; orig. an aristocrat (who had 'blue blood'), blue noses passed the repressive 'blue laws' that restricted the morals of many states.

blue papers n. (UK prison use) the papers that signify the imminent release of a prisoner serving a life sentence *LL*.

blue pencil v. to censor, to edit by cutting; fr. trad. colour of the editor's pencil.

blue vein n. an erection; fr. that vein that runs up the penis *Newman:3*.

blue-eyed soul n. (musical use) a style of popular music in which white performers performed soul songs, usually the province of Black performers; most popular in 1960s *Capital Radio 1983*.

blue-eyed soul brother/sister n. (US Black use) any white who is accepted as genuinely friendly towards Blacks *Folb*.

blues n. 1. (Aus. use) the police; fr. their uniforms *Humphries*; 2. amphetamines; fr. 'Purple Hearts', a popular variety *c*1965; 3. (orig. Black but now general use) misery, depression, unhappiness, etc.; 4. (West Indians use) a shebeen, an illegal drinking club or a party where drink is sold without a licence *Powis*.

bluey n. 1. (UK criminal use) lead;

2. (orig. Aus.) a red-headed person *Powis*.

bluff n. (lesbian use) a female homosexual who can alternate between active/passive roles; fr. butch and fluff (qqv) *Stanley*.

blunt n. a cannabis / marijuana joint made of buds rolled in a tobacco leaf, taken from the wrapper of a Phillies Blunt cigar; thus adv. 2. blunted: intoxicated with cannabis.

blunt n. (drug use) any drug available in a blunt-ended capsule.

BMOC (acro.) Big Man On Campus *Junker*.

BMW abbr. of 'black man's wheels', the popular BMW motorcar; the actual name is Bayerische Motor Werke.

BO juice (US campus use) deodorant; fr. body odour *Underwood*.

boarding house n. a prison (fr. the old nickname for New York City's Tombs prison).

boar's nest n. 1. anywhere, orig. a logging or mining camp, where only men live or only men are admitted; 2. an untidy room or house.

boasie a. (Jamaican) proud, boastful, showy; comb. of English 'boastful' and Yoruba *bosi* 'proud and ostentatious' *Thelwell*.

boat n. (rhyming sl.) boat-race = face *Norman:3*.

boat n. (US Black use) the vagina *Klein*.

bob a nob n. one shilling each; used when estimating the cost of meals, outings, tickets, etc.

bob and weave v. to avoid direct action, either confrontation, explanation, aggression, etc.; fr. boxing use *PT*.

Bob Hope n. cannabis; fr. rhy. sl. = dope.

bob up v. to appear (unexpectedly) *Wodehouse:GB*.

bobbish a. healthy, in good spirits, well set up, cheery *Wodehouse:AAG*.

bobbitt v. to sever the penis, usu. of one's husband or boyfriend, in retribution for some unacceptable behaviour, typically physical abuse or adultery.

bobbles n. (US Black use) gaudy, flashy, ostentatious jewellery; fr. 'baubles' *Klein*.

bobby n. a British policeman; fr. Sir Robert Peel who established the force in 19th C. *Mandelkau*.

bobby dazzler n. anything or person seen as exceptional, wonderful.

bobby soxer n. teenage US girl, wearing (short) bobby-socks; orig. describing the fans of Frank Sinatra in 1940s and thus girls of late 1940s, 1950s who enjoyed pop music and its ancillary pleasures.

bobkhes n. fr. Yiddish: 'goat droppings'; an absurd idea, an insulting sum, price or proposition, esp. in show business use *Rosten*.

Bob's your uncle (cp) everything will be absolutely fine; there'll be no worries; fr. the apparently nepotistic choice by Tory leader Robert Cecil of his nephew Arthur Balfour as Chief Secretary for Ireland in 1900, a decision that was both surprising and unpopular *A. J. Langguth, 'Saki', 1981*.

Boche n. (derog.) German *BvdB*.

bod n. (abbrev.) body *McBain:1*.

bod a. (US campus use) outstanding, exceptional *Underwood*.

bodacious a. a general intensifier, usu. defined as extreme, arrant, phenomenal. Although the term gained a new lease of fashionable life in the early 1990s, it dates back to US dial. c.1845, when it was presumed to be a mix of bold + audacious. The variation boldacious can be found in Devonian dial. 19th C.

bodger a. aka: *bodgie*: second-rate, worthless; fr. SE *bodge*: to mend badly, to patch up *Baker*.

bodgie n. (Aus. use) male equivalent to UK *teddy boy*; fr. bodger (qv) *Ready*.

body n. (UK police use) a person, esp. a suspect or wanted criminal *Newman:2*.

body and soul lashing n. (nautical use) a piece of rope tied around a sailor's oil-skins to provide a grip for rescuers if he fell overboard; also, on sailing ships, extra binding to keep the wind out of one's clothes *Channel 4 TV 1983*.

body lover n. a homosexual who prefers rubbing and fondling a body than anal penetration or fellatio *Legman*.

body queen n. (homosexual use) one who primarily looks for partners who specialize in body-building *Stanley* .

body-snatching (journalistic use) getting hold of a major source for an important story and holding on to them, usually in a luxury flat or five-star hotel, in order to get the story from them and ensure that no other paper can track them down (cf: baby-sitting) *'World In Action', Granada TV, 1983*.

BOF abbr. boring old fart.

boff n. a laugh, a joke; usu. show business use *Variety: passim*.

boff v. **1.** to copulate *'Hill Street Blues', Thames TV, 1983*; **2.** to hit, to assault *Runyon:1*.

boffin n. **1.** any form of scientific expert; **2.** spec. Scotland Yard fingerprint expert *Neaman & Silver*.

boffo superb, magnificent, excellent; usu. show business use *Goldman*.

boffola n. a laugh, esp. a loud 'belly laugh'; usu. show business use (cf: boff) *Variety: passim*.

bog n. lavatory (cf: dike) *Sharpe:1*.

bog v. to wet the end of a cigarette while smoking it.

bog bamboo n. the penis.

bog in v. (Aus. use) **1.** to start a task enthusiastically; **2.** to eat heartily; **3.** not to stand on any ceremony *Wilkes*.

bog off v. to go away; usually as a dismissive excl.: 'Bog off!'.

bogart v. to hold on to a marijuana joint (qv) for longer than one's companions feel is fair; allegedly from the greediness in this area ascribed to the film star Humphrey Bogart *'Easy Rider', directed P. Fonda*,

D. Hopper, 1969.

bogblocker n. a general term to denote anything particularly unpleasant; the image is of some obstruction, probably faecal, blocking a bog (or lavatory).

bogbrush n. a cropped, spiky haircut; supposedly resembling a lavatory brush.

bogey n. aka: *bogie* policeman, detective *Norman:2.*

boghopper n. a peasant, an unsophisticated rural person (cf: bogtrotter).

bogroll n. lavatory paper.

bogtrotter n. (derog.) Irish person *BvdB.*

bogue n. (drug use) the sickness that follows an addict's withdrawal from regular narcotic use *Algren.*

bogue a. (US teen. use) (abbrev.) bogus; fake, uncool (qv) *Sculatti.*

bogus a. a general term of disapproval: unpleasant, undesirable, untrustworthy.

boho n. (abbrev.) bohemian, eccentric *Wolfe:2.*

bohunk n. (derog.) a Slav; thus an oafish, dull, if muscular person (cf: honkie) *BvdB.*

bohunkus, bohunky n. the buttocks.

boil off the stomach v. to vomit copiously.

boiled a. drunk *Dickson.*

boiler n. an old woman, often 'old boiler', without any remaining sexual appeal; fr. the old tough hens only used for boiling (cf: chick) *Powis.*

boilermaker n. beer with a whiskey chaser; the traditional US workingman's drink. *W Kennedy 'Legs'.*

boilerplate n. standard practice; used by lawyers – the regular clauses in any contract – or media – the basic syndicated wire service stories used throughout the US newspaper system *Vidal.*

boiling out n. a scolding, a telling-off.

boilover n. (Aus. use) in sport, spec. horse-racing, an upset – the failure of a favourite to win *Wilkes.*

boing-boing n. tourist; implying the twanging of a rubberneck (qv) *Price:3.*

boink n. v. see: bonk *Morgan.*

boko n. the nose *Topper (comic) passim.*

bold as brass a. arrogant, impudent, outspoken, shameless.

boldacious a. (US Black use) excessive behaviour – over-aggressive, arrogant, unrestrained, etc. – that is inappropriate for a given situation; fr. SE *bodacious Klein.*

bollixed up ruined, messed up, performed very badly; US sp. of UK *bollocksed up Rawson.*

bollock n. (UK 'society' use) ball (hunt, charity, etc.); fr. pun on the mild obscenity *Barr.*

bollock naked aka: *stark bollock naked*: totally naked, and thus revealing one's genitals.

bollocking n. a severe telling off *Powis.*

bollocko a. naked, fr. bollock naked (qv) *Powis.*

bollocks! excl: rubbish, nonsense.

bollocksed up UK version of US bollixed up (qv).

bolshie a. uncooperative, subversive, Left-wing; fr. Russian Bolsheviks.

BOLTOP acro. *better on lips than on paper* (written over an X, meaning a kiss) (cf: NORWICH, SWALK) *Partridge:5.*

bomb n. (theatrical use) **1.** (UK) a major success; **2.** (US) a disaster, a flop *Goldman;* **3.** (Aus. use) a dilapidated, run-down old car *Wilkes.*

bomb n. drug use: see bomber *Larner.*

bomb off v.i. to fail to work, esp. of a computer program *Underwood.*

bombed a. **1.** drunk *Higgins:1;* **2.** intoxicated by a given drug *Powis.*

bomber n. (drug use) a very large and potent cannabis joint (qv) *Major.*

bomber n. (abbrev.) black bomber, a variety of amphetamine in a black capsule *Green:1.*

bombosity n. the buttocks.

bombshell n. a shock, a surprise, usu. unpleasant; thus *drop a bombshell*: to deliver such a shock.

bonaroo (US prison use) fr. Fr. 'bon' = good *Chandler: Notebk.*

bonce n. head; created by 19th-C. schoolboy who took word fr. *bonce*: a large marble *Performance*.

bonds n. (pimp use) the clothes with which a pimp bedecks his working girls; and, since his money has paid for them, 'binds' the girls to him *Neaman & Silver*.

bone n. 1. $1.00 *Himes:1*; 2. the erect penis.

bone v. to drive fast *Ice T:3*.

bone carrier n. a gossip, a rumour-monger.

bone down v. to have sexual intercourse.

bone gobbler n. one who performs oral sex.

bone phone n. the penis.

bone up (on) v. to learn, to revise.

boned hit hard on the head; from the hard skull that is battered *Powis*.

bonehead n. fool, dullard, idiot *Farrell*.

boner n. 1. an erection (cf: hard-on) *Price:2*; 2. (school use) a mistake.

bones n. (derog.) a Black person.

bones n. 1. dice; esp. in 'roll them bones!'; fr. material originally used in making dice *Hotten*; 2. (US college use) 1. marijuana cigarettes (cf: joint); 2. nickname for Yale U. ultra-secret, ultra-Establishment society 'Skull & Bones' (cf: spook) *Bernbach*.

bone-shaker n. a decrepit vehicle with, *inter alia*, inadequate springs, thus jolting its passengers.

boneyard n. a cemetery *Chandler:LG*.

bong n. a bowl-shaped pipe used for smoking marijuana or hashish *Cypress Hill*, 'Black Sunday' (1993).

bongo lips n. (derog.) a Black person (cf: boot lips).

bonified (US Black use) competent, qualified, the right man for job; fr. Fr. *bon* = good *Klein*.

bonk n. v. sexual intercouse; to have sexual intercourse (cf: screw and other 'sex as carpentry' synonyms).

bonkers stupid, insane, eccentric

Capital Radio 1983.

bonzer a. good, thus extremely, very *Humphries*.

boo n. marijuana (cf: bu) *Price:2*.

boob n. 1. a fool, an idiot; fr. *booby* 'Yellow Submarine', film 1968; 2. (UK criminal use) a prison *Obs. 1981*.

boob v. to make a mistake, to blunder.

boob play n. a foolish action, an error, a blunder (cf: boob) *rr*.

boo-boo n. poss. fr. Yiddish *bulba* 'potato': a blunder, usu. embarrassing *Rosten*.

booboos n. (derog.) a Black person.

boobs n. breasts; fr. obsolete *bubbies Higgins:1*.

boob-tube n. television; fr. the alleged mental state of regular watchers *Hoffman:a*.

booby wagon n. (cf: black maria 1.).

booby-hatch n. aka: *booby hutch*: mental hospital; the first poss. fr. Coney Hatch, the second poss. fr. mad March hares.

boocoo / bocoo a. very much, extremely; used as a general intensifier; fr. Fr. 'beaucoup' = very much and imported to US by returning US soldiers who picked it up from the Francophone Vietnamese *Morgan*.

boocoodles n. many, a good deal (cf: boocoo).

boodle n. money *L. Charteris 'The Saint' books: passim*.

boodle bag n. a purse.

booferbox n. large radio/tape recorder/stereo particularly popular among ghetto youths (cf: Third World briefcase, ghetto blaster) *C. Clarke*.

boofhead n. fool, idiot, simpleton *Baker*.

boog a. (derog.) Black, Negro (cf: boogie) *Algren*.

boogaloo v. to dance; orig. Black use *Hoffman:a*.

boogie n. (derog.) Black *Price:1*.

boogie v. 1. spec. to dance (cf: boogaloo); 2. to enjoy oneself, have a party, a good time *Price:1*.

boogie box n. see ghetto blaster, wog box.

boogie-woogie v. (US Black use) to leave, to depart *Klein*.

boojie n. (US Black use) (derog.) a bourgeois Black; fr. bourgeois *Price:3*.

book n. 1. a magazine, a periodical; mainly illiterate use; the bound variety are presumably an unknown quantity *Ian Dury, 'Razzle'*; 2. (Black pimp use) a supply of names and addresses of clients (cf: working from a book) *Milner*.

Book n. the oral tradition that forms the basis of Black pimping; a good deal has been encapsulated in *'Pimp: The Story of My Life'* by Iceberg Slim, 1967 *Milner*.

book v. 1. to arrest, thus write down in a police charge book *Capital Radio 1983*; 2. to note *Newman:1*; 3. (abbrev.) bookmaking *Higgins:3*.

book it v. (US campus use) to study assiduously *Underwood*.

book the joint v. (US teen. use) to look over a place, to check it out (qv) *Pond*.

book up v. (US campus use) to study hard (cf: book it) *Underwood*.

booked a. fatally ill.

bookful n. (US cant) a life sentence (cf: do the book, — and cover).

bookie n. (abbrev.) bookmaker *Performance*.

boola-boola (US use) a. college chauvinism; fr. college sports cheer 'boola-boola' *Price:3*.

boolhipper n. (US Black use) a leather coat *Major*.

boom box n. see ghetto blaster, wog box *Morgan*.

boom-boom n. (US juv. use) excrement *Neaman & Silver*.

boomer n. 1. (Aus. use) anything considered exceptionally large or strong; fr. orig. use: a large kangaroo *Wilkes*; 2. (US use) a transient worker, a migrant; thus *boomer reporter*: a journalist who works on papers all over the country, never keeping one job for too long *Gruber*.

boondock v. (US campus use) to neck, to park (qv) (cf. boonies, 2.).

boondoggle n. a waste, of time, of money, of energy; esp. used by US govt. for a project that is considered to waste tax dollars *Green:2*.

boong n. (derog. Aus. use) Aborigine *Humphries:2*.

boonie n. a peasant, a country person; fr. *boondocks*: USMC use for hard rural areas *Price:2*.

boonie hat n. (US milit. use) soft hat worn by troops *Del Vecchio*.

boonie rat n. (US milit. use) an infantryman, a foot soldier, who fights and patrols through the jungles, swamps, etc. *Del Vecchio*.

boonies n. (abbrev. boondocks) 1. (US milit. use) the field, the bush, the jungle; anywhere the troops operate that is not designated a firebase, a basecamp or occupied by civilians; fr. Tagalog *bundok*: mountain *Del Vecchio*; 2. (US campus use) rural areas, the countryside – not necessarily rough or unpleasant *Underwood*.

boopety a. arrogant, self-important.

boose n. the mouth.

boost v. to steal from large stores; fr. boost = raising up, which the booster (qv) does with the goods *Breslin*.

booster n. something exceptional of its type (cf: buster).

booster n. a shoplifter on a large and professional scale *Grogan*.

boot n. 1. (US milit. use) any new recruit in the US armed forces; thus *boot camp*: basic training camp; *boot second lieutenant*: newly commissioned 2nd Lieut., etc.; fr. leggings worn by recruits to USN during training *Del Vecchio*; 2. (US Black use) a fellow black (usu. derog.); poss. fr. black boots? *Jones*; 3. dismissal from a job; usu. as 'get the boot'.

boot v. (US campus use) to vomit *Bernbach*.

boot around v. to kick, usu. in a fight *Runyon*.

boot lip n. (derog.) a Black person (cf: bongo lips).

boot out v. to throw out, eject *Price:2*.

bootchkey, butchski n. a Czech immigrant (cf: chesky) (fr. Czech *pockej*: wait, used by Czech youngsters while playing games and thus adopted as generic by early Eastern European immigrants to US).

booted (US campus use) 1. expelled; 2. vomited *Bernbach*.

boot-hill two-step n. diahorrea. (fr. SE boot-heel + two-step).

bootlicker n. a cowardly, obsequious person; one who curries favour, who sucks up (qv) **Seale**.

booty n. (US Black use) 1. the female; 2. spec. the vagina *Folb*.

booty bandit n. (derog.) a homosexual male.

booty-buffer n. 1. sodomite; 2. homosexual *Kurious: A Constipated Monkey (1994)*.

booze n.v. drink; to drink.

booze artist n. a drunkard.

booze belly n. a fat stomach, created by excessive drinking (cf: beer gut).

boozed a. drunk *Dickson*.

boozed up a. drunk *Dickson*.

boozer n. a public house *Powis*.

booze-up n. a drinking session *Tidy*.

bop n. 1. a dance; 2. (US Black use) foolish talk, prattle (cf: bebopper) *Folb*.

bop v. 1. to fight *Salisbury*; 2. hit; 3. to walk in a carefree, bouncy way *Price:2*; 4. to have sexual intercourse *Morgan*.

bop around v. to keep moving, to wander about rather than stay put.

bop one's baloney v. to masturbate (cf: beat one's meat, bash one's bishop, etc.) *Morgan*.

bop out v. to faint.

bo-peep n. (rhyming sl.) sleep; fr. the nursery rhyme character who lost her sheep while sleeping *Wright*.

bopper n. (abbrev.) teenybopper (qv) *Farren*.

boppers n. (US campus use) shoes *Underwood*.

bopping club a street gang who have regular fights with opponents *Salisbury*.

bopping gang n. street gang who are active fighters (cf: bopping club) *Jones*.

boracic a. (rhyming sl.) boracic lint = skint = out of funds *Payne*.

borax n. (US use) rubbish, lies, exaggeration; fr. cheap and shoddy material peddled by immigrant Jews.

borders n. (drug use) non-proprietory capsules of barbiturate powder sold on the black market and with inference of having been made up on the US/Mexico border *Folb*.

bore stiff v. to bore completely; stiff = corpse-like.

bore the pants off v. to bore completely and totally.

born with burnt feet phr. illegitimate (cf: bred in the ditch, have calluses on one's feet).

borrachio, borracho a. n. a drunkard; thus a. drunk (fr. Sp. *borracho*: a drunkard, drunk).

borrow v. (UK police use) to arrest; a suspect is 'borrowed' from his family and friends (cf: claim) *Laurie*.

Borscht Belt n. (show business use) a circuit of predominantly Jewish hotels in the Catskill Mts, New York State; the musicians and comedians who perform there have named them for the favourite Jewish/Russian beetroot soup *Goldman*.

bosh n. nonsense, rubbish; Turkish wd. = worthless *Hotten*.

bosom friend n. a pack of money kept for security inside her brassiere by a woman while she is travelling.

boss a. excellent, wonderful *Gothic Blimp Works no.4*.

Boss Charley n. (US Black use) the white, esp. those in authority *Bruce:2* (cf Mr Charlie).

boss dog n. an important person, or one who poses as such (cf: big dog).

boss player n. (Black pimp use) a thoroughly experienced, professional, worldly-wise pimp who may even transcend pimping for superior occupations; can be applied to any admirable figure outside the pimp milieu *Milner*.

boss trick n. good customer *Maledicta*

(cf: boss; trick).

boss-eyed a. squinting.

boss-lady, boss-woman n. a wife who dominates her husband (cf: boss-man).

bossy-barefoot n. one who is dedicated to telling others what to do.

bot v. (Aus. use) to scrounge; thus *on the bot*: scrounging *Wilkes*.

bother n. trouble, difficulties; thus *in bother Laurie*.

botheration! mild exclamation of annoyance that precludes anything more lurid and thus taboo *Rawson*.

bottie n. (nursery use) the bottom, the buttocks.

bottle n. courage, bravery *Griffiths*.

bottle v. to collect money from a busker's audience.

bottle and glass n. (rhyming sl.) = arse, the buttocks *Cole*.

bottle baby n. an alcoholic tramp whose life has destroyed his sanity and reduced his mental age to that of an infant *Schulberg*.

bottle blonde n. one whose blonde hair is only dyed and comes not from nature but from a bottle *London Weekend Television 1983*.

bottle it v. see: bottle out *Robins:1*.

bottle out v. to be a coward, to run away, to back down from a challenge; to lose one's bottle (qv) *Griffiths*.

bottler n. 1. (UK use) a coward, someone who bottles out (qv); 2. (Aus. use) anyone outstanding, either in a positive or negative manner, tho' usu. congratulatory.

bottom burp n. a fart; generally a children's usage, but popularized on BBC-TV's *The Young Ones*.

bottom drawer n. wherever an engaged girl starts collecting the necessities of her trousseau.

bottom line n. the end result, the final assessment; fr. Yid. *di untershte sture* to denote the final profit/loss figure on an account *Vidal*.

bottom man n. the submissive partner in a homosexual sado-masochist couple *Jay & Young*.

bottom woman n. (Black pimp use) the most reliable and experienced of a pimp's stable of prostitutes *Shulman*.

bottoms n. (US Black use) the least pleasant, the poorest part of a given ghetto or inner-city area *Klein*.

bottoms up! a popular toast before drinking; the bottoms are those of the glasses as the drinks are emptied into the drinkers' mouths.

bought it killed, esp. in battle; an abbrev. of 'bought the farm' *Sharpe:1*.

bougie a. (abbrev.) bourgeois: taking on the attitudes and lifestyle of the middle classes (cf: boojie) *Price:2*.

boulevard boy n. a Los Angeles rent-boy (qv) who works Sunset or Hollywood Boulevard *Maledicta 9*.

bounce n. 1. (US criminal use) arrest and subsequent trial *Dunne*; 2. (UK criminal use) fiddling and dishonest practice – adjusting invoices, stealing stock, etc. – by retail shop employees *Powis*.

bounce v. 1. to pay a cheque, knowing that one has insufficient funds in one's bank account; for the bank to refuse to honour that cheque, marking it 'return to drawer'; 2. to throw out; of a party, a place of entertainment, etc.; 3. to dismiss from a job *Thompson:J*.

bouncer n. a large, tough man employed to keep order in given premises – often a pub, club, concert hall, etc. (cf: bounce v. 2) *Powis*.

Bouncing Betty (US milit. use) a mine that springs a metre in the air prior to exploding; also known as *old step and a half* from the distance a soldier can cover between triggering the mine and being killed by it *O'Brien*.

bounty bar n. the UK version of the US Uncle Tom (qv); a black man or woman who is black on the outside but white inside.

bourbon a. (US teen. use) hazy, spaced out (qv), unable to focus mentally *Sculatti*.

bovver n. fr. Cockney pron. bother; fighting, disturbance, esp. that caused by skinhead youths (cf: aggro) *Robins:1*.

bovver boots n. high-laced boots

preferred as footwear by skinhead youths; usu. merchandised under the brandname 'Dr Martins'.

bow and arrow n. **1.** (rhyming sl.) sparrow *Jones:J.*; **2.** derog. a Native American Indian.

bowel off v. to have an attack of diahorrea.

bowl n. (drug use) a pipe used for smoking marijuana *Del Vecchio*; **2.** derog. a Native American Indian.

bowlegged a. (US prison use) concurrent, referring to a sentence (cf:wild) *Morgan.*

bowler-hatted a. retired from active service and given a desk job in Whitehall *Green:2.*

bowsered a. drunk *Dickson.*

bow-wow n. juv. or facetious use: a dog.

box n. **1.** the vagina *Keyes*; **2.** the penis *Stanley*; **3.** (US prison use) a safe *Chandler: Notebk.*; **4.** a guitar *Powis*; **5.** television, fr. goggle box (qv) *Powis*; **6.** tape deck; fr. box = guitar *Underwood.*

box cars (gambling use) the point of twelve in craps dice *Chandler:Notebk.*

box clever v. to carry out any enterprise smartly and efficiently; fr. boxing use.

box lunch n. cunnilingus (cf: box 1) *Keyes.*

boxcar n. **1.** a large foot; **2.** a large, clumsy person.

boxed a. drunk *Dickson.*

boy n. (homosexual use) a male prostitute *Legman.*

boy n. **1.** champagne; allegedly fr. Edward VII's habit of merely saying 'Boy!' to an attendant page who automatically brought him a glass of that wine *A. Binstead, 'Pitcher in Paradise', 1903*; **2.** (drug use) heroin (cf: girl) *Green:1.*

boy in the boat n. (lesbian use) the clitoris *Maledicta.*

boy racer n. a daredevil young car driver; the term implies disdain for such puerile antics.

boy-ass n. a boy who exists simply as a sex object for his homosexual partners

Legman.

boyo term of address, usu. Irish or (cliché) Welsh.

boysie n. general term of address to a male; S. London use *BBC-1 TV series 'Only Fools & Horses' passim.*

Boystown n. (homosexual use) the predominantly gay neighbourhood in West Hollywood (cf: Swish Alps) *White.*

boystown sound music popular in gay discos *K. Wilson.*

bozo n. **1.** fool, idiot *San Francisco Comic Book no.2*; **2.** tough, a thug *Farrell.*

brace and bits n. (US rhyming sl.) female breasts, plus pun on brace = pair *Neaman & Silver.*

brace of shakes at once, immediately, usu. *in a . . .*

bracelets n. (UK criminal use) handcuffs *LL.*

bracer n. a quick drink, intended to brace up the drinker prior to what may be a difficult undertaking *Southern & Hoffenberg.*

brackers a. out of cash, impoverished; an abbrev. of the rhy. sl. boracic (qv).

brag the potatoes v. to say grace before a meal (cf: talk to one's plate).

brahma a. anything good, enjoyable, attractive; fr. Hindu deity and Indian Army use *Dury.*

Brahms and Liszt n. (rhyming sl.) = pissed = drunk *name of wine bar in Covent Garden, London.*

brainchild n. an idea, an inspiration.

brains n. (UK police use) the CID; usu. ironic *Powis.*

bran up v. eat.

brand X n. (US Black use) marijuana *Folb.*

brannigan n. **1.** a (drunken) spree; **2.** a fight (cf: donnybrook).

brass n. **1.** money; esp. Northern UK use: 'where there's muck there's brass' and similar homilies *Thames TV series 1983*; **2.** audacity, gall, cheek; **3.** a prostitute; fr. rhyming sl. *brass nail* = tail (qv) *Performance*; **4.** (abbrev.) brasshat (qv).

brass a. out of cash, impoverished; the

'a' is short since it is an abbrev. of the rhy. sl. boracic, pron. brassic.

brass balls n. anything severely challenging, esp. in a 'masculine' context *Powis*.

brass monkey weather extremely cold temperature; fr. cp 'cold enough to freeze the balls off a brass monkey' *Whitcomb*.

brass tacks n. (rhyming sl.) facts; usu. in 'let's get down to brass tacks' and as such almost SE.

brass up v. to hand over money (cf: brass).

brassed off a. irritated, fed up, annoyed *LL*.

brasshats n. senior officers – both police and milit. use *Newman:1*.

brassy a. of a woman: showy, flashy, ostentatious; implies a superficial bright, hardness, but also possible prostitution (cf: brass 3).

brat pack n. the original brat pack were the youthful Hollywood up-and-comers of the mid-1980s; the term is now applicable to any selection of successful young hopefuls – novelists, chefs, black success stories ('black pack') whatever. Taken presumably from Hollywood's Holmby Hills Rat Pack, a coterie of movie stars and singers led by Humphrey Bogart in the Fifties. *Green:3*.

bread n. **1.** money fr. Yiddish *broyt Price:2*; **2.** (derog.) a Black person.

bread and bread don't make a sandwich phr. the reply given by one effeminate gay man when partnered with another; a parallel phrase is 'I'm a pouf, not a lesbian.'

bread and butter n. **1.** (rhyming sl.) gutter *Jones:J*; **2.** one's basic income and the work that provides it *Bruce:2*.

bread and butter column (journalistic use) a column fuelled in the main by press agent handouts and similar varieties of free publicity for those who send it to the writer; such a column harms no one, puffs a great many and keeps the writer off the breadline *Bruce:2*.

bread and butter letter n. a letter of thanks sent to one's hostess shortly after having enjoyed her hospitality.

bread and cheese v. (rhyming sl.) sneeze *Jones:J*.

bread and lard a. (rhyming sl.) hard *Franklyn*.

bread and skip n. an inadequate meal: eg. 'bread and molasses, and skip the molasses' (cf: bread and with it).

bread and with it n. a light meal: eg. 'a loaf of bread and (something else) with it' (cf: bread and skip).

bread hooks n. the hands (cf: biscuit hooks, lunch hooks).

bread is not done, one's phr. to describe one who is considered mentally deficient (cf: half-baked).

breadbasket n. the stomach, fr. boxing use *Wright*.

bread-cutter, bread-grinder n. a tooth.

breadhead n. an individual who is interested primarily in acquiring money; coined during the anti-money Sixties; fr. bread + head (qqv).

break n. an escape from prison *Waits*.

break v. (journalist use) to happen; a story 'breaks'.

break a leg! (theatrical use) trad. term of encouragement to a fellow actor prior to their going on stage; the direct 'good luck' is paradoxically considered very bad luck *Green:2*.

break an ankle v. (euph.) to become pregnant out of wedlock; orig. 18/19th C. UK, now survives mainly in US *rawson*.

break down v. (US Black use) to explain; to put the listener right *Folb*.

break it down v. (Aus. use) to give in, to desist *Wilkes*.

break it off v. (US Black use) to have sexual intercourse.

break it up! general admonition to move on, break up a meeting – of several people or a couple.

break one's arm v. to boast.

break one's ass v. **1.** to beat up someone; **2.** to hurt oneself; **3.** to work very hard *Price:2*.

break one's balls v. to attack, to

complain, to nag; thus *ball-breaker*: the 'castrating female' who nags constantly and undermines the male concerned *Bruce:2*.

break one's chops v. **1.** to talk incessantly; **2.** to make a great fuss about something *Price:2*.

break one's ear v. to interrupt, to chatter continually *McBain:1*.

break one's luck (prostitute use) to encounter the first customer of the day *Milner*.

break one's (own) neck v. to get married.

break squelch v. (milit. use) to break radio silence and start transmitting *Del Vecchio*.

break up v.t., v.i. **1.** to collapse in laughter; **2.** to cause someone else to laugh heartily.

break weak v. to act in a cowardly manner.

break wide v. (US Black use) to lose interest.

breaker n. **1.** Citizen's Band radio enthusiast *CB*; **2.** UK police use: shop-/housebreaker *Laurie*.

break-in n. (Valley Girls (qv) use) someone who is leaving *Pond*.

breaking n. **1.** (abbrev.) break dancing: dance style perfected in New York's South Bronx slums; dancers spin, whirl and twist, pivoting on heads, elbows, knees, etc.; performed to rap DJs (qv) *ES 21/9/83*; **2.** (abbrev.) breaking and entering (cf: B&E) *Newman:1*.

breaks n. luck, chance, opportunities; either *good breaks* or *bad breaks* 'Requiem for a Heavyweight', Channel 4, 1983.

breath and britches n. an unpleasant, untrustworthy person (cf: all mouth and trousers).

breathe down one's neck v. **1.** to be physically close; **2.** to be in hot pursuit, or in competition.

bred in the ditch a. phr. illegitimate (cf: born with burnt feet).

breechy a. (of a woman) immoral (fr. dial. breachy: (of cattle) liable to break through the pasture fence).

breed n. (abbrev.) half-breed, derog. term for American Indian *BvdB*.

breed a scab (on one's nose) v. to stir up trouble for oneself.

breeders n. (homosexual use) married homosexuals who produce children *Jay & Young*.

breeze n. **1.** simplicity, easy, no problems *Humphries:2*; **2.** (US Black use) a relaxed person.

breeze along v. to visit, with inference of casual, unplanned dropping in *Humphries:2*.

breezer n. (Aus. use) a fart *Neaman & Silver*.

breezy a. bright and cheery *Wodehouse:AAG*.

brekker n. breakfast; fr. Oxford '-er' endings of 1920s *Wodehouse:PB*.

brew n. a pot of tea *Bleasdale*.

brew n. beer, ale; spec. in UK: Carlsberg Special brew, poss. the strongest canned beer on sale in UK *Greaser Comics*.

brew v. (drug use) to prepare heroin for injection by heating with water in a spoon or bottle cap (cf: cook) *Klein*.

brew up v. to make tea.

brewer's droop n. temporary impotence due to the effects of alcohol on the erectile tissue *Humphries*.

brewski n. (US campus use) beer *Bernbach*.

brick n. **1.** a reliable, kind, selfless person; fr. the solidity of the object *Vidal*; **2.** (drug use) one kilo (2.2 lbs approx) of marijuana (cf: key) *Green:1*.

brick it v. to be terrified, very nervous; fr. shit bricks(qv).

brickie n. (abbrev.) bricklayer *Wilkinson*.

bricks n. **1.** the city streets, thus **2.** the urban environment in general (cf: pavement); **3.** a street prostitute's beat.

Bridewell v. (spec. Liverpool police use) a police station, esp. the cells it contains; fr. St. Bride's Well, 19th-C. prison in London *Bleasdale*.

brief n. **1.** a barrister; whose legal commissions are his/her briefs

Newman:1; **2.** (UK police use) a warrant to arrest or search *Powis*.

brierpatch child n. an illegitimate child.

brig n. prison; esp. US milit. use *Wodehouse passim*.

bright n. (US Black use) a light-skinned black person *Klein*.

brill! (abbrev.) brilliant! *Lucien Green passim 1983*.

brilliant n. (homosexual use) an obviously, exaggeratedly homosexual man *Legman*.

bring down n. anything depressing, either person or circumstance *Burroughs:1*.

bring down v. **1.** to attract; to make move in one's direction *Bruce:2*; **2.** to depress; fr. drug use.

bring home the bacon v. to deliver whatever was requested and required *Wodehouse:AAG*.

bring it in v. (poker use) for the player with the lowest exposed card to commence betting at the start of a round *Alvarez*.

bring one up v. (US Black use) to criticize, to tell off *Folb*.

bring oneself off v. to masturbate *Neaman & Silver*.

bring out v. (gay use) to recruit a rent-boy (qv) *Maledicta 9*.

bring the house down v. to delight, to gain overall approval; fr. theatrical use.

briny n. the sea; fr. the salt water.

brisket n. the human chest.

Bristol City (rhyming sl.) = titty = female breasts (cf: Bristols) *Cole*.

Bristols n. (fr. rhyming sl.) Bristol bits = tits = breasts *Norman:3*.

britannia metal n. **1.** the erect penis (cf: English sentry); **2.** something fake, sham.

bro n. (US Black use) (abbrev.) brother; a fellow black *Del Vecchio*.

broad n. **1.** a male homosexual prostitute; fr. broad = woman *Legman*; **2.** a woman *Big Ass Comics 1*.

broad in the beam a. fat, overweight, esp. around the buttocks; fr. naut.

description of a ship.

broads n. playing cards *Powis*.

broadsman n. a card sharp *Powis*.

broke a. out of funds, impoverished, poor *Performance*.

broke to the wide a. aka: *broke to the world*: absolutely penniless.

broke up a. **1.** injured, hurt; **2.** depressed, badly upset.

broken stick n. an unreliable person.

broker n. someone who is usually broke (qv), a poor person *Runyon*.

brolly n. umbrella *Capital Radio 1983*.

bronco n. a young man, a novice in the gay world and thus somewhat rough; fr. Western use *Legman*.

Bronx cheer n. a loud, derisive noise, imitative of a fart (cf: raspberry) *Neaman & Silver*.

Brooklyn butterflies n. cockroaches *O'Rourke:1*

Brooklyn Indian n. a Jew.

broom v. to disappear quickly; fr. the image of sweeping away *Chandler: Notebk*.

brooming off (taxi-driver use) illegal practice by cabbies whereby they refuse any fares other than those they consider maximally profitable, despite the regulation that they must take whatever fare presents itself; the rejected fare is 'swept' along to the next cab *Powis*.

brothel creepers n. suede shoes, often in lurid colours, with extra thick rubber soles, esp. popular among rock 'n' roll fans of 1950s (and in 1980s revival).

brothel stompers n. (US campus use) see brothel creepers, although these 'respectable' versions have no great thickness of sole *Bernbach*.

brother n. (US Black use) form of address to fellow black male (cf: bro) *Himes:1*.

brothers n. Black people; orig. in 1960s Black radical use, now used by both black and white speakers with only residual polit. overtones *Higgins:2*.

brougham n. (US Black use) an elegant, expensive and prized motor car; fr. the smart carriages of 19th C. named for Lord Henry Brougham (1778–1868) *Klein*.

brown v. see: brown-nose.

brown v. (homosexual use) to perform anal intercourse *Legman*.

brown bomber n. **1.** (Aus. use) a parking policeman *Ready*; **2.** a laxative pill *Pearce*.

brown eye n. **1.** the anus; **2.** anal intercourse (cf: ring, brown).

Brown Family n. generic term for homosexuals; mainly obs.; referring to the predeliction for anal intercourse (cf: brown, brown eye, etc.).

brown hatter n. a homosexual *Cole*.

brown noser n. anyone who pays excessive court to authority – at school, in work, etc. (cf: ass-kisser, -licker) *Junker*.

brown stuff n. (drug use) opium *Burroughs:1*.

brown tonguer n. see brown noser *Private Eye 1985*.

brown wings (Hells Angels use) anilingus or anal intercourse *Mandelkau.* (cf: black, red wings)

brownbag v. to drink liquor from a bottle 'hidden' in the bag in which one purchases it from the liquor store; necessary in US states where drinking in the street is illegal *R. Stone, 'A Flag for Sunrise', 1981*.

brownbagger n. an office worker (cf: dinner-pailer, nine-to-fiver).

browncoat n. (taxi/police use) the junior examiner at the Police Public Carriage Office in London (cf: whitecoat) *Powis*.

browned off irritated, annoyed; fr. accumulation of brown rust on fatigued or worn out metal *Norman:2*.

brownie v. see: brown-nose.

brownie n. a shot of whisky *Private Eye passim*.

Brownie point n. a commendation awarded to the Girl Guides' junior branch and thus usu. a sarcastic and backhanded form of compliment when handed out by adults *Underwood*.

browning n. anal intercourse; mainly obs. (cf: brown, brown eye, etc.)

Jay & Young.

Browning Family n. the world of homosexuals (cf: Brown Family) *Legman*.

Browning Sisters n. homosexuals in general (cf: Brown Family) *Legman*.

bruiser n. thug, spec. a boxer *Schulberg*.

brummy a. (Aus. use) second-rate, tawdry; fr. SE *brumagem Humphries:2*.

Bruno n. (US college use) Brown University *Bernbach*.

brush n. (Aus. use) a female; fr. pubic hair thereof *Wilkes*.

brush ape n. a hill-billy, a peasant.

brush colt n. an illegitimate child (cf: catch colt).

brush one's teeth v. (US Black use) to perform cunnilingus *Folb*.

brush-off v. to ignore, to treat contemptuously, to dismiss *Hotten*.

Brussels sprouts n. (rhyming sl.) Scouts *Jones:J*.

b.s. (abbrev.) bullshit *Del Vecchio*.

BSHs (acro.) *British Standard Handfuls*, cod-officialese to denote the female breast *Powis*.

btm n. coy abbrev. for bottom = posterior.

bu n. (drug use) marijuana (cf:boo) *Sanders:2*.

bub n. boy; used as derog. form of address, implying youth, insignificance, etc. *Motor City Comics*.

bubble n. the female breast.

bubble n. (ski use) aka *egg*: telecabin *Barr*.

bubble n. (UK prison use: rhyming sl.) bubble and squeak = speak = information *Obs. 1981*.

bubble and squeak n. (rhyming sl.) a Greek *Cole*.

bubbled betrayed, informed against; fr. rhyming sl: bubble and squeak: to speak *Newman:1*.

bubble-gum (music business use) catchy, simplistic pop music aimed specifically at the pre-pubescent and early teenage female market, all, allegedly, prime consumers of bubble gum.

bubblegum machine n. 1. the flashing lights on top of a police car; thus 2. the vehicle itself.

bubble-gummer n. a young girl, aged 10–14 *Jenkins*.

bubblehead n. foolish, careless person, with a brain full of air. (cf: airhead) *Esq 1983*.

bubbly n. champagne *Vidal*.

bubby term of address, mix of buddy + baby (qqv) *Price:3*.

bubele n. general affectionate term of address (fr. Yiddish *bubele*: little grandmother).

bubonic (teen use) a. extreme, notably powerful.

buck v. 1. to desire, to work towards, aim for *Price:1*; 2. to avoid, to resist.

buck n. (Liverpool police use) a tearaway, a young, aggressive criminal *James MClure, 'Spike Island', 1980*.

buck n. 1. (abbrev.) buckshot, used to load shotgun shells *Higgin:1*; 2. (US prison use) a priest *Chandler: Notebk*; 3. a dollar; $100 *Laugh In The Dark*.

buck and a half n. $150 *Higgins:2*.

buck fever n. nervousness in the face of an unknown or new situation that may render one incapable of action (fr. hunting j.).

buck private n. (US milit. use) a private soldier who is 'bucking for' promotion; thus occas. other ranks in a similar position, eg: *buck colonel*, who wishes to be a general.

buck up v. 1. to encourage, to cheer up; 2. as excl: cheer up! *Norman:2*.

bucket n. an old car; fr. abbrev. rust bucket *Ice T:3*.

bucket n. 1. (homosexual use) the anus *Legman*; 2. (Can. prison use) county prison; fr. rhyming sl. bucket and pail *Caron*.

bucket v. (Aus. use) to disdain, to denigrate, to despise *Wilkes*.

bucket (down) v. to rain very heavily.

bucket job n. (UK criminal use) aka: *bucket gaff*; a fraudulent company *Powis*.

bucket-fed a. spoiled, over-indulged (fr. farming j.).

buckle my shoe n. a Jew (fr. rhy. sl.

cf: box of glue, fifteen-two, five to two, four by two, half past two, kangaroo, pot of glue, quarter to two, sarah soo).

buck naked a. (orig. US) naked.

bucko a. aggressive, overbearing, domineering *Wodehouse: JM*.

buck's night n. (Aus. use) a stag party, the party thrown for a bridegroom on the eve of his wedding *Bickerton*.

buckshee a. free, gratis; fr. *baksheesh*: a tip (Persian for a gift, a present); picked up by Middle East and Indian imperial troops and thus brought West *Wright*.

buckwheat n. (US Black use) a light complexioned black person *Folb*.

buckwheat crop n. a marriage that takes place when the bride is already pregnant.

bucky a. out of order, not working.

bud n. 1. a young, pubescent girl *Wolfe:2*; 2. (Valley Girls (qv) use) marijuana; emphasizing its herbal origins *Harpers/Queen 1983*.

bud sesh n. (US teen. use) getting together to smoke marijuana; fr. buddy session *Pond*.

buddha n. marijuana; thus bud-sack: a container for marijuana *Dre*.

buddhahead n. derog. an Oriental person.

buddy n. friend, acquaintance *Laugh In The Dark*.

buddy-buddy a. exceptionally and overtly friendly, prob. insincerely so *Bruce:2*.

buddy-gee n. (US Black) a friend.

buddyseat n. pillion seat on a motorcycle *Selby:1*.

budgie n. (UK criminal use) a talkative person, esp, in police use, a minor informer; fr. the budgerigar, a popular UK cage bird, which can be taught to speak *Powis*.

buf n. (Valley Girls (qv) use) an attractive male; fr. 'beautiful' or 'beautiful fellow' *Pond*.

buffalooed adv. coerced, crushed; metaphorically run down by a herd of buffaloes.

buffer n. genial old fool, a description more affectionate than critical *Hotten*.

buftie-boy, bufty n. (Sc. use) homosexual *Welsh:1* (cf: battie-boy).

bufu a. (Valley Girls (qv) use) homosexual, fr. buttfucker *Harpers/Queen 1/83*.

bug n. 1. an enthusiast, a fan, a devotee, who has a 'bug' in his/her head *Runyon*; 2. (Can. prison use) homemade water heater for making coffee *Caron*; 3. (espionage use) any form of electronic surveillance gadget *Higgins:5*; 4. an insane, unstable person; fr. 'bugs in the head' and thus the unstable mobster Benjamin Siegel (1906–47) earned the nickname 'Bugsy' *Stone*.

bug v. 1. to tap a telephone *Greenlee*; 2. to annoy, irritate *Price:2*; 3. to walk slowly, lethargically.

bug dust n. something of little value or importance, esp. as 'that's a load of bug dust!'

bug juice n. (Can. prison use) depressant drug used for controlling violent or non-cooperative prisoners *Caron*.

bug out v. to leave, to run away 'Banty Raid', cartoon, *Thames TV 1983*.

bug pass n. (Can. prison use) a prisoner so deranged that he is no longer responsible for his actions *Caron*.

bug trap n. (US cant) a bed.

bug-eyed a. drunk; one's eyes are popping like those of some insects *Dickson*.

bugger n. fr. SE synonym for sodomite: a person, esp. *silly bugger*, *daft bugger*, etc; not necessarily perjorative.

bugger! syn. for damn! (qv) (cf: buggeration, botheration, etc.).

bugger (it) up v. to make a mess of , to blunder *Higgins:2*.

buggeration! general excl. of annoyance (cf: botheration).

buggerlugs n. general term of (affectionate) address, usu. among men *Waterhouse*.

bugger's grips n. the brushed back 'wings' of hair that adorn the temples of many upper class Englishmen; coarse rumour imputes these as the handholds for those who are positioning such partners ready for anal penetration *K. Payne*.

bugger's woods n. an out of the way place, an unimportant place. (fr. boogerman or bogeyman).

bugging adv. going crazy, suffering mental stress.

Buggins turn a sinecure that comes to all members of a given committee, board of directors, etc. so long as they remain members of that group and, in due course, inevitably take their turn at a given task.

bughouse n. 1. a jail; 2. a hospital, esp. a mental hospital; 3. an outside lavatory; 4. see: fleabag.

bughouse a. insane, crazy *Schulberg:2*.

bughutch n. tatty, rundown, dirty cinema (cf: fleapit) *Waterhouse*.

bugle n. the nose; through which one blows.

bugle duster n. handkerchief *Humphries*.

buick v. to vomit; fr. the noise of the vomiting (cf: hughie, ralph) *Bernbach*.

build pigpens v. to deceive, esp. for a merchant to cheat a customer. (fr. the practice of woodcutters who pile the wood on their carts in the shape of a pigpen, thus making the pile, which is hollow, appear larger than it is).

built n. an attractive woman with a noticeably good figure *Breslin*.

built a. a well muscled man, poss. referring spec. to his penis. (cf: hung) *Price:1*.

built like a brick shithouse a very strong, muscled man, who resembles a squat, four-square, solid edifice.

buke v. to sodomise.

bull n. 1. (abbrev.) bull-dyke = lesbian *Dunne*; 2. policeman, fr. Ger: *bulle*: (sl.) policeman or poss. Sp. sl. *bul*: policeman *Fiction Illus. 3*; 3. (US criminal use) a veteran, long-term convict *Dunne*.

bull and cow n. (rhyming sl.) row *Powis*.

bull dagger n. a masculine lesbian (cf: bull-dyke) *Jones*.

Bull Durham! excl. euph. bullshit (qv).

bull fuck n. gravy.

bull gang n. a team of manual labourers.

bull session n. (US use) sitting around gossiping, often of men rather than woman (cf: bull) *King*.

bullcrap n. see: bullshit *Southern*.

bulldog n. (US newspaper use) the first edition (c.12 midnight) of a morning paper; the first (late morning) edition of an evening paper *Fiction Illus. 3*.

bulldog v. (US prison use) to harass, whether verbally or physically.

bulldogger n. (US Black use) a violent person.

bull-driver n. a peasant, a farmer.

bull-dyke n. a masculine lesbian; usu. an unpleasant, excessively man-hating one (cf: bumper) *Big Ass Comics 1*.

bullet n. (poker use) 1. an ace *Uris*; 2. (US prison use) a one-year sentence *Morgan*.

bullet-proof a. immune, irrefutable.

bull-fiddle n. the double-bass *Some Like It Hot, directed Billy Wilder, 1959*.

bull-goose n. the leader, the boss.

bullpen n. 1. sport: the bench on which the batting team in baseball sit when not performing; 2. police use: the holding cage in a precinct house *Himes:1*; 3. any enclosure – college dormitory, factory changing room, etc. – where a group of men associate, gossip, etc.

bullsh n. (abbrev.) bullshit (qv) *Humphries*.

bullshit n. rubbish, nonsense, lies *Price:2*.

bullshit v. to tell lies, to tease, to confuse with false information.

bullshit artist n. anyone with a good line of persuasive, if insincere patter *Underwood*.

bull-shy a. timid, nervous.

bully! (excl.) wonderful, excellent, fine! *PT*.

bully beef n. (UK prison use; rhyming sl.) chief (officer) (cf: corned beef) *Norman:1*.

bully for you! (excl.) well done! congratulations; usu. ironic/sarcastic use.

bullyrag v. to bully, to pressurize, to taunt *PT*.

bum n. 1. the buttocks *Payne*; 2. spec. a tramp, a vagrant *Powis*; 3. (derog.) term of abuse for anyone unpleasant *Laugh In The Dark*; 4. (boxing use) a poor, incompetent fighter *Heller*; 5. a promiscuous girl, fr. bum: tramp (vagrant) used as tramp (promiscuous woman) *Bruce:2*.

bum a. useless, second rate, poor, inferior, etc; fr. bum = vagrant, tramp, etc. *Algren*.

bum v. 1. to wander around; 2. to beg *Price:3*.

bum bandit n. homosexual.

bum banditry n. homosexuality.

bum deal n. a poor bargain, a mistaken agreement; fr. bum, a.

bum map n. (US banking use) a cheque that is returned to drawer *Breslin* (cf: bounce 1).

bum steer n. 1. spec. a false clue, thus; 2. a mistake, the wrong direction *Humphries*.

bum trip n. see: bummer 1.

bum wad n. lavatory paper (cf: bum fodder).

bumba, bumpa n. (US Black) the buttocks.

bum-boy n. (derog.) homosexual male; fr. bum = buttocks.

bumchat v. to make statements to a woman with the sole interest in her seduction *S. Ford*.

bumf n. paperwork, fr. abbrev. bumfodder, orig. Second World War milit. sl. *Dickson*.

bumface n. general term of disdain; usually only used by children.

bum-fluff n. very light growth of hair on the face of a boy who is on the verge of shaving.

bumfodder n. 1. lavatory paper; 2.

trashy literature, only good for use as 1; 3. tabloid newspapers.

bum-freezer n. a short jacket that stops short of covering the buttocks; orig. describing an Eton jacket, latterly the 'Italian' styles of 1950s and thence any short (men's) jacket *Whitcomb*.

bumfuddled a. confused, mixed up (cf: bamboozle).

bummed out a. 1. suffering from a bummer (qv) *McFadden*; 2. drunk *Dickson*; 3. depressed, miserable *Maupin:3*.

bummer n. 1. (drug use) an unpleasant drug experience, esp. while using LSD *Green:1*; 2. any unpleasant experience *Hoffman:a*.

bump n. spontaneous, cursory sexual intercourse *Klein*.

bump v. 1. to dismiss an employee; 2. to increase wages or, in gambling use, a bet.

bump into v. to meet by accident.

bump off v. to murder *Sharpe:1*.

bump one's gums v. to argue.

bump start v. to get something started with a sudden, violent gesture or action (whether physical or metaphorical) (cf: kick start).

bump uglies v. to have sexual intercourse.

bumper n. 1. (cant) a pickpocket's assistant who bumps into the victim *Neaman & Silver*; 2. a masculine lesbian *Legman*; 3. (Aus. use) cigarette butt (cf: not worth a bumper) *Wilkes*.

bumper head n. one who performs oral sex.

bumpers n. breasts *Neaman & Silver*.

bumpy n. the buttocks.

bum-rap v. to slander, to attack verbally, to catcall *Bruce:2*.

bum's rush n. forcible ejection, esp. from a bar or club *Goldman*.

bumsky a. second-rate, inferior.

bum-sucker n. sycophant, crawler (cf: ass-kisser, -licker, brown-noser).

bun in the oven pregnant *Humphries*.

bunch v. to leave a job, to leave something unfinished (cf: bunk off).

bunch of fives n. the fist *Hotten*.

bunch punch n. (US campus use) group sex in which a number of males have sex with one female (cf: gangbang) *Underwood*.

bunchy a. chubby.

bunco n. (criminal use, esp. US) fraud; fr. *banco*, first used in US c.1870 *Powis*.

bunco artist n. a confidence trickster *Wodehouse:PGM*.

bunco squad n. (US police use) a special squad devoted to combating confidence tricksters (cf: bunco, pussy posse).

bunco-steerer n. (US criminal use) a member of a confidence trickster gang who persuades a victim to take part in the current swindle they are using to make money.

bundle n. a large amount of money *Grogan*.

bung n. 1. aka: *bunghole*; the anus *Legman*; 2. a lump, a swelling.

bung v. 1. pass, throw *Payne*; 2. to protrude, to stick out (cf: bung n. 2.).

bung n., v. a bribe, to offer or give a bribe; usu. of police (UK) (cf: sling) *Powis*.

bung ho! a toast when drinking; also synonym for 'goodbye' *Pynchon*.

bungalow v. (US milit. use in Vietnam) to live with; fr. shack up (qv) *Neaman & Silver*.

bungalow bill n. a man who is either not very intelligent ('nothing up top') or endowed with large genitals ('it's all down below'); the phrase, for whichever reason, became associated with one of actress Joan Collins' well publicized escorts, one Bill Wiggins.

bunged up a. stuffy, blocked, esp. of one's nose during 'flu or a cold.

bunghole n. see: asshole *Price:3*.

bunghole v. to sodomize *Bukowski:1*.

bunfight n. a tea party, esp. with image of children struggling for sticky buns.

bungo n. (West Indian use) (derog.) crude, boorish, ignorant black person *Thelwell*.

bungs up a. very drunk, rolling drunk

(fr. naut. j. bungs up: a vessel that is rolling in a heavy sea to such an extent that the bungs in her planking are visible).

bungy n. an eraser, a rubber; usu. school use.

bunk n. 1. nonsense, rubbish; fr. bunkum *Sanders:2*; 2. uncool (qv).

bunk a. fake, counterfeit (cf: bunco) *Morgan*.

bunk down v. to sleep *Humphries:2*.

bunk into v. to meet by accident.

bunk off v. to play truant, usu. UK schoolchildren (cf: hop the wag).

bunk up n. sexual intercourse *Norman:1*.

bunker n. a sodomite; fr. bugger (qv) *Legman*.

bunkum n. nonsense, rubbish *Neaman & Silver*.

bunkum town n. that area of the town where the poor live.

bunny n. 1. (fr. rhyming sl.) rabbit (and pork) = talk *Newman:2*; 2. (US Black use) a promiscuous woman, whose habits emulate the preoccupations of rabbits *Klein*.

buns n. the buttocks *Vidal*.

buns n. (Aus. use) a tampon; from the term jam buns; thus to 'have the buns on': to be menstruating (cf: have the painters in, have the rag on, etc).

bunty n. a small, middle-aged woman, implying one's affection for a woman so-titled *Powis*.

buoyant a. drunk; 'my teeth are floating' *Dickson*.

buppie acro. a black upwardly mobile young professional (cf: yuppie).

burbed-out (US middle-class) conventional, poss. fr. Burberry coat *Price:3*.

burbs n. abbrev. for suburbs.

burg n. a town, a city; fr. German *Big Ass Comics 1*.

burglar n. corruption of *bugger* (cf: bunker) *Legman*.

burgle v. to sodomize; fr. SE *bugger Neaman & Silver*.

burgoo n. fr. Hindustani: porridge or soup *P. MacDonald, 'X v. Rex', 1933*.

buried (US prison use) held

incommunicado *Chandler: Notebk.*

burk v. to vomit; to break wind.

burly a. (US teen use) hard to achieve, challenging (physically or mentally).

BURMA acro. *be undressed, ready, my* angel: written on envelopes of love letters (cf:BOLTOP, NORWICH, SWALK) *Partridge:5*.

burn n. a love-bite (cf: hickey).

burn n. (UK prison use) a smoke, a cigarette *LL*.

burn v. 1. to cheat, defraud, fail to pay a debt *Bruce:2*; 2 (spec. drug use) to sell cut or second-rate drugs *Caserta*; 3. to betray sexually *Two Lane Blacktop, 1971*; 4. (US campus use) to grade harshly *Underwood*; 5. to annoy, to infuriate, to embarrass *Pond*; 6. to recognize *Higgins:1*; 7. (UK criminal use) to open a safe using oxyacetylene cutting equipment *LL*.

burn artist n. a con-man, a cheat esp. in the drug world where he/she will either sell second-rate drugs, or take a buyer's money and vanish without delivering the goods (see burn 2.).

burn down v. 1. to shoot, to kill; 2. to overdo, to use to excess *Burroughs:1*.

burn one's foot v. to become pregnant (cf: break one's leg, stub one's toe).

burn one's shoulder v. to be drunk; with a cigarette? by falling on the stove? *Dickson*.

burn rubber v. to drive a car very fast; fr. the smoking tyres *Tuff Shit Comics*.

burn up v.t. to annoy, to irritate (cf: burnt at) *Runyon:1*.

burn up one's tail v. to work extremely hard.

burn with a low blue flame v. to be extremely drunk; fr. image of lighting the alcohol fumes pouring from one's mouth *Neaman & Silver*.

burned at annoyed with *McFadden*.

burnie n. (drug use) a half-smoked marijuana cigarette *De Lannoy & Masterson*.

burning down habit an extremely heavy addiction to narcotics (cf: oil burner habit) *Burroughs:1*.

burnout n. one who has exhausted their capabilities; one who can no longer function efficiently within their own job or discipline *Price:3*.

burnt n. (fr. rhyming sl) burnt cinder = window (pron. winder) *Norman:2*.

burnt adv. (US teen use) terrible, hopeless.

burnt a. (US campus use) disappointed, esp. sexually *Underwood*.

burnt offering n. joking description of any food which has been burnt on the stove.

burnt out adv. referring to the victim of excess, too much drink and/or drugs, all of which has taken its toll both physically and, esp. mentally.

burn-up n. fast riding of a motorcycle, esp. used by outlaw bike riders, Rockers, etc. *Mandelkau*.

buroo n. unemployment office, Labour exchange; fr. bureau.

burrhead n. derog. a Black person (cf: burrheaded).

burst n. a spree, a party with much eating and drinking *Tidy*.

burst v. to beat up; usu. as a threat 'I'll burst him!'.

burst one's bubble v. (US campus use) to humiliate; to deflate someone's ego *Underwood*.

burton n. (rhyming sl.) Burton-on-Trent = rent *Powis*.

bury the brisket v. to have sexual intercourse (cf: hide the salami).

bury the tomahawk v. to have sexual intercourse (cf: shoot, stab in the thigh).

bus n. an automobile.

bush n. 1. the female pubis *Dunne*; 2. (drug use) marijuana, esp. as in Congo bush, African bush, etc. *Green:1*; 3. an important person, or one who likes to pose as such (cf: bushwa, push). 4. (abbrev.) bush league (qv) *Higgins:1*.

bush around v. to consider, to ponder over.

bush baby n. an illegitimate baby (cf: baby in the bushes, woods colt).

bush league 1. (baseball use) second rate teams, leagues, players; 2. amateur, unprofessional, unsophisticated.

bush patrol n. 1. sexual by-play, and thus; 2. sexual intercourse *Neaman & Silver* (cf: bush 1).

bush telegraph n. a network of gossip, rumours which brings news (often inaccurate) before the official sources.

bushed exhausted, tired out; as if one had been wandering, lost, through the woods *Higgins:5*.

bushel and peck n. (rhyming sl.) the neck (cf: Gregory Peck) *Cole*.

busher n. an amateur, an unsophisticated person (cf: bush league).

Bushey Park n. (rhyming sl.) a lark, thus a joke *Jones:J*.

bushwa aka: *bushwah, booshwa, booshwah, boushwa(h)*; euph. bullshit *Rawson*.

business end n. that part (practical or metaphorical) that really matters.

business girl n. prostitute (cf: working girl) *Powis*.

business, the n. 1. the best, the peak of excellence; often found as 'do the business' (although 'do one's business' is a colloquial euphemism for defecate.); 2. what is required or necessary.

bust n. 1. (US Black use) the police; fr. 2. an arrest *Folb*; 3. a failure *Runyon*.

bust v. 1. to smash, to break up *Mandelkau*; 2. to hit (with the fist) *Goulart*; 3. to arrest; spec. to catch in possession of drugs *Price:1*; 4. to demote; often found as 'bust down (to)'.

bust a grape v. (US Black use) to engage in any form of hard, productive work *Klein*.

bust a gusset v. to break down with laughter, to lose control, to make a superlative effort.

bust a gut v. to exert oneself strenuously.

bust caps v. 1. to fire a weapon whether in military or civilian (usually

criminal or police) use. *Ice T:3*;
2. (drug use) to inject a narcotic (cf: cap).

bust one's ass v. work exceptionally hard *Higgins:3*.

bust one's buttons v. to strain onself physically or emotionally.

bust one's chops v. see: break one's chops.

bust one's hump v. to work very hard *Higgins:1*.

bust one's nuts v. 1. see: bust a gut; 2. to have sexual intercourse, to come to orgasm.

bust one's nuts v. see: bust a gut.

bust rhymes v. to work as a rap DJ or MC (qqv); also 'bust rhythms' *Ice T:1*.

bust some booty v. (US Black use) to perform sexual intercourse (cf: booty) *Folb*.

bust (someone) up v. to beat up, to hurt in a fight *Jones*.

bust this! excl. (US use) now look here! *T 8/4/91*.

bust up v. to end a love-affair.

busted a. 1. see: bust v 3; 2. without money *Heller*.

Buster general US mode of address to any male.

buster n. 1. a person, often an old and cantankerous one *Wodehouse:AAG*; 2. something exceptional of its type; 3. a dandy; 4. a large or full grown child.

busting desperate; fr. bursting *Humphries:2*.

bustle-punching (UK police use) the action of the *frotteur*: using the anonymity of a dense crowd to rub one's penis against the nearby buttocks of defenceless women *Powis*.

bust-out n. an enormous feast (cf: blow-out) *Goldman*.

bust-out a. an intensifying adjective: extreme, tremendous, great, etc. *Bruce:2*.

busy n. a CID officer, a detective, as opposed to *flattie* (flatfoot, qv), the regular policeman *Powis*.

busy as a one-armed paper-hanger (cp) denotes extreme activity.

butch n. a masculine lesbian: or masculine male homosexual, opp. of femme (qv) *Jay & Young*.

butcher n. an inefficient surgeon, esp. one who practises cosmetic work *P. Roth, 'Goodbye Columbus', 1959*.

butchers n. 1. (fr. rhyming sl.) butcher's hook = a look *Norman:2*; 2. (Aus. use; fr. rhyming sl.) butcher's hook = crook (qv) = ill, sick. *Humphries:2*.

butt n. 1. cigarette end *Price:1*; 2. (abbrev.) buttocks *Bukowski:2*.

butt in v. to interfere, to make a nuisance of oneself; fr. pushing forward like a charging bull.

butt out! (excl.) go away, leave me alone, etc. (cf: butt).

butt pussy n. the anus.

butt slut n. (derog.) a homosexual male, usu. taking a passive role (cf: slut-puppy).

butt-fuck v. to subject to anal intercourse *Jay & Young*.

butt-plunger n. (pimp use) a man who inserts a dildo into his own anus then walks around naked while the prostitute looks on *OUI 8/75*.

butter n. (US Black use) 1. a woman; 2. spec. buttocks *Folb*.

butter baby n. (US Black use) a sexy, well-built female *Folb*.

butter one's corn v. to masturbate.

butter skin n. money (cf: buckskin).

butter up v. to flatter, to ingratiate oneself *Neaman & Silver*.

butter-and-egg man n. (US use) a small-town success, often a farmer who produces such commodities, who attempts to pass for a sophisticate in the big city *C. Connolly, Journals, ed. D. Pryce-Jones, 1983*.

butterball n. an overweight young person *Whitcomb*.

butterbox n. 1. (derog.) a Dutchman; fr. his country's product *BvdB*; 2. a fop (fr. 1703); thus effeminate male *Humphries*.

butterboy n. a novice, in whose mouth butter would not melt; esp. a young policeman or a newly qualified taxi-driver *Powis*.

buttercup n. an effeminate male homosexual *Legman*.

buttered a. (US Black use) well turned out, elegant *Klein*.

buttered bun n. a girl who has had intercourse with one man and is about to repeat this immediately with a new partner. (cf: crumpet) *S. Hutt*.

buttered scone (bingo rhyming sl.) 1 (cf: Kelly's eye) *Wright*.

butterhead n. (US Black use) a Black who, for whatever reason, is considered an embarrassment to his race *Major*.

butterflies in one's stomach nerves, apprehensions, tension.

butterfingers n. one who cannot grasp anything properly when thrown to him/her.

butterfly n. (US Black use) an over-dressed, flashy person *Klein*.

buttfucker n. one who indulges in anal intercourse.

buttinski n. one who intrudes, interferes; fr. butt in + suffix-ski *Schulberg*.

button n. 1. policeman; fr. those upon his uniform *Chandler:LG*; 2. the clitoris *Neaman & Silver*; 3. the chin, esp. in *on the button*: a blow square on the chin and thus: exactly, perfectly, quite correctly *Farrell*.

button man n. (US Mafia use) a lower echelon member of a Mafia family (cf: soldier).

button mob n. a large group of uniformed police, esp. at a demonstration, a royal appearance, etc. *Powis*.

button one's lip v. to be quiet, to stop talking.

button up v. 1. (abbrev.) button one's lip (qv); 2. to close, to shut down, (govt. use) to withold information *PT*.

button-down a. conforming, straight (qv); fr. the button-down collared shirts from Brooks Brothers (New York) that are the uniform of the US business establishment *McFadden*.

buttoner n. (UK criminal use) the member of a gang running a game of three-card monte (qv) who persuades passers by to bet on the inevitably fraudulent game; fr. buttonhole *Powis*.

buttons n. brains, native wit; esp. as phr. doesn't have all (his/her) buttons, doesn't have a full row of buttons, has a few buttons missing, has lost his/her buttons: is not very intelligent.

butty n. 1. a friend, a 'mate'; usu. Northern UK use; 2. a sandwich; fr. 'buttered bread'; thus *jam butty*, *chip butty*, etc.

buy n. (drug use) the purchase of a given drug.

buy v. to accept, to believe *The Roches, 'Nurds'*.

buy a ticket v. (US Black use) aka: *buy a wolf ticket*: to call one's bluff, to take on a challenge *Folb*.

buy the farm v. 1. to accept whatever is offered without query; to be conned or hoaxed; fr. image of a simple country person ensnared into a bad purchase by a smooth salesman *'Hill Street Blues', Thames TV, 1983*; 2. to die *Rawson*.

buy the ring v. to perform anal intercourse (cf: bit of ring) *Folb*.

buyer n. (UK criminal/police use) a receiver of stolen goods (cf: fence) *Powis*.

buzz n. a telephone call (cf: bell) *Wodehouse:AAG*.

buzz n. 1. a rumour *Norman:2*; 2. a pleasant sensation from taking a given drug, esp. barbiturates or cannabis *Grogan*.

buzz v. (US teen. use) to drive around town in one's car, looking for amusement (cf: cruise) *Pond*.

buzz around like a blue-arsed fly v. to be excessively busy; often to the detriment of others.

buzz off! (excl.) go away! *McBain:1*.

buzz the nab v. (Valley Girls (qv) use) to leave, to escape a situation; fr. buzz (drive around) and nab (abbrev. nabes: the neighbourhood) *Pond*.

buzzard n. an old and unattractive person (cf: buffer) *Folb*.

Buzzard's Row n. the poor area of a town. (fr. Buzzard's roost: the coloured area of town, itself fr. the slaughterhouse area, where buzzards gathered to eat the discarded entrails).

buzzer n. police badge.

BVDs n. underwear, from the popular brand name.

by George! mild excl.

by jingo! euph: by Jesus! *Rawson*.

by Jove! (euph.) by God! *Rawson*.

BYO (Aus. use) (abbrev.) Bring Your Own; refers to bringing drinks to a party or an unlicensed restaurant; sometimes BYOG: Bring Your Own Grog *Bickerton*.

C

C n. **1.** $100; fr. century. thus *C-note*:$100 dollar bill (cf: G) *Chandler: LG*;**2.** (drug use) cocaine (cf: H) *Burroughs: 1*.

cab joint n. a brothel recommended by cabbies *Maledicta 9*.

cabbage n. cash, banknotes (cf: lettuce) *Klein*.

cabbage leaf, cabbage leaves n. **1.** see: cabbage; **2.** large ears.

cabbagetown n. **1.** derog. the German immigrant section of a town (cf: Kraut); **2.** the poor area of town.

caboose n. the buttocks; fr. the cow-hide container stretched across the rear of the chuck wagon, when full it hangs down behind the wagon *Rawson*.

cack n. a small child.

cackle one's fat v. to brag, to boast.

cad n. (US Black use) (abbrev.) Cadillac *Klein*.

cadaver cadet n. a necrophile.

caddy n. (abbrev.) Cadillac.

cade n. a spoilt child (fr. dial. cade: a lamb that has been rejected by its mother and reared as a pet)

caff n. corruption of *café*, usu. cheap and cheerful *Payne*.

caflugalty, cafugelty n. a row, an argument.

cag out v. to break down, to stop working.

Cain and Abel n. (rhyming sl.) table *Wright*.

cake n. (US Black use) money *Shulman*.

cakehole n. the mouth, usu. abbrev.

hole (qv).

cakes n. female breasts *Higgins: 5*.

cakewalk n. anything considered very easy (cf: piece of cake).

calaboose n. fr. Sp *calabozo*: gaol; mainly US South/Western use *Runyon*.

calamity jane n. a nagging woman, a pessimist, a worrier.

calf n. a coward.

calf n. **1.** 50p.; fr. rhyming sl: cow and calf = half = half a pound, orig. 10/–, now 50p *LL*; **2.** (US Black use) a Cadillac *Folb*.

calf v. to vomit.

Cali n. the state of California.

California bankroll n. (Black and gambling use) a show bankroll in which the one large-denomination note is exhibited on the outside, concealing a quantity of small bills; a general slur to which all states, i.e. *Michigan bankroll*, are variously subject, depending on a speaker's prejudice *Folb*.

California house n. an outside privy.

call v. (Aus. use) to vomit, abbr. of call for Hughie, call for Ralph (qqv).

call for hughie v. (UK 'society' use) to vomit (cf: cry hughie) *Barr*.

call for Ralph v. to vomit.

call it a day v. to stop, to go no further, to express satisfaction with progress.

call one out v. to challenge to a fight *Folb*.

call the punches v. see: call the shots *dl*.

call the shots v. to dictate a course of action, to say what should happen; fr. dice gambling use *McFadden*.

call-boy n. a male prostitute who can be hired on the phone. fr. call-girl (qv) *Jay & Young*.

call-girl n. a female prostitute who can be hired by telephone (cf: call-boy).

call-house n. a brothel – homo- or heterosexual – that takes 'orders' for sex on the phone; previously the 'call' referred to the fact that girls could be 'called' for their services by the attendant customers *Legman*.

calluses on one's feet, have v. to be born illegitimate (cf: born with burnt feet) (the phr. describes a child that is born less than nine months after its parents were married; such a child has calluses from making the usual nine-month 'journey' in a somewhat shorter time).

camel jockey n. derog. a Syrian, an Indian (from India) (cf: sand scratcher)

camp v. to act ostentatiously and outrageously in a homosexual manner; though by no means restricted – verbally or physically – to the gay world *Jay & Young*.

camp as a row of tents a. extremely, ostentatiously camp (qv).

can n. 1. buttocks *Legman*; 2. (drug use) quantity of marijuana (approx. 1oz) (cf: lid) *Folb*; 3. (US cant) a safe *Caron*; 4. prison *Higgins: 1*; 5. lavatory.

can v. 1. to stop (a noise, an action, etc.) *Underwood*; 2. to dismiss from a job, to throw out, to ignore; fr. can=buttocks *Farrell*.

can I speak to you? (UK criminal use) acknowledged code between a newly arrested criminal and his arresting officer; the topic of their conversation would be the possibility and quantity of a bribe which would secure the villain's freedom or at least a reduction in the charges (cf: do you drink?) *Powis*.

can of worms n. an unpleasant, complex and unappetizing situation

Variety 1983.

can opener n. (US cant) any tool used for the breaking open of a safe and invaluable when explosives would lead to discovery *Runyon*.

can you see green in my eyes? (S. Afr. use) do you think I'm lying? *Marcuson*.

Canadian bacon n. (gay slang) an uncircumcised penis.

canal boat n. 1. (rhyming sl) the Tote *Jones: J*; 2. a large foot or shoe.

Canaries n. Norwich City Football Club.

canary n. 1. (UK cant) an informer; thus *sing like a canary*: to inform without restraint *Cole*; 2. (show business use) a female singer, usu. fronting a band.

cancel one's ticket v. to murder, to assassinate *Rawson*.

cancer stick n. a cigarette.

candy n. (US Black use) 1. heroin, but see nose-candy; 2. sexually desirable person of either sex; 3. (drug use) any drug in capsule form *Folb*.

candy-ass n. weakling *Price: 2*.

candy-butt n. young, inexperienced male (cf: candy-ass) *Folb*.

candyman n. (US Black use) a man who sells drugs, women and any other desired commodity for a pleasant life. (cf: candy, nose-candy) *Klein*.

candy-striper n. US hospital voluntary auxiliary workers; fr. striped dresses they wear *Price: 2*.

canned a. drunk; fr. canned up, and thus turned to liquid (?) *Dickson*.

cannibal n. one who indulges in oral sex *Major*.

cannibal n. v. an act of mutual and simultaneous fellatio and cunnilingus (cf: sixty-nine); thus also used as a verb. *AS 60.1 (1985)*.

cannon n. 1. a large gun *rr*; 2. the penis *Klein*; 3. (US) a pickpocket; because he 'shoots at' a victim (?) *Chandler: Notebk*.

canoodle v. to cuddle, to neck (qv) *Rawson*.

can't find one's ass with two hands (cp) to be very drunk *Dickson*.

can't hit a lick (US Black use) the inability to succeed in a given aim, esp. that of making money either legally or otherwise; fr. musical use *Klein*.

can't hit the ground with his hat a. (cp) extremely drunk *Dickson*.

can't see through a ladder a. (cp) extremely drunk *Dickson*.

can't win 'em all (cp) denoting commiseration over a disaster or disappointment, sometimes, but not necessarily, involving actual competition *Wodehouse: GB*.

Canuck n. (derog.) Canadian *BvdB*.

canyon n. the vagina (cf: yodel in the canyon) *Folb*.

cap n. 1. (abbrev.) capsule: containing a narcotic, usu. heroin. *Payne*; 2. (US Black use) cunnilingus; a strained parallel to head (qv) *Klein*.

cap v. 1. to transfer bulk drugs (in powder form) into capsules for sale *Green:1*; 2. to kill, to shoot dead.

cap on v. to attack someone verbally, to discredit someone *Folb*.

cape of good hope n. (rhyming sl.) soap *Jones: J*.

capeesh? excl. do you understand?; fr. Italian 'capito' = I understand.

caper n. a large scale crime, usu. involving a great deal of elaborate planning and aimed at very large sums of money, expensive pieces of jewellery, etc. the supposed lack of violence in such enterprises lent them this somewhat jovial, jokey air *Powis*.

capped a. shot dead.

capper n. an anecdote that steals the limelight from a previous anecdote; a punchline *Bruce: 1*.

capping n. (US Black use) the ritual exchange of verbal insults (cf: dozens).

Captain Cook n. (rhyming sl.) 1. a look *Humphries*; 2. a book *Jones: J*.

capture n. an arrest and conviction for a crime *Norman: 1*.

caput finished, over, ruined, etc; fr. Ger. *kaputt*; done for.

car park n. (rhyming sl.) a nark = an informer *Powis*.

caravan v. (US teen. use) to drive cars in groups and to perform a variety of elaborate manoeuvres on the street *Folb*.

card n. a character, a noticeable person, a likeable eccentric *Jones*.

card v. (US campus use) to request proof of age (in a bar) by producing one's identification card *Underwood*.

Cardboard City n. the cardboard box 'homes' that are used as shelter by the homeless; the original Cardboard City was situated on London's South Bank, but rising homelessness has meant that the term now applies to any such gathering.

cark v. (Aus. use) to die; fr. dial. cark or kark meaning to caw like a crow, thus the assoc. is with a carrion bird.

carked a. (Aus use) ruined, destroyed, exhausted (cf:cark).

Carl Comedian n. (US campus use) derog. dismissal of a raconteur whose jokes and stories fail to make the desired impact *Bernbach*.

Carl Rosa n. (rhyming sl.) a poser, anyone pretending to be something that he/she is not; thus *the old Carl Rosa*: fraud *Powis*.

carn n. money; prob. fr. coin = money.

carnales n. Mexican equivalent of homeboy (qv) *Morgan*.

carney n. a carnival worker *Waits*.

carnies n. (Aus. use) (abbrev.) carnations *Humphries: 2*.

carpenter's dream n. an available girl; 'flat as a board and easy to screw' *Price: 1*.

carpet n. (UK prison use) a three months' sentence; fr. the earlier assumption that prison workshops took just 90 days to produce a particular type of regulation size carpet *Norman: 1*.

carpet v. to reprimand, to criticize, to tell off, esp. in milit. use; the miscreant stands on the carpet in front of the superior's desk *Hotten*.

carpet biter n. one who becomes so enraged as to start chewing at the carpet.

carpetbag v. 1. (US student) to attempt to make a good impression, usu. on one's teachers, by pretending to have an all-consuming interest in a given subject; thus 2. to deceive (fr. SE carpetbagger: a derog. description applied, after the American Civil War, to immigrants from the Northern into the Southern States, whose 'property qualification' consisted merely of the contents of the carpet-bag which they had brought with them. Hence, applied to all Northerners who went south and tried, by a variety of deceitful tricks, to obtain political influence, esp. by claiming an interest in local areas of which, in fact, they had no real knowledge).

carpy (UK prison use) fr. *carpe diem* ('make the most of the day' Lat.): to be locked away in one's cell at night *LL*.

carriage trade n. the upper classes; usu. ironically; fr. earlier divisions of transport *Chandler: LG*.

carrot crunchers n. visitors to London from the provinces and the countryside (cf: swedes) *Powis*.

carry v. to carry arms *Higgins: 1*.

carry a bone v. to gossip, to spread rumours.

carry a case v. (US criminal use) to be out on bail *Klein*.

carry a torch v. to mourn a dead love affair; to feel love without it being returned *Vidal*.

carry ballast v. to hold one's liquor.

carry on v. to have an adulterous relationship *Major*.

carry the can (for) v. to take the blame that should be another's.

carrying see: holding *Major*.

carry-on n. a commotion, an exciting event, a disturbance; often in phr. a *right/real carry-on Hotten*.

carry-out n. a cafe which specializes in food that can be packed and taken away for eating elsewhere *Jan Harold Brunvand, 'The Vanishing Hitchhiker', 1983*.

cart v. to carry, to drag; thus *cart away*, *cart out*, etc.*Higgins: 1*.

cartnapping (retail industry use) the stealing of supermarket and self-service store trolleys *Dickson*.

carve a slice v. take a portion of the profits *Waits*.

carve-up n. 1. any situation in which one feels oneself unfairly deprived of a desired aim or object; 2. (UK prison/criminal use) a share-out of loot, profits, etc. (cf: carve a slice) *LL*.

carvie n. (UK prison use) one who helps carve-up, share, a ration of tobacco; a prisoner may take on a regular 'carvie' for periods of his sentence *LL*.

carving knife n. (rhyming sl.) wife *Jones: J*.

cas a. (Valley Girls (qv.) use) term of general approval for favoured clothing; abbrev. of casual *Pond*.

cas (pron. cazz) a. abbrev. of casual = satisfactory; thus good.

case n. (UK criminal use) a brothel *Powis*.

case v. 1. to look over, to appraise, esp. prior to a robbery as in *case the joint Runyon*; 2. (UK prison use) to discipline, to put on report *LL*.

case card n. the last card of the four available of each denomination to appear in the deal; thus *case ace*, *case deuce*, etc. *Algren*.

case dough n. (US prison use). limited money *Chandler: Notebk*.

case it around v. (Valley Girls (qv.) use) 1. to check out (qv.) a place or situation (cf: case); 2. to move on to a new activity *Pond*.

case out v. 1. to join forces for any undertaking; 2. (excl.) go away! *Algren*.

case over v. to assess; to judge the quality; to look at *Price: 3*.

case the joint v. to survey a house, shop, etc. with a view to subsequently robbing it *Caron*.

caser n. 1. five shillings, fr. Yiddish kesef: silver *Norman: 4*; 2. (UK prison use) a prison officer notorious for excessive discipline (cf: case 2) *LL*.

cash and carried (rhyming sl.) married (cf: cut and carried) *Jones: J*.

cash in one's chips v. to die; fr. gambling use, the action one takes on leaving a game *Humphries: 2*.

cash one's last check v. euph. to die (cf: cash in one's chips).

cashed up (Aus. use) wealthy, well-off, albeit temporarily *Wilkes*.

Caspar Milquetoast n. aka: *Casper Milktoast*: a cowardly, weak person. fr. the central character in the cartoon 'The Timid Soul' created by H. T. Webster, first pub. in New York *World*, 1924 *Waits*.

casper n. (US Black use) a particularly light-skinned black person *Folb*.

cassava (UK Black use) woman; fr. the West Indian foodstuff.

cast v.t. (UK police use) to be discharged fr. the police force *Laurie*.

cast nasturtiums v. joking corruption of cast aspersions.

cast the net v. (US pimp use) for a pimp to employ an experienced prostitute to lure a new girl into joining his stable (qv.) *Klein*.

Casuals n. working class UK youth who dress in the designer-labelled clothing of their society peers but whose accents and lifestyles remain resolutely proletarian *Harpers/Queen 8/83*.

cat n. a person, usu. male; from jazz use c.1950s poss. fr. 'alligator', early Black use for worldly, smart, sophisticated male, abbrev. to gator, gate, cat (?) *Price: 2*.

cat v. to vomit *R. Kipling, 'Stalky & Co', 1908*.

cat and mouse n. (rhyming sl.) house *Jones: J*.

cat around v. 1. (US campus use) to wander purposelessly about *Underwood*; 2. to search for a sexual partner (abbrev.) tom-cat (qv.) *McFadden*.

cat in a sack n. something to suspect or be wary of; thus buy a cat in a sack: to buy something that one has not actually inspected

cat on a hot tin roof, like a phr. nervous, agitated (cf: hen on a hot griddle)

catbird n. a mischievous or cunning person.

catbird seat n. a privileged or advantageous position; the image is of a cat looking down on a targetted bird.

catch n. the number of clients a prostitute has serviced within a given time *Klein*.

catch v. to take the passive role in sexual intercourse (cf: govern) *AS 60.1 (1985)*.

catch v. 1. to attend, esp. a performance; 2. to notice, to appreciate.

catch a buzz v. (lesbian use) to masturbate with an electric vibrator *Maledicta*.

catch a cold v. 1. to get into trouble, poss. through impetuousness; 2. to lose out financially, poss. after purchasing a supposed 'bargain' which proves to be otherwise.

catch colt n. an illegitimate child (cf: brush colt).

catch one's death v. to catch a bad cold or 'flu.

catch one's tit in a wringer v. to find oneself in trouble, in an unpleasant situation. The most famous use was during the Watergate Affair when a leading figure suggested that were Katherine Graham, prop. of the Washington *Post*, to permit revelations on White House involvement, she would 'catch her big fat tit in a wringer' *Higgins: 2*.

catch some rays v. 1. to sunbathe *Junker*; 2. Valley Girls (qv.) use: goodbye; a feasible alternative farewell in sun-drenched California *Pond*.

catcher n. one who plays the passive role during sexual intercourse *AS 60.1 (1985)*.

catfish death, have a v. to drown oneself.

Catfish Row n. the Black area of a town.

cathouse n. brothel *Price: 1*.

catnip n. (drug use) inferior or fake marijuana *Folb*.

catnip, not know v. to lack common sense.

cats and kitties n. (rhyming sl.) = titties = breasts *Neaman & Silver*.

cat's pee, cat's piss n. any form of weak alcoholic drink.

cat's pyjamas n. anything exceptional, superlative. (cf: the bee's knees).

cat's whisker, to a phr. very well, exactly, perfectly.

cat's whiskers n. see: cat's pyjamas.

catting (US Black use) (abbrev.) tom-catting: looking for female company and/or conquests *Jones*.

cattle car n. (US Navy use) equivalent of Black Maria or paddy wagon (qqv.) used by the USN's Shore Patrol *Pynchon*.

catty-cat n. (US Black use) the vagina (cf: pussy) *Folb*.

caught in a snowstorm under the influence of cocaine (cf: snow) *Chandler: Notebk*.

caught short 1. desperate to visit a lavatory as soon as possible; 2. (euph.) expecting a child out of wedlock.

caught with one's trousers down surprised in an embarrassing position, or, on a metaphorical level, caught without adequate defences or preparation.

cauliflower n. (abbrev.) cauliflower ear, the sign of a boxer whose ears have taken too many punches to retain their original shape.

caution sign n. (US Black use) anyone who dresses in an excessively gaudy and vulgar manner, with many clashing bright colours *Folb*.

cavalier n. an uncircumcised penis, or the boy who has one (usu, school use) (cf: roundhead).

cavvy n. marijuana.

CB abbrev. cock and balls; used in S&M (qv) contact ads to advertise 'cock and balls torture' *SMD*.

CCW (US police use) (acro.) Carrying a Concealed Weapon *Klein*.

cecil n. (US prison use) cocaine (US pron. *seesul* thus cf: C) *Chandler:*

Notebk.

celebrity fucker n. anyone who courts the famous with the hope of enjoying some proxy fame (cf: groupie) *Wolfe: 2*.

cell task n. (UK prison use) ironic reference to the official cell tasks set prisoners; in fact a pin-up picture whose real life incarnation would obviously make a preferable 'task' to that set by the authorities *LL*.

cement kimono n. (US gangster use) a method of disposing of a corpse by placing inside a barrel filled with wet cement and tossing the resultant lump into a river. (cf: wooden overcoat) *rr*.

cement overcoat n. see: cement kimono *Alvarez*.

cement-head n. (US teen. use) a gullible, conventional person *Sculatti*.

central cut n. the vagina *Klein*.

centre man n. (US prison use) a sycophantic prisoner, who hangs around the centre of the goal where the staff tend to be found *Neaman & Silver*.

century n. $100 or £100 (cf: C) *Major/ LL*.

cereb n. (US campus use) (abbrev.) cerebral: one who works exceptionally hard *Bernbach*.

certain age n. (euph.) middle-aged or older; usu. of women.

CG (contact ads use) abbrev. cross gender *SMD*.

cha-cha v. (US Black use) to have sexual intercourse; fr. the dance *Folb*.

chair n. (abbrev.) the electric chair *Higgins: 1*.

chalfonts n. haemorrhoids; fr. rhy sl: Chalfont St Giles = piles.

chalice n. aka. *chillum*: a pipe used for smoking marijuana; when used by Rastafarians it takes on a sacred and ritualistic role, thus the 'religious' name *Thelwell*.

chalk n. 1. (US Black use) a white person *Folb*; 2. (rhyming sl.) Chalk Farm = arm *Powis*.

chalk eater n. (gambling use) a horse race better who always plays the short priced favourites; fr. the chalk used to write up the odds on the bookmaker's slate *Runyon*.

chalkie n. (Aus. use) school-teacher, who wields it *Wilkes*.

champagne trick n. a particularly wealthy/generous client for a prostitute (cf: trick) *Neaman & Silver*.

chance one's arm v. to take risks; fr. boxing use.

chancer n. anyone who risks their luck, usu. foolishly *Payne*.

changes n. any alteration in one's mental/emotional state; thus *go through changes*, *put through changes* (qqv.) *Major*.

chapper n. (UK criminal use) a policeman, fr. Yiddish *Powis*.

charge n. 1. drugs in general, spec. marijuana *Norman: 2*; 2. the effect of a given drug (cf: high) *De Lannoy & Masterson*.

charge n. (drug use) marijuana *Green: 1*.

charge (one) off v. 1. to end a relationship; 2. to ignore someone one knows well.

charged (up) adv. 1. intoxicated by alcohol; 2. intoxicated by drugs (cf: charge)

charged (up) intoxicated by cannabis (cf: charge) *Powis*.

charity girl n. (US use) a promiscuous girl who 'gives it away for free' *Neaman & Silver*.

charity moll n. (Aus. use) an amateur prostitute, or a professional who undercuts her peers *Wilkes*.

Charlie n. 1. (drug use) cocaine *Burroughs: 1*; 2. see: Mr Charlie.

charlie n. (Aus. use) 1. a prostitute; 2. a lesbian *Baker*.

charlie a. 1. wary, fr. charley: a watchman (1812) *Norman: 2*; 2. (UK 'society' use) flashy, ostentatious, not socially acceptable *Barr*.

Charlie Ronce n. (rhyming sl.) a ponce (cf: Joe Ronce) *Dury*.

Charlie Whitehouse n. a chamber pot.

charlies n. breasts; fr. Aus. rhyming sl. Charlie Wheeler = Sheila = a girl and thus her distinguishing

characteristic *Dunne*.

Charlie's dead (school use) your slip is showing.

charming wife n. (rhyming sl.) a knife *Powis*.

charver v. to make love; fr. Parlyaree (theatrical slang.) chauvering: sexual intercourse; poss. fr. Fr. *chauffer*: to heat up *Norman: 2*.

chase a rabbit v. euph. to go to the lavatory.

chase the dragon v. to smoke heroin, sucking up the smoke of the drug which is burned on a piece of kitchen foil; the heated heroin liquifies and flows across the paper, gradually giving off smoke which is sucked into the smoker's lungs by a tube, also usually made of kitchen foil; the 'dragon' underlines the Oriental origin of much of the heroin found in the UK *Green: 2*.

chassis n. the female figure; thus *classy chassis*: an attractive figure, and thus an attractive woman; fr. motoring use *Neaman & Silver*.

chat n. verbal skills, fluency, articulacy, the ability to charm a victim with words alone *Norman: 2*.

chat up v. to attempt the first, verbal stages of seduction.

chateaued a. (UK 'society' use) very drunk (on wine); puns on shattered and chateau *Barr*.

chatter box n. (US Black use) 1. record player; 2. telephone *Klein*.

chaw-mouth n. 1. a talkative person; 2. derog. an Irishman.

chazerai n. fr. Yiddish *chazer* a pig: a pigsty, a mess; cheap, worthless, rubbish *McBain: 1*.

cheap a. mean, miserly, grasping *Higgins: 5*.

cheap Charlie n. (US milit. use) any soldier who is less than generous when drinking in a bar, etc. *Del Vecchio*.

cheapie n. a mean person *Higgins: 3*.

cheapskate n. a mean, ungenerous person *Runyon*.

cheat the starter v. to have a child out of wedlock; to become pregnant prior to the wedding *Neaman & Silver*.

cheaters n. glasses, spectacles
  Runyon: 1.

check in v. 1. to die (cf: cash in one's
  checks, check out, 2.); 2. to go to bed.

check out v.t. to kill; fr. check out:
  leave a hotel, depart *Price: 2.*

check out v. 1. to look over, sum up
  Price: 2; 2. to die *Dunne.*

check you later phr. see you later,
  goodbye.

cheder n. a prison cell, fr. Yiddish
  cheder a small room, or a study *Powis.*

cheeb n. (US Black use) marijuana.

cheerio 1. goodbye; 2. a toast (cf:
  cheers).

cheers 1. one of the most common
  toasts before drinking; 2. thank-you;
  3. goodbye (cf: cheerio).

cheese n. a light-skinned Black
  person.

cheese n. 1. aka: *head-cheese*:
  smegma that accumulates around the
  uncircumcised penis *Legman*; 2. (US
  teen use) the best of a given type or
  style (cf: big cheese) *Sculatti.*

cheese v. to play up to, to toady to (cf:
  eat cheese).

cheese v. 1. to ejaculate *Klein*; 2. to
  break wind (cf: fart) *Dunne.*

cheese it! stop it! formerly Aus. cant
  but latterly general use, esp. by
  schoolchildren *Baker.*

cheesecake n. 1. a pin-up girl (cf:
  beefcake) *San Francisco Comic Bk
  no. 2*; 2. easy, simple, no problems
  Higgins: 1.

cheesed off miserable, annoyed, fed
  up *Humphries.*

cheese-eater n. an informer; fr. euph.
  for rat: an informer *Grogan.*

cheesehead n. idiot, fool.

cheesy a. 1. (street gang use) disloyal
  Salisbury; 2. false, hypocritical; fr. the
  'say cheese' ritual for the summoning
  up of instant false smiles for the
  camera *Norman: 2.*

Chelsea smile n. a knife slash that
  runs from the corner of the mouth up
  and across the cheek; such cuts are
  inflicted on rival supporters by Stanley
  knives wielded by the more violent
  section of the fans of Chelsea FC *L*
  Green.

cherries n. (rhyming sl.) cherry hogs
  = dogs = greyhound racing tracks
  Powis.

cherry n. 1. a female virgin; thus *bust a
  cherry*: to deflower; 2. (homosexual
  use) anally virgin *Legman*; 3. virgin;
  thus *harvest the cherries*: to take a
  youth and have his virginity taken
  Price: 1; 4. (US milit. use) a fresh
  troop, one who has yet to be 'blooded'
  in combat *Del Vecchio.*

cherrypop v. to seduce and deflower
  virgins, usu. females.

cherry-picker n. 1. a large, hooked
  nose; 2. a pointed shoe.

cherry-picking (business use) the
  reviewing of a number of competing
  ideas prior to selecting those most
  useful/profitable for one's own ends.

cherry-top n. 1. a police car with a red
  light on its roof; thus 2. a policeman.

chevy n. (rhyming sl.) chevy chase =
  face *Powis.*

chew v. 1. to talk; 2. to embarrass; 3.
  to argue, to protest.

chew (it) over v. to discuss, to
  consider, to ponder (cf. bite the bait).

chew down v. to haggle, to bargain
  with.

chew face v. (US college use) to kiss
  Bernbach.

chew one's balls off v.t. to reprimand
  severely.

chew one's bit v. 1. to be anxious or
  upset; 2. to argue or talk loudly.

chew one's tobacco twice v. to be
  mean, to be tight-fisted.

chew out v. to tell off, to harangue
  Higgins: 1.

chew the fat v. to converse, to talk
  over; fr. rhyming sl. = have a chat
  Runyon.

chew the rag v. see: chew the fat
  Runyon.

chewers n. teeth, real or false.

chewing, chewings n. 1. food; 2. a
  telling off, a scolding (cf: chew out).

chewing match n. an argument.

Chicago bankroll see: California
  bankroll *Folb.*

Chicago lightning gunfire *Chandler:*

Notebk.

Chicago piano n. a Thompson sub-machine-gun, which achieved notoriety as the preferred weapon of Chicago gangsters in 1920s and later *Fiction Illus.* 3.

Chicago typewriter n. a Thompson sub-machine-gun,

chichi n. the female breast, fr. Mexican *Morgan*.

chichi a. 1. aka *shishi*: homosexual *Stanley*; 2. affected, pretentious, 'pretty-pretty'.

chick n. a girl: fr. chicken, lively, perky and 'good enough to eat'; the opposite of cat (qv.) *Powis*.

chicken n. 1. a coward; fr. that bird's alleged characteristic *Salisbury*; 2. (US Black use) 1. unattractive old woman; 2. an aggressive woman (NB: both uses are direct reverse of usual white equivalents; cf: bad) *Folb*; 3. underage boys (cf: mystery) *Jay & Young*.

chicken coop n. 1. a police car or patrol wagon; 2. an outside lavatory.

chicken feed n. derisorily small amounts; of money or anything else *Himes: 1*.

chicken fucker n. general derog. term; often intensified by comb. bald-headed chicken-fucker.

chicken hawk n. an older male homosexual with a preference for young boys (cf: chicken queen) *McFadden*.

chicken out v. to be scared, to be too frightened to act *Farren*.

chicken queen n. older homosexual male who prefers sex with teenage boys (cf: chicken hawk) *Jay & Young*.

chicken ranch n. a brothel, fr. a house in Gilbert, Texas, where poor farmers once paid for their pleasures with chickens *Neaman & Silver*.

chicken run n. teenage virility ritual involving the driving of two cars at high speed towards each other, or towards a dangerous obstacle: the first one to turn aside or brake is 'chicken' *'Rebel without a Cause'*, directed N. Ray, 1955.

chicken's neck n. a cheque; rhy. sl.

chickenshit cowardly, fearful *Higgins: 1*.

chickie n. a warning of the impending approach of authority — whether policeman, parent or teacher — and thus a command to stop whatever one is doing that might cause that authority to act against one (cf: keep chickie).

chi-ike v. to tease, to fool, to deceive *Sillitoe*.

chili n. (derog.) a Mexican; thus *chili*- as prefix to anything supposedly Mexican; fr. popular Mex. food.

chili chump n. aka: *chili pimp* (US Black use) a pimp who has only one girl working for him; an inexperienced pimp *Klein*.

chilichoker n. a Mexican *Morgan*.

chill n. death, assassination; fr. the cold corpse *Fiction Illus.* 3.

chill v. to murder, to assassinate.

chill out v. to calm down, to control one's emotions; originated by black US teenagers, the term has now spread to the UK, and is used by both blacks and whites *Pond*.

chilling adv. relaxing, acting in a cool (qv) manner (cf: chill out).

chilly a. 1. emotionless, detached (cf: arctic, cool); 2. cold-blooded; 3. skillful, competent at a given task or profession (cf: cool).

chilly most n. (US Black use) a relaxed, composed person.

chimney n. (US Black use) a hat, fr. the chimney's position on top of the house *Major*.

chin music n. conversation, chatter, talk.

china n. (rhyming sl.) china plate = mate = best friend *Powis*.

Chinaman n. one who has political influence.

chinch n. a bedbug *Major*.

chinchilla n. the vagina (cf: beaver).

Chinee n. complementary ticket *Runyon*.

Chinese a. one of the racial stereotypes used in many contexts: the Chinese eye-shape, plus the supposed cunning of the wily Orientals always has 'Chinese' implying something slightly out of true, either physically, ethically, or otherwise (cf: French).

Chinese n. a Chinese meal, often a take-out. (cf: Indian)

Chinese brown n. a form of heroin.

Chinese chance (US use) no chance whatsoever, no luck; fr. gold rush use, when Chinese worked otherwise abandoned claims *New York restaurant name, c.1982*.

Chinese cut n. a stroke that sends the ball in quite another direction from that in which the batsman aimed; 'Chinese' implying 'slanted' as in the racial clichés of oriental eyes *BBC Radio 3 1983*.

Chinese duckets n. complimentary tickets to a theatrical or sporting event (cf: Chinee) *Runyon*.

Chinese fire drill bedlam, chaos *Stone*.

Chinese No. 3 a variety of heroin, processed in Hong Kong and imported by Chinese smugglers. (cf: chase the dragon).

Chinese rocks n. a form of heroin.

Chinese white n. a form of heroin.

chinfest n. any meeting at which there is a good deal of talking and gossip.

chingazo n. fr. taboo Sp. 'a fuck': sexual intercourse *Folb*.

Chink n., a. Chinese *Price: 2*.

Chink chow n. Chinese food *Underwood*.

chinky a. (US campus use) stingy, mean; fr. the tightness of one's wallet and pockets *Underwood*.

CHINS (US prison use) (acro.) *Children In Need of Supervision* (cf: MINS, PINS) *Neaman & Silver*.

chintzy a. stingy, mean.

chinwag n. a chat, a conversation *Humphries*.

chip v. (US criminal use) to carry out a small crime with only minimal profits *Klein*.

chip in v. to join in, to contribute; fr. poker use *Price: 2*.

chip one's teeth v. to talk, esp. to excess or angrily.

chipper a. cheerful, lively, perhaps

slightly drunk *Neaman & Silver*.

chippie n. 1. carpenter, esp. theatrical, movie use *Wilkinson*; 2. a promiscuous woman; a prostitute *Waits*; 3. (abbrev.) fish and chip shop.

chippie v. to fool sexually; to betray *Waits*.

chippy n. a prostitute who does not really work at it full-time, a promiscuous young girl. *Price: 1*.

chippy v. to use narcotics, esp. heroin, only on an irregular basis rather than to be a habitual addict.

chippy on v. to cheat on one's wife or husband with a new sexual partner *Bruce: 2*.

chips n. buttocks *Selby: 1*.

chisel v. to cheat, thus *chisel out of*: to defraud *Greaser Comics*.

chiseller n. a cheat, a thief *Greaser Comics*.

Chi-town n. Chicago, Illinois *Ice T:2*.

chiv n. a knife; fr. Romany *Powis*.

chiva n. heroin *Morgan*.

chizz v. (school use) to cheat, to swindle; fr. chiseller (qv).

choco abbrev. of chocolate (qv); and as such a derog. term (generally among middle/upper class speakers) for a black person.

chocolate n. a black person.

Chocolate City n. the Black ghetto; any concentration of Blacks *Price: 2*.

chocolate (stuff) n. (drug use) heroin (cf: tootsie roll) (fr. colour and consistency of Mexican heroin).

choff v. food; fr. chow (qv.) + scoff (qv.) *Sanders: 2*.

choice a. excellent, first-rate *Pond*.

choirboys n. (US police use) innocent, novice policemen who work strictly by the rulebook *'Hill Street Blues', Thames TV, 1983*.

choke n. a Mexican (cf:chillichoker) *Morgan*.

choke a darkie v. (Aus. use) to excrete *Humphries*.

choke off v. 1. to upbraid, to reprimand; 2. to silence (in mid-flow) *Wodehose: AAG*.

choke the chicken, choke the chook v. to masturbate.

choke up v. to give unwillingly, esp. to pay a long-standing debt (cf: cough up).

choked a. upset, annoyed, depressed, having 'a lump in one's throat' *Performance*.

choked down (US Black use) well dressed, poss. fr. choker: a tie, thus one who wears a tie must look smart *Folb*.

choker n. a disappointment, an annoyance (cf: sickener) *Norman: 3*.

chokes and croaks (US campus use) course in first aid and safety education *Dickson*.

chokey n. 1. (UK prison use) punishment cells *Norman: 1*; 2. prison *Dury*.

chokka aka: *chokker*: full to the brim; fr. choc full, choc a bloc *Capital Radio 1983*.

Cholo aka *Chico*: see *bato Folb*.

cho-mo n. (US cant) a child molester (fr. abbr. child molestor).

chompers n. teeth, both genuine and false. (fr.SE chomp: to chew).

choof v. to leave, to go away; fr. UK early 20th C *teuf-teuf*: goodbye (?) *Baker*.

chook n. (Aus. use) a chicken *Humphries*.

choose off v. (US Black use) to challenge to a fight *Folb*.

choose up v. (US prison use) for an experienced inmate to select a newcomer as a homosexual partner, whether or not the latter agrees to act as one *Klein*.

choosing money n. (US pimp use) the voluntary donation of her earnings by a ho (qv.) to a pimp whom she wishes to start acting as her own pimp *Shulman*.

chop n. 1. (Aus. use) share, portion *Wilkes*; 2. food.

chop n. abbrev. of chopper 1. (qv).

chop chop quickly, fast; fr. Chinese pidgin *Dunne*.

chop cotton v. to work hard.

chop suey n. a person of mixed ancestry. (fr. SE chopped up + chop suey: a dish of stir-fried meat and vegetables, created by Chinese chefs for their Western customers; not part of Oriental cuisine, it was seen as adequate for the Western palate; the orig. Chinese is *shap sui*: mixed bits).

chop the clock v. (car sales use) to tune back the mileometer in order to fool a customer into thinking a vehicle is less old than it actually is *J. Updike, 'Rabbit is Rich', 1982*.

chopper n. a Thompson sub-machinegun, usu. gangster use (cf: Chicago piano, typewriter) *rr*.

chopper n.1. a helicopter *M. Herr, 'Dispatches' 1978*; 2. a cut down, 'chopped' motorbike, spec. a Harley-Davidson, preferred for speed and style by outlaw motorcycle gangs, i.e. Hells Angels *San Francisco Comic 3*.

choppers n. teeth.

chopping sticks (bingo rhyming sl.) 6 *Wright*.

chops n. lips. mouth; fr. animal use and thus usu. derog *Sillitoe*.

chopstick n. slightly derog. Asian person *Folb*.

chosen a. (US prison use) selected, like it or not, as the homosexual lover (cf: punk) of an older, tougher inmate (cf: choose up) *Klein*.

chow n. food, esp. in an institutional setting, ie army messhall, prison, etc.; fr. Chinese *O'Brien*.

chowder-head n. (US teen use) see: cement-head *Sculatti*.

chow-hound n. (US milit. use) any serviceman who is especially keen on his food, runs to head the messhall queue, etc. *AS 41 (1966)*.

christen v. to mark or otherwise damage, esp. of a dog that reveals its lack of house-training.

Christer n. (derog.) an overly religious person, esp. a proselytizing teetotaller.

Christmas! (euph.) Christ! *Rawson*.

Christmas hold n. (Aus. use) a squeeze of one's opponent's testicles; fr. pun on 'hand full of nuts (testicles)', a popular Yuletide pleasure *Wilkes*.

Christmas tree n. (drug use)

1. stimulant (deximal spansules)
2. depressant (butabarbital (Tuinal))
Klein; 3. a heavily over-made or over-dressed woman.

Christopher Columbus! (euph.)
Christ! *Rawson*.

chrome dome n. (orig. US) a bald head, thus a bald-headed person.

chromo n.2. an ugly, distasteful person *Runyon: 1*; 2. (Aus. use) a prostitute.

chronic, the n. premium grade cannabis/marijuana *Dre*.

chubb v. (UK prison use) to lock up; fr. trade name of the locksmith *LL*.

chubby-chaser n. a man who prefers (unfashionably) plump or even fat women *M. Innes 1983*.

chubette n. a fat girl (cf: bimbette).

chuc n. (abbrev.) Pachuco = Mexican-American *Farina*.

chuck n. a verdict of not guilty: chucked out of court *Newman: 3*.

chuck v.1. to vomit; 2. to throw *Performance*; 3. to end an affair, to reject a lover.

chuck a cheesy n. (Aus. use) to grin.

chuck a dummy v. to vomit.

chuck horrors n. see: chucks *Algren*.

chuck it in v. to give up, esp. of a job. or as excl. *chuck it in!* stop it! *Griffith*.

chuck up the sponge v. to give in, to surrender; fr. boxing use *Neaman & Silver*.

chuck wagon n. 1. a small restaurant or café; 2. a buffet.

chuck you, Farley! joking expletive, fr. 'fuck you, Charley!'

chucker-out n. a staff member at pubs, dance-halls, concert-halls and similar places of public entertainment to eject, by force if necessary, rowdy and undesirable people (cf: bouncer) *Dickson*.

chucklehead n. dolt, simpleton, fool.

chucks n. 1. Converse All-Star baseball boots; signed by designer Chuck Taylor *Jay & Young*; 2. the craving for food that hits a heroin addict once he has withdrawn from using the drug – which on the whole destroys the appetite during its regular

use. *Burroughs: 1*.

chuff n. (homosexual use) pubic hair *Maledicta*.

chuff euph. fuck (mainly used in the North of England).

chuffed a. very pleased, delighted, happy *Barr*.

chug v. (abbrev.) chug-a-lug: to drink, esp. to down in one gulp or without putting down the glass *Price: 2*.

chummy n. (UK police use) address of anyone to whom the policeman is talking; a suspect *Laurie*.

chummy a. friendly; fr. chum *Higgins:2*.

chump n. anyone gullible, easily taken in *Milner*.

chump job n. respectable, low-paying regular work (cf: nine to five) *Milner*.

chump off v. (US Black use) to look down on, to disdain *Klein*.

chump-change a. second rate, inferior, good only for fools *Price:2*.

chump v. to trick, to deceive, to make someone a chump (qv) *Thompson:J*.

chumpy a. naive, stupid, gullible.

chunder v. (Aus. use) to vomit; according to Barry Humphries, the great popularizer of the word in his 'Barry Mackenzie' strip in *Private Eye* and on film, fr. nautical shout of warning 'watch under!'; Wilkes (op cit) also offers rhyming sl. fr. Chunder Loo of Akin Foo = spew = vomit; Chunder Loo featured in long-running series of ads for Cobra boot polish c.1910 *Humphries*.

chungo bunny n. (derog.) Black person; mispron. of jungle bunny (qv) *Higgins:1*.

chunk n. (Can. prison use) a handgun *Caron*.

chunk v. (US Black use) to discard, to throw away; fr. chuck (qv) *Klein*.

church is out phr. everything is finished, no alternative is available.

church key n. a can opener *Greaser Comics*.

church mouse n. (homosexual use) a homosexual who frequents crowded churches in order to fondle any potential sex partners *Legman*.

chutzpah n. fr. Yiddish: gall, cheek, outrageousness, audacity *Rosten*.

ciggy n. abbr. cigarette.

cinch n. a simple, easily attained thing; fr. *cinch*: grip tightly, thus something one can grasp easily *Grogan*.

circle jerk n. joint masturbation, often in competition, by a group of boys, poss. sitting in a circle *Morgan*.

circus n. a sex-show *Legman*

Circus cowboys n. rent boys (qv) who congregate in and around Piccadilly Circus, London.

— city a fantasy place that acts as an intensifier for a given adjective or phrase; thus *nowhere city*, *forget-it-city*, *fun city*, etc. *Bruce:2*.

city slicker n. (derog.) a city person.

civvie n. a civilian, thus termed by members of the forces, the prison service, police, etc.

civvy street n. the world of civilian life, usu. service use.

claim v. (UK police use) to arrest (cf: borrow) *Laurie*.

clam n. 1. (UK use) a tight-lipped person; 2. (US use) a mean person.

clam up v. to stop talking, to become deliberately secretive *Goulart*.

clam-digger n. 1. the hands; 2. the nickname of the inhabitants of various towns in NE US.

clams n. dollars *Dunne*.

clap n. venereal disease *Price:1*.

clap trap n. a brothel where one might contract venereal disease (cf: clap).

clapped out a. worn out, useless; esp. of machinery, cars, etc. fr. clap (qv) and its deleterious effects, even on such things as could not possibly contract it *Capital Radio 1983*.

clapping for credit (US campus use) music appreciation course *Bernbach*.

claret n. blood *Performance*.

class act n. an impressive performance, both literally and metaphorically.

classic a. (US campus use) anyone or anything that is regarded as out of the ordinary, eccentric; inference is one of

ironic appraisal *Bernbach*.

clean a. 1. (Black pimp use) dressed in the height of current male fashion, perfectly groomed *Milner*; 2. beyond any possible suspicion, guiltless *Higgins:1*; 3. not using any form of drug; not currently addicted *Higgins:1*; 4. (criminal use) without any form of incriminating identification; not carrying a gun *Grogan*.

clean one's clock v. to beat up severely.

clean one's plow v. to thrash, to beat severely; thus clean one's plow off: to come to the end of one's patience (cf: clean one's clock).

clean out v. (gambling use) to take all of an opponent's money. (cf: take to the cleaners) *Powis*.

clean shot n. good luck, favourable opportunity *Higgins:1*.

clean the pipe n. to perform oral sex.

clean to the bone a. (US Black use) aka: *fonky to the bone*, *mod. . .*, *ragged. . .*, *silked. . .*, *tabbed. . .* exceptionally well dressed *Folb*.

clean up v. 1. (Black use) to make excuses; to form an alibi *Milner*; 2. to do very well out of a project; esp. in gambling use. (cf: take to the cleaners) *Pearce*.

clean up on to deal with successfully *Schulberg*.

clean up the kitchen (homosexual use) to practise cunnilingus *Legman*.

clean up the walls v. (US Black use) to chatter, to gossip, to talk nonsense *Seale*.

clear cut (US Black use) 1. stylish clothes; 2. pure drugs *Klein*.

clear off v. to leave, to depart, esp. as excl. *clear off*! *Manser*.

clearly a. (Valley Girls (qv) use) totally, maximally, perfectly, etc. *Pond*.

clear-up n. (UK police use) the identification and capture (ideally) of a known villain *Laurie*.

clem n. derog. a farmer, a peasant (cf: rube) (fr. proper name Clarence).

clever a. (Aus. use) in good health, in

order, working well, etc., thus *not too clever*: generally negative response to 'how are you', 'how is it', etc. *Ready*.

clever clogs n. a slightly derogatory description (usu. used by children) of anyone considered notably clever (often 'too clever for their own good').

click v. to work out exactly as planned; like a perfectly designed machine *rr*.

click with v. to get on well, usu. with someone of the opposite sex *Wodehouse:AAG*.

clickers n. false teeth.

clickety-click (bingo rhyming sl.) 66.

cliff-hanger n. any suspenseful, threatening situation, although usu. one from which one is eventually delivered; fr. movie description of such silent-era serials as 'The Perils of Pauline' (starring Pearl White) in which the heroine, at an episode's end, was often literally hanging from a cliff *McFadden*.

climb all over v. 1. to attack verbally; to reprimand; 2. to maul sexually, usu. spoken by a female of a male.

climb the rigging v. to lose one's temper, fr. RN use *Green:2*.

climb the walls v. to approach insanity through nerves, irritation, tension, etc.

climbing trees to get away from it aka: *got to swim underwater to get away from it; so busy I've had to put a man on to help*: (Aus. male cp) in answer to query 'getting any?' (qv) *Neaman & Silver*.

clincher n. the ultimate solution, the culmination *Schulberg*.

clink n. prison; fr. the name of the Southwark gaol, demolished in the 18th C. *Sillitoe*.

clinker n. a piece of excrement adhering to the anus.

clip v. 1. to hit, to tap sharply *Runyon:1*; 2. to defraud, to steal from (cf: welch, rip off) *Higgins:1*; 3. to kill, to murder *Morgan*.

clip-joint n. a club or similar place of entertainment where the customers are deliberately and systematically

defrauded under the guise of charging them for their pleasure *Norman:2*.

clipped a. circumcised (cf: roundhead).

clippie n. a bus conductress, who once clipped tickets.

clipping (UK criminal/police use) posing as a prostitute, obtaining the money, but absconding before intercourse takes place (cf: murphy game) *Powis*.

clit n. (abbrev.) clitoris *Southern & Hoffenberg*.

clithopper n. (lesbian use) a promiscuous lesbian *Maledicta*.

clitty n. the clitoris *Fiesta Magazine XIII:6*.

clobber n. fr. Yiddish (?); clothes *Norman:2*.

clobber v. to hit *Newman:1*.

clobber one with v. to force an unpleasant/unwanted task or duty on someone.

clobbered a. drunk *Dickson*.

clock n. the face *Sillitoe*.

clock v. 1. to see, to recognize, to notice *Payne*; 2. to hit *Price:2*.

clock a daffy v. (S. Afr. use) shoot a line (qv), tell a deceitful story with the intention of tricking the hearer *A. Marcuson*.

clock and a half? (taxi-driver use) the attempt by a crooked cabbie to get an innocent, usu. foreign, fare to pay an extra 50% of what is registered on the clock; some pretext may be put forward, but often just the phrase, delivered with confidence, is sufficient *Powis*.

clock in v. to arrive; fr. industrial time-keeping practice *Wodehouse:GB*.

clocker n. (drug use) a dealer of crack (qv) cocaine; thus clocking: working as a crack dealer. (fr. SE clock: a time piece; the need for the drug and the appearances of the dealer both seem to occur at regular intervals).

clodpoll n. fool, incompetent *Dickson*.

clompers n. false teeth (cf: chomper).

clone n. 1. (gay use) general

description of gay men who posed as one of a variety of super-masculine stereotypes, eg. truck driver, military man, cowboy, etc. The style was epitomized by the members of the 1970s disco group Village People; **2.** (computer use), a machine that resembles the industry standard, and which will perform all the same functions, but which is cheaper, and may be assembled from parts supplied by less reputable manufacturers; clones are invariably of IBM machines, usually the 'AT' model. *Green:3*.

clonk n. **1.** a blow, a hit; **2.** a noise of one hard object striking another (cf: clunk).

clonk v. to hit (cf: clunk).

close, but no cigar (cp.) commiserating with a 'near-miss' or a good try; fr. fairground use: the pitchman rewarded successful punters (qv) with cigars *C. Colegrave*.

closed swinging n. (sex industry use) swapping parties in which only husband-and-wife partnerships take part; no singles are allowed to unbalance the situation (cf: open swinging, swinging) *SMD*.

closer n. (horse-racing use) a horse on whom the odds shortened drastically in the minutes prior to the race, but which still failed to win *Bukowski:1*.

closet a. secretive, clandestine, hidden; fr. homosexual use.

closet case n. (homosexual use) a homosexual who finds it difficult or impossible to admit his sexuality in public *Jay & Young*.

closet queen n. see: closet case *Stanley*.

cloth-ears n. general term of abuse, esp. to someone who at first seems to not have heard one's comment *Capital Radio*1983.

clothes n. (NY police use) (abbrev.) plain clothes; a detective *'Serpico', directed Sidney Lumet, 1973*.

clotheshorse n. an exquisitely well-dressed, fashionable person, although the implication is that beyond such

perfection lies little else.

cloud n. a Black person, esp. a crowd of Black people (cf: smoke).

Cloud 9 paradise; anywhere exceptionally pleasant *Major*.

clout n. **1.** influence, esp. in politics; one who 'packs a punch' in government *PT*; **2.** a stupid, oafish person (cf: clod); **3.** a philanderer.

clout v. to steal *Higgins:3*.

clown n. fool, idiot; generally derog. application *Price:2*.

clown around v. to play the fool *Heller*.

cluck n. a dull, stupid person; with the brains of a chicken *Junker*.

clucky a. (Aus. use) pregnant; ref. is to a broody hen *Neaman & Silver*.

clue one in v. to explain, to offer information *Greenlee*.

clueless a. stupid, ignorant, incompetent.

clunk n. a fool, an idiot.

clunk v. to hit, to strike.

clunker n. worn-out, useless car *The Collected Trashman 1969*.

cluster-fuck n. **1.** orgy; **2.** gang rape (cf: gang bang) **3.** a group of indecisive people, unable to decide on what to do next *S. Prosser*.

clutch n. (UK 'society' use) a dance (the activity, not the event) *Barr*.

Clydesdale n. (US use) an attractive male, invariably a WASP (qv).

C-note n. $100 bill (cf:C) *Fiction Illus.3*.

CNR strawberries n. (Can. prison use) prunes *Caron*.

coal n. a dark-skinned Black person (cf: cheese).

coal burner n. a white man or woman who enjoys sexual relations with a black man or woman *Maledicta*.

coal-scuttle blonde n. a Black woman.

coat and badge v. (rhyming sl.) to cadge; usu. in 'on the C. and B.'; fr. Doggett's Coat and Badge, awarded to Thames watermen who, with this prize, had the right to charge higher fares in their mid-19th-C. heyday *Cole*.

Coat-hanger n. (Aus. use) the Sydney

Harbour Bridge; fr. its shape *Wilkes*.

cob v. to take, to steal (cf: cop).

cobber n. (Aus. use) friend, mate; fr. UK dialect *cob*: to take a liking to someone; like the other great clichéd Aus. word bonzer (qv) (cf:ripper) cobber is now nearly defunct *Ready*.

cobbler n. (US cant) a forger, esp. of passports, currency and stocks and bonds *Neaman & Silver*.

cobblers! (rhyming sl.) cobblers awls = balls (qv) = rubbish! *Powis*.

cobitis n. (UK prison use) loss of appetite, poss. fr. eating too many prison loaves ('cobs') *LL*.

cobs n. testicles; fr. cobblers (qv).

cock n. 1. general term of address, esp. Cockney use; in itself an abbrev. of Cockney *Wright*; 2. the penis.; UK and northern states of US; 3. the vagina: southern states of US (cf: nuts 2) *Grogan*; 4. US southern campus use: a woman, viewed solely as a sexual object *Underwood*; 5. a man who is easy to sponge on; spec. one who buys more than his necessary share in a pub *Powis*; 6. nonsense, rubbish; also *load of old cock*.

cock v. to knock out (cf: cold-cock]

cock a deaf 'un v. to pretend to be deaf, or at least to ignore by 'not hearing' the speaker *Norman:2*.

cock a snoot at v. to disdain, to ignore, to turn up one's nose. .

cock and hen (bingo rhyming sl.) 10 (cf: Downing Street) *LL*.

cock and hen n. £10 *EN 1957*.

cock block v. (US Black use) to ruin another man's sexual activities by stealing his girl, interrupting his seduction etc. *Folb*.

cock cheese n. smegma.

cock doctor n. venerealogist *Higgins:1*.

cock it up v. 1. (UK use) to blunder, to make a mistake; 2. (Aus. use) for a woman to offer herself sexually in an obvious manner *Wilkes*.

cock linnet n. (rhyming sl.) minute *Jones:J*.

cock movie n. pornographic film

Simmons.

cock off v. to fail, to blunder *Higgins:1*.

cock one's pistol v. to surprise, to astonish; esp. in phr. 'That cocks my/his pistol'.

cock pluck v. (US Black use) see finger-fuck *Folb*.

cock rock n. heavy metal music with even more than the usual macho strutting and posturing.

cock sparrow n. (rhyming sl.) barrow *Jones:J*.

cock up v. to make a mess of; to blunder.

cockamamy a. confused, ludicrous, fake, fraudulent, absurd *Rosten*.

cock-brain n. a foolish young man.

cocked a. drunk (cf: half-cocked).

cock-eyed a. 1. very drunk, fr. the inability to coordinate physically that accompanies such a state *Farrell*; 2. eccentric, odd; out of true, at an angle *Wodehouse:JO*.

cock-hound n. (US Black use) a man devoted to sex before all things; fr. the Southern use of cock as vagina rather than penis *Milner*.

cockle and hen (rhyming sl.) ten, usu. £10 (cf: cock and hen) *Cole*.

cockroach n. a despicable person.

cockroach business n. a small, mean enterprise.

cockroach joint n. lowest, filthiest possible café or restaurant.

cocksman n. 1. an exceptionally virile man *Price:1*; 2. (US Black use) a male prostitute *Major*.

cocksucker n. 1. spec. fellatrix; 2. generally abusive term. (cf: motherfucker) *Price:2*.

cocktease v. to lead on in a sexual manner but never to permit actual intercourse. Thus one who does this is a *cockteaser* (cf: pricktease, -teaser) *Price:2*.

cocky general term of address to a man *Wodehouse: MOJ*.

coco n. (abbrev.) coconut: head *Runyon:1*.

cocoa n. derog. a Black person, esp. light-skinned.

coconut head n. **1.** a fool; **2.** derog. a Black person.

coconuts n. (drug use) cocaine *De Lannoy & Masterson*.

cocooning n. (US use) staying at home with one's family.

COD abbr. (sex industry use) a male whore; abbrev. cock on delivery *Maledicta 9*.

Codfish Flats n. the poor area of town (cf: Catfish Row).

codger n. a fellow, a man; usu. in 'old codger' with the implication of crotchety old age *Hotten*.

codology n. the practice of teasing; fr. cod: to tease, to hoax *Sex Pistols, 'Dead Horse', 1979*.

cods n. **1.** testicles; orig. Middle Eng. usage *Humphries*; **2.** a mess (cf: ballsup, cockup).

cod's roe n. (rhyming sl.) = dough (qv) = money *Wright*.

codswallop n. nonsense, rubbish, drivel.

coffee and cocoa (rhyming sl.) say so; thus cp: I should cocoa (esp. in 'Billy Cotton Band Show' BBC Light Prog. 1950s) *Cole*.

coffee coolers n. (US Black use) the lips.

coffee grinder n. old and unstable propellor-driven aeroplane *Higgins:3*.

coffeeand n. (abbrev.) **1.** coffee and cakes: the cheapest meal available in a café or diner; thus, in context, referring to cheap, minimal, second-rate: *coffeeand role* in the theatre is a small part that will pay for little more than snacks *Selby:1*; **2.** coffeeand habit (drug use) a smalltime heroin habit, adopted either through grim self-control or simple poverty.

coffeeand pimp n. a smalltime pimp, whose girls barely make him a living, let alone provide the high style to which he should aspire *Green:2*.

coffee-break parole n. (US prison use) nickname for a Special Circumstances release; so called because they are granted very quickly *Morgan*.

coffeehouse v. (poker use) to bluff a rival verbally rather than by betting *Alvarez*.

coffee-strainer n. a bushy moustache.

coffin-dodger n. an old person, prob. ill *Welsh:1*.

coffin nail n. a cigarette, presumably from nicotine's cancerous potential *Uris*.

cognoscenti n. (homosexual use) the world of homosexuals, its style, language, ethos, etc. *Legman*.

coil one's ropes v. to die (cf: give up the ship, keel over, lose the number of one's mess, sling one's hook, slip one's cable).

coin n. money *Variety 1983*.

coin v. to make a great deal of money.

cojones n. (Sp.) testicles; used both to mean the physical organ and the metaphorical courage, and in both cases a synonym for balls (qv); popularized first by the works of Ernest Hemingway and latterly by Puerto Rican immigrants to US *Rawson*.

coke n. cocaine (cf: C, Charlie, girl, etc.) *Milner*.

coke stare n. (US Black use) the evil eye; a deliberately aggressive and unpleasant look *Folb*.

cold a. (of a cheque) fraudulent, worthless (cf: catch a cold, have a bad cold).

cold adv. dead.

cold a. adv. **1.** (sporting use) out of form, below par *Sanchez*; **2.** (US teen. use) unpleasant, difficult, unnecessary; and by bad = good thus: excellent, first rate, superb *E. Beyer*; also used adverbially as in 'cold chillin' (cf: stone) *Ice T:1*.

cold n. (butchers' sl.) frozen, thus imported meat *Cole*.

cold as a cocksucker's knees phr. extremely cold.

cold case n. (US Black use) a very bad situation *Folb*.

cold in hand a. (US Black use) without money, broke (qv) penniless (cf: cold, catch a cold, have a bad cold) *Major*.

cold meat n. a corpse; thus *cold meat box*: a coffin; *cold meat cart*: hearse.

cold potato n. someone or something judged to be worthless, insignificant or boring.

cold shot n. (US Black use) unnecessary and aggressive behaviour *Folb*.

cold shoulder v. to ignore, to snub.

cold storage n. 1. death; 2. a prison.

cold turkey n. withdrawal from heroin addiction without any assistance from medication *Grogan*.

cold-cock v. to knock out unconscious. (cf: cold-deck) *Grogan*.

cold-cunt v. (lesbian use) to ignore, to brush off; fr. cold shoulder (qv) *Maledicta*.

cold-deck v. to knock unconscious; fr. knock cold (qv) and deck (qv).

collar n. (drug use) the strip of paper wrapped around a dropper to ensure a tight fit with the needle *Burroughs:1*; 2. an arrest *Goldman*.

collar v. (US Black use) to understand; thus 'collar the jive': to understand every aspect of a situation (cf: colly).

collar a hot v. (US Black use) to eat a meal (cf: collar a nod).

collar a nod v. (US Black use) to sleep (cf: collar a hot).

collar and tie n. a masculine lesbian; fr. the use of men's clothing *Legman*.

collect v. (Aus. use) to be hit by, to collide with, usu. of a car *Wilkes*.

college n. gaol *Runyon*.

college hill n. that part of a town or city where the rich live.

collegiate fucking (homosexual use) body to body rubbing (cf: Princeton rub) *Jay & Young*.

collie n. (Jamaican use) marijuana, ganga; thus *collie-man*: ganga seller *Thelwell*.

collies n. heroin *Welsh:1* (fr. colly-wobbles).

colly v. (US Black use) to understand, to comprehend *Major*.

colly-wobbles n. feelings of tension, fear or sickness, usu. seen as stemming from the stomach *Hotten*.

Colonel Sanders n. see: chicken hawk; the name, quite possibly libellous, puns on the Colonel's internationally franchised product.

color-blind a. one who is given to stealing.

colours n. (Hells Angel use) the emblems of the Hells Angels, ie an embroidered patch of a winged skull wearing a motorcycle helmet, the name Hells Angels, the name of the chapter (town, etc.), the letters MC: motorcycle club *Thompson*.

colt n. an illegitimate child (cf: brush colt, catch colt, field colt, filly, woods colt).

Comanche n. (gay use) a man who uses cosmetics (cf: Indian, warpaint).

comb the kinks out of v. to correct errors in another's views or actions; to 'set straight'.

combo n. 1. a group of musicians; abbrev. combination; 2. (criminal use) combination lock (on a safe) *Bukowski:1*.

comboozelated a. (US campus use) drunk *Underwood*.

come n., v. an orgasm; to achieve orgasm; thus *come a river*: for a woman to have multiple orgasms *Price: 2*.

come a cropper v. to suffer an accident, usu. a fall *Wodehouse:CW*.

come a purler v. to fall down, to trip over an obstacle, usu. sustaining some form of injury *Wodehouse:AAG*.

come across v. 1. to pay-up, esp. reluctantly *Wodehouse:AAG*; 2. to deliver, to surrender, esp. sexually *Humphries*.

come and get it! (ex milit. use) general cry indicating that a meal is ready.

come and go a. easy going; thus come and go party: an informal party, 'open house'.

come around v. 1. euph. for menstruate; n. 2. menstruation.

come clean v. to confess, to make an admission (cf: make a clean breast of) *Gruber*.

come down v. to occur; to turn out.

come down v. for the effect – good or bad – of a given drug to end.

come down in a pile v. to die.

come down on aka: *come down fonky*, *come down hard*: to talk to severely, to criticize heavily; to assault *McFadden*.

come in one's pants v. to behave in an exaggerated, over-excited manner; the image is of extremely premature ejaculation.

come it v. to act aggressively, often with no grounds for so doing *Hotten*.

come off it! stop it! don't keep trying that line, etc. *Manser*.

come on n. patter, sales or seduction talk, a line (qv) *M. Jagger, K. Richard, 'I'll Take You To The Top', 1982*.

come on v. to appear; esp. 'come on tough, come on nasty' etc. *Safire*.

come on like gangbusters v. to come on strong (qv); fr. US radio serial of 1940s which featured hard-hitting, intrepid crimefighters *Bruce:2*.

come on strong v. to make one's presence and opinions felt *Thompson*.

come on to v. to approach reasonably aggressively; to solicit *Jay & Young*.

come one's cocoa 1. to ejaculate, and thus 2. (UK police/criminal use) to inform or to confess one's crimes *Powis*.

come one's fat v. see: come one's cocoa *Powis*.

come one's guts v. (Aus. use) to give information to the police (cf: come one's cocoa, fat).

come one's lot v. see: come one's cocoa *Powis*.

come out v. to declare oneself as a homosexual; fr. coming out of the closet (qv) *Jay & Young*.

come sick v. euph. to menstruate.

come the big note v. (Aus. use) to boast, to set oneself as a richer/more important person than is true (cf: big-note artist) *Wilkes*.

come the old acid v. to act contrarily, aggressively, to argue *Austin*.

come the old soldier v. to deceive another for one's own benefit, esp. to avoid an unpleasant task; a veteran, supposedly, knows every trick when it comes to avoiding onerous duties *Wright*.

come the raw prawn v. to act resentfully or unpleasantly; to be rude *Humphries*.

come the tin soldier v. see: come the old soldier *Powis*.

come through v. take over in an emergency; carry out requirements *Higgins:1*.

come to a sticky end v. to meet great misfortune, esp. a violent death or a gaol sentence; usu. said of a person already condemned as 'a bad lot'.

come to one's milk v. to yield to authority, to accept orders when facing no alternative.

come undone v. to find oneself in difficulties *Safire*.

come unglued v. to become mentally and emotionally unstable *Neaman & Silver*.

come unstuck v. see: come undone.

come up v. (US Black use) to grow up.

come-along n. (police use) a chain manacle *Stone*.

come-freak n. anyone who is obsessed with physical sex and the delights thereof (cf: come, v) *Shulman*.

come-on boy n. a male prostitute who entices a client and then, instead of sex, has him beaten and robbed by a confederate (cf: murphy game) *Legman*.

come-on girl n. an immoral woman.

come-too-soon n. an illegitimate child.

come-you-all n. a ruckus, a large-scale fist-fight, a brawl.

comer n. an ambitious, go-ahead person, 'the coming man' *Dunne*.

comics n. (US milit, use) topographical maps *Del Vecchio*.

Commie n. (abbrev.) Communist (cf: reds) *Vidal*.

commo n. (US milit. use) (abbrev.) communication *Del Vecchio*.

Commo n. (Aus. use) Communist; commie refers to those who live in rural communes *Ready*.

commode-hugging drunk (US campus use) extremely drunk, to the point of hugging the lavatory bowl and vomiting within (cf: drive the porcelain bus, etc.) *Underwood*.

completely a. (Valley Girls (qv) use) all purpose term of approval (cf: clearly) *Pond*.

compo n. (Aus. use) workers' compensation, payment for time lost after an injury at work *Ready*.

con n. 1. (abbrev.) confidence man, confidence trick/game *Powis*; 2. (abbrev.) convict; thus *ex-con*: former prisoner *Price:2*.

con v. to fool a victim in one or another form of confidence trick *Powis*.

con and coal n. (rhyming sl.) the dole *Wright*.

con artist n. confidence trickster, fraud (cf: artist) *Bleasdale*.

Conan Doyle n.,v. (rhyming sl.) 1. boil (on the neck); 2. to boil (a kettle) *Jones:J*.

conch n. (US campus use) (abbrev.) conscientious: a devotedly hard worker (cf: cereb, grub, etc.) *Bernbach*.

concrete overcoat, concrete slippers n. a supposed gangland method of murder: the victim's feet are dunked in quick-drying concrete; he is then dumped into a river or overboard from a boat; the irremovable weight ensures his drowning *Welsh:2*.

condo n. (abbrev.) condominium *McFadden*.

confusion n. (UK Black use) a street fight, a riot *Powis*.

conk n. 1. nose *Humphries*; 2. head *Waits*; 3. fr. congolene, a fiery liquid used in the artificial straightening of naturally kinky black (Negro) hair: hair that has been thus treated *Goldman*.

conk v. to hit, to knock out *Selby:1*.

conk out v. to collapse, to break down, to malfunction *Wolfe:2*.

conk-buster n. (US Black use) 1. a difficult problem; 2. an intellectual; 3. cheap liquor.

conker n. 1. a very hard blow; 2. an old, unreliable car, prone to breaking down (cf: clunker).

conkhouse n. (US Black use) the head (cf: conkpiece).

conkpiece n. (US Black use) the head (cf: conkhouse).

connect v. 1. to obtain drugs, usu. by keeping a specific appointment with the connection (qv) *Burroughs:1*; 2. to achieve sexual fulfillment AS 60.1 (1985).

connection n. 1. a supplier of drugs *Grogan*; 2. the person with whom one achieves sexual fulfillment.

Connie n. (abbrev.) Lincoln Continental *Higgins:2*.

cono n. (New York Sp. use) cunt; thus, girls in the context of potential seduction *Pynchon*.

cons n. 1. (prison use) (abbrev.) convicts *Cole*; 2. (UK police use) (abbrev.) previous convictions *Laurie*.

Cons basketball shoes; fr. trade name 'Converse All-Stars' (cf: chucks) *Price:3*.

contract n. a paid assignment to murder a given victim, thus, *take out a contract on Higgins:1*.

convictitis n. (UK prison use) the illusion, fostered by too long a career in the prison service, that every prisoner is about to attack one for no other reason than that one is a warder *LL*.

convincer n. a weapon (cf: keeper).

cooch n. liquor (cf: hooch).

cook v. to tamper with, to falsify; thus 'cook the books', 'cook the accounts' *Hotten*.

cook v. for a musician or group of musicians to be playing in harmony and particularly creatively.

cook v. (drug use) to prepare a narcotic (esp. heroin) for injection by heating a solution of powder and water for use in a syringe *Tuff Shit Comics*.

cook a mark v. (cant) to calm down one's victim when he has been stripped of his money, possessions, etc. *Neaman & Silver*.

cook, get oneself a v. (of a man) to get married.

cook one's goose v. to give someone their due deserts *Farrell*.

cook up v. (drug use) to prepare an injection of a narcotic drug, usu. heroin, by heating a measure of the powdered drug plus some water in a teaspoon or bottle cap *Welsh:1* (fr. SE).

cooker n. (drug use) a container, usu. a bottle cap, in which the mixture of heroin and water can be heated prior to drawing it into a syringe and thence injecting it into one's arm *Larner*.

cookie n. (US Black use) see: oreo.

cookie n. an attractive woman. fr. cookie=biscuit, a common example of the equation of sex and food in sl.

cookie pusher n. a young man who errs to the 'feminine side of life' – tea parties, conversation, the niceties of dress and of gossip, art rather than sport, etc; fr. the cakes that such men are continually passing around such tea parties *Green:2*.

cookies n. any form of desired object: sex or money *Milner*.

cooking a. responsive, appreciative, esp. of an audience *Bruce:1*.

cool n. 1. (street gang use) a temporary armistice between opposing gangs *Salisbury*; 2. temper, poise, attitude to life and ability to deal with it *Price:2*.

cool v. to calm down, to deal with a problem *Goldman*.

cool a. calm, self-possessed, aware, sophisticated *Price:2*.

cool cat n. a sophisticated, competent, unruffled, able person (cf: cat) *Squeeze, 'Cool for Cats', 1980*.

cool head n. (US campus use) a calm, unflappable person *Underwood*.

cool it v. calm down; often as excl. 'cool it!' *Underwood*.

cool off v. 1. to become bored *Burroughs:1*; 2. to calm down.

cool out v. to calm down *Price:2*.

cool the rock v. (Valley Girls (qv) use) to calm down, to restrain one's excessive behaviour *Pond*.

cooler n. 1. (US Black use) a funeral home (cf: chill, cold meat) *Klein*. 2. punishment/solitary confinement cells *Caron*.

coolie n. (street gang use) any youth unaffiliated to a gang *Salisbury*.

coon n. (derog.) (abbrev.) racoon; a Black person *Price:2*.

Coon bottom / Coon Town n. Black community within an urban area.

coon-lover n. see: nigger-lover *Breslin*.

coop n. prison *Wodehouse:MS*.

coop v. (US police use) to sleep while on duty – in a motel room or similar hideaway *'Hill Street Blues', Thames TV, 1983*.

coot n. 1. (US campus use) the vagina; 2. (US campus use) females considered solely as sexual objects *Underwood*; 3. a fool, a simpleton; usu. as old coot, silly old coot, etc.

cootie n. 1. (US Black use) an inexperienced, naïve young person, keen to improve his/her status *Klein*; 2. a body louse; a bedbug.

cooze n. 1. vagina, thus derog. euph. for cunt (qv) *Stone*; 2. by extension, female (usu. promiscuous) *Schulberg*.

cop n. (abbrev.) copper (qv).

cop v. 1. spec. to buy drugs. cf: score 2. obtain, purchase *Price:2*; 3. (UK criminal use) to receive bribes, esp. of a policeman *Powis*; 4. (US pimp use) to seduce a girl, spec. with the intention of making her into a ho (qv) *Shulman*.

cop a bird v. to fellate (cf: bird) *Legman*.

cop a cherry v. to take a girl's virginity (cf: cherrypop).

cop a dose v. to catch venereal disease *Humphries*.

cop a drop v. (UK police use) to accept a bribe. (cf: bung) *Laurie*.

cop a feel v. to indulge in some form of petting, but not intercourse

Higgins:1.

cop a heel v. **1.** (US cant) aka: *cop and heel* to run off, to escape *Klein*: **2.** (US prison use) to attack fr. behind *Chandler: Notebk*.

cop a moke v. (US prison use) to escape, to go on the run *Neaman & Silver*.

cop a packet v. to gain a great deal, poss. more than one bargained for this can either be good – more money than expected – or bad – a longer gaol sentence than feared *LL*.

cop a plea v. (US criminal use) to plead guilty to a lesser charge in return for the dropping of a major one (cf: cop out 2) *Dunne*.

cop a slave v. (US Black use) to work, to go out and find work (cop the slave).

cop a squat (US Black use) sit down, make yourself at home *Klein*.

cop a tube (surf use) to catch a perfect wave *Pond*.

cop an attitude v. (US Black use) to take a negative stance on a given topic; to make one's own position adamant despite prevailing opinions and pressures *Klein*

cop and blow v. **1.** (Black pimp use) to exploit an unsatisfactory prostitute for as much money as possible before discarding her *Shulman*; **2.** (US teen use) to make a purchase and then leave; of fast food, drugs, prostitutes, etc. *Sculatti*.

cop it v. usu. abbrev: cop it hot: to get into trouble, to suffer in a given way, spec. *cop a packet*: to be severely wounded or hurt.

cop one's joint v. to perform fellatio *Goldman*.

cop out v. **1.** to avoid a problem or a difficult situation; to run away; to give up trying; **2.** (US criminal use) to use legal plea bargaining to plead guilty to a lesser charge in return for having a major one dropped *Klein*.

cop out on v. to inform against *Bruce:2*.

cop shop n. police station (cf: bill shop).

cop some z's v. to sleep *Milner*.

cop the lot v. to gain everything *Performance*.

copacetic, copasetic a. excellent, first rate. (? fr. Chinook jargon *copasenee*: 'everything is satisfactory', esp. as originally used on the waterways of Washington state. Other etys. include: the painfully contrived phr. 'the cop is on the settee', i.e. the cop is not paying attention, which elided into copacetic and was supposedly used as such by US hoodlums; an unknown Italian word; the Fr. *coupersetique* fr. *couper*: 'to strike', thus 'striking' or 'worth a strike'; the Yiddish phr. *hakol b'seder*: 'all is in order' or, earlier, *kol b'tzedek*: 'all with justice').

Copenhagen capon n. (gay use) a transsexual; the reference is to the pioneering operation undergone in Denmark by Christine Jorgensen.

Copenhagen, go to v. phr. (gay use) to have a sex-change operation.

copout n. a coward, a runner away from problems, a weakling *Underwood*.

copper n. **1.** a policeman; from the copper badges carried by New York City's first policemen, c. 1850 *Grogan*; **2.** (US prison use) good conduct marks; a prisoner who gains such marks is considered to resemble a policeman.

copper v. to inform.

copper jitters n. (drug/criminal use) excessive fear of the police, verging on obsession *Burroughs:1*.

copper nob n. a red-headed person.

copper-hearted a. (US prison use) an informer by nature *Chandler: Notebk*.

copping n. (UK criminal/police use) the practice by bent (qv) policemen, of taking bribes from criminals, either to turn a blind eye when necessary, to drop charges, lose evidence, etc. *Powis*.

copping clothes n. (US pimp use) particularly smart, legitimate suit of clothes, worn specifically to entice and seduce potential hos (qv) *Shulman*.

cor! aka: *gor*: euph. for God, as in *cor blimey*: God blind me! *Wright*.

cordwood n. 1. a rustic, a farmer; 2. a kitchen match; 3. a toothpick.

corked a drunk *Dickson*.

corker n. anything excellent, superlative, first rate *Mortimer*.

corksacking (euph.) cocksucking (qv); coined by Anthony Burgess in *NYT* 1972.

corn on the cob n. (US Black use) sexual intercourse in which the partners are partially clad *Klein*.

cornball a. naïve, unsophisticated (cf: corny) *Grogan*.

cornhole v. to have anal intercourse *Jay & Young*.

cornpone n. a person obviously from the South of the US; fr. the food of the same name *Major*.

corn-bread a. plain, simple, down-to-earth.

corned drunk; fr. corn whiskey *Runyon*.

corner v. aka *lawing* (UK criminal use) 1. a confidence trick whereby shoddy goods are sold by pretending they are in fact high-grade stolen property and playing on the 'thrill' some people derive from such a purchase; 2. arranging to sell stolen goods and then having fake 'policemen' break in, confiscate the goods and threaten the victim with charges of receiving; these charges can, naturally, be dropped in return for a bribe which is arranged by a fake 'solicitor' who makes sure there is no real police involvement by assuring the victim that he has no rights in law and that paying and shutting up is the best thing to do *Powis*.

corner cowboys n. idlers who while away their days standing and gossiping on street corners *Schulberg*.

corny a. sentimental, naïve, unsophisticated; all such characteristics are attributed to country folk, surrounded by cornfields.

corporation cocktail n. coal gas bubbled through milk, a down-and-out alcoholic's tipple, although in an age of North Sea gas this drink is redundant.

corpse v. (theatrical use) to cause (intentionally or not) a fellow performer to forget their lines and/or laugh on stage *Green:2*.

corrode v.i. (US campus use) to be overcome with disgust or repulsion *Underwood*.

corroded a. (US Black use) unappealing, unattractive *Folb*.

COs n. (taxi driver use) police officers who specialize in checking on laws that affect cabs and their drivers *Powis*.

cossie n. (Aus. use) swimming costume *Humphries:2*.

cost ya! (abbrev.) it will cost you something: ie don't ask for favours, but most things can be done – for a price *LL*.

cot-case n. (Aus. use) an invalid *Humphries:2*.

cottage n. (UK homosexual use) anywhere male homosexuals gather for sex; often a public lavatory (cf: glory hole).

cotton n. 1. (drug use) small piece of material through which heroin has been sucked up into a syringe and which can be boiled, when no better supplies exist, to extract one final emergency fix (qv) *Burroughs:1*; 2. (US Black use) female pubis *Folb*.

cottontop n. 1. a person with light-coloured hair, a white blond; thus 2. a Swede.

cotton-pickers n. the hands.

cotton-picking a. derog. term of abuse implying second rate, vulgarity, etc. *Selby:1*.

couch potato n. one who is addicted to watching television and who does this while lying on the couch, as inert and braindead as a potato *Green:3*.

cough v. to confess, to inform.

cough drop n. a 'character', a 'card' (qv) *Wodehouse: MOJ*.

cough up v. to reveal, to hand over (objects or information).

couldn't fight one's way out of a paper bag (cp) implying physical weakness on the part of the subject.

couldn't knock the skin off a rice-

pudding (cp) contemptuous dismissal of a weakling, or supposed weakling.

couldn't organize a fuck in a brothel (cp) utterly incompetent.

couldn't run a piss-up in a brewery (cp) an individual of such minimal competence that even provided with everything necessary to achieve a given aim, that aim remains beyond him/her.

council houses n. (rhyming sl.) trousers *Powis*.

country cousin n. (rhyming sl.) a dozen *Jones:J*.

county hotel n. (US cant) a county jail.

couple freak n. (contact ads) couple seek a man to join them in sex *SMD*.

couple of chips short of a fish dinner phr. not very intelligent; one of a number of phrases meaning stupid and punning on 'not all there' (cf: few snags short of a barbie, five annas short of the rupee, not having both oars in the water, not playing with a full deck, not quite there, not the full quid, one sandwich short of a picnic, one shingle short, only eighty pence in the pound, ten pence short of the full quid, two bricks short of the load, two pence short of a bob, two wafers short of a communion).

coupon n. (Sc. use) face *Welsh:1*.

courage bump n. acne. (fr. dial. courage: sexual desire; the assumption is that the emergent sexuality of the adolescent male manifests itself in infected pimples).

cousin n. (homosexual use) the lover of another homosexual *Legman*.

cousin sis n. urination. (fr. rhy. sl. cousin sis = piss (qv)).

cousin up v. to curry favour, to toady. (fr. supposed intimacy of cousins).

cove n. a person, a man; fr. Romany *Wodehouse VGJ*.

cover one's ass v. to look after oneself *Higgins:1*.

cover the sheet v. (US police use) to make one's arrest quota *Neaman & Silver*.

cover the waterfront v. 1. euph: to menstruate; 2. euph. to change a baby's nappy or diaper.

cover-up n. an alibi, concealment, usu. illegal or at least unethical.

cow n. an obese, unattractive female.

cow jockey n. a farmer, a rustic.

cowabunga! (surf use) excl. of pleasure, victory (over the waves), etc. *Green:2*; the term gained a whole new currency, especial among the pre-teens, with the popularity c.1990 of the Teenage Mutant Ninja Turtles, where it featured heavily. Its ultimate origin seems to have been in Howdy Doody, a US children's television programme of the Fifties, in which 'Cowabunga!' was the greeting exchanged by 'Buffalo Bob' and 'Chief Thunderthud'.

cowboy n. 1. (US Black use) see *bad-ass nigger Folb*; 2. a tradesman who ignores the basic ethics and business standards of his peers but aims only for money; thus *cowboy builder, cowboy plumber* etc *Bleasdale*.

Cowboy City n. (US trucker use) Cheyenne, Wyoming *CB*.

cowlick n. a hairstyle, smoothed down over the forehead, that looks as if a cow had licked it into place (cf: duck's arse, *DA*).

cowpoke n. cowboy *Chandler:LG*.

cow's n. (rhyming sl.) cow's calf = half = ten shillings *Norman:2*.

cowyard confetti n. (Aus. use) euph. for bullshit (qv) *Wilkes*.

cozzer n. policeman; fr. Heb. *chazer*: pig, thus harking back to *Lexicon Balatronicum* (1815) at least *Newman:1*.

CPT n. an hour or two later than the prescribed time, sooner or later. (fr. abbr. colored people's time: the stereotype is that Blacks have a less immediate sense of time than their white peers)

crab v. to spoil, to upset, to ruin *rr*.

crab-apple two-step n. diarrhoea (cf: green-apple quickstep).

crabby a. nagging, cantankerous *Higgins:2*.

crack v: insert '1.' before def; insert '2. to break wind.' after def.

crack n. 1. a joke; 2. a try, a chance *Price:2*; 3. a remark *Runyon:1*; 4. vagina; 5. a purified and potent form of cocaine which is smoked rather than snorted; crack, a mixture of cocaine, baking powder and water, is heated and the resultant pellets are smoked through a small glass pipe. Its strength, alleged addictiveness and destructive popularity have made it a major source of social disruption *Morgan*.

crack v. 1. to work something out, to find a solution; 2. to hit *Price:2*; 3. to break wind.

crack a bottle v. to have a drink *Hotten*.

crack a cherry v. to take a girl's virginity (cf: cop a cherry, etc.) *Grogan*.

crack a fat v. (Aus. use) to achieve erection *Humphries*.

crack a stiffie v. to get an erection (cf: crack a fat; stiffie).

crack a tube v. (Aus. use) to open a can of beer *Humphries:2*.

crack ho n. (US Black use) a girl who will offer sex in return for crack (qv) cocaine (cf: ho).

crack house n. a room or whole house in which users gather to take crack (qv) (cf: shooting gallery).

crack it v. to achieve a successful (from the male point of view) seduction *Ready*.

crack on v. to tell tales, to boast *Waterhouse*.

crack one up v. to make someone laugh *Price: 3*.

crack one's face v. aka: *crack a smile*: to laugh, to smile.

crack something up v. to promote an event, object, idea, etc.

crack the books v. to open books, thus to read *Vidal*.

crack up n. a nervous breakdown, a mental collapse *F. Scott Fitzgerald, bk title, 1936*.

crack up v. 1. to laugh uproariously *Goldman*; 2. to crash – a car, an airplane, etc. *Heller*.

crack wise v. to make a 'clever' comment that impresses no one (cf: wiseguy) *McFadden*.

cracked a. insane, crazy, eccentric *Bleasdale*.

cracker n. 1. poor Southern US white farmer *Bruce:1*; 2. an attractive (young) female; usu. as in 'a little cracker'.

cracker-ass n. a skinny person.

crackerbarrel a. homespun philosophies; fr. the cracker (biscuit) barrel that could once be found in every US small town general store, surrounded by ageing sages offering the wisdom of their lifetimes (cf: scuttlebutt).

crackerjack a. 1. excellent, first class, superlative *Vidal*; 2. fake, make-believe.

crackers a. mad, crazy *Humphries*.

crackle n. (UK criminal use) banknotes, usu. £5 and up *LL*.

cracko n. a madman, a lunatic (cf: crackpot) *Shulman*.

crackpot n. an eccentric *Dury, 'Laughter', 1981*.

cracky (euph) Christ (cf: crikey) *Rawson*.

cradle-snatcher n. an older person, usu. a woman, who prefers affairs with people substantially younger than they are.

crag n. (US campus use) irritable, nagging woman *Underwood*.

cramber v. to defecate *M. Storey*.

cramp n. (euph) Christ, usu. as in mild oaths (cf: crackers, cracky, crikey, criminy, cripes).

crank n. 1. any form of amphetamine drug; such drugs 'crank up' one's bodily motor *Thompson*; 2. the penis.

crank v. (Valley Girls (qv) use) all-purpose word; 'like you crank yourself together or you crank to school, or you crank up the radio . . .' *Pond*.

crank it out v. to write (usu. rubbish) more from duty than pleasure or interest; to be a hack writer *Higgins:5*.

crank up v. to inject narcotics with a hypodermic syringe *Caron*.

crankpot n. a mean, ill-tempered individual (cf: barmpot)

cranky hatch n. (US cant) see: booby hatch, crazy alley.

crap n. **1.** spec. excrement; **2.** rubbish, nonsense, anything useless *Bruce:1*.

crap v. **1.** to go to the lavatory, defecate; **2.** *crap around*: fool about, tell deliberate lies *Dunne*.

crap out v. **1.** to fail, to go wrong, to blunder; fr. the losing throws in dice *Laugh in the Dark*; **2.** to collapse, to become exhausted, to fall asleep *Goldman*.

crapbrain n. general term of abuse, based on alleged stupidity of the recipient *'Hill Street Blues', Thames TV, 1983*.

craphat n. derogatory description used by British paratroop regiments to refer to any soldiers other than themselves *Green:3*.

craphouse n. **1.** lavatory; **2.** any unpleasant, dirty place; **3** (show business use) a small, unfashionable venue *Bruce:2*.

crapper n. **1.** lavatory (cf: crap) *May*; **2.** the anus, the buttocks *Rawson*.

crappo a. disgusting, appalling (cf: crappy) *Price:3*.

crappy a. unpleasant, disgusting, vile, revolting; fr. crap (qv).

crap-shoot n. any situation in which luck, not judgement, is of paramount importance; fr. gambling game of craps.

crash n. (Aus. use) an excretion *Ready*.

crash v. **1.** to sleep, collapse exhausted, spec. after a bout of heavy drug (esp. amphetamine) use; orig. from Royal Navy slang 'crash the swede': to sleep; as such it migrated first to Aus. then to US and finally back to UK *Lou Reed, 'Take a Walk on the Wild Side', 1972*; **2.** (abbrev.) gate-crash: to appear uninvited at a given party or other function *Wodehouse:AAG*; **3.** (UK police use) to drop enquiries into a given case

Powis.

crasher n. **1.** an uninvited guest at a party; **2.** someone who collapses from fatigue *Thompson*; **3.** a bore *Obs. 1983*.

crash-hot (Aus. use) first rate, excellent.

crash-pad n. a flat or house in which any passing friends or strangers can find a bed at short notice (cf: crash) *Uneeda Comix*.

crawfish n. (US campus use) a stingy, mean person *Underwood*.

crawfish v. **1.** to grovel, to abase oneself before another *N. Mailer, 'The Naked and the Dead', 1947*; **2.** to back down, to renege on a previous statement, committment; fr. the movements of the fish *Chandler:LG*.

crawling a. infested with insects or vermin.

crazy **1.** keen on, enthusiastic. esp. as *crazy for Price:2*; **2.** (excl.) wonderful, amazing, etc.; mainly used in beatnik/ bop jazz era of 1940s/50s.

crazy alley n. (US prison use) a special part of a prison used for insane prisoners *Chandler: Notebk.*

crazy for extremely enthusiastic.

crazy house n. lunatic asylum, mental hospital *Dunne*.

crazy-ass a. insane, utterly eccentric *Burroughs:Jr.*

creaker n. (US Black use) an old person.

cream n. semen.

cream v. **1.** to destroy, to beat up comprehensively, to overcome easily *Price:2*; **2.** to win a sporting competition decisively *Higgins:5*; **3.** to achieve orgasm.

cream one's jeans v. to ejaculate spontaneously (while dressed) on seeing a supremely erotic sight; often used only figuratively and meaning over-excited, even if not erotically *Humphries*.

cream puff n. (derog.) a homosexual or a generally weak man *Schulberg:2*.

cream puff freak n. (pimp use) a client who likes to throw gooey cakes at a girl and thus achieve sexual arousal *OUI 8/75*.

creamie n. an attractive and sexually malleable female *Bleasdale*.

creaming n. (UK criminal use) stealing from one's employer, usu. on a small, but protracted scale *Powis*.

creamstick n. (US Black use) the penis (cf: cream, n.) *Klein*.

crease v. to beat severely *Austin*.

crease up v. to collapse with laughter.

creased a. exhausted, tired out.

cred a. adv. literally an abbrev. of credible / credibility, the term as used in the 1980s by young people (and those who purvey their material wants) meant acceptable on a street (qv) level, unaffected by puffery, artistic pretentiousness and similar negative trappings.

creep n. an unpleasant person, poss. inference of some physical peculiarity, criminality *Price:2*.

creep v. 1. to forego one's pride and beg unashamedly; to curry favour, to suck up to (qv) (cf: bootlick); 2. (US pimp use) for a prostitute to distract her trick (qv) while an accomplice slips into the room and rifles his wallet; since he always has to pay in advance, he won't check his money till they have parted *Shulman*; 3. to perform a theft, esp. the activities of a sneak thief *Norman*; 4. (US campus use) to go out on the town *Underwood*.

creep joint n. a particularly filthy brothel.

creep on v. (US Black use) 1. to cheat, esp. sexually; 2. to sneak up on someone, with the intention of attacking them physically; 3. to follow.

creeper n. (US Black use) an adulterous or cheating lover.

creeper n. (UK cant/police use) a sneak thief *Cole*.

creeping and tilling (US Black use) diverting a store cashier's attention while a confederate opens and robs the till *Klein*.

creeping Jesus n. a whining, sneaking person.

creepshow a. awful, disgusting; from the horror movie title.

creepsville n. any unappealling place *Underwood*.

creepy a. unpleasant, suspicious, menacing *Higgins:5*.

creepy-crawly n. an insect; usu. juv. use.

crew n. 1. a gang, usu. football supporters, who engage in fights with rivals *Robins:1*; 2. originally used in US by young blacks to denote a teen gang, spec. of rap singers, break dancers or graffiti, the term has crossed the Atlantic and now, in UK use, both black and white means simply a gang.' (cf: posse) *Wild Style, film, 1983*.

crib n. 1. a small, cheap brothel; fr. early 19th C. use: a room, a lodging *Salisbury*; 2. a safe *Chandler: Notebk*; 3. house, apartment, anywhere one lives *Price:2*; 4. (student use) examination or other aids which help with answers to homework, or actual cheating in exams.

crib v. (student use) to cheat.

crib man n. (US cant) one who specializes in breaking into houses and apartments *Neaman & Silver*.

cribsheet n. see: crib.

crikey! (excl.) euph. for Christ! *Humphries*.

Crimea n. (rhyming sl.) beer *Wright*.

crimey n. (US criminal use) partner in crime, accomplice *Morgan*.

criminey! (euph.) Christ! *Rawson*.

Crimson n. (US college use) Harvard University *Bernbach*.

crinched a. (US campus use) bent, dented; fr. crimped + pinched *Underwood*.

crinkle top n. (US Black use) a female with an Afro (qv) or natural (qv) haircut *Folb*.

crip n. (US campus use) anything easy, esp. of a given college course.

cripes! (euph.) Christ! *Rawson*.

crispy n. (Valley Girls (qv) use) anyone whose faculties seem impaired by an excess – of drugs, drink, etc – and is thus 'burnt out' *Pond*.

crispy adv.(US teen use) hungover.

criss cross v. (US Black use) to

deceive or cheat; development of double-cross *Klein*.

croak v. **1.** to die *Humphries*; **2.** to kill *Rawson*.

croaker n. **1.** doctor *Chandler: Notebk*; **2.** one who talks too lengthily and too loudly; **3.** a pessimist; **4.** one who backs out of undertakings they have promised to perform.

crock n. **1.** a hypochrondriac, a malingerer; **2.** a drunkard; **3.** a broken-down or mechanically unreliable car (cf: junker); **4.** (abbrev.) crock of shit: useless, unpleasant event or experience *Price:2*.

crock of shit n. see: crock.

crocked a. drunk *Klein*.

crocko a. drunk *Dickson*.

crombie n. overcoat, fr. trade name of a particular coat, particularly beloved by skinheads (qv) of late 1960s.

cronky a. (Aus. use) corrupt, dishonest, lying; fr. racing use *Humphries*.

crook **1.** defective, useless, unpleasant (of people) *Humphries*; **2.** ill *Humphries:2*.

crooked on (Aus. use) averse to, hostile to (cf: crook) *Wilkes*.

crop n. (US campus (spec. U. of Arkansas) use) fifth of a gall. of wine *Underwood*.

cross v. (abbrev.) double-cross: to betray, to let down *Schulberg*.

cross bar hotel n. (US use) prison *Neaman & Silver*.

cross man n. (US Black use) anyone who manipulates others for his own advantage; fr. double-cross *Klein*.

cross up v. to betray, to double-cross *Chandler:LG*.

cross-eyed a. drunk *Dickson*.

cross-talk v. (US Black use) to interrupt another speaker.

crossways, crosswise adv. **1.** in a bad humour; **2.** disagreeing with.

crotch n. a woman; a concentration on her physical sexuality *Higgins:3*.

crotch cheese n. unwashed vaginal secretion found in less than ideally

clean females (cf: headcheese) *Klein*.

crow n. **1.** an unattractive woman *Runyon:1*; **2.** (UK criminal use) a lookout man in a street game of three-card monte (qv) *Powis*.

crow eaters n. (Aus. use) South Australians *Bickerton*.

Crow Jimism the reverse of anti-Black discriminatory Jim Crow laws (qv); thus guilt-induced affection for and fascination with Blacks by white liberals *Bruce:2.*

Crow MacGee a. (US prison use) no good, unreal, false *Chandler: Notebk*.

crowd pleaser n. (US police use) the officer's gun; an ironic use *Neaman & Silver*.

crown v. to hit over the head *Goulart*.

crown jewels n. male genitals *Stanley*.

crud n. **1.** spec. dried semen, on the body, clothes or bedlinen; **2.** any disease; **3.** dirt, in general *Selby:1*; **4.** an unappealing person *Underwood*.

cruddy a. useless, no good, lousy, second rate *Price:3*.

crude a. (US Black use) worthless, excess and as such useless *Klein*.

crude n. (US police use) a tip-off from an informer; as opposed to a communication, a complaint from a member of the public *Neaman & Silver*.

cruise a. (Valley Girls (qv) use) easy, simple, useful; describing anything suitable for cruising (cf: cruise) *Pond*.

cruise v.t. to approach someone obviously with sexual intent; both for commercial or non-commercial purposes *A. Hanson*.

cruise v. **1.** spec. to search for sexual contacts by walking specific streets, areas, etc. **2.** to drive around, often along a town's main street, surveying the situation, looking for friends, girls to pick up, etc. *Tuff Shit Comics*.

cruisemobile (Valley Girls (qv) use) any favoured car *Pond*.

cruiser n. **1.** prostitute *Higgins:1*; **2.** a marked police car that patrols given streets.

cruising for a bruising adv. phr. **1.**

looking deliberately to cause trouble, *Ice T:2*; **2.** acting in such manner that will get one into trouble, usually of a physically harmful nature.

crumb crusher *n.* (US Black use) a baby who is just learning to eat solids *Klein*.

crumbly *n.* (UK 'society' use) an older person, c.50–70 (cf: wrinkly, dusty) *Barr*.

crumbs! (euph.) Christ! usu. child use only, prob. the mildest of such euphemisms.

crumb-snatcher *n.* see: crumb crusher *Folb*.

crumbum *a.* useless, awful, second rate, inferior *Price:3*.

crumby *a.* see: crummy *a. Sillitoe*.

crummy *a.* **1.** second-rate, inferior, unpleasant *Burroughs:1*; **2.** infested with lice.

crummy *n.* (logger use) pickup trucks that transport loggers to and from camps *Wolfe:2*.

crumpet *n.* a girl or woman; example of sex/food equation (cf: bit of crackling, cookie) *Humphries*.

crunch *n.* the ultimate aspect of a given situation, a more aggressive and crisis laden bottom line (qv); often in 'when it comes to the crunch . . .' *Dickson*.

cruncher *n.* (Aus. prison use) a small-time criminal *Neaman & Silver*.

crunchy *n.* a vegetarian / New Age devotee *S Prosser*.

crush *n.* **1.** a sexual interest in someone *The Roches, 'Nurds'*; **2.** (lesbian use) the vagina *Maledicta*.

crush out *n.* (US cant) a means of obliterating the body and the evidence of a murder by putting the corpse into a car and the car through a junkyard crushing machine *Neaman & Silver*.

crusher *n.* **1.** a boor, an intruder; **2.** one who persists in making unwanted advances to women.

crust *n.* cheek, audacity, nerve *Wodehouse passim*.

crust of bread *n.* (rhyming sl.) the head (cf: loaf of bread) *Franklyn*.

crusty *n.* a member of the underclass

of the punk (qv) scene, who adopt deliberately filthy clothing (hence their 'crustiness'), live communally (often in squats) or on the streets, enjoy an excess of drink and drugs and generally set out to appall their less extreme peers.

crutch *n.* see: roach clip *Folb*.

cry hughie *v.* to vomit; fr. alleged noise the vomiting makes: herwaaagghh!! (cf: cry ralph, cry ruth) *Billy Connolly passim*.

cry ralph *v.* to vomit; fr. alleged sound of being sick (cf: cry huey, cry ruth) *Billy Connolly passim*.

cry ruth *v.* to vomit *Humphries*.

cry Uncle! *v.* to beg someone to stop an action, to surrender *Jay & Young*.

crying *a.* general intensifier; esp. in crying shame (n) *Algren*.

crystal *n.* powdered Methedrine *Goldman*.

cs (abbrev.) chickenshit (qv) (cf: bs) *Rawson*.

Cuban pumps *n.* (gay use) heavy boots *Maledicta 9*.

Cubans *n.* see: Cuban pumps.

cube *n.* (drug use) morphine; fr. the shape of bulk supplies *Green:1*.

cuckoo *a.* crazy, eccentric, insane *Heller*.

cuddle and kiss *n.* (rhyming sl.) miss, thus a girl *Jones:J*.

cuff *v.* **1.** to hide a cigarette or marijuana joint (qv) inside the cupped fingers *Larner*; **2.** (US Black use) to hit, to fight *Folb*; **3.** to place on credit (cf: on the cuff) *Bukowski:6*.

cuff it *v.* to extemporise, to respond to a situation spontaneously *C. Spicer*.

cuffs *n.* (UK police/criminal use) (abbrev.) handcuffs *LL*.

cuffs and collars pubic hair that matches the colour of the visible hair; thus ostensibly proving that a woman is not dyeing her hair *Price:2*.

cull *n.* (US campus use) **1.** a socially unacceptable person; **2.** spec. fraternity use: anyone rejected for membership in fraternity/sorority; fr. hunting/countryside use *Underwood*.

cull bird *n.* (US campus use) any

female considered socially/physically unacceptable *Underwood*.

culo n. buttocks, behind; fr. Sp. *Morgan*.

culture fruit n. see: African golf ball.

culture-vulture n. anyone who battens on to the prevailing cultural trends in order to debase and exploit them for economic gain, irrespective of the aesthetic loss involved *Hoffman:a*.

cum n. semen.

cum v. to achieve orgasm; often found as alternative to come (qv) to enhance the sexual aspect of the otherwise common word *Bukowski:2*.

cum chum n. (derog.) a homosexual male.

cum drum n. a condom with a reservoir for semen (cf: cum).

cum freak a man obsessed with sexual gratification (cf: cock hound) *Folb*.

cunt n. 1. the vagina; fr. Middle Eng. orig., but taboo since 15th C.; among many (obs.) euphemisms is 'the divine monosyllable'; 2. a fool, a dolt, an unpleasant person – of either sex (cf: prick).

cunt positive (lesbian use) the concept of appreciating the vagina despite its secondary image in a phallocentric world *Jay & Young*.

cunthound n. a man who is obsessed with sex and seduction.

cuntlapper n. 1. general term of abuse *Higgins:3*; 2. spec. cunnilinctor *Legman*.

cup of tea n. personal preference; ie: - 'she's my cup of tea . . .' etc.

cupcake n. 1. spec. the female breast *Higgins:4*; 2. an attractive (young) female.

cupcakes n. (derog.) a homosexual male.

cuppa n. aka: *cupper*: a cup of tea *Performance*.

curly (one) n. a tricky problem, a challenge.

curly wolf n. a tough, tricky character; fr. qualities of the animal.

currant bun n. (rhyming sl.) the sun *Cole*.

curse n. (euph.) menstrual period 'Serpico', directed S. Lumet, 1973.

cushions n. the buttocks.

cushty n. first rate, excellent, enjoyable; widely popularized by the TV series *Only Fools and Horses* (cf: cushy).

cushy a. soft, comfortable, easy, etc. *LL*.

cuss out v. to curse; to attack verbally, to criticize *Seale*.

custard and jelly n. (rhyming sl.) telly = television *Jones:J*.

custards n. (Aus. use) pimples, acne; fr. pus such eructations contain *Ready*.

cut a. drunk; fr. *cut one's leg*, a facetious ref. to a staggering drunk.

cut n. 1. (US sporting use) a pre-arranged point at which a group of competitors or recruits to a team are reduced by those who fail to achieve a given standard; thus *make the cut*: to continue on the team, in the competition, etc.; 2. a share, of profits, of loot, of the proceeds of a robbery, etc.

cut v. 1. for a manager or agent to take a percentage of a client's money, esp. in boxing use *Heller*; 2. to dilute a drug with some adulterant *Larner*; 3 (US campus use) to have sexual intercourse *Underwood*.

cut a gut v. to make a mistake, esp. an embarrassing one.

cut a hog v. 1. see: cut a gut; ; 2. to fail in a task, esp. when it is beyond one's abilities.

cut a melon v. to divide up, esp. the spoils of a large coup or a crime.

cut a side v. 1. (US Black use) to have sexual intercourse; 2. (musician use) to record a song, one side of a 45 rpm or a number of songs, one side of a 33 rpm record.

cut a slice (off the joint) v. to have sexual intercourse (male point of view).

cut and carried a. (rhyming sl.) married (cf: cash and carried) *Jones:J*.

cut down to size v. to reduce a person's (high) opinion of him/herself to a realistic estimate.

cut it v. to manage, to deal with (difficult) situations *Price:2*.

cut it out! just stop that! *Manser*.

cut it up v. to have an uproarious good time; 'cutting the rug' *Thompson:J*.

cut loose v. 1. to terminate, to let go, to get rid of *Milner*; 2. to abandon restraints, either in one's action or, in an argument, in one's language and abuse.

cut no ice v. make no impression, fail to impress *Austin*.

cut off at the pass v. to intercept, to ambush: metaphorically as well as physically; fr. the cliché of many Westerns 'I'll cut them off . . .' *PT*.

cut one's eyes v. 1. (US Black use) to look suspiciously, to look askance at; 2. to glance at, to look at furtively.

cut (out) v. to leave *Selby:1*.

cut that out! (excl.) stop doing that! *rr*.

cut the buck v. to work hard (fr. dial. cut the buck: to dance vigorously, itself fr. buck and wing).

cut the cake v. (US Black use) to get married.

cut the cake v. (US Black use) to deflower a virgin *Klein*.

cut the crap! (excl.) don't try to fool me! stop talking rubbish! etc. *Southern & Hoffenberg*.

cut the fool v. (US Black use) to act the fool, to play tricks.

cut the mustard v. to come up to a given standard *Dury*, 'Laughter'.

cut the rug v. to dance.

cut up v. 1. to divide, esp. money, loot *Higgins:1*; 2. (US Black use) to complain.

cut up rough v. to react unpleasantly, to become annoyed *Wodehouse:VGJ*.

cut up rusty v. see: cut up rough.

cut up touches v. (US cant) 1. to reminisce over old successes, major villanies, etc. 2. to share out the spoils of criminal acts.

cut-buddy n. (US Black use) a close friend.

cut-rate a. cheap, unsatisfactory, limited.

cutchie n. (Jamaican use) a pipe used for smoking ganja, marijuana *Thelwell*.

cutesie a. excessively sweet, cloying.

cutesie-pie 1. see: cutesie; 2. an attractive female, usu. young, poss. a given male's girlfriend.

cutie n. pretty young girl *Capital Radio 1983*.

cuts and scratches n. (rhyming sl.) matches *Jones:J*.

cutter n. a revolver, which 'cuts down' its targets.

cutthroat n. see: badass nigger *Folb*.

cutty n. (US Black use) a friend, a close intimate *Folb*.

cuz (US Black use) fr. abbrev. cousin: form of address between black males *Folb*.

CYA (US civil service use) (abbrev.) *Cover Your Ass* (qv): the basic admonition to anyone, at any level, working in government.

cyclops n. (US Black use) a television (cf: one-eyed monster).

CYT abbr. cute young *t*hing.

D

D n. (Aus. use) (abbrev.) detective *Wilkes*.

da n. 1. (abbrev.) *d*uck's *ass*: a style of haircut popular in 1950s but still found *White*; 2. (US campus use) (abbrev.) *d*umb *ass* = fool, idiot *Underwood*.

dabs n. fingerprints *Powis*.

dachsie n. (abbrev.) dachshund *Barr*.

D & D a. 1. (police use) *d*runk and *d*isorderly; 2. *d*eaf and *d*umb.

dad- (euph.) God; thus *dad-blamed*, *dad-blasted*, etc.: all reasonably mild exclamations.

dad and dave v. (Aus. use)
1. (rhyming sl.) to shave *Bickerton*;
2. fr. popular 1930s radio serial
concerning various aspects of rural
Aus. life: hayseed, peasant,
unsophisticated person *Wilkes*.

dad-gummed a. euph. for God-
damned; similar terms include: dad-
blasted, dad-binged, dad-fetched,
dad-gasted, dad-goned, dad-rotted,
dad-snatched.

daddy n. 1. (UK prison use) a leader –
through intimidation and other
influence – of the inmates in a Borstal
(cf: baron) *R. Minton, 'Scum', 1981*;
2. a masculine lesbian (cf: papa)
Legman; 3. (US Black use) form of
address to a black male; *daddy-o* (qv)
beloved of 1950s white beatniks is now
obs. *Himes:1*; 4. the supreme
example, the most important/
powerful/well-known, etc.; often as
the daddy of them/us all.

daddy one n. (US Black use) a lover
or any man who provides for a given
woman *Folb*.

daddy-bag n. the testes and the
scrotum.

daddy-o term of address; orig. black
use, then permeated white beatnik
and latterly hippie culture, generally
obs. now *Bukowski:1*.

daffadown dilly (rhyming sl.) silly (cf:
daffy) *Jones:J*.

daffy a. eccentric, foolish; esp. in *daffy
about*: madly in love with *Runyon*.

daft a. foolish, silly *Dury, 'Do It
Yourself', 1979*.

dag n. (Aus. use) 1. unenterprising
person, a coward; 2. a card (qv), a
character *Humphries*.

dagger n. see: bull-dagger.

dago n. (derog) Italian (US), South
American (UK), Mexican.

Dago n. (US trucker use) San Diego,
California *CB*.

Dago Centre n. see: Dago town.

dago red n. cheap, rotgut red wine,
usu. drunk by alcoholics; orig. the
cheap home-produced red wine made
by Italian families and merchandized,

during Prohibition, by Italian
gangsters.

Dago Town n. the Italian or Puerto
Rican area of a US town or city.

dagwood n. an extra-large sandwich.
(fr. the character Dagwood Bumstead
in Chic Young's syndicated cartoon
strip *Blondie*, launched in the US in
1930).

daily n. 1. (abbrev.) daily help,
charwoman; 2. (fr. rhyming sl.) *Daily
Mail* = tail = rear end; thus *up one's
daily*: following close behind
Newman:1.

Daily Getsmuchworse n. the *Daily
Express Private Eye passim*.

Daily Mail n. 1. (rhyming sl.) tail =
buttocks *Powis*; 2. (rhyming sl.) tale,
thus a lie *Jones:J*.

daily-daily n. (US milit. use) anti-
malaria pills that must be taken every
day; pun on berri-berri (?)
Del Vecchio.

dairies n. (US Black use) the female
breasts; fr. lactation *Folb*.

daisy n. 1. anything particularly
appealing, excellent; 2. a male
homosexual; 3. (US Black use) a
housewife *Klein*.

daisy chain n. a circle of people,
hetero- or homosexual, all linked
physically in mutual sex acts
Legman.

daisy roots n. (rhyming sl.) boots
*L. Donegan, 'My Old Man's a
Dustman', 1960*.

daks n. (Aus. use) trousers; fr. trade
name Daks, popular trouser tailors
Ready.

damage n. the cost; usu. in 'what's the
damage?' *Humphries:2*.

damager n. (boxing and theatrical
use) joke corruption of word manager,
implying his alleged effect on those
whose livelihoods are in his hands
Powis.

dame n. woman; often with the
implication of promiscuity *McBain:1*.

damn all nothing, absolutely zero,
etc.; euph. fuck all (qv) *Manser*.

damn tootin' absolutely, completely
accurate, no doubt at all *Farrell*.

damned clever, these Chinese (cp) remarking on some particularly ingenious invention; the attribution is less to the skill of the Chinese than to their supposed wiliness.

damp n. the vagina *Southern & Hoffenberg*.

damper n. **1.** a small safe, a cashbox *Runyon:1*; **2.** (Can. prison use) solitary confinement, punishment cells *Caron*; **3.** anything which diminishes pleasure, which 'dampens' the warmth of one's emotions.

dance v. to steal from first or higher floors; dance implies Fred Astaire, thus stairs, up which the villain must climb *Powis*.

dance in the hog trough v. for an older sister to be left unmarried when her younger sibling has found a husband; occas. also used of boys.

dance on one's lips v. to hit in the face; to kick *Folb*.

dance on the mattress v. to make love; to have sexual intercourse *Klein*.

dancers n. the feet.

dandy a. attractive, first-rate, excellent; a general term of approbation *Jenkins*.

dang a. (euph.) damn *Rawson*.

Danish pastry n (gay use) a transsexual; from the pioneering operation undergone in Denmark by Christine Jorgensen.

dap a. (US Black use) (abbrev.) dapper, well-dressed; *dap to a tee*: very well dressed *Folb*.

dap n. (US milit. use) a ritualistic handshake, differing as to unit, involving much slapping of palms, snapping of fingers, etc. (cf: give some skin, etc.) *Del Vecchio*.

daps n. gym shoes, tennis shoes *K. Morris*.

darbies n. (UK police/criminal use) handcuffs; fr. a moneylender's bond of particular severity known as 'Father Darby's bands' *LL*.

Darby Kelly (rhyming sl.) belly, often as 'Darby Kel' *Powis*.

dark meat n. Blacks, esp. as sex objects (cf: white meat) *White*.

darkie n. (derog.) Black person *P. Tinniswood, 'The Home Front', 1983*.

darkness at noon (US campus use) the slide shows that form the basis of lectures in Art History *Bernbach*.

darktown n. the Black area of a town or city.

darn (euph.) damn; thus varieties incl. *goldarn*, *gosh darn* (both using euphs. for 'God') *Rawson*.

darry n. (UK prison use) a look; fr. 19th C. *derrey*: an eyeglass *LL*.

dash n. (Nigerian use) bribery; the money paid as a bribe *ST 6/2/83*.

dash! general euph, both for fuck (qv) damn (qv) etc.; fr. the — that a less candid age would use for the printed obscenity; thus *dash it*, *dashed*, etc. *Manser*.

dash in the bloomers n. sexual intercourse, usu. quick and adulterous *Higgins:5*.

date n. (Aus. use) the anus, the backside as a whole; fr. dot *Wilkes*.

date v. **1.** (Aus. use) to goose (qv) someone; fr. date, *n* (qv) *Wilkes*; **2.** to have an affair with someone, to be 'going out with' on a number of pre-arranged days *Price:2*.

daughter n. a male homosexual brought into the gay world by a homosexual friend *Stanley*.

daughter (UK Black use) any young woman, irrespective of relationship. *Robins*.

Davy Jones' locker n. a watery grave; fr. at least 1774.

daylight v. (US Black use) to enlighten, to explain *Klein*.

de facto n. (Aus. use) one of the two partners in an unmarried but steady relationship; from the Latin meaning in fact (as opposed to de jure: in law) *GQ magazine 3/92*.

dead a. **1.** of glasses or bottles: empty *Biff Comix, 1981*; **2.** finished, lost, spec. arrested, captured *Higgins:3*; **3.** absolutely, extremely, very *Performance*.

dead as a dodo a. absolutely dead, utterly irrelevant (of information, news); fr. the bird last seen alive in Mauritius in the 1680s.

dead cert n. absolute certainty, esp. in race course betting *Sillitoe*.

dead duck n. a complete, irredeemable failure *Vidal*.

Dead End Street n. the vagina *Maledicta*.

dead from the neck up a. anyone considered particularly stupid.

dead man's shoes (US Black use) anything that one would rather not have to experience but which probably cannot be avoided *Klein*.

dead marine n. (Aus. use) an empty bottle (cf: dead soldier) *Wilkes*.

dead meat n. 1. a corpse; 2. a stupid, dull person *Klein*.

dead pigeon n. a guaranteed and absolute failure, often in context of a forthcoming election *Vidal*.

dead presidents n. dollar bills (cf: Abraham Lincoln, portrait of Madison).

dead set a. (Aus. use) absolute, perfect, exact, ideal, etc. *Humphries:2*.

dead set on a. fascinated by, obsessed with, in love with.

dead shot n. (US Black use) the insertion of the penis into either the vagina or anus *Klein*.

dead soldier an empty bottle.

dead time n. (US prison use) any time spent in prison which does not actually diminish one's sentence *Klein*.

dead to rights a. 1. certain, sure; 2. caught in the act (cf: bang to rights) *Algren*.

dead to the wide aka: *dead to the world*; utterly and completely exhausted *Sillitoe*.

dead 'un n. (Aus. use) in horse-racing, a mount that seems not to have been raced to its full capacity *Wilkes*.

deadass n. an utterly boring, useless person.

deadbeat n. a failure, a down-and-out *Fiction Illus.3*.

deadeye n. the anus *Klein*.

dead-eye dick n. (homosexual use) one who performs anal intercourse fr.

nickname for a superlative marksman *Legman*.

deadhead a. useless, spec. non-participant *Higgins:3*.

deadhead n. 1. a fool; 2. a lazy worthless person; 3. a follower of the US rock band, the Grateful Dead.

deadhead v. to ride for free; to drive a cab, airplane, etc. without its usual load, passengers, etc. *Higgins:4*.

deadpan a. expressionless, fr. dead+pan (face) *Howard*.

deadpan v. to speak without expression, esp. in a situation that would normally demand some emotion *Price:3*.

deal v. to sell drugs, esp. marijuana (cf: connect) *Green:1*.

Dear John n. a letter concluding a relationship, usu. sent by the woman and received by the man, often in prison or serving in the forces *Pearce*.

death! (US school use) excl. of approval or admiration *E. Beyer*.

death on a. dealing very strictly and severely with employees, business partners, etc. *Klein*.

de-bag v. to remove someone's trousers, usu. as a somewhat heavyweight joke; fr. *bags*: trousers 19 C.-mid 20 C.; now obs. except in some (public) school use *Dickson*.

debs n. (street gang use) the girl-friends or girl members of a street gang *Salisbury*.

debut n. first homosexual experience *Jay & Young*.

debutante n. someone new to the gay life *Jay & Young*.

deck n. 1. floor, the ground; fr. USN/USMC use *Norman:2*; 2. (US contruction work) the roof of a building, or its highest floor at a given stage of building *Price:2*; 3. (drug use) a measure of heroin (cf: bag) *Larner*.

deck v. to knock on to the ground *Bukowski:7*.

deck ape n. (US navy use) deck hand *Pynchon*.

deck up v. (drug use) to portion out large measures of heroin into small portions (cf: deck, bag) *Larner*.

decoke v. (motorist use) to clean the spark plugs of accumulated carbon.

decorate the mahogany v. to lay down money, whether for gambling or in payment of a bill.

deeache n. (backsl.) head *Cole*.

deek v. (Sc. use) to watch, to see *Welsh:1* (cf: decko).

deelo n. (backsl.) old *Cole*.

deelo nam n. (backsl.) old man *Cole*.

deenach n. (backsl.) hand *Cole*.

deep six v. 1. (naut. use) to throw overboard S. *Llewellyn, The Worst Journey in the Midlands, 1983*; 2. to get rid of, to abandon *Waits*.

deepthroat v. to take the entire length of the penis into one's mouth – and thus down one's throat – during fellatio *Morgan*.

def a. perfect, excellent, first-rate (cf: rad, safe) *Ice T:1*.

defug v. (UK 'society' use) to open the doors/windows in order to get some fresh air into a musty/smoke-filled room *Barr*.

dehorned a. demoted, deprived of a position of power or authority.

dekko n. a look, a view; fr. Hindustani *dekho*, a look *Humphries*.

Delhi belly n. food poisoning, epitomized in diarrhoea, suffered by tourists in India. Other localized versions of this problem include Cairo crud, Gyppie tummy, Rangoon runs, Hong Kong dog (cf: Montezuma's revenge) *Rawson*.

delok n. (butchers' backsl.) cold, ie. frozen/imported meat *Cole*.

delonammon n. (backsl.) old woman *Powis*.

demo n. (abbrev.) demonstration (of a political or pressure-group nature).

Denmark, go to v. phr. (gay use) to have a sex-change operation (cf: Copenhagen, go to).

Denmark, something's rotten in phr. (gay use) referring to someone who is presumed to have had a sex change; from Shakespeare's *Hamlet* Act I, Scene iv.: 'Something is rotten in the state of Denmark' (cf: Copenhagen capon, Danish pastry).

dep n. 1. (police/criminal use) (abbrev.) deposition *Mortimer*; 2. (UK prison use) (abbrev.) deputy governor *LL*.

dep n., v. (abbrev.) deputy; to act as deputy *Capital Radio 1983*.

depresso a. (US teen. use) depressing *Price:2*.

deputy do-right (US Black use) the police *Folb*.

Derby Kelly n. (rhyming sl.) belly (cf: Darby Kelly) *Franklyn*.

deri n. derelict house or other dwelling *Robins:1*.

dero n. (Aus. use) a derelict person, a down-and-out *Wilkes*.

derry n. see: deri.

destroyed (drug use) extremely high (qv) (cf: wasted) *Folb*.

dethroned a. (homosexual use) a queen (qv) who has been ejected from the public lavatory where he is looking for sex. (cf: abdicated). *Legman*.

detox n. (abbrev.) detoxification after a period of drug addiction *Jay & Young*.

deuce n. 1. two dollars *Fiction Illus.3*; 2. (drug use) two pills *Folb*; 3. (US prison use) a two-year sentence *Morgan*.

deuce 25 aka *deuce and a quarter*: a Buick 225; any car with 225 hp engine *Folb*.

Deuce, the n. New York's 42nd Street, between 7th and 8th Avenues (until the shutting down of many porno cinemas and bookstores in the early 1990s this was the centre of midtown vice; in 1994, with renovation apparently suspended, it still had the crime, esp. crack (qv) dealing, but none of the redeeming glamour that even briefly before, had harked, however marginally, back to the old 42nd Street).

deuce-deuce n. a .22 revolver or pistol.

devil n. (US Black, esp. Black Muslim, use) white person *Folb*.

devil had an auction, like the phr. a remark offered when faced with a particularly untidy house.

devil's half-acre n. 1. a rough or unworkable piece of land; 2. the rough area of a town.

dew n. (US milt. use) marijuana *Del Vecchio*.

dewdrop n. a drop of mucus lodged at the opening of a nostril and hanging there prior to removal.

dex n. (abbrev.) dexedrine, a form of amphetamine drug *Green:1*.

dexy n. see: dex *Green:1*.

DFFL (acro.) *Dope Forever, Forever Loaded*: a popular patch worn by Hells Angels, hippies, etc. *Thompson*.

dialogue n. (Valley Girls (qv) use) a conversation; esp. one person's monologue *Harpers/Queen 1/83*.

diamond a. first rate, excellent.

diaper n. (US Black use) a sanitary towel; fr. usual use: nappy *Folb*.

dibs n. money *Runyon*.

dibs on trad. expression claiming a share of, or the next turn with a given article *Uris*.

dick n. 1. a detective *Fiction Illus.3*; 2. the penis *Price:2*; 3. (US teen. use) an unattractive male, esp. one who has an overly high self-image *Pond*.

dick v. to have intercourse, fr. male point of view. *Shell*

dick around v. to waste time, to dither.

dick gun n. (milit. use) gun for firing rubber bullets; which look extremely phallic *A.F.N. Clarke, 'Contact', 1983*.

dick peddler n. aka: *prick peddler*: a male prostitute who will only take active roles with his clients *Legman*.

dick teaser n. see: prick teaser.

dicked a. assured of success; fr. *dick* = penis, thus image of potency *Underwood*.

dickery n. (rhyming sl.) dickery dock = clock *Powis*.

dickhead n. a fool, an incompetent; a general term of abuse (cf: dick) *Bleasdale*.

dickless tracy n. (US cant) woman police officer; fr. puns on dick = detective (qv) and cartoon strip 'Dick Tracy' *Neaman & Silver*.

dickory dock n. (rhyming sl.) cock =

penis *Cole*.

Dick's hatband, tight as a. phr. very mean.

dickty a. (US Black use) snobbish, haughty *Major*.

dicky a. out of order, sub-standard, not working as it should *Humphries:2*.

dicky diddle 1. n. urine, 2. v. to urinate.

dicky dirt n. (rhyming sl.) shirt 'Dickie Dirts': chain of cut-price shirt and jeans shops in late 1970s London.

dicky up v. to adorn (oneself), to dress up (cf: dike down).

dicky-bird n. (rhyming sl.) a word *Norman:1*.

dicky-licker n. (derog.) a homosexual *Legman*.

did I ever! general expression of intensification, ie: I certainly did! usu. in answer to a question.

did I fuck! excl. of negation, eg: 'Did I steal that car, did I fuck!'; similarly *will I fuck!* = no I certainly won't.

diddicoi n. a gypsy; fr. Romany *Powis*.

diddies n. breasts; mispron./dial. use of titties (qv).

diddle v. 1. to molest sexually; 2. to have sexual intercourse; 3. to cheat, to defraud *Hotten*.

diddler n. (Can. prison use) child molester *Caron*.

diddley-hop n. (street gang use) a top gang fighter *Larner*.

diddley-poo n. excreta; usu. children's use *Rawson*.

diddley-shit a. minimal, small, insignificant *Uneeda Comix*.

diddley-squat n. nothing, zero; thus *it don't mean diddley squat*: it is totally irrelevant, unimportant *Morgan*.

diddums (nursery use) term of soothing affection use by parent to child

diddy-bag n. aka: *ditty-bag* a small bag for various trifles, mainly US milit. use.

diddy-bop 1. (Black use) pretentious Black person, pretending/trying to identify with whites *Morgan*; 2. naïve, immature Black; 3. Black bourgeois

Greenlee.

diddy-bopping (milit. use) walking carelessly (cf: diddy-bop) *Baker*.

didies n. underpants *King*.

didn't ought n. (rhyming sl.) port (wine) *Powis*.

dido n. (US police use) a minor complaint by one officer against another *Runyon*.

die v. (show business use) for a performance to fail, to fall flat; esp. of a comedian who does not amuse *T 12/9/83*

diesel/diesler n. **1.** an overtly masculine lesbian *Goldman*; **2.** (UK prison use) prison tea; it tastes like derv *Obs. 1981*.

diesel-dyke n. see: diesel 1. *Bruce:2*.

dig n. a sex show, fr. Black sl. *dig*: to look, to notice *Legman*.

dig v. appreciate, enjoy; from jazz fan use referring to music c. 1950s *Price:2*.

dig in v. to eat heartily; often as exhortation: 'dig in!'

dig in the grave n. (rhyming sl.) a shave *Cole*.

dig you later phr. see you later, goodbye.

digger n. **1.** an Australian; fr. form of address used by miners in Aus. gold-fields of 19th C., spread after Aus. participation in First World War *Baker*; **2.** (Can. prison use) solitary confinement, punishment block *Caron*.

digits dealer n. (US cant) numbers racketeer *Neaman & Silver*.

dike n. **1.** see: dyke *Bruce:2*; **2.** (Aus. use) a lavatory, esp. a communal urinal use by schoolboys, soldiers, etc. (cf: bog) *Wilkes*.

dildo n. a fool, an incompetent, from the lack of autonomous competence of the sexual aid so named *Harpers/Queen 8/83*

dill n. (Aus. use) a fool *Humphries;* the UK use may also be attributed to an abbrev. of the 'silly' name Dilbert (slightly transformed by the comedian Lenny Henry into his bumptious character 'Delbert Wilkins').

dillo n. (backsl.) old *Powis*.

dilly n. anything outstanding or remarkable; often used ironically *Thompson:J*.

dime n. **1.** (in general US use) the number ten (cf: nickel); **2.** (gambling use) $1000 *Alvarez*; **3.** (US prison use) 10-year prison sentence.

dime bag n. (drug use) $10 worth of a given drug (cf: nickel bag) *Green:1*.

dime, get off the v. to leave, to run off.

dime-a-dozen a. common, undistinguished; fr. the cheapness of such items *Vizinczey*.

dinah n. nitroglycerine; fr. dynamite *Chandler:Notebk*.

din-din n. (juv. use) dinner.

dinero n. money; fr. Sp. *Goulart*.

ding n. **1.** (Aus. use) derog. term for foreigners, esp. Italians and Greeks *Wilkes*; **2.** (Aus. use) (abbrev.) wing-ding (qv.) *Wilkes*.

ding v. **1.** to knock down; **2.** to beg; **3.** to break *Wolfe:7*.

dingaling n. **1.** (US Black use) the penis *Chuck Berry, song title 'My Dingaling', 1978*; **2.** idiot, fool *Underwood*.

dingbat n. a fool, an idiot *Higgins:4*.

ding-dong n. **1.** (rhyming sl.) a fight *Jones:J*; **2.** penis *Lou Reed, 'Sister Ray', 1968*.

ding-dong v. to annoy, to irritate.

dinge n. a Black; fr. dingey: shabby, grimy *Chandler:1*.

dinge queen n. a homosexual who prefers black partners *Stanley*.

dinger n. (Aus. use) anus, buttocks *Wilkes*.

dingleberries n. pieces of excreta clinging to the hairs around an inadequately cleansed anus *Green:2*.

dingo v. (Aus. use) to act in a particularly cowardly and treacherous manner, to exhibit the mannerisms of the dingo, the native Aus. dog, a despised creature *Wilkes*.

dingo's breakfast n. (Aus. use) 'a piss and a look around' (cf: Mexican breakfast).

dingus n. **1.** penis *Neaman & Silver*; **2.** thingummijig, whatchamacallit, etc.

TZ.

dingy a. (US campus use) silly, foolish (cf: dingbat) *Underwood*.

dining at the Y v. perform cunnilingus; fr. the conjunction of the thighs, plus a pun on the YMCA/ YWCA *Humphries*.

dink n. 1. an Oriental, esp. Vietnamese (cf: gook) *Higgins:1*; 2. the penis, esp. of a small boy (cf: dingus); thus 3. derog. term for a person.

dink-do (bingo rhyming sl.) 22 *Wright*.

dinki-di a. (Aus. use) real, genuine, fr. dinkum (qv.) *Humphries*.

dinkum a. (Aus. use) honest, genuine; esp. as *fair dinkum*: fair play, on the level; fr. UK dial. dinkum: fair share of work *Humphries*.

dinky n. (UK 'society' use) a large car; deliberate understatement and ref. to defunct brand of toy cars *Barr*.

dinky (acro.) *dual income no kids yet*: a social acronym (see: buppie, lombard, yuppie) created to describe the ideal couple of the booming 1980s. *Green:3*.

dinky one's slinky v. to masturbate.

dinner pailer n. a regular working man or woman (cf: chump 2., working stiff).

dinners n. the female breasts.

dino n. tramp, hobo, layabout *Algren*.

dinosaur n. (US Black use) 1. the penis *Folb*; 2. an ageing rock star, usually of the 1960s or early 1970s vintage. Such stars, and their bands, won't lie down and subsist gracefully on their royalties; instead they continue to stage concerts, make albums, tour the world and generally refuse to act their age.

dip n. 1. (abbrev.) dipshit (av.) *Underwood*; 2. a pickpocket *Powis*.

dip v. to eavesdrop, to butt into another's conversation.

dip it v. see: dip one's wick *Dunne*.

dip one's wick v. to have sexual intercourse (of a male) *Humphries*.

dip the bill v. to take a drink *Chandler:Notebk*.

dip the fly v. (US Black use) to have sexual intercourse *Folb*.

diphead n. see: dipshit *Underwood*.

dipping in business (US Black use) interfering in affairs that are none of one's concern *Klein*.

dipping in the bush v. to engage in cunnilingus *Klein*.

dippy a. crazy, eccentric, insane.

dipshit a. (derog.) second rate, inferior *Price:2*.

dipso n. (abbrev.) dipsomaniac; alcoholic *Fiction Illus.3*.

dipstick n. (euph.) dipshit (qv.) *Stone*.

dirt n. information, not necessarily, but often scurrilous; often as 'what's the dirt on. . .?' (cf: dish the dirt).

dirt n. a male or female prostitute who steals from their clients *Maledicta 9*.

dirt farm n. (US Black use) any centre for (malicious) gossip (cf: dish the dirt) *Folb*.

dirt road n. the anus *Sanders:2*.

dirt tamper n. one who practises anal intercourse *Legman*.

dirtbag n. general term of opprobrium *Morgan*.

dirties n. diarrhoea; sometimes modified as to source, eg. green-apple dirties.

dirty a. (drug use) currently addicted to drugs (cf: clean).

dirty a. (UK criminal use) dubious, unsafe, to be avoided ; the opposite of kosher (qv).

dirty dishes n. (UK cant) planted incriminating evidence *Neaman & Silver*.

dirty dowager n. (homosexual use) an unkempt, ill-preserved older queen (qv.) *Legman*.

dirty dozens see: dozens *Folb*.

dirty great a. to imply great size in a given context; the most common use of *dirty* as an intensifier.

dirty leg n. a promiscuous girl *Jenkins*.

dirty look n. a disapproving glance or stare.

dirty money n. money that is considered not to have been earned honourably or respectably.

dirty old Jew (bingo use) 2 (cf: me and you).

dirty pool n. unfair, duplicitous *Jay & Young*.

dirty weekend n. a weekend spent either with one's lover (in the absence of one's spouse) or with one's spouse but mercifully relieved of one's children.

dirty whore (bingo rhyming sl.) 34.

discombobulate v. to discomfit, to perplex ('jocular use' *OED*) *Higgins:5.*

discover one's gender v. to come out (qv.); to accept one's homosexuality *Legman.*

dish n. 1. an embarrassing story about a given subject's life *White*; 2. an attractive female. (cf: crumpet, cookie, etc.); 3. something one likes, something suited to one's taste (cf: cup of tea).

dish v. to hurt, to stop another's plans, to frustrate.

dish it out v. to hand out, usu. punishment, blows, abuse, etc. *rr.*

dish out gravy v. (UK criminal/prison use) to hand out particularly severe sentences *LL.*

dish queen n. a homosexual who enjoys slandering his peers (cf: dish the dirt) *Stanley.*

dish the dirt v. to gossip maliciously, to slander *Selby:1.*

dishy a. attractive, pretty.

dishybilly a. undressed, not fully dressed, dishevelled. (fr. Fr. *déshabillé*: undressed).

diss v. abbrev. of disrespect; to slander, to attack verbally. *Ice T:3.*

ditch v. 1. to throw away, to dispense with, to abandon – both persons and things *Price:2*; 2. to leave in a hurry; 3. to play truant from school.

ditso a. useless, second rate, no good *Price:2.*

ditty-bop see: diddy-bop *Price:3.*

ditz / ditso n. 1. a fool, an idiot *Morgan*; 2. something excellent.

ditzy a. first-rate, excellent, exceptional.

div n. a weakling *Dury*; 2. something excellent.

dive v. to perform cunnilingus *Legman.*

dive into the dark v. (US Black use) to have sexual intercourse *Klein.*

dive into the sky v. to penetrate the anus with one's penis *Klein.*

divine right n. (US Black use) the police *Folb.*

divvy n. (abbrev.) dividend; the annual financial share-out by a co-operative society.

divvy up v. (abbrev.) to divide up, usu. illicit profits *Wodehouse:PGM.*

dj (abbrev.) *d*inner jacket.

DJ (abbrev.) *d*isc jockey *Capital Radio passim.*

DM (abbrev.) Doc Martens: a heavy boot favoured first by working men, then by skinheads and latterly by fashionable girls.

do n. 1. a party, a celebration, dinner, etc; often reasonably formal *Pynchon*; 2. (US Black use) (abbrev.) hair-do *Folb*; 3. excrement, usu. animal (cf: doggie-do, doo-doo); 4. (US Black use) processed or straightened hair (cf: conk).

do v. 1. to consume a given drug: ie *do coke* (qv.), etc. *Jay & Young*; 2. to copulate with a girl or woman; 3. to sue, to take to court, to charge with a crime; thus 'X was done for taking and driving away', etc. *Bleasdale*; 4. to assault.

do a Bertie v. (UK police/criminal use) to turn Queen's evidence against one's accomplices; fr. a criminal turned confessor: Bertie Smalls *Powis.*

do a bit v. 1. (US prison use) to serve a prison sentence; 2. show business: to perform a routine on stage *Goldman.*

do a bunk v. run off, escape, go into hiding *Sillitoe.*

do a crib v. (US criminal use) to break and enter premises for the purpose of robbery (cf: crib) *Klein.*

do a dry waltz with oneself v. to masturbate *Algren.*

do a fair lick v. to run fast *Sillitoe.*

do a foreigner v. for men contracted to one job to take time off illegally to tackle another, more lucrative one *Bleasdale.*

do a freeze v. (Aus.) to be ignored, to

be overlooked.

do a job v. (criminal use) to commit a crime, esp. a robbery.

do a job on v. 1. to beat up; 2. to make someone the victim of a confidence trick or allied hoax or deception.

do a Melba v. (Aus. use) to announce, with great fanfare, one's imminent retirement, only to return, time and time again, for another 'farewell' – a practice of the late Dame Nellie Melba (1861–1931) and many other 'showbiz greats' *Wilkes*.

do a mischief to v. (UK criminal use) to harm, to beat up.

do a number v. 1. (drug use) to make and smoke a marijuana or hashish cigarette; 2. make a fuss, become emotional, subject to emotional blackmail or at least some form of moral/friendship/ethical pressure; often *do a number on Dickson*.

do a powder v. see: take a powder *LL*.

do a runner v. (UK criminal/police use) to abscond from the police or to be on the run, prior to possible capture by the police *Powis*.

do a solid v. perform a great favour *Price:2*.

do a thing v. (drug use) to inject oneself with heroin *Klein*.

do a ton v. to drive a motorcycle or car at one hundred mph.

do as you like n. (rhyming sl.) a bike = bicycle *Powis*.

do bandies v. (US teen use) to perform feats of physical daring, esp. when one dares one's companions to follow suit.

do brown v. to deceive, to take in, to surprise; fr. cooking use *Hotten*.

do down v. to take advantage of someone, esp. financially or by talking behind their back in a derogatory way.

do in v. 1. to inject a narcotic drug *Burroughs:Jr*; 2. to kill, thus *do oneself in*: commit suicide *McBain:1*; 3. to wear out.

do in the eye v. to cheat.

do it for myself v. (taxi-driver use) to

take a (usually bargain) fare without putting it on the clock and thus having to pay it to the cab company *Price:2*.

do it like Mommy v. to act in a domesticated manner – doing the housework, shopping, etc. *Sculatti*.

do it on one's head v. aka: *do it on one's dick/prick*: to endure any challenging situation esp. a prison sentence with no difficulty *Grogan*.

do (it) up right v. to carry out fully and correctly, to achieve a set objective *Southern*.

do one's block v. to lose one's temper *Humphries*.

do one's do v. to do what is necessary, do what one must do.

do one's dough v. to lose one's money, to spend up.

do one's head v. (US campus use) to take a given, preferred drug *Underwood*.

do one's nut v. see: do one's block *Powis*.

do one's (own) thing v. to behave as dictated by one's personal beliefs, wishes, idiosyncrasies, etc. *Wolfe:2*.

do one's stuff v. to perform as one is expected; to do one's duty; to exhibit a given speciality *Fleetwood Mac, 'Rumours', 1976*.

do oneself in v. to commit suicide; to put oneself in a deliberately unpleasant situation/position *Neaman & Silver*.

do over v. 1. to beat up *Austin*; 2. to cheat, to defraud.

do skippers v. to sleep around on floors, sofas; to have no permanent home *Norman:2*.

do the business v. to fulfill a promise, to act as expected, often in a sexual context.

do the dirty on v. to treat badly, to betray a trust, to cheat.

do the do v. (US Black use) to have sexual intercourse *Folb*.

do the full sesh v. (Valley Girls (qv) use) to indulge completely, to take to the limit; sesh = (abbrev.) session *Pond*.

do the lolly v. (Aus. use) lose one's

temper, lose control of one's emotions, senses *Wilkes*.

do the milk route v. (sex industry use) to tour bus stations or other such places very late at night or very early in the morning looking for trade.

do the nasty v. to have sexual intercourse *F. Zappa, 'Brown Shoes Don't Make It', 1966*.

do the natural thing v. (US Black use) to have sexual intercourse *Folb*.

do the party v. (UK criminal use) a stage in a game of three-card monte (qv.) whereby one of the gang apparently bets and wins (posing as just another bettor), thus encouraging the real victims to put down their cash *Powis*.

do the pussy v. (US Black use) to have sexual intercourse (cf: pussy) *Folb*.

do time v. serve a prison sentence *Higgins:1*.

do up v. 1. to inject a narcotic; 2. to deal with; esp. to beat up *Norman:2*.

do what? excl. 'what did you say?', 'please repeat the question'.

do you need a boy? (drug use) surreptitious request for heroin (cf: boy) *De Lannoy & Masterson*.

do you think I'm made of money? aka: *I'm not made of money!* cp: admonishing someone – usu. a wife or child – who is spending the breadwinner's hard-earned cash with excessive abandon.

DOA a. (police use) (abbrev.) *Dead On Arrival Dunne*.

dob in v. (Aus. use) 1. to betray, to inform against; 2. to contribute (financially); 3. dob oneself in: to let oneself in for problems *Humphries:2*.

dobe n. a cigarette or cigar butt.

dock v. to cut; use. in *dock one's pay*: retain a portion of one's wages; fr. SE *dock*: slicing off a dog's tail *Seale*.

dock asthma n. (UK police use) ironic reference to the gasps of alleged 'surprise' from the accused when the police produce their evidence in court *Powis*.

Dr Feelgood n. a doctor who obliges

patients – often showbusiness or entertainment celebrities – with amphetamines or narcotics which, despite their user having no real medical need for them, guarantee 'good feelings' *Blacker*.

Dr Thomas n. (US Black use) a middle-class Black aspiring to white status; as Uncle Tom but with professional qualifications *Folb*.

doctor's orders (bingo use) 9; fr. the Army's No. 9 pills, or the nine months of pregnancy *Wright*.

do-dad n. any object or gadget without a specific name *TZ*.

doddle n. anything absolutely simple or easy to achieve *Norman:2*.

dodge n. a trick, a gimmick, a means of avoiding problems, esp. those encountered in work *Thompson:J*.

dodgy a. dubious, unreliable: temporarily the cp (with its antonym 'swinging') of comedian Norman Vaughan, compere of TV's 'Sunday Night at the London Palladium'.

dodo n. an idiot, a dullard; fr. 'dead as a dodo' *Klein*.

does a bear shit in the woods? Is the Pope a Catholic? cp. the implication is don't ask me stupid questions, of course it/they does/do. The phrase is also found reversed, ie. 'Does the Pope shit in the woods…?'.

does your mother know you're out? (cp) sarcastic comment to a person whom the speaker feels should be elsewhere, due to immaturity, foolishness, inexperience, etc.

doesn't have a pot to pee in (cp) very poor.

doesn't know enough to come in out of the rain (cp) someone who is exceptionally stupid *Heller*.

dog n. 1. (rhyming sl.) dog and bone = phone *Capital Radio 1983*; 2. (derog.) an untrustworthy, vicious, traitorous, completely venal man *Milner*; 3. weakness, cowardice *Higgins:3*; 4. unattractive woman *Price:1*; 5. (commercial use) anything that remains hard to sell, used by antique trade, auto business (esp.

second hand cars), etc. *AS 41 (1966)*;
6. (Aus. use) an informer *Wilkes*;
7. euph. for dog excrement, thus
'there's dog all over the pavement';
8. style, esp. if affected or pretentious,
thus 'put on dog': to act in such a
manner; 9. (US Black campus use) a
novice, similarly used are canine,
hound, pup, puppy; 10. (US Black
use) lust, sexual desire; 11. the hardest
part of the job (once done all that is
left is the tail).

dog v. 1. to pursue, to hunt down
(usually with sexual intent) *Ice T:2*; 2.
a form of planned voyeurism/
exhibitionism: couples arrange to
meet (in their cars) in a selected
carpark; some have intercourse while
others watch *I Jackson*; 3. (US cant) to
cheat; 4. to betray, to inform against;
5. to act in a menial capacity.

dog and bone n. (rhyming sl.)
telephone *Jones:J*.

dog around v. 1. to live a promiscuous
life (cf: cat, v.) *Price:3*; 2. (US campus
use) to neglect one's academic work
Underwood.

dog doctor n. a second-rate or
incompetent doctor, fig. 'only fit to
work with animals'.

dog food n. (US Black use) heroin.

dog fuck n. sexual intercourse in
which entry is made from the rear.

dog it v. 1. to dress up; fr. put on the
dog (qv); 2. to malinger, to act lazily
(cf: dog around 2) *Higgins:4*;
3. (gambling use) to act weakly, to be
a loser, to lack winning spirit; fr.
abbrev. underdog (cf: pooch) *Alvarez*.

dog juice n. (US Black use) cheap
liquor *Folb*.

dog tag n. a legitimate prescription
for otherwise illegal narcotics; for a
dog to be 'legal' (not a stray) it must
have a labelled collar *AS 41 (1966)*.

dog turd n. a large cigar.

dog wagon n. 1. a small café or
restaurant sited in a converted vehicle:
the quality of food is generally poor; 2.
see: black maria.

dog watch n. (broadcasting use)
programmes that are broadcast after

midnight; orig. nautical use
AS 41 (1966).

dog-ass a. inferior, second-rate,
unpleasant *Jenkins*.

dog-end n. the last fraction of a
cigarette. (cf: butt) *Norman:2*.

dog-face n. infantry soldier *Grogan*.

dog-food (drug use) heroin *Folb*.

dogged out a. dressed up.

dogger out n. (UK criminal use) a
lookout man *AS 41 (1966)*.

doggie n. (abbrev.) dog-face (qv.)
Selby:1.

doggie bag n. a bag provided by some
retaurants for customers to take home
left-overs, ostensibly for later
consumption by their pet dog
AS 41 (1966).

doggie (doggy) -do n. (euph.) canine
excrement.

doggie-fashion n. see: dog fuck.

doggone general US intensifier (cf:
ruddy, bleeding, etc.) *Rawson*.

doggy a. 1. (US Black use) hard,
mean, thoughtless *Folb*; 2. (US Black
use) obsessed with sex, lecherous; 3.
fashionable; 4. lazy, sluggish.

dog-knotted for two lovers to be
locked together during intercourse
because of a vaginal muscle-spasm
brought on by a sudden shock
Sharpe:1.

dogmeat n. a worthless, despicable
person *Morgan*.

dogpatch n. (derog.) a small town or
hamlet (fr. Dogpatch, the hill-billy
settlement in which the syndicated
cartoon strip *Lil Abner* takes place).

dogs n. 1. (fashion use) badly designed
garments *AS 41 (1966)*; 2. shoes;
coined by US sportwriter Tad Dorgan
(d.1929) in NY *Evening Journal*
AS 41 (1966); 3. the feet *Runyon*.

dog's ballocks n. (journalistic use) the
printed symbol :- (cf: dog's cock)
AS 41 (1966).

dog's cock n. (journalistic use) a
printed exclamation mark, thus !
(cf: dog's ballocks) *Green:2*.

dog's dinner n. a distasteful mess (but
cf: dressed up like a dog's dinner)
Legman.

dog's nose n. (US criminal use) a paid informer *AS 41 (1966)*.

dog's tail, not by a phr. not by a long way, in no way.

dogs of war n. mercenary troops; fr. F. Forsyth bk title, in turn fr. W. Shakespeare *Julius Caesar*.

dogsbody n. any member of an organization who takes on all the menial and tedious tasks, often working for any senior person who gives out instructions *Dickson*.

dogswatch n. (journalistic use) a shift on a newspaper running fr. 9–12 midnight; fr. nautical use *AS 41 (1966)*.

do-hickey n. any nameless small object (cf: do-dad).

doing a hundred (US Black use) to be in good shape, to be doing well; fr. one hundred per cent (qv) *Major*.

doings n. whatever objects are required to perform a given job.

doing the dutch v. (Can. prison use) to commit suicide *Caron*.

doing-up n. the wilful destruction of property as part of a gang war *Performance*.

do-it fluid n. (US Black use) liquor.

do-jigger n. (US use) the penis *Neaman & Silver*.

dole-bludger n. (Aus. use) one who claims unemployment benefit either when work is available or while actually employed in 'the Black Economy'; the Aus. equivalent to UK 'dole scrounger' (cf: bludger) *Wilkes*.

doley n. (Aus. use) aka: dolie: anyone drawing unemployment benefit *Wilkes*.

doll n. 1. an attractive (young) woman *Runyon*; 2. (US campus use) a conceited young woman *Underwood*.

Doll City n. (US teen. use) a conventionally pretty girl (cf: doll) *Sculatti*.

doll up v. to dress up a person or an object *Uneeda Comix*.

dolly n. 1. (abbrev.) dolly-bird; a pretty young girl, but particularly popular in 1960s 'Swinging London' *Keyes*; 2 (drug use) (abbrev.) Dolophine, a

synthetic morphine *Goldman*.

dollar n. five shillings, and thus obsolete outside films, books, etc. of a pre-metric era; fr. a time when exchange rate was four US $ to a £ sterling.

dollface n. an attractive girl, or boy; often used as form of address 'Hey, dollface!'

dolly boy n. see: rent boy (cf: dolly girl) *Maledicta 9*.

Dolly Varden n. (rhyming sl.) the garden; fr. Charles Dickens character *Powis*.

DOM n. (acro.) *D*irty *O*ld *M*an; poss. an actual or alleged child molester but usu. any older man who makes obvious his preference for girls younger than he might be expected to pursue *Barr*.

dom (abbrev.) (sex industry use) dominatrix.

dome n. (orig. US) the head.

dominicker 1. n. a coward (cf: chicken); 2. a person of mixed race, esp. of Black, Indian and White ancestry; 3. v. to back down, to act in a cowardly manner (cf: chicken out) (fr. SE dominicker: the Dominique fowl or any other chicken with mottled or barred plumage; the dominicker rooster was believed always to back down when challenged by another rooster).

donah n. 1. attractive woman; fr. parlyaree (a form of theatrical/circus sl. deriving fr. Italian *donna*: a woman); 2. (criminal use) the 'lady', the queen in a game of three card monte *Powis*.

donald abbrev. sexual intercourse; fr. rhy. sl. Donald Duck = fuck (qv).

done a. 1. cheated (cf: ripped off) *Wilkinson*; 2 beaten up, assaulted *LL*.

done for a. without a chance, hopeless, defeated, lost, abandoned.

done in a. very tired, exhausted.

done like a dinner (Aus. use) see: done to a turn *Wilkes*.

done over worsted, put at a disadvantage, forced to lose out in a disagreement or struggle.

done thing n. whatever is currently accepted by a given group of people – professional, social, economic, etc.

done to a turn worsted, beaten, at a disadvantage; with image of being spit-roasted and defenceless.

done up a. 1. exhausted (cf: done in); 2. beaten up, badly injured, also as 'done up like a kipper'; 3. very drunk; 4. out of order, not working; 5. dressed up, esp. as 'done up to the nines'.

done up like a kipper 1. beaten up; 2. caught red-handed by the police; ambushed during a crime *Cole*.

dong n. the penis *Price:2*.

donkey drop n. (cricket use) a full toss *M. Meyer (ed.), 'Summer Days', 1983*.

donkey-dick n. a notably large penis; thus donkey-dicked.

donkey-lick v. (Aus. use) to trounce, to beat comprehensively *Wilkes*.

donkey-rigged a. in possession of a notably large penis.

donkey's years a very long time; fr. the length of a donkey's ears and the addition of an extra 'y'.

donnybrook n. a fight, a riot, a noisy brawl; fr. notorious Donnybrook Fair in Eire at which such events were a regular feature.

Dons n. Wimbledon Football Club *BBC-1 TV passim*.

don't argue n. (Aus. use) in rugby football, a straight-arm hand-off; fr. illus. in the trademark of Aus. company J. C. Hutton pty. Ltd *Wilkes*.

don't ask me statement of ignorance or lack of interest in a previous query.

don't be funny (cp) don't be stupid (cf: don't make me laugh).

don't call us, we'll call you (cp) semi-joking phr. of dismissal; fr. trad. theatrical use by producers/directors to auditioning actors whom, of course, they never do call *Manser*.

don't do anything I wouldn't do! (cp) exhortation to anyone who is leaving, esp. on holiday or in search of similar supposed pleasures; the inference is usu. sexual *Del Vecchio*.

don't fancy yours! joking reflex comment when two young men see two girls, irrespective of real charms *L. Deighton, Close-Up, 1974*.

don't get your bowels in an uproar (cp) don't make so much (unnecessary) fuss.

don't give a monkey's couldn't care less *Austin*.

don't give a rap (for) couldn't care less; fr. *rap*: halfpenny (orig. a form of small counterfeit coins in Ireland 18th C.) *Hotten*.

don't give a tuppenny fuck couldn't care less.

don't give me that (cp) you can't fool me (cf: tell it to the Marines) *Manser*.

don't have a clue has absolutely not the slightest idea *Wodehouse:AAG*.

don't hold no air (US Black use) to have little impact or effect on either people or event *Folb*.

don't just stand there – do something! (cp) urging a quantity, if not a quality of action.

don't know one's ass from a hole in the ground to be particularly stupid *R. Newman, 'Rednecks'*.

don't know shit from Shinola haven't the first idea about a given topic, to be particularly wrong in an opinion; Shinola is a black shoe polish *Price:2*.

don't know (someone) from a bar of soap (Aus. use cp) implying absolute lack of acquaintance with a person mentioned or seen *Wilkes*.

don't know whether you're coming or going utterly confused, lost, disorientated.

don't make a production out of it (cp) 'don't make a mountain out of a molehill'.

don't make it a federal case don't make a minor problem into a major one *McBain:1*.

don't make me laugh (cp) don't be stupid, ridiculous (cf: don't be funny).

don't mind me (I only live/work/etc. here) (cp) a resentful *cri de coeur* from a speaker who feels his/her territory is being taken over by strangers.

don't shoot the pianist he's doing his best (cp) self-explanatory *Capital Radio 1983*.

don't spend it all at once (cp) usu. on handing over a small amount of money, in payment of a debt, etc.

don't strain yourself! (derisory cp) addressed to anyone deemed to be failing conspicuously at pulling their weight.

don't take any wooden nickels (cp) look out for yourself.

don't worry – it may never happen (cp) usu. offered as advice to someone looking especially miserable or worried.

donut bumper n. (derog.) a lesbian (cf: bumper).

doob n. amphetamine; the term originated with the Mods of the early 1960s and then spread among other users (cf: speed).

doo-dads n. morsels, pieces, odds and ends *White*.

doodah n. **1.** anything for which one cannot remember the name; **2.** an emotional crisis, a nervous, tense state *Wodehouse:AAG*.

doodle the penis *Rawson*.

doodler n. a lazy person, an idler.

doodley-shit n. worthless rubbish, trash (cf: diddley-squat, etc.) *Farina*.

doo-doo n. **1.** excrement, usu. animal (cf: do, doggie-do), thus fig. **2.** trouble, difficulties, esp. 'deep doo-doo': serious trouble (cf: in the shit).

doofus (US campus use) odd, strange, eccentric *Underwood*.

doog a. (backsl.) good *Cole*.

doog eno (butchers' backsl) good one *Cole*.

doog gels (butchers' backsl.) good legs (of a passing woman) *Cole*.

doo-hickey n. anything to which one cannot immediately put a name, a thingammijig.

dooky n. excrement *Sanders:2*.

doolally a. mad, eccentric; fr. Indian Army Deolali sanatorium in Bombay *Waterhouse*.

doonups n. (butchers' backsl.) pounds *Cole*.

doorknob n. **1.** a doughnut; **2.** the head; **3.** the female breast.

doorstep child n. an illegitimate child.

doorstepping (journalistic use) hanging around on the doorstep, or some similar venue, of the possible and much sought after source of a major story *'World in Action', Granada TV, 1983*.

doover n. (Aus. use) penis *Humphries*.

doozy n. something outstanding of its type.

dope n. **1.** drugs *Price:1*; **2.** a fool, a dunce *Breslin*; **3.** information *Major*.

dope v. **1.** to drug; **2.** spec: to work out the potential of a racehorse prior to making one's bet *Runyon:1*; **3.** to drink to excess.

dope a. very good, excellent; from a mix of dope = drugs and dope out (qv) *Ice T:1*.

dope out v. to work out; esp. in working out possible winners in a horserace *Gruber*.

dope stick n. a marijuana cigarette.

dope the ponies v. to work out possible winners amongst competing racehorses *Gruber*.

doped a. drunk.

doper n. a drug user, no specific choice required.

dopey a. dull, stupid, vapid *Bruce:2*.

do-rag n. (US Black use) the scarf or similar cloth that is used to bind up one's newly-straightened process (qv.) hairstyle *Klein*.

do-re-mi n. money *Thompson*.

dorf n. (US campus use) a fool, an eccentric *Underwood*.

Dorian love n. (gay use) homosexuality.

do-right boys n. the police, esp. the highway patrol.

do-right man n. a conformist, esp, one who follows rules within an institution *Klein*.

dork n. the penis; thus *dork-brain*: derog. description *Hiassen*.

dorky a. (US campus use) odd, weird, bizarre (cf: dork) *Underwood*.

dorm n. (school use) (abbrev.) dormitory.

Dorothy's friends n. homosexuals; fr. 'Dorothy', the character played by Judy Garland (1922–69), still a deity to large parts of the gay world, in *The Wizard of Oz* (1939) *H. Page*.

dos a reno n. (butchers' backsl.) a sod *Cole*.

dose n. venereal disease *Norman:2*.

dosed up a. suffering from venereal disease.

dosh n. money; the term became increasingly popular during the 1980s; poss. from the earlier term doss = place to sleep, and by extension the money needed for accommodation.

doss n. a place to sleep, a bed *R. Graves, 'Goodbye to All That', 1929*.

doss down v. to fall asleep, usu. on floor or similar temporary accommodation *Norman:3*.

dosser n. tramp, vagrant, a homeless person *Wilkinson*.

doss-head n. fool, idiot, simpleton *Welsh:1*.

dosshouse n. lodging house, night shelter or similar refuge for tramps, vagrants, etc. *LL*.

dot n. (lesbian use) the clitoris *Maledicta*.

dotty a. eccentric, odd; fr. *dotty on one's pins*: unsteady on one's legs, and thence in one's brain *Wodehouse:MS*.

doty a. senile, weak-minded (through old age) (cf: crumbly) (fr. dial. doty: old wood that is crumbling away, but poss. abbr. SE dotage: feeble-minded old age).

double a. qualifying adj. that intensifies another adj: double-good, double-quick (qv), etc.

double v. (abbrev.) double-date: two couples going out together *Price:1*.

double carpet n. (UK prison use) six months imprisonment (cf: carpet) *Powis*.

double guts n. a large stomach, a pot belly.

double quick extremely fast *Dury*.

double sawbuck n. $20 *Chandler:*

passim.

double shot n. two ejaculations of semen *Klein*.

double-bagger n. (Valley Girls (qv.) use) an intensely unappealing person (cf: bag your face, bag lady) *Pond*.

double-clutch v. (drug use) to take more than one's share of a communally smoked marijuana cigarette; US grass (qv.) smokers ritually take only one puff before passing on their cigarette (cf: bogart) *Folb*.

double-doored a. (Can. prison use) from both ends *Caron*.

double-dooring (US criminal use) a method of defrauding hotels whereby one arrives like any normal guest at the front door, but leaves by the back door – any form of illegal departure, leaving one's cases (filled with stones or telephone directories, etc.) *Breslin*.

double-headed a. (US Black use) very clever, exceptionally intelligent; also as four-headed, two-headed.

double-life man n. a bisexual *Legman*.

double-nickel n. (US trucker use) the freeway where there is a speed limit of 55 mph *Higgins:4*.

double-o v. to stare at, to look over, to check; the 'o' in question is an eye *Schulberg*.

double-shuffle n. a quick getaway.

double-whammy n. intensifier of whammy (qv.).

double-X n. something superlative, outstanding. (fr. racetrack j: double-X: the horse most likely to win, thus the optimum bet).

douchebag n. derog. term of general abuse; from the apparatus used for douching *Price:2*.

dough n. money *Price:1*.

dough-boy n. (US milit. use) a US soldier, orig. in Mexican War c.1847 in the flour and rice-based concoction that was a staple; subsequently replaced by GI, grunt, boonierat, etc. (qqv.).

dough-pop v. to defeat completely *Jenkins*.

douse the Edisons v. (US teen. use) to turn off the lights; fr. Thomas Alva Edison (1847–1931) *Sculatti*.

dowager n. (homosexual use) an elegant older queen (qv.) *Legman*.

down a. **1.** depressed; **2.** knowledgeable, aware, prepared *Folb*.

down n. (drug use) heroin.

down in the dumps miserable, unhappy, gloomy (cf: in the pits) *rr*.

down the drain lost, wasted, useless.

down the hatch! popular toast prior to taking a drink *Chandler:LG*.

down the pan wasted, lost, abandoned; the pan is that of the lavatory.

down the plug see: down the drain.

down there n. coy reference to the vagina *Waterhouse*.

down to responsibility *Powis*.

down to Larkin free; esp. of a round of drinks that are on the house (qv.) *Powis*.

down under n. Australia; supposedly sited 'underneath' the UK on the globe *Capital Radio 1983*.

downer n. **1.** barbiturate, tranquilizer. *Green:1*; **2.** depressing, worrying situation. *Underwood*.

down-home a. pertaining to the customs, attitudes and general lifestyle of the US South; thus, unsophisticated, rural *Wolfe:6*.

Downing Street n. (bingo use) 10 (cf: cock and hen); fr. the residence of UK Prime Ministers at 10 Downing Street, London SW1.

the Dozens aka: *Dirty Dozens*: a ritual game of testing a rival's emotional strength by insulting his various relatives, especially his mother, and taking similar insults in return (cf: signify) *Himes:1*.

drack n. (Aus. use) **1.** rubbishy, worthless goods; fr. Yiddish *dreck* = dirt *Baker*; **2.** an unattractive woman *Wilkes*.

draftnik n. (US campus use) one who has avoided the military service conscription; one of the -nik suffix words that developed post 1957 with the launch of the Russian Sputnik, the first of which was beatnik (qv.)

Underwood.

draftpak n. (Sc. use) an habitual drunkard *Welsh:1* (fr. draftpak: take-away packs of draft beer available over the bar in Scottish public houses).

drag n. **1.** dressing in the clothes of the opposite sex. orig. theatrical use and stressing the drag of a long dress along the floor, as opposed to tight-fitting trousers *Jay & Young*; **2.** a puff of a cigarette *Price:1*; **3.** a disappointment, a pity, a nuisance, a bore *Price:1*; **4.** a motor car; orig. a four-horse coach *Norman:3*; **5.** a street, thus *main drag*: the main street *Wright*; **6.** influence, pull *rr*; **7.** (US milit. use) the final man in a platoon, bringing up the rear of a moving column (cf: point, stackman) *Del Vecchio*.

drag v. **1.** (UK police use) to steal from cars *Laurie*; **2.** to waste time, to idle, usu. as drag around.

drag one's tail v. to mope around, to look miserable; fr. a dog with its tail down.

drag the chain (Aus. use) orig. for a shearer who lagged behind the others; latterly a drinker who fails to keep up with the rest of his companions *Wilkes*.

drag the rag v. to hurry up.

drag-ass a. tedious (of a thing); lazy (of a person) *Price:2*.

drag-dyke n. 'masculine' lesbian who chooses to dress in male clothing; the reverse of the usual drag (qv) *Jay & Young*.

draggy a. **1.** boring, of people and events; **2.** unwell, sickly-looking.

drag-queen n. a feminine homosexual who prefers to dress as a woman *Stanley*.

Drain n. (London Transport use) the Waterloo and City Line *ES 1983*.

drake n. a cigar or cigarette end (cf: duck).

drama queen n. anyone considered to be making an excessive fuss, or 'making a mountain out of a molehill'; the use of 'queen' suggests its origins in homosexual slang, but the term is widespread today.

drapes n. clothes *Folb*.

drat (euph.) damn *Rawson*.

dratsab n. (backsl.) bastard *Cole*.

draw a blank v. to have no luck, to receive no reply to a request; fr. card playing use.

draw the crabs v. (Aus. use) to attract unwelcome attention, to draw enemy fire (actual or metaphorical) *Wilkes*.

draw the crow v. (Aus. use) to come off worst, usu. in a share-out or division of spoils. labour, prizes, etc.; fr. story in which a number of game birds and one crow were on offer and one hapless person 'drew the crow' *Wilkes*.

draw water v. to have influence.

dread n. adj. **1.** used as a noun, a generic term for any Rasta man. **2.** Used as an adjective, it implies seriousness, importance – whether positive or negative. There is an overtone, as in Babylon (qv), of a Biblical element.

dream box n. (US Black) the head.

dream on! a dismissive exclamation *L Green*.

Dream Street n. 47th Street, New York City, betw. 6th & 7th Aves.; home of the stage door to the Palace Theatre, HQ of American vaudeville. Coined by Damon Runyon *Fiction Illus.3*.

dreamboat n. a particularly attractive man or woman; the fuel of one's fantasies *Chandler:LG*.

dreck n. fr. Ger. 'dung' **1.** spec. excrement; **2.** anything worthless, second rate, rubbishy *Schulberg:2*.

dredge-heads n. habitual drinkers, who drink up the dregs in every glass *Price:3*.

drench one's gizzard v. to drink heavily (cf: wet one's whistle).

dress down v. to tell off, to reprimand, to criticize.

dressed (US Black use) a car filled with every conceivable decoration, gimmick, and similar flashy adornment *Klein*.

dressed to the nines a. dressed up to the height of fashion.

dressed (up) like a deacon, dressed (up) like a (nigger) preacher a. phr. dressed up, in one's best clothes.

dressed up like a dog's dinner a. dressed in the height of chic and fashion (but cf: dog's dinner) *AS 41 (1966)*.

dressed up like a pox doctor's clerk a. (Aus. use) flashily dressed, over-dressed *Humphries*.

dressed up like a sore finger, dressed up like a sore thumb, dressed up like a sore toe phr. (Aus./NZ/US) over-dressed, flashily dressed (cf: dressed up like a pox-doctor's clerk).

dress-up n. (pimp use) client who enjoys dressing up in the prostitute's clothes and makeup; may provide his own wardrobe *OUI 8/75*.

dreykop n. a trickster, a fraudsman, fr. Yiddish, lit. 'twisted head' *Powis*.

dribble n. meaningless chatter.

dribbles n. euph for dribbling shits: incontinence, diarrhoea.

drift v. to leave, to depart, esp. as command: Drift!: go away.

drill v. to shoot (dead); fr. drilling a hole.

drink n. **1.** the ocean, the sea; fr. Second World War RAF use *Dickson*; **2.** a bribe, a sum of money that would supposedly purchase 'a drink', but usu. much larger. *Newman:1*; **3.** a tip, a commission, a bonus *Performance*.

drink v. (UK police/criminal use) to be susceptible to bribery; thus code between newly arrested criminal and policeman 'Do you drink, officer?' (cf: can I speak to you?) *Powis*.

drink at the fuzzy cup v. (US Black use) to engage in cunnilingus *Folb*.

drink of black coffee n. a severe reprimand, a telling off (like the coffee, the scolding is strong, 'hot' and bitter).

drink with the flies phr. (Aus.) to drink by oneself.

drinker n. an after-hours drinking club *Newman:1*.

drip n. **1.** venereal disease, spec. gonorrhoea; **2.** a weakling, a spineless person.

drip it up v. to purchase on extended credit, to use hire purchase (cf: on the drip) *BBC Radio 4, 1983*.

dripping a. (UK 'society' use) gutless, cowardly, weak (cf: drip) *Barr*.

dripping for it sexually eager *Maledicta*.

drippy a. weak, ineffectual.

drive n. (US Black use) a highway.

drive bananas v. to drive mad, to infuriate (cf: go bananas).

drive on (US Black use) to hit hard and without warning *Folb*.

drive one up the wall v. to infuriate, to annoy intensely, fig. to the point of insanity (cf: climbing the walls).

drive one's hos v. (US Black use) to keep one's stable (qv) of prostitutes hard at work, observing one's rules and earning plenty of money *Klein*.

drive the porcelain bus v. (US campus use) to vomit; spec. when hugging the circular lavatory (steering wheel-shaped) bowl and vomiting therein *Bernbach*.

drive-by n. (US use) a gang killing that is effected when the gunmen drive by their target and pepper him/her with shots; such murders are mainly associated with the teenage gangs of Los Angeles *Green:3*.

drivers n. (US campus use) legs *Underwood*.

drobe n. (US Black) clothes. (abbr. wardrobe).

drongo n. (Aus. use) a fool, fr. 1920s racehorse that consistently finished last or thereabouts in 37 races, and was used as a name for a slow-witted figure in polit. cartoons in the Melbourne *Herald Humphries*.

droob n. (Aus. use) a useless, foolish, depressing person *Wilkes*.

droodle v. to wander aimlessly, to laze around.

droop n. 1. a dull, ineffectual or unpleasant person (cf: drip); 2. a feeling of unhappiness, depression, also the droops (cf: down).

droopy a. unpleasant, dull, weak (cf: drippy).

drop n. 1. (US Black use) an orphan *Major*; 2. delivery, usu. of stolen goods, contraband, etc. *Payne*.

drop v. 1. to knock down *Humphries*; 2. to lose money *Higgins:3*; 3. (drug use) to consume pills or any drug that can be taken orally *Green:1*.

drop a beast v. (UK 'society' use) to fart *Barr*.

drop a brick v. to make an error, a mistake, esp. verbally.

drop a clanger v. to make a social error, the awfulness of which reverberates around the assembled gathering.

drop a dime v. to inform; from the act of making a telephone call. *Hiaasen*.

drop a lug v. (Black pimp use) to confront someone either as to his character or his actions *Milner*.

drop a thumper v. to break wind (cf: fart) *May*.

drop dead a. extreme; esp. as in drop dead beautiful.

drop dead! excl. of dismissal (cf: go to hell!).

drop game n. (US criminal use) a confidence trick whereby the victim is persuaded to pay money for a wallet, supposedly found and filled with money, but actually planted by the con-man *Klein*.

drop hairpins v. (homosexual use) to reveal one's sexual preferences by dropping broad hints. (cf: drop one's beads) *Stanley*.

drop it! (excl.) change the subject, stop talking that way, etc. *Himes:2*.

drop off the twig v. to die; as if one were a bird *Humphries:2*.

drop one in it v. to put someone deliberately into difficulties; 'it' is trouble, but the inference is also of excrement.

drop one out v. (police use) to dismiss from a list of possible suspects; to let off *Newman:2*.

drop one's beads v. (homosexual use) accidentally to reveal one's homosexuality by a slip of the tongue or other blunder (cf: drop hairpins) *Stanley*.

drop one's bundle v. (Aus. use) to panic, to lose (emotional) control *Wilkes*.

drop one's cookies v. to lose one's temper, to lose control, to be overcome with emotion (whether positive or negative).

drop one's gear v. (Aus. use) to undress (of a female) *Ready*.

drop one's load v. (US Black use) to reduce tension by having sexual intercourse (cf: empty one's trash) *Klein*.

drop out v. to die.

drop sticks v. (UK cant (West Indian use)) pickpocketing *Cole*.

drop the cue v. to die; fr. billiards (cf: take the last count, strike out, etc.) *Rawson*.

drop the hook on v. to make an arrest *Chandler:LG*.

drop the pill on v. (US criminal use) to execute in the gas chamber *Morgan*.

drop trou v. (US campus use) (abbrev.) drop one's trousers; a classier version (supposedly) of mooning (qv) *Bernbach*.

dropout n. a dull, boring person.

dropped (US campus use) unofficially but dedicatedly engaged to be married; fr. traditional gift by the man of a pendant or drop, bearing his initials *Underwood*.

dropper n. 1. a paid killer *Chandler: Notebk*; 2. an eye-dropper used by narcotics addicts as a makeshift syringe when custom-built hypodermics are unavailable *Lou Reed, 'Heroin', 1967*; 3. (UK criminal/ police use) a passer of dud cheques *Powis*.

drops n. 1. money left in pre-arranged (secret) places for bribes, pay-offs, shares of a robbery, etc.; 2. the weekly housekeeping money for one's wife *Powis*.

dropsy n. a bribe.

drove a. very angry, infuriated.

drug p.ppl. of drag (qv): exhausted, disinclined, bored; thus 'I'm too drug to go out tonight . . .' *Sculatti*.

druggie n. 1. (abbrev.) drugstore owner, druggist *Goldman*; 2. (derog.) (and rarely used by anyone involved with drugs) a drug user.

drugstore (catering use) the trolley which holds the restaurant's cutlery *Breslin*.

drugstore cowboy n. a man, usu. a youth, who frequents drugstores for no other reason than meeting his friends, gossiping and wasting time *Farrell*.

drum n. 1. house, home *Griffiths*; 2. (Can. prison use) cell *Caron*.

drummed up artificially inflated, made to appear more important than reality allows *PT*.

drummer n. (US use) a salesman; fr. 'drumming up trade' + drum = house (which he visits) *Algren*.

drumming (UK criminal use) posing as a door-to-door salesman to tour houses and thus check out which ones are empty and thus ripe for robbery *Powis*.

drumstick case n. (US Black use) rape *Klein*.

drumsticks n. (US Black use) well-rounded thighs of an attractive woman *Klein*.

drunk as a . . . bastard, bat, beggar, besom, big owl, boiled owl, brewer's fart, a cook, a coon, a coot, a cooter, a dog, a fiddler, a fiddler's bitch, a fish, a fly, a fowl, a Gosport fiddler, a hog, a king, a little red wagon, a log, a lord, a monkey, a Perraner, a pig, a piper, a poet, a rolling fart, a sailor, a skunk in a trunk, a sow, a swine, a tapster, a tick, a top, a wheelbarrow.

drunk tank n. (US use) short-term lockup for a night's drunk arrests prior to sending them to court.

drunk to the pulp (US Black use) drunk to the point of passing out *Klein*.

drunky a. drunken; esp. with given name, 'Drunky John', etc. *Dickson*.

druthers n. an alternative choice, a preference; fr. 'I'd rather . . .' *Algren*.

dry Dutch courage n. narcotics; a contemporary play on the traditional 'wet' Dutch courage (qv) which refers to alcohol.

dry land n. (US Black use) all clear; safety *Klein*.

dry up v. to stop talking, to refuse to give information (to the police) *Klein*.

dry-fuck v. to simulate intercourse by rubbing one's clothed body against that of one's partner.*Bukowski:7*.

dry-hump v. see: dry-fuck.

dry-snap v. to fire a gun that is either empty, or does not have a round ready in the barrel *Higgins:2*.

DS abbrev. *drug squad Guardian 6/6/87*.

D/T abbrev. (contact ads) dirty talk *SMD*.

d.t.s (acro.) delirium *tremens*; see: the shakes *Himes:1*.

dub n. (US campus use) 1. cigarette *Underwood*; 2. a failure, an incompetent, a novice.

dub up v. to lock up in a cell *Norman:2*

dubber n. (US campus use) cigarette (cf: dub) *Underwood*.

dubbies n. female breasts *Farina*.

dubee n. aka: doobie (drug use): a marijuana cigarette *Folb*.

Dublin University graduate n. a particularly stupid person; an unexceptional example of the clichéd condemnation of the Irish as fools *Powis*.

ducat n. a ticket, for theatre, sporting event, etc. (cf: ducket) *Schulberg:2*.

duchess n. a girl who is making money in films *Chandler: Notebk*.

Duchess of Fife n. (rhyming sl.) wife (cf: dutch) *Cole*.

duck n. 1. (US cant) a gullible fool; 2. a cigarette or cigar end (cf: drake).

duck v. 1. usu. in *to fuck, suck and duck*: to bend over preparatory to anal intercourse *Legman*; 2. to avoid *Higgins:5*.

duck butter n. 1. semen; 2. smegma.

duck out v. 1. to avoid *Salisbury*; 2. to leave '*The Blue Parrot*' (film), 1953.

duck shoot n. (milit. use) a simple operation, 'like shooting ducks on a pond' *Wolfe:5*.

duck soup n. anything simple, easy; any person easily persuaded or victimized *Runyon*.

ducket n. a ticket (cf: ducat) *Runyon:1*.

ducket v. (Can. prison use) to be placed on report for punishment by the governor; fr. docket *Caron*.

duckies n. (US Black use) money *Klein*.

ducks n. term of address, generally affectionate or friendly *Sillitoe*.

duck's ass see: d.a.

duck's butt n. (US Black use) female with unkempt hair *Folb*.

duck-shoving n. (Aus. use) fighting for status, rank, position, esp. in polit. terms *Wilkes*.

ducky 1. term of address (cf: ducks); 2. a. sweet, delightful, charming; an example of the apparent charm (cf: chick) of farmyard animals.

dud n. a failure *Jay & Young*.

dud v. to dress up, to dress smartly.

dude n. 1. a man *Grogan*; 2. (US campus use) a thing *Underwood*; the term gained a whole new currency, especial among the pre-teens, with the popularity c.1990 of the Teenage Mutant Ninja Turtles, where it featured heavily.

dudes n. men, people *Price:2*.

dudley n. (US teen. use) a failure, a loser; fr. dud (qv) *Pond*.

duds n. clothing *Vidal*.

due (police use) due to be arrested – as part of the everyday problems of a regular, known criminal – irrespective of whether the person in question had actually committed the crime of which he was suspected *Newman:1*.

duff a. useless, broken down *Austin*.

duff n. buttocks *Rawson*.

duff v. to blunder, to make a mess of *Underwood*.

duff around v. to sit about, to act lazily; fr. duff (qv) *Higgins:5*.

duff over v. see: duff up.

duff up v. to beat up *Sharpe:2*.

duffer n. 1. (US prison use) bread; fr. UK prison: food, esp. pudding *Chandler: Notebk*; 2. an incompetent, foolish person *Price:3*.

dufus n. 1. an eccentric, foolish or gauche person *Morgan*; 2. a thingummyjig.

dugs n. female breasts *Wolfe:2*.

duji n. (drug use) heroin *Rattray*.

duke v. to fight with the fists *Bruce:2*.

duke in v. to fool, to truck.

duke it out v. to fight with fists *Price:2*.

Duke of Kent n. (rhyming sl.) rent *Powis*.

Duke of York n. (rhy. sl.) **1.** to talk; **2.** to walk; **3.** a fork.

dukes n. fists *Runyon*.

dukie n. (US Black use) excretion; thus *dukie hole*: the anus *Klein*.

dumb a. stupid *Price:2*.

dumb as four o 'clock phr. very stupid.

dumb bunny n. a fool.

dumb sock n. **1.** a fool; **2.** (derog.) a Swede or any Scandinavian immigrant.

dumb-ass a. stupid, unintelligent *Jenkins*.

dumb-bell n. idiot, fool *Wodehouse:AAG*.

dumbo n. a fool, a dullard (cf: dum-dum, lamebrain, etc.).

dum-dum n. fool, idiot (cf: dumbo, dummy) *Bruce:2*.

dummy n. **1.** a wallet *Norman:2*; **2.** (Can. prison use) bread *Caron*; **3.** a deaf mute *Powis*; **4.** a fool, an idiot *Dunne*.

dummy up v. to stop talking; to keep quiet *Pearce*.

dump n. an unpleasant, disgusting and unappealing place *Wilkinson*.

dump v. **1.** to knock down; fr. dump on the floor *Selby:1*; **2.** (US campus use) to defecate *Underwood*.

dump on v. to impose oneself on another person *McFadden*.

dump one's load v. to vomit.

dump truck n. (derog. male use) a car full of lesbians *Stanley*.

dunderhead n. fool, idiot, incompetent.

dunking n. having sexual intercourse; the image is of dunking doughnuts or biscuits in coffee.

dunnee n. (Aus. use) lavatory *Humphries*.

dunnigan worker n. a thief who

hangs around public lavatories, hoping to steal from discarded coats, or take parcels, etc. that have been put down *Chandler: Notebk*.

dust n. see: angel dust.

dust v. to kill; to murder *Morgan*.

dust off, give one the v. to ignore, to snub (cf: give one the brush).

dust one v. (US Black use) to knock down, to beat up *Folb*.

dustbin lids n. (rhyming sl.) kids = children *Jones:J*.

dust-off n. (US milit. use) medical evacuation of casualties by helicopter *Del Vecchio*.

dust-up n. a fight *J. Mortimer, 'Rumpole & the Golden Thread', 1983*.

dusty a. (US Black use) unclear, unable to predict the future *Klein*.

dusty n. (UK 'society' use) very old person, 70 yrs and onwards (cf: wrinkly, crumbly) *Barr*.

dusty bread n. (US Black use) a conventional, conservative girl *Klein*.

dutch n. wife; fr. rhyming sl: Duchess of Fife (qv).

Dutch n. (rhyming sl.) dutch plate = mate *Powis*.

dutch v. **1.** to speak emphatically; **2.** to ruin another's business, social standing, enjoyment, etc. with deliberate malice; **3.** to bet in such a way that the bank is broken.

Dutch bath n. a very cursory wash.

Dutch courage cowardice that, fortified by generous quantities of alcohol, becomes (temporary) bravery; coined during various UK-Holland wars of 18th C. *Safire*.

Dutch dumplings n. (gay use) the buttocks.

Dutch girl n. a lesbian; punning on the 'dikes' (see: dyke) of Holland.

Dutch, go v. phr. **1.** to share (usu. the price of a meal); **2.** to commit suicide.

Dutch kiss n. a kiss in which both participants grab the other's ears.

Dutch nickel n. a kiss (cf: yankee dime) (in racial sterotyping Dutch = thief, therefore such a kiss has been 'stolen').

Dutch treat n. an outing, visit to a

restaurant, etc. in which costs are
shared equally – ie there is no 'treat' at
all in the sense of one party being
entertained at the other's expense
Safire.

Dutch uncle n. one who talks severely
and critically, who lays down the law;
usu. as *talk like a Dutch uncle*.

Dutchman, I'll be a a phr. that
underlines the improbability of the
preceding statement; usu. following a
conditional 'If that's. . . then I'll
be. . .'.

DV (US Black use) (abbrev.) Cadillac
Coupe *De Ville Folb*.

dweeb n. an idiot.

DX (US milit. use) (abbrev.) direct
exchange; also, to discard or dispose
of, ultimately to kill *Del Vecchio*.

dyke n. lesbian *Jay & Young*.

dyke down v. (US Black use) to dress
smartly *Klein*.

dynamite a. 1. excellent, wonderful,
first-rate; often as excl.' 2. undiluted
drugs *White*.

E

E abbrev. ecstasy (qv), the popular
nickname of the hallucinogenic drug
MDMA methylene
dioxymethamphetamine (cf: acid,
adam).

eager beaver n. an excessively
earnest, keen person whose efforts are
sometimes more notable for their
sound and fury than their actual
usefulness.

ear-basher n. a bore, a loudmouth
who refuses to stop talking *'Minder',
Thames TV, 1980*.

ear-bender n. a chatterer, a bore (cf.
ear-basher).

earhole v. to listen: to overhear
Norman: 2.

ear-jerker n. (film use) a film in which
the main attraction is the volume and
predominance of the music; on the
model of tear-jerker (qv.) *T 25/3/83*.

earl v. to vomit (cf: hurl); thus 'go to
see Earl', 'Earl's knocking at the door'
(cf: hughie, ralph).

early a. (US Black use) up to date
Klein.

Early Battersea n. vulgar, tasteless
decor (cf: Jewish Renaissance, Jewy
Louis).

Early Eclectic n. vulgar, tasteless
decor.

Early Hallowe'en n. vulgar, tasteless

decor.

Early Homosexual n. vulgar, tasteless
decor.

early out n. (US milit. use) any
serviceman who has 150 days or less
remaining of his active service duty
Del Vecchio.

early riser n. (US prison use) an
inmate who is granted an early parole
Klein.

early variety n. an illegitimate child.

early-bird a. first of the day, ie:*early
bird matinée Waits*.

earn v. (UK criminal use) to make a
dishonest profit from a given crime
Powis.

earner n. 1. (UK cant) any job or plan
that pays well, almost invariably
criminal *Payne*; 2. (UK police use) a
bribe, often paid as regularly as more
legitimate wages *Newman: 1*.

ears chewed down, get one's v. to
be scolded severely.

ears knocked down, get one's v.
see: ears chewed down, get one's.

ears lowered, get one's v. to get a
haircut.

earth (backsl.) three *Cole*.

earwig n. a lookout, one who listens
for approaching steps, then checks
their owner before admitting him/her
Performance.

earwig v. (rhyming sl.) to twig = to understand *Jones: J.*

ease it v. (UK prison use) to relax, to let up on some form of crime or rule-breaking *LL.*

east and west n. (rhyming sl.) vest *Wright.*

east and west, east and west and crooked phr. disorderly, confused (cf: galley-west, high, west and crooked)

East Jesus n. an out-of-the-way place, a small town.

easter egg n. a woman wearing too much make-up.

easy a. 1. sexually available, esp. in *easy lay*; 2. equivocal, not caring one way or another when faced with a given choice.

easy as kiss my arse very simple indeed.

easy as pie very simple.

easy as taking candy from a baby aka: . . . *money from a child* cp: very simple, almost criminally so *'1-2-3', Len Barry, 1965.*

easy as winking see: easy as pie.

easy game n. see: easy ride *Klein.*

easy ride n. sexually available female.

easy rider n. 1. (US Black use) a sexual athlete; 2. a pimp, a kept man; 3. a guitar; 4. a girl who agrees to sex on the first date. 5. any 'outlaw' motorcyclist; fr. film title 1969 *Underwood.*

easy street n. a secure, comfortable life; a situation free of problems, esp. material ones (cf: sitting pretty).

easy stuff n. see: easy ride *Klein.*

easy-peasy very simple; usu. juvenile use S. Lewellyn, *'The Worst Journey in the Midlands', 1983.*

eat v. aka: *eat pussy, eat out*: cunnilingus *Price: 2.*

eat a pumpkin through a knot hole, to be able to v. to have buck teeth; also as 'eat an apple through a knot hole', 'eat corn-on-the-cob through a picket fence'.

eat at the Y v. to perform cunnilingus; the Y refers both to the spread legs, and to the YMCA / YWCA.

eat cheese n. (US Black use) to toady to, to ingratiate oneself with.

eat crow v. to suffer humiliations and insults without responding in kind *Goldman.*

eat dirt v. to retract a previous statement, usu. incurring humiliation and embarrassment by so doing *Underwood.*

eat hair pie v. to perform cunnilingus *Legman.*

eat it v. (euph.) eat shit (qv.) *Higgins: 5.*

eat jam v. to lick the anus *Legman.*

eat my shorts! (US campus use) derogatory, dismissive phrase drop dead, go to hell, etc. (shorts, in US, are underpants); the phrase moved into the mainstream with the success of television's cartoon family, The Simpsons, whose renegade son Bart took it as his personal catchphrase *Bernbach.*

eat one's ass off v. to criticize severely, to punish heavily *Chandler: LG.*

eat one's hat v. to go back on one's words, esp. to admit that a public statement was in fact wrong.

eat one's heart out v. to be consumed by jealously *Neaman & Silver.*

eat one's meat v. to fellate *Goldman.*

eat out v. to perform cunnilingus.

eat peas out of a bottle, not have enough sense to v. to be very stupid.

eat pound-cake v. (homosexual use) to suck a partner's anus *Legman.*

eat pussy v. to perform cunnilingus (cf: eat, pussy).

eat razor soup v. to say something cheeky or impertinent (cf: who slept in the knifebox?).

eat shit v. to suffer and accept humiliation; to humble oneself, usu. to attain a desired goal *Vizinczey.*

eat supper before you say grace v. to conceive a child before one gets married.

eat the greaser v. to swallow one's

words, to recant (cf: eat one's hat) (fr.
dial. greaser: a lump of salt pork used
to grease the bars of a griddle).

eat up v. to enjoy immensely.

eating 1. bothering, usu. as in *what's
eating you/him/etc.*; 2. consumed by an
obsession *Runyon*.

eating tackle n. teeth.

eats n. food *Price: 2*.

ebony n. (US Black use) the
quintessence of black sensibility *Klein*.

ebony a. general reference to any
black person; thus 'ebony chick' and
'ebony pigeon': black girls.

ecky n. see ecstasy *Welsh:2*.

ecstasy n. a slang term for the drug
known offically as MDMA or
methylene dioxymethamphetamine.
Ecstasy existed in the 1960s, as one of
many synthetic hallucinogens, but
only reached its apotheosis as the acid
(qv) of the late 1980s. *Independent on
Sunday 3 June 1990*.

Edgar Britt n. (Aus. use) rhyming sl.
see Jimmy Britt (qv.) *Wilkes*.

edge n. (US Black use) a knife; thus
'pack an edge': carry a knife.

edge n. tension, usu. creative;
concentration *Higgins: 3*.

edge city n. the extremes of
experience, whether spiritual,
physical, drug induced or whatever;
usu. with overtones of fear and
challenge (cf: — city) *Wolfe: 2*.

Edie n. a prostitute (working
Piccadilly, Bayswater Rd and other
cheap streets) (cf: Tom n.).

Edmundo n. (rhyming sl.) Edmundo
Ros (Latin American band leader) =
boss *Payne*.

Edna! (UK criminal use) rhyming sl.
Edna May = on your way! *Powis*.

E-ed, E'd a. under the influence of
ecstasy (qv) *Welsh:1*.

eel juice n. liquor *Chandler: Notebk.*

eel out v. to avoid a problem, esp. in a
deceitful, self-serving way.

eemosh n. (backsl.) home *Cole*.

eenin (backsl.) nine *Cole*.

eeson n. (backsl.) to have a look *Cole*.

eevach a kool v. (backsl.) to have a
look *Cole*.

eevige v. (backsl.) to give *Cole*.

eff off! (euph.) fuck off! *Rawson*.

effing (euph.) fucking *Dury*.

effing and blinding using obscenities,
'bad language' *T. Parker, People of
Providence (1984)*.

egg v. to move carefully, quietly.

egg n. a 'henpecked' husband.

egg n. 1. a person, usu. qualified as
good egg, bad egg, etc. *Farrell*; 2. (US
campus use) a conspicuously studious
and intellectual student; abbrev.
egghead (qv.) *Underwood*.

egg in the nest (US Black use) to be
pregnant *Klein*.

egg roll n. (derog.) a Korean
immigrant to the US.

egghead n. intellectual, anyone
considered to work with brain rather
than brawn *Motor City Comics*.

eggplant n. a Black person.

eggs in the basket n. (homosexual
use) testicles *Legman*.

ego trip n. self-aggrandisement,
boastfulness, egocentricity; fr.
Freudian ego + drug culture trip (qv.)
Underwood.

EGYPT (acro). eager *to* grab your
pretty *tits*: written on envelopes of
love letters (cf: BURMA,
NORWICH, SWALK) *Partridge:5*.

Egyptian queen n. (gay use) a
homosexual black man, particularly if
he is stately and proud.

eightball n. 1. (derog.) Negro, Black;
fr. colour of the 8 ball in pool *Farrell*;
2. a conventional, law-abiding person
Farrell.

eight-pager n. small, illustrated eight-
page pornographic booklet in which
popular characters – Popeye, Mickey
Mouse, Blondie, etc. – were crudely
pastiched in erotic scenarios far
removed from their everyday antics,
(cf: Tijuana bible).

80-90 n. euph. amongst New York
Hasidim: *putz* = prick; fr. numerical
values '80' + '90' that are ascribed to
Hebrew letters 'pay' and 'tzadik' that
are in themselves a euph. for 'putz'
Safire.

eighty-six v. to throw out, fr. rhyming

sl.: eighty-six = nix = nothing *Price: 2*

elbow v. to get rid of, to dismiss (cf: big E) *Farren*.

elbow bender n. a serious drinker.

elbow grease n. physical effort, fr. the movement of an elbow when its arm is rubbing or polishing hard.

elbow shaker n. (US Black use) one who reminds others of a forgotten or overlooked fact or event by digging them in the ribs *Klein*.

electric a. weird and wonderful, marvellous *Powis*.

elephant n. 1. (rhyming sl.)Elephant and Castle = asshole (pron. arssle) = anus *Powis*; 2. a clumsy, awkward person.

elephant's trunk a. (rhyming sl.) drunk *Dury*.

elevated a. drunk; 'high' *Dickson*.

eleven-bravo (US milit. use) an infantryman; fr. 11-B, the number of his MOS (military occupational speciality), his army job description *Del Vecchio*.

Eli n. (US college use) Yale Universities, thus *Elis* members of Yale *Bernbach*.

elly-bay n. (Pig Latin) the belly *Runyon*.

elrig n. (backsl.) girl *Cole*.

elwoff n. (butchers' backsl.) fowl *Cole*.

emag n. (backsl.) game, usu. as a term of disgust or disappointment: 'what's your game?' etc. *Powis*.

embalmed a. very drunk *Neaman & Silver*.

embalming fluid n. whisky (cf: conversation fluid).

emok nye (backsl.) come in *Cole*.

empty one's trash v. (US Black use) to have sexual intercourse; spec. to ejaculate (cf: drop one's load) *Neaman & Silver*.

encore (UK 'society' use) fr. Fr. 'more', used to mean wonderful, very good.

end n. that area of a football stadium, behind the respective goals, traditionally reserved for the hard-core supporters of home and away

teams and the scene of most fighting *Robins:1*.

end of the ball-game n. death; one of a number of games-playing/sporting metaphors for life's termination. (cf: cash in one's chips; struck out; throw in the sponge; etc., etc.) *Rawson*.

end over appetite phr. head over heels (cf: ass/arse over appetite).

end-around n. the result, the final assessment, the bottom line (qv.) *Higgins: 1*.

enforcer n. (gay use) a lesbian who keeps the other girls in line.

English culture sex advertisements: bondage and discipline (cf: French, Greek culture, etc.) *Neaman & Silver*.

English guidance (commercial sex use) bondage and discipline; fr. the popular assumption that all Englishmen enjoy such activities *Rawson*.

English martini n. (gay use) tea; especially when spiked with gin.

English method n. (gay use) homosexual intercourse against the thighs (cf: Princeton first year).

English muffins n. (gay use) a boy's buttocks.

English sentry n. (gay use) the erect penis.

eno (backsl.) one *Cole*.

enob n. 1. (butcher's backsl.) bone *Cole*; 2. the penis, using 'bone' as synonym *Rawson*.

enough to make a black man choke adj. phr. unpalatable; usually said of food and medicines.

entertain the general v. to menstruate.

enthroned (homosexual use) a homosexual who looks for sex in public lavatories; fr. queen (qv.) (cf: abdicated, dethroned) *Legman*.

eppes, eppis, eppus pron., n., a., adv. 1. something, a little; 2. a somebody; 3. quite, perhaps, maybe, for some inexplicable reason; 4. debatable, worthless, unsatisfactory; 5. nothing. (fr. Ger. *etwas*: something, thence Yiddish *eppes*; like many Yiddish terms *eppes* is capable of many uses, often ironic, and all dependent on context. It entered the slang vocabulary via the underworld, which used it to mean low-class or worthless. Subsequent meanings have developed since).

equalizer n. a gun; reduces all before it to the same abject level *Runyon*.

erase v. to murder, to kill (cf: rub out) *Rawson*.

-erino suffix applicable to various words, generally implying intensification, further excellence, appeal, etc.

——eroo sfx. intensifier, implying a greater flamboyance or exaggeration; allied to a variety of terms, eg. floperoo, smackeroo, stinkeroo.

Errol Flynn (rhyming sl.) chin *Cole*.

esaff n. (backsl.) face *Cole*.

esclop n. (backsl.) the police *Powis*.

eskimo (US derog.) a Jew (cf: Ikey-Mo) *Rosten*.

esky n. (Aus. use) a portable drinks cooler, popularly filled with beer for cricket watching, etc; fr. eskimo, and thus chilliness *Ready*.

ethno n. (Aus. use) immigrants to Australia, of various ethnic persuasions *Wilkes*.

Ethy meat n. a black woman; fr. abbr. of Ethiopian.

-ette all-purpose diminutive, often applied to otherwise unsuitable words.

euchred (Aus. use) exhausted, destitute; fr. card-game 'euchre' (orig. US) in which, if a player chooses to play a given round and fails to take 3 tricks, he/she is 'euchred' (*OED*) *Wilkes*.

European accentuation n. (gay use) a tapered body with jutting buttocks.

eve n. the hallucinogen MDEA, a type of ecstasy (qv) (cf: adam).

even Steven fair shares.

ever so very much; usu. in 'thanks ever so!' and certainly not 'U' speech *Manser*.

everything but the kitchen sink an

undertaking that requires whatever is available, no matter what it is, relevant or not.

evif (backsl.) five *Cole*.

ex! (juv. excl.) (abbrev.) excellent; used in UK prep schools (cf: brill) *Lucien Green*.

ex n. (abbrev) ex-husband, ex-wife, ex-lover: the other half of a lapsed relationship *McFadden*.

excuse my French! genteel euphemism automatically offered after the speaker has sworn in public; as ever, Anglo-Saxons blame the French for anything remotely 'dirty' *Dunne*.

exercise the ferret v. to copulate *Humphries*.

expat n. (abbrev.) expatriate; applied to UK citizens living abroad.

extract the Michael v. consciously 'genteel' version of take the micky (qv.)

exxes (backsl.) six *Cole*.

eye n. (US prison use) **1.** detective; fr. logo of Pinkerton's detective agency; **2.** a warder *Chandler: Notebk*.

eye doctor n. (homosexual use) one who practises anal intercourse *Legman*.

eyeball v. to stare at *White*.

eye-eye! look at that!, what's all this! take a look around, etc. *LL*.

eyeful n. an attractive female.

eye-opener n. **1.** the first drink of the day. (cf: phlegm-cutter); **2.** a surprise, a shock, not necessarily unpleasant *Bukowski: 1*.

eyes n. nipples or female breasts *Neaman & Silver*.

eyes like pissholes in the snow deeply sunken eyes, often bloodshot to boot; poss. the result of an excess of alcohol.

Eyetie n. (derog.) Italian, fr. exaggerated 'Italian' pronounciation *Humphries: 2*.

eyewash n. rubbish, nonsense.

F

faastie a. (Jamaican use) rude, impertinent, impudent; fr. Surinam Creole *fiesti – nasty Thelwell*.

fab a. (abbrev.) fabulous; excl. of approbation, first popularized by the Beatles c.1963 but still used, often with an ironic intonation *Vidal*.

face n.1. a person; esp. in police use, a known criminal *Griffith*; 2. a person, spec. a fellow mod (qv) c.1962; now the name of a 'style' magazine which, twenty years later, promotes much the same sartorial and ethical attitudes as did the mods in their day.

face n. general term of greeting, eg. Hello, face.

face artist n. (US criminal sl.) a fellator *Legman*.

face fungus n. beard and/or moustache *Humphries*.

face the nation v. (US Black use) to engage in cunnilingus *Klein*.

face-ache n. joc. form of address, despite apparent rudeness of the phrase; the ache presumably comes fr. laughter.

faced (US teen. use) extremely drunk; euph. fr. shit;faced (qv) *Bernbach*.

face-fucking n. fellatio in which one partner lies on his/her back with opened mouth *Jay & Young*.

facer n. a problem, an obstacle – both unexpected; anything that one must face up to *Laurie*.

facial n. (pimp use) a client who likes the prostitute to sit on his face, sometimes after she has inserted a suppository or even when she is having intercourse with another man *OUI 8/75*.

factory n. (UK police use) a large, forbidding Victorian police station in the London Metropolitan area *Powis*.

fade n. 1. (US Black use) a Black who immerses him/herself into the white world, and thus 'fades away' *Major*; 2. (US Black use) (derog.) a White person.

fade v. 1. to put at a disadvantage; fr. dice use, implying that the shooter can match any throw that comes up *Breslin*; 2. to leave; to vanish *Goldman*; 3. (US Black use) to drop a topic of conversation; to change an unpalatable subject *Klein*; 4. to die; 5. to surpass, to dismiss, fr. poker use. *Dre*.

faded boogie n. (US Black use) a black informer; a black who apes whites and loses his own ethnicity *Major*.

fading game n. (gambling use) a dice game in which players bet against each other rather than against the bank or house as in a casino (cf: head and head game) *Runyon: 1*.

fag n.1. (abbrev.) faggot (qv) *Jones*; 2. cigarette; 3. a bore, a chore; one is 'fagged out' (qv).

fag v. to supply with a cigarette; to smoke a cigarette [fr. fag].

fag (along) v. to move quickly, to leave in a hurry.

fag hag n. 1. a woman, prob. heterosexual, poss. ageing, who courts and indulges the company of male homosexuals *Jay & Young*; 2. a heterosexual male, irrespective of age, who prefers the company of homosexuals to that of his preferential peers *Price: 3*.

fag hots n. (homosexual use) cheap pornography aimed at the male homosexual readership *Maledicta*.

fag tag n. (US campus use) see fruit loop (qv) *Bernbach*.

fag your face! (Valley Girls (qv) use) general term of dislike, euph: go fuck yourself! (cf: fug, bag your face) *Pond*.

fag-end n. 1. the butt of a cigarette; 2. a fragmentary part of a speech or conversation which one might overhear, just as it tails off (cf: pick up fag-ends).

fagged out exhausted; fr. corruption of SE *fatigued* (?) *Wright*.

faggot n. a homosexual; prob. orig. 17th C. *faggot*: a promiscuous woman, thus playing on effeminacy and the multiple couplings of some homosexuals *Price: 2*.

faggotter n. (US Black use) a pimp who specializes in selling the services of male homosexual prostitutes *Klein*.

faggy, faggoty a. (orig. US) effeminate, homosexual.

fagola n. homosexual (cf: faggot) *Vidal*.

fair crack of the whip! (Aus. excl.) be fair! *Humphries*.

fair crow n. (Aus./NZ) something inexpressibly tedious or baffling. (fr. Aus. phr. draw the crow: to get the worst share or the worst job in a given situation; the crow is a bird of traditionally bad omen).

fair dinkum! (Aus. excl.) honest! really! *Humphries*.

fair dos (Aus. use) general statement of agreement, acceptance.

fair enough! statement of acceptance, agreement *Baker*.

fair go n. (Aus. use) any situation which meets basic requirement of fairness to all without fear, favour or prejudice; fr. a call in a game of 'two-up' that indicated all relevant rules were satisfied and that the coins could be spun *Wilkes*.

fair one n. a street gang fight conducted under some sort of mutually recognized rules *Salisbury*.

fair pop n. a good opportunity, a fair chance.

fair shake n. (abbrev.) fair shake of the dice (qv) *Bruce: 2*.

fair shake of the dice! (Aus. excl.) be fair!

fair-haired boy n. see: white-haired boy *Heller*.

fairy n. homosexual male *Jay & Young*.

fairy snuff! corruption of 'fair enough' *Wright*.

fake it v. to pretend *McFadden*.

fake on one v. (US Black use) to ignore *Folb*.

fake-ass a. fraudulent (cf. wack-ass).

fall v. (US criminal use) to be caught in illegal activities and subsequently arrested, tried and convicted *Klein*.

fall apart n. to collapse emotionally; to lose control of one's feelings '*Total Eclipse of the Heart*', Bonnie Tyler, 1983.

fall by v. to visit without prior warning; to drop in *Folb*.

fall guy n. a patsy (qv); a victim who is chosen or forced to suffer punishments or difficulties that are in fact due to another person *Chandler: LG*.

fall in v. 1. to go to bed; 2. (US Black use) to arrive (cf: fall by, fall up).

fall money n. (US prison use) bail and legal fees; just in case one 'takes a fall' (qv) *Chandler: Notebk*.

fall off the back of a lorry ironic reference to goods that are obviously stolen; they didn't fall, 'they were pushed'.

fall off the roof v. 1. to be sexually incapacitated; 2. to be menstruating.

fall off the wagon v. to resume drinking after a period of abstinence *Neaman & Silver*.

fall out v. 1. to be overcome with laughter; 2. to lose control of a situation; 3. to fall asleep.

fall up v. (US Black use) to arrive, to turn up (cf: fall by).

fallen off the wagon a. drunk (cf: on the wagon) *Dickson*.

false face n. (US campus use) a hypocrite, an insincere person *Underwood*.

falsies n. a padded brassiere that accentuates the shape and dimensions of otherwise diminutive female breasts *Howard*.

family n. an intimate, either related in fact or emotionally *Powis*.

family jewels n. 1. the male genitalia (cf: crown jewels); 2. (CIA use) any secrets the revelation of which would embarrass and thus 'hurt' the agency and thus the USA *Green: 2*.

famous last words! (cp) don't you be so sure; offered to a speaker who has just made an absolute promise as to some future event.

fan v. 1. to flaunt oneself deliberately to gain sexual interest *Major*; 2. to conduct a search of a suspect's clothes *Runyon*; 3. to pick pockets *Powis*; 4. to move around quickly, to run (cf: turn on the fan).

fan one's ass v. (US Black use) to

move one's buttocks in an exaggerated manner with the deliberate intention of attracting one's audience sexually; usu. of homosexuals (cf: fan one's pussy) *Klein*.

fan one's pussy v. (US Black use) a female version of the male fan one's ass (qv) *Klein*.

fancy crib n. (US Black use) a fashionable, chic, well designed home (cf: crib) *Klein*.

fancy Dan n. 1. a flashily dressed man, a dandy; 2. a ladies' man; 3. a showy but ineffective sportsman or worker.

fancy dude n. anyone who acts in a superior or pretentious manner.

fancy man n. a male lover, not always adulterous, but usu. referring to a married or older woman rather than a girl *Sillitoe*.

fancy pants n. an overdressed male, erring towards the effeminate in this preoccupation.

fancy pants v. to act suspiciously or uncharacteristically nervously, coyly *Chandler: Notebk*.

fang v. (Aus. use) to demand money; (cf: put the bite on) *Wilkes*.

fanny n. 1. lies, a cover story *Newman: 1*; 2. (US) the buttocks *Jay & Young*; 3. (UK) the vagina *Keyes*; 4. nonsense, thus fanny merchant: all talk and no action.

fantabulous a. incredibly wonderful; fr. comb. of fantastic + fabulous *Underwood*.

fantail a. (US prison use) a highly promiscuous prison homosexual (cf: fan one's ass) *Klein*.

far and near n. (rhyming sl.) beer *Wight*.

far gone a. drunk *Dickson*.

far out! (excl.) amazing! remarkable! wonderful! fr. the mental 'space' entered under the influence of hallucinogenics *SF Comics*.

farblondjet a. confused, lost, astray (fr. Yiddish *farblondzhen*: to lose one's way, to go astray).

farchadet a. confused, befuddled (fr. Yiddish *fartschadat*: confused, itself fr. Slavic *chad*: smoke, daze).

fare n. a prostitute's client; someone who 'pays for a ride' *Norman: 2*.

farm n. mental hospital *Dunne*.

farm v. (US campus (spec. University of Arkansas) use) to drink alcohol (cf: crop) *Underwood*.

farmer n. (US Black use) recently arrived Southern farm workers who persist in their country ways despite the pressing sophistication of the Northern cities *Klein*.

farmers n. haemorrhoids; fr. rhy. sl. Farmer Giles = piles.

farmer's haircut n. a short haircut that leaves a white strip of skin showing between the bottom of the hair and the tanned portion of the neck.

farmer's time n. thirty minutes ahead of actual time.

Farmington n. (US campus/prep school use) Miss Porter's School (for girls), Farmington, Conn. *Bernbach*.

farmisht a. confused, mixed up. (fr. Yiddish *farmisht*: confused).

farputst a. dressed up. (fr. Yiddish).

farshtinkener a. stinking. (fr. Ger. *verstinken*: stink up).

fart n. fool, unpleasant person, often older than the speaker; fr. the bodily function (cf: cunt, prick, etc.) *Underwood*.

fart v. to break wind *Higgins: 1*.

fart around v. waste time *Higgins: 1*.

fart box n. the buttocks.

fart off v. see; fart around.

fartarse around v. see: fart around.

farting spell 1. a short space of time; 2. as 'have a farting spell': to lose one's temper, to lose control.

fartknocker n. an obscure person.

fart-sack n. a bed.

fast 1. amoral, illegal, corrupt; 2. of a woman: promiscuous *Klein*.

fast black n. (UK 'society' use) a black London taxi *F. Fogarty*.

fast lane n. the active, competitive and ruthless world fought over by those of ambition and intent *Vidal*.

fast mover n. (US milit. use) the 1400 mph F-4 fighter bomber *Del Vecchio*.

fast talking Charlie n. (US Black use)

a Jew (derog.) (cf: Mr Charlie) *Folb*. •

fast track n. (US pimp use) those streets or blocks in a city where prostitutes work; spec. the East Coast cities as opposed to the slower California West *Shulman*.

fast-fuck n. 1. sexual intercourse that, through various circumstances, has to be hurried and brief; 2. of a man: one who is unable to delay his own orgasm until his partner is satisfied too; a premature ejaculator *Klein*.

fat a. (US Black use) pregnant *Klein*.

fat cat n. any successful, wealthy, influential person *Hoffman: a*.

fat chance! not a hope! no chance at all! *PT*.

fat city n. (US campus use) the process of gaining weight or the state of being fat *Underwood*.

Fat City n. success, wealth; often fr. criminal activities *Higgins: 3*.

fat knot n. (US Black use) a substantial roll of dollar bills *Klein*.

fat lip n. unpleasant talk *Major*.

fat nuts, have v. (US Black use) to use violence, to be a violent person.

fathead n. fool, idiot, often used affectionately as well as derog. *Wodehouse: PGM*.

father and mother of . . . general intensifier; usu. 'of a thrashing' or 'of a row'.

father and mother stuff n. (street gang use) attacking 'civilians' – non-gang members, women, children, the old *Salisbury*.

fatmouth a. braggart, noisy, loud-mouthed (qv) *Higgins: 1*.

fatmouth v. to argue, to answer back, to be cheeky *Folb*.

fats or fems n. (homosexual use) (abbrev.) fat or effeminate homosexuals, as described in gay ads *Jay & Young*.

fatso n. general derog. term addressed to a fat person *Chandler: LG*.

fave a. (abbrev.) favourite.

fave rave n. (teen. use) most favoured person, most enjoyable experience, preferred food, etc., etc.

fay n. (US Black use) (abbrev.) ofay

(qv).

faygele, feygele n. a male homosexual. (fr. Yiddish *feygele*: little bird + FAG; Yiddish *Feygel* is also a girl's proper name).

feather v. to curry favour with, to toady to.

feather up v. to prepare to fight (fr. the action of birds).

featherbed n. an extremely fat person.

featherbedding n. (industrial use) the practice of making things easy for union members, of handing out easy 'jobs for the boys' *Green: 2*.

featherhead n. one who takes foolish chances.

feather-legged a. terrified, extremely frightened.

feathermerchant n. a physical weakling *Uris*.

feathers n. a bed; thus 'a date with the feathers': bedtime; 'hit the feathers': go to bed.

feathers in one's hair, have v. to be sleepy.

feature v. to note, to pay attention to; often. as phr. 'feature this'.

feature with v. (Aus. use) to seduce a compliant female; coined by Barry Humphries for his strip character 'Barry Mackenzie' *Humphries*.

fed up a. irritated, annoyed, bored; intensified as *fed up to the back teeth*.

feeb n. 1. (abbrev.) feeble, thus, a feeble, useless person; 2. (butchers' backsl.) beef *Cole*.

feed box n. the mouth.

feed one a line v. to deceive through a cunning story, excessive charm, any verbal facility *Junker*.

feed one stuff v. (US Black use) to deceive; to pass on false (and self-serving) information *Klein*.

feed one's face v. 1. to stuff oneself with food; 2. to indulge in oral intercourse *Klein*.

feed the bears v. (CB use) to pay a parking fine, to get a parking ticket (cf: bear) *CB*.

feed the fishes n. 1. to die by drowning; 2. to vomit.

feed the kippers v. to vomit over the side of a ship.

feed the worms v. to die.

feedback n. response, usu. negative or problematic *Higgins: 2*.

feel a draught v. (US Black use) to sense racial antagonism in one's conversation or dealings with whites *Major*.

feel froggy v. (US Black use) to feel like fighting (cf: froggy) *Folb*.

feel good v. to feel mildly drunk.

feel like death warmed up v. to feel absolutely appalling; often used by those suffering fr. hangovers.

feel one's collar v. (UK criminal/police use) to arrest, to place under suspicion; fr. the physical act of grabbing a villain *Newman: 1*.

feel one's oats v. to feel like sex.

feel up v. to engage in the manual stimulation of a girl *Higgins: 1*.

feeling funny phr. drunk, out on a spree.

feeling no pain a. drunk *D. Leitch*.

feeling right royal a. drunk *Dickson*.

feet in the trough, have one's phr. to have a well-paid, undemanding job, esp. one earned through connections or corruption.

felch queen n. homosexual who is stimulated by fecal matter *Stanley*.

felony shoes n. (US use) any brand of the high-priced trainers (Nike, Adidas, etc.) worn by teenagers. The term is implicitly racist, suggesting that the black teenagers who particularly favour such footwear are de facto up to no good. (cf: airs)

fem n. see: femme *Klein*.

femme n. 1. effeminate homosexual male *Jay & Young*; 2. a feminine lesbian.

fence n. 1. (Aus. use) a procurer of the sexually complaisant for such customers who prefer something out of the ordinary *Baker*; 2. a receiver and seller of stolen property; thus *to fence* (cf: placer) *Caron*.

fence parole n. (US prison use) attempting an escape by climbing the prison fence or wall; such efforts, inevitably, lead to death *Morgan*.

fence rail n. a very thin person.

ferminster n. a devoted nay-sayer, one who consistently opposes. (fr. dial. fornenst: opposite).

ferryboat n. a large, clumsy shoe (cf: canal boat).

fetch n. (US Black use) an illegitimate or abandoned child.

fetched a. euph. for damned.

few snags short of a barbie, a phr. (Aus.) eccentric, crazy; one of several phr. dealing with someone who is 'not all there' (cf: couple of chips short of a fish dinner, two sandwiches short of a picnic, etc.)

fey n. aka: *fay*: abbrev. of ofay (qv) *Burroughs: 1*.

F/F (contact ads use) abbr. fistfucking (qv) *SMD*.

F-40s (drug use) seconal; fr. pharmaceutical identification stamped on the capsule *Folb*.

fhb (cp) (abbrev.)*family hold back*; often used by mother when there is only enough food to feed the guests properly.

fib v. to lie, usu. children's use *Dunne*.

ficky-fick n. sexual intercourse, usu. in pidgin sl.

fiddle-britches n. anyone who is too clever for their own good.

fiddle-fart around v. (US campus use) to waste time, to shirk duties *Underwood*.

fiddlestick n. the penis.

fiddlesticks! (excl.) nonsense! rubbish!; earlier use meaning 'the penis', makes it a euph.

field nigger n. (US Black use) working class, street blacks, as opposed to Black bourgeoisie; fr. slavery era distinction betw. field and 'house' slaves *Seale*.

field of wheat n. (rhyming sl.) street *Jones: J*.

fiend on v. (US Black use) to show off, to outdo a rival *Folb*.

fifi water n. (US prison use) aftershave *Morgan*.

FIFO acro. fit in or fuck off, a phr.

commonly used in situations where conformity is valued over and above creativity.

fifty cent bag n. (drug use) $50 worth of marijuana (cf: dime bag. nickel bag) *Folb*.

fifty: fifty usu. *50:50* alternating fellatio and sodomy between the same partners *Legman*.

fight one's hat v. to struggle uselessly. (fr. proverb: if the hat fits, wear it).

fight one's head v. to be impatient or restless. (fr. western j. 'fight the head': of horse that tosses its head in an attempt to throw off the harness or dislodge the bit).

fighting clothes on, have one's phr. to be ready to quarrel, to be spoiling for a fight.

FIGMO (acro.) *fuck it, got my orders* (cf: FUBAR, FUBIS, SNAFU, etc) *Partridge:5*.

figure v.i. to consider, to feel, to estimate; fr. totting up numbers *Runyon*.

figure v.t. to consider, to think of a person or object as; usu. *figure/ for . . . Runyon*.

figure out v. to work out, to understand *Price: 2*.

file v. (Black pimp use) an instruction to a prostitute to take note of present mistakes so as to avoid them in future; a parody of business use in the 'oldest profession' *Klein*.

fill in v. beat up *Welsh:1*.

fill one in v. to explain, to give details *Wodehouse: PGM*.

fill one up v. (US Black use) to gratify and satisfy completely; with obvious sexual overtones, although sex need not enter the pleasure *Klein*.

fill one's shirt v. to eat heartily.

filling station n. (US Black use) a liquor store *Folb*.

filling station n. (derog.) urban description of a small town.

film for your brownie n. toilet paper; punning on brownie = camera and = anus.

filth n. the police, esp. the CID

Performance.

filthy a. a general intensifier, eg. filthy rich, filthy temper (cf: stinking).

fimpted a. (US Black use) very ugly.

fin n. 1. (US Black use) a female hip that resembles in its opulent curve the fins on a 1950s model automobile *Klein*; 2. a five dollar bill, abbrev. of finnif (qv) *Chandler: Notebk*.

fin up (US prison use) a sentence of five years to life *Chandler: Notebk*.

financial a. (Aus. use) in credit, in the black, solvent *Bickerton*.

find the lady n. (criminal/gambling use) the three-card trick, three-card monte (qv), usu. played on the street; the 'lady' being a solitary queen alongside two nondescript cards.

fine and dandy n. (rhyming sl.) brandy *Jones: J*.

fine as frog hair phr. to be feeling very well or very cheerful (cf: froggy).

fine as wine (US Black use) any particularly attractive male or female *Folb*.

finger n. 1. (UK police use) an unpopular person; fr. finger = informer (qv) *Laurie*; 2. an informer *Runyon*.

finger v. to inform, to point out, to tip off *Runyon*.

finger artist n. (US Black use) a lesbian *Major*.

finger pie n. manually stimulating the female genitals (cf: hair pie) *The Beatles, 'Penny Lane', 1967*.

finger-fuck v.1. manual stimulation of the female genitals *Higgins: 1*; 2. manual stimulation of a male's anus *Jay & Young*.

finger-pointing n. the making of (false) accusations *PT*.

finicky a. the manner of an obsessive, petty person, concerned with minutiae and as such often irritating to others.

fink n. 1. company policeman, spy; 2. police informer *Higgins: 2*; both terms, 1. chronologically preceding 2. come from *Pink*, an abbrev. for *Pinkerton*, the detective agency recruited to help break strikes.

finnif $5.00; fr. Yiddish: 'five'

Runyon: 1.

finsburies n. (film/TV use) arc light; fr. rhyming sl. Finsbury Park = arc *Franklyn*.

fire v. **1.** in sport, to work/play at maximum capacity; fr. an engine which is 'firing on all cylinders'; **2.** (US Black use) to strike a blow *Seale*.

fire away to start, usu. as excl. start what you're doing, say your piece, etc. *Manser*.

fire into v. to approach sexually, to pick up, to seduce *Welsh:2*.

fire on v. (US Black use) disparage, ridicule (cf: blaze on) *Folb*.

fire on all cylinders phr. to work properly; thus 'fire on one cylinder': to work badly.

fire power n. (US Black use) physical strength and ability *Folb*.

fire up v. (drug use) **1.** To pump the blood and heroin mixture out of the hypodermic into the vein or muscle *Klein*; **2.** to light a marijuana cigarette *Folb*; **3.** (US Black use) to excite sexually; to anger, to arouse emotionally *Klein*; **4.** (US campus use) to have sexual intercourse *Bernbach*.

firebug n. arsonist *Higgins: 4*.

fire-eater n. a noticeably courageous person; with the supposed daring of the performer.

firkin a. (euph.) fucking *Fiesta magazine passim*.

firm n. a criminal gang, large or small *Performance*.

first base n. (teen. use) initial advances on a girl; usu. implying the caressing of some part of the body or even the removal of some clothing; such a base is always above the waist. Thus *second base*: similar explorations below the waist; such progress derives fr. baseball *Waterhouse*.

first bird n. (UK prison use) one's first experience of a prison sentence (cf: bird) *LL*.

first cab off the rank (Aus. use) the speediest one to react, the first one off the mark *Wilkes*.

first cracker out of the box at once, immediately *Wodehouse: MOJ*.

first skirt n. (US milit. use) senior officer in Women's Army Corps (cf: top brass) *Neaman& Silver*.

first-nighter n. (US Black use) a one-time sexual encounter, unlikely to be repeated *Klein*.

firsts n. (US Black use) any blacks who are the first to take on a specific job in a formerly all-white world *Major*.

fish n. **1.** (derog.) woman, fr. alleged smell of the vagina; **2.** (Can./US prison use) a new inmate; **3.** a prison homosexual *Caron*.

fish a. fresh, uninitiated, new, etc. *'The Mean Machine' dir. Albert S. Ruddy*.

fish 'n' chip mob n. (Sandhurst use) unfashionable regiments and thus anyone considered socially unacceptable *Barr*.

fish or cut bait (cp) either carry out what you're doing or let someone else more competent get on with it while you take a secondary role (cf: shit or get off the pot) *PT*.

fish queen n. any man, homo- or heterosexual, who enjoys cunnilingus (cf: fish 1) *Legman*.

fisherman's daughter n. (rhyming sl.) water, that which one drinks, rather than lakes, rivers, seas, etc. *Wright*.

fish-hooks in one's pockets, have phr. to be particularly mean and miserly.

fishing fleet n. (UK 'society' use) those girls who visit Hong Kong, and once many more centres of the British Empire, esp. India, in the hope of catching a rich husband *Barr*.

fishy n. suspect, dubious; fr. the smell of rotting fish *SF Comics*.

fist v. see: fist-fuck *White*.

fist junction n. (US Black use) that point of confrontation at which a physical fight takes over from mere words *Folb*.

fist one's mister v. to masturbate.

fist-fuck v. **1.** (homosexual use) to insert one's hand and forearm into the partner's anus or vagina *Jay & Young*;

2. to masturbate.

fit a. tired out, exhausted *Underwood*.

fit a. good-looking *D Robins*.

fit n. see: works *Klein*.

fit n. (US Black use) a suit of clothes (fr. abbr. outfit).

fit as a Mallee bull (Aus. use) extremely healthy, in perfect physical condition *Wilks*.

fit to be tied furious, enraged, in need, therefore, of restraint *Vidal*.

fit to bust emotionally moved, either to rage or ecstasy, depending on context *Prices: 3*.

fit up n. any temporary structure, esp. a stage, boxing ring, etc. which can be assembled, then knocked down for assembly at another venue *Newman: 1*.

fit up v. to incriminate by using false evidence, both physical and verbal. (cf: stitch up, frame) *Newman: 1*.

five and dime a. insignificant, paltry; fr. small shops of the same name *Folb*.

five in the South (gambling use) the point of five in craps dice *Chandler: Notebk*.

five to two n. (rhyming sl.) a Jew (cf: four by two) *Cole*.

five-day wonder n. (UK police use) a graduate of the special course at Bramshill Police College (cf: Shake 'n' Bake, etc.) *Laurie*.

five-finger discount n. (US Black campus use) the act and proceeds of shoplifting *Klein*.

Five-finger Mary n. one's hand, as used for masturbation (cf: Mrs Hand . . .' shake hands with the wife's . . ., etc.) *Dunne*.

fix n, v **1.** an injection of narcotics; to inject narcotics *Price: 1*; **2.** any corrupt deal, a bribe, a favour, etc.; thus *to put the fix in*: to ensure a plan or event favours whoever has paid the bribe, arranged the deal, etc.

fix up v. see: fit up *Laurie*.

fixing to v. to be about to do something, to intend to do something *Country Joe MacDonald, 'Feel Like I'm Fixin' to Die Rag', 1967*.

fizgig n. (Aus. use) a police informer *Baker*.

fizzing a. (euph.) fucking, mainly teen. use *Waterhouse*.

fizzle n. a failure

flabbergast **1.** n. an awkward clumsy person; **2.** v. to astound, astonish, to confuse; thus **3.** a. flabbergasted: astonished, exhausted, annoyed or disgusted; **4.** euph, for damned (poss.fr. SE flabby or flap + aghast; it was first mentioned in the *Annual Register* (1772) as a new piece of fashionable slang; possibly of dialectal origin; the *English Dialect Dictionary* has it as a Suffolk word while Scot. has 'flabrigast': to boast extravagantly and 'flabrigast it': worn out with exertion).

flach (backsl.) half *Cole*.

flack n. (show business use) publicity man; press agent; fr. the barrage of anti-aircraft fire – that assailed Second World War bombers; also poss. fr, the 'flags' that such people wave for their product *Goldman*.

fladge n. (abbrev.) flagellation, only when used in a sexual context (cf: B&D, English culture).

flag v. (homosexual use) to attract a stranger with the eyes or with a slight gesture of the head *Legman*.

flag is up, the n. (of a woman) she is menstruating (cf: fly baker, fly one's flag, fly the red flag).

flag-waver n. an assistant to the boss, who communicates with the rest of the workforce.

flak n. interference; annoyance, problems *The Roches, 'Nurds'*.

flak catcher n. a civil servant, or similar figure in private industry, whose task is to intercept complaints, queries and similar problems coming from the public, before such problems reach his superiors *Wolfe: 4*.

flake n.**1.** a boring, unappealing, incompetent, undesirable person *Price: 3*; **2.** (US police use) see accommodation collar *Neaman & Silver*.

flake v. (US police use) to plant evidence *Neaman & Silver*.

flake off v. (US campus use) to depart, to go away *Underwood*.

flaked out a. exhausted *Humphries*.

flako a. drunk; fr. flaked out (qv) *Dickson*.

flaky a. second-rate, unreliable, distasteful, possibly eccentric person. (cf: flake).

flaky ho n. (pimp use) an unstable, unreliable prostitute whose desire for clients and money is undermined by her inability to maintain a good front and economic and social discipline*OUI 8/75*.

flame v. (homosexual use) 1. to look exaggeratedly 'feminine' in dress and style *Jay & Young*; 2. spec. to wear makeup *White*; both meanings fr. 19th-C. *flamer*: a conspicuous person who 'burns brightly'.

flamer n. (US prep school use) anyone who commits a major social error; thus the error itself; such blunders mean that one 'goes down in flames' *Bernbach*.

flaming a. mild perjorative, euph. fucking *Wright*.

flaming 1. speaking incessantly and obsessively on a particular topic of little interest to anyone but oneself; or to talk arrant and apparent nonsense about an otherwise interesting subject; possibly from gay use 'flame' = to act conspicuously. 2. more recently, the practice of using computer bulletin boards and other communications links to circulate obscene messages, pictures, etc.

flannel n. rubbish, nonsense; albeit plausible rubbish *Neaman & Silver*.

flannel v. to talk nonsense in a soothing, plausible manner, esp. for the purposes of charming a woman one wishes to seduce.

flannel feet n. 1. a large foot; 2. a clumsy person.

flap n. 1. panic, excitement, commotion, ex milit. use since First World War *Powis*; 2. excrement, esp. animal (cf: flop).

flap one's chops v. to talk incessantly, to gossip (cf: flapping at

the jibs).

flap shot n. in pornographic still or moving pictures: close-up shot of the labia and open vagina *Green: 2*.

flapdoodle n. nonsense, rubbish (cf: baloney) *Wolfe: 2*.

flapjaw n. a noisy talker, a braggart.

flapper n. 1. (US Black use) the mouth; 2. (US black use) the penis *Klein*; 3. a large foot or the shoe that encases it.

flapping at the jibs (US Black use) to talk wildly, out of control, in a panicky, unrestrained manner; fr. flapping at the jaw/jowls/lip etc. *Seale*.

flapping track n. a small, unlicensed race track for horses or dogs *T. 13/3/84*.

flaps n. ears, usu. large ones *Powis*.

flaptabs n. ears *Sillitoe*.

flash a. ostentatious, showy *Norman: 2*.

flash n. 1. (UK criminal use) a large bundle of notes; esp. when used in a three card monte (qv) game to entice poss. victims *Powis*; 2. the initial physical effects of an injection of narcotics *Southern*; 3. brief glimpse, esp. when offered to a man by a woman inadvertently revealing her thighs, breasts or genitals. *rr*.

flash v. 1. to show off, usu. one's material possessions and gross self-esteem; 2. (US campus use) to vomit *AS 50 (1965)*; 3. to expose one's genitals *Bruce: 2*.

flash as a Chinky's horse (Aus. use) see flash as as rat with a gold tooth.

flash as a rat with a gold tooth (Aus. cp) extremely ostentatious *D. Leitch*.

flash case n. (US Black use) a satchel or bag that contains illegal drugs or any other contraband; fr. 18th C. (and later) use of *flash*; pertaining to criminality *Klein*.

flash of light n. (rhyming sl.) a sight *Cole*; 2. a spendthrift, one who shops ostentatiously.

flash on v. to have a sudden inspiration, memory, moment of absolute comprehension, etc. *McFadden*.

flash roll n. a sum of money that is revealed as proof that a given person, esp, a narcotics dealer or other criminal, is willing to do business; the money is 'flashed' (qv) before the client (cf: flash case).

flash the ash v. to hand around one's pack of cigarettes *Cole*.

flash the range v. (US prison use) the scanning of the area outside one's cell by using a small hand mirror to catch any reflections of approaching warders, etc. *Klein*.

flash up n. (of a woman) to dress showily, to use an excess of cosmetics.

flasher n. 1. an exhibitionist *Powis*.

flash-tail (US Black use) a female prostitute *Klein*.

flat a. (Aus. use) (abbrev.) flat out: exhausted, worn out *Humphries: 2*.

flat n. the truth. (fr. abbr. flat truth).

flat fuck n. (lesbian use) sexual relations between two women, rubbing bodies together (cf: dry fuck) *Maledicta*.

flat joint n. a crooked gambling game or casino; orig. fair/carnival use, when a *flat* was a crooked or doctored 'wheel of fortune'.

flat top n. (navy use) an aircraft carrier.

flatbacker n. (Black pimp use) a prostitute who specializes in quantity rather than quality in her clients *Milner*.

flatfoot n. policeman, detective *Fiction Illus. 3*.

flat-footed adv. plainly, firmly, without adornment.

flat-footed a. 1. (of food) plain, devoid of any further cooking or mixing; 2. (of a person) unprepared, caught unawares.

flat-footed in the corn-field a. utterly unsophisticated, completely ignorant.

flatlander n. an outsider, an incompetent person (lit. one who comes from the flatlands, the plains and thus seen as inferior by those who live in the mountains).

flats n. 1. playing cards; 2. plastic credit cards *Powis*.

flatten v. to knock down *Humphries*.

flattie n. see: flatfoot; (cf: busy) *Powis*.

flavour of the month phr. a derisory reference to a contemporary and, it is presumed, short-lived fashion or fad.

fleabag n. 1. a cheap, sordid hotel *Runyon: 1*; 2. (pimp use) an old, worn out prostitute who is forced to seek equally run down clients, often on Skid Row or in cheap hotels, etc. *OUI 8/75*; 3. (US Black use) troublesome, difficult person who tends, like fleas, to follow around and keep irritating the individual who has been made subject of his/her woes *Klein*.

fleapit n. cheap, tawdry, rundown cinema *Waterhouse*.

fleas and ants n. (rhyming sl.) pants *Wright*.

fleece v. to rob; esp. in a crooked sideshow or gambling game fr. the shearing of sheep (both actual and figurative).

fleshpot n. (US Black use) a woman, viewed strictly as a sex object *Klein*.

flesh-presser n. a politician who attempts to curry favour with the voters by shaking as many hands, kissing as many babies and patting as many backs as he can reach in a campaign (cf: glad hand).

flick n. 1. a knife with a spring-loaded blade; 2. a razor blade with one side taped for holding as a weapon *Folb*.

flick v. (US Black use) to fail deliberately to turn up for work or school (cf: bunk off) *Klein*.

flick my bic v. (US Black use) suggestion to a woman that she should stimulate one's genitals with her hand; *bic* = a popular pen. *Klein*.

flicks n. the movies, the cinema; orig. *flickers*, denoting the slight jerkiness of early pictures *Humphries*.

flim-flam n., v. a confidence trick, a criminal hoax, to perpetrate such a trick or hoax *Morgan*.

flint n. (US Black use) a cigarette lighter *Klein*.

Flip n. (derog.) Filipino *Bukowski: 2*.

flip a. nonchalant, unconcerned, in control; abbrev. flippant *Price: 2*.

flip n. (US Black use) a passive homosexual.

flip v. to lose control (cf: freak) *Price: 2*.

flip! excl. a euph. for fuck (qv).

flip for v. to become fascinated, obsessed by.

flip one's lid v. see: flip one's wig *Neaman & Silver*.

flip one's wig v. to lose one's temper; to lose one's sanity *Schulberg*.

flip oneself off v. (Aus. use) to masturbate *Wilkes*.

flip out v. see: flip.

flip the bird v. (US campus use) to make an obscene gesture (cf: give the finger) *Underwood*.

flip-flop n. (US prison use) an individual who first gains parole and then returns to the same jail after breaking the terms of that parole or committing a new crime *Klein*.

flip-flop v. to change direction; fr. computer use.

flip-out n. an eccentric, a madman *Thompson*.

flipping a. (euph.) fucking; esp. in *flipping heck*: fucking hell!

flipwreck n. (Aus. use) a person who has (supposedly) masturbated themselves into physical and mental decline; pun on shipwreck *Wilkes*.

flit n. a homosexual *P. Wickham*.

flivver n. an automobile, spec. a Model T Ford *Runyon:1*.

floater n. 1. (homosexual use) a gay prostitute who works only in towns where he is unknown and does not live *Legman*; 2. a (social) error, a *faux pas* *Wodehouse:MOJ*.

flock n. see: stable *Klein*.

flog v. to sell; currently non-specific, but orig. with criminal overtones *Performance*.

flog one's mutton v. to masturbate (cf: bang the bishop, flog the log, etc.).

flog the log v. to masturbate *Junker*.

flood v. (US Black use) to have an erection, the penis 'floods' with blood *Folb*.

floor v. 1. to accelerate the car – by pressing the relevant pedal down, thus *four on the floor*: a gearshift on the floor of the car, instead of on the steering wheel *Price:3*; 2. to defeat utterly; fr. boxing or wrestling imagery.

floosie n. see: floozie *Southern & Hoffenberg*.

floozie n. a promiscuous young girl *McBain:1*.

floozie a. 1. showy, stylish; 2. over-dressed, over-made-up; 3. silly or light-headed.

flop n. 1. a cheap room or bed; 2. a drunk passed out and as such a possible victim for a robber (cf: lush-roller); 3. (UK criminal/police use) anywhere a thief or gang can leave the loot so as to avoid detection during the immediate aftermath of a crime *Powis*; 4. (US prison use) the rejection of one's application for parole (cf: knockback); 5. see: wake-up; 6. excrement, esp. cow-flop; 7. a weak, flabby person; 8. a fat, ungainly, slovenly person, esp., a woman (cf: floppy); 9. a dull, unpleasant person, a misfit, a failure; 10. (orig. US) a failure, esp. of a film or stage play.

flop v. 1. to collapse, to fail, esp. of a stage entertainment or similar undertaking; 2. to fall asleep, to go to bed.

flophouse n. a lodging house or night shelter for tramps, down-and-outs, alcoholics, etc. *LL*.

flopover v. to assume a position with the buttocks in the air or with the body bent at 45° and the hands thus supported by the knees, either of which will permit the easy introduction of the penis into the anus or vagina *Klein*.

flopped out a. exhausted, tired out.

floppy n. a fat, ungainly, slovenly person, esp. a woman (cf: flop 8.).

flopper n. anyone who fakes an accident in order to make a fraudulent insurance claim; the image is of someone deliberately 'flopping' down in front of a car.

flopsweat n. (show business use) the nervousness and tension (and sweat) that overcome a performer at the thought of failure (a flop) on stage *Green:2*.

Florida n. (US prison use) the solitary confinement/punishment block, fr. the siting of such cells in the warmest areas of the prison, often underground *Klein*.

flossed up a. of a woman, made up (cf: tarted up) *Powis*.

flounder n. (rhyming sl.) flounder and dab = cab = taxi *Laurie*.

flounder mouth n. a person with a notably large mouth. [fr. SE flounder: a fish with a large mouth]

flour mixer n. (rhyming sl.) *shikse* (Yiddish) = Gentile girl *Powis*.

flowery n. (rhyming sl.) flowery dell = cell (though usu. peter, qv) *Powis*.

flub v. 1. to botch, to bungle, to make a mess of; 2. to confuse; 3. to waste time, to fool around.

flub the dub v. 1. (orig. milit. j.) to shirk; to evade one's duties; 2. to blunder, to fail in a task.

flubdub v. to mess around, to waste time (cf: flub).

flue n. (UK prison use rhyming sl.) screw = prison officer *LL*.

fluence n. (abbrev.) influence: delicate, subtle influence, either in business/polit./etc. manipulation or in actual physical acts, ie. the spinning of a cricket ball; also implication of *fluency D. Leitch*.

fluff n. 1. (US Black use) the vagina *Folb*; 2. young, attractive, but empty-headed girl (cf: airhead, bimbo) *Chandler: Notebk*; 3. the passive partner in a lesbian couple (cf: femme) *Stanley*.

fluff v. to make a mistake, esp. in theatrical use.

fluff off v. to avoid work, to shirk.

fluke (orig. US campus use) v. 1. to fail; 2. to steal; 3. to back out, to renege on a promise; n. 4. a failure, a worthless person or thing.

flummox v. to fool, to confuse, to overcome (by trickery), to avoid, to disappoint.

flunk (out) v. to fail an examination *Greenlee*.

flunky n. a condom *Welsh:1*.

flush n. the lavatory *Higgins:3*.

fluter n. a fellator (cf: skin flute) *Legman*.

fly a. smart, sharp, perspicacious; the term, quite independently, is popular among US blacks, where it means the same; thus *fly boy*; not usu. very complimentary *Powis*.

fly a flag v. to betray one's personality, esp. in a situation, eg. prison, where such honesty may be foolish.

fly a kite v. 1. usu. with *go. . .*: a suggestion that an unwanted person should go away; 2. to present a false front, a deceitful line of talk in order to persuade one's victim that one's intentions are other than that which they really are; 3. to pass a dud cheque *Norman:2*.

fly by the seat of one's pants v. to fly an aircraft using natural ability and daring rather than instruments and technology *BBC-1 TV 1984*.

fly girl n. (US/UK Black use) a smart, attractive girl. *IceT:2*.

fly off the handle v. to lose control, to become extremely angry *Farrell*.

fly the coop v. to leave, poss. suddenly; fr. avian habits *Price:2*.

fly the red flag v. to be menstruating (cf: have the flag out, flying baker, put one's flag out).

fly to flinders v. to lose one's temper.

fly up v. to go to bed (fr. the action of chickens in 'flying up to the roost').

flyblow v. to gossip maliciously about an absent third party, to attack behind one's back.

flyboy n. a pilot, civil or military; usu. with slight implication of disdain or dislike *Bukowski:1*.

fly-by-night n.a. dubious, crooked, criminal; esp. of a businessman who takes one's money but fails to provide any or at least adequate recompense

Humphries:2.

flying a. exhilarated by using a drug (cf: high) *Higgins:1.*

flying blind a. drunk *Dickson.*

flying fuck phr. an all-purpose negative epithet; usu. in comb., eg. (not) give a flying fuck, (go) take a flying fuck.

flying saucer n. a diaphragm *Junker.*

fly-over people inhabitants of those states of the USA over which one passes in an airplane flying from Coast to Coast; formerly 'middle America' *Wolfe:8.*

FNG (milit. use) (abbrev.) *Fucking New Guy,* used of new arrivals in a squad, platoon, etc. *O'Brien.*

fodder n. (UK 'society' use) well-cooked food; referring back to the stables that so many such speakers know and love *Barr.*

fog v. to shoot *Chander: Notebk.*

foggy a. confused, not very intelligent.

Foggy Bottom n. the US State Department; derived both fr. the name of an area of Washington, DC, and from the 'foggy' obfuscations produced by its bureaucrats.

foghorn n. 1. the nose (cf: hooter); 2. one who talks too loudly.

fold v. 1. (journalist use) for a magazine or newspaper to cease from publication *J. G. Dunne, 'Quintana and Friends', 1981;* 2. (poker use) to throw in one's hand; both uses imply the folding up and putting away of clothing *Alvarez.*

fold one's ears v. to lecture or advise someone at great and serious length *Major.*

fold out v. to go to bed (one unfolds a bedroll).

fold up v. to collapse, to surrender; both defeats are under unbearable pressure; fr. poker use (cf: fold).

folding stuff n. cash money *Humphries.*

Follies n. (UK prison use) the Quarter Sessions *LL.*

follow one's nose v. (US Black use) to lead a law-abiding life, whatever

temptations may exist to the contrary *Klein.*

fonfen n. the line (qv) created by con-men to further a given fraud or trick; fr. Yiddish *Powis.*

fonk (Black pimp use) the negative aspects of funk (qv) *Milner.*

fonk v. (US Black use) to show off, to upstage others (cf: fiend, front off, high sign, style).

fonked out heavy (US Black use) very well dressed *Folb.*

fonky positive or negative intensifier depending on context; thus exceptionally good or bad; smelling sweet or vile, etc. *Folb.*

foodie n. (euph.) gourmet, one of a self-elected circle of London eaters, devoted to the best and newest in eating and drinking; coined by *Observer* food writer Paul Levy, 1981.

fool n. 1. anyone excessively enthusiastic about a given activity or topic; thus *dancing fool, singing fool; writing fool* (drug use): a doctor who will write as many prescriptions for narcotics as there are people requesting them *Burroughs:1.*

fool v. to curry favour with.

fool around v. to conduct a promiscuous sex life; thus *let's fool around:* a suggestion by one of a couple that they should abandon speech for (sexual) action *Higgins:5.*

fool away v. to waste time or resources, to fritter away.

fool's gold n. (US criminal use) fake jewellery *Klein.*

foop v. 1. (US campus use) to engage in homosexual acts fr. reverse of *poof* (?) (qv) *Underwood;* 2. (US Black use) to dance uninhibitedly.

foop n. see: fooper.

fooper n. (US campus use) a homosexual *Underwood.*

foot soldier n. a male homosexual prostitute who 'walks the street'.

football n. (drug use) a measure of one half grain of a narcotic *Goldman.*

foot-in-mouth disease n. aka: *dontopedology:* the continual problem of making grossly tactless or embarrassing statement *Neaman & Silver*.

footling a. incompetent, inadequate, mediocre *Wodehouse:AAG*.

footslogging hard, exhausting and protracted walking, orig. First World War milit. sl. *Wodehouse:AAG*.

footy n. football.

foozle, fuzzle n. **1.** a conservative, an old fogey, one who is behind the times; **2.** one who is easily tricked.

for a motherfucker (US Black use) an intensifying expletive: 'he has guns for a motherfucker': he had a great many guns; 'I'm throwing bricks for a motherfucker'; I'm throwing bricks continually and passionately, etc. *Seale*.

for crying in the beer excl. euph. for for Christ's sake (cf: for crying out loud).

for crying out loud! (euph.) for Christ's sake! *Manser*.

for days! (homosexual excl.) implies shock or amazement; fr. concept of having sex on and on for days *Stanley*.

for keeps for the duration, for a long time, for ever *Price:2*.

for real honest, sincere, to be taken at face value *Junker*.

for sure (Valley Girls (qv) use) certainly, definitely, absolutely *Harpers/Queen 1/83*.

for yonks for ages, for a very long time; poss. fr. eons *Barr*.

forbidden fruit n. an underage sexual partner (cf: jail bait).

forget it! (excl.) implies absolute dismissal of a suggestion, a concept.

forget you! (US teen. use) impossible, out of the question, no way (qv) *Pond*.

fork! (excl.) give!; thus *fork out, fork over*: to pay, to hand over money *Powis*.

fork n. (US cant) pickpocket *Neaman & Silver*.

fork out v. to pay, to donate *Hotten*.

fork over v. to hand over, to give out *Sanders:2*.

forks fingers *Powis*.

form n. previous convictions. fr.

horse-racing use (cf: previous) *Dury*.

Fort Bushy (homosexual) the pubic hair *Maledicta*.

forty n. (US Black use) a large bottle of beer. (fr. its contents: forty ounces of beer).

forty acres n. extremely large feet.

forty miles from nowhere phr. far from what the speaker considers 'civilization', deep in the countryside.

forty miles of bad road phr. a very unattractive person, sight or situation.

Forty-Deuce (US con-man use) 42nd Street fr. 8th Avenue to Times Square; the centre of New York's tourism/nightlife/underworld *Shulman*.

forty-eight (milit. use) forty-eight hour leave pass *Waterhouse*.

foul up v. to ruin, to destroy, to blunder *Higgins:3*.

four by two n. (rhyming sl.) (derog.) Jew *Humphries*.

four sisters on thumb street (US Black use) masturbation (cf: Mrs Hand and Her Five Daughters) *Folb*.

four-eleven-forty-four (4-11-44) n. (UK Black use) the penis *Neaman & Silver*.

four-eyes (derog.) anyone who wears glasses; overtones also of distrust of anyone 'intellectual' *Sillitoe*.

4-F useless, inferior, weak; fr. milit. specification for anyone unfit to serve *Uris*.

4-F Club Find 'em, Feel 'em, Fuck 'em and Forget 'em: the axiom for macho US youth; Mae West in *I'm No Angel* (1933) tells her maid to 'find 'em, fool 'em and forget 'em' when it comes to men *Junker*.

four-flusher n. a cheat, a scrounger, one who fails to pay due debts; fr. poker use: a real flush requires five cards of the same suit, four is merely a bluff *Higgins:4*.

four-letter man n. **1.** (UK 'society' use) an unpleasant person; the four letters are perhaps s-h-i-t or c-u-n-t *Barr*; **2.** (US use) both as **1.** and as h-o-m-o (cf: three-letter man) *Neaman & Silver*.

four-letter words n. (euph.)
obseenities, notably cunt, fuck, shit,
etc.; thus six-letter. . .: bugger; and
ten-letter: cocksucker, etc. (qqv).

fourth of July n (rhyming sl.) tie
Wright.

fox n. (Black use) a girl, a woman
Milner.

foxed a. drunk *Dickson*.

foxy a. sexy, usu. Black use, but
whites also *Price:2*.

FP (UK criminal use) False Pretences,
fraud *LL*.

frag n. (US milit. use) (abbrev.) a
fragmentation grenade *Del Vecchio*.

frag v. (US milit. use) the practice, as
the US morale in Vietnam declined, of
soldiers assassinating unpopular or
incompetent officers and NCOs by
tossing a fragmentation grenade at
them during the heat of battle
Del Vecchio.

frail n. girl, woman *Sharpe:1*.

frail eel n. (US Black use) an
attractive woman.(cf. frail).

fram v. to beat, to strike, to attack.

frame n. (UK police use) the general
situation, esp. that surrounding the
suspects in a given crime (cf: in the
frame) *Laurie*.

frame v. to trap a suspect (poss.
innocent) by creating false evidence,
witnesses etc. (cf: frame-up) *Fiction
Illus.3*.

frame-up n. the concoction of criminal
guilt or charges *Performance*.

frances n. the buttocks (cf. fanny).

frank and fearless n. (UK 'society'
use) a discussion; fr. diplomatic/
journalistic hyperbole/hypocrisy
Barr.

franzy house n. **1.** a brothel; **2.** an
insane asylum (fr. dial franzy: frenzy).

fratting essentially abbrev. of
fraternize, but used as euph. for
fucking (qv) *Rawson*.

frazzling a. general intensifier.

freak n. **1.** any person considered odd
by the speaker; **2.** an obvious user of
drugs, esp. cannabis and
hallucinogens; **3.** (US milit. use) aka:
freq radio frequency *Del Vecchio*;

4. (Black pimp use) anyone with
eccentric sexual tastes, habits; esp.
one who enjoys sex for its own sake
and does not ask for cash, a perversion
in pimp ethos *Shulman*; **5.** similar to 4.
but used generally to describe anyone
(usually female) who enjoys sex and is
keen to pursue it. *Ice T:1*.

freak v. (abbrev.) freak out: to worry,
to disturb, to cause severe anxiety (the
extent of the disturbance varies totally
as to context): orig. 1960s drug/hippie
use.

freak fuck n. any variation on
'straight' heterosexual intercourse
Folb.

freak off v. **1.** to offer sex for free, no
cash required; **2.** to furnish a room or
apartment; 'freak' here implies one's
own tastes, but in interior decoration
and not sex *Milner*.

freak out n. **1.** spec. any unpleasant
experience caused by drug use,
esp. with LSD; **2.** anxiety, ranging
from twinges of fear to a full
nervous breakdown, varying as to
context.

freak trick n. (US prostitute use) any
customer who requires out of the way
sex or who attacks the girl physically
Neaman & Silver.

freaking (euph.) fucking (qv) *Wolfe:8*.

freaky a. odd, bizarre, unnerving
Grogan.

freckle n. (Aus. use) anus *Humphries*.

freckle-puncher n. homosexual; from
freckle = anus (cf. dung-puncher).

Fred n. (Aus. use) the average
Australian (cf: Alf, ocker, Roy)
Wilkes.

Fred's n. (UK 'society' use) nickname
for Fortnum & Mason, the country's
leading caterers, of Piccadilly, London
Barr.

free for all n. (US campus use) a
sexually available female *Underwood*.

free ride n. an easy time *PT*.

free shot n. the unpaid for services of
a prostitute *Klein*.

free show n. the inadvertent
revelation by a woman of her body – in
all or part – glimpsed by a passing

male (cf: flash).

free-base v. a method of intensifying the effect of cocaine by heating it in combination with ether or other chemicals prior to inhaling it.

freebie n. **1.** (prostitute use) giving one's sexual services without making a charge; **2.** any free sample, free trip, esp. press tours, promotions, etc.

freelance v. for a girl to work as a prostitute without being committed to a pimp *Morgan*.

freeload v. **1.** to enjoy for free the pleasures that are made available to a celebrity or at an important event but become equally available to anyone who cares to struggle hard enough to grab them; **2.** in general use to define the taking of any benefits for which one has not made due efforts to deserve *O'Brien*.

freeloader n. a parasite, esp. those who form a celebrity's entourage and enjoy the crumbs from his/her various tables *Jenkins*.

Freeway Freddie n. (US Black use) any police in a patrol car *Folb*.

freeze n. cocaine; from the effects of the drug when inhaled or rubbed on the gums.

freeze v. **1.** to become silent, to quieten down, to refuse to answer questions or make conversation *Greenlee*; **2.** to intimidate.

freeze on v. to ignore, to snub, to reject *'Hill Street Blues'*, *Thames TV, 1983.*

French a. a racial stereotype used in various contexts: the English (and thus US) belief in 'gay Paree' and its supposedly sex-obsessed denizens has long equated 'French' with sexy or, pejoratively, pornographic and 'dirty' (cf: Chinese).

french v. to fellate.

French active n. the passive (sucked) partner in fellatio *Jay & Young*.

French art n. fellatio.

French article n. a French prostitute.

French bathe v. phr. (gay use) to use perfumes as a deodorant in lieu of bathing.

French by injection a. (gay use) said of anyone considered particularly well versed in fellatio.

French culture fellatio, obs. except in homosexual contact advertisements (cf: English culture, Greek culture) *Jay & Young.*

French dip n. (gay use) vaginal precoital fluid.

French dressing n. (gay use) semen.

French embassy n (gay use) a YMCA where homosexual activity is extensive and unchecked.

French head job n. fellatio.

French inhale v. (US use) to blow out smoke through the nose.

French joke, tell a v. phr. (gay use) oral stimulation of anus.

French kiss n. a deep kiss, using the tongue as well as lips (cf: soul kiss) *Jay & Young.*

French kiss filter n. (gay use) any filter-tipped cigarette.

French language expert n. (gay use) a fellator.

French language training n. (gay use) teaching fellatio.

French leave n. absenting oneself from a job or duty without prior permission *Higgins:4.*

French lessons, take phr. to contract venereal disease.

French letter n. contraceptive sheath *Sharpe:1.*

French love n. fellatio.

French passive n. the fellator *Jay & Young.*

French photographer n. (gay use) homosexual photographer.

French postcard n. (gay use) an exciting, prospective sexual partner.

French prints n. (gay use) unusual heterosexual pornography.

French revolution n. (gay use) the movement for homosexual rights.

French screwdriver n. a hammer (cf: Birmingham screwdriver, Jewish screwdriver).

French, speak v. phr. to indulge in unconventional sexual play.

French stuff n. (gay use) 1: pornography 2: any unusual sex activity.

French tickler n. a contraceptive sheath with extra protrusions for added stimulation *Sharpe:1*.

Frencher n. a male with a perverse sexual appetite.

Frenchery n. a brothel.

French-fried ice cream n. (gay use) semen.

Frenchie n. 1. a contraceptive sheath; fr. French letter (qv); 2. a french woman *Sharpe:2*.

frenchified a. sexually talented; usu. said of a woman.

Frenchman n. one who offers fellation to others for cash *Bukowski:1*.

frenchy n. 1. a contraceptive sheath, fr. French letter (qv); 2. a foolish man; 3. a flighty woman.

Frenchy n. a Frenchman, or a person of French descent.

fresh a. 1. familiar, cheeky, over-intimate *Higgins:1*; 2. (US Black use) smart, on the ball, aware, attractive - a general term of approval varying as to context. *Ice T:1*.

fresh fish n. new young whore (cf: fish).

fresh hide n. (US Black use) a new lover or sexual partner; fr. hide: skin (usu. of an animal) *Folb*.

fresher n. (student use) a student in his/her first term at a university; one of the last survivors of the Oxford '-er' suffix of the 1920s, which once offered 'Pragger Wagger': the Prince of Wales, 'wagger pagger bagger': waste paper basket, etc.

fress v. fr. Yiddish 'eat': to perform either form of oral intercourse, usu. cunnilingus *Goldman*.

frick and frack n. (US Black use) the testicles *Folb*.

fricking a. (euph.) fucking (qv) *Heller*.

fried a. (drug use) extremely high (qv) *Folb*.

fried, dyed, swooped to the side (US Black use) straightened Black hair which is attempting to emulate the texture and even colour of a white person's hair *Folb*.

friend form n. (US prison use) official papers that must be completed to

facilitate outside visitors to the inmates *Klein*.

friend in need n. (US Black use) sarcastic reference to anyone who is continually looking for loans, free handouts, etc. *Klein*.

friendlies n. (milit. use) one's allies or those troops in one's own forces. Thus *friendly fire*: artillery or small-arms fire coming from one's own, misdirected side *Del Vecchio*.

frig v. 1. (euph.) to fuck; orig. euph. for masturbate *Powis*; 2. to mess around, to fiddle about (cf: diddle, futz).

frigging a. (euph.) fucking (qv) *Price:2*.

frighteners n. threats, violence, anything that will terrify a given person into doing what is required; thus *to put the frighteners on*: to intimidate, to harass *Performance*.

frilly a. (of a woman) one who puts on airs, who acts arrogantly.

frip n. (US campus use) a weak, ineffectual person *Underwood*.

'Frisco speedball n. drug cocktail containing LSD, cocaine and heroin *Green:1*.

frisk v. 1. (police use) to search, for weapons, illicit drugs, stolen goods, etc. *Selby:1*; 2. (police use) to search a suspect, usu. briefly *LL*.

'Fro n. (US Black and campus use) (abbrev.) Afro: Black (and white) hairstyle where normally short, curly black hair is allowed to grow out in a bush around the head, supposedly in the style of one's African forbears.

Frog n. (derog.) French person *BvdB*.

frog n. 1. (banking use) a cheque that is returned to drawer (cf: leaper, bum map) *Breslin*; 2. (rhyming sl.) frog and toad = road *Powis*; 3. (Aus. use) a contraceptive sheath; fr. French letter (qv) *Wilkes*.

frog and toad n. (rhyming sl.) road *London Transport poster 1983*.

frog up v. (US Black use) to cheat, to confuse, to trick. (fr. stereotype of the French as cunning and deceitful).

froggy a. (US Black use) aggressive,

belligerent, keen to fight; keen to start 'jumping' *Folb*.

front n. 1. a respectable appearance; a mask for illegal activities *rr*; 2. (criminal use, esp. pimps, con-men) anything one needs – fancy clothes, a clever line of patter, a personal style, a mental attitude – for the successful promotion of one's game (qv) (cf: more front than Brighton Beach) *Milner*.

front v. 1. (Aus. use) to appear in front of *Wilkes*; 2. to advance either money or any other commodity (esp. drugs) as a loan or a sample of goods on offer; when buying drugs the seller may ask for the money to be 'fronted' so he in turn, can make a bulk purchase from his superior in the sales chain *Morgan*.

front door n. (US Black use) the female genitals; as opposed to back door (qv) *Klein*.

front line n. (UK Black use) that area of a city where the Black community is most likely to clash with the forces of white law and order; All Saints Road, Notting Hill, Railton Road, Brixton, etc.

front one off v. (US Black use) 1. to reveal information about another person that puts that person in an embarrassing or otherwise difficult position *Klein*; 2. to be attracted to the company of another person not so much for their personality as for the outward show and physical beauty in the reflected glory of which one can bask *Shulman*.

front street n. (US Black use) the main street of a town; that street on which most of the (illegal) action takes place (cf. fast track) *Klein*.

fronts n. (US Black use) clothes, esp. suit or jacket *Folb*.

front-wheel skid n. (rhyming sl.) (derog.) Yid = Jew *Powis*.

frosty n. a chilled glass or can of beer *Humphries*.

fruit n. a male homosexual *Selby:1*.

fruit fly n. a woman who enjoys the company of homosexual rather than

heterosexual males (cf: fag hag) *Stanley*.

fruit loop n. (US campus use) the small loop (ostensibly for hanging the shirt when no hanger is available) on the upper back of many shirts; such a loop, supposedly, can be used to hold a victim ready for buggery (cf: bugger's grips) *Bernbach*.

fruitcake n. an eccentric, a peculiar person; fr. 'nutty as a fruitcake' (cf: nuts) *Dunne*.

fruity a. sexually aroused; the fruit is 'ripe' for enjoyment.

fry v. (criminal use) to be electrocuted in the electric chair *Himes:1*. (cf: bake)

fry one's hair v. (US Black use) to straighten one's hair (cf: conk).

F/S (contact ads use) face sitter *SMD*.

F-60s (drug use) histadyl fr. pharmaceutical identification stamped on the capsule.

F-66s n. (drug use) tuinal, fr. pharamaceutical identification stamped on the capsule.

fubar (milit. use) (acro.) fucked *up* beyond *all* recognition *Uris*.

fubis (US milit. use) (acro) *f*uck *y*ou *b*uddy, *I*'m *s*hipping out (cf: I'm all right, Jack).

fuck n. 1. sexual intercourse; 2. a person, ie dumb fuck, crazy fuck, etc.

fuck v. 1. to have sexual intercourse; 2. an expletive, ie: fuck off, get fucked, etc.

fuck a duck! general expletive *Newman:1*.

fuck about v. 1. to annoy, to irritate *Welsh:1*; 2. waste time; n. 3. a time waster (cf: fuck off, n.).

fuck book n. pornography (cf: stroke book, eight-pager, etc.) *Pearce*.

fuck (it) up v. to make a mistake, to err, to blunder *Higgins:1*.

fuck like a bunny v. to copulate enthusiastically; thus fuck like a mink; (Aus. use) fuck like a rattlesnake (cf: shag like a. . .); fuck like a stoat; all generally have a female subject except for rattlesnake (cf: snake).

fuck me! exclamation of surprise, astonishment (cf: fuck my old boots!).

fuck my old boots! excl. denoting

one's astonishment; orig. milit. use (cf: fuck me!).

fuck off! excl. either aggressive — 'go away!' — or jocular — 'don't be silly!' — according to context; often compounded to fuck off out of it!

fuck off n. a lazy or inefficient person, who prefers to 'fuck off' rather than work.

fuck off v. 1. intr. to waste time, to idle. 2. to leave, to go away; 3. trans. to annoy; phr. 4. 'fucking off' wasting time, acting lazily.

fuck (one's)/(the) arse off 1. v.i. to copulate enthusiastically; 2. v.t. to make one's partner the object of such enthusiastic or aggressive love-making. Both generally have a male subject (cf: fuck like a bunny).

fuck (one's) brains out v. see: fuck (one's) arse off.

fuck over v. to hurt emotionally; to act cruelly, to interfere, to mess around with, to adulterate (ideas/objects) *Caserta*.

fuck pad n. (orig. US) a room or apartment which a man keeps for seductions and sex.

fuck that for a lark! (cp) don't expect me to get mixed up; that's a stupid idea, etc.

fuck the dog v. to waste time (cf: screw the pooch).

fuck truck n. (Aus. use) any vehicle, usu. a small van (possibly with a mattress in the back), in which a young man hopes to seduce girls (cf: passion wagon, shag wagon).

fuck up (one's) pussy v. (US black use) to interfere with a rival, or a companion's efforts at seducing a given female.

fuck with v. to mess about with, to interfere, to become involved with *Morgan*.

fuck you, Jack, I'm all right! (cp.) unalloyed selfishness; thus film title *I'm All Right, Jack*, 1958 (cf: fubis).

fuckarse n. general term of contempt (cf: fuckhead, fuckwit).

fuckdust n. general term of abuse (cf: fuckarse).

fucked a. 1. ruined, spoilt; 2. unhappy, wretched.

fucked off phr. annoyed, furious (cf: hacked off, pissed off, ticked off).

fucked up a. 1. (drug use) extremely stoned (qv); 2. (US milit. use) wounded or killed *Del Vecchio*.

fucked up and far from home in an utterly awful situation, miserable and lonely.

fucker n. 1. one who fucks; 2. general term of abuse, e.g. 'You stupid fucker!'; 3. a man, a fellow, with no particular abuse intended (cf: bugger n. 2.).

fuckfaced a. blear-eyed, half-awake *Price:2*.

fuck-film n. a pornographic film; (cf: skin-flick).

fuckhead n. idiot, moron, fool, etc. *Bruce:2*.

fucking a. adj. form of fuck (qv).

fucking A/fuckin' A excellent, first rate *Price:3*.

fucking ada! exclamation, usu. implying disbelief, displeasure *Dury, 'Laughter'*.

fucking off wasting time, idling, lazing about *Seale*.

fuck-knuckle n. (Aus. use.) a fool, an incompetent.

fuckpig n. general term of derision; the implication is of grubbiness.

fuckpump n. a married man.

fuckstick n. the penis *D Atyeo*.

fuckup n. a failure, a loser.

fuckwit n. general term of derision; the implication is of stupidity.

fucky a. nubile, ostensibly sexually enthusiastic; usu. of a female.

fuck-your-buddy week n. phr. a moment or act of betrayal; usu. as 'it's fuck-your-buddy...': *T J Williams The Glory Hole (1977)*.

fuddy-duddy n. fussy, pernickety, narrow-minded person, often with assumption of their being old *Southern & Hoffenberg*.

fudge! usu. 'oh fudge!': euph. for fuck (qv) (cf: sugar) *Rawson*.

fudge-packer n. (derog.) a homosexual male (cf: mud-packer).

fug v. (euph.) fuck (qv); coined by N. Mailer in *The Naked and the Dead*, 1949.

full a. drunk *Wilkes*.

full as a . . . boot, bull, fiddler, goat, googy egg, goose, lord, tick; a variety of similes to describe the state of extreme drunkenness.

full as a fairy's phone book a. (Aus. use) (poss. one-off for 'Sir Les Patterson'): extremely drunk; thus also *full as a state school hat rack, full as two race trains, full as a seaside shithouse on Boxing Day Humphries:2*.

full as an egg a. very drunk *Franklyn*.

full as the family po a. (Aus. use) extremely drunk *Wilkes*.

full bird n. (US milit. use) a full Colonel *Higgins:5*.

full buf n. (Valley Girls (qv) use) dressed up in one's finery, 'dressed to kill' *Pond*.

full feather n. 1. one's best clothes (cf: full buf); 2. in top condition.

full house both syphillis and gonorrhoea *Powis*.

full moon n. (as used by women) menstruation.

full of beans enthusiastic, excited, cheerful *Wodehouse:AAG*.

full of it (euph) full of shit (qv) *Gruber*.

full of piss and vinegar healthy in mind and body, full of energy and elan.

full of shit lying, spinning a line, telling tales, a generally unpleasant person or experience.

full scream (US Black use) total commitment; no holds barred *Klein*.

full sheet n. (UK prison use) a report against an officer for a serious offence against a prisoner *LL*.

full to the gills a. drunk *Dickson*.

full tour n. (US teen. use) a tedious experience (cf: three-hour tour) *Sculatti*.

full two bob n. (Aus. use) worthwhile, as good as advertised *Humphries*.

FUMTU acro. fucked up more than usual (cf: snafu).

fun v. to joke with, to tease *Morgan*.

funbag n. a woman, with an assumption of sexual availability.

funch n. sexual liasons at lunchtime, fr. fuck (qv) + lunch; the trad. genteel term is *matinee* (cf: nooner) *Rawson*.

fungus n. see: face-fungus *Norman:2*.

funk n. cowardice, terror; thus *to funk it*: to avoid an issue or an act through fear *McFadden*.

funker n. a weakling, a coward *Barr*.

funky a. (Black use) refers to 1. sweat generated during sex; 2. the odour of the female genitals; 3. anything basic, elemental, earthy (cf: fonky) *Milner*.

funnies n. (abbrev.) funny papers = comic strips in daily/weekly newspapers *Dunne*.

funny a. 1. tipsy, slightly drunk; 2. homosexual, effeminate (cf: funny man).

funny farm n. a mental hospital *Napoleon XIV*, 'They're Coming To Take Me Away, Ha! Ha!', 1966.

funny man n. (US Black use) a homosexual male *Klein*.

funny money n. (criminal use) counterfeit money.

funny pages n. those pages which newspapers reserve for comic strips *PT*.

funny papers n. (US milit. use) topographical maps (cf: comics) *Del Vecchio*.

funny peculiar or funny ha-ha? (cp) asking the speaker whether 'funny' means odd or amusing *Manser*.

funt n. fr. Yiddish: one pound sterling.

fur n. the vagina (cf: beaver, pussy) *Underwood*.

furburger n. the vagina, esp. during the act of cunnilingus since then it is 'eaten' (qv) *Humphries*.

furphy n. (Aus. use) a groundless rumour; fr. one Furphy, the proprietor of sanitary carts used by the Australian forces in the First World War; the gossip and chat around these carts developed into the general word (cf: scuttlebutt) *Humphries:2*.

furry hoop n. vagina *Humphries*.

fuss v. to quarrel, to pick a fight.
fuss up v. to agitate, to annoy, to irritate, to disturb.
fussbudget n. **1.** a particularly fussy person (cf: fuss-pot); **2.** a bad-tempered person; also as fuss-bug, fuss-butt, fuss-button, fuzz-button, fuzzy-dud.
fusspot n. a notably fussy person (cf: fussbudget).
futy n. the vagina *Maledicta*.
futz n. **1.** spec: the vagina; **2.** euph: fuck (qv) *Rosten*.

futz (around) v.i., v.t. to waste time, to mess around, to trifle with. (fr. Ger. *furzen*: to fart or Yiddish *arumfartzen zikh*: to fart around; the term is also a euph. for fuck around).
fuzz n. policeman; poss. fr. fuss, since a detective makes a 'fuss' over criminality *Grogan*.
fuzz-brained a. stupid.
fuzzburger n. see: furburger *Simmons*.
fuzzy cup n. (US Black use) the vagina *Klein*.

G

G n. **1.** (abbrev.) grand = thousand (usu. dollars or pounds) (cf: K, C) *Runyon*; **2.** (drug use) one grain, usu. of morphine *Burroughs:1*; one gram, usually of heroin or cocaine; **3.** (US Black use) (abbr.) gangster (cf: OG) *Dre*.
g n. (US Black use) (abbrev.) goodies: the female genitals; the vagina *Folb*.
g a. (US teen. use) (abbrev.) gross (qv) *Pond*.
gab v. to talk; fr. 18th C. Scottish *gab* = mouth *Caserta*.
gab-box n. the mouth (cf: gab).
gabby a. talkative *Runyon:1*.
Gabriel n. (UK prison use) the chapel organist; fr. his angelic namesake *LL*.
gabriel n. (music use) a trumpet player; fr. the archangel who announces the 'last trump' *Major*.
gadgy n. (gay use) a rent boy's client; fr. Romany 'gorgio' = a non-Gypsy male, and thus a 'straight' (qv) in the sexual context (cf: john, trick) *Maledicta 9*.
gaff a. excellent, simple; fr. gaffer 1 *Higgins:3*.
gaff n. **1.** a gimmick, a hidden trick; fr. Fr. *gaffe*: a social error *Bruce:2*; **2.** house, home. orig. a fair, then a cheap music-hall or theatre *Performance*.

gaffer n. **1.** the boss; **2.** spec. the manager of a circus; thus **3.** the 'straight' front man for any form of fraud or marginal business. *Higgins:3*.
gaffle v. to snatch, to round up; poss. fr. 'gaff' as in landing a fish *Morgan*.
gag v. **1.** to make a joke; fr. 'choking' with laughter **2.** to choke *Price:2*.
gag me with a spoon! (Valley Girls (qv) use) an expression of disgust *Harpers/Queen 1/83*.
ga-ga n. **1.** inexperienced, immature homosexual; **2.** homosexual foreplay *Legman*.
gaga a. crazy, eccentric *Higgins: 5*.
gage n. see: gauge *Southern*.
galah n. (Aus. use) a fool, fr. the rose-breasted grey backed Aus. cockatoo 'much given to chatter' *Humphries*.
galah session n. (Aus. use) an interval set aside regularly on the Flying Doctor radio network for anyone who wishes to exchange news and gossip rather than make emergency calls; fr. the 'chattering' galah (qv) *Wilkes*.
Galilee stompers n. (gay use) sandals (as worn by Jesus Christ).
gallon head n. (US Black use) **1.** a person with a large head; thus, traditionally **2.** an intelligent person *Klein*.

gal's at the stockyards phr. a woman is menstruating.

gam n. leg, usu. female; fr. Fr. *jambe*: leg *Runyon:1*.

gam v. 1. to fellate, fr. *gamahuche* (mainly 19th C.) *Keyes*; 2. (US Black use) to boast, to show off; fr. 18/ 19th C. *gammon*: to tell tall tales, to hoax, to flatter insincerely *Major*.

Game n. (abbrev.) pussy game: prostitution *Milner*.

game n. (US Black use) any means whereby one attempts to gain economic, psychological or other advantages over a rival or victim *Shulman*.

game v. any attempt to manipulate humanity for one's own ends, usually financial ones; to trick, to deceive *Milner*.

game room n. (S&M (qv) use) a torture chamber (cf: toys).

gammy a. lame, crippled; as in 'gammy leg', etc.

gander n. a look, a survey; fr. the bird's long neck *Runyon*.

gander-gut n. one who is thin and awkward; similar are 'gander-legged', 'gander-shanked'.

gang-bang n. 1. multiple rape of a woman *Price:2*; 2. (US Black use) a fight *Folb*.

gangbanger n. (US use) member of a teenage gang. *Ice T:3*.

gang-shag n. 1. (white use) see: gang-bang; 2. (US Black use) a riotous, noisy party *Major*.

gangster v. (US cant) to take by force.

gangster n. (US Black use) 1. marijuana; 2. a troublemaker; 3. an aggressive, abusive person *Folb*.

gangster doors n. (US Black use) a four-door saloon *Folb*.

gangster ride n. (US Black use) an old-fashioned, large, poss. black car *Folb*.

gangster walls n. (US Black use) white-walled tyres *Folb*.

ganja n. aka: *ganga, gunja*: marijuana, spec. that grown in Jamaica *Green:1*.

gannet n. a glutton, a heavy eater; fr. the bird, orig. nautical use *LL*.

gansta n. (orig. US Black use) (cf: G., gangbanger, O.G.) 1. the 'outlaw' lifestyle paraded by black youths in ghettos of the US and, latterly, the UK; thus: gangstarap, the music that originates in and epitomises this lifetyle, typically focussing on drugs, sex and guns.

gaol break n. (film use) time off from shooting for a meal break *Chandler: Notebk*.

gaolbait n. a girl under the age of consent, with whom intercourse, even when mutually desired could legally lead to imprisonment for statutory rape *Norman:2*.

gaolbird n. a convict, or a former prison inmate *Price:3*.

gaolhouse lawyer n. (US/UK prison use) any inmate who has used his incarceration to study law, both for his own use and to advise other prisoners. Can also be used in derog. sense to imply amateurishness and interference.

gape n. (US Black use) anyone who is not part of the hip subculture and who thus 'gapes' in wonder/horror at its antics *Klein*.

garbage n. nonsense *Jay & Young*.

garbage mouth n. a regular, even obsessive user of obscenity/profanity *Underwood*.

garbage wagon n. a motorcycle that still retains its basic style and specifications, prior to being adapted to outlaw motorcycle gang use (cf: chopper) *Thompson*.

garbo n. 1. (film use) a snobbish, standoffish person; fr. the actress Greta Garbo (1905–) whose most famous (if mythical) line declared 'I want to be alone' *Chandler: Notebk*; 2. (Aus. use) garbage man, dustbin man *Humphries:2*.

garbroth n. any poor or worthless; often in phr. 'mean as garbroth', 'poor as garbroth' (lit. broth made from the gar(fish), generally seen as the food of the very poorest and as such not properly fit for human consumption).

garden n. (homosexual use) pubic hair (cf: grass, lawn) *Maledicta*.

garden gate n. 1. (rhyming sl.) magistrate *Jones:J*; 2. (bingo rhyming sl.) 8 (cf: Harry Tate).

garden house n. an outside lavatory, a privy.

garden of Eden n. (US Black use) the vagina *Klein*.

gardening (cricket use) for the batsman to pat down supposed imperfections in the grass around his crease so as to ensure that the ball cannot take an awkward bounce *BBC Radio 3 1983*.

gargle n. a drink.

garmouth v. to boast, to brag, to make empty threats (fr. SE gar: a fish that is generally considered not worth eating other than in the direst extremity).

gas n. (US Black use) a processed haircut.

gas n. 1. (US campus use) idle or boastful talk *AS 50 (1965)*; 2. a good time, plenty of fun; usu. Irish use, esp. in 'a great gas'.

gas v: 1. to enjoy, to have a good time *Folb*; 2. to chatter, to talk inconsequentially and continually; to offer only 'hot air' *May*.

gas and run v. to have one's car filled by a garage attendant, then drive off before he can obtain your money in payment *Whitcomb*.

gas-guzzler n. the traditionally enormous US automobile, profligate of petrol and dwarfing its European rivals; symbolic of the 1950s, out of favour in the energy-conscious '70s, but currently staging a renaissance (cf: boat).

gash a. spare *LL*.

gash n. 1. spec. vagina; 2. any girl or woman *Higgins:1*.

gash-eater v. one who performs cunnilingus *Legman*.

gassed a. drunk *Schulberg*.

gassy a. talkative.

gat n. a pistol or revolver; poss. fr. Gatling gun (?) *Sharpe:1*.

Gate n. (abbrev.) Notting Hill Gate,

London W11.

gate fever n. (UK prison use) the nervous feeling that overtakes many prisoners as their sentence draws to its close *Cole*.

gate, give one the v. to throw out, to reject, to dismiss

gatemouth n. (US Black use) a gossip, a loudmouth *Major*.

gauge n. a shotgun (fr. abbr. twelve gauge).

gauge n. (drug use) marijuana *Green:1*.

gaum, gaumhead n. a fool, a clumsy oaf (fr. dial. gaum: to stare vacantly); thus gaumy a. stupid, clumsy.

gawd n. (mispron./euph.) God.

gawdelpus n. an irritating or helpless person; often used of a child: 'you 'orrible little gawdelpus!'; fr. 'God help us'; unstated is 'what shall we do about you?'

gawp v. to stare *Algren*.

gay a. homosexual; (with the decline of derog. terms, such as queer, gay is nearly SE) *Stanley*.

gay and frisky n. (rhyming sl.) whisky *Cole*.

gayola n. (US cant) payoffs and bribes made to police to permit running of gay clubs fr. payola (qv) *Neaman & Silver*.

gazlon n. (UK criminal use) a small time, poss. timid thief, fr. Yiddish *gozlin*: a swindler, an unethical person *Powis*.

gazooney n. see: gonsil *Legman*.

gazoopie n. aka: *gazupie*: a sex show *Legman*.

gazump v. (usu. estate agent use) to accept a stated price for one's property and then to raise that price, using as a threat, a supposed, but usu. non-existent 'offer' from elsewhere; alternatively the seller accepts one price and then, tempted by a genuinely greater offer, dumps the first buyer without sorrow or ceremony (cf: gessump).

gazungas n. breasts *Neaman & Silver*.

GB (abbrev.) goofball (qv) *Major*.

GBH n. (drug use) GHB or gamma hydroxybutyrate (a pun on legal j.

GBH: grievous bodily harm; developed in the US as an anaesthetic it was picked up by body-builders as a growth-hormone stimulant; its pleasurable side-effects brought it into recreational drug use, but these too have led to its being banned).

GBH (UK police/criminal use) (abbrev.) *G*rievous *B*odily *H*arm *LL*.

gd (abbrev./euph.) god *d*amned *Bukowski:1*.

gear a. excellent, wonderful, just right; fr. 'that's the gear': that's the stuff, and at peak popularity one of the Beatles' supposed favourite words; currently used somewhat ironically (cf: fab).

gear n. **1.** spec. drugs; **2.** a given object or objects, things *Performance*.

gear up v. to prepare oneself mentally and physically for dealing with the day; fr. motor car use *White*.

geared a. (US criminal use) sexually aberrant *Legman*.

gee v. (US Black use) to have sexual intercourse; poss. fr. gee up, thus ride taken in a sexual sense *Klein*.

gee man n. (Aus. use) one who 'gees up' the potential customers into a sideshow, strip club, etc. (cf: amster) *Baker*.

gee up v. to provoke trouble deliberately, to tease maliciously *LL*.

gee willikins! mild, euphemistic excl.; usu. US juv. use.

geechie a. (US Black use) unintellibible; fr. *geechie* the creole spoken by the inhabitants of the South Sea Is. off Georgia: gullah *Folb*.

gee-gees n. horses, esp. those on racecourses; thus *play the gee-gees*: to gamble on horseraces.

geek n. **1.** a carnival freak who specialized in biting the heads off live chickens *SF Comics*; **2.** (Valley Girls (qv) use) a vulgar lower class youth, fr. carnival use (qv) *Harpers/Queen 1983*; **3.** a generally unpleasant person, irrelevant of class. *Teenage Mutant Ninja Turtles passim*.

geek v. (Aus. use) to stare at, to look at (cf: gig) *Ready*.

geepie n. (pron. with hard 'g') a youthful hipster (cf: teenybopper) *Sculatti*.

geese n. (derog.) Jews *Runyon*.

geetoh n. GTO, a motor car *Higgins:1*.

geetus n. **1.** money; **2.** power; also as geedus, geetas, geetis, geets.

geewillies n. see: willies *Morgan*.

geeze v. to inject narcotics; thus *geezed*: under the influence of narcotics; *geezer*: an injection of narcotics, the equipment with which one injects *Grogan*.

geezer n. a man. fr. 19th-C. dialect *Performance*.

gelt n. fr. Yiddish: money; fr. Ger: gold *Norman:2*.

gen n. information, facts; fr. RAF 'general information' *Humphries*.

gendarmes n. fr. Fr: policemen *Runyon:1*.

gender-bender n. synonym for transvestism or transexuality, bending or eroding the line between the two sexes; the term was popularized during the rise to fame of the pop star Boy George, whose outrageous clothes and ostentatious make-up managed to disturb many observers. *Observer 30/12/84*.

generic n. (derog.) a Black person (cf: off-brand) (fr. SE generic: not marked with the producer's brand-name, and available at a lower price because of plain, cheap packaging).

George n. (air crew use) the automatic pilot in milit. and civil aircraft. Fr. Second World War cp: 'let George do it I can't be bothered' *Green:2*.

George called phr. indicating that a woman is menstruating.

George Washington n. a one dollar bill (cf: Abraham Lincoln, portrait of Madison).

georgia v. see: georgy *Major*.

georgy v. (US Black use) **1.** to trick or take advantage of a victim by using a variety of sexual lures; **2.** to hire a prostitute and then leave without paying *Himes:2*.

geri n. (abbrev.) geriatric, a derog.

term for the old (and middle-aged) (cf: wrinklies).

german bands n. (rhyming sl.) hands *Jones:J*.

German helmet n. (gay use) the glans penis.

German marching pills n. (gay use) amphetamines, esp. methedrine (a German invention).

German silver n. anything that is sham, fake.

gertcha! fr. get along with you *Capital Radio 1983*.

gessump v. (UK prison use) to acquire anything by fraud or a confidence trick; (cf: gazump) *LL*.

gestaps n. (US Black use) the police; fr. *geheime staatspolizei*, the Gestapo, the internal police force used by the German Nazi regime 1933–45 *Folb*.

get! (excl.) go away! *Goulart*.

get n. 1. idiot, fool, poss. fr. *get*: child (one of his begetting) *Bleasdale*; 2. the profit, the take, the booty of a robbery.

get v. as in *get yours*, *get theirs*, etc., to die, usu. by accident or through violence *Wolfe:5*.

get a bang out of v. to enjoy, to derive pleasure from, to get a thrill.

get a bee in one's bonnet v. to become obsessed by a given topic; also *have a bee . . .*

get a capture v. (UK cant) to be arrested *Norman:1*.

get a fourpenny one v. to suffer physical harm, to be beaten up, spec. hit in the face.

get a glow on v. to get drunk; fr. the reddening of some drinkers' faces *Dickson*.

get a guernsey v. (Aus. use) to gain approval, to do well; fr. the award of one's team 'guernsey' (like the UK 'get one's colours', 'get one's cap') that marks one's selection to a given team *Wilkes*.

get a hair up one's ass v. to be in a bad temper *Price:3*.

get a haircut v. (US Black use) to be cheated, robbed or in some way made to suffer by a woman *Major*.

get a hump on v. to hurry, to exert oneself (cf: bust one's hump).

get a jag on v. to get drunk *Dickson*.

get a kick out of v. to enjoy, to appreciate (cf: kick) *Bruce:2*.

get a line on v. to understand (cf: line) *PT*.

get a load of v. to notice, to look at deliberately; usu. in a sexual context, 'get a load of that!', and used betw. males *Manser*.

get a load on v. to become drunk *Schulberg*.

get a shot of leg v. (US Black use) to have sexual intercourse *Folb*.

get a snootful v. to be drunk (cf: snoot) *Dickson*.

get across v. 1. to irritate, to annoy; (US Black use) 2. to succeed; 3. to seduce; 4. to acquire status; *Folb*.

get along with you! (excl.) implying general disbelief of the previous speaker *Manser*.

get an earful v. listen to *Capital Radio 1983*.

get an edge on v. to drink steadily, not to outright drunkenness, but to preserve a feeling of general inebriation *Higgins:5*.

get away with murder v. to flout all proprieties with absolute success; to achieve the otherwise unacceptable *Higgins:4*.

get away (with you)! (excl.) don't try to fool me; don't tell lies, don't make me laugh, etc.; fr. SE meaning of physical movement *Breslin*.

get behind v. 1. to make a commitment to an idea, a job, a person, etc. *Milner*; 2. to understand; fr. hippie/drug use of 1960s *McFadden*.

get Chinese v. (US campus use) to succumb heavily to a given drug, usu. marijuana; the inference is the deviousness of the Chinese stereotype, rather than the presence of opium. *Bernbach*.

get clear v. to work out a given situation to its logical conclusion; fr. Scientology *clear*: the ultimate state of those who subject themselves to a scientology course *McFadden*.

get cold feet v. to become scared, to back down on a previous promise or statement; the cold comes when one 'tests the water' of a situation and finds it chilly *Higgins:1*.

get cracking v. to start work, to get on with anything speedily and efficiently; fr. cracking a whip over one's team of horses *Humphries*.

get down v. (US Black use) 1. to concentrate; 2. to commit oneself; 3. to do something especially well; 4. as an excl.; this is popular when shouted between the lines of a disco record *Folb*.

get down dirty v. (US Black use) to become abusive, to cause trouble *Folb*.

get down fonky v. see: get down dirty *Folb*.

get down from the Y v. (US Black use) to fight *Folb*.

get down shitty v. see: get down dirty *Folb*.

get down with v. (US Black use) to become involved with; to enjoy *Folb*.

get gay with v. to tease, to provoke, to be flippant *Chandler:LG*.

get her! excl. of derision, mockery (both affectionate and otherwise); orig. homosexual use, 'her' being someone acting exceptionally affectedly, but now general use *Thames TV 1984*.

get high behind v. 1. to hurry up, to get off to work; 2. to become impatient, to get angry.

get his v. to die, usu. violently; poss. abbrev. 'get his deserts'.

get home with the milk v. to stay out all night and return only at dawn.

get hot under the collar v. to become increasingly ill-tempered *Neaman & Silver*.

get in bad (with) v. to earn disfavour, to get into trouble.

get in deep v. to become heavily involved; usu. in either crime or love 'The Stone Killer', film, 1973.

get in line v. to conform.

get in one's eye v. (US Black use) to

beat up *Folb*.

get in one's hair v. to annoy, to irritate; the image is of lice.

get in the buggy v. to comply with requirements, to act as ordered (cf: stay on the wagon).

get in the collar v. to start working, to work hard; thus also 'fill one's collar', 'go up against the collar'.

get into v. to penetrate either the vagina or anus *Legman*.

get into v.t. to become involved in something.

get into one's pants v. to seduce *Bukowski:1*.

get into one's ribs v. to borrow money; one's wallet is carried in a pocket near the ribs *Wodehouse:PGM*.

get it? do you understand? esp. referring to the point of a joke *T 1983*.

get it in the neck v. 1. to be killed; 2. to be punished severely; to suffer badly.

get it off one's chest v. to confess, to unburden oneself *Wodehouse:AAG*.

get it on v. to take positive action *Greenlee*.

get it on (with) v. to have sexual intercourse *McFadden*.

get it to the T v. succeed absolutely and perfectly *The Who, 'Quadrophenia', 1973*.

get it together v. 1. to start a sexual relationship; 2. to make a decision, to take action; 3. to pull oneself together, to stop vacillating, etc.

get it up v. 1. to achieve erection; thus, 2. to maintain enthusiasm for a given idea, situation etc. (cf: hard-on for) *Higgins:5*.

get jack of v. (Aus. use) to resent, to be bored, with, fed up with *Humphries:2*.

get knotted! (excl.) go away, stop bothering (me); euph., get fucked *Manser*.

get loose v. to relax (cf: hang loose).

get lost! fr. Yiddish *ver farvalgert*: disappear, move on, go away *Rosten*.

get low v. (US campus use) to smoke marijuana; a reverse pun on usu. 'get high' (qv) *Bernbach*.

get more ass than a toilet seat to have an extensive and varied sex life *'The Deer Hunter', dir. M. Cimino, 1979*.

get next to (US Black use) to become lovers, to seduce *Capital Radio 1984*.

get off v. (drug use) to experience the effects of a given drug; fr. 'taking off' and getting 'high' (qqv) *Larner*.

get off on v. to enjoy *McFadden*.

get off one's back v. to stop annoying someone; to stop nagging or otherwise irritating *Big Ass Comics 1*.

get off one's case v. to desist from harassing, to stop annoying *McFadden*.

get off with v. to seduce, to pick up and poss. go to bed with.

get on v.t. (US Black use) to pursue a given goal, aim *Klein*.

get on one's tits v. to irritate, to annoy *Bleasdale*.

get on one's wick v. to irritate, to annoy; fr. rhyming sl., Hampton Wick = prick = penis (qv) *Neaman & Silver*.

get one at it v. to tease, to drive into a fury *Norman:1*.

get one going v. 1. to drive someone into a temper, to make one lose control through teasing; 2. to drink heavily; 'one' = a drinking session *Dickson*.

get (one) wet v. (NZ) to gain an advantage over someone.

get one's act together v. to calm down; to plan sensibly, to state a goal and aim for it *McFadden*.

get one's ashes hauled v. to have sexual intercourse; ashes a mispron. of ass (?) *Keyes*.

get one's ass in a sling v. to get into bad trouble, physical or otherwise *Higgins:4*.

get one's ass in gear v. to hurry up, to stop wasting time, to put some effort and commitment into one's activities, to start doing something useful and positive (cf: get one's act together) *Uris*.

get one's back v. to look after, lit., to

see that nobody is attacking from behind. *Dre*.

get one's back up v. to annoy, irritate, infuriate; fr. the feline habit of bristling the fur when annoyed or frightened *Sillitoe*.

get one's bowels in an uproar v. to become excited, agitated *Schulberg:2*.

get one's cards v. to be dismissed from work; the cards in question are Insurance Cards, P45 forms, etc.; thus to *give one one's cards*: to dismiss *LL*.

get one's collar felt v. (UK criminal use) to be arrested *LL*.

get one's cookies v. to have sexual intercourse *Higgins:2*.

get one's dander up v. to lose one's temper; poss. fr. Romany *dander*: to bite *Neaman & Silver*.

get one's end away v. to have sexual intercourse *Humphries*.

get one's end in v. see: get one's end away *Wilkes*.

get one's feet muddy v. to have been in criminal trouble *Powis*.

get one's feet under the table v. to establish friendly relations; of a man, to start living with a woman.

get one's finger out v. to stop dawdling and lazing about and begin some constructive activity *Waterhouse*.

get one's goat v. to annoy someone; fr. the goat's propensity to butt when in a bad temper (?) *Neaman & Silver*.

get one's greens v. to have sexual intercourse; poss. fr. obs. *garden*: female genitals (cf: garden of Eden) *Rawson*.

get one's gun off v. to reach orgasm *Pearce*.

get one's head down v. to have some sleep *Newman:2*.

get one's head together v. to sort oneself out; to calm down *Wilkinson*.

get one's hooks on v. to grasp, to grab, to obtain; esp. when the object is most desired or currently held by a rival. (cf: hooks) *Wodehouse:GB*.

get one's jollies v. to enjoy oneself; to have sex *Goldman*.

get one's knickers in a twist v. to

become excessively agitated over a problem or situation, to worry to extremes.

get one's leg over v. to seduce *May*.

get one's nose cold v. (drug use) to sniff cocaine, which has a numbing quality, esp. if, as more than likely, it has been adulterated with procaine or novocaine.

get one's nuts off v. to achieve orgasm, poss. through masturbation *Southern & Hoffenberg*.

get one's oats v. to gain sexual release.

get one's pratt v. to irritate, to tease.

get one's respect v. (US Black use) to ensure that one is treated in the manner to which one feels one should be accustomed, esp. in prison *Klein*.

get one's rocks off v. 1. to enjoy oneself; 2. to have sexual intercourse *Higgins:1*.

get one's shit together v. see: get one's act together *Jay & Young*.

get one's shoes full v. to become drunk *Dickson*.

get one's skates on v. to hurry up, to stop wasting time.

get one's tail-feathers up v. to get annoyed, to lose one's temper (cf: lower one's feathers).

get one's thing off v. (US Black use) to gain pleasure from any given act *Klein*.

get one's wings v. 1. (drug use) to start using heroin *Grogan*; 2. (Hells Angels use) to be initiated into an outlaw motor cycle club (cf: red wings, brown wings) *Thompson*.

get over v. (US Black use) to achieve a given goal *Klein*.

get rooted! (Aus. use) excl. of strong protest; euph. Fuck off! get fucked! *Baker*.

get shot of v. aka: *get shut of* to get rid of something/someone *Sillitoe*.

get smart v. act in an arrogant manner, usu. as 'Don't get smart with me' *Welsh:1*.

get some v. to have sexual intercourse; thus: *getting any? Higgins:1*.

get some big leg v. aka: *get some cock, get some pussy, get some tail, get some soft leg*: to have sexual intercourse *Folb*.

get some brown v. aka: *to get some brown sugar; get some duke*: have male homosexual intercourse *Folb*.

get some cold comfort v. (necrophile use) to have sexual relations with a corpse.

get some ink v. to receive newspaper/magazine coverage for one's actions, speech, etc. *Higgins:5*.

get straight v. (US campus use) to sober up, either from drink or drugs *Underwood*.

get stuck into v. 1. to start a fight; 2. to start any form of activity; the implication is one of enthusiasm and activity.

get stuffed! (excl.) euph. for get fucked! *Manser*.

get stupid v. (US teen use) to attend a party *T 8/4/91*.

get the ass v. (US campus use) to lose one's temper; to become annoyed (cf: get the red ass) *Underwood*.

get the bass out of one's voice v. (US prison use) to stop acting aggressively.

get the bird v. to be jeered, mocked, etc.; esp. theatrical use and dating back to 16th C.; fr. the hissing noise that geese, and an unappreciative audience can make.

get the Book v. (UK prison use) 1. to become religious while serving one's sentence; 2. for a Prison Officer to be disciplined for internal offences, usu. suspended pending an inquiry *LL*.

get the boot v. to be thrown out; both of a place or of employment (cf: get the chop).

get the bullet v. see: get the boot, get the chop, etc.

get the bum's rush to be thrown out.

get the chop v. 1. to be dismissed from one's job; 2. to be killed.

get the drawers v. (US Black) to have sexual intercourse.

get the drop on v. to obtain an (unfair) advantage over someone fr.

drop = knock down (qv).

get the fat off v. (Aus. use) to relieve someone of their money, usu. by some form of trick or con-game *Humphries:2*.

get the fuck out!, get to fuck out! intensifier of 'go away' (cf: fuck off, v.).

get the glory v. (UK prison use) to become suddenly and fervently religious while serving one's sentence *LL*.

get the hell out of Dodge v. (US campus cp) to leave, to depart; 'if you don't want to stay here, then get the hell . . .' *Underwood*.

get the lead out! hurry up, stop dawdling, get on with it! *'Minder', Thames TV, 1983*.

get the message v. to appreciate, to understand; orig. jazz use, but now general.

get the needle v. to be extremely annoyed *Norman:2*.

get the order of the boot v. to be sacked from work; fr. Order of the Bath.

get the picture v. to understand, to appreciate.

get the red ass v. to bear a grievance *Jenkins*.

get the slingers v. to be thrown out, dismissed from a job *Norman:3*.

get the wind up v. to become nervous; fr. 'get the wind up one's trousers' *Wodehouse:GB*.

get them in v. to order a round of drinks; esp. as excl. get them in! *Waterhouse*.

get this! (excl.) now listen! this is amazing!, etc. *Capital Radio 1983*.

get to v. 1. corrupt, bribe, influence *Heller*; 2. to effect, to influence emotionally *McFadden*.

get to first base v. make some preliminary headway in seduction (cf: first base).

get tore in v. (Scottish use) to fight vigorously *G. MacDonald Fraser, 'McAuslan in the Rough', 1974*.

get under one's skin v. 1. to annoy, to irritate; 2. to fascinate, esp.

sexually; both meanings fr. insect infestation.

get up n. 1. (US prison use) the date of one's release given by a parole board, and thus the day on which one 'gets up' in prison but goes to bed free (cf: wake-up, n.) *Klein*; 2. lies, a ruse, a subterfuge; something 'got up' to allay suspicions/enquiries *Newman:1*.

get up and go n. (orig. US) energy, ambition, drive.

get up there v. to grow old.

get weaving v. to stop wasting time, to hurry up, etc. *Manser*.

get wet v. to murder, to kill (fr. espionage j. 'get wet': to kill).

get with v. to understand; to join in; to accept the majority line.

get-along n. a leg, esp. in phr. a hitch in one's get-along: a limp.

getting any? popular greeting between men; the 'any' in question is, of course, sex *BBC-1 TV 1983*.

getting off at Redfern (Aus. use) coitus interruptus; Redfern is the station immediately before Sydney Central (cf: getting out at Gateshead) *Wilkes*.

getting out at Gateshead coitus interruptus; spec. used by natives of Newcastle-upon-Tyne, Gateshead being the station previous to their own (cf: getting off at Redfern) *Wilkes*.

getting the mohawk (US teen. use) building up one's irritation into a genuine bad temper *Sculatti*.

gfu (milit. use) (acro.) general fuck-up (cf: snafu) *Rawson*.

ghetto blaster n. large stereo tape recorder plus radio carried by ghetto youths (cf: Third World briefcase, wog box) *Capital Radio 1984*.

ghetto star n. (US gang use) a leading gangster (cf: G, O.G.).

ghinny n. (derog.) Italian (cf: guinea) *Higgins:1*.

ghost v. (UK prison use) to move a prisoner from one gaol to another during the night, both departure and arrival taking place when the other prisoners are locked in their cells *Obs. 1981*.

ghosting (US milit. use) idling, avoiding duties (cf: Goldbrick) *Del Vecchio*.

GI haircut n. a very short hair cut, imported into civilian life by former soldiers.

gib teenuck n. (backsl.) (derog.) big cunt *Cole*.

gib teesurbs n. (backsl.) big breasts (of a passing female) *Cole*.

gift of the gab articulateness, charm, persuasiveness *Wright*.

gig n. **1.** spec. a musical performance at a given venue; **2.** a job. *Price:2*; **3.** (street gang use) an event, a party *Salisbury*; (Aus. use) **4.** a fool, an idiot *Ready*; **5.** a look, a glance *Wilkes*.

gig v. **1.** (Aus. use) to look at, to stare (as in obs. UK school sl: *giglamps*: spectacles) *Ready*; **2.** (music business use) to play at a given venue, to perform *May*; **3.** to cheat, to swindle; **4.** to irritate, to annoy.

giggle-house n. (Aus. use) mental hospital, lunatic asylum *Wilkes*.

gigo (acro.) garbage *in*, garbage *out*: cp implying that one cannot expect poor input to produce, by some magic, excellent output; fr. computer jargon.

gigolo v. (US Black use) to steal a friend's lover; to cheat on one's lover or partner *Folb*.

gimme cap n. a baseball cap carrying the logo of a sports team, manufacturer or other commercial institution. (fr. SE give me; the practise of emblazoning objects with a logo and offering them free in order to spread the brand's name began with cigarette papers which were given away free with the purchase of loose tobacco; buyers would demand 'Give me. . .' a pack of papers, a cap or whatever is on offer).

gimp n. courage, bravery, spirit, thus gimpy: brave, spirited.

gimp n. **1.** spec. a cripple; thus **2.** an incompetent, a useless person, a loser *Price:3*.

gimp v. (US campus use) to ruin, to spoil *Underwood*.

gimped in (US campus use)

irregularly shaped, dented *Underwood*.

gimped up (US campus use) confused, at a loss, mixed up *Underwood*.

gimpy a. **1.** crippled; **2.** botched, second rate *Underwood*.

gin v. (US Black use) **1.** to thrash, to beat; **2.** to fight, to scuffle.

gin and fuck-it n. a girl, usu. foreign au pair or tourist, who can allegedly be seduced for the price of a drink in certain pubs where such pick-ups congregate.

gin and Jaguar belt n. (UK criminal/police use) the wealthy Home Counties areas around London, esp. ripe for robbery *Powis*.

ginch n. **1.** vagina *Junker*; thus **2.** an attractive female *Wolfe: 2*.

ginchy a. attractive, sexy (cf: ginch 2).

ginger n. **1.** (rhyming sl.) ginger beer = queer = homosexual *Powis*; **2.** (Aus. use) a prostitute who robs her customer of his wallet (cf: murphy game) *Wilkes*.

gin-jockey n. (Aus. use) a white man who enjoys sexual relations with Aborigine women (cf: gin-shepherd) *Wilkes*.

gink n. a useless, stupid person *Wodehouse: passim*.

ginnal n. (Jamaican use) trickster, confidence man *Thelwell*.

ginney n. see: guinea *Dunne*.

ginormous a. incomparably huge; fr. RAF sl. great +*immense* + *enormous*.

gin-shepherd n. a white man who attempts to prevent miscegenation between his peers and Aborigine women (cf: gin-jockey) *Wilkes*.

ginzo n. (derog.) Italian (cf: guinea) *Higgins:1*.

gippy tummy n. see: gyppy tummy.

girl n. **1.** (drug use) cocaine (cf: boy) *Green:1*; **2.** (US Black use) general form of address between two women, neither of whom need, chronologically, to be a girl (cf: man).

girl's blouse n. see: big girl's blouse.

GIs n. diarrhoea/dysentery suffered by

US troops on foreign duties (cf: Delhi belly, Montezuma's revenge) *Rawson*.

gissa job! (cp) fr. dial., give me a job, used by character 'Yosser Hughes' in A. Bleasdale's 'Boys from the Blackstuff', 1982 *Bleasdale*.

gissum n. see: gizzum.

git n. see: get.

git-down time n. the start of a prostitute's working 'day', when she 'get's down to business' *Shulman*.

git-'em-up guy n. a hold-up man; a robber; fr. demand 'get your hands up!' *Runyon*.

git-go n. the beginning *Milner*.

gitty-gap n. (US campus use) a thing *Underwood*.

give! (excl.) explain! confess! *Rosten*.

give a blow v. to blow marijuana smoke directly from the cigarette into someone else's mouth, achieved by reversing the joint in one's own mouth and blowing (cf: shotgun) *Milner*.

give a body v. (UK police use) to inform, to betray the names of one's criminal associates; usu. as exhortation 'Go on, John, give us a body' (and we'll be kinder to you) *Cole*.

give a break v. to give a chance, to let off, to excuse, to give an opportunity.

give a damn v. to care.

give a flying fuck, couldn't v. couldn't care less *Price:2*.

give a leg-up v. to help someone over an obstacle, wall, etc.; both physical and figurative *Wodehouse:PGM*.

give a little leg v. to confuse, to tell tales *Higgins:2*.

give a shit v. to care, but also, not to care, ie: 'I could give a shit' (cf: give a damn) *Price:2*.

give a squeeze v. (UK cant) to give a chance (to) *Cole*.

give a stuff v. see: give a shit *Humphries*.

give a tumble v. to try out, to experiment *Powis*.

give bellows v. to get rid of, to send away.

give cone v. (Valley Girls (qv) use) to fellate; fr. licking an ice-cream cone

Pond.

give head v. to perform oral intercourse *Goldman*.

give (her) a length v. to make love to a woman.

give (her) one v. to have sexual intercourse.

give it a fly v. (Aus. use) see: give (something) a burl *Wilkes*.

give it a go v. make an attempt, give it a try *Capital Radio 1983*.

give it a whirl v. try something out.

give it all that v. to boast, to show off *Powis*.

give it the gun v. to accelerate, to drive a car fast *rr*.

give it the herbs v. (Aus. use) to accelerate a car *Wilkes*.

give it up (homosexual use) an aggressive demand from one male that another accept his advances, esp. in gaol *Klein*.

give it to v. (US criminal use) to murder, to execute *Bruce:2*.

give jiggs v. to keep a lookout; (abbrev.) *jiggers!* look out! run for it! *Farrell*.

give laldie, give laldy v. (Sc. use) to enjoy greatly, to peform enthusiastically *Welsh:1* (fr. dial laldy: to punish).

give one a bell v. to call on the telephone (cf: give one a buzz) *Humphries:2*.

give one a buzz v. to call someone on the telephone (cf: give a bell) *Wodehouse:AAG*.

give one a coating v. (UK police use) to give one a reprimand *Powis*.

give one a piece of one's mind v. to tell someone off severely *Neaman & Silver*.

give one a song and dance v. to tell fanciful tales for the purpose of confusing or tricking the listener *Chandler:LG*.

give one a tumble v. to go to bed with someone *Runyon:1*.

give one Larry Dooley v. (Aus. use) to beat someone, to punish *Wilkes*.

give one rocks v. to excite sexually, spec. to make a man have an erection

Bukowski:1.

give one some curry v. (Aus. use) 'to make things hot' for someone, to attack (verbally or physically) *Wilkes.*

give one some stick v. to encourage action by making threats.

give one the belt v. to get rid of, to throw out *Norman:2.*

give one the blacks v. to ignore, to cut, esp. when snubbing a former friend.

give one the brush v. to ignore, to snub; fr. *brush*: (abbrev.) brush off *Dunne.*

give one the bullet v. to dismiss from employment, to throw out *Norman:2.*

give one the business v. 1. to have sexual intercourse *Neaman & Silver*; 2. to tease, to taunt, to put at a disadvantage by one's own actions *Dunne.*

give one the chop 1. to kill or otherwise dispose of a person; 2. to fire from a job.

give one the creeps v. to worry, to perturb, to disgust *Price:2.*

give one the finger v. to make a manual gesture (the raised middle finger in the US, the 'V-sign' in the UK) to imply derision and disdain *McFadden.*

give (one) the foot v. to throw out, to oust, to reject (cf: give one the boot).

give one the glad eye v. to give someone of the opposite sex a glance that implies sexual attraction.

give one the highball v. to reject, to brush off, esp. to end a relationship or love affair.

give one the leather v. to kick a person *Runyon:1.*

give one the leg v. see: pull one's leg *Higgins:4.*

give one the office v. (UK prison use) to initiate a new prisoner into the rules and regulations, official and unofficial, of prison life *LL.*

give one the old boracic v. to deceive, to tell tales; prob. fr. Aus. *poke borak*: to hoax, to confuse the credulous; itself fr. barrack: to jeer.

give one the pink slip v. to hand

over, to cede ownership of something to another person; fr. the pink slip which in the US proves ownership of a given car *Wodehouse:AAG.*

give one the pip v. to irritate intensely *Wodehouse:AAG.*

give one the runaround v. to deceive, to delay, to put off, to avoid – all such efforts usu. in order to give oneself some form of advantage, breathing space, etc. *Thompson.*

give one what for v. to give someone a hard time, to tell off severely, to beat, esp. of an errant child.

give one's arse a chance v. derog. comment aimed at a talkative person; usu. prefaced by 'Why don't you shut up and. . .' *Powis.*

give one's best shot v. to make one's best efforts; often as 'give—one's best shot' *Whitcomb.*

give over! stop it! almost always northern UK use.

give props v. (US Black use) to applaud, to praise, to acknowledge as good.

give some body v. to accede to sexual advances *Klein.*

give some plank v. (US Black use) see: give some skin.

give some skin v. (US Black use) ritual palm slapping that forms greeting between Blacks or Black and knowledgeable white (cf: slap five).

give some spli v. (US Black use) see give some skin *Klein.*

give (something) a burl v. (Aus. use) to give it a try *Humphries.*

give the business v. 1. to kill *Rawson*; 2. to deceive, to bamboozle.

give the chop v. to destroy, to abandon, to stop, to cut off *Dunne.*

give the dog a bone v. to have sexual intercourse *Squeeze, 'Cool for Cats', 1983.*

give the drummer some v. see: give some skin *Major.*

give the duke v. to slow hand-clap as a sign of disapproval of a given sporting event; fr. duke=hand *Heller.*

give the eye v. to appraise sexually *Selby:1.*

give the finger v. to make a
derogatory gesture by raising the
middle finger in the direction of the
person targeted; the meaning is 'fuck
off' (cf: flip the bird).

give the green light v. to give
permission, to allow; fr. traffic lights/
railway signals *Wodehouse:AAG*.

give the gun v. to accelerate a motor
car.

give the heat v. to murder, to kill (cf:
heat) *Rawson*.

give the Man the play v. (US Black
use) to inform (cf: Man) *Folb*.

give the once-over v. to look over, to
assess *Price:3*.

give the rap v. to murder, to kill
Rawson.

give the works to v. 1. to harm; from
actual murder to mere beating up *rr*;
2. to make an effort in a given context,
whether selling an item, shooting a
line (qv), criticizing, etc.
Chandler:LG.

give them away with a pound of tea
ironic reply by criminal to questions
referring to the origins of obviously
stolen goods in his possession *Powis*.

give one's face v. to permit
oneself to indulge in oral intercourse
at the insistence of a partner *Klein*.

give up rhythm v. (US Black use) for
a woman, using body language, to
indicate her sexual availability to a
man with whom she is walking or
dancing *Shulman*.

give up the store v. to surrender, to
give in *PT*.

gizmo n. 1. (drug use) the
paraphanalia used for injecting
narcotics; 2. any (small) thing for
which one has temporarily forgotten
the correct name, a gadget, a
thingumijig *TZ*.

gizzum aka: *gissum*: semen *Price:1*.

glad eye n. a glance of sexual interest;
thus *give the glad eye*: to appraise
sexually (cf: hard eyes).

glad hand v. to welcome
enthusiastically, even excessively and
very likely insincerely; often used of
politicians and similar professional

charmers. fr. the outstretched hand of
greeting (cf: flesh-presser).

glad rags n. one's best and prob.
gaudiest clothes.

glads n. (Aus. use) (abbrev.) gladioli
Humphries:2.

glamour puss n. an ostentatiously
well-dressed, lavishly made-up, etc.
woman.

Glasgow kiss n. a head butt (cf:
Chelsea smile, Gorbals kiss).

glass n. (US criminal use) a diamond;
thus *genuine glass*: very high quality;
fake glass: worthless *Klein*.

glass jaw n. (boxing use) a
conspicuously weak jaw which breaks
or fractures when hit and loses its
possessor his fights *Dunne*.

glassed (UK criminal use) cut in the
face or body by a jab or slash from a
broken bottle *Powis*.

glasshouse n. prison, (esp. UK milit.
use) fr. glass-roofed North Camp
military prison at Aldershot
Wodehouse passim.

gleep a cage v. (US cant, motorcycle
gang use) to steal a car
Neaman & Silver.

glim n. a lantern; esp. a dark lantern
used by thieves *Norman:2*.

glimmer n. a beggar *Powis*.

glitterati n. those fashionable writers
and academics and sundry critics, etc.
who have transcended their usual
obscurity into the dubious limelight of
the New York and London gossip
columns *Safire*.

glitzy a. fashionable, sophisticated,
chic; glamorous + ritzy (qv) *T 8/9/83*.

globetrotter n. (drug use) a narcotics
addict who is continually on the move
Major.

glom v. aka: *glaum*: to grab, to steal
Chandler: Notebk.

glory hole n. 1. the vagina *Stanley*;
2. (homosexual use) a hole cut in the
side of a public toilet cubicle; one man
pushes his penis through while
another, anonymous, man fellates him
Jay & Young.

glossy n. (abbrev.) glossy magazine;
usu. expensive women's fashion

magazines – *Vogue*, *Harpers/Queen* (which has called itself 'the non-drip glossy, punning on both drip = weakling, dullard, and gloss paint), etc. a descendant of the earlier *slicks*.

glut n. (abbrev.) glutton (qv) *Legman*.

glutton n. (homosexual use) a man obsessed with sex to the exclusion of other considerations *Legman*.

glutton for punishment n. (homosexual use) a fellator who continues sucking the penis even when orgasm has been reached *Legman*.

G-man n. FBI agent, fr. Government-man *Runyon:1*.

GMBU (acro.) *G*rand *M*ilitary *B*alls-*U*p (cf: GMFU) *Mortimer*.

GMFU n. (UK 'society' use) *G*rand *M*ilitary *F*uck-*U*p (cf: GMBU) *Barr*.

gnarly a. (Valley Girls (qv) use) general term of disapproval, disappointment, annoyance *Pond*.

gnat's eyebrow n. something very small; also as gnat's balls, gnat's bristle, gnat's eye, gnat's heel, gnat's prick; esp. in phr. e.g. 'down to a gnat's eyebrow': to the finest detail; 'sharp enough to split the hair on a gnat's ass': extremely fine.

gnat's piss n. derog. description of any liquid, but esp. alcohol, that is weak, thin, tasteless, etc.

gnaw the 'nana to perform fellatio *Humphries*.

go v. to say, to talk; 'I go "How are you" and he just goes "Lousy". . .' *Pond*.

go a bundle on v. to support whole-heartedly. fr. the betting of one's whole 'bundle' (bank-roll).

go a million v. (Aus. use) to be utterly lost, in a totally hopeless position, at a total disadvantage *Wilkes*.

go ahead up v. (US Black use) to take part in some form of activity with another person *Folb*.

go all over town with v. see: around the world *Legman*.

go all the way v. a man who 'goes all the way' achieves satisfactory seduction; the woman who does so is willing to permit it *Rawson*.

go (and) jump in a lake! (euph.) go to hell! (qv) *Manser*.

go and see a man about a dog v. (cp) an excuse to facilitate one's leaving; often when needing to visit the lavatory.

go and take a running jump (at yourself) aka: *go and take a flying fuck*: epithet of dismissal and distaste.

go ape v. to lose control, esp. of one's temper *Selby:1*.

go around the block v. to gain experience 'Hill Street Blues', Thames TV, 1983.

go bananas v. 1. to lose emotional control, to become obsessed by *Morgan*; 2. to delight in something absolutely, usu. ≃ over *Underwood*.

go bark at the moon (excl.) go away! get lost! fuck off! *Simmons*.

go belly up v. (US use) to die; a dead fish floats belly up on the water *Neaman & Silver*.

go bent v. (UK police use) for a witness to retract a previous statement (that helps the prosecution) (cf: bent) *Laurie*.

go bent on v. to let down; to desert *Norman:2*.

go boil your head! (excl.) generally dismissive, euph. for go to hell! (qv).

go Borneo v. (US campus use) crazily drunk; fr. presumed antics of the 'Wild Man of Borneo' *Bernbach*.

go case v. to sleep with *Norman:1*.

go chase yourself! excl. (Aus.) go away!, euph. go to hell! (qv).

go cold on v. to lose one's initial enthusiasm for a proposition, activity, etc.

go crackers v. to go mad, become insane, eccentric.

go crawl back in your hole! hostile phr. used when requesting someone to be quiet (and go away).

go down v. 1. (US street gang use) to attack a rival gang *Salisbury*; 2. to happen, to take place *McFadden*.

go down in flames v. to fail to complete a task, despite one's best efforts *Safire*.

go down like a lead balloon v. to find

no favour whatsoever; usu. of an idea
or suggestion.

go down (on) v. to practise oral
intercourse, for either sex (cf. blow,
eat) *Higgins:2*.

go down on v. to cause someone
trouble, to harm someone *Stone*.

go down south v. see: go down (on)
Powis.

go down the drain v. see: go down
the plughole.

go down the plughole v. to be
wasted, to be lost for ever; like
bathwater.

go down the road v. to pursue a
given policy or course of action, even
if it proves unpleasant *PT*.

go down the tubes v. to fail badly; to
collapse completely.

go fish v. (homosexual use) an
effeminate man, wishing to imply his
approximation of a woman during sex,
might claim 'I just go fish', ie: turn into
a girl (cf: fish) *Legman*.

go for v. 1. to accept, to believe
Higgins:1; 2. attack; 3 to find sexually
or otherwise attractive or appealing
Howard.

go for broke to commit oneself
unreservedly; esp. in gambling or
betting context (cf: shit or bust).

go for it! (US campus use) general
exhortation to those present, urging
them to act crazily, the intention being
thus to have extreme fun *Bernbach*.

go for one's tea v. to die *Powis*.

go for the doctor v. (Aus. racing use)
for one rider and his mount to move
significantly ahead of the field *Obs.
3/7/83*; 2. (Aus. use) in gambling, to
bet all one's money *Wilkes*.

go for the whole shot v. make an
absolute commitment; indulge oneself
completely *McFadden*.

go for veg v. (US campus use) to
become drunk *Underwood*.

go from the fists v. aka: *go from the
shoulders*, *go from the Y*: to fight.

go fuck a duck excl. of dismissal (cf:
go milk a duck!, go to hell!).

go halves v. to share, to divide
equally.

go hang v. 1. to go wrong, to collapse
(of a plan), to fail *PT*; 2. (euph.) go to
hell; thus 'tell him to go hang!'

go haywire v. to lose control, to go
mad; poss. fr. the baling wire used by
US farmers to mend implements that
have gone wrong *Bukowski:2*.

go Hollywood v. to sodomize; fr. the
cinematic capital, where it presumed
such excesses are quotidian pleasures
Neaman & Silver.

**go in and out like a fiddler's
elbow** v. phr. to copulate
enthusiastically and energetically.

go in the tank v. (boxing use) to lose a
fight deliberately; fr. tank =
swimming pool (cf: take a dive)
Dunne.

go in the water v. (boxing use) to lose
a fight deliberately; fr. take a dive (qv)
Dunne.

go into a flat spin v. to lose
perspective and orientation, to be
come very confused; fr. flying use.

go like a bat out of hell v. to move
exceptionally fast.

go like a bomb v. 1. to go very fast;
2. to work out very successfully (cf:
bomb).

go like hot cakes v. of a product or
commodity: to sell out quickly.

go like the clappers v. to run very
fast; rhyming euph. for go like hell:
clappers = bell, rhymes with hell.

go milk a duck! excl. of dismissal,
euph. for 'go fuck a duck'.

go nap on v. 1. (UK use) to commit
oneself fully; fr. gambling use: to bet
all one's assets, 2. (Aus. use) usu. in
negative sense: 'don't/doesn't/etc. go
nap. . .': to dislike, to avoid *Wilkes*.

go off v.t. to find a person or object
unappealing, distasteful, tedious. usu.
when one's feelings have been more
positive before *Griffith*.

go off half-cocked v. to talk foolishly,
esp. when under the influence of one's
emotions or of drink or drugs.

go off the boil v. 1. to lose impetus, to
lose enthusiasm; 2. to calm down
Wodehouse: AAG.

go off the deep end v. to lose control,

to become extremely angry, depressed, to show any extreme of emotion *Jay & Young*.

go off the rails v. to err, to make a mistake *Wodehouse: PGM*.

go on about v. to nag, to complain continually and habitually, to make a lengthy fuss.

go on, twist my arm (cp) a joking pretence that the speaker has to be persuaded into doing something that is in fact very appealing and will require no second thoughts on doing it.

go one-on-one v. to have a direct confrontation with another person.

go out poncing v. (UK police use) for vice squad officers actively to search the streets for working ponces *Laurie*.

go out with v. (UK police use) to share totally in a fellow officer's operations; the inference is that all the 'real' police work takes place out 'on the streets' *Laurie*.

go over the hill v. 1. (prison use) to escape; orig. escaping fr. outdoors work gangs, using hills as cover from one's pursuers *Neaman & Silver*; 2. to get married.

go overboard v. to commit oneself completely, often as 'go overboard for . . .' *'Serpico', directed S. Lumet, 1973*.

go phut v. to collapse; fr. noise a bursting balloon makes *Wodehouse: AAG*.

go round with v. to fight with *Jones*.

go spare v. to lose one's temper: to act crazily. *Norman: 2*.

go steady v. to maintain a regular relationship *The Beach Boys, 'I Get Around', 1964*.

go straight v. give up crime *Higgins: 2*.

go the big spit v. to vomit *Humphries*.

go the hang-out road v. to tell the complete truth; fr. 'let it all hang out' (qv) *PT*.

go the knuckle v. (Aus. use) to have a fist-fight *Wilkes*.

go the limit v.1. see: go for broke; 2. to have sexual intercourse *Rawson*.

go the whole shot v. see: go for broke.

go through changes v. to undergo alterations in one's emotional or mental state or attitudes; development of hippie/drug use of 1960s (cf: put through changes) *Major*.

go through like a dose of salts to go very fast, to move very quickly.

go through the card v. to cover comprehensively and completely; fr. betting use, to bet on every horse in a given race *Powis*.

go through the flint mill phr. to endure a series of problems, to suffer badly.

go to bat v. to take action, to involve oneself with a specific task or job, to take a stance; fr. baseball (or cricket in UK) use *Higgins: 4*.

go to blazes! excl. of dismissal, both of the person and his/her opinion or statement, fr. euph. of go to hell (qv) – where the fires of perdition burn.

go to buggery! general excl. of dismissal; syn. for go to hell (qv).

go to bye-byes v. (juvenile use) to go to sleep.

go to hell! general excl. (cf: go to blazes).

go to Mexico v. to become drunk; for US teenagers brief trips across the border usu. implied non-stop excess *Dickson*.

go to pieces v. to collapse emotionally.

go to sleep v. to die; perhaps the ultimate of such euphemisms, and equally popular when 'putting an animal to sleep' *Higgins: 1*.

go to the dogs v. to decline socially; to become rundown, dirty and turn into a tramp.

go to the pack v. (Aus. use) to decline – socially, economically, etc. (cf: go to the dogs) *Dennis*.

go to the races v. to die; fr. racing use (cf: throw up the cards, pegged out, etc.) *Rawson*.

go to town v. to make a great fuss, to concentrate on; fr. a rural sensibility that equates such efforts with urban life *Performance*.

go under one's neck v. (Aus. use) to usurp another's privileges; to stop someone else's intended actions *Wilkes*.

go under the house v. (Black use) to perform cunnilingus *Legman*.

go up v. (abbrev.) go up the river (qv) *Himes: 1*.

go up the old dirt road v. to practise sodomy *Legman*.

go up the river v. to go to gaol; fr. the Hudson River which leads to Sing-Sing, New York State's major prison.

go up the wall v. to lose one's temper (cf: climb the walls) *Green: 2*.

go upside one's head v. (US Black use) hit in the face, beat up *Folb*.

go way down South in Dixie v. (homosexual use) to perform ani- or cunnilingus *Legman*.

go west v. to die; to end, to collapse; for one's 'sun to set' *Weight*.

go with v. 1. to accept and act upon given plan or suggestion; 2. to have an affair/relationship with someone *White*.

go with the flow v. to accept a situation and make no attempt to alter it; to act passively. a mass popularization of therapist Carl Rogers' dictum on 'floating with a complex streaming of experience' which was not so simplistic *Price: 2*.

go-around, give one the v. (orig. US) to reject, to avoid, to jilt.

goat n. nickname for a GTO automobile *Morgan*.

goat roper n. a peasant, a rural person, an unsophisticated person.

gob n. mouth.

gob v. to spit *Wolfe:8*.

gob job n. fellatio (cf: blow job, head).

gobble v. to fellate *Legman*.

gobble box n. (US campus use) television set (cf: goggle box) *Underwood*.

gobble the goo v. to fellate *Legman*.

gobby a. see: gabby *BBC-1 TV 1983*.

gobshite n. a fool, a dupe.

God forbids n. (rhyming sl.) kids, children *Powis*.

God slot (TV use) that period of early Sunday evening TV viewing set aside by law for mandatory, if marginal, religious broadcasting. *Green:2*.

godawful a. especially appalling *Price: 2*.

goddam a. generally derog., to intensify one's dislike of a given person, object, etc. *McBain:1*.

goddie n. (backsl.) dog *Cole*.

god-help-us n. aka *gawdelpus* (qv): a difficult person, often a mischievous child *Wodehouse: MS*.

God's in heaven (bingo rhyming sl.) 7 *Wright*.

God's own medicine n. (drug use) morphine (cf: mother nature's own tobacco) *Algren*.

goer n. a promiscuous, sexually available female *'Monty Python's Flying Circus'*, BBC-2 1969.

gofer n. assistant, errand boy, anyone who is told to 'go fer . . .' some requirement *Price:2*.

goggle (at) v. to stare (at) *Wodehouse: AAG*.

goggle box n. the television *May*.

goggy n. a school child who has been rejected by its fellows; (cf: gunk, spod, Wendy, zoid) *Maledicta 9*.

gogo n. the buttocks.

going down happening *Price:2*.

going for pinkslips racing cars with the winner gaining the other's vehicle; the pink (insurance) slip is proof of ownership.

goitre n. (UK criminal use) a bulging wallet full of notes; fr. the physical ailment *Powis*.

gold n. money; fr. *gelt* (qv) *Burroughs:1*.

gold dust n. (drug use) heroin, presumably the Chinese (brown) variety, but also fr. the high price *Underwood*.

gold watch n. (rhyming sl.) Scotch whisky; orig. the rare *waterbury watch* (19th-C. use) *Powis*.

Goldberg n. (US Black use) any Jew, esp. the shopowners of Harlem and other ghettoes *Milner*.

goldbrick n. a shirker, a loafter, a lazy person; fr. trick of selling a supposed (in fact painted) gold brick to the gullible, thus getting money without working for it *Uris*.

gold-digger n. (orig. US) a young woman, typically from the chorus line, who swaps sexual favours for the monetary and material gifts of a (usually) older lover (cf: bimbo).

golden doughnut n. (Aus. use) the vulva *Wilkes*.

golden duck n. (cricket use) to be given out at the first ball of one's innings.

golden girl n. (drug use) particularly high grade cocaine (cf: girl) *Folb*.

golden oldie n. anything vintage but still valued; spec. rock 'n' roll records of 1950s/early 1960s.

golden shower urolagnia *Shulman*.

golden shower queen homosexual who enjoys being urinated on *Stanley*.

golly! (euph.) God, extra-mild euph., usu. child use only *Wodehouse:AAG*.

gollywhopper n. an outstanding example of its kind; similarly gollsocker, gollybuster.

go-long n. (US Black use) consequences, inevitable developments, circumstances; thus 'caught in the go-long': to be a victim of circumstances.

go-long n. (US Black use) the police truck in which arrested people are taken to the local cells (cf: paddy wagon, hurry-up) *Major*.

GOM n. see: God's Own Medicine.

gome n. (US campus use) a devotedly hard worker *Bernbach*.

gomer n. a fool, a rustic simpleton (fr. the proper name Gomer Pyle, a fictional fool; but cf: gaum).

gone a. 1. insane, crazy, bizarre *Runyon*; this predates, and poss. outlives, 2. (Jazz/beatnik use) weird and wonderful, lost in music, drugs, etc; esp. *gone cat*.

gone for a Burton gone away, esp. absent presumed dead; fr. Second World War RAF use; the 'Burton' is a particular beer *Powis*.

gone on obsessed by, esp. when in love *Goulart*.

gone to pot of a person: fallen in status, leading a degenerate life; of a thing: broken down, ceased from functioning properly or well *Hotten*.

gonef aka *gonnif*: fr. Yiddish: a thief *Rosten*.

goner n. a doomed person, anyone who cannot avoid an unpleasant fate *Big Ass Comics 1*.

gong n. (milit. use) a medal.

goniff n. aka: *gonef*, thief, fr. Yiddish *Schulberg*.

gonk n. (UK prostitute use) contemptuous description of a client; fr. large cuddly figures momentarily popular in 1960s *Powis*.

gonner n. see: goner *T 12/9/83*.

gonsil n. (US tramp sl.) a young, homosexual sidekick who accompanies a tramp *Legman*.

gonzo a. finished, defeated, useless; fr. gone + zo (cod-Italian suffix) *Higgins:5*.

goob n. (US campus use) a small mole, spot or similar skin blemish, fr. goober = peanut *Underwood*.

goober n. 1. (US campus use) a small child; fr. goober = peanut = a given small object or person *Underwood*; 2. the penis *Rawson*; 3. an idiot, a fool, an incompetent *Pond*.

gooberhead n. a general derog. term, typically describing an eccentric, a fussy person, one who drives badly (cf: dickhead, goober 2.).

good hair n. (US Black use) straight, soft hair, the opposite of bad hair.

good news n. an acceptable person, event, etc.; general term of approval *Barr*.

good ole boy n. 1. a Southern man of any age who conforms to the prevalent cultural standards *White*; 2. (US preppie (qv) use) a student who is considered of the right type by his peers *Bernbach*.

good on you! (Aus. use) general expression of approbation, thanks, etc. *Ready*.

good people n. 1. spec. former

criminals (US) who have retired from their various specialities; **2.** one's peers *Maurer*.

good shot good try, even though one may have failed.

good stuff n. (US Black use) **1.** sexually sophisticated; **2.** effective, pleasant drugs; **3.** success in a confidence trick, in deception *Klein*.

good time n. **1.** (US prison use) the penis *Higgins:1*; **2.** (US Black use) an especially acceptable, likeable person *Klein*.

goods n. (US criminal use) **1.** stolen goods, contraband *Klein*; **2.** information, usu. to be used in an unfriendly manner towards its subject *Morgan*.

good-time n. (Can. prison use) time off for good behaviour *Caron*.

good-time Charlie n. a playboy, a dissolute man (cf: champagne Charlie 2).

gooey n. a pretty girlfriend.

goof n. an eccentric, crazy person; fr. dial. *goof*: a fool *Thompson:J*.

goof v. to blunder, to make a mistake *Goldman*.

goof bender n. letting one's hair down, acting absurd just for fun *Price: 3*.

goof butt n. (drug use) a marijuana cigarette (cf: goof ball).

goof off v. to act lazily, to mess around instead of working *SF Comics*.

goof on v. to laugh at, to find amusing *Goldman*.

goofball n. a barbiturate; a tranquilizer *De Lannoy & Masterson*.

goofed a. inebriated with a given drug; esp. barbiturates (cf: goofball) *Selby: 1*.

goofer n. a homosexual prostitute who will take active roles in fellatio or anal intercourse.

goofy a. stupid, uncoordinated, inept *Wodehouse: YMS*.

goo-goo eyes n. an amorous glance directed at a loved, or hopefully soon to be loved one.

gook n. **1.** (US campus use) dull, stupid, foolish person; poss. fr. milit.

use in Vietnam *Underwood*; **2.** (derog.) Oriental; originated by US troops in Korean War, perpetuated in Vietnam and thus spread into non-milit. use *Del Vecchio*.

goolies n. testicles; fr. *gullies*; marbles.

goombah n. a thug, a gangster; fr. Italian: godfather, one of the names (cf: M. Puzo, *The Godfather*, 1969) used for a leader of the Italian-American Mafia *Grogan*.

goon n. **1.** thug (cf: heavy); **2.** spec. non-union labour used for strike breaking, intimidation, etc. *Tuff Shit Comics*.

goon squad n. a group of thugs, usu. organized for a specific purpose – strike-breaking, extortion, etc.

goop n. fool, idiot *Wodehouse: YMS*.

goopy a. **1.** sticky; **2.** lacking in energy, exhausted.

goose n. **1.** (US campus use) a socially unacceptable person; a fool *Underwood*; **2.** a Jew.

goose v. **1.** to poke a finger into the anus or vagina to surprise or poss. titillate the recipent of such attentions *Selby: 1*; **2.** to press, to push; **3.** to accelerate a car; thus **4.** 'goose up': to move forward a short distance.

goose egg n. **1.** a large bruise that comes up on the head after striking it, or being struck a blow; **2.** an illegitimate child.

goose's neck n. (rhyming sl.) cheque *Jones: J*.

goosetown n. the poor part of town; also as goose flat, goose hollow, goose nibble.

goosy a. nervous, jittery, on edge.

goozlum n. any viscous, treacly substance, often describing a food.

gopher n. see: gofer *Chandler: LG*.

gor blimey! (excl.) fr. God blind me *Wodehouse: AAG*.

Gorbals kiss n. head butt (cf: Chelsea smile, Glasgow kiss).

Gordon & Gotch n. (rhyming sl.) a watch; fr. firm of book and periodical importers *Jones: J*.

Gordon Bennett! (excl.) euph. for

gor blimey (qv) from US racing gambler of 19th C. *Payne*.

gorge out v. (US campus use) spec. description by students of Cornell University for those among them who leap to their deaths from a nearby bridge and into the gorge below *Neaman & Silver*.

gorilla n. 1. (business use) a monster success, a smash hit *Safire*; 2. (US prostitute use) a customer who likes to beat up his girl *Shulman*; 3. a thug, a muscleman, a hoodlum *Fiction Illus. 3*.

gorilla v. (US Black use) to use violence; to rape *Folb*.

gorilla in the washing machine v. (US Black use) to perform cunnilingus *Folb*.

gorilla pimp n. (US Black use) a pimp who controls his girls by threats and actual violence (cf: sugar pimp) *Milner*.

gorp v. to eat nosily, greedily.

gosh! (euph.) God! extra-mild euph., usually used only by children.

go-sign, give the v. to dismiss, to reject, to brush off.

got up a. dressed up particularly smartly for some occasion *White*.

got up like a pox-doctor's clerk (cp) describing someone who is very smartly (too smartly?) dressed.

got your eye full? (cp) addressed to someone who is staring, with undoubted suggestion that they should stop at once; this can be followed with 'want a picture?'

goths n. a subgroup of punk (qv) rock fans who dress in austere black and enjoy a suitably grim, joyless music.

gouchy adv. (Sc. use) depressed *Welsh:1*.

gourd n. 1. (esp. drug use) the head, (cf: out of one's gourd); 2. (US campus use) a stupid, empty-headed person *Underwood*.

govern v. 1. to take the active role in sexual intercourse (cf: catch); 2. to engage in sado-masochism (see: S&M (qv)) *AS 60.1 (1985)*.

governor n. (UK police use) general

address to a senior officer within the same squad *Laurie*.

goy n. (Yiddish) gentile; pl: *goyim Norman: 3*.

grab n. (UK prison use) pay *LL*.

grab v. 1. to arrest *Higgins: 1*; 2. to appeal to *People's Comics*.

grab one's dick v. (US Black use) to boast, to brag.

grab-all n. a greedy person.

grab-ass v. to play around, to mess about *Stone*.

grab-bag n. a random collection of items, ideas, people, etc. *Thompson*.

grabbers n. fingers *Sillitoe*.

grab-it-and-growl n. a diner, a lunch counter; also grab-it-and-gallop.

graduate v. (US Black use) to increase, through knowledge and sophistication, one's status within the ranks of one's peers in the streets and the criminal milieu *Klein*.

graft n. 1. corruption; 2. the proceeds of corruption, political/criminal payments, etc.; both meanings stem fron SE graft: work, occupation; 3. efforts, hard work; usu. physical, labouring work *Sillitoe*.

graft v. to work hard, to make an effort, to struggle *Powis*.

grafter n. a hard worker, one who perseveres fr. graft 3.

grand n. thousand (usu. dollars or pounds) (cf: G, K).

grand bag n. (homosexual use) a large scrotum *Legman*.

grand duchess n. 1. a female heterosexual who occupies a pride of place in a homosexual male coterie; 2. an experienced, older, sophisticated male homosexual *Stanley*.

Grand Tour n. (US campus use) the traditional tour undertaken by recently graduated US college students in Europe; fr. the earlier practice of England's young aristocrats *Bernbach*.

grandstand v. to make oneself conspicuous. *White*.

granny n. (UK criminal use) a legitimate business that serves only as a front for criminal activities *LL*.

granny v. to defeat comprehensively, to allow one's opponent no score at all *Welsh:1*.

granny grunt n. **1.** a stomach ache, menstruation; also: granny chills, granny rag; **2.** a fussy person (though not necessarily female or old) (cf: grunt); **3.** (US Black use) a mythical figure to whom otherwise unanswerable questions are referred.

granny rag n. home-made tampons, made of pieces of cloth (cf: granny grunt).

grape n. any form of liquor, wine and spirits *Chandler: Notebk*.

grapes n. **1.** (USAF use) the deck crew, wearing purple uniforms, who work on aircraft carriers *Wolfe:6*; **2.** (US Black use) the female breasts *Folb*.

grapevine n. a network of unofficial sources, rumours, half-truths, etc. which seems to spread the news around a given circle or group faster than any sanctioned announcement (cf: bush telegraph).

grass n. **1.** marijuana *Price: 2*; **2.** (homosexual use) pubic hair (cf: garden, lawn) *Maledicta*; **3.** (rhyming sl.) grasshopper = copper = informer *Performance*.

grass v. to inform, tell tales, betray *Norman: 1*.

grass-eater n. (US police use) a policeman who, while still corrupt, remains satisfied with what perks – materials and financial – his beat offers rather than canvassing for extras (cf: meat-eater) *Green: 2*.

grassfighter n. (Aus. use) anyone known for losing their temper and brawling in public, presumably in grassy areas *Neaman & Silver*.

gravestones n. **1.** prominent front teeth; **2.** false teeth.

graveyard shift n. (industrial use) the overnight shift, the late shift *Green: 2*.

graveyard stew n. milk toast (such toast is generally given to the ill, thus the idea that once his or her appetite has been reduced to such a meal the sufferer has nowhere to go but the graveyard).

gravy a. wonderful, excellent, perfect *Underwood*.

gravy n. money *Higgins: 2*.

gravy train n. a simple, heavily profitable situation from which one can benefit easily *Sharpe: 1*.

gray a. (Black use) any white person *Milner*.

grease n. **1.** (homosexual use) any form of lubricant – KY Jelly, etc. – that facilitates anal intercourse *Klein*; **2.** (abbrev.) greasers: motorbike riders, aka Rockers, as opposed to Mods *Mandelkau*; **3.** protection money *Chandler: Notebk*; **4.** (US campus use) a meal, food *Underwood*.

grease v. **1.** to corrupt, to bribe, to smoothe over problems, esp. fr. authorities *Fiction Illus*. *3*; **2.** to kill, esp. military use (cf: grease-gun) *Del Vecchio*.

grease the gash v. (of a woman) to masturbate.

greaseball n. derog. description of any Latin race: Greeks, Puerto Ricans (cf: spic), various South Americans, etc. *Price: 2*.

grease-gun n. an automatic weapon *Higgins: 3*.

greaser n. **1.** a 1950s Teddy Boy, his hair larded with Brylcreem or similar unguent; **2.** a motorcycle gang member (cf: rocker); **3.** (US campus use) an old-fashioned person, whose style harks back to 1950s youth cults.

greaser n. (derog.) Mexican; and other Latin races *BvdB*.

greasy corner n. any poor area or settlement, esp. that occupied by Blacks and poor Whites.

greasy spoon n. a cheap cafe or restaurant; fr. the state of its cutlery and the texture of its product *Farren*.

greasy spot on the road n. (derog.) a small town or hamlet (cf: wide place in the road).

Great Scott! euph. for Good God! *Rawson*.

great shakes a. very good, admirable *Price: 3*.

grebo n. a British youth cult featuring

a cultivatedly sordid appearance, a
boorish manner and devotion to heavy
metal music; poss/ fr. 'greb', a general
term of abuse used in North of
England schools since 1930s.

greefo n. aka: *griefo*, *greapha*:
marijuana *De Lannoy & Masterson*.

Greek a. anal intercourse; often used
on a prostitute's bill of sale *Price: 2*.

Greek v. (gay use) to engage in
pederasty.

Greek culture n. anal intercourse,
usu. in homosexual advertisement use;
fr. the ethnic cliché that categorizes all
(ancient) Greeks as sodomites (cf:
English culture, etc.) *Jay & Young*.

Greek love n. (gay use) pederasty.

Greek side n. (gay use) the buttocks.

Greek way n. (gay use) pederasty.

green a. naïve, innocent,
unsophisticated *Sillitoe*.

green n. aka: *long green*: dollar bills
Price: 1.

green hornet n. (Canadian cant) a
Toronto motorcycle policeman; fr.
cartoon superhero *Neaman & Silver*.

green house n. (drug use) a place
known for selling drugs, esp. green-
coloured marijuana *Klein*.

green niggers n. Irishmen; similar
inferior status to black 'niggers' but
'green' (Irish) rather than black
Price: 2.

green thumb n. (US Black use)
someone who has the knack of making
money; fr. the more usual gardeners'
'green fingers' *Klein*.

green welly brigade n. the rural
upper classes; fr. the green wellingtons
(rather than the more common black
variety) that such people are prone to
wear.

green-ass a. naïve, inexperienced (cf:
green) *Algren*.

greenbacks n. dollar bills *Himes: 2*.

greener n. (abbrev.) greenhorn (qv)
Algren.

greenhorn n. a novice, an
unsophisticated person, esp. a new
immigrant or a new arrival in the city
from the country *Farrell*.

greenie n. (US campus use) beer,

spec. Heineken lager which comes in
predominantly green-labelled bottles
or cans *Bernbach*.

greenies n. (UK 'society' use) money;
like so many similar class usages, the
-ie suffix underlines the lifelong
addiction to nursery language (cf:
greenbacks) *Barr*.

greens n. (rhyming sl.) greengages =
wages *Powis*.

Gregory Peck n. (rhyming sl.) the
neck *Cole*.

grey n. dull, boring, earnest, hard-
working, esp. university use.

grey ghost n. (Aus. use) a parking
policeman, who superseded the brown
bomber (qv) *Wilkes*.

grief n. misery, problems, troubles.

grief v. (US campus use) to trouble, to
bother, to annoy *Underwood*.

griff n. information, news; fr. *griffin*:
orig. denoting a newcomer to the
Indian Army or Civil Service and a
greenhorn (qv) in general *LL*.

grifter n. swindler, confidence man
Fiction Illus. 3.

grill v. to interrogate *X*.

grind n. 1. hard, continuous, wearing
work, esp. academic work *Price: 3*;
2. a hard worker at school *Junker*.

grind v. 1. to rub one's body,
especially the genital area against
one's partner while dancing; 2. to have
sexual intercouse *Price: 2*.

grind house n. 1. a cinema; 2. a
second-rate cinema, rarely showing
any first-run feature films.

grinder n. a large sandwich made of
two slabs of bread cut lengthwise from
the loaf and containing a variety of
ingredients (cf: submarine).

gringa n. (Sp.) white woman *Vidal*.

gringo n. (derog. Sp.) white man, usu.
Mexican use, referring to white
Americans *Vidal*.

gripples n. (US Black use) the anus
Klein.

grisly a. (US teen. use) awful,
disgusting, generally distasteful *Pond*.

gritch v. (US campus use) to nag, to
complain; fr. gripe + bitch
Underwood.

gritchy a. (US campus use) irritable, grouchy *Underwood*.

grizzle v. to whine, to cry slightly but continually; usu. of a child.

groaty a. (US teen/campus use) disgusting, unpleasant; fr. grotesque (cf: grotty, grody) *Underwood*.

groceries n. the vagina (one of many sl. sexual words with 'edible' connotations, cf: lollipop, jelly roll, hair pie, etc.) *Maledicta*.

grockle n. (UK 'society' use) **1.** a tourist; the term originated in the West Country, specifically in Torbay, where a local remarked that the stream of visitors to the town resembled little Grocks, or clowns, but spread throughout Britain's holiday resorts where the local people thus derided the flocks of annual visitors to their area. *J Meades* **2.** in 'society' use, the term means simply outsider, with overtones of unpleasantness and yobbery *Barr*.

grody a. (Valley Girls (qv) use) disgusting, unpleasant; fr. grotty (qv), in its turn fr. grotesque *Harpers/ Queen 1/83*.

grody to the max a. (Valley Girls (qv) use) extremely, even more, disgusting (cf: grotty, max) *Harpers/ Queen 1/83*.

grog n. (Aus. use) alcohol, usu, beer; fr. 18th C. *grog = rum Humphries*.

groggy a. weak, unsteady, semi-conscious; fr. orig. meaning of drunken *Wright*.

groid n. (US southern campus use) (derog. abbrev.) Negroid: Black student *Underwood*.

groin n. (UK criminal use) aka: *groyne*: any ring containing a gemstone; esp. a diamond *Powis*.

grok v. to appreciate, to understand and experience completely, usu. *grok the fullness*; popular hippie and mystic use *R. Heinlein, 'Strangers in a Strange Land'*.

groove n. **1.** a way of life, of thinking and dealing with people, events, etc. *Randy Newman, 'Trouble in Paradise', 1983*; **2.** a delight, a pleasure, anything enjoyable *Southern & Hoffenberg*.

groove behind v. to enjoy or appreciate a given situation or other stimulus *Farina*.

groove on v. see: groove behind *McFadden*.

grooved very pleased, very happy *Bruce: 2*.

groover n. person, neutral when coined in the 1960s but currently slightly derisory *Welsh:1*.

groovy a. **1.** delightful, wonderful, pleasant, enjoyable, etc.; **2.** (Valley Girls (qv) use) passé, out of date, esp. when referring to the tastes and styles of the 1960s, during which time **1** was the only accepted meaning *Pond*.

grope v. to fondle a potential partner in order to assess response to one's advances *Stanley*.

gross a. disgusting; esp. in US teen and campus use *Underwood*.

gross out v. to disgust, to shock *Jay & Young*.

grotty a. disgusting, unattractive, fr. grotesque; especially popular during the Beatlemania era of the early 1960s (cf: groaty, grody) *Payne*.

grouch-pot n. a grumpy, irritable person (cf: fuss-pot).

ground n. (UK police use) a given police officer's area of operations (cf: manor, patch) *Laurie*.

ground rations n. (US Black use) sexual intercourse *Major*.

Ground Zero n. the basic position; the start; the essentials; fr. military use *Higgins: 5*.

grounded a. to be stopped from enjoying some normal right or pleasure; teenage use, fr. aerospace: aircraft that cannot fly *Price: 2*.

group grope n. an orgy *Stanley*.

grouper n. see: groupie *Wolfe: 2*.

groupie n. young girl who associates herself with rock bands, offering her body for their celebrity *J. Fabian & J. Byrne, book title, 1969*.

grouse a. (Aus. use) wonderful, attractive, excellent – all-purpose term of approval *Wilkes*.

grouse gear n. (Aus. use) teen expression for particularly attractive female *Ready*.

grove (p.ppl. to groove) to have taken great pleasure in something *Sculatti*.

grow horns v. (US campus use) to become angry; the horns of a bull rather than those of a cuckold *Underwood*.

growler n. (US campus use) lavatory *Underwood*.

grub n. (US campus use) a hard worker, one who works to the exclusion of other interests *Bernbach*.; **2.** (Aus. use) dirty, unkempt person; fr. grubby *Humphries: 2*; **3.** food; used since mid-17th C. *Price: 2*.

grub v. to beg, to scrounge *Selby: 1*.

grubber n. **1.** (US campus use) a disgusting, filthy person; fr. grubby *Underwood*; **2.** (Aus. use) a hospital, spec. a vagrants' casual night shelter; poss. link to US campus use *Wilkes*.

grubbies n. (US campus use) dirty, greasy old clothes *Underwood*.

grubble v. to rummage around, to search at random *Sanders: 2*.

grubstake n. enough money to buy one a meal (cf: grub).

grumble and grunt n. (rhyming sl.) cunt (qv) = female genitals *Franklyn*.

grunch! (US campus use) general excl. of annoyance or disgust; prob. fr. grunge (qv) *Underwood*.

grunge n. a style of music and among its followers, of dress, that originated in a number of Seattle rock bands, notably Nirvana. The music features heavily distorted guitar and angst-ridden lyrics; the clothes are essentially a mix-and-(not necessarily)-match selection of junk store castoffs and/or army surplus.

grunge n. sticky, dirty, unpleasant substances *Underwood*.

grunge v. **1.** to whine, to complain; **2.** to assault, to attack, to terrify *Sanders: 2*.

grungy a. dirty, messy, unappetizing, unappealing *Junker*.

grunt n. an ill-tempered, constantly complaining person (cf: granny grunt).

grunt n. a US Marine private soldier, supposedly fr. such a soldier's endless complaining; the Vietnam era successor to the doughboy (qv) *Webb*.

grunter n. (Aus. use) prostitute; fr. the (simulated) grunts of passion with which she embellishes her services (?) *Wilkes*.

grunters n. old people out of sympathy with current youth enthusiasms (cf: wrinklies, crumblies, etc.) *ES 11/5/83*.

G-string n. (US Black use) any device – tampon, towel, etc. – used to staunch flow of menstrual blood *Klein*.

gub n. (Aus. Aborigine use) white man (cf: Mr Gub) *Wilkes*.

gubbins n. indefinite noun for any nameless object.

Gucci n. (US Black use) a poser (fr. brandname Gucci: much beloved by those who rate their own value in terms of those designer labels they can flaunt).

guck n. any form of sticky substance; ointment, cream *Performance*.

gucky a. (UK 'society' use) sickening, likely to make one vomit (of an event or person as much as of a food or drink) *Barr*.

Gucky n. (UK 'society' use) deliberate mispronunciation of Gucci, a favourite designer label for such speakers *Barr*.

guff n. **1.** (UK prep school use) a fart *Barr*; **2.** lies, nonsense, twaddle *Runyon*.

guinea a. Italian (derog.) (cf: ghinny, ginny) *Price: 2*.

guinea pig n. (US criminal use) an informer, a stool pigeon (qv) *Klein*.

guinea stinker n. a cheap, malodorous cigar supposedly preferred by Italian-Americans (cf: guinea, ghinny, etc.) *Goldman*.

guineas n. (US campus use) money; fr. obs. UK denomination of £1 1 shilling *Underwood*.

guinzo n. Italian (derog.) (cf: guinea) *Price: 2*.

gully dirt n. a worthless, contemptible person, one who fails to fit the local norms; esp. in phr. 'sorry as gully dirt'.

gully jumper n. a farmer, a peasant (cf: apple knocker, clodhopper).

gum heel n. (US prison use) policeman (cf: gumshoe, rubber heels) *Chandler: Notebk*.

gum things up v. to make a mess (of pre-arranged plans); to ruin a satisfactory situation by one's interference *Wodehouse: PGM*.

gum up the works v. see: gum things up.

gum-bumping n. arguing.

gumby n. a fool, an idiot; from the character in television's 'Monty Python's Flying Circus'.

gumdrop n. (drug use) barbiturate, spec. seconal; any kind of drug available in pill or capsule form *Folb*.

gump n. a fool; thus gump-headed: foolish. (fr. Yorks dial gump: homely, parochial, awkward, well-meaning; gump was adopted as a trademark by the 20th C. comedian Norman Wisdom).

gumption n. intelligence, natural wit, shrewdness; fr. 18th-C. dial: *gawm*: understanding, which also gives *gormless*: stupid, doltish *Wright*.

gumshoe n. A (private) detective; fr. supposedly rubber-soled shoes used for creeping around on investigations *Chandler: passim*.

gumshoe v. to creep around, esp. used of policemen or private detectives (cf: gumshoe, n.) *Schulberg*.

gun 1. (drug use) a hypodermic syringe; 2. the penis *J. Hendrix, 'Hey Joe', 1966*.

gun v. to rev an engine hard *Griffith*.

gun for v. 1. to look for someone with the intent of creating some form of confrontation; from the Western gunfighter usage of one man pursuing another; 2. to be sexually interested in a person.

Gunga Din n. (rhyming sl.) chin (cf: Errol Flynn) *Wright*.

gunge n. a sticky mess, poss. when in the form of gravy or sauce, but equally often merely resembling such foods *Barr*.

gung-ho a. enthusiastic, usu, aggressively so; often describing soldiers or sportsmen; fr. Chinese *keng ho*: awe-inspiring, (lit. more fiery) *Whitcomb*.

gunk n. 1. a schoolchild who has been rejected by its fellows, (cf: goggy, spod, Wendy, zoid) *Maledicta 9*; 2. a fool, a dullard (cf: gonk).

gunner n. the shooter in a game of dice craps *Runyon: 1*.

Gunners n. Arsenal Football Club.

gunny n. 1. (drug use) marijuana *Folb*; 2. (US milit. use) gunnery sergeant.

gunny sack a. valueless, of little importance; thus (US cant) 'gunny sack charge': an arrest on an insignificant charge that will not stand up in court.

gunsel n. see: gonsil.

guntz n. the whole lot; fr. German *ganz Norman, book title, 1962*.

gunzel v. (US Black use) to fight; fr. misreading of gonsil (qv) *Folb*.

gurgle n. liquor.

gussied up adv. dressed up, esp. for a night out (cf: dolled up, duded up, togged up).

gut n. 1. an easy task; fr. college use (qv) *Price: 2*; 2. (US campus use) an easy course *Farina*.

gut it v. (US campus use) to stay up all night working without any amphetamines for stimulation but purely through strength of will and character; fr. guts – bravery, rather than gut – simple *Underwood*.

gutless a. cowardly *Tidy*.

guts n. 1. courage, bravery *Larner*; 2. stomach *Price: 2*.

gutshoot v. to shoot in the stomach *Higgins: 3*.

gutso n. (derog.) a fat person.

gutstick n. (US Black use) the penis *Klein*.

gutsy a. brave (cf: guts).

gutted a. (UK prison use) sick and tired, fed up, deeply disappointed, utterly depressed; from 'sick to my guts', the term originated in jail use, but has become hugely widespread over the past decade *Observer 1981*.

gutty a. (UK police use) tedious, irritating, hard to tolerate *Laurie*.

Guv n. (abbrev.) Guvner (qv) or governor (qv).

guvner n. (UK police use) address by any rank to their immediate superior from sergeants upwards '*The Sweeney*', *Euston Films, 1974, etc*.

Guy n. (rhyming sl.) Guy Fawkes = a walk *Powis*.

guy n. a general term of address, originally among young UK blacks, and now in general teen use.

guyver n. (Aus. use) flattery, insincerity, pretence *Wilkes*.

Guz (Royal Navy use) abbrev. guzzle: Devonport, the naval home port where sailors can eat and drink without restrictions *BBC-1 TV 1984*.

guzzle v. 1. to eat or drink messily or noisily; 2. to choke *Runyon: 1*; 3. to indulge in foreplay *Runyon: 1*.

gynae n. (abbrev.) gynaecologist *Barr*.

gyp n. a cheat, one who fails to pay his due debts; abbrev. of gypsy and as such an ethnic slur *Goulart*.

gyp v. to cheat, to swindle *rr*.

gyp joint n. anywhere, esp. a club, bar, etc., where the unwary will be swindled (cf: clip-joint, gyp).

Gyppy tummy n. stomach troubles, diahorrea; orig. that contracted in Egypt, but now extended to any such problems that UK tourists experience abroad or in ethnic restaurants at home (cf: Montezuma's revenge).

gypsies n. (sex industry use) prostitutes who travel around for trade, or live in trailer parks.

gypsy's n. (rhyming sl.) gypsy's kiss = piss = urination *Powis*.

gypsy's warning n. no warning at all.

gyrene n. (US milit. use) a Marine *Uris*.

H

H² (US preppie (qv) use) hot and heavy (of sexual or romantic partnerships) *Neaman & Silver*.

habe n. (abbrev.) habeas corpus: an order compelling its subject to attend court *Higgins:1*.

habit n. drug addiction *Grogan*.

hack n. 1. (Oxford University use) undergraduates who attempt to maximize their chances of a job by creating for themselves the best possible sounding curriculum vitae while still at the university *Harpers/Queen 8/83*; 2. (US use) a taxicab *Fiction Illus.3*; 3. a reporter, a journalist; formerly derog., but recently popular, if tongue-in-cheek *P. Howard, The Times*; 4. (US/Can. prison use) a prison guard *Caron*.

hack v. 1. to irritate, to annoy *Underwood*; 2. (US campus use) to

vomit; fr. SE *hack*: to cough *Underwood*.

hack around v. 1. to joke, to tease *Higgins:1*; 2. to waste time *Higgins:3*.

hack it v. to manage, to bear a difficulty, to solve a problem; fr. physically hacking one's way through *Stone*.

hack one's mack v. to masturbate.

hacked a. very angry *Goldman*.

hacker n. 1. taxi-driver *Goulart*; 2. run of the mill, average person; fr. hack-work *Higgins:3*.

hackie n. (US use) taxi-driver *Chandler:LG*.

hackles, go through the v. to suffer, to endure an excess of bad luck (cf: go through the flint mill) (fr. SE hackle: a flax-comb, an instrument set with parallel steel pins for splitting and combing out the fibres of flax or hemp).

had a. **1.** seduced, debauched; **2.** fooled, defrauded, conned (qv) *Algren: 2.*

had it up to here to be exasperated, to lose all one's patience.

had it with to be annoyed with, to lose patience with: 'I've had it with you', etc. *McFadden.*

haint'ing-ain'ting n. a rustic, a peasant. (fr. rustic pron. of SE hasn't as hain't and isn't as ain't).

hair n. (US campus use) courage, masculine prowess; thus, *to show hair*: for a sportsman to play aggressively and well *AS 50 (1965).*

hair and hide, hide and hair phr. everything, entirely, completely.

hair crossed, have a v. to be over-sensitive, to be touchy (cf: all hair by the nose, hair up one's ass).

hair in the butter n. a delicate situation (cf: fly in the ointment).

hair of the dog n. a further drink of what one was drinking on the previous night in the hope of getting rid of the hangover that the initial drinking has caused; 'the hair of the dog that bit you' *Runyon:1.*

hair on it, have v. (of a joke) to be old, to be out of date, no longer to be funny.

hair pie n. the vagina; fr. the pubic hair, plus pun on 'hare'; an example of sex = food (cf: finger pie) *Morgan.*

hairbag n. an unpleasant, disgusting and unappetizing person *'Hill Street Blues', Thames TV, 1983.*

hairball n. general term of derision; see: hairbag.

haircut n. (UK prison use) a short term of imprisonment; in a local gaol from a few weeks up to 2 or 3 months; in a convict gaol fr. 3 to 5 yrs. *LL.*

haired up adv. annoyed, furious, upset.

hairy n. (Glasgow use) a poor female; the premise is that a better off woman would wear a hat and hide her hair *G. Macdonald Fraser, 'McAuslan in the Rough', 1976.*

hairy a. (US campus use + UK general) dangerous, exciting *AS 50 (1965).*

hairy-assed a. **1.** madly, wildly, extremely; **2.** overtly, aggressively masculine *Higgins:1.*

half elision of 'half-past. . .' in telling the time: 'half-ten', 'half-four', etc.

half a bar n. formerly 10 shillings, thus currently 50p *Powis.*

half a cock n. £5, fr. cock and hen (qv), rhyming sl: £10 *LL.*

half a crown (bingo use) 26, fr. old coinage 2/6 *Wright.*

half a mo wait a moment, hang on (qv); fr. half a moment.

half a sheet n. see: half a bar.

half a stretch n. (UK criminal use) six months imprisonment *Norman:2.*

half a yard n. $50 *Caron.*

half and half a. (US campus use) **1.** bisexual (cf: AC/DC) *Underwood*; **2.** (sex industry use) fellatio plus full intercourse (see: around the world).

half pint n. see: half portion *Schulberg:2.*

half seas over a. drunk; orig. nautical use; prob. fr. image of half-submerged in liquor.

half step v. (US Black use) to act in an inappropriate or ineffectual manner *Folb.*

half the bay over a. drunk *Dickson.*

half your luck! (Aus. use) excl. signifying envy/jealousy of the person addressed *Ready.*

half-assed a. incompetent, second rate *Higgins:1.*

half-baked incompetent, inadequate, below a given standard *Obs. 6/2/83.*

half-brass n. a woman who associates with the prostitute milieu but is not a working girl herself *LL.*

half-cock at less than full speed, with less than total commitment, effort, etc; fr. mechanical use.

half-cocked a. second-rate, not fully capable, unfinished *Dury.*

half-cut a. more than mildly drunk but not yet incapable.

half-gone a. drunk.

half-high a. tipsy, mildly drunk (cf: half cut).

half-inch v. (rhyming sl.) to pinch = to steal *Cole*.

half-iron n. a man who enjoys the company but not the specific predelictions of homosexuals; fr. iron hoof = poof (qv) *LL*.

half-lo (US drug use) (abbrev.) half-load: 15 bags (qv) of heroin, a typical purchase made by a small pusher (qv) *J. Breslin, 'Forsaking All Others', 1982*.

half-man n. (US Black use) half a bottle of spirits, esp. whisky.

half-ounce v. (rhyming sl.) to bounce = to cheat, to shortchange *Cole*.

half-past two n. (rhyming sl.) a Jew *Franklyn*.

halfpenny dip n. (rhyming sl.) a ship *Jones:J*.

half-portion n. a diminutive person *Wodehouse:AAG*.

half-saved n. an eccentric, a fool *Obs. 6/2/83*.

half-way house (bingo use) 50; there are 100 numbers available to the caller.

half-wide a. reasonably intelligent, aware of what goes on and thus, in certain contexts, corruptible (cf: wide boy) *Newman:1*.

halvsies n. see sixty-nine *AS 60.1 (1985)*.

ham and egger n. an ordinary, run of the mill person *Higgins:1*.

ham hocks n. (US Black use) aka: *hocks*: female legs, ankles *Folb*.

hambone a. referring to Blacks *Morgan*.

hambone n. the penis; other 'butcher-related' terms include: beef, beef bayonet, butcher, crimson chitterling, dark meat, gooser, goose's neck, live sausage, meat, mutton dagger, pork sword, sausage, schnickel, schnitzel, tubesteak, turkey neck, white meat.

hambone v. 1. (Aus. use) for a man to strip off his clothes in public, prob. at a drunken party *Ready*; 2. to live frugally.

hammer n. 1. (US trucker use) the accelerator *Higgins:4*; 2. (US Black use) very attractive black girl *Major*.

hammer v. 1. (driving use) to drive at maximum speed; thus *put the hammer down*: to drive fast, to accelerate *Humphries:2*; 2. to beat up, to hurt physically.

hammer ass v. to work very hard *Higgins:1*.

hammer man n. (US Black use) an authoritarian figure *Major*.

hammered a. drunk.

hammered down a. stunted, short and squat, insignificant.

hammerhead n. (US campus use) anyone stupid and obstinate *Underwood*.

hammers n. (US Black use) female thighs *Folb*.

Hammers n. West Ham Football Club.

Hampsteads n. (rhyming sl.) Hampstead Heath = teeth *Cole*.

Hampton n. (rhyming sl.) Hampton Wick = prick = penis *Powis*.

Hampton rock n. (rhyming sl.) cock = penis *Cole*.

hand fucking n. (US Black use) male masturbation (cf: hand shandy).

hand gig n. (homosexual use) a homosexual prostitute who specializes in masturbating his clients or joining in mutual masturbation with them *Legman*.

hand in one's dinner pail v. 1. to die; 2. to resign from one's job *Wodehouse:PGM*.

hand job n. masturbation, often offered in a prostitute's price list *Price:2*.

hand shandy n. the act of masturbation.

handbag v. to attack, esp. of a woman. (fr. the ideologically inspired aggressiveness of the former British Prime Minister Margaret Thatcher, who was seen, cartoonishly, as hitting opponents with her omnipresent handbag.)

-handed a. (police/criminal use) the size of a firm (qv) of criminals can be two-, three-, four, team- or mob-handed.

handful n. 1. (prison use) five year

sentence *LL*; **2.** £5 *EN 12/11/57*.

hand-gallop v. to masturbate *Higgins:2*.

handkerchief head n. (US Black use) a subservient, role-playing, white stereotypical black woman, the female version of a Tom (qv) (cf: Aunt Jemima) *Folb*.

handle n. name, nickname, or title, now esp. fr. Citizen's Band Radio use, but in prison use at least c.1950 *Capital Radio 1983*.

handmedowns n. second-hand clothes, either given free or bought at a second-hand shop.

hand-reared a. possessed of a large penis *B. Aldiss, 'The Hand-Reared Boy', bk title*.

hands off (your) cocks, feet in (your) socks! (cp) jocular wake-up cry, orig. RAF, but general in services, institutions, and similar sites of dormitory accommodation *'Serpico', dir. S. Lumet, 1973*.

handsome a. excellent, wonderful; general term of approval (cf: sweet) *Cole*.

handy a. useful, admirable.

hang n. (US Black use) a job; which supports one's living *Major*.

hang v. turn, as in *hang a left*, etc. *Higgins:1*.

hang a Lilly v. to turn left (cf: hang a Louie) *Underwood*.

hang a Louie v. to turn left *Underwood*.

hang a Ralph v. aka hang a Ralphie: to turn right *Underwood*.

hang a U-ie n. make a U-turn *Humphries:2*.

hang about v. see: hang around.

hang about! (excl.) wait a minute, don't go!

hang around v. to wait about, to linger in one place *Wilkinson*.

hang black v. (US Black use) to associate primarily, if not wholly, with one's Black peers.

hang down n. the penis (cf: hang out).

hang in n. influence.

hang in there v. to maintain a

position, usu. with implication of pressures to surrender *Manser*.

hang it all on one's back v. (of a woman) to display one's wealth through extravagant dress and jewellery.

hang it up v. to give up trying, to accept defeat, to acknowledge that a target will never be achieved *Klein*.

hang loose v. **1.** relax, take things as they come; **2.** (excl.) relax! enjoy yourself! don't worry! (cf: hang tough) *McFadden*.

hang one on v. **1.** to hit someone, to have a fight *Farrell*; **2.** to be drunk *Dickson*.

hang one out to dry v. to treat particularly harshly; to make an example of an individual *Dunne*.

hang one to the all v. to punish severely *Underwood*.

hang one's lip v. to be in a bad temper, to sulk.

hang out v. to meet, to collect together at a regular venue (cf: hang around).

hang out n. a place where a given group tend to meet *The Collected Trashman, 1969*.

hang the moon v. to be very important; thus phr. 'think one hung the moon': to think very highly of someone.

hang tough v. to behave in an aggressive, tough manner; to persist in a course of action whatever the problems (cf: hang loose).

hang up v. to distress, to annoy *Keyes*.

hang up n. problem, delay, neurosis *Yellow Dog Comics 22, 1972*.

hang up one's harness v. (US western use) aka: *hang up one's tackle* to die *Adams*.

hang up one's hat v. (US western use) to die *Adams*.

hangers n. breasts *Price:2*.

hanging-up n. (taxi-driver use) the refusal of some drivers to take fares as they appear at a rank, and instead to hold back until something lucrative – a trunk-laden tourist, etc. – turns up *Powis*.

hankiehead n. see: towelhead (cf: raghead).

hankypanky n. trickery, deceit; esp. of a sexual nature *Sanders:2*.

ha'penny n. the pudendum *Neaman & Silver*.

happening a. (Valley Girls (qv) use) fashionable, chic, up to the minute *Harpers/Queen 1/83*.

happy as a box of birds a. (Aus.) in very high spirits.

happy as a pig in shit (cp) utterly contented.

happy as Larry (Aus. use) perfectly happy, quite content *Lawson*.

happy bag n. (UK criminal use) the bag in which a shotgun is carried on an armed robbery; the gun makes the victim 'happy' to pass over his money *ST 3/4/83*.

happy hour n. orig. US, now general: a period, one or poss. two hours, when a pub or bar offers drinks at half price, usu. about 6 pm; the assumption is that those customers who arrive for the cheap drinks will become sufficiently tipsy to stay on for the more expensive ones.

happy wagon n. see: black Maria.

happy water n. alcohol, liquor.

harbour light (rhyming sl.) all right; usu. as 'all harbour' *Cole*.

hard n. 1. an erection *Bukowski:1*; 2. a thug, a hoodlum *Keyes*.

hard bit n. (US prison use) an unpleasant time in prison due to one's personality, one's crime (which may alienate other prisoners) inability to adapt, etc. *Klein*.

hard case n. a tough, ruthless person *Norman:2*.

hard money n. cash, coins, change *Klein*.

hard one (necrophile use) a corpse that is still in the stage of rigor mortis.

hard stuff n. 1. spirits, as opposed to beer *Humphries*; 2. (drug use) hard drugs, ie. narcotics, as opposed to soft, ie. tranquillizers, cannabis, etc. *Klein*.

hard time v. a prison sentence that a prisoner finds difficult to undergo

Higgins:2.

hard way n. (gambling use) the making of an even point in a dice game by throwing a pair rather than two separate numbers *Runyon*.

hard-ass a. tough, no-nonsense, uncompromising.

hard-boiled a. tough, mean, unpleasant; as in the lengthily cooked egg *R. Goulart, The Hard-Boiled Dicks', bk title, 1967*.

hardcore a. serious, experienced, full-time *Grogan*.

hardcore n. 1. the strongest varieties of pornography, usually featuring at the least uncensored still or moving pictures of intercourse, plus such personal choices as paedophile shots (see: kiddie porn), bestiality, S&M (qv), etc. 2. the American branch of punk rock; '-core' is an all-purpose rock music suffix: it includes 'thrashcore', 'grindcore' ('If you worship nonsense Heavy Metal bands, like whacking out 30 minute long songs with wind down riffs and useless guitar wanking, plus crave to be "hip" and have journos licking your scrotum, call yourself Grind Core.') and 'grunge core' ('Much the same as above [grindcore] with absolutely zero musical skill and unwashed underwear'), and dancecore. *Britcore: The Street Suss Encyclopedia (1990)*.

hard-down 1. a. real, true, genuine; 2. adv. really, truly, genuinely.

harder than pulling a soldier off your sister phr. very difficult indeed.

hardeyes n. unpleasant look, disapproving stare (cf: glad eye) *Higgins:1*.

hardhead n. 1. (Aus. use) a villain, a criminal *Ready*; 2. see: bad-ass nigger (although such a name does reinforce one white cliche: that one can never knock out or hurt a black man by hitting him on his head, since it is too solid to damage) *Folb*.

hard-leg n. (US Black use) a man who devotes all his time and energies to pursuing the street life and the world of strictly male endeavour – pimping, hustling (qv), etc. *Klein*.

hardmouth v. see: badmouth *Folb*.

hard-nose n. (gambling use) a bettor who will never let himself become excessively in debt to his bookmaker *Bukowski:1*.

hard-nose a. tough, uncompromising (cf: hard-ass) *Price:2*.

hard-on n. 1. an erection: *to have a hard-on for*: to want something very much; to like or dislike a person particularly *Price:2*; 2. term of address, usu. sarcastic and referring to someone's high self-esteem; fr. have a hard-on for (qv) *'Serpico', dir. S. Lumet, 1973*.

hardrock a. see: hardcore *Morgan*.

hard-talk v. to employ pressure tactics in a sales pitch *Bruce:2*.

hard-up a. impoverished.

hardware n. (criminal/police use) guns, ammunition.

harelip v. to destroy, to disfigure, to discomfit; esp. in phr. 'harelip the government', 'harelip the governor'.

haricot n. (Aus. rhyming sl.) haricot bean = queen = homosexual *Humphries*.

Harlem credit card n. a piece of hose used to syphon petrol from another car into the tank of one's own.

harmola n. second-rate boxer; the suffix -ola tends to imply some jocularity, in this case to the fighter's potential for causing harm *Schulberg:1*.

harmony hair spray n. the act of ejaculating into a woman's hair; fr. the popular hair spray of the same name *Cole*.

harness bull n. uniformed police officer; the 'harness' is the Sam Browne some forces in the US favour *Chandler*.

harnessed, get oneself v. to get married.

Harolds n. knickers, fr. rhyming sl.? *Humphries*.

harp n. Irish person *Higgins:3*.

harpic a. crazy, insane; from the eponymous lavatory cleanser, which uses the advertising slogan 'Clean round the bend'.

harpoon n. a hypodermic syringe, as used by drug addicts (cf: works).

Harrow drive (cricket use) a shot that while aimed in one direction goes in quite another one, often for a boundary *BBC Radio 3, 1983*.

Harry —ers verbal style orig. in services, affected in 1950s by 'society' and now widespread if obs.: various words prefixed by 'Harry' and suffixed by 'ers'; eg: Harry flakers (tired out, cf: flaked), Harry crashers (asleep, cf: crash out) etc. etc.

Harry Randall n. (rhyming sl.) candle; fr. UK music hall comedian, c.1900. *Wright*.

Harry Tate 1. (bingo rhyming sl.) 8; 2. late (Tate was a comedian popular 1900–1910) *Wright*.

Harry Wragg n. (rhyming sl.) fag (qv) = cigarette; fr. 1930s jockey and trainer *Franklyn*.

harvest moon n. (rhyming sl.) (derog.) coon = black person.

Harvey Nichol n. (rhyming sl.) a pickle = a problem, a difficult situation *Jones:J*.

Harvey Nichols n. (rhyming sl.) pickles; fr. the Knightsbridge store *Jones:J*.

has-beens n. (rhyming sl.) greens; usu. prison use *Cole*.

hash n. (abbrev.) hashish *Higgins:2*.

hash v. (US campus use) to wait on tables in college or local cafeteria/bar, usu. as part-time job to help pay for fees; abbrev. *sling hash*: to work as a waiter/waitress in a café *Underwood*.

hash up v. to plan (cf: cook up).

hashover n. the after-effects of an evening's heavy indulgence in smoking hashish; fr. drinkers' hangover *Sanders:2*.

hash-up n. a meal, usu. of whatever ingredients are available, or of reheated, re-cooked left-overs.

hassle n. a problem, a nuisance, anything requiring irritating effort *Price:2*.

hassle v. to annoy, to nag; to pressurize *Vidal*.

hat n. a contraceptive.

hat time n. (US Black use) the end of a day's work, thus used as syn. for Goodbye. (fr. US prison farm j. hat time: the moment when the captain takes off his hat and waves it to signal the end of the chain gang's working day).

hat up v. (US Black use) to leave, to exit *Klein*.

hatched, matched and dispatched the Births, Marriages & Deaths announcements in *The Times*; listings under Adoptions were proposed as *attached Barr*.

hatchet job n. **1.** (journalist use) a particularly vicious piece of writing, criticizing a person or artistic endeavour; **2.** (US campus use) a broken date *Underwood*.

hatchet man n. **1.** (criminal use) a man who is used to punish, or even murder selected victims on the orders of his boss; **2.** anyone who takes on, or is told to take on unpleasant tasks, such as, in a company, firing members of staff, broaching distasteful but necessary topics, etc.

hatchi n. (lesbian use) the vagina *Maledicta*.

haul ass v. to leave, to escape, to run off *Wolfe:2*.

haul off v. to get ready; often as 'haul off and...'.

haul one's own ashes v. to masturbate. (cf: get one's ashes hauled).

have v. (UK police use) to believe, to accept *Laurie*.

have a bash v. to make an attempt.

have a bellyfull (of) v. to lose patience, to become infuriated by irritating repetition; fr. mental, rather than physical satiety.

have a brass neck v. to be impudent, rude.

have a buzz on v. to be drinking, and mildly intoxicated but not drunk *Neaman & Silver*.

have a calf v. to lose control, to have a emotional fit (cf: have kittens).

have a cob on v. to be in a bad temper, to become annoyed.

have a crack v. to attempt, to have a try *Higgins:3*.

have a cut off the joint v. to have sexual intercourse (fr. male point of view).

have a dash v. (abbrev.) have a dash of lavender: to be marginally homosexual *Legman*.

have a down on v. to feel hostile towards, to be prejudiced against.

have a field day v. for a task or problem to turn out infinitely simple; to have great and unopposed success; fr. hunting/shooting use *PT*.

have a few too many v. to be drunk *The Who, 'Tommy', 1969*.

have a hard-on for v. **1.** to care deeply about, to be extremely concerned about. **2.** to dislike intensely, of both persons and objects; fr. the sexual use, describing the erect penis (cf: hard, hard-on) *Higgins:1*.

have a heat on v. to be drunk *Runyon*.

have a hit on v. (business use) (of a project/person) to make an impact; to come into conflict *Safire*.

have a lam on v. to be in a bad temper *Welsh:1*.

have a lash v. to take part in, to make a try at *Wilkes*.

have a line on v. to understand, to know what is happening; fr. racing use, the *line*: the daily details of the horses running and the odds on them *Higgins:2*.

have a little visitor v. to have a period; genteel euph.

have a mad on (with) v. to be annoyed (with) *Goulart*.

have a moustache v. to perform cunnilingus; fr. female pubic hair *Legman*.

have a pop (at) v. to try, to make an attempt *Wodehouse:MOJ*.

have a ring through one's nose v. (US Black use) to be obsessed, to the point of foolishness, with one other person, usu. a lover, by whom one can be led *Folb*.

have a screw loose v. to be slightly

eccentric, not altogether in control
Southern & Hoffenberg.

have a shot at v. 1. (UK use) to make
an attempt, to have a try; 2. (Aus. use)
to make a sneering remark in
someone's direction *Wilkes*.

have a shot in the locker v. to
maintain one's potency or ability,
sexual and otherwise.

have a skinful v. to be very drunk
Humphries.

have a slash v. to urinate *Humphries*.

have a soft spot for v. to favour
someone, even if such favouritism is
neither sensible nor approved.

have a stick up one's ass v. to be
totally and irredeemably boring; such
a stick would render one physically,
and thus mentally, rigid *Simmons*.

have a stiff one on the rocks v.
(necrophile use) to have intercourse
with a corpse.

have an in v. to have special contacts,
in criminal use, to have such contacts
within a place – ie, a bank – that is to
be robbed *Powis*.

have another guess coming phr. to
be wrong, to be mistaken.

have beans up one's nose v. to have
ulterior motives, to act in a deceptive
or dishonest manner (cf: put beans up
one's nose).

have big eyes v. to be particularly
interested *Southern*.

have by the short and curlies v. to
have at an extreme disadvantage, to
control completely; fr. idea of
grasping one's pubic hair *May*.

have by the short hairs v. see: have
by the short and curlies.

have down chill v. to know something
thoroughly (cf: have cold).

have eyes for v. desire, wish for, usu.
sexually *T 11/5/83*.

have eyes for fluff (gay use) for a
'masculine' lesbian to be looking for a
femme (qv).

have had one's chips v. to have died;
fr. poker use.

have it away v. 1. to escape (from
prison); 2. to copulate.

have it away with v. 1. to copulate

with a given person; 2. to steal a given
object.

have it coming v. to deserve, to
merit, usu. 'it' is unpleasant
Thompson:J.

have it covered v. (US Black use) to
have a situation well under control
Folb.

have it in v. to have sexual intercourse
Mortimer.

have it knocked v. to have a problem,
and esp. life in general, absolutely
under control.

have it off v. 1. (UK criminal use) to
carry out a successful crime *Powis*;
2. (UK police use) to make a
successful raid and arrest *Newman: 2*;
3. to copulate *Norman:2*.

have it on one's dancers v. (UK
criminal use) to run away, to escape
(cf: have it away) *Powis*.

have it out v. to force a confrontation;
to fight *Mandelkau*.

have it taped v. to have something
worked out, assessed fully, etc; orig.
milit. use: fr. tape measure.

have kidney trouble v. (homosexual
use) to frequent public lavatories for
sex *Legman*.

have kittens v. to worry to excess, to
throw a fit, to succumb to one's
emotions, often through worry or fear;
fr. the nervousness of a pregnant cat.

have off v. (UK police use) to arrest;
'off the streets' *Laurie*.

have one cold v. to have at one's
mercy, to have at a disadvantage.

have one mapped v. to have
someone completely and accurately
assessed; to work out another's
movements and attitudes *Klein*.

have one on v. to deceive, to tease, to
delude *Keyes*.

have one over v. to seduce, to deceive
Powis.

have (one) over v. to cheat, to
defraud, to trick *Griffith*.

have one over a barrel v. to put at a
great disadvantage; to inconvenience
deliberately.

have one's act together aka: *have
one's act down, have one's game*

uptight, have one's shit together/down, etc., to be in full control of a given situation, whether emotional, social, sexual, financial, whatever *Folb*.

have one's back v. to take care of, to look after, from the image of guarding one's back from attack *Dre*.

have one's back teeth afloat v. to be very drunk.

have one's cock caught in a zipper v. to be in very bad trouble *Higgins:2*.

have one's foot in the road phr. to spend a good deal of time away from home, to travel frequently.

have one's foot on the rail phr. to drink heavily.

have one's greens v. to have sexual intercourse (cf: greens) *Mortimer*.

have one's guts for garters v. to punish comprehensively; to hurt.

have one's head up one's ass v. to be completely and deliberately stupid *Price:2*.

have one's heart in one's boots v. to be depressed, frightened.

have one's heart in one's mouth v. to be terrified, to be very apprehensive.

have one's porch light out v. to be stupid, mentally deficient *Higgins:4*; thus the reverse, 'put on one's porch light': to sit up and take notice *Morgan*.

have one's nose in the air v. to act in a snobbish, superior manner (cf: high-hat) *Neaman & Silver*.

have one's nose open v.t. (Black pimp use) 1. to produce sexual excitement in another person *Morgan*; 2. to be infatuated with another person; both uses imply heavy breathing *Milner*.

have one's number v. to understand another person absolutely, for all their possible evasions and excuses (cf: peep one's hole card) *Stone*.

have one's pots on v. to be drunk *Runyon*.

have oneself v. (US Black use) to masturbate.

have papers v. (US Black use) to be legally married *Folb*.

have smallpox v. (US cant) to be wanted on an arrest warrant *Neaman & Silver*.

have some rabbit in one v. (US Black/criminal use) 1. to be an habitual absconder from institutions or situations *Pearce*; 2. to be sexually active *Klein*; both meanings derive fr. the alleged obsessions of rabbits.

have someone on v. to trick, to hoax, to lie *Humphries*.

have something going v. to be involved in a close relationship, usu. sexual *Folb*.

have the (dead) needle v. to be very angry.

have the drop on v. to place someone else at a disadvantage, in any confrontation, physical, mental, financial, etc.

have the flag out v. to have one's menstrual period.

have the goods on v. see: have the drop on; with the added inference that the goods (qv) in question relate to ueful information *Morgan*.

have the hots for v. to desire sexually *Price:3*.

have the painters in v. (US use) to have one's menstrual period *Neaman & Silver*.

have the rag on v. 1. spec. to have a menstrual period *Bruce:2*; 2. to act foolishly, eccentrically, to be annoyed *Higgins:1*.

have the slows v. (drug use) to be very high (qv); life outside one's head seems to crawl by *Folb*.

have too much on one's plate v. to be overburdened; esp. with work or commitments.

have two left shoes v. (US Black use) to be absolutely wrong *Klein*.

have whiskers v. to be old, to be out of date *Goulart*.

have you got a coat? (UK police use) have you settled on a suspect who can be realistically arrested? *Laurie*.

have-to n. anything inescapable, esp. something that is forced upon one by social convention; thus 'have-to wedding': a wedding that is arranged after the putative bride is found to be pregnant.

Hawaiian disease n. (gay use) the absence of women, or 'lakanuki'.

Hawaiian eye n. (gay use) the anus; the reference is to the television detective series of the same name.

Hawaiian time n. flexible time, a general disregard for punctuality; thus similarly Alaska time, Jewish time, Indian time.

hawk v. to irritate, to annoy (cf: hack).

hawk v. (US Black use) to keep a suspicious and close watch on *Klein*.

hawk one's brown v. to work as a male prostitute (cf: brown).

hawk one's fork v. (Aus. use) to work as a prostitute; the 'fork' is the juncture of the legs and thus the vagina *Humphries:2*.

hawk one's mutton v. to work as a prostitute (either sex) *Norman:2*.

hawk one's pearly v. to act in a promiscuous manner, to offer one's body for sexual enjoyment *Sharpe:2*.

hawkshaw n. (esp. West Indian use) a detective; fr. 'Hawkshaw the Detective' created by Henry Cecil Bullivant in such books as *The Ticket-of-Leave Man* (1935), etc. *Powis*.

hay n. 1. a small sum of money; usu. as 'that ain't hay', remarking on a substantial sum *Wodehouse:PGM*; 2. marijuana *De Lannoy & Masterson*.

hay eater n. (US Black use) a white person *Major*.

haybag n. a fat, poss. drunken old woman *Runyon:1*.

haymaker n. a swinging punch which counts more on energy and ire than on skill and direction; once such a blow landed, the recipient would 'hit the hay' (qv) *Farrell*.

hayseed n. a farmer, a simple peasant, poss. with hair still filled with hay.

HBI (UK police/criminal use) (abbrev.) House Breaking Implements *LL*.

he can put his shoes under my bed any time phr. a complimentary reference (by a woman) to an attractive male.

he doesn't know if he's Arthur or Martha phr. a reference to a man who is still ambivalent about his own sexuality.

he who smelt it, dealt it (cp) often used as the answer to who cut the cheese (qv) disclaiming all responsibility for having farted.

—head sfx. 1. in a variety of combs. in which —head is linked to a noun to create a term meaning fool or idiot, such usages date back to the 17th C.; the implication is that the head is shaped like or otherwise resembles the noun and the usages include airhead, beefhead, blockhead, bonehead, boofhead, bubblehead, bughead, cabbage-head, cement-head, chowder-head, chucklehead, coconut head, cotton head, deadhead, dickhead, diphead, doughhead, dumbhead, fathead, fuckhead, gourd-head, hammerhead, hulver-head, jolt(er)-head, lighthead, loggerhead, lunkhead, meathead, muddle-head, muffin-head, musclehead, mutton-head, noddy-head, nut-head, peahead, pestlehead, pinhead, poophead, prawnhead, prick-head, pudding-head, rattle-head, sheep's-head, stupe-head, thickhead, toolhead, weather-head, wethead; 2. an habitual user, a devotee, usu. of a given drug or of drink in general, typically a-head, acid-head, boozehead, hooch-head, hop-head, jickhead, juice-head, liquor-head, lush-head, pill-head, piss-head, pot-head, rumhead, slophead, smack-head, sophead, sot-head, weed-head, winehead (cf: —artist); 3. (US derog.) a person of a specific (and alien) ethnic origin: typically, buddhahead, burrhead, coconut head, fish-head, gig-head, handkerchief-head, jug-head, kinky-head, nappy-head, nubbin head, onion-head, pepper-head, potato-head, towelhead, whisky-head.

head n. 1. (US campus use) a person;

fr. 1960s hippie use *Underwood*; **2.** the regular user of any kind of drug: *pot head*, *acid head*, etc. *Wolfe:2*; **3.** oral intercourse, usu. fellatio, but also cunnilingus; **4.** a hangover; thus 'I've got an awful head this morning' (cf: hair of the dog).

head and head game n. (gambling use) a dice game in which players bet against each other rather than against a bank (as in a casino game) *Runyon:1*.

head cook and bottle-washer n. a general factotum who may in fact carry out neither of these duties *A. Green*.

head hunt v. **1.** (US Black use) to look for trouble, to start a fight *Folb*; **2.** (business use) to recruit executives, often by poaching them, offering massive inducements, from rival companies *ST 6/3/83*.

head hunter n. one who performs oral sex.

head up adv. in direct confrontation *Klein*.

head-banger n. **1.** a psychotic, a randomly, obsessively violent person; someone who lacks control of their temper *Wilkinson*; **2.** in music business, a fan of loud, monotonous, 'heavy metal music', usu. a denim-clad, patch-bestrewn youth who plays a make-believe (or even cardboard) guitar and shakes his head violently as he watches or listens to his heroes.

headcase n. an eccentric, a bizarre person.

headcheese n. **1.** (cf: duck butter); **2.** (US Black use) pork luncheon meat.

heading n. using the top of the head to butt someone in a fight (cf: nutting) *LL*.

headlight n. a light-skinned Black person (cf: high yellow).

headlights n. **1.** the female breasts *Neaman & Silver*; **2.** spectacles, glasses, esp. tinted or dark glasses.

headshrinker a psychiatrist, psychoanalyst, etc. (cf: shrink) *Caron*.

heads up! excl. by lookouts for illegal street traders or street gamblers to

warn of an approaching policeman *Powis*.

hear (it) on the street v. to pick up a rumour, to hear the latest gossip.

hearse n. **1.** an ambulance; **2.** a large automobile.

heart n. (street gang use) courage, bravery, spirit *Salisbury*.

heart of oak (rhyming sl.) broke (qv) *Powis*.

heat n. **1.** weapons, arms *Greenlee*; **2.** pressure, esp. on criminals from the police *Fiction Illus.3*; **3.** (drug use) the heating of powdered heroin prior to smoking it (cf: chase the dragon) *'Hill Street Blues', Thames TV, 1983*; **4.** popularity (cf: hot).

Heat n. the police *Goldman*.

heater n. a pistol, revolver (cf: heat) *Wodehouse:PGM*.

heat's on the police are enforcing exceptional pressure on the community *C. Himes, bk title*.

heave v. to vomit; fr. the sensation in one's stomach *Bernbach*.

heave-ho n. rejection, ejection *Wodehouse:PGM*.

Heavens to Betsy! excl. of shock, horror, surprise *Higgins:4*.

Heavens to Murgatroyd! see: Heavens to Betsy!.

heaver n. (US Black use) a self-styled great lover, esp. of the more earthy, animalistic type (cf: stud) *Klein*.

heavy n. a thug, a villain; esp. in cinema and theatre.

heavy a. **1.** (drug use) a hard drug – heroin, cocaine – rather than a soft one – cannabis, etc. *Burroughs:1*; **2.** intense *Price:2*; **3.** frightening, threatening; **4.** thuggish, violent; **5.** meaningful, important, emotionally strong; a general intensifier, esp. loved by late 1960s hippies and radicals, varying as to context *Hoffman:a*.

heavy v. to threaten, to menace.

heavy date n. a more than usually important meeting with one's boyfriend/girlfriend *R. Wild*.

heavy manners n. (UK Black use) any form of oppression or repression experienced by blacks (esp. at the hands of the police).

heavy mob n. **1.** a gang of thugs *Norman:2*; **2.** (police use) physically tough officers used in violent situations; **3.** (UK police use) officers from the Flying Squad and, formerly, the Special Patrol Group *Powis*.

heavy-duty a. tough, unpleasant *Price:2*.

heavyweight n. an important person with power and influence *Jenkins*.

Hebe n. a Jew; fr. Hebrew *Price:1*.

heck (euph.) hell *Seale*.

he'd fuck anything with a hole in it phr. said of an indiscriminately promiscuous male.

hedge n. (UK criminal use) the crowd that gathers round an illicit street game of three-card monte (qv) *Powis*.

hedgehog n. (US campus use) male derog. term for unattractive female (cf: dog) *Underwood*.

heebie-jeebies n. unpleasant fantasies, nameless terrors, anything the mind can conjure up to produce nerves and fear *Hoffman:a*.

heel n. **1.** spec. a petty criminal; **2.** a dishonest, untrustworthy person *Humphries*; either fr. 'down-at-heel' or the image on an unwanted person, continually at one's heels.

heel on v. (US Black use) to leave, to depart *Klein*.

heeled a. **1.** armed *Grogan*; **2.** rich; abbrev., well-heeled.

heifer n. (US Black use) an unattractive, obese woman (cf: cow); **2.** (US campus use) any female *Underwood*.

heifer-dust n. **1.** nonsense, rubbish (cf: bullshit); **2.** (Aus.) a girl or woman (cf: heifer).

heinie n. **1.** the buttocks; fr. euph. diminutive of hind end or hinder parts *Neaman & Silver*; **2.** a very short haircut.

Heinie n. (derog.) German *Stone*.

heinie highway n. the anus (cf: hershey highway).

Heinz n. **1.** (UK bookmaker use) any combination bet; fr. the '57 Varieties' *Wall St. Jour. 10/5/67*; **2.** a mongrel.

heist n. a robbery; fr. hoist *Grogan*.

Helen, Helena n. euph. for hell and used in various mild oaths; also as Helen Blazes, Helen Maria, Helena Montana

hell n. (US Black use) an expert, an admirable or impressive person.

hell for breakfast, hell-bent for breakfast phr. rushed, hurriedly, at top speed (cf: hell-bent for election).

hell to breakfast, from phr. **1.** in all directions, everywhere; **2.** decisively, violently; **3.** for a long time, for a long distance.

Hell Week n. (US campus use) period of initiation for pledges to a college fraternity *Farina*.

hellacious a. (US campus use) wonderful, amazing, extraordinary *Underwood*.

hell-bent for election phr. hurriedly, recklessly.

heller n. (US campus use) exciting, dramatic party; fr. 'hell-of-a' good time *Underwood*.

hellified a. extreme, excessive.

Hello, John, got a new motor? cp of 'alternative' comedian Alexei Sayle, coined c.1980 and parodying the many 'Johns' and 'Jack the Lads' of London's East End and its Essex overspill *A. Sayle, 'The Train to Hell', 1984*.

hell's a-popping, hellzapoppin' phr. (orig. US) general phr. of intensification, implying aggression, chaos, forcefulness.

hell's bells! mild. excl. *Wodehouse:AAG*.

hell's bottom, hell's hollow, hell's point n. any disreputable or out of the way area (cf: hell's half acre).

hell's teeth! excl.; see hell's bells *Manser*.

hems n. (abbrev.) haemorrhoids *Klein*.

hen n. a woman; term of address in Central Scotland to a woman *J. Boyle, 'A Sense of Freedom', TV film, Channel-4 1983*.

hen on a hot griddle, like a phr. in an agitated or nervous manner (cf: cat on a hot tin roof).

hen party n. a women-only get-together; the opposite of a stag party (for men) but generally devoid of the drunken excess.

hen-headed a. stupid, foolish, scatter-brained.

hen-pecked a. a man, usu. married, who is persecuted by the woman with whom he lives.

Henry! excl. a mild oath, euph. for hell! (qv).

Henry n. (drug use) heroin *Green:1*.

hep a. aware, informed, sophisticated, in the know (cf: hip).

hep n. (abbrev.) hepatitis *Hoffman:a*.

her indoors n. the wife; coined by Leon Griffiths in the *Minder* series on Thames TV, 1979 onwards *Payne*.

herb n. (drug use) marijuana, esp. Jamaican term *Green:1*.

Herbert n. a simple person; thus *Herbert music*: music hall jokes mixed with rock music *G 28/3/83*.

herbs n. (Aus. use) speedy, powerful, responsive to the accelerator (of a car) *Humphries:2*.

herder n. (US prison use) a prison guard *Chandler: Notebk*.

here we go (again) (cp) often stated with some resignation and implying distaste for some form of repetitious activity, speechifying, etc.

here's how! popular toast when drinking *Manser*.

here's looking at you a toast before drinking, immortalized (and clichéd) after Humphrey Bogart's rendition in *Casablanca*, 1941.

here's mud in your eye! a toast when drinking *Schulberg*.

Hershey highway n. the anus.

he-she n. homosexual male (cf: omee-palone) *Shulman*.

hex n. a curse, s spell; fr. Yiddish *hexe*: witch.

Hey Rube! 1. a call for help; 2. a fight, orig. between circus/carnival people and local townspeople. 'Hey Rube' was the traditional rallying cry of circus or carnival employees when faced with any trouble from locals

Pynchon.

H/H abbr. (contact ads use) high heels *SMD*.

hi-de-hi. . .ho-de-ho popular style of greeting, and the requisite response; orig. 1940s, but real popularity arrived with BBC-TV's eponymous situation comedy, set in a 1950s holiday camp.

hick n. any inhabitant of the countryside, a peasant, a farmer; fr. late 17th C. meaning: an easy victim to card-sharpers, and thus usu. a rustic *White*.

hickey n. a love bite, usu. on the neck *Junker*.

hickory v. to whip, to thrash.

hickory-dock n. (rhyming sl.) clock *Cole*.

hicktown n. a small town (cf: hicksville, jaytown).

hide n. 1. a girl, usu. considered as a sex-object; 2. an old crone, a hag, an ugly old woman.

hide n. 1. (music use) drums; fr. their skins *Major*; 2. the human skin, thus one's life, esp. in 'save one's hide', etc. *PT*.

hide the salam v. (US preppie (qv) use) (abbrev.) hide the salami: to have sexual intercourse; usu. as in *to play hide. . .* also as *hide and salam* fr. W. Allen, *Annie Hall*, 1976 *Bernbach*.

high a. intoxicated with drugs or drink. or, poss, religious/spiritual enthusiasm *Underwood*.

high and goodbye n. (US Black use) unreliable person (poss. hi – hello – and goodbye?) *Folb*.

high as a cat's back a. drunk (cf: high).

high as a fiddler's fist phr. drunk (cf: high).

high as a kite a. very drunk; fr. rhyming sl. tight = drunk *Cole*.

high as Lindbergh phr. drunk (cf: high).

high as ninety a. drunk (cf: high).

high as the hair on a cat's back phr. very expensive.

high diver n. cunnilinctor *Legman*.

high flier, high flyer n. an important person, or one who poses as such.

high flying n. immorality, hedonism, extravagance.

high game v. (Black pimp and conman use) giving the mark (qv) less than he pays for but leaving him believing he actually had more than the basic price *Milner*.

high monkey-monk see: high mucky-mucky *Dunne*.

high mucky-muck n. a superior person, usu. derog.; prob. fr. Chinook jargon: *hiu muckamuck*: plenty food, denoting a powerful member of a tribe *Runyon*.

high nose n. arrogance, snobbery.

high on oneself phr. conceited, arrogant, snobbish.

high on the hog living a comfortable, secure and well-off life; fr. the area of the choicest cuts of pork and its by-products (cf: life of Riley) *Price: 3*.

high roller n. a heavy gambler *Fiction Illus. 3*.

high sign n. a warning, a recognition signal, a secret sign.

high, wide and handsome a. happy, pleasant, carefree, performing well and easily.

high yellow n. aka: *high yaller*: a Mulatto woman or girl *Himes: 1*.

high-brow n. an intellectual or anyone the speaker considers to be one.

higher than a cat's back phr. very tall.

Higher-Higher n. (US milit. use) the high command *Del Vecchio*.

highfalutin a. snobbish, pompous.

high-five v. to greet by raising the arm and ritualistically slapping each other's palm. *Morgan*.

high-hat v. to act in a superior manner towards another, to put on airs *Mandelkau*.

high-hat, high-hatter n. (orig. US) 1. a member of the social élite (cf: fancy pants, silk stockings); thus 2. an arrogant, superior person, a snob; a. 3. high-hatty, high-hatted: snobbish, stuck up.

highpockets n. a tall man *Uris*.

high-siding (Black use) showing off, bragging, often in the ostentatious display of jewellery, flashy clothes and cars, etc. *Milner*.

high-steppin' a. see: high-siding.

hightail (it) v. to leave quickly, to run off, to escape.

high-toned a. superior, stand-offish *Tennessee Ernie Ford, '16 Tons', 1956*.

high-up n. the boss, the leader; anyone senior, more powerful than the speaker.

high-wall job n. (UK criminal use) breaking and entering a factory or any similar building surrounded by a high wall (cf: second storey man) *Sillitoe*.

hike v. raise *Variety 19/1/83*.

hincty a. 1. suspicious *Chandler: Notebk*; 2. snobbish; 3. (US Black use) derog. ref, to any Black abandoning racial pride for attempts to ape white manners/styles.

hindside n. the buttocks, the posterior (cf: backside).

hindside of nowhere n. a particularly out of the way place.

hindside-backaways, hind-side backwards adv. back to front.

hindside-before adv. back to front.

Hindustani jig n. (gay use) anal intercourse.

hinge-jaw n. one who talks too much.

hinges n. the joints of the human body, thus phr. 'one's hinges are creaking': one is getting old.

hinges of hell phr. general phr. of intensification, esp. 'as black as the hinges of hell', 'hot as the hinges of hell'.

hip a. sophisticated, *au fait*, aware, in tune with events, ideas and situations. as abbrev. for hipster (qv) the word had a more specific meaning to jazz/beatnik buffs of 1950s, but now the general use is predominant *Price: 2*.

hip v. to initiate, to explain *Goldman*.

Hip City (US Black use) Cleveland, Ohio *Klein*.

hip deep to a tall Indian phr. very deep, often used of water, snow (cf: knee-high to a grasshopper).

hipidity n. (US campus use) hippie (qv) *Underwood*.

hipped on adv. interested in, obsessed by.

hippie n. 1960s teen cult member, preaching a philosophy of 'love and peace', backed by wide spectrum drug usage, esp. of cannabis and hallucinogens.

hippo n. a mild depression. (fr. abbr. hypochondria).

hips up (on one's shoulders), get v. (US Black use) to get upset, annoyed, hurt.

hipster n. the epitome of the 1950s Bohemian stance: the quintessence of cool (qv), in full retreat from emotional display, hymned by bop music and lulled by heroin into complete disaffiliation from humanity; currently merely historical.

hipsters n. the accumulations of fat around the thighs and stomachs of the overweight (cf: bagels) *Neaman & Silver*.

Hiram n. a rustic, a peasant (cf: Clem, Rube).

hired gun n. (business use) an executive who is hired for the performance of a particiularly tough task; fr. imagery of cinema Westerns; the task performed, he may well 'ride off into the sunset' (cf: headhunter) *Kidder*.

hissy n. a tantrum, an outburst of bad temper.

hist v. see: heist *Runyon*.

hit n. 1. a murder, esp. a gangster killing; 2. a puff on a marijuana cigarette. *SF Comics*; 3. a portion of any drug: a tablet of amphetamine or barbiturate; a line of heroin or cocaine, etc.; 4. (rhyming sl.) hit and miss = kiss *Powis*.

hit v. 1. to pay *Higgins: 1*; 2. to adulterate drugs prior to selling them (cf: cut) *Higgins: 1*; 3. arrive at *Runyon*; 4. to rob, to hold up *Higgins: 1*; 5. to inject narcotics; spec. for the drug to register its immediate effect on the user *Goldman*.

hit a bull in the ass, not be able to phr. to be clumsy or inept, esp. to be a poor marksman, other combs

include '. . .with a bass fiddle', 'with a handful of peas', 'with a handful of tapioca', 'with a shovel' (cf: couldn't hit a barn door).

hit a knot v. to snore.

hit and missed a. (rhyming sl.) (always in full) pissed (qv) = drunk *Powis*.

hit for v. 1. to purchase, esp. of drugs *Dre*; 2. to borrow money, thus 'hit for a loan' *Welsh:1* (cf: hit on).

hit for six v. to assert oneself decisively in an argument; to destroy any form of opposition; fr. cricket use.

hit her up v. to accelerate, to go fast.

hit it off v. to establish a relationship, to become friendly, to get on well *Sillitoe*.

hit me! (gambling use) invitation to the dealer to give one another card.

hit me and cut the rap! (US teen use) stop talking and just do what you came to do, give me what I want, etc. (cf: beat about the bush) *Sculatti*.

hit on v. 1. to approach, usu. against the subject's wishes *Goldman*; 2. to seduce; in pimp use, to attract a woman to one's team of prostitutes *Milner*.

hit (one) up v. (US Black use) to approach, to speak to, to question.

hit skins v. to have sexual intercourse (cf: bump bellies).

hit some shit v. (US Black use) to encounter problems *Folb*.

hit the ball v. 1. to leave quickly (cf: ball the jack); 2. to work hard, to be diligent at a job.

hit the books v. (US campus use) to study hard *Underwood*.

hit the bottle v. to drink heavily *Algren*.

hit the breeze v. to depart, to travel, to run fast.

hit the bricks v. 1. exit, leave for the street, start walking; 2. spec. to be discharged from a gaol sentence.

hit the deck v. 1. to fall down; 2. to throw oneself deliberately to the ground *Mortimer*.

hit the gas v. to accelerate in a motorcar *Selby: 1*.

hit the ground with his hat, not be able to phr. **1.** general. phr. implying incompetence; **2.** to be extremely drunk.

hit the hay v. to go to sleep *Runyon*.

hit the high spots v. to go out for an evening's dining and dancing.

hit the jug v. to drink heavily *Dickson*.

hit the mainline v. to inject narcotics *Chandler: LG*.

hit the road v. to leave, to set out on a journey *Eagles, 'Desperado', 1975*.

hit the roof v. to explode with temper, to become extremely annoyed *Fiction Illus. 3*.

hit the sack v. to go to sleep (cf: sack out) *Bruce: 1*.

hit the sauce v. see: hit the bottle.

hit the shucks v. to go to bed, to go to sleep (cf: hit the hay, hit the sack, hit the tick).

hit the trail v. to leave *Chandler: LG*.

hit the wind v. (US Black use) to leave quickly, to run away *Klein*.

hit-and-get n. (US conman use) the passing off of a con-trick in a town and then immediately 'getting out' of that town and starting over again *Thompson: J*.

hitch n. (US milit. use) a term of enlistment in one of the US armed forces *Stone*.

hitched a. married.

hitch-hiker on the Hershey highway n. a homosexual male.

hit-head n. a crack (qv) user *Shell* (cf: hitter).

hitman n. an assassin, usu. employed by some variety of organized crime. (cf: hit, v.).

hitter n. **1.** a success, a star, usu. with overtones of violence, criminality *Price: 1*; **2.** a crack (qv) user (cf: hit-head) *Shell*.

hive off v. (Aus. use) to leave *Ready*.

hiver n. (derog.) a person with AIDS *Welsh: 1* (fr. acro. HIV + sfx. -er).

ho n. Black pron. of *whore*: a prostitute *Milner*.

ho stroll n. (US Black pimp use) the street or streets in a given town or city where prostitutes work regularly *Klein*.

Hoboken n. **1.** an insignificant, out of the way place; **2.** hell. (fr. proper name of Hoboken, New Jersey).

hobosex n. sex with a number of strangers in a short period of time; from hobo = tramp; thus hobosexual: one who enjoys such random adventuring.

hock v. to pawn; thus *in hock Higgins: 3*.

hockshop n. the pawnbroker's shop.

hocky n. dog excrement *Neaman & Silver*.

hocus-pocus n. **1.** drugged alcohol; **2.** marijuana *Snoop Doggy Dogg 'Doggystyle' (1993)*.

hog n. **1.** penis *Higgins: 1*; **2.** (US campus use) male term for an unattractive female (cf: dog) *Underwood*; **3.** (drug use) pig tranquillizer, PCP, phencyclidine (cf: angel dust) *Green: 1*; **4.** (drug use) anyone who uses more narcotics than does the speaker *Burroughs: 1*; **5.** (Hells Angels use) a motorcycle (usu. Harley-Davidson) modified and cut down for outlaw gang use (cf: garbage wagon); **6.** (Black use) any automobile, esp. a Cadillac *Milner*; **7.** a miser, a mean person.

Hogan's ghost! (Aus. use) general expression of amazement *Bickerton*.

hog-caller n. a loud and piercing scream, akin to those used by farmers calling their pigs *Bukowski: 1*.

hoggish a. **1.** greedy, avaricious; **2.** stupid.

hogwash! (excl.) nonsense! rubbish! *Jay & Young*.

hog-whimpering adv. extremely drunk.

ho-hum a. non-committal, inconclusive *Jay & Young*.

hoist v. (UK criminal use) **1.** to shoplift *Powis*; **2.** hoist (a few) to have a drink/drinks.

hoister n. (UK criminal use) **1.** a pickpocket; **2.** a shoplifter *Powis*.

hoity-toity a. aloof, snobbish; fr. haughty *Esq. 6/83*.

ho-jo n. (abbrev.) Howard Johnson's

motel *Higgins: 2*.

hokey a. fake, false; fr *hokum McFadden*.

hokey-pokey n. any form of trickery, swindling, something underhand, duplicitous. (fr. 17th C. SE hocus pocus: the name of a juggler (and, apparently, as the assumed name of a particular conjuror) derived from the sham Latin formula employed by him, which ran '*Hocus pocus, tontus talontus, vade celeriter jubeo*'; despite 17th C. Protestant suggestions, the term is not linked to the '*Hoc est corpus*' of the Roman Catholic Eucharist).

hold everything! see: hold it!

hold it down! excl. be quiet!

hold it! (excl.) stop what you're doing; be quiet, etc. *Seale*.

hold one's head v. (US Black use) to be patient, to restrain oneself.

hold one's horses v. to slow down, to show restraint.

hold one's mud v. to keep one's own counsel, to keep quiet *Morgan*.

hold one's noise v. to stop talking *Wilkinson*.

hold paper on v. stand as a creditor to someone *Dunne*.

hold the baby v. **1.** spec. from stock market use: purchasing stocks which one then cannot sell; **2.** to be left to clear up a problem, to take an (unpleasant) responsibility *Performance*.

hold the bag v. (cant) for a villain to be left with full responsibility for a crime in which his associates have not been legally involved '*Serpico*', directed *S. Lumet, 1973*.

hold the can v. to take responsibility, usu. unwanted (cf: hold the baby 2) *Humphries: 2*.

hold the phone v. wait, delay, 'hang on'; fr. telephone use *Capital Radio 1983*.

hold your water! (excl.) wait a minute, don't get excited, etc. (cf: hold one's horses) '*The Mean Machine*', directed *Albert S. Ruddy*.

holding in possession of drugs

Burroughs: 1.

hold-out n. (pimp use) an unprofessional, undisciplined prostitute (cf: flaky ho) *OUI 8/75*.

hole n. **1.** (abbrev.) cakehole = mouth; esp. on *shut one's hole Performance*; **2.** (US prison use) the punishment cells; **3.** see: ho *Milner*; **4.** the vagina *Folb*; **5.** (derog.) a passive homosexual male; **6.** sexual intercourse, thus 'get one's hole': to have sex.

hole card n. a secret, which can be either a weakness which, once discovered, can be exploited or a hidden strength; fr. poker use; thus peep one's . . . (qv) *Runyon*.

hole in one! (excl.) absolutely correct! fr. golf use *Payne*.

hole in the ground, not know from a phr. (orig. US) general phr. implying ignorance of a given person; variations include a hole in the fence, a hole in the road, a hole in a tree (cf: not know one's ass from a hole in the ground).

hole in the wall a. second-class, inferior, small-time (qv) *Whitcomb*.

hole up v. to settle, to take up residence; poss. but not definite inference of hiding away, taking refuge *Wolfe: 2*.

holes & poles n. (US campus use) sex education classes *Jay & Young*.

HOLLAND acro. hope *our love lives and never dies*: written on envelopes of love letters (cf: BURMA, NORWICH, SWALK) *Partridge:5*.

holler v. to shout, to scream *Higgins: 1*.

holler copper v. to inform *Runyon*.

hollow n. in a variety of combs, describing an area of a town; usu. referring to poor or foreign groups: e.g. Dead Man's Hollow, Frog Hollow, Irish Hollow, Piggy Hollow, Punkin Hollow, Skunk Hollow, Sleepy Hollow, Smoky Hollow, Snuff Hollow.

hollow tooth n. (UK police use) New Scotland Yard, fr. it's being 'rotten inside', ie, corrupt *Powis*.

Hollywood swoop n. (US Black use) an automobile manoeuvre whereby one cuts in front of another vehicle, stopping one's own car and thus forcing, the other vehicle to halt, à la TV police chase sequences. *Folb*.

hols n. (abbrev.) holidays *Capital Radio 1983*.

holy cats! excl. of surprise, dismay, alarm *Rawson*.

holy cow! excl. of surprise *Rawson*.

holy cripes! general excl. of surprise, alarm, etc. (cf: cripes) *Rawson*.

holy friar n. (rhyming sl.) a liar *Jones: J*.

Holy Joe n. 1. anyone of a religious bent; 2. spec. a clergyman, esp. in services or in goal. *LL*.

holy mackerel! mild excl; see holy smoke, Moses, etc. *Manser*.

holy Moses! see: holy smoke *rr*.

holy smoke! excl. of surprise, shock, wonder, etc. *rr*.

Home and Colonial n. (UK police use) London-based Regional Crime Squad which includes officers from the Metropolitan (home) and provincial (colonial) forces *Powis*.

home and dry safe and sound.

home squeeze n. see: main squeeze *Folb*.

homeboy, homegirl n. (US Black use) 1. someone who stays mainly at home *Morgan*; 2. a neighbourhood person; 3. a good friend (cf: Yiddish *landsman*) *X*.

homeland n. (US Black use) the Black area of a city (cf: homeboy, homey).

homes n. affectionate diminutive of homeboy (qv); usually as term of address, eg. 'Hey, homes…' *Morgan*.

homey n. affectionate diminutive of homeboy (qv) *Ice T:1*.

homie n. 1. a homosexual; 2. (US Black use) see: homey.

hominy gazette n. (Aus. prison use) internal prison rumours; fr. the main constituent of prison meals (cf: bush telegraph) *Neaman & Silver*.

homo n. (abbrev.) homosexual *Price: 2*.

hon (abbrev.) honey, general term of endearment, affection *rr*.

honcho n. leader, employer, boss, the head person of any job or other situation; orig. US forces use in Korea *Higgins: 1*.

honcho v. to lead, to direct others in a task or plan.

hone v. 1. to pine for, to yearn after; 2. to look for, to search out.

honest? do you really mean it?; are you joking? etc.

honey n. 1. a girl, a woman *Higgins: 1*; 2. a mistress *Higgins: 1*; 3. (US campus use) female term for endearing, attractive male *Underwood*.

honey cart n. (airline use) disposal vehicles that flush out the lavatories of airliners (cf: honey wagon) *Green: 2*.

honey dipper n. (US milit. use) a latrine cleaner; fr. *honey*; excrement and urine *Neaman & Silver*.

Honey Hill n. the poor area of a given town.

honey house n. a privy or outside lavatory.

honey (it) up to v. to toady to, to act the sycophant, to flatter (cf: honey, honeyfuggle).

honey wagon n. (US agricultural use) a manure cart used for cleaning out barns (cf: honey cart) *Neaman & Silver*.

honey, honeydew n. excrement, faeces, ordure (whether animal or human).

honeyfuck v. 1. to have sexual intercourse in innocent/idyllic circumstances; 2. to have sex with a pre-pubescent girl.

honeyfuggle v. (euph.) honeyfuck (qv).

honeymoon n. (drug use) the early use of heroin, during which period the user can stop without any real physical or mental pain; prior to actual addiction *De Lannoy & Masterson*.

honeymoon cystitis n. a vaginal infection that supposedly stems from intensive intercourse, which in turn is supposedly the staple of honeymooning couples.

honeypot n. the vagina *Southern & Hoffenberg*.

honk n. (abbrev.) honkie (qv) *Burroughs: Jr*.

honk v.i. (US campus use) to be sexually aroused *Underwood*.

honk on v. (US campus use) to go away; to leave one alone *Underwood*.

honker n. **1.** penis *Jay & Young*; **2.** (Valley Girls (qv) use) anyone considered odd, ecentric *Pond*.

Honkers n. Hong Kong, usu. amongst UK ex-patriates stationed or working in Far East *P. Theroux, 'Saint Jack', 1973*.

honkie n. a white person; fr. hunkie: orig. name for Poles who worked in Chicago stockyards *Price: 2*.

honky-tonk n. **1.** a seedy bar which may also offer music, gambling, whores; fr. the honky-tonk piano that was often a feature of such establishments; **2.** the late Dick Emery used *hello honky-tonk(s)* as a cp but it may not survive his death.

honyok n. rustic, peasant *Gruber*.

hooch n. alcohol, liquor; fr. Alaskan Indian *hoocheno*: liquor *Chandler: LG*.

hood n. **1.** (Aus. surfer use) the police *Humphries: 2*; **2.** an enemy agent; used passim by John le Carré in his fiction, but like other similar usages, either already espionage sl. or soon to become such (cf: babysit, mole).

hood n. (abbrev.) hoodlum = gangster, thug *Fiction Illus. 3*.

hood n. (US Black use) abbrev. neighbourhood *Boyz 'N' the Hood, title, 1991*.

hoodoo v. to cheat, to deceive, to take advantage of.

hoody n. a hooded sweatshirt, as worn by many rappers (qv) as a semi-uniform.

hooey n. rubbish, nonsense.

hoof n. the human foot.

hoof it v. **1.** to walk on foot; **2.** to run *Farrell*.

hoof out v. to throw out, to expel.

hoofer n. dancer *Bruce: 1*.

hoofing (show business use) dancing *T 15/3/83*.

hoo-ha n. nonsense, rubbish, twaddle *Humphries: 2*.

hook n. **1.** (US campus use) the telephone *Underwood*; **2.** (US milit. use) (abbrev.) hook-up: radio *Del Vecchio*; **3.** (US Black use) Jew (derog.) fr. popular stereotype of hooknosed Semites, see hooknose *Folb*; **4.** (abbrev.) hooker (qv); **5.** the pickpocket who actually steals the wallet, money, etc. rather than his various accomplices (cf: wire) *Chandler: Notebk.* **6.** (US police use) anyone with sufficient power and clout (qv) to influence police management decisions, esp. in the giving to specific officers of choice assignments *Neaman & Silver*.

hook v. **1.** to addict to drugs; **2.** to engage in prostitution; **3.** to arrest, to catch in a crime *Higgins: 1*; **4.** to fool, to practice a confidence trick upon.

hook down v. to swallow *Wolfe: 2*.

hook joint n. a brothel where the prostitutes are likely to cheat their clients.

hook, line and sinker n. absolutely, completely fr. fishing imagery.

hook shop n. a brothel; fr. hooker (qv) *Goulart*.

hooker n. prostitute. fr. the redlight area of New York in 19th C: Corlear's Hook *Price: 2*.

hooking (UK police use) the practice of a dishonest informer who attempts to smear honest policemen and drag them into his own problems for his own ultimate benefit *Powis*.

hooknose n. (derog.) a Jew *Farrell*.

hooks n. human hands *Algren*.

hooky a. illegal, bent (qv); from hook = steal.

hoon n. (Aus. use) a procurer of prostitutes, but not a pimp to a specific girl or girls *Baker*.

hoop n. (US prison use) sodomy (cf: ring) *Legman*.

hoopdie swoop v. (US Black use) to move in on and pick up a man or woman with great speed and efficiency *Folb*.

hoopla n. fuss, commotion *Grogan*.

Hooray (abbrev.) hooray Henry (qv).

Hooray Henry n. aka: *Hoorah Henry*:rich young man given to much public exhibitionism, drunkenness and similar anti-social activities, all based on an excess of snobbish self-esteem *Runyon*.

hooroo! (Aus. use) goodbye *Ready*.

hoosegow n. prison; fr. Sp. *juzgado*: a tribunal or court of justice *Wodehouse passim*.

hoot n. 1. (Aus. use) money, wealth *Wilkes*; 2. a most amusing experience *White*.

hoot v. 1. to laugh loudly; 2. (Aus. use) to smell badly, to stink *Ready*.

hootch n. (US milit. use) in Vietnam, any form of shelter from a peasant hut, to a bunker, to an office building *Del Vecchio*.

hootenanny n. an imaginary object (cf: dingus, thingummibob, thingummijig); 2. a general term of abuse; 3. nonsense, rubbish, anything insignificant, euph. for a damn, and used similarly, e.g. I don't give a hootenanny (cf: hoot).

hooter n. 1. nose; 2. (drug use) a marijuana cigarette.

hoowah n. whore fr. New York pron. *Price: 2*.

hop n. (US/Aus./N.Z.) beer.

hop n. heroin, opium *Chandler: 2*.

hop it! (excl.) go away, run along, etc. *Manser*.

hop joint n. a room or apartment where patrons gather to smoke opium or take heroin (cf: shooting gallery) *Runyon: 1*.

hop on a babe v. (US campus use) to have sexual intercourse; the inference is that the man, lacking greater finesse, has made a pounce (prob. when drunk) to initiate the activity *Bernbach*.

hop the coop v. to escape, from any form of confinement, not necessarily prison *Chandler: LG*.

hop the twig v. to die (cf: drop off the twig).

hop the wag v. to play truant from school (cf: bunk off) *Powis*.

hope-to-die a. (US Black use) closest, most trusted, best; fr. affirmation 'Hope to die if . . .' *Folb*.

hophead n. (drug use) 1. spec. heroin addict; 2. user of any drug *Thompson*.

hopped up a. 1. spec. of a car which has been improved beyond its basic specifications; 2. excited *Price: 2*; 3. under the affect of narcotics *Morgan*.

Hopping Sam (US milit. use) see Bouncing Betty *Rawson*.

horizontal rumble n. (US campus use) sexual intercourse (cf: rumble) *Bernbach*.

Horlicks n. (UK 'society' use) a mess *Barr*.

horn n. 1. the nose; 2. telephone *McFadden*; 3. (US milit. use) a radio handset *Del Vecchio*; 4. an erection *Higgins: 1*.

horn v. to inhale a narcotic *Goldman*.

horn in v. to interfere, to butt in, to intrude *Farrell* .

horn movie n. pornographic film *Simmons*.

horny a. sexually eager, aroused *Price: 1*.

horrors n. unpleasant experiences – usu. paranoid fantasies – brought about occasionally by the effects of smoking cannabis *Keyes*.

horry n. (Aus. use) (abbrev.) horizontal; copulation *C. Clarke*.

hors d'oeuvres n. (drug use) barbiturates or amphetamines; a prelude to harder (qv) pleasures *Folb*.

horse n. 1. heroin *Grogan*; 2. (Can. prison use) a smooth piece of wood with a string attached *Caron*; 3. (rhyming sl.) horse and trap = clap = venereal disease, spec. gonorrhoea *Powis*.

horse apple n. a piece of horse excrement found lying in the road, thus also horse biscuit, horse doughnut, horse dumpling (cf: alley apple).

horse around v. to joke, to mess

about; fr. horse-play *Higgins: 3*.

horse laugh n. a bad joke; hollow laughter *Chandler: LG*.

horse piss n. weak coffee (cf: gnat's piss).

horsefeathers (euph.) horseshit (qv) *Rawson*.

horseman n. (Can. prison use) a Mountie, a member of the Royal Canadian Mounted Police (RCMP) *Caron*.

horseplayer n. a gambler on horseraces *Bukowski: 1*.

horses n. (abbrev.) horsepower *Selby: 1*.

horse's ass fool, idiot *Farrell*.

horse's hangdown n. fool, idiot (cf: horse's ass) fr. the animal's penis, thus prick = fool *Higgins: 4*.

horseshit n. rubbish, nonsense (cf: bullshit) *Bruce: 2*.

horsewomen n. masculine lesbians *Legman*.

horsey adv. 1. amorous, lustful, frolicsome; 2. impatient, rude, peremptory.

hose v. (homosexual use) to sodomize.

hose down v. (milit. use) to fire at, usu. with automatic weapons or aircraft weapons *Wolfe: 5*.

hostie n. (abbrev.) air hostess (cf: stew) *Humphries: 2*.

hot a. 1. urgent, fresh *SF Comics*; 2. wanted by the police, suspect; 3. stolen (goods); 4. (sporting use) playing well, on top form *Sanchez*; 5. (gambling use) enjoying a run of luck *Southern*; 6. angry, annoyed *Jenkins*; 7. sexy, sexually available; 8. attractive, pleasurable; general term of approval.

hot n. a hot meal.

hot v. to indulge in hotting (qv) *Ind. 3/9/91*.

hot as floogies n. extremely hot.

hot belly n. a Mexican (cf: pepper belly).

hot box n. the female genitals.

hot chair n. the electric chair *Sillitoe*.

hot cross bun (rhyming sl.) on the run *Cole*.

hot dog n. successful gambler *Higgins: 3*.

hot foot n. see hot-foot v.

hot for a. enthusiastic, keen on *Thompson*.

hot lot n. (UK police use) the flying Squad, or the defunct Special Patrol Group *Powis*.

hot meat injection n. sexual intercourse.

hot on see: hot for *Seale*.

hot pants 1. worried, anxious *Higgins: 2*; 2. sexually eager *Chandler: LG*.

hot poop n. the latest news or gossip.

hot potato n. a problem, a difficult person, a trying situation; anything those concerned would prefer not to handle *Uris*.

hot seat n. 1. the electric chair (cf: hot chair, hot squat); 2. an unpleasant situation, esp. in a courtroom or public enquiry *PT*.

hot shot n. the substitution of battery acid for white powdered heroin; when injected by the addict it causes instant death and leaves no trace *Grogan*.

hot squat n. the electric chair.

hot stuff form of address, often implying that the person in question has a higher opinion of him/herself than does his/her audience *Price: 3*.

hot to trot n. enthusiastic for sex *McFadden*.

hot walker n. (horse race use) a groom who walks a horse in order to cool it down after a race *Higgins: 1*.

hot-ass a. superlative *Shell*.

hotch v. to swarm with, to burst with *Welsh:1* (fr. Sc. dial. hotch).

hot-dog v. to chase, to harass.

hot-dogger n. (US teen/campus use) 1. a show-off, a braggart; 2. a successful, talented individual *Underwood*.

hot-foot v. to rush around; poss. fr. *hot foot* n., malicious trick played on an unsuspecting sleeper; matches are thrust end-first into the gap between upper and sole of the shoe (or between naked toes if vulnerable); these matches are lit and the shoe 'catches fire' or the flesh is painfully singed *Humphries: 2*.

hothead n. anyone quickly inspired to rage, a short-tempered person *Safire*.

hot-fling n. (US Black use) an exciting sexual encounter with a new partner *Klein*.

hot-knife v. to smoke cannabis from heated knives; the fumes are then sucked up through a broken-off milk-bottle neck. *Guardian 6/6/87*.

hot-pillow joint n. a cheap hotel which rents out its room by the hour to prostitutes and their clients or to (illicit) lovers (cf: no tell hotel, no-tell motel).

hots n. **1.** sexual desire *Price: 2*; **2.** (US campus use) electric hair rollers *Underwood*.

hot-shit a. see: big deal *Patti Smith, 'Piss Factory', 1976*.

hot-shot n. an important, influential person *Chandler: LG*.

Hottentot apron n. (lesbian use) elongated labia *Maledicta*.

Hottentots n. the buttocks; from the nakedness of these African natives.

hotter n. one who indulges in hotting (qv) *Indep 3/9/91*.

hottie n. (abbrev.) hot water bottle *Humphries: 2*.

hotting n. the vogue term (in late 1991) for what used, prosaically, to be known as joy-riding, or, in legal parlance, taking and driving away. The term comes from the slang 'hot', meaning both stolen and speedy. The 'hotter' steals a high performance car, drives it off and, often to the cheers of an appreciative crowd, puts it, and his own driving skills through their paces, emphasizing skids, spins and hand-brake turns – the stuff of movie car-chases. *Indep. 3/9/91*.

hot-wire v. to start a car without an ignition key by making the required connection between two wires *Higgins: 1*.

hound dog n. **1.** one who hangs around when he or she is not wanted; **2.** a person of mixed race.

house n. (abbrev.) whore-house or

house of ill-repute, a brothel *Heller*.

House n. the most popular form of contemporary dance music, originated at Chicago's Warehouse Club and spread across the Western world; a direct descendant of disco, it features similarly mindless rhythms and banal lyrics, with the sole difference that electronic special effects – synthesizers, sampling, drum machines – have replaced the original instrumental playing. (cf: acid house). *Green:3*.

house v. (UK police use) to trace a person or any suspicious or wanted object to a given place *Powis*.

house mother (sex industry use) a madame.

house nigger n. (US Black use) a black employed, often as the 'token nigger', in a mainly white organization; fr. slavery difference between house and field niggers (qv) *Klein*.

house party n. (US Black use) a party held in a private house, for which an admission fee (to cover food and drink) is paid (cf: rent party).

house split n. the management's share in a brothel or casino.

how are they hanging? jocular male to male greeting; 'they' are testicles (cf: getting any?) *Schulberg: 2*.

how does that grab you? (cp) what do you think of that? (slightly aggressive inference, a challenge is assumed) *McFadden*.

how d'ye do n. (rhyming sl.) shoe *Cole*.

how high is a Chinaman? (cp) the answer to a statement or question which the speaker considers to be absurd or unanswerable; a pun on supposed Chinese name *How Hi*.

howl v.t. (US preppie (qv) use) to mock, to tease; fr. the 'howls of derision' that accompany this *Birnbach*.

how's about how about; adopted almost as his own property by disc jockey Jimmy Savile, who also talks not of boys and girls but of 'guys and

gals' *BBC-1 TV, 'Top of the Pops',
passim.*

how's it hanging? greeting: what are
you up to, how are you, etc. (cf: how
are they hanging) *Price: 1.*

how's tricks? greeting, (cf: what's
happening) *Greaser Comics.*

hoy v. (Aus. use) to call; fr. the excl.
hoy! Ready.

H/T abbr. head trip.

hubba! hubba! US teen term of
approval, esp. when directed at a
passing girl *Firesign Theatre, 'How
Can You Be in Two Places at Once,
When You're Not Anywhere At
All', 1970.*

hubbie n. (abbrev./corruption)
husband *May.*

huck n. a Black person (cf:
huckleberry).

huckleberry n. nickname for a Black
person (cf: huck).

Huey n. (US milit. use) UH-1
helicopter *Del Vecchio.*

hully n. (US Black use) especially fat
person *Folb.*

hum n. euph. for hell.

humbug n. (US Black use) 1. a fight;
2. anything worrying or complicated
or both; 3. a false arrest.

humbug v. (US Black use) to fight, to
act tough; thus humbugger: a thug, a
fighter; humbugging: fighting,
brawling.

humdinger n. a remarkable and
excellent event *Wodehouse: JO.*

hummer n. 1. (UK cant) an arrest on
trumped up charges; fr. humbug
Neaman & Silver; 2. something
exceptional of its type (fr. abbr.
humdinger).

humongous a. enormous, outsized,
huge *'Mad Max 2', film, 1982.*

hump n. euph. for damn, e.g. 'I don't
give a hump'.

hump v. 1. to have sexual intercourse
Price: 2; 2. to carry (heavy) objects;
esp. in milit. use: patrolling with a
heavy pack, weapon, supplies, etc.;
esp. popular in Aus. *O'Brien*; 3. to act
lazily, to loaf around, to be idle.

hump 'em and dump 'em popular

male cp suggesting seduction and then
abandonment are best ways of relating
to women (cf: 4-F Club) *Vidal.*

humper n. a carrier of heavy objects,
esp. in rock music use for those who
lift band's equipment.

humpty n. sexual intercourse (cf:
rumpy-pumpy).

humpty a. sexually excited.

humpy n. (Aus. surfing use) an ideal
surfing wave; its back is suitably
'humped' *Humphries: 2.*

Hun n. (derog.) German *BvdB.*

hun n. (abbrev.) hundred: $100
Milner.

hung a. having a large penis *Price: 1.*

hung for a. (US teen. use) in need of,
lacking *Sculatti.*

hung for bread a. impoverished, out
of money *Bruce: 2.*

hung like a horse a. a well-endowed
male.

hung up a. 1. obsessed *Underwood*;
2. delayed *Caserta.*

hung up on a. obsessed with; esp. in
love with someone *Norman: 3.*

hungry a. 1. ambitious, enthusiastic,
driven; 2. (UK police use) an officer
who is extra-keen to make arrests
Laurie.

hungry croaker n. (drug use) a doctor
who for one reason or another is
willing to prescribe drugs for any user
who asks for them (cf: writing doctor)
Klein.

Hungry Hill n. the poor area of a
town; variations include Hungry
Gulch, Hungry Hollow, Hungry
Ridge, Hungry Street, Hungry-go-
naked Place, Hunger Street.

hunk n. an attractive, rugged, well-
built male; possibly somewhat
unintelligent (cf: beefcake)
Underwood.

hunkie n. see: honkie.

hunko a. short, stocky physique
Price: 1.

hunky a. strong, attractive, well-built
man *Jay & Young.*

hunky-dory a. excellent, first rate, all
as it should be *David Bowie, album
title.*

hunt v. (Aus. use) to drive away, to chase off *Wilkes*.

hunyak n. 1. an immigrant from central or eastern Europe, e.g. a Hungarian or Pole (cf: bohunk, hunk, hunky); 2. see: honyok.

hurrah n. a boisterous party; a ruckus.

hurrah v. 1. to tease, to harass; 2. to cause a commotion, to raise a ruckus.

hurrah clothes n. one's best clothes, one's 'Sunday suit'.

hurl v. (Aus. use) to vomit *Humphries*.

hurricane lamp n. (rhyming sl.) tramp *Cole*.

hurry-up n. a police patrol car *Norman: 2*.

hurry-up wagon n. (UK criminal use) a Black Maria or police van *LL*.

hurt v. (street gang use) to wound severely: to kill *Salisbury*.

hurt for v. to want something desperately, usu. to alleviate current unhappiness *Underwood*.

hurtin' for certain a. (US Black use) ugly *Folb*.

hurting a. 1. generally miserable; 2. (drug use) urgently needing narcotics to sustain one's regular dosage *Higgins: 1*; 3. (Black pimp use) in financial difficulties *Milner*.

hurting dance n. sadness, frustration, jealousy, usu, in a relationship where A has B 'doing a hurting dance' *Price: 2*.

hurting for a. in great need of, desperate for *Higgins: 1*.

husband n. the supposedly 'aggressive' partner of a homosexual couple *Legman*.

hush money n. a bribe paid to ensure that embarrassing facts are suppressed *Higgins: 3*.

hush up v. to keep secret, to hide *Wodehouse: MOJ*.

hush-hush a. most secret, undercover *Vidal*.

husky n. a tough male, a thug *Howard*.

hustle n. any get-rich-quick scheme; a means of seduction *Higgins: 1*.

hustle v. to offer a sale of drugs to a person *Carson*.

hustler n. 1. gambler or player of pool, bowling, etc. who uses skill and possibly cheating to make a living against lesser opponents *Price: 1*; 2. a prostitute of either sex *Price: 2*; 3. (US campus use) a male who succeeds in his conquests of females *Underwood*.

hydraulic n. (Aus. use) a light-fingered person, who'll 'lift anything that isn't nailed down' *Wilkes*.

Hymie n. derog. term for a Jew; fr. the stereotypical Jewish name Hyman.

hype n. 1. (abbrev.) hypodermic syringe, thus; 2. a heroin addict *Grogan*; 3. (pimp use) a prostitute who works simply to support her narcotic addiction *OUI 8/75*.

Hype n. aka: *the Bill*: the short change swindle in which the criminal persuades a shopkeeper that he has paid with a larger denomination note than he actually has, thus gaining extra change *Burroughs: 1*.

hype v. 1. to promote a person or commodity through an excess of overzealous, grandiose publicity, esp. in rock business use, fr. hyperbole; 2. (US Black use) to outsmart, to make a fool of *X*.

hyped adv. high on drugs *Shell*.

hyper a. (abbrev.) hyperactive: tense, over-emotional, betraying one's feelings, esp. towards an attractive person *McFadden*.

hypo n. (drug use) (abbrev.) hypodermic syringe (cf: works) *Algren*.

I

I am sure (Valley Girls (qv) use)
(abbrev.) I am sure that you are
wrong/ that I don't want to do what
you suggest / etc.; intensified as *I am
so sure Pond*.

I can't handle this (teen. use) general
term of apprehension,
disentanglement from a difficult
situation; popular among drug users
who are finding a given experience too
intense *Pond*.

I could do that a favour (cp)
remarked by a man of a passing
female; the 'favour' would of course
be sexual.

I couldn't care less statement of
absolute disinterest, although the
opposite sentiment, albeit hidden,
may be the true one.

I don't believe this! excl. of disbelief
that extends beyond mere lack of
simple credence into a denial that one
could ever have landed in such a mess,
that others could have created such
horrors, that such stupidity could
exist, etc. *Safire*.

I don't give a fuck intense version of I
couldn't care less (qv).

I don't know (teen. use) all-purpose
term that is used less as a definite
statement than as an alternative to 'er'
or 'Y'know' as a sentence-breaker;
usu. pron: I dunno *Pond*.

I hear you a 'deeper' way of saying 'I
understand', 'yes'; one supposedly
'hears' with every fibre of one's being
McFadden.

I should be so lucky! (cp) initimating
envy on behalf of a speaker who has
just been informed of another's luck;
the word-pattern implies Yiddish
origin.

I should cocoa! (cp) (esp. popular in
BBC Radio 'Billy Cotton Bandshow'
1950s): you must be joking, don't
make me laugh, etc. fr. rhyming sl:
cocoa = say so. *Powis*

I suppose n. (rhyming sl.) nose
Capital Radio, 1983.

I wouldn't kick her out of bed phr.
referring to an attractive woman; a
comment usually made by one of a
group of young men observing a
passing female (cf: don't fancy yours).

I wouldn't know statement of
dismissal, uninterest (cf: don't ask
me).

**I wouldn't trust him/her as far as I
could throw him/her** (cp) implying
absolute lack of faith in its object.

ice n. diamonds *Wodehouse, bk. title,
'Ice in the Bedroom', 1961*.

ice v. to murder, to kill (cf: chill)
Stone.

ice cream freezer n. (rhyming sl.) a
geezer = a male person *Powis*.

iceberg n. 1. an unemotional person
Folb; 2. (Aus. use) anyone who enjoys
an early morning swim in the icy ocean
waters *Wilkes*.

iced a. (US prison use) in solitary
confinement *Major*.

iced to the eyebrows a. extremely
drunk *Chandler: LG*.

icing expert n. (homosexual use) a
fellator *Legman*.

icky a. distasteful, nauseating,
unpleasant, esp. in juv. use. *Rosten*.

icky-poo a. (children's use) disgusting,
nasty, unpleasant, usu. with overtones
of stickiness *Higgins: 5*.

ID v. (police use) to identify
Newman: 1.

IDB (UK 'society' use) (acro.) *I*n
*D*addy's *B*usiness; used by young men
to describe their occupation *Harpers/
Queen 8/83*.

iddy (boy) n. derog. name for a Jew;
fr. abbrev. of yid (qv).

idiot board n. (TV use) the cue cards
used as prompts for a TV performer;
ths cards are held up by the *idiot girl
Green: 2*.

idiot box n. the television, implying
that TV watchers are less than
normally intelligent *Underwood*.

idiot oil n. alcohol *P J O'Rourke 'Give War a Chance'* (1992).

idrin (UK Black use) lit. brethren, therefore one's 'brothers', usually in Rastafarian use.

if it moves, salute it; if it don't paint it (milit. cp) supposedly the advice for a successful services career.

if you can't beat 'em, join 'em (cp) a statement of cynical resignation, not to mention the justification for a number of otherwise self-abasing acts.

if you can't do the time, don't do the crime (UK cant cp) self explanatory (cf: time) *Cole*.

iffy marginal, not wholly acceptable, unpalatable *Newman: 3*.

ig v. to ignore deliberately, to snub (cf: diss).

ig man n. (US Black use) (abbrev.) ignorant man *Klein*.

ignant a. (US Black use) ignorant, stupid person; fr. pron.

ikey mo n. (derog.) a Jew; fr. Isaac Moses *Humphries*.

ill a. uncool(qv), unpleasant *Ice T:1*.

I'll be blowed! general excl. of surprise, shock, etc.

I'll eat my hat! statement of utter disbelief: if such and such is true/ happens, the . . .; the most famous instance of the phrase was uttered by a BBC commentator at the 1938 FA Cup Final who promised, 'If there's a goal now, I'll eat my hat.' There was, and to his credit, he did.

I'll freeze, Bill (US teen. use) cp: thank you, but no; a polite rejection of an offer or suggestion *Sculatti*.

ill piece n. (homosexual use) an unattractive and (therefore) unpopular homosexual *Stanley*.

illegitimis non carborundum (cp) don't let the bastards grind you down; the 'Latin' translation is hardly accurate.

illin' adv. acting in an uncool (qv) or unpleasant manner *Beastie Boys No Sleep Till Brooklyn* (1986).

illy-whacker n. (Aus. use) a professional confidence man, esp. the itinerants who follow fairs and country shows; fr. spieler (qv) *Wilkes*.

ILUVM (acro.) *I Love You Very Much*: written on envelopes of love letters (cf:BOLTOP, NORWICH, SWALK) *Partridge:5*.

in a coon's age over a very long period; fr. the lifespan of a racoon *Runyon*.

in a fix a. pregnant.

in a jam in trouble, facing a problem *Higgins: 3*.

in a jiffy very quickly, in a moment *Performance*.

in a minute phr. (US Black use) phr. of farewell, goodbye.

in a mucksweat frightened, flustered, under tension.

in a pickle in a mess, in difficulties *Hotten*.

in a pig's ass (excl.) completely impossible, absolutely not! *Price: 2*.

in a pig's ear see: in a pig's ass *'Minder', Thames TV 1983*.

in a pig's eye see: in a pig's ass.

in a spot in trouble, in difficulties; (abbrev.) in a spot of bother.

in a twitter nervous, worried; fr. Second World War RAF sl. *twittering ringpiece*: a state of extreme nervousness *Wodehouse: AAG*.

in and out like a fiddler's elbow (cp) rapid and enthusiastic copulation.

in and out man n. (UK criminal use) a thief who burgles a house when an opportunity arises, rather than making elaborate plans, etc. *EN 12/11/57*.

in bondage (US Black use) indebted to, under the control of; with a biblical inference *Klein*.

in dock out of work, out of circulation; fr. naut: dry dock where ships are laid up for repairs *Norman: 3*.

in dutch in trouble, out of favour *Farrell*.

in front in advance, beforehand (cf: front, v.) *Bruce: 2*.

in hock indebted to, owing (both money and metaphorical debts) *Algren: 2*.

in hot ashes adv. **1.** nervous, exciting, apprehensive; **2.** in trouble.

in like Flynn a dead certainty, esp. in

areas of sexual conquest; fr. the alleged sexual prowess of the actor Erroll Flynn (1909–59).

in lumber adv. in trouble.

in mourning (UK 'society' use) dirty fingernails, thus edging the hands, like mourning paper, in black *Barr*.

in one's birthday suit (euph.) naked *Rawson*.

in one's corner on one's side; fr. boxing use.

in one's cups a. drunk *Neaman & Silver*.

in orbit a. drunk; extremely high (qv) *Dickson*.

in pig a. pregnant *N. Mitford, 'The Pursuit of Love', 1945*.

in queer Street in trouble, esp. financial *Powis*.

in Shit Street in difficulties, facing problems, etc.

in shtuck aka: *in shtook*: fr. Yiddish: in trouble *'Minder', Thames TV, 1980*.

in spades to the greatest extent; very much, extremely – any form of intensifier; fr. card use *Runyon: 1*.

in the altogether a. naked *Rawson*.

in the bag a. drunk *Higgins: 4*.

in the bag certain, easy, no problem *Higgins: 3*.

in the barrel (US business use) actually fired already or likely to be fired from one's job.

in the box seat (Aus. use) in full control, in a position of dominance, power; box seat = driving seat in a (horse-driven) coach (cf: in the driving seat) *Wilkes*.

in the buff a. naked; fr. the colour of 'white' flesh *Neaman & Silver*.

in the cellar (sports use) at the bottom of a league or similar points table; Wodehouse favours 'down among the wines and spirits' (generally obs. now): miserable, feeling low, down in the dumps *Bukowski: 2*.

in the chair buying a round of drinks; fr. chairing a meeting *'Only Fools and Horses', BBC-1 TV 1983*.

in the closet 1. spec. for a homosexual to hide his sexual predelictions; 2. to hide away *Higgins: 2*.

in the club a. pregnant; the club in question is the 'pudding club'.

in the death in the end *Norman: 2*.

in the dog-house out of favour, in disgrace; supposedly consigned to the dog's kennel rather than one's hearth and home *AS 41 (1966)*.

in the driving seat in control, running things, on top of a situation; fr. the controlling position in a vehicle (cf: in the box seat).

in the frame (UK criminal/police use) under suspicion, usu. with some grounds, of having committed a given crime; fr. racetrack use, the frame holds the numbers of the winning horses in a race; and, from villain's point of view, implying a frame-up (qv) *Mortimer*.

in the hole (gambling use) in debt, owing *Seale*.

in the house adv. both lit. present and fig. aware, on the ball etc. *Dre*.

in the money rich, successful in a wager; fr. racing use: those horses that finish 1–2–3 'run in the money', thus paying out to those who bet on them *Wodehouse: MOJ*.

in the peek n. (UK prison use) in an observation cell, into which a man is placed if, for instance, he has smashed up his cell or shown similar signs of instability *LL*.

in the pink a. extremely fit, well and cheerful; fr. abbrev. in the pink of condition *Dunne*.

in the pits a. depressed, miserable (cf: down in the dumps) *Neaman & Silver*.

in the pudding club pregnant (cf: bun in the oven).

in the rude a. (genteel euph.) naked *Joe Orton, 'Entertaining Mr Sloane', 1964*.

in the saddle performing sexual intercourse, usu. of a male who is 'riding' *Dunne*.

in the soup a. in trouble, in difficulties.

in the stretch almost complete; fr. racing use: the stretch: the last part of the course *Grogan*.

in the tank a. drunk *Dickson*.

in the wrapper a. very drunk
Higgins: 5.

in your eye! (US campus use) term of
general derision, dismissal, contempt
Bernbach.

incoming n. (milit. use) hostile fire,
esp. shellfire, that is aimed at and
bombarding the speaker *Del Vecchio*.

indian n. an Indian meal; often a take-
out. (cf: Chinese)

indian n. (gay use) a man who uses
make-up (cf: warpaint).

Indian, dead as a wooden a. phr.
dead.

Indian giver n. one who first gives,
then takes way the gift *Morgan*.

Indian rug n. (gay use) a cheap wig
done in braids (cf: rug).

indian up v. to sneak up without
alerting one's targets.

Indians, give it back to the v. phr.
said if anything fails or breaks.

indoor money n. (UK criminal use)
reserve cash for use in day to day life,
rather than the proceeds of a given
robbery *Newman: 1*.

industrial debutante n. a prostitute
who specializes in attending US
business conventions *Rawson*.

info n. (abbrev.) information *rr*.

ink n. **1.** (US Black use) cheap wine
Major; **2.** a mention in the
newspapers; fr. the printers' ink used
Dunne.

ink v. to sign a contract *Higgins: 5*.

inked a. (Aus. use) drunk
Neaman & Silver.

inky-dinky n. (US Black use) a
particularly dark American black
Major.

inner man n. the stomach, one's
appetite (for food) *Neaman & Silver*.

inside in prison *Caron*.

inside man n. (UK criminal use) in a
three-card monte (qv) team, one of
the shills (qv) who pose as normal
bettors but act only to encourage the
real victims of the game *Powis*.

instant boot camp n. (US campus
use) the act of vomiting; fr. boot (qv)
and the military training 'boot camp',
a notably vile environment *Bernbach*.

interior decorating n. (UK 'society'
use) sexual intercourse during the day
Barr.

international milk thief n. (UK
police use) ironic term for any petty
villain *Powis*.

interrupter n. (UK police use) a court
interpreter *Powis*.

into 1. interested in, involved with;
2. owing money to *Higgins: 1*.

irey a. (Jamaican (Rasta) use)
powerful and pleasing *Thelwell*.

iris out v. to leave unobtrusively; fr.
film use: the contracting of the picture
to the dimensions of a small dot and
thence a blank screen
Wodehouse: PGM.

Irish a. a general racial epithet; the
Irish seem eternally condemned as
slow-witted, bungling peasants; thus
Irish — will invariably imply such
negative qualities (cf: Chinese,
French, etc.).

Irish apple n. a potato; also Irish
apricot / grape / lemon.

Irish beauty n. a woman with black
eyes.

Irish buggy n. a wheelbarrow (cf:
Irish local).

**Irish by birth but Greek by
injection** n. a male homosexual (cf:
Greek).

Irish clubhouse n. (gay use) a refined
house of prostitution.

Irish confetti n **1.** (gay use) semen
spilled extravaginally; **2.** bricks., esp.
as thrown during riots.

Irish dip n. (gay use) sexual
intercourse.

Irish draperies n. (gay use) Pendulous
breasts.

Irish fortune n. the vagina.

Irish hoist n. a kick in the behind.

Irish horse 1. (US use) tough,
undercooked salt beef; **2.** (gay use) an
impotent penis.

Irish jig n. (rhyming sl.) **1.** wig *T 26/9/
83*;**2.** cig (arette) *Wright*.

Irish lace n. a spider's web.

Irish legs n. heavy female legs.

Irish local n. a wheelbarrow (cf: Irish
buggy).

Irish marathon n. an extended session of lovemaking.

Irish promotion n. (gay use) masturbation.

Irish rise n. sexual detumescence.

Irish root n. the penis.

Irish screwdriver n. a hammer (cf: Birmingham screwdriver, Jewish screwdriver).

Irish shave n. the act of defecation.

Irish shift n. (US use) a more than routinely hypocritical action by a politician.

Irish toothpick n (gay use) the erect penis.

Irish turkey n. (US use) corned (UK: salt) beef and cabbage.

Irish wake n. any boisterous occasion, not necesarily a wake as such

Irish wedding n. (gay use) masturbation.

Irishman, potato-fingered n. clumsy person; from alleged predilection of the Irish for potatoes.

Irishman's dinner n. a fast.

Irishman's pocket n. (US use) a pocket that is both large and empty.

iron n. **1.** (rhyming sl.) iron hoof = poof = homosexual *Scaffold*, 'Thank You Very Much', 1967; **2.** gun *Higgins: 2*; **3.** a motor car 'The Killers', directed Don Siegel, 1964.

iron butterfly n. a hypodermic syringe, made of metal and glass (its curved finger-holes are the 'wings' of the butterfly), rather than the plastic used in modern disposables *Morgan*.

iron cross n. (US Black use) extremely unfavourable circumstances from which it is hard to extract oneself *Klein*.

iron tank n. (rhyming sl.) bank *Jones: J*.

irvine n. (US Black use) the police *Folb*.

Irving n. (US use) a dull, uninformed, obnoxious person (cf: Melvin) *Neaman & Silver*.

Island n. the Isle of Wight, thus HMP Parkhurst which is situated there.

island-hopping n. the practice amongst (rich) tourists of touring around the islands of the West Indies, the Aegean Sea or similar hot and inviting spots.

Isle of Wight (rhyming sl.) all right *Powis*.

issue n. (Aus. use) everything, the lot, all there is *Ready*.

it derog. reference to a casual, picked up partner, as opposed to a lover *Legman*.

it n. (US Black use) the quintessence of black being, spirit, sensitivity, etc.

it looks like rain (cant cp) an arrest – poss. of the speaker – seems likely *Neaman & Silver*.

it takes two to tango (cp) sexual intercourse, esp. adulterous, requires two people, not just a lustful male.

Italian airlines n. (gay use) walking.

ITALY (acro.) *I Trust And Love You*: written on envelopes of love letters (cf:BOLTOP, NORWICH, SWALK) *Partridge:5*.

item n. a couple; fr. such fashionable couples being items for newspaper gossip columnists *Price: 3*.

it'll all come out in the wash (cp) problems, etc., will all be made clear in due course, no matter how daunting at present.

it's a breeze (rhyming sl.) it's easy *Cole*.

it's one o'clock at the water-works (coy cp) your fly is undone *Rawson*.

it's the beer talking (cp) the excuse, usu. in a public house, for breaking wind.

it's your baby (cp) that's your problem *Manser*.

it's your corner it's your turn to pay, usu. in a pub *Powis*.

it's your little hip pocket (US Black use) you're in very great trouble *Himes: 2*.

Ivan n. a generally stupid East European person; fr. popular Russian name *Powis*.

ixnay prep. no; fr. dog Latin and thus the reverse of 'nix' *Morgan*.

J

j n. (drug use) (abbrev.) joint (qv).

jack a. flashy, ostentatious (cf: new jack) *Dre*.

jack n. 1. (rhyming sl.) jack and jill (usu. pl) = pills: the pills of heroin in which the drug is issued to registered addicts in the UK *Green*; 2. (abbrev.) blackjack *Runyon*; 3. a detective, orig. northern dial., now general *Powis*; 4. (rhyming sl.) jack tar = bar *Powis*; 5. general term of address to a man '*Hill Street Blues', Thames TV, 1983*; 6. (Aus. use) venereal disease *Wilkes*; 7. mugger, thief; abbrev. jack roller *Ice T:3*.

jack v. to steal *Morgan*.

Jack and Jill n. (rhyming sl.) hill, bill, till, pill *Cole*.

jack around v. 1. mess about, usu. with sexual, adulterous overtones *Jenkins*; 2. (US campus use) to tease *Underwood*.

jack in the box v. (US criminal use) to break and enter a house, apartment *Klein*.

jack in the box (US Black use) the state of having one's penis inside one's partner's vagina *Klein*.

jack it in v. stop doing something; to give in *Dury, 'Do It Yourself'*.

jack job n. (US campus use) unfair treatment *Underwood*.

Jack Jones n. (rhyming sl.) alone *Cole*.

jack of (Aus. use) bored with, tired of, etc.

jack off v. 1. (drug use) to pump backwards and forwards with the plunger of the hypodermic without finally injecting the blood and heroin mix into the arm; fr. both the up and down gesture of masturbation, and the figurative 'jacking off' instead of reaching a climax *Klein*; 2. to masturbate (cf: jerk off) *SF Comics*.

jack roller n. a thief who specializes in attacking the vulnerable: drunks, vagrants, etc. *Shulman*.

jack shit absolutely nothing; always used with a qualifying negative vb., *you don't know jack shit about . . .* etc. *Underwood*.

Jack the Lad n. a show-off; anyone particularly pleased with himself and keen on ensuring everyone knows it *Dury*.

Jack the Ripper n. (rhyming sl.) a kipper; fr. the 19th-C. mass-killer; also kippers are slit open *Wright*.

jack up v. 1. (drug use) to inject narcotics (cf: jack off); (US Black use) 1. to assault, to attack; 2. to have sexual intercourse *Folb*; 4. to interrogate (by the police); to stop and search *Seale*.

Jack-a-dandy n. (rhyming sl.) brandy *Cole*.

jackanape n. (US Black (radical) use) an undisciplined albeit enthusiastic member of a radical movement; one who finds it hard to put the general good before his/her own pleasures; fr. SE use, orig. one who acts like an ape. *Seale*.

jackdaw n. (rhyming sl.) jaw *Jones: J*.

jacked (Aus. use) angry, annoyed, fed up *Bickerton*.

jacked out (US campus use) annoyed, irritated, angry *Bernbach*.

jacked up a. 1. (US teen. use) upset, anxious, waiting anxiously for time to pass *Sculatti*; 2. (Aus. use) infected (usu. with venereal disease) *Wilkes*.

jacket n. 1. (drug use) (abbrev.) yellow jacket = nembutal, a tranquilizer *De Lannoy & Masterson*; 2. (US police use) the file on a given criminal, recording previous convictions, etc. (cf: form) *Algren*.

jacking off (gambling use) 1. racking up the pool balls; 2. shaking dice with a movement that might be seen as resembling masturbation (cf: jack off, v.) *Klein*.

jack-off n. derog. form of address; lit: masturbator *Bruce: 1*.

jacks (rhyming sl.) jack's alive = five, thus £5.00 *Norman: 2.*

Jack's alive (rhyming sl.) five *Cole.*

jacksie n. anus, usu. in *up your jacksie*: derog. response to an unpalatable idea or opinion *May.*

Jack-sprat n. fat.(fr. rhy. sl.).

jag n. a breakdown, an emotional collapse; often as a crying jag: lengthy and profound sobbing *Jay & Young.*

Jag n. (abbrev.) Jaguar motor car.

jailbait n. an underage sexual partner; used of either sex, although more commonly of teenage girls.

jailing adv. (US prison use) accustoming oneself to life in jail and adapting one's lifestyle to make one's time there as tolerable as possible *Morgan.*

jake all right, OK, satisfactory *Farrell.*

jake flake n. (US Black use) anyone interested in themselves above anything or anyone else *Klein.*

jakes n. lavatory; orig early 16th C., when SE *Wolfe: 2.*

jalobies n. nipples *Morgan.*

jalopy n. a (decrepit) car *Waits.*

jam n. 1. a problem, a difficult situation; usu. *in a jam Chandler: LG*; 2. (Black use) cocaine; 3. semen *Jagger & Richards, 'Some Girls', 1977*; 4. (homosexual use) a heterosexual male; 5. foreplay between two homosexual men *Legman*; (US Black use) 6. the vagina; 7. an attractive woman *Folb.*

jam v. 1. for musicians to play together without set scores or arrangement for the pleasure and the spontaneous music thus created *Price: 2*; 2. (Black pimp use) to sniff cocaine *Milner*; 3. (US teen. use) to leave, to exit fast *Pond*; 4. to arrest; to put in an unfavourable position *Klein*; 5. to ruin, to make a mess of *Algren.*

jam fag n. a homosexual with no other sexual interests *Legman.*

jam house (Black pimp use) a place where cocaine can be both purchased and then snorted in convivial surroundings *Milner.*

jam it v. to drive a car or bike fast

Thompson.

jam it! threatening exclamation, abbrev. of *jam it up your ass Bukowski: 1.*

jam jar n. (rhyming sl.) motor car *Capital Radio 1983.*

jam one up v. (US Black use) 1. to rape; 2. to beat, to overpower; 3. to talk forcefully *Folb.*

jam roll n. (rhyming sl. UK prison use) parole *Obs. 1981.*

jam tart n. (rhyming sl.) sweetheart, thus girlfriend *Cole.*

Jamaica discipline n.(gay use) a wife's denial of sexual favours to her husband.

Jamdung n. (Jamaican) Jamaica; fr. *jam*: press, *dung*: down; refers to oppression of the Jamaican proletariat *Thelwell.*

jamming a. exciting *Shell.*

jammy n. 1. tampon, *Beastie Boys*; 2. (US Black use) the penis *Ice T:1.*

jamoke n. fellow, person, man *Higgins: 4.*

jam-pot n. the anus *Legman.*

jam-rag n. a tampon or protective towel.

jane n. a girl, a woman *Grogan.*

jap n. (derog.) a Black person.

jap v. (street gang use) to ambush one's rivals; fr. Japanese attack on Pearl Harbor (?) *Salisbury.*

JAP n. (acro.) Jewish American Princess: a rich, spoiled Jewish girl *Rosten.*

Japanese triad n. sexual relations between one women and two men.

Japwise adv. not fully informed.

jar n. (drug use) a quantity of pills, usu. 500/1000 (cf: lid) *Folb.*

jarhead n. an alcoholic, a heavy drinker *'Hill Street Blues', Thames TV, 1983.*

jarred a. drunk *Dickson.*

J. Arthur n. (rhyming sl.) J. Arthur Rank (for the cinema magnate, 1888–1972) = wank = masturbate, thus, by extension, a fool *Powis.*

jasper n. (US Black use) a lesbian, fr. white *jasper*: man, guy *Folb.*

java n. (US/Can use) coffee. thus also

obs. *jamoke*: strong black coffee, fr. Java + Mocha (two brands) *Caron*.

jaw v. to talk.

jawbone v. to talk, to chatter *Grogan*.

jawbreaker n. a word that the speaker considers so long or complex that its pronunciation threatens to be harmful.

jazz n. idle chatter; slightly deceptive conversation *Greenlee*.

jazz v. (US Black use) to have sexual intercourse *Folb*.

jazz around v. lead a fast life, mainly in pursuit of sex *Pynchon*.

jazz up v. to brighten up, to improve, to make more gaudy *Jay & Young*.

jazzy a. bright, colourful.

JD (acro.) *J*uvenile *D*elinquent *Grogan*.

jeepers creepers n. euph. for Christ; usu. as mild oath.

jeeter n. derog. a rustic, a peasant. (fr. Jeeter Lester, the poor white peasant protagonist of Erskine Caldwell's novel *Tobacco Road* [1932]).

jeff v. (US Black use) to use a given line of talk to deceive or seduce another person; thus *tight jeff*: well-rehearsed patter, *slack jeff*: spontaneous ad libbed chatter *Klein*.

jel n. (Valley Girls (qv) use) an appalling, unacceptable person; fr. jello (jelly) -brain *Pond*.

jellied a. under the influence of tranquilisers *Welsh:2*.

jello squad n. (US campus) an imaginery gathering or club of all those students considered beyond the social pale of their peers on campus *Underwood*.

jelly n. (UK cant) (abbrev.) gelignite *Powis*.

jelly baby n. secretions from the anus or vagina during/after intercourse *Klein*.

jelly, jellies n. temazepam, a tranquiliser; usu. found in the plural *Welsh:1*.

jelly roll n. (US Black use) the female genitals *Folb*.

jelly sandwich n. (US Black use) sanitary napkin *Folb*.

jellybox n. the vagina *Southern & Hoffenberg*.

jellyfish n. a weak, ineffectual, cowardly person *Stone*.

Jem Mace n. (rhyming sl.) face; fr. prizefighter, 1831–1910 *Wright*.

Jemima n. (gay use) Black woman's pudendum; from Aunt Jemima, the stereotypical black 'mammy'.

jemmy n. (UK criminal use) a short housebreaker's crowbar.

jerk n. a fool, an idiot, a failure; orig. fr. jerk off (qv) but such onanistic inference is generally irrelevant *Price: 2*.

jerk around v. to waste one's time, to irritate; fr. jerk off, v. *Bruce: 2*.

jerk off v. 1. spec. to masturbate; 2. to mess around, to waste time, energies *Price: 2*.

jerk one's chain v. to annoy, to distract forcefully; as an owner drags on a dog's lead to control it *Higgins: 1*.

jerking each other off phr. indulging in mutual flattery; the image is of mutual masturbation (cf: up each other).

jerking the gherkin masturbation *Humphries*.

jerk-off n. (derog.) useless person; lazy incompetent (cf: jack off).

jerkwater a. 1. small time, second rate, mediocre; fr, jerkwater town (qv) *Thompson: J*; 2. slow-witted, foolish.

jerkwater town n. a small, insignificant town; known only for its water tower and trough from which a train could scoop water from between the tracks without actually stopping (cf: tank town) *Runyon*.

jerry a. aware, knowledgeable, informed; fr. 19th C. UK verb: to recognize, to discern, detect *Runyon*.

Jerry n. (derog.) German *Sillitoe*.

jerry n. a chamber pot; fr. jereboam, usu. a double-magnum of wine *Hotten*.

jessie n. a weakling, an ineffectual person (cf: big girl's blouse, nellie).

Jesus H. Christ! general excl., the H. is redundant other than for rhythm

'Hill Street Blues', Thames TV, 1983.

Jew/Jewish the Jew as a racial stereotype requires greater space than available here, as do the arguments pro/con the inclusion of such vilifications; in short Jew = money to his gentile peers (unlike the Scot who equals money but inventive/brave/etc. with it) and the words below bear this out (cf: Chinese, French, Irish, etc.).

jew n. a mean person, a skinflint.

jew v. (derog.) to cheat financially *Goldman*.

Jew canoe n. 1. (US use) a Cadillac *Dunne*; 2. (UK 'society' use) a Jaguar *Barr*.

Jew joint n. (US use) a second-hand clothes store.

Jew sheet n. (gay use) Account, often imaginary, of money lent to friends.

Jew Town n. (US use) Jewish community within an urban area.

Jew York n. (UK 'society' use) (derog.) New York; fr. large Jewish population therein (cf: Yidney).

Jew's lance n. (gay use) Jewish circumcised penis.

Jewish airlines n. (gay use) walking (cf: Italian airlines).

Jewish by hospitalization adj. phr. (gay use) circumcised but not Jewish.

Jewish compliment n. (gay use) a circumcised penis.

Jewish corned beef n. a circumcised penis.

Jewish foreplay n. the man pleads for sex, his partner refuses all physical contact.

Jewish lightning n. (derog.) deliberate arson in order to gain the insurance on an otherwise unprofitable business.

Jewish National n. (gay use) a circumcised penis; the reference is to the Hebrew National brand of kosher salami.

Jewish overdrive n. freewheeling down hills to save petrol (cf: Mexican overdrive).

Jewish penicillin n. chicken soup.

Jewish piano n. (derog.) cash register *Powis*.

Jewish Renaissance n. (gay use) over-elaborate furniture in doubtful taste (cf: Jewy Louis).

Jewish typewriter n. (derog.) a cash register *Powis*.

Jewy Louis n. (UK 'society' use) (derog.) flashy, vulgar style of interior decoration, poss. featuring (fake) Louis XV, XVI furniture *Barr*.

jib v. (US Black use) to talk; poss. fr. 19th C jib: underlip; also fr. flapping jibsail on a ship (?) *Seale*.

jib-jibe n. (US Black use) talk that goes in one ear and out the other *Klein*.

jiblet n. (drug use) barbiturate *Folb*.

jibone n. aka: *jabone* 1. a greenhorn (qv), an innocent, a newly-arrived immigrant; 2. a heavy, a thug, a muscleman; as which 1 was often used *Price: 2*.

jick head n. (US Black use) a drunkard; fr *jiggins*: a fool (?) *Major*.

jiffy n. a very short time *Humphries*.

jig n. (abbrev.) jigaboo (qv) *Dunne*.

Jig Town n. Black community within an urban area (cf:jig).

jigaboo n. aka: *zigaboo*; derog, term for a Black person; fr. alleged 'natural rhythm' which has Blacks jigging around.

jig-a-jig n. sexual intercourse; often found in pidgin slangs.

jig-chaser n. a white person who pursues the company of Blacks.

jiggered 1. (euph.) damned; with some feeling of confusion also *Rawson*; 2. exhausted, worn out *Keyes*; 3. drunk *Dickson*.

jiggery-pokery n. tricks, deceit, lies, underhand activities in general; fr. Scots *jouk*: a trick.

jigglers n. (UK criminal use) skeleton keys for use on pin tumbler locks; fr. sleight-of-hand required to turn lock *Powis*.

jill off v. (lesbian use) to masturbate, the 'feminized' jack off (qv) and the other of the nursery rhyme characters *Maledicta*.

Jim n. (US Black use) title for a fellow Black man, usu. as shorthand for making gesture of friendship *Bruce: 2*.

jim n. (US Black use) jewellery, diamonds; fr. gem *Klein*.

Jim Crow a. white racist discrimination vs. Blacks and the Jim Crow laws that embody it; fr. early 19th C. Kentucky plantation song with chorus 'Jump Jim Crow' and a blackface entertainer Thomas Dartmouth Rice who performed it c.1829 *W. Safire, 'Safire's Political Dictionary', revised edn., 1978*.

Jiminy Cricket (euph.) Jesus Christ! *Rawson*.

jim-jams n. (abbrev.) pyjamas, usu. children's use *Humphries: 2*.

jimmies n. (Aus. use) a fit of nerves; see Jimmy Britts *Wilkes*.

jimmy n. 1. (rhyming sl.) jimmy riddle (qv) *Payne*; 2. US version of jemmy (qv); see: jammy *Dre*.

Jimmy Britts n. (Aus. use; rhyming sl.) the shits = terrified, scared, fr. Britt, a boxer who toured Australia during the First World War *Bickerton*.

Jimmy Hix 1. (UK criminal use; rhyming sl.) fix = injection of narcotics *LL*; 2. (gambling use) the point of six in craps dice *Chandler: Notebk*.

jimmy o'goblins n. money.

Jimmy Riddle n. (rhyming sl.) piddle = urinate.

Jimmy Skinner n. (rhyming sl.) dinner *Wright*.

Jimmy Woodser n. (Aus. use) anyone who drinks alone; or a drink that is taken by oneself *Lawson*.

jims n. (UK prostitute use) men who like to watch prostitutes at work (or just 'dirty old men' in sex bookshops, etc.) but offer no actual sexual threat *Powis*.

jing-jang n. (lesbian use) the vagina *Maledicta*.

jinny n. a speakeasy or unlicensed drinking place; fr. gin available there *Chandler: Notebk*.

jive v. to lie, to confuse, to tease; thus *jive about with*; to play with, to mess around *Price: 2*.

jive a. fake, phoney, deceitful, unappealing *Greenlee*.

jive and juke v. (US campus use) to have a very good time *Underwood*.

jive hand n. (US Black use) an undesirable situation which puts one person at an unfair disadvantage; one is dealt 'a bad hand' *Klein*.

jive-ass a. derog. term of abuse; (cf: jive) *Jones*.

jizz n. see: jizzum.

jizzum n. 1. energy, strength; 2. semen.

J/O abbr. (contact ads use) jerk off (qv), thus masturbate *SMD 154/N2*

J/O scene n. (homosexual use) (abbrev.) jerk off (qv); mutual masturbation *Jay & Young*.

joanie a. (Valley Girls (qv) use) out of date, unfashionable *Pond*.

joanna n. (rhyming sl.) piano *Cole*.

job a. (UK police use) anything involved in police work, ie: 'a job dog', 'a job car', etc.; all police work is known as 'the job' and the magazine of the Metropolitan Police is 'The Job' *Laurie*.

job n. 1. (US campus use) bowel movement *Underwood*; 2. (criminal use) the committing of a given crime, often with a qualifying name, thus 'The Barclays Bank job', etc. *Mortimer*.

job v. (Aus. use) to hit, to beat up *Wilkes*.

jobbed a. (UK cant) framed up on false evidence (cf: flake, verbal) *Neaman & Silver*.

jobbers n. (taxi-driver use) freelance, journeymen cabbies who hire their vehicle and work on the clock (qv) *Powis*.

jobbie n. (Scots use) a turd. *Tootie Fruttie BBC2 TV 1988*.

jobsworth n. minor factotum whose only status comes from enforcing otherwise petty regulations, fr. 'more than my job's worth to let . . .' *Farren*.

jock n.1. (US campus and sports use) a sportsman; fr. the athletic supporter 'jock strap' worn by such performers *Underwood*; 2. (abbrev.) disc jockey *Harry Chapin, 'I Am The Morning*

DJ'; **3.** (abbrev.) jockey *Higgins: 1.*

Jock n. a Scot *Payne*.

jock v. (US Black use) to steal *Ice T:2.*

jock major n. (US campus use) to major in physical education *Simmons*.

jocker n. one who practises anal intercourse *Legman*.

jockey n. **1.** a masculine lesbian *Legman*; **2.** any form of driver, esp, cabs, buses; **3.** a worker in a given job: *swab jockey*: washer-up; *pump jockey*: petrol pump attendant *Dunne* etc.

jockey v. to struggle for a place, esp. the lead in a race; fr. racecourse use *Selby: 1.*

jocks n. **1.** sportsmen; **2.** the practitioners of various jobs, ie: *construction jocks*, etc. *Higgins: 1.*

jocksniffer n. a (presumably male) sports groupie who likes to hang around sports stars (jocks, qv). *Higgins 'Victories' 1989.*

jodrell abbrev. the act of masturbation; fr. rhy. sl. Jodrell Bank = wank (qv).

Jody n. (US Black use) mythical seducer 'Joe de (the) grinder' who specializes in married women or those with boyfriends; also derided by US troops, prisoners and other isolated men, as the lover who takes the 'girl you've left behind' *Klein*.

joe n. **1.** coffee; fr. Java (qv) *Schulberg*; **2.** an ordinary person, as in *college joe*, etc. (cf: Joe Blow) *Teresa*.

Joe Baxi n. (rhy. sl.) a taxi *Welsh:1.*

Joe Blake n. (rhyming sl.) cake *Wright*.

Joe Blakes n. (Aus. use, rhyming sl.) snakes (which one sees) and thus = delirium tremens.

Joe Blow n. an average member of the public.

Joe Bonce n. (rhyming sl.) a ponce, a procurer of prostitutes (cf: Charlie Ronce) *Cole*.

Joe Cool n. a mythical character who embodies whatever qualities are currently seen as cool (qv) *Welsh:1* (cf: Johnny Cool, Mr Cool).

Joe Gurr n. (rhyming sl.) stir = porridge = prison *Wright*.

Joe MacBride n. sexual intercourse

Welsh:1 (fr. rhy. sl. Joe McBride = ride (qv).)

Joe Public n. the general public (cf: Mr Average) *T 3/3/83.*

Joe Ronce n. (rhyming sl.) ponce, procurer (cf: Joe Bonce, Charlie Ronce) *Cole*.

Joe Strummer n. something unpleasant or disappointing *Welsh:1* (fr. rhy. sl. Joe Strummer = bummer (qv); Strummer is best-known as a member of the early punk band, The Clash, c.1977]

joes n. (Aus. use) a fit of depression *Dennis*.

joey n. (UK prison use) any form of contraband – letters, parcels, etc. – smuggled into a prison *LL.*

joey n. a weakling, fr. rhy. sl. Joey Hunt = cunt = foolish, inadequate person.

john n. **1.** (homosexual use) an older man who supports a younger one without actually sharing a long-term relationship with him *Stanley*; **2.** the lavatory *Price: 2.*

John n. **1.** (prostitute use) a client *Selby: 1*; **2.** any anonymous male; ex *John Doe*, police, legal jargon for anonymous male suspect, victim, etc. *Fiction Illus. 3*; **3.** general term of address, irrespective of actual name; ie 'Hello, John, got a new motor', etc. *Norman: 2.*

John Bull (Aus. use; rhyming sl.) full, thus drunk *Humphries*.

John Hancock n. signature; fr. the particularly large signature of J.H. on the US Declaration of Independence 1776.

John Henry n. (US Black use) a hard-working black man, tough and indomitable in the face of appalling challenges *Major*.

john hop n. (Aus. use; rhyming sl.) cop = policeman *Neaman & Silver*.

John Law n. policeman, esp. a senior one *Powis*.

John Q. Public n. the average, law-abiding citizen.

John Selwyn Gummer n. (rhy.sl.) bummer (qv).

John Thomas n. the penis
Humphries.

john-john (UK Black use) motor car
D Robins.

Johnny—— used as a prefix, as in
Johnny-darkie, Johnny-gyppo, etc.;
these days tends be used facetiously/
ironically.

Johnny at the rat hole n. an
exceptionally enthusiastic, greedy
person *Runyon*.

Johnny Bliss n. (Aus. use; rhyming
sl.) piss = urination *Wilkes*.

Johnny Horner n. (rhyming sl.)
corner *Jones: J*.

Johnny-be-good n. (US Black use)
the police *Folb*.

Johnny-come-lately n. a novice, an
unsophisticated person, a recent
arrival or recruit *Bruce: 2*.

johnson n. the penis.

join the great majority v. to die; all
the dead of thousands of years of
humanity *Neaman & Silver*.

joint n. **1.** a marijuana or hashish
cigarette *Price: 2*; **2.** (US use) prison
Milner; **3.** any place, esp. a bar or club
Breslin; **4.** the penis *Goldman*; **5.** (US
Black use) an artistic creation,
typically a record or film (coined by
film-maker Spike Lee who credits his
films 'Another Spike Lee Joint'; now
used by many rap (qv) artists to
describe their records and tapes).

jointman n. (Can. prison use) any
prisoner who behaves like a guard
Caron.

jo-jos n. (Can. prison use) a bulky coat
without pockets *Caron*.

joker n. a man, a person; usu. with
implications of incompetence *Price: 2*.

jolly d. (public school use) wonderful,
excellent, fantastic.

jolly for polly a. phr. sexually
available; fr. rhy. sl. polly = lolly =
cash *Maledicta 9*.

jolt n. an injection of a narcotic
Goldman.

Jonathan Ross n. drink, spec. beer
Welsh:2.

jones n. **1.** a heroin habit (qv) *Grogan*;
2. as a metaphor from 1. an obsession

with (something) *Ice T:1*.

josh v. to tease.

joskin n. old man, old gaffer *Runyon*.

journo n. (Aus. use) journalist *Ready*.

joxy n. (lesbian use) the vagina
Maledicta.

joy n. (drug use) marijuana *Folb*.

joy bang n. (drug use) an occasional
injection of a narcotic by anyone who
is not addicted.

joy buzzer n. (lesbian use) the clitoris
Maledicta.

joy juice n. (US campus use) beer
Underwood.

joy pop n. see: joy bang *Algren*.

joy trail n. the vagina *Dunne*.

jubbies n. breasts.

Judas Priest! general excl., euph. for
Jesus Christ! 'Hill Street Blues',
Thames TV, 1983.

Judy n. girl, woman, mainly Liverpool
dial. *Keyes*.

Judy with the big booty n. (US
Black use) a fat female *Folb*.

jug n. **1.** prison; thus *jugged*: in prison
Wodehouse: AAG; **2.** a drink, esp. a
pint of beer *Norman: 2*; **3.** a bank
Caron.

jugged a. imprisoned *Chandler: LJ*.

jughead n. a drunkard.

jugs n. breasts; by the use of physical
resemblance, large breasts *Price: 2*.

jug-up n. (Can. prison use) mealtime
Caron.

juice n. **1.** interest on a debt or loan (cf:
vigorish) *Higgins: 3*; **2.** influence:
political, criminal, anything involving
corruption, pay-offs, favours *Bruce: 2*;
3. spec. electricity (theatre, TV, film
use); **4.** enjoyment, satisfaction,
stimulation *Price: 2*; **5.** alcohol *Powis*.

juice v. **1.** to bribe, esp. in context of
organized crime paying off the
authorities *Chandler: LG*; **2.** to add
interest to a loan, debt *Higgins: 3*.

juice house n. (US Black use) liquor
store *Folb*.

juice man n. (US cant) the collector of
loans for an illegal loan shark (qv)
Neaman & Silver.

juiced a. drunk
Gothic Blimp Works no 4.

juice-freak n. (US campus use) cf. juice-head *Underwood*.

juice-head n. a heavy drinker, an alcoholic.

ju-ju n. (drug use) 1. any drugs in capsule form; 2. marijuana cigarettes *R. Chandler, 'Farewell My Lovely', 1940*.

juke v. (US campus use) 1. to dance; 2. to have a good time (at a party); both fr. juke box, but itself fr. juke: cheap, raucous music played at similarly inclined roadhouses, cafés and brothels (cf: jive and juke) *Underwood*.

jumbo a. very large. (fr. proper name Jumbo: the first elephant to be exhibited at London's Regent's Park Zoo and subsequently a star of Barnum & Bailey's Circus).

jump n. the beginning, the outset *Goldman*.

jump v. 1. to ambush, to make a surprise attack *Mandelkau*; 2. to have sexual intercourse *Powis*.

jump bad v. to misbehave *Price: 2*.

jump bail v. (criminal/police use) to leave the country and thus avoid a possible prison sentence while remanded on bail prior to one's trial *Wodehouse: MOJ*.

jump down one's throat v. to become furious with someone, often for no apparent reason.

jump salty v. to be annoyed, irritated; to take offence *Waits*.

jump steady n. (US Black use) alcohol, which ensures that one keeps 'jumping' *Folb*.

jump the gun v. to act prematurely; fr. sporting use: in a false start a competitor will set off before the starting pistol has been fired *Manser*.

jump the last hurdle v. to die; fr. racing/running use (cf: take the long count, etc.) *Rawson*.

jump the rails v. to lose control, to disappear; fr. horseracing use *Chandler: LG*.

jump up and down v. (US Black use) to have sexual intercourse *Folb*.

jumped up a. conceited, arrogant; the implication is of one who no longer 'knows their place'.

jumper n. (UK cant) a jump lead carried by criminals to start stolen cars without using an ignition key *Powis*.

jumping a. lively, energetic, exciting *McFadden*.

jumping cat n. (US Black use) 1. a sophisticated, poised older person; 2. anyone successful in their occupation, legitimate or criminal *Klein*.

jump-up man n. see: jump-up merchant *Powis*.

jump-up merchant n. one who steals fr. lorries, trucks, etc. *Norman: 2*.

jumpy a. nervous, irritable *Higgins: 1*.

Junction n. the area of South London near Clapham Junction railway station *Nell Dunn, 'Up The Junction', (1965)*.

jungle n. 1. derog. a Black person (cf: jungle bunny); 2. that area of a town or city where tramps and vagrants congregate; also as hobo jungle; thus jungle buzzard: one who frequents such centres.

jungle bunny n. (derog.) Black person; fr. alleged origins in the jungle *Price: 1*.

jungle juice n. any form of strong, home-distilled liquor, often made of jungle-grown fruits and plants, herbs, etc. by soldiers with no 'regular' drinks.

jungle meat n. (gay use) a Black man's penis.

jungle mouth n. (US campus use) bad breath *Underwood*.

jungly a. (UK 'society' use) disorganized, chaotic, less than smart *Barr*.

junior jumper n. (US Black use) a juvenile (under 16) who commits rape and robbery (cf: R&R) *Neaman & Silver*.

junk n. 1. any unspecified objects, poss. worthless; poss. merely dismissive *Goulart*; 2. (drug use) heroin *Goldman*.

junk v. to reject, to throw away, to abandon *Bruce: 2*.

junk food n. the products of the

burgeoning world of 'fast-food' restaurants such as McDonalds, Burger King, Spudulike, etc. etc.; the implication, and to many palates, the actuality, is that such food is indeed junk, ie: rubbish.

junk hawk n. a heroin user whose entire existence centres on the drug *Grogan*.

junker n. a near-derelict but just driveable second-hand car; one step from the junkyard *Burroughs: Jr*.

junkette n. a young junkie (qv) girl *Morgan*.

junkie n. heroin addict *Price: 2*.

just a tick wait a moment *K. Waterhouse, 'In The Mood', 1983*.

just like mother makes it (cp) perfect, ideal; often, but not necessarily referring to food or drink *Wodehouse: MOJ*.

just quietly (Aus. use) strictly between you and me *Wilkes*.

just seven (gambling use) the point of seven in craps dice *Chandler: Notebk*.

just the job see: just the ticket.

just the ticket perfect, ideal, exactly as desired and required *ES 19/5/83*.

just what the doctor ordered anything perfect, ideal, excellent; with extra implication of acting as a cure for previous problems.

juvie n. (US criminal use) Juvenile Hall; reform school *Major*.

K

K 1. (civil service use) (abbrev.) Knight; 2. (abbrev.) kilo-: use of the prefix denoting 'one thousand' as one thousand dollars; of late K has replaced the former equivalent G (qv) *Higgins: 1*.

kab edis n. (butchers' backsl.) backside or rump, both human and as a cut of meat *Cole*.

kak v. to vomit *Sanders: 2*.

ka-ka n. (juv. use) excrement *Neaman & Silver*.

kaker n. fr. Yiddish 'excrement':
1. anything unpleasant or distasteful;
2. cannabis (cf: shit) *Cole*.

kale n. money; its 'green-ness' connotes the vegetable (cf: cabbage, lettuce) *Farrell*.

kalied a. drunk.

Kanaka n. Hawaiian *BvdB*.

kanga n. a pneumatic drill; orig. fr. *kangaroo shit*, because it jumps up and down *Cole*.

kangaroo n. (rhyming sl.) a Jew.

Kangaroo Valley Earls Court, London; base for many expatriate Australians *Humphries*.

Kansas City roll n. see: California roll X.

Kansas yummy n. any young woman who proves hard to seduce; she need not necessarily come from Kansas, but the implication is of small-town/rural innocence and morality.

kaput a. out of order, not working (fr. Ger. *kaputt* and Fr. (*être*) *capot*: (to be) without tricks in the card-game of piquet).

kark v. see: cark.

karsy n. aka: kazi: spec. lavatory; thus any messy unappealing place that resembles one *Performance*.

kasj see: cas *Morgan*.

kate and sidney (rhyming sl) steak and kidney *Jones: J*.

kate karney n. (rhyming sl.) the army *Jones: J*.

kaycuff foe! (backsl.) fuck off! *Cole*.

kaylack v. (backsl.) talk *Cole*.

kaynab n. (butchers' backsl.) bank *Cole*.

kayrop n. (butchers' backsl.) pork *Cole*.

kazoo n. anus, buttocks; often in *up the kazoo Rawson*.

KB (UK prison use) (abbrev.)

knockback (qv).

kecks n. knickers *Keyes*.

keel n. the buttocks; fr. nautical use *Neaman & Silver*.

keel over v. to collapse, to fall over; fr. nautical use *Austin*.

keen a. competent, appealing (in clothing), sharply dressed, etc. *Klein*.

keeper n. any form of weapon (cf: convincer).

keep a stiff lip v. (US Black use) to keep quiet, to maintain a secret *Klein*.

keep ahead of the game v. to have a given situation under control *Folb*.

keep banker's hours v. to act lazily; fr. the relatively brief periods during which a bank remains open for public business *Neaman & Silver*.

keep cave v. (UK school use) to keep a lookout, fr. Lat. *cave* = beware.

keep chickie v. to maintain a lookout (during a crime) *Grogan*.

keep mum v. to keep quiet; thus 1940s exhortation to secrecy: 'be like Dad: keep Mum' *Powis*.

keep nit v. (Aus. use) to act as lookout *Wilkes*.

keep on the straight and narrow v. to maintain a regular, law-abiding life.

keep one's cool v. to remain calm, despite circumstances to the contrary *McFadden*.

keep one's dick in one's pants v. to act calmly; often as 'Keep your dick...', and meaning calm down (cf: keep one's pants zipped) *Higgins:4*.

keep one's ear to the ground v. to be on the lookout, to take note of developments *Schulberg: 2*.

keep one's end up v. to do one's duty, to carry out one's share; fr. cricket use.

keep one's hair on v. to keep calm, to keep one's temper.

keep one's nose clean v. to lead a law-abiding, upright life; to avoid dangerous temptation; to resist interfering in things that are not one's business *Chandler: LG*.

keep one's pants zipped v. to retain control over one's ambitions, desires, conversation, etc.; such temptations

are not always sexual *Higgins: 5*.

keep one's pecker up v. to stay cheerful, despite possible adversity; 'never say die!' (cf: pecker) *Hotten*.

keep oneself to oneself v. to lead a solitary life; to resist interfering in the business of others.

keep shoatie v. (Scots use) to keep a lookout *Welsh:1* (cf: keep chickie).

keep stum(m) v. to keep quiet, to say nothing (cf: stumm & crum).

keep tabs on v. to keep under surveillance, to take note of *Higgins: 1*.

keep taking the tablets (cp) carry on with one's prescribed medicine; used in response to a statement that implies madness or eccentricity on behalf of the speaker *Manser*.

keep the ball rolling v. to maintain the progress of a situation *A. Powell, title of 4 vols of autobiography, 1976/82*.

keep the cap on the bottle v. to suppress the publication of facts/information deleterious to oneself *PT*.

keep the cork on v. to maintain control of one's emotions *Thompson: J*.

keep the lines open v. to maintain communication; fr. telephone lines *McBain: 1*.

keep-up n. (US Black use) anyone who looks after the home, spec. a maid *Klein*.

keester n. see:keister *Bruce: 2*.

keister n. 1. the anus, buttocks *Legman*; (US cant) 2. a safe; 3. a burglar's bag of safe/house-breaking tools.

keks n. trousers *Welsh:1* (cf: kicksies).

kelly's eye (bingo use) 1 (cf: buttered scone).

kelt n. (US Black use) a white person *Major*.

kerb-crawling v. to drive a car slowly along the pavements of areas where prostitutes are known to operate and thus to make a pick up; this practice all too often leads to punters (qv) approaching quite innocent women.

kerfuffle n. a fuss, a row, a flap (qv).

kerried a. exhausted, tired out; fr. rhy.sl. Kerry Packered = knackered (qv).

Kevin n. a derogatory description (used by the middle classes) of working-class youths whom they regard as overly flashy and socially unacceptable (cf: Sharon).

key n. (drug use) one kilo of marijuana or hashish *Green: 1*.

key in v. to focus on; fr. film use, the key light focusses directly on a single actor *Price: 3*.

K-factor n. (skiing use) (abbrev.) Kraut-factor; the number of Germans visible on the slopes *Barr*.

KG (US police use) (acro.) *K*nown *G*ambler *Neaman & Silver*.

khyber n. (rhyming sl.) khyber pass = ass = buttocks *Powis*.

ki n. (UK prison use) cocoa; fr. nautical use *LL*.

KIA v. (US milit. use) to shoot dead or otherwise kill in combat; fr. milit. j. abbrev. *K*illed *I*n *A*ction *Del Vecchio*.

kibitz v. to watch (a gambling game) and to comment/advise but not to participate; fr. German *Kiebitz* a lapwing, a noisy and inquisitive bird. In German *kiebitzen* means to look over a cardplayer's shoulders *Rosten*.

kibitzers n. spectators in a gambling club or casino who do not play but watch and/or advise those who do; thus any non-participating adviser/observer *Performance*.

kick n. 1. the sensation any place or situation produces *Burroughs: 1*; 2. pocket esp. in trousers *Wodehouse: TJ*.

kick v. to stop taking an addictive drug; fr. kick the habit (qv) *Bruce: 2*.

kick about v. to make a fuss, to complain; fr. kick up a fuss *Farrell*.

kick around v. to hang about, to wander aimlessly.

kick ass v. 1. to beat up someone; to fight; 2. (US campus use) to have a good, if boisterous time *Underwood*.

kick down (to) v. to give (something) to.

kick in the ass n. see: kick in the pants.

kick in the pants n. 1. a setback, a grave disappointment; 2. anything that urges one on to greater effort, commitment, etc.

kick it v. (US Black use) to talk, to chatter, to gossip (cf: kick it around).

kick it v. to associate with.

kick it! general exhortation, often in the context of playing music.

kick it around v. to talk, to gossip.

kick (it) around v. to discuss, to debate a topic *PT*.

kick off v. to die *Higgins: 3*.

kick (one) into touch v. to dismiss, to reject *Welsh:1*.

kick (something) off v. to start, to set in motion *Greenlee*.

kick start v. to set going with an initial sudden impetus; from the kick-starting of a motorbike.

kick the bucket v. to die *Sillitoe*.

kick the gong around v. 1. to use drugs, esp. heroin/morphine *Chandler: Notebk*; 2. to masturbate.

kick the habit v. to stop taking an addictive drug, usu. heroin *Bruce: 1*.

kick the stuffing out of v. to maltreat, to beat up severely *Farrell*.

kick the tin v. (Aus. use) to make a financial contribution *Wilkes*.

kick (to) v. (US black use) to inform, explain, tell.

kick up daisies v. to die (cf: push up daisies).

kick upstairs v. to promote an official or executive who cannot actually be dismissed but whose value in his/her current role is no longer useful to the organization *Capital Radio 1983*.

kickback n. commission on a payment made by the payee to the customer; usu. a genteel euph. for bribe *Price: 2*.

kicker n. the last, most problematical piece of information *Fiction Illus. 3*.

kick-off n. the beginning, the start; fr. soccer use *Wodehouse: MOJ*.

kicks n. thrills, pleasure *Higgins: 2*.

kicksies n. trousers *Hotten*.

kid v. to tease, to joke with, to pretend, to fool *Higgins: 1*.

kid stuff 1. kiddie porn (qv); 2. the

children who are exploited in such pornography.

kiddie porn n. pornography that features the sexual exploitation of young (sometimes very young) children. The practice has been going on very many years, the term emerged into wider use during the mid-1980s.

kiddiwink n. a young child.

kiddo n. a child; esp, as a greeting: 'Hey, kiddo' *C. MacInnes, 'Absolute Beginners', 1959*.

kidney n. the female womb *Klein*.

kidney wiper n. the penis; obvious extension of kidney (qv).

kid-simple n. (homosexual use) an obsessive lover of young boys *Legman*.

kife n. a bed *Powis*.

kike n. (derog.) a Jew; poss. rhyming with Ike (cf: Ikey Mo); or fr. Yiddish *kikel*: a circle, the mark used by some illiterate Jewish immigrants – rather than a cross – when signing papers at Ellis Island, NYC, c.1900 *Higgins: 3*.

ki-ki n. 1. bisexual; 2. a homosexual who is equally happy in active or passive sex roles *Stanley*.

Kilburn n. (rhyming sl. UK police use) Kilburn Priory = diary, spec. that used by an officer for writing up evidence that will be given in court *Powis*.

kill v. 1. to convulse with laughter, to bowl over, to surprise *Goldman*; 2. (theatre/TV/film use) to turn off a given light or lights *Green: 2*; 3. to finish, esp. a drink.

kill one's dog v. to drink heavily *Dickson*.

kill some babies v. to masturbate.

killer a. (US teen. use) wonderful, amazing, etc. (cf: kill 1) *Pond*.

killing a. (UK 'society' use) very funny; thus 'that really kills me' etc. *Barr*.

killing floor n. (US Black use) anywhere used for the purpose of sexual intercourse *Folb*.

killout n. (US Black use) a fascinating person, enthralling topic or thing *Major*.

kimible n. (US Black use) the exaggerated, identifiable pimp walk poss. fr. (arms) akimbo *Klein*.

kindness n. (US Black use) a sexual favour; thus, *to do a kindness*: to indulge sexually *Klein*.

king a. (Aus. surf use) excellent, wonderful, perfect *Humphries: 2*.

king n. (Aus. use) (abbrev.) kinghit: a knockout punch or blow *Wilkes*.

King Dick a. (rhyming sl.) thick (qv) = stupid, dull *Wright*.

kinky a. odd, bizarre, eccentric, spec. sexually perverse *Performance*.

kip n. 1. a bed; 2. the place where one sleeps, one's home; both uses fr. orig. 18th C. a brothel *Norman: 2*.

kip v. to sleep *Norman: 2*.

kipe v. (US campus (spec. University of Arkansas) use) to steal *Underwood*.

kiphouse n. see: dosshouse *LL*.

kipper n. (Aus. use) (derog.) Englishman; fr. the herring which, after processing, has become 'two-faced with no guts' *Wilkes*.

kishke n. fr. Rus: intestine; the guts *Rosten*.

kiss v. 1. (US teen. use) (abbrev.) kiss goodbye: reject, do without, etc. *Sculatti*; 2. to fellate or perform cunnilingus *Legman*.

kiss ass v. to be subservient, sycophantic *Jones*.

kiss goodbye v. to reject, to do without.

kiss my arse! general cp. of contempt or dismissal *J. Joyce, Ulysses, 1922*.

kiss my tuna! (Valley Girls (qv) use) all-purpose excl. of rejection; tuna = vagina and the implication is that the oral sex that is invited is *de facto* distasteful *Pond*.

kiss of death n. a person or object contact with whom or which invariably proves fatal – metaphorically if not practically.

kiss off n. conclusion, farewell, termination (usu. with sense of one party compelling it on the other) *Jay & Young*.

kiss off v. to reject, ignore, spurn, toss aside *Higgins: 5*.

kiss one's ass goodbye v. to give up completely; to abandon all hope.

kiss one's ring v. to fawn, to act the sycophant, to toady.

kiss the dog v. (US cant) for a pickpocket to steal from the person with whom he/she is face-to-face *Neaman & Silver*.

kiss the porcelain god v. (US campus use) to vomit (cf: drive the porcelain bus) *Bernbach*.

kiss the worm v. to fellate *Legman*.

kisser n. 1. the mouth *Wright*; 2. the whole face *Runyon*.

kissyface n. (US teen/campus use) the act of kissing *Underwood*.

kite n. 1. (Can. prison use) a contraband letter or note smuggled in/out of gaol. *Caron*; 2. (US prison use) any form of written document, memo, etc. used within a gaol *Folb*; 3. a dud cheque; thus *kiting*: passing dud cheques for fraud; a bouncing (qv) cheque 'flies away' *Norman: 2*; 4. (US campus use) an inveterate drug user, who stays 'high as a kite' *Underwood*.

kitted up a. dressed, clothed *Humphries*.

kitty n. the vagina (cf: pussy).

kitty-cat n. (US Black use) 1. a Cadillac; 2. a female (cf: pussy) *Folb*.

Kiwi n. New Zealander; fr. the national bird.

kleenex n. a juvenile used for sex, because 'You pick it up, blow, and throw it away'.

klick n. (US milit. use) a kilometre *Del Vecchio*.

kludge n. anything thrown together more by luck than judgement and with little style or sophistication, though sufficient workability for those who assembled it; fr. computer jargon *Kidder*.

klutz n. fr. Ger 'a log': a stupid, clumsy person *Grogan*.

knacker v. to harm, to ruin *Tidy*.

knackered a. worn out, exhausted; fr. SE: horse-butcher *Wilkinson*.

knackers n. testicles *T 13/7/83*.

knee v. (abbrev.) knee in the testicles.

knee trembler n. sexual intercourse when both partners are standing up; popular with cheap prostitutes or with couple who have nowhere to lie down *Norman: 2*.

kneecap v. an extra-legal 'punishment' esp. beloved of and poss. introduced by the IRA, whereby victims are shot through the kneecaps and, while painfully crippled, are not actually killed. *Humphries: 2*.

knees up n. a party, a celebration, fr. Cockney popular song 'Knees Up Mother Brown!'

knee-high to a grasshopper phr. (orig. US) very short (cf: knee-high to a tall Indian).

knee-slapper n. an uproarious joke, the term is often used ironically.

kneel at the altar v. (US prison sl.) to fellate *Legman*.

knicker bandit n. a criminal who steals women's underwear from washing lines.

knickers! excl. meaning rubbish! piss off! (qv), etc.; general negation of the preceding speaker's opinion, demand, etc. *Powis*.

knight of the golden grummet n. (US criminal sl.) one who enjoys anal intercourse; fr. naut. grummet = rope ring; gold = excrement *Legman*.

knob v. to have sexual intercourse; the term is almost invariably used of men (cf: bang, bonk, screw).

knob cheese n. see: cock cheese.

knob polisher n. a young male whore.

knob-end n. general derog. term *Welsh:1* (cf: dickhead).

knobs n. 1. the female breasts *Folb*; 2. (US Black use) stylish, up to date shoes with shined toecaps *Seale*.

knock n. (Aus. use) a promiscuous female *Wilkes*.

knock v. 1. (UK criminal use) to cheat, to defraud, to con (qv) *LL*; 2. to criticize *Higgins: 3*; 3. to have sexual intercourse *Keyes*; 4. (US Black use) to kill *Klein*.

knock about v. to travel around rather than settle down *Sapper*, *'Jim Maitland', 1923*.

knock at the door (bingo rhyming sl.) 4 *Wright*.

knock back v. 1. to drink, esp. to finish off a drink *Welsh:2*; 2. to reject *Humphries:1*.

knock back n. a rejection *Humphries*.

knock cold v. to knock unconscious (cf: cold-cock).

knock down drag out n. a vicious fight in which one participant is knocked unconscious *White*.

knock for a loop v. to surprise completely, to devastate *Heller*.

knock it off v. stop doing something *Dury, 'Do It Yourself'*.

knock it on the head v. to stop doing something; to finish a task; fr. the final blow of a hammer that drives in a nail (?).

knock it out v. 1. (US Black use) to have sexual intercourse; 2. (journalism use) to write something quickly, with neither style nor concentration.

knock off v. 1. (criminal use) to steal; 2. (police use) to arrest; 3. to seduce *Powis*.

knock off a piece to seduce a girl, piece is abbrev: piece of ass (qv) *Schulberg*.

knock on together v. to have an affair *Sillitoe*.

knock one's block off v. to injure physically, usu. in form of a threat: 'I'll knock . . .'

knock out v. 1. to impress, to overwhelm, to delight *Keyes*; 2. to earn a given sum of money; ie 'knocking out £200 per week' etc.

knock over v. to rob, usu. with violence; of person or places *Tuff Shit Comics*.

knock the bejazus out of v. see: knock the stuffing out of.

knock the dust off the old sombrero v. to perform oral sex.

knock the stuffing out of v. to beat severely.

knock them cold v. aka: *knock them dead* for a performer or performance to devastate an audience with its excellence.

knock up v. to make pregnant *Price: 2*.

knockabout man n. (Aus. use) pickpocket *Baker*.

knockback n. (UK prison use) the rejection of one's application for parole (cf: flop).

knocked a. under control, at one's mercy: 'I've got it knocked'.

knocker n. 1. a critic *Keyes*; 2. a gambler who refuses to pay his debts (which cannot be enforced legally in the UK) *Performance*.

knockers n. breasts *Tidy*.

knocking-shop n. a brothel *Hotten*.

knock-off n. a fake, a copy; used in fashion trade – cheap copies of 'model' garments – in antiques – cheap reproductions – etc.

knock-out n. a surprise *Wright*.

knock-out! (excl.) wonderful! perfect! *Capital Radio 1983*.

know how many beans make five v. to be alert, to be aware of given facts/ information.

know one's number v. to understand another person, to assess a situation (cf: peep one's hole card) *Heller*.

know one's onions v. to be well informed, to be aware.

know the dish v. (US Black use) to be aware of the embarassing truth *Shell*.

know the ropes to understand how to do a given task, fr. sailing use.

know the words and music v. (homosexual use) to understand and partake in the gay sub-culture *Legman*.

know what time it is v. to be au fait, aware, streetwise (qv) *Ice T:2*.

know what's what v. to be aware of the facts, abreast of a situation.

know where the bodies are buried v. to have special knowledge of a situation, esp. of its less appealing side, that gives one power over those who nominally control it; the threat, rather than the use of blackmail *Wodehouse: PGM*.

know-it-all n. (derog.) 1. a clever person, esp. one who is 'too clever for their own good'; 2. a braggart, a show-off.

knuckle n. a fight, violence; fr. the fist

used therein *Robins:1.*

knuckle down v. to succumb, to surrender (cf: knuckle under) *Hotten.*

knuckle sandwich n. a blow from a fist *Humphries.*

knuckle under v. to surrender, to accept something one dislikes but is not strong enough to fight; one falls beneath a rival's knuckle (qv) *Schulberg.*

knucklehead n. derog. term of abuse, description for any foolish, stupid, slow person; the knuckles pressed to the forehead imply the intensity of thought *Folb.*

knucks n. (abbrev.) brass knuckles, worn over the fist to ensure victory in a fistfight *Farrell.*

Kojak v. (US teen. use) to find a parking space in an area where such discoveries are at best rare; fr. US TV show 'Kojak' whose eponymous hero seems to possess this facility *ad nauseam Sculatti.*

Kojak with a Kodak n. (CB use) policeman manning a radar speed trap; fr. popular TV show and make of camera *CB.*

kong n. (US Black use) home-distilled whisky; fr. King Kong (film 1933) and thus denoted great strength *Major.*

konk v. (Black use) to straighten one's otherwise naturally curly hair (cf: process) *Selby: 1.*

kook n. an eccentric, albeit an acceptable one *Morgan.*

kooky a. odd, eccentric (with overtones of charm) *Goldman.*

kool tou! (backsl.) look out! *Cole.*

kosher a. 1. honest, legitimate, above-board; fr. Yiddish: according to the Jewish dietary laws, thus kosher meat, etc. *Runyon;* 2. (gay use) circumcised.

kosher delicatessen n. (gay use) Israel.

kosher dill n. (gay use) circumcised penis.

kosher style a. (gay use) circumcised (cf: kosher 2.).

KP n. (Aus. use) common prostitute *Baker.*

Kraut n. (derog.) a German; fr *sauerkraut*: a form of pickled, shredded cabbage, beloved of the nation *Higgins: 2.*

krazin n. (US campus use) a load of utter rubbish; absolute nonsense *Simmons.*

Kremlin n. (UK police use) New Scotland Yard *Powis.*

Kreskin v. (US teen. use) to prophesy, to work out intuitively, to foresee; fr. US TV magician 'Kreskin' *Sculatti.*

kurve n. prostitute; fr. Yiddish kurveh *Powis.*

kvetch n. to complain, to delay, to nag, fuss; fr. Ger. squeeze, press *Rosten.*

kylege (UK Black use) money *D Robins.*

L

labonza n. the buttocks; the pit of the stomach *Neaman & Silver.*

labour n. (abbrev.) labour exchange: the employment exchange, the job centre *Norman:2.*

lace curtain n. (homosexual use) a long foreskin *Legman.*

lace curtains n. the genitalia of an uncircumcised male *Stanley.*

lace-curtain Irish n. genteel petit-bourgeois Irish-Americans; who adorn their windows with such items *Bruce:2.*

laced a. drunk; one's blood is 'laced' with alcohol *Dickson.*

laddish a. macho, loud, displaying the various characteristics of the young man or 'lad'.

la-di-dah n. (rhyming sl.) a cigar *Powis.*

la-di-dah a. **1.** stuck up, arrogant, snobbish; **2.** effeminate, affected, a sissy *Humphries:2*.

ladies n. (Black pimp use) prostitutes *Milner*.

lady n. (pimp use) sophisticated, classy prostitute whose talents mean she can make her own rules as to those she sleeps with and what she charges for the pleasure *OUI 8/75*.

Lady Five Fingers n. masturbation (cf: Mrs Hand . . .).

lady killer n. a sexually successful man; sometimes, however, only in his own eyes *Thompson:J*.

lady lover n. a lesbian *Legman*.

Lady Muck n. any stuck-up woman; the class is irrelevant – the pretentions are the point.

Lady Snow n. (US Black use) a respected upper-class white woman *Klein*.

lag n. a convict, a prisoner (cf: lagging) *Norman:1*.

lagging n. (UK criminal use) **1.** any prison sentence; **2.** a sentence of more than two years imprisonment; both fr. orig. meaning: transportation to the penal colonies *Norman:2*.

lagging station n. (UK prison use) a long-term prison *Obs.1981*.

lahteeache (backsl.) all right *Cole*.

laid back n. soothing, peaceful, passive, calm; used both of people and music; fr. the physical position (cf: mellow) *White*.

laid out (US Black use) well-dressed *Klein*.

laid to the bone (US Black use) clothes cut so well that they seem pasted to the wearer's figure *Klein*.

laid to the natural bone (US Black use) naked *Folb*.

lair n. (Aus. use) a show-off, an extrovert *Ready*.

lairize v. (Aus. use) to brag, to boast, to show-off *Wilkes*.

lairy a. (Aus. use) flashy, ostentatious, vulgar, showy; fr. lair (qv) *Dennis*.

lakes n. (rhyming sl.) Lakes of Killarney = barmy = mad *Powis*.

Lakes of Killarney n. see: lakes *Cole*.

lamb n. a young homosexual boy (cf: chicken) *Legman*.

lamb-time n. (US teen. use) spring *Sculatti*.

lame n. (abbrev.) lame-brain (qv).

lame a. **1.** drunk *Dickson*; **2.** lacking in cool *G. Green*.

lame duck n. (US polit. use) a President who has been defeated in November's election but will not actually leave his office – in which his decisions are *de facto* irrelevant – until January; this usage can extend to any similarly-placed officials *Green:2*.

lame-brain n. an incompetent, a fool *Price:2*.

lamp v. to look at, to assess visually; fr. 19th C. *lamp*: eye *Farrell*.

Lancashire lasses n. (rhyming sl.) glasses (spectacles) *Franklyn*.

landsman n. a fellow-countryman; fr. Yiddish, thus spec. a fellow Jew (cf: paisan).

lard-ass n. **1.** a lazy, good-for-nothing person *Bukowski:1*; **2.** an overweight person *Uris*; both miscreants sit on their posterior and do nothing but cultivate 'lard'.

lare n. (Aus. use) a ruffian, a tearaway (qv); fr. abbrev. of larrikin.

lark n. **1.** any form of activity, occupation *Norman:3*; **2.** a game *Performance*.

lash-up n. a home-made assembly, essentially amateur, but quite adequate for a limited period; refers to material objects, organizations, ideas, etc. *Higgins:5*.

latch on to v. **1.** to understand, to grasp *Sillitoe*; **2.** to take hold of, to attach oneself to *Thompson:J*.

later! (abbrev.) see you later; goodbye *McFadden*.

later for that phrase of dismissal; I can't be bothered (now) *Seale*.

Latin mystery n. a doctor's prescription.

laughing gear n. the mouth.

laughing tackle n. the mouth.

launder v. to 'de-criminalize' corruptly or illegally gained money by 'washing' it through a casino till or a bank. The 'dirty' notes, etc. are deposited and 'clean' cash is issued, without the taint of scandal (cf: dirty money) *PT*.

laundromat n. any situation, often a game of chance, in which illicit money can be laundered (qv); pun on the do-it-yourself laundry shops *Alvarez*.

lavender a euph. for homosexuals and anything referring to them *Legman*.

lavvy n. abbr. lavatory *Welsh:2*.

law n. the police *Norman:2*.

lawing n. see: corner 2 *Powis*.

lawn n. (homosexual use) pubic hair; if the pubic hair is shaved, a *mowed lawn* (cf: garden, grass) *Maledicta*.

lay n. 1. sexual intercourse; 2. a person with whom one makes love, usu. as a *good lay* or a *bad lay*, etc. *Price:2*.

lay v. 1. to make love to *Price:2*; 2. (US Black use) to over-indulge in drugs or drink to such an extent that one is laid on one's back *Klein*.

lay a rap on v. (orig. US) to persuade.

lay an egg v. to fail completely, esp. show business use; *Variety* headlined the morning after the 1929 Crash: 'Wall Street Lays an Egg' *Goldman*.

lay back aka: *lay low, lay up* (US Black use) 1. to relax; 2. to do nothing specific; 3. to have sexual intercourse *Folb*.

lay dead v. (US Black use) to do nothing, to stop everything *Folb*.

lay down n. (UK police use) a remand in custody *Powis*.

lay down v. to give in to another, to accept *Folb*.

lay down merchant n. one who specializes in passing forged banknotes *Norman:2*.

lay down one's knife and fork v. to die (cf: hand in one's dinner pail) *Neaman & Silver*.

lay for v. to wait for someone (invariably with the intention of harming them) *Morgan*.

lay in v. (US prison use) to stay in one's cell at any time when one might usually be out of it *Klein*.

lay into v. to attack physically.

lay (it) on the line v. to be absolutely honest; to declare one's feelings, one's

attitude *Junker*.

lay it out v. (lesbian use) to admit and poss. flaunt one's sexual preference (cf: lay (it) on the line) *Maledicta*.

lay off! a warning: keep away! stop doing a given action.

lay on v. 1. to give, esp. of drugs; 2. to provide; 3. to tell, to impose facts upon *Jay & Young*.

lay out v.t. to knock someone out in a fight.

lay rubber v. to drive off at speed, spinning the wheels as one accelerates away.

lay some on me! (US Black use) invitation to swap ritual handslaps as form of black-to-black greeting *Klein*.

lay some pipe v. to have sexual intercourse.

lay the leg v. (US prison use) to sodomize *Legman*.

lay the lip v. (US prostitute use) to fellate *Legman*.

lay the scene on v. to explain, to outline a situation (cf: scene) *Bruce:2*.

lay tight v. (US Black use) to stay calm, to retain one's grip of a situation *Klein*.

lay up v. to hide; to rest *Grogan*.

layabout n. a voluntarily unemployed male, usu. involved in some minor criminality *Norman:2*.

lay-by n. (Aus. use) a deposit on and the subsequent purchasing by instalments of a given article in a shop *Ready*.

layin' and playin' (US Black use) to be idling around the house, usu. with one's woman *Klein*.

LB n. (drug use) one pound weight, fr. 1 *lb*. (cf: OZ) 'Hill Street Blues', *Thames TV, 1983*.

LD (US Black use) (abbrev.) Cadillac *El*dorado *Price:2*.

lead down v. (milit. use) to fire at; fr. lead bullets.

lead on, Macduff (cp) exhorting someone else to take the initiative; a corruption of 'lay on, Macduff' in Shakespeare's *Macbeth*.

lead up the garden path v. to trick, to deceive deliberately, to tease.

lead-foot v. to move slowly and clumsily *Fiction Illus.3.*

lead-pipe cinch n. absolute certainty *Algren.*

lean and linger n. (US rhyming sl.) finger *Runyon.*

lean green n. (US teen. use) money (cf: green, greenbacks) *Sculatti.*

lean on v. to pressurize, to persuade, poss. with violence or threats of violence *Vidal.*

lean over backwards v. to make every effort towards a given end; the inference may be altruistic or self-aggrandising.

leaning house n. (US Black use) a brothel or a place where illicit meetings, drug sales, etc. take place *Klein.*

leap and you will receive (US Black use) ritual challenge to a fight, ie: come and get it! *Folb.*

leaper n. **1.** (drug use) any form of stimulant, amphetamine, etc. *Green:1*; **2.** a dud cheque, drawn against inadequate funds (cf: bounce) *Breslin.*

leapfrog n. (pimp use) a client who hires a number of prostitutes to play leapfrog while he watches (and masturbates) *OUI 8/75.*

Leaping Lena (US milit. use) see Bouncing Betty *Rawson.*

learn a new way v. turn to homosexuality *Higgins:1.*

leary a. aka: *leery*: bright, alert, intelligent; thus suspicious of someone *Newman:1.*

leather n. **1.** (homosexual use) the anus *Legman*; **2.** a wallet *Runyon:1.*

leather v. **1.** to beat, to kick *Hotten*; **2.** (homosexual use) to perform anal intercourse *Legman.*

leather medal n. (US sports use) the booby prize, the wooden spoon (qv).

leather piece n. (US Black use) any garment, esp. coat, made of leather *Wolfe:4.*

leatherneck n. a Marine, both UK and US use; early US marine uniforms had a leather neckband.

leave before the gospel v. to practise

coitus interruptus (cf: get out at Gateshead; get off at Redfern) *Neaman & Silver.*

leave for dead v. to defeat absolutely; to leave far behind in any form of competition.

leave it out! stop doing that! *Dury, 'Do It Yourself', 1979.*

leave off! (excl.) stop it! (esp. in sense of stop telling lies) *Newman:1.*

lech n. **1.** (abbrev.) lecher; **2.** sexual desire; fr. lechery *Stone.*

Lee Marvin a. starving *Welsh:1* (fr. rhy. sl. with proper name Lee Marvin, US film star 1924-87).

leech n. a parasite, a sponger; fr. the blood-sucking creature *Larner.*

leeky store n. (US Black use) liquor store *Folb.*

leery a. **1.** bad tempered, disagreeable, cheeky *Powis*; **2.** cunning, underhand (cf: leary) *Keyes.*

left off! (US campus use) (excl.) jokey reversal of more generally popular right on! (qv) *Underwood.*

lefthanded a. undesirable, unpleasant, evil; the lit. translation of Lat. *sinister.*

lefty n. **1.** a left-handed person; **2.** a political radical, of left-wing ideology.

leg n. (US campus use) (abbrev.) dirty leg (qv) *Underwood.*

leg art (newspaper use) pictures of women revealing their legs (cf: cheesecake).

leg it v. to run away *Newman:1.*

leg man n. a man who prefers a woman's legs to any other part of her anatomy (cf: ass man, tit man).

leg opener n. a drink given to a girl in the hope of getting her drunk enough for seduction *Humphries.*

leg work n. **1.** (US tramp use) to have intercourse between the thighs or the buttocks (but without actual penetration of the anus) *Legman*; **2.** any job that requires a great deal of walking *Fiction Illus.3.*

legal eagle n. a lawyer, the implication is of an astute one; technically rhyming sl.

leggner n. (UK prison use) a twelve month sentence, pun on stretch (qv) a leg *LL*.

leggy a. of a girl with particularly attractive legs; esp. loved by tabloid newspapers who offer 'leggy lovely' as a noun.

legit a. (abbrev.) legitimate; and as such the description of anything that, in context, might be considered as otherwise; thus *on the legit*: conducting an honest life/business, etc. *Algren*.

legless a. drunk; to the extent of falling over.

legover n. sexual intercourse; back formation from get one's leg over (qv).

legs eleven (bingo use) 11.

legs up to her arse (cp) male description of a woman with exceptionally long (and attractive) legs.

leg-shake artist n. (Aus. use) a pickpocket *Baker*.

lemon n. 1. (US Black use) a light-skinned black person *Major*; 2. anything undesirable, esp. females; fr. sourness of the fruit *Wodehouse:MOJ*.

lemon curd n. a turd; both as the actual object and as a derogatory term for a person.

lemon squeezer n. a man; fr. rhy. sl. = geezer (qv).

leo-time n. (US teen. use) August, fr. astrological sign 'Leo' *Sculatti*.

les n. (abbrev.) lesbian *Norman:2*.

lesbo n. (abbrev.) lesbian *Legman*.

leso n. (Aus. use) lesbian, *Wilkes*.

let it all hang out v. (hippie, currently new therapy use) to cast aside any restraints, to do what one wants, to act from the heart *Blacker*.

let it ride v. to ignore, to forget; fr. dice gambling where a winning bet is not picked up from the table but left to be gambled again *Howard*.

let me hold some change (US Black use) please give me some money *Seale*.

let off a little nigger v. (derog.) to act in a crazy, uninhibited way, to let off steam.

let one have it v. to kill, esp. with gunfire *rr*.

let one's game slip v. (US Black use (though, general use also)) to lose control of a situation, a plan, an objective, etc. *Folb*.

let one's hair down v. (homosexual use) to relax one's inhibitions; poss. in homosexual use prior to more widespread use *Legman*.

let the dog see the rabbit (cp) give someone a chance to get on with a given task.

let the tail go with the hide phr. to ignore small details while concentrating on the overall picture.

letch n. (abbrev.) lecher *Bukowski:2*.

let's be having you! (cp) time to start work, get out of bed, etc. *Manser*.

let's boogie (US teen. use) let's go, let's be off *Pond*.

lettuce n. money (cf: cabbage, kale) *Humphries*.

level v. to admit, confess; to be honest *Runyon:1*.

Levy v. (rhyming sl.) Levy and Frank = wank = masturbate *Powis*.

lewdie n. a married woman who frequents singles' bars looking for brief encounters. *AS 60.1 (1985)*.

lezzie n. (abbrev.) lesbian.

LF see: long firm *Powis*.

LF gear n. the proceeds of a long firm (qv) fraud, sold off at greatly reduced prices; sometimes, to tempt those who find such sales romantic, perfectly legitimate, if shoddy, goods are advertised as 'LF gear' *Powis*.

libber n. a feminist, a member of the Women's Liberation Movement; usu. derog. (male) use *Shulman*.

liberate v. to steal; fr. 1960s radical use, on the Proudhon principle that 'property is theft' but likewise with a degree of irony/self-mockery given the 1960s obsession with 'freedom' and 'the revolution'; with further irony, the 'radical' use stems fr. Second World War 'liberating forces' who 'freed' commodities as well as people

Payne.

lick n. **1.** a blow; **2.** (rock music use) a particular phrase of music, ie *guitar lick*.

lick v. to defeat, to beat *Wright*.

lick my froth! (Valley Girls (qv) use) general term of abuse, dismissal (cf: kiss my tuna!) *Pond*.

lickety-split anything fast; some onomatopoeic overtones.

licking n. a beating, a defeat *Tidy*.

lid n. (drug use) quantity of marijuana, approx 22 gms; fr. the quantity of the drug that fills a popular tobacco tin lid *Green:1*.

lie doggo v. to remain hidden and quiet; like a stalking dog *Powis*.

Life n. (US Black use) the subculture of crime, pimping, drug dealing, etc. that makes up the alternative world of the streets *Milner*.

life of Riley n. the good life; the materially satisfactory life, a comfortable existence *Price:3*.

lifeboat n. (US prison use) a pardon, the commutation of a sentence *Chandler: Notebk*.

lifer n. **1.** (prison use) anyone serving a life sentence *BBC-TV 1983*; **2.** (US milit. use) a career soldier; also used as derog. term for anyone who appears excessively keen on milit. discipline and its administration to his peers *Stone*.

lift v. **1.** to arrest, esp. N. Ireland use by both Army and police *Wilkinson*; **2.** (criminal use) to steal.

lift one's game v. (US pimp use) to improve one's situation – financially, emotionally, intellectually, etc. *Shulman*.

ligger n. a hanger on; spec. in entertainment industry: a freeloader (qv). fr. *least important guest* (?) or linger: hang around, or the Banffshire dialect 'lig' meaning to gossip, or to talk too much. The term became widespread in the early 1970s, but goes back at least to 1960 when Colin MacInnes used it in his essay 'The Other Man' *NME*.

light v. (US Black use) to enlighten

someone with general or specific knowledge *Klein*.

light into v. to attack verbally, to criticize, to nag *rr*.

light of love n. (UK prison use; rhyming sl.) Gov = prison governor *LL*.

light off v. to have an orgasm *Higgins:2*.

light out v. to leave, to run away, to escape.

lighten up v. (US Black use) to calm down, to cease from an action *Folb*.

lights on but there's nobody home phr. insane, or at least mentally deficient; vacant. *Talking Heads 'Swamp'*.

lightweight n. an insignificant person, a weakling. *McFadden*.

like all-purpose, absolutely meaningless interj. that breaks a sentence but has no effect on the meaning: 'it's, like, cold . . .', 'I feel, like, sick', etc.; orig. in beatnik/jazz worlds c.1950s *Pond*.

like a bat out of hell moving very quickly.

like a dose of salts very quickly; usu. *go through (you) like a . . .*

like a good 'un enthusiastically, keenly *Norman:2*.

like a nigger girl's left tit derog. phr. neither right nor fair.

like a rat up a drain very quickly; usu. in sexual context: *up that like a . . . Humphries*.

like a spare prick at a wedding (cp) absolutely useless; the assumption is that only the bridegroom is necessary *Barr*.

like billy-o most enthusiastically, strenuously, speedily: general expression of energy or effort.

like crazy intensely, excessively, obsessively, etc. *PT*.

like fuck **1.** excl. of denial or negation, usu. as 'like fuck I will!' (cf: like hell!); adv. **2.** intensely, very much *Welsh:1*.

like hang phr. (Aus./NZ) general intensive phr.

like it or lump it v. to accept a

situation, willingly or not; often as *well, you'll have to . . .*

like nobody's business very well, excellently, very quickly.

like taking candy from a baby (cp) extremely easy *Wodehouse:MOJ*.

like winking very quickly *Hotten*.

likkered a. drunk; fr. 'liquored' *Dickson*.

Lilley and Skinner n. (rhyming sl.) dinner *Powis*.

Lilly (drug use) seconal, fr. manufacturer's name on the pill.

lily n. 1. anything remarkable or particularly outstanding (cf: lulu) *Runyon*; 2. an effeminate male; 3. a homosexual who fears to reveal his sex life; *Legman*; 4. (US Black use) a white person *Folb*.

Lily Law n. the police *Maledicta 9*.

Limbo Room n. (Can. prison use) a place where corporal punishment is administered to prisoners *Caron*.

Limey n. English person; (abbrev.) lime-juicer (obs); fr. the former habit of serving UK sailors lime-juice as a preventative against scurvy *Price:2*.

limo n. (abbrev.) limousine; esp. in show business use.

limp-dick n. a. an inadequate person, a weakling; also used adjectivally.

line n. 1. (drug use) a portion of heroin or cocaine scraped into a line across a mirror in order for it to be sniffed into the nostril *Green:1*; 2. (drug use) a small marijuana cigarette; 3. a smooth verbal style aimed at seduction or at persuading someone else to accept an idea or plan; esp. in sexual or business contexts.

line up on v. (homosexual use) to gang-fellate or sodomize *Legman*.

linen n. (rhyming sl.) linen draper = newspaper *Norman:2*.

lines n. (US Black use) 1. words in general; 2. persuasive patter aimed at seduction *Folb*.

line-up n. 1. a police identification parade *Price:2*; 2. gang-rape *Salisbury*.

lion's lair n. (rhyming sl.) chair

Wright.

lip n. 1. cheek, back-talking *Norman:1*; 2. lawyer; fr. concept of his 'talking back' (as in cheekiness) in defence of his client *Chandler: Notebk*.

lip dancing n. oral sex.

lip off v. to talk rudely, cheekily, provocatively *Dunne*.

lipkisser n. a man who enjoys cunnilingus *AS 60.1 (1985)*.

lippy n. (abbrev.) lipstick *BBC-TV 1982*.

lippy a. cheeky, verbal, talkative, loudmouthed (cf: lip) *Jenkins*.

LIQ (US Black use) (abbrev.) *LIQ*uor store *Folb*.

liquid cosh n. (UK prison use) major tranquillizers used to restrain (for short- or long-term periods) rebellious or 'difficult' prisoners *Cole*.

liquid laugh n. vomit *Humphries*.

liquid lunch n. a meal that consists (almost) entirely of alcohol *Humphries:2*.

liquor's talking a situation in which indiscretions and/or garrulous speech are put down to drunkenness *Dickson*.

lit 1. see: lit up; 2. (US Black use) to be shot *Klein*.

lit to the gills a. drunk *Dickson*.

lit up a. drunk.

lit up like a Christmas tree a. very drunk *Dickson*.

lit up like Broadway a. aka: *lit up like Times Square*: very drunk *Neaman & Silver*.

lit up like Main street a. very drunk *Dickson*.

little black book n. the volume in which every bachelor supposedly keeps lists of available and willing female company.

little boy blue n. (US Black use) the police; fr. uniform colour *Folb*.

Little Eva n. (US Black use) a loud-mouthed white girl *Major*.

little green men n. a popular description of the putative inhabitants of outer space.

little jobs n. (children's use) urination (cf: big jobs) *May*.

little Joe n. (gambling use) the point of four in craps dice *Algren*.

little Josie (gambling use) the point of four in craps dice *Chandler: Notebk.*

little madam n. a young girl who acts, and considers herself, both older than her years and superior to her peers *Humphries:2*.

little man n. see: little man in the boat *Klein*.

little man in the boat n. (US Black use) the clitoris *Klein*.

little Miss Roundheels n. a promiscuous girl *Thompson:J.*

little office n. (euph.) lavatory *Humphries:2*.

little people n. (US milit. use) in Vietnam, the enemy; fr. the stature of the Vietnamese *Del Vecchio*.

little pretty n. (US Black use) an attractive male *Folb*.

little sister n. aka: *little pal*: the vagina *Maledicta*.

little stranger n. an unborn foetus; often illegitimate or of unknown paternity *Vidal*.

lit-up (US milit. use) under fire *Del Vecchio*.

Litvak n. a Jew whose family come fr. Lithuania and as such considered lower-class by Polacks (qv) *Goldman*.

live a. (US teen. use) excellent, wonderful; thus *a live one*: an admirable person or object *Pond*.

live high on the hog v. to live in general and to eat in particular with great self-indulgence *Neaman & Silver*.

live it up v. to have a good time, to enjoy oneself *Capital Radio 1983*.

live one n. 1. (cant) the ideal victim for a proposed hoax, fraud, etc. *Selby:1*; 2. (homosexual use) a generous rich client for a prostitute *Legman*.

living end n. the extreme, the absolute limit.

living off the tit living in luxury, over protected; 'breast-fed' *Higgins:2*.

Lloyd n. (rhyming sl.) Harold Lloyd = loid (qv); fr. the silent-film star, (1893–1971) *Powis*.

load n. (US Black use) 1. the intense urge to have sex; 2. a large amount of semen in the testes; 3. heavy responsibility *Klein*.

load of reg load of rubbish, nonsense; fr. milit. reg: (abbrev.) regimental: stickler for discipline, esp. petty, nonsensical rules *Cole*.

loaded a. 1. drunk; 2. intoxicated with a given drug *Jay & Young*; 3. rich, either in actual cash or simply, esp. in prison use, in possessions such as tobacco *Norman:3*.

loaded for bear fully prepared for all problems, esp. the hardest ones. fr. hunting use: bear-shooting requires heavy armament *Higgins:4*.

loaded to . . . sl. synonyms for drunk, incl: . . . *the barrel*, . . . *the earlobes*, . . . *the gills*, . . . *the guards*, . . . *the gunnels*, . . . *the hat*, . . . *the muzzle*, . . . *the Plimsoll Mark*, . . . *the tailgate*. *Dickson*.

loadsa- an all-purpose prefix that simply means 'plenty of'. It has been applied to various nouns, notably loadsamoney, meaning grossly and flashily wealthy, a term that was created as the name of a character – a cockney plasterer – created by comedian Harry Enfield on the television programme 'Saturday Night Live'. This grotesque figure, waving his money and preaching the gospel that 'Wad is God' was designed to mock contemporary excess, especially as perceived as a creation of the Thatcherite 1980s. *Green:3*.

loaf n. head, esp. brains, intelligence; thus *use one's loaf*: to act sensibly; fr. rhyming sl. *loaf of bread* = head *Performance*.

loan shark n. the supplier of private loans at maximum interest *Higgins:3*.

lob n. 1. a dull, stupid person; fr. Yiddish *lobbas*: rascal *Runyon:1*; 2. penis *Selby:1*; 3. (UK prison use) pay *LL*.

lob in v. (Aus. use) to arrive, to turn up *Wilkes*.

lobster n. (US Black use) a rich person *Klein*.

lobster shift n. the evening shift after the day workers have gone off *Price:2*.

loc v. (US Black use) **1.** to act in a crazy way; **2.** to smoke marijuana *Dre*.

loc up v. (US Black use) see loc 2.

lock v. (US pimp use) to ensure a ho's (qv) fidelity (emotional and economic) to a given pimp (cf: bonds) *Shulman*.

lock assholes v. to fight *Price:2*.

lock into v. to become part of a plan, a group, etc; to join.

loco a. insane, crazy; fr. locoweed: a narcotic weed that affects cattle in South-West US *People's Comic*.

locoweed n. marijuana. fr. the plant that affects cattle (cf: loco) *Southern*.

locs n. (US Black use) sunglasses.

Lofty nickname for both very tall and very short men; for the latter see BBC-TV series 'It Ain't 'Alf 'Ot, Mum' 1970s passim.

log n. the penis *Kurious: A Constipated Monkey (1994)* (cf: flog the log).

loid n. (abbrev.) celluloid (often actually plastic, as in a credit card): pieces of plastic used to slip open Yale-style locks when housebreaking (cf: Lloyd) *Powis*.

lollied informed against, grassed (qv); poss. fr. *lollypop* = shop (qv) *Powis*.

lollies n. female breasts; which can, like the sweet, be sucked.

lollipop n. (US Black use) a sucker (qv) who has been 'sucked', ie: taken advantage of *Klein*.

lollipop man/woman n. a man or woman who supervises children crossing the road near a school; fr. the sign on a pole which they carry, and their role in tending children.

lolly n. money *Performance*.

lolly v. (prob. rhyming sl.) lollypop = shop = inform to police *Newman:1*.

lollygag v. to waste time doing nothing but standing around chattering about little, and going nowhere *Greenlee*.

Lombard acro. *l*oads *o*f *m*oney *b*ut *a* right *d*ickhead: one of a rash of acronyms (cf: buppie, dinky, yuppie) coined during the mid-1980s; this one described many of the newly rich young men who populated the City of London *Green:3*.

Lombard Street to a China orange (cp) the longest possible odds.

lone wolf n. a solitary person, usu. male; he may enjoy many acquaintances and be by no means a recluse, but permits no one to penetrate his façade.

loner n. a solitary person, not necessarily lonely, who prefers to work and live alone *Grogan*.

long bit n. (US prison use) a term of imprisonment over 38 months which must be completed prior to becoming eligible for parole *Klein*.

long con n. any trickery and cheating that is carefully planned for perfect execution (cf: short con).

long firm n. (UK criminal/police use) a fraudulent scheme whereby a firm is set up, small orders placed and paid for to establish good credit; then a massive order is made, its contents quickly sold off, often below par, and the firm vanishes, the warehouse is shut down and the debts, this time huge, are never paid. *J. Pearson, 'The Profession of Violence'*.

long green n. money, fr. colour of dollar bills.

long johns n. long woollen winter underwear, combinations.

long (thin) streak of piss n. an unflattering description of a tall, thin person.

long time no see (cp) I haven't seen you for a long time.

long-hair n. a hippie (qv) among whose 'badges' was extra-lengthy hair *Stone*.

long-haired a. intellectual, aesthetic; always derog. use, fr. the apparent necessity for the cultured to abandon the 'short-back-and-sides' cut; thus *long-haired music*: the classics, etc.

longshot n. a slim chance; fr. gambling use, a bet laid at long odds on an unlikely contender *Shulman*.

long-tailed 'un n. large denomination

sterling note, £10, £20, £50 *Powis*.

long-winded a. (homosexual use) a man who takes a long time to reach orgasm *Legman*.

loo n. the lavatory.

looey n. (US milit. use) (abbrev.) lieutenant (pron. 'lootenant') *Uris*.

loogan n. idiot, fool, incompetent *Runyon*.

looie n. (US milit. use) lieutenant (pron. 'lootenant') *Jones*.

look sharp v. 1. to hurry up, to get on with; 2. to dress smartly, fashionably (cf: sharp) *J. Jackson, LP record title, 1979*.

look what the wind's blown in (cp) facetious greeting to a new arrival, or remark to a companion concerning that arrival.

looker n. 1. an attractive woman *Bukowski:7*; 2. (pimp use) a client who wishes only to look at a prostitute, usually naked, and occasionally fondle her breasts; 3. a voyeur *OUI 8/75*.

lookism n. (homosexual use) evaluating a stranger purely on the basis of their physical appeal or lack of it *Jay & Young*.

looks like a wet weekend (Aus. cp) used by a girl announcing, or a boy registering the onset of a menstrual period *Neaman & Silver*.

looks like he wouldn't piss if his pants were on fire (cp) describing someone monumentally stupid *Thompson:J*.

looks like he/she lost a pound and found sixpence (cp) of anyone who looks notably downcast.

loon n. a fool, an idiot; such people are supposedly 'moonstruck', fr. Lat. *luna*: moon *Higgins:5*.

loon about v. to act crazily, irresponsibly *Mandelkau*.

loon pants n. trousers featuring exaggerately flared bottoms, esp. beloved of early 1970s hippies; ads in *Melody Maker* passim.

loony a. eccentric, insane (cf: loon) *Wodehouse: JO*.

loony bin n. mental hospital or similar

institution *Price:2*.

loony doctor n. psychoanalyst, psychiatrist, etc. *Wodehouse: COJ*.

loony farm n. see: loony bin.

loony tune n. a crazy person; from the series of film cartoons created by the team of Hollywood animators Hanna–Barbera, fittingly the term was popularized by another Hollywood star, Ronald Reagan, to describe such figures as Libyan leader Colonel Gaddaffi.

looped a. (US campus use) drunk, fr. obs. *loop-legged Underwood*.

loop-the-loop n. (rhyming sl.) soup *Powis*.

loop-the-loop n. sixty-nine (qv).

loopy a. eccentric, crazy *Price:3*.

loose cannon (on a rolling deck) n. an unstable person, one who may well be dangerous to his fellows *Morgan*.

loose ends n. (US Black use) spare money available for loans *Klein*.

loose link n. (US Black use) an informer.

loot n. money *Selby:1*.

Lord love a duck! mild. excl. of surprise, etc. *Wodehouse:MOJ*.

Lord Lovel n. (rhyming sl.) shovel: only US use now *Wright*.

Lord Mayor v. (rhyming sl.) to swear *Jones:J*.

Lord Muck n. a hypothetical aristocrat, snobbish and conspicuous in his contempt for lesser mortals, but (since he is Lord *Muck*) in fact no better than they are.

lose one's bottle v. to back down, to turn cowardly (cf: bottle).

lose one's britches v. to lose a good deal of money, usu. through betting (cf: lose one's shirt).

lose one's cool v. to lose one's dignity or self-possession, to lose one's temper (cf: freak out) *SF Comics*.

lose one's doughnuts v. (US campus use) to vomit (cf: blow one's doughnuts) *Bernbach*.

lose one's gender v. (homosexual use) to abandon homosexuality for the safer world of heterosexuality *Legman*.

lose one's lunch v. (US campus use) to vomit (cf blow one's lunch) *Bernbach*.

lose one's marbles v. to go mad, lose control *Higgins:3*.

lose one's rag v. to lose one's temper *P. MacDonald, 'X v. Rex', 1933*.

lose one's rudder v. to be drunk; and thus lose one's sense of direction *Dickson*.

lose one's shirt v. to lose a good deal of money, usu. through gambling or other speculation (cf: lose one's britches).

lose the ball v. to find oneself in an increasingly difficult situation; to lose control of one's life, work, relationships, etc. fr. sporting use *Safire*.

Lou Reed n. amphetamine *Welsh:1* (fr. rhy. sl. Lou Reed = speed (qv); Reed is best-known as lead singer of the late 1960s band The Velvet Underground).

loudmouth n. 1. a braggart, a boaster; 2. spec: a lawyer *Higgins:4*.

lounge lizard n. a smooth and highly plausible fortune- or sex-hunter who works his charms in the lounges of hotels; an adventurer (cf: saloon bar cowboy).

louse one up v. to cause a person difficulties, to cause trouble *rr*.

louse up v. to make a mess of, to ruin; usu. deliberately.

lousy with full of (a given commodity, type of person, etc); fr. orig. milit. (First World War) ref. to infestations of lice *Wodehouse:PGM*.

love chocolate n. a white person who specializes in black partners (cf: love vanilla). *AS 60.1 (1985)*.

love dove n. (drug use) a variety of ecstasy (qv) which is branded with a small dove of peace.

love handles n. the spare tyre (qv) of flesh around a portly stomach that may be seen in a kinder light by those who appreciate the Rubensesque figure (cf: bagels) *Bernbach*.

love it to death v. to enjoy or to love to extremes; in ironic use, to deplore

Price:2.

love juice n. (US Black use) semen *Klein*.

love vanilla n. a black person who specializes in white partners (cf: love chocolate). *AS 60.1 (1985)*.

lovely n. a pretty young girl; fr. SE adj. use.; esp. popular with tabloid press, seaside entertainers, etc.

lovely grub! (cp) implies approval of whatever is being considered, whether actual food or not.

low Greek n. (gay use) heterosexual intercourse; 'high' Greek uses the anus – the vagina is 'lower' down the body.

low in the saddle a. drunk, and thus slumped over *Dickson*.

low neck and short sleeves n. (homosexual use) a circumcised penis *Legman*.

low rent a. cheap, unappealing, distateful, unfashionable *Wolfe:5*.

lowdown n. privileged information, intimate details *Gruber*.

lower the boom (on) v. to reprimand severely; to put an end to someone's misbehaviour; fr. USN use *Green:2*.

lowlife n. a criminal, or someone who may well be.

lowlife a. (US Black use) unpleasant, aggressive *Folb*.

lowride v. to cruise the streets in a lowrider (qv) *Ice T:3*.

lowrider n. a customized car which has been 'chopped and channelled' to lower the suspension and give it a generally sleeker look *Morgan*.

lox jock n. (derog.) a Jew; fr. *lox* = smoked salmon, supposedly a favourite Jewish dish *Dunne*.

LTR (abbrev.) *L*iving *T*ogether *R*elationship: marriage in all but the legalities *McFadden*.

lubricated a. drunk (cf: neck oil) *Dickson*.

luck into v. to come up with a stroke of luck *Breslin*.

luck out v. to strike lucky *Higgins:3*.

lucozade n. (rhyming sl.) spade (qv) = black person *'Minder', Thames TV 1983*.

Lucy Law n. (homosexual use) police *Stanley*.

lucy locket n. (rhyming sl.) a pocket *Jones:J*.

ludes n. (abbrev.) quaalude; methaqualone *White*.

lug n. 1. ear; fr. Scots dial. *Powis*; 2. large, stupid man; lug: to drag, to haul; such a heavyweight would need to be dragged along, mentally or physically *Tuff Shit Comics*.

luggage n. (US teen. use) bags under the eyes *Sculatti*.

lugger n. 1. (US criminal use) in a shoplifting team (cf: booster) the accomplice (usually two) who helps the actual thief remove the stolen goods from the store *Breslin*; 2. (Can. prison use) a smuggler of contraband in/out of the prison *Caron*.

lukshen n. an Italian, as used by Jews (cf: spaghetti) (fr. Yiddish *lokshen*: noodles).

lulu n. 1. anything remarkable, exceptional, wonderful; 2. an ironic use of 1: a disaster, an abject failure *Tuff Shit Comics*.

lumber v.t. to persuade, to trick *Norman:2*.

lumbered burdened with, trapped *Keyes*.

lummel excl. of surprise, wonder, shock, disbelief; fr. 'Lord love me!' *Wilkinson*.

lump v. to hit someone over the head with a lump of stone or a brick *Selby:1*.

lumpy chicken (US milit. use) fr. loud and clear *Del Vecchio*.

lunch n. oral intercourse (cf: eat, fress).

lunch at the lazy Y v. to perform cunnilingus; the Y refers both to the spread legs, and to the YMCA /

YWCA (cf: eat at the Y).

lunch hooks n. fingers *Algren*.

lunchbox n. (US campus use) a simpleton *Underwood*.

lunchy a. (US campus use) 1. dull, stupid, absent-minded; fr, out to lunch (qv); 2. carefree, light-hearted, jokey; 3. unfashionable, out of style *Underwood*.

lunger n. a mouthful of spit and mucus *Wolfe:8*.

lungs n. female breasts *Jenkins*.

lunk n. oaf, curmudgeon; (abbrev.) lunkhead (qv) *Waterhouse*.

lunkhead n. absolute fool, idiot, incompetent *Morgan*.

lurk n. (Aus. use) dodge, racket or scheme; fr. 19th-C. UK cant: to pretend some form of distress in order to raise money from the credulous *Humphries*.

lurkola n. (Aus. use) fr. lurk (qv) homegrown version of US/UK payola (qv) *Baker*.

lurky a. (US campus use) seedy, untrustworthy, weird *Underwood*.

lush n. 1. a drunkard; fr. Lushington; 2. alcohol *Selby:1*.

lush v. 1. to become drunk; 2. (abbrev.) lush-roll (qv) *Hotten*.

lush it around v. to become drunk *Farina*.

lush it up v. see: lush it around.

lushed a. drunk (cf: lush).

lush-roll v. to rob a drunk; fr. lush (qv) *Selby:1*.

lush-worker n. one who robs drunks, esp. in subways *ST 1983*.

lust dog n. (US campus use) male term for allegedly promiscuous female *Underwood*.

lyricsing (UK bl.) chatting up, sweet-talking *Robins*.

M

M n. (drug use) (abbrev.) morphine (cf: GOM) *Green:1*.

M & Ms n. (drug use) barbiturates, amphetamines, drugs available as pills; fr. US sweet (like UK 'Smarties') name *Folb*.

M and S nickname for Marks & Spencer group of department stores; alternative, considered more vulgar: *Marks* or *Marks and Sparks* (the firm's house magazine is called *Sparks*).

MA n. (US milit. use) (abbrev.) Mechanical Ambush: any US set booby trap *Del Vecchio*.

ma aka: *mother*: a derog. title put before a man's name to imply his homosexuality *Legman*.

Ma and Pa store n. small corner store selling necessities; traditionally owned and run by a family *Rosten*.

Mac general term of greeting in USA; no specific ref. to Scotsmen implied *Southern & Hoffenberg*.

mac out v. (US teen. use) to overeat, to gorge oneself, esp. on junk food (qv); fr. McDonald's hamburger chain, and their major seller: the Big Mac *Pond*.

macaroni n. **1.** (rhyming sl.) pony = £25 *Jones:J*; **2.** (US Black use) the middle man, usu. a pimp, who stands between the john (qv) and the ho (qv) *Klein*.

macaroni with cheese n. a hustler (qv) who involves himself in a wide variety of activities – pimping, drug-selling, gambling games, etc. (cf: macaroni) *Klein*.

macer n. a thief, a villain, fr. early 19th C. *Powis*.

machine n. (US campus use) a motorcycle *Underwood*.

macing n. cheating, esp. at three-card monte (qv) *Powis*.

mack a. (Black pimp use) anything pertaining to a pimp: pimp shoes, etc. *Milner*.

mack n. (US Black use) a seductive line (qv) used with the intention of charming a member of the opposite sex (cf: mack, a.) *Folb*.

Mack man n. a black pimp; fr. Fr. argot *maquereau*, lit. mackerel, pimp; thus *hard-mack*: a pimp who rules through threatened or actual violence; *sweet mack*: a gentle pimp who prefers to use charm, aka *sugar pimp Milner*.

mack on v. aka: *mack to*: to attempt the seduction of a given person *Folb*.

mackery n. pimping *Algren*.

macking making verbal advances to someone of the opposite/same sex with a view to seduction *Jones*.

mad a. (Aus. use) generally intensifying adj. of approval: 'you mad bastard', etc. *Ready*.

mad as a cut snake (Aus. use) completely deranged, utterly furious *D. Leitch*.

mad as a wet hen (cp) extremely angry.

mad dog v. (US Black use) to stare at intensely and threateningly. (fr. SE mad dog, such animals fix their targets with an unwavering, aggressive stare).

mad minute n. (US milit. use) a weapons free-fire test and practice session *Del Vecchio*.

mad money n. saving set aside for some spontaneous, unscheduled expenditure, usu. on pleasure *Austin*.

Madam n. the proprietor of a male or female brothel *Legman*.

madam n. nonsense, rubbish, esp. in *load of old. . .*

made (US Black use) one who has had their hair straightened, usu. of females *Major*.

made man n. (US criminal use) a formally initiated member of the US Mafia *Teresa*.

Maggie's Drawers n. (US milit. use) flag waved on a rifle range to signal 'target missed' *Uris*.

maggie's pie n. (US Black use) the female pudendum (cf: magpie's nest)

Klein.

maggot n. 1. the penis; 2. (US Black use) (derog.) a White person.

magic a. excellent; a term that has spread from London working-class use into far wider currency.

magoozlum n. rubbish, trash; poss. fr. Hollywood use of *magoo*: the gooey ingredient of 'custard pies' *Chandler:LG.*

magpie's nest n. (US Black use) the female pudendum *Klein.*

maharishee n. (drug use) marijuana; fr. Maharishi Mahesh Yogi, popular 1960s guru for the Beatles and other hippies (qv) *Folb.*

mahogany flat n. (US Black use) an expensive, well-furnished and situated apartment or home *Klein.*

main n. (abbrev.) mainline (qv) *Burroughs:Jr.*

main bitch n. 1. aka: *main ho*, main stuff: (Black pimp use) the favourite prostitute among those a pimp controls; 2. (general use) a man's favourite girlfriend *Folb.*

main chance n. the principle opportunity one may have for making money, attaining a goal, taking advantage of one's rivals, etc; thus one who has *an eye for the main chance*: a smart operator (qv).

main drag n. the main street *Runyon.*

main man n. best friend, most important person *Price:1.*

main squeeze n. most favoured person, usu. lover *Price:2.*

main stem n. 1. (US Black use) the élite, the upper class; 2. see: main drag.

mainline n. the vein into which an addict injects narcotics *Lou Reed, 'Sister Ray', 1968.*

mainline v. to inject narcotics directly into a vein (skinpop) *Southern.*

mainliner n. a drug addict who injects narcotics into the vein *Fiction Illus.3.*

major a. (US teen. use) all-purpose term of great approval (cf: serious) *Pond.*

make n. (police use) an identification *McBain:1.*

make v. 1. to attain a given goal: *make the team, make a club,* etc.; 2. to seduce; 3. to recognise *Morgan*; 4. to attend, to go to *Bruce:2*; 5. to seduce (cf: put the make on).

make a beeline for v. to go directly towards; not really based on nature, however.

make a bomb v. to become very rich.

make a car v. to break into parked cars in order to steal any valuables left inside them *Burroughs:1.*

make a clean breast of v. to confess, to own up unreservedly; fr. 'getting it off one's chest' (cf: come clean).

make a dead set for v. to make it clear to someone that he/she is the object of one's affections.

make a dog's dinner out of v. to make an appalling mess.

make a Federal case (out) of v. to take very seriously, esp. when speaker feels the problem is really minor, 'to make a mountain out of a molehill'; in the US legal system, the Federal legislature often implies greater severity *Schulberg.*

make a killing v. to make a profit by gambling; whether at the races, on the stock-market, in a casino, etc.

make a pass v. 1. attempt to harm, attack; 2. see: make a play for *Higgins:3.*

make a play for v. to make sexual advances towards a member of the opposite (or the same) sex, to attempt seduction *rr.*

make a run v. to go out buying a given commodity, esp. drugs, but also groceries, liquor, etc. *Jones.*

make a sandwich v. a sexual position in which two men have simultaneous vaginal and anal sexual intercourse with the same woman. *Folb.*

make book v. to run a bookmaking operation *Dunne.*

make change v. (US Black use) to work or otherwise obtain money for staying alive *Major.*

make for a stash v. stealing the drugs another addict has hidden and using them oneself *Burroughs:1.*

make ignorant v. (UK criminal use) to irritate, to annoy *Powis*.

make it v. **1.** to be successful *Grogan*; **2.** to have sexual intercourse *Higgins:1*; **3.** to move, to get on, to depart *Jones*.

make like v. to imitate; thus *make like a chicken*, etc. *Major*.

make one v. **1.** (prison use) to plan and effect an escape *Obs. 1981*; **2.** (general cant) to put together plans for a crime, esp. a robbery, then carry out that crime *Newman:1*.

make one out v. to plan an escape from prison *Newman:3*.

make one right v. (US Black use) to feel good, esp. as a result of drug use *Folb*.

make one's bones v. (US Mafia use) to arrange and carry out one's first contracted murder *M. Puzo, 'The Godfather', 1969*.

make one's rep v. (criminal use) to establish oneself as a successful, respected criminal *A. Karpis, 'The Alvin Karpis Story', 1971*.

make out v. **1.** to succeed; **2.** to seduce a woman; **3.** to indulge in a variety of sexual foreplay, petting but not necessarily intercourse *SF Comics*.

make out artist n. a man renowned for his sexual prowess *NYRB 17/3/83*.

make pee-pee v. to urinate, usu. children's use *Bukowski:1*.

make the fist v. (US radical, esp. Black radical use) to make the Black Power sign of the clenched fist *Folb*.

make the legal move v. (US teen. use) to get married *Sculatti*.

make the scene v. **1.** understand, appreciate a situation, experience *Lou Reed, 'Run, Run, Run', 1966*; **2.** to go somewhere (cf: scene) *Bruce:2*.

make whoopee v. to go out on a spree, to enjoy oneself uproariously (cf: go on a tear, take a flyer).

makings n. (drug use) the tobacco, cannabis and cigarette papers required for the production of a joint (qv).

malco n. abbrev. of malco-ordinated and as such a general term of abuse;

(cf: mong, spaz) *L Green*.

malflor n. (US use) a lesbian; fr. Puerto Rican/Sp. *Maledicta*.

mall rat n. (US use) a young person who spends their time hanging around shopping malls.

mallet n. (US Black use) the police; fr. their repressive role *Folb*.

mama . n. **1.** (Hells Angel use) the girls who ride with the Hells Angels, available for communal sex and allied indignities, aside from the *old ladies*, the actual girl-friends of the riders; the term is abbrev. of the phrase 'Let's go make someone a mama' *Thompson*; **2.** a feminine lesbian (cf: papa) *Legman*.

mammy-jammer n. (euph.) motherfucker (qv) *Major*.

mammy-rammer n. (euph.) motherfucker (qv) *Jones*.

mammy-tapper n. (euph.) motherfucker (qv) *Jones*.

mams n. (S. Afr. use) breasts; fr. mammaries *Neaman & Silver*.

man n. **1.** a drug dealer *Goldman*; **2.** the police *Larner;* **3.** a criminal boss; **4.** any superior figure; esp. used by prisoners of their warders or of whites by blacks *Seale*.

man a-hanging n. (US Black use) a person in trouble *Klein*.

man in the boat n. (US Black use) the clitoris *Klein*.

man with a paper ass n. (US Black use) anyone who is all talk and little or no action; fr. the empty mouthings embodied in the Maoist 'paper tiger' *Folb*.

man with fuzzy balls n. (US Black use) a white man; there is a theory that fuzz (qv) = police derives from this *Folb*.

manhole n. (US Black use) a hangout (qv), esp. for men only *Klein*.

manky a. unpleasant, disgusting, poss. smelly, poss. fr. Fr. *manqué*: lost *Dury, 'Do It Yourself', 1979*.

manor n. area of operations; home base, usu. police use *Payne*.

mantee n. a masculine lesbian *Legman*.

manto n. a woman, a girl (poss. fr. dial manto: a lady's gown, itself fr. Fr. *manteau*: a gown; thus fig. its wearer).

map n. the human face *Wodehouse:CW*.

maps n. (musician use) sheet music *Major*.

maracas n. female breasts, fr. musical instrument *Maledicta*.

mare n. ill-tempered, unpleasant woman (cf: cow, bitch) *Powis*.

mariweegee n. (drug use) marijuana; fr. pron. *Folb*.

marj n. aka: *marge*: (abbrev.) margarine *'Fiesta' magazine 10/83*.

mark n. a sucker, the potential and actual victim of a conman *Caron*.

mark up v. to bruise, to leave scars after a fight *Performance*.

mark one's card v. to explain, to point out, to warn *Newman:1, Norman:2*.

marker n. 1. (US Black use) the bait that lures a victim into some form of swindle or other fraud *Klein*; 2. an IOU for a gambling debt *Higgins:3*.

marks n. (drug use) see tracks *Burroughs:1*.

Mars Bar n. (rhy.sl.) a scar *Welsh:2*.

marv n. (US teen. use) a highly intelligent person, a scholar; fr. marvellous *Pond*.

marvy a. (abbrev.) marvellous, usu. teen. use.

Mary! homosexual exclamation; orig. Elizabethan use, abbrev. Virgin Mary *Stanley*.

mary n. marijuana *Bukowski:1*.

Mary Ann n. (rhyming sl.) hand *Cole*.

Mary Ellen n. (Liverpool use) market women; spec. women who work as cleaners on liners, etc. *Bleasdale*.

mary poppins n. breasts *T. Wolfe, NY 'Herald Tribune Sunday Magazine', 1965*.

mary warner n. marijuana, cannabis; fr. pron. *Green:1*.

maryanne n. (drug use) marijuana *Green:1*.

maryjane n. marijuana. cannabis *Jay & Young*.

Masers n. (abbrev.) Maserati

Higgins:5.

mash it on me v. (US Black use) 1. to give one what one is due; 2. to pass over stolen or contraband goods *Klein*.

mash the fat v. (US Black use) to have sexual intercourse *Folb*.

masher n. a man who forces his unwanted attentions on women; generally obs.; poss. fr. Romany *mash*: to lure, entice *Bruce:2*.

massive a. (Valley Girls (qv) use) term of great approval (cf: awesome) *Harpers/Queen 1/83*.

massive n. see posse.

master a. (US Black use) the absolute best.

master-dog n. (US Black use) the supreme authoritarian figure (usu. a white man) within a institutional hierarchy *Klein*.

mat n. (US Black use) one's regular sweetheart, one's wife *Major*.

match n. (drug use) (abbrev.) matchbox, approx. half ounce of marijuana (cf: lid) *Folb*.

matchbox n. 1. see: match; 2. (criminal use) an easily robbed target; no stronger than matchwood *Klein*.

mate n. friend *Griffith*.

mauler n. brass knuckles (cf: maulers) *Chandler:LG*.

maulers n. hands *Wright*.

mauley n. signature, fr. maulers (qv) *Powis*.

maven n. expert, connoisseur; fr. Yiddish *Rosten*.

maw n. (US Black use) 1. mouth; 2. vagina *Klein*.

max v. to give the maximum *Morgan*.

max out v. to indulge to extremes *Channel-4 TV 1983*.

maxed out a. very drunk (cf: max out) *Dickson*.

maximum n. (US prison use) the longest time one must serve of an indeterminate sentence *Klein*.

maxing v. relaxing *T 8/4/91*.

Mayfair Mercenary n. a girl whose indeterminate class is transcended by her beauty and her ambition to frequent the wealthy salons of Mayfair and similar smart environs; often the 'mistress', 'girl-friend' or 'companion' of the men in the same places; coined by P. York in *Harpers/Queen* c.1980.

mazel n. (Yiddish) luck (always good).

mazuma n. money; fr. Yiddish *Wodehouse passim*.

M/C seeks singles phr. (contact ads use) husband likes to watch other men have intercourse with his wife *SMD*.

McAlpine fusilier n. Irish labourer working for the construction firm McAlpines, or any similar firm *Powis*.

McCoy (abbrev.) the real McCoy (qv) *Chandler: Notebk*.

McMuff n. the vagina.

MCP (abbrev.) *M*ale *C*hauvinist *P*ig; much beloved by early 1960s/70s feminists but now obs. other than amongst tabloid journalists and late arrivals *McFadden*.

McQ abbr. meaningful quickie; brief but enjoyable sexual intercourse *AS 60.1 (1985)*.

me and you (bingo rhyming sl.) 2 (cf: dirty old Jew) *Wright*.

meal ticket n. anyone who provides money or a livelihood for someone else – who thus needs to make less effort for themself *Payne*.

mean a. aggressive, unpleasant; also used positively, on 'outlaw' premise of bad = good (cf: bad, vicious, etc.) *Price:2*.

mean enough to kill his grandmother derog. phr. describing a notably unpleasant person; variations include 'push his grandmother downstairs', 'rob his grandmother's grave', 'steal the pennies off his grandmother's eyes', 'take the fillings out of his grandmother's teeth'.

meaner than cat shit a. (derog.) description of an notably unpleasant person; euph. alternatives incl. cat dirt, cat dung, cat manure, cat's tail [fr. SE mean: aggressive, unpleasant + cat shit].

mean-hair a. (homosexual use)

unpleasant, cruel *Thompson*.

meany n. a mean, tight-fisted person; usu. juv. use *Goulart*.

measure one's dick v. to put under suspicion, to check records on a suspect *Higgins:1*.

meat n. 1. a man; usu. a powerful man; 2. the penis; 3. prey, as in 'he's my meat' referring to a potential victim; 4. the vagina *Price:2*.

meat market anywhere that people – homo- or heterosexual – gather for the primary purpose of finding sexual partners (often used in universities to describe first-year parties) *Stanley*.

meat rack n. (homosexual use) any place where homosexuals display their charms to potential tricks (qv) or trade (qv); one London 'rack' is in Piccadilly Circus, next to the County Fire Office *White*.

meat shot n. in pornographic still or moving pictures, a close-up of the genitalia, male or female.

meat wagon n. (UK prison use) a wagon for conveying prisoners to and from court, police stations, prisons, etc. *Norman:1*.

meat whistle n. the penis.

meat-eater n. (US police use) a policeman who, not content with such payoffs, bribes and perks that are freely offered, actively compels people to offer him such monies (cf: grass-eater) *Green:2*.

meathead n. general term of abuse; implying that mere flesh, rather than brains, occupies one's skull *'Hill Street Blues', Thames TV, 1983*.

mechanic n. a card sharp *Breslin*.

meddle v. (US campus use) 1. to have sexual intercourse; 2. to be intimate, but not spec. on a sexual level *Underwood*.

medico n. doctor *Wodehouse:AAG*.

meet n. 1. (abbrev.) meeting; appointment; 2. spec. a meeting for the purchase of drugs *Payne*.

meg v. (film use) to direct a film; fr. *megaphone*, a vital part of the director's armoury in the days of silent films *Variety passim*.

mega a. (US teen. use) superlative, extra-special, etc. *Pond*.

megabucks n. enormous sums of money, usu. in context of film or book deals; on model of nuclear *megadeath*: 1m deaths *Vidal*.

megger n. (film use) film director, fr. use of megaphone by directors during silent film era (cf: meg) *Variety passim*.

megsmen n. petty criminals and cheats, orig. *magsman*: card sharp, fr. mid-19th C. *Powis*.

mellow a. calm, peaceful, unconcerned with the material or painful; (cf: laid back) a state often induced by smoking cannabis *White*.

mellow n. (US Black use) a favourite boy/girlfriend; a good friend of either sex *Folb*.

mellow out v. to calm down (oneself or others); to relax mentally *White*.

mellow yellow n. 1. (US Black use) a Mulatto girl *Folb*; 2. (drug use) a variety of LSD, poss. obs. *Green:1* fr. song title by Donovan 1967.

melted a. drunk *Dickson*.

melted butter n. (US Black use) an attractive female, esp. a Mulatto, and thus fr. skin tone *Folb*.

Melvin n. a dull, tedious, and otherwise distasteful person (cf: Irving) *Neaman & Silver*.

member n. (US Black use) a fellow black person *Folb*.

Memphis Glide n. a style of dancing *Price:2*.

mensch n. fr. Yiddish: a 'real man'; implication is of character and integrity rather than sexual or physical prowess *Bruce:2*.

mental a. insane, crazy, out of one's mind *Sillitoe*.

mental job n. one who is, or potentially might be insane *Rawson*.

Merc n. (abbrev.) Mercedes Benz *Performance*.

Mercedes n. (US Black use) an elegant woman with good looks and an attractive figure; fr. the automobile of the same name and status *Folb*.

merchant n. a person, esp. a specialist in some kind of trade or profession, often criminal; synonym for general use of artist (qv) *Norman:2*.

merchant banker n. (rhy. sl.) = wanker (qv) (cf: J Arthur).

mercy! homosexual excl., overtones of (campy) 'Southern belle' *Stanley*.

mercy Mary! homosexual excl. of surprise *Stanley*.

merry-go-round n. (US Black use) anyone who is attempting to deceive or swindle another person *Klein*.

mesc n. (abbrev.) mescalin *McFadden*.

meshugge n. fr. Yiddish: crazy, obsessed, weird *Rosten*.

mess about v. 1. to indulge in varying degress of sexual intimacy (cf: mess around); 2. to waste time, wander off the subject, distract one's attention, etc.' epitomized in Kenneth Williams' cp 'Stop messing about!' used in various Kenneth Horne BBC-Radio comedy shows and in 'Carry On. . .' films since.

mess around v. (US campus use) to have sexual intercourse *Underwood*.

mess one's mind v. to disturb and harm emotionally *M. Jagger & K. Richard, '19th Nervous Breakdown', 1966*.

mess over v. to harm, to interfere with someone, to annoy *Seale*.

mess up v. to assault; to ridicule *Folb*.

mess with v. 1. to use; 2. to become involved with *Grogan*.

mess with nature v. (US Black use) to lose one's potency, esp. through excess use of narcotics or alcohol *Folb*.

messed up (drug use) extremely intoxicated by a given drug (cf: wasted, wrecked, destroyed, etc.) *Folb*.

Met. n. (UK criminal/police use) (abbrev.) Metropolitan Police (serving London) *Newman:1*.

meter thief n. (UK police use) term of contempt for petty villain who steals from gas/parking meters, etc. *Powis*.

meth n. (abbrev.) methedrine *Higgins:1*.

metho n. (Aus. use) metholated

spirits, beloved by extreme alcoholics *Humphries:2*.

me-tooing following suit, climbing on a bandwagon *Higgins:5*.

Mexican n. cheap, second rate; the stereotype of Mexicans in the US is uniformly negative.

Mexican airlines, to fly v. phr. (gay use) to smoke marijuana; from the fact that much marijuana smoked in the US is grown in Mexico.

Mexican athlete n. (US use) an unsuccessful candidate for a college/school sports team.

Mexican breakfast n. (US (Texas) derog.) a cigarette and a glass of water, ie: nothing nourishing at all *Safire*.

Mexican Buick n. (US use) a Chevrolet; fr. respective status of the cars.

Mexican carwash n. (US use) washing the car by leaving it out in the rain.

Mexican cigarette n. (gay use) poorly made marijuana cigarette.

Mexican credit card n. see: Harlem credit card.

Mexican dragline n. (US use) a shovel or spade.

Mexican green n. (drug use) a grade and type of marijuana *Green:1*.

Mexican jeep n. (US use) a donkey.

Mexican jumping bean n. (gay use) amphetamine.

Mexican muffler n. (US use) a home-made silencer made from a tin can stuffed with steel wool which is then attached to the car's exhaust pipe.

Mexican nightmare n. (gay use) gaudy ceramic crockery; typical of that sold to tourists in Mexico.

Mexican nose guard n. (US use) a jock strap or athletic supporter.

Mexican overdrive n. (US use) coasting or free wheeling in order to save petrol.

Mexican promotion n. (US use) a better job but one which brings no increase in salary; aka Mexican raise.

Mexican schlock n. (gay use) any art in poor taste; typically that sold to tourists in Mexico.

Mexican stand-off n. any situation in which neither party is willing to back down from a stated position but simultaneously neither party has a superior edge; the result is that both parties give in and walk off *Green:2*.

Mexican toothache n. diarrhoea, often contracted on a foreign holiday (cf: Delhi belly, gippy tummy, Montezuma's revenge).

Mexican two-step n. see: Aztec two-step.

Mexican window-shade n. venetian blinds.

mf (abbrev.) *motherfucker* (qv).

mic n. (drug use) (abbrev.) microgram, the basic measurement of LSD; an average LSD trip (qv) requires approx 250 mics *Hoffman:a*.

Mick n. Irish person; fr. Michael, a common Irish name (cf: Paddy) *Higgins:3*.

mick n. (Aus. use) Roman Catholic; fr. use of Mick as an Irish and thus often RC person (qv) *Wilkes*.

mickey n. 1. a small bottle of wine or spirits *Folb*; 2. (abbrev.) Mickey Finn (qv).

Mickey Dee's n. (US Black use) McDonald's hamburger restaurants.

Mickey Finn n. a knockout drug, poss. chloral hydrate, mixed into an unsuspecting victim's drink; fr. an eponymous saloon keeper of Chicago, c.1896–1906. *Wodehouse:MOJ*.

Mickey Mouse a. second rate, badly made, artificial *Price:2*.

Mickey Mouse n. (theatrical rhyming sl.) the house, the audience *Jones:J*.

middle leg n. the penis *Neaman & Silver*.

middle finger n. a prostitute's trick that ensures each client arrives at a speedy orgasm and the girl can maximize her nightly earning potential *Klein*.

middle-cut n. (US Black use) the vagina *Klein*.

midnight n. (US Black use) a particularly dark black person *Folb*.

miffed a. annoyed; fr. 17th C. *miff*: a petty quarrel.

mike-mike n. (US milit. use) one millimetre *Del Vecchio*.

mileage n. **1.** experience; **2.** a criminal record *Shulman*.

military medium (cricket use) gentle, medium paced bowling which goes straight up and down the wicket *BBC Radio 3 1983*.

milk v. to defraud, to extract money from *Higgins:1*.

milk and water a. weak, diluted, adulterated; 'milk and water socialism', etc.

milk bottles n. the female breasts; other milk-related terms include: air the dairy, cream-jugs, dugs, feeding bottles, jugs, jujubes, milk can, milkers, milkshop, milkwalk, milky way, pap feeder, udders.

milkers n. female breasts; (cf: norks) *Rawson*.

milko n. (Aus. use) a milkman *Humphries:2*.

milksop n. coward, weakling *Dickson*.

mill n. (abbrev.) million, usu. dollars *Higgins:3*.

Miller time n. a period of relaxation, the end of the working day (fr. the advertisements for Miller Lite Beer, which promote the end of the day as 'Miller time').

million n. a sure bet, fr. 'a million to a bit of dirt' *Norman:2*.

million dollar wound n. (US milit. use) any wound that guarantees the victim a passage out of a war zone and back to the USA; equivalent to UK *Blighty wound* in First World War *O'Brien*.

miln up v. (UK prison use) to lock into a cell; fr. name of a popular locksmiths *LL*.

Milwaukee goitre (US use) a beer belly; fr., *inter alia*, 'Schlitz: the beer that made Milwaukee famous' as did the many beers brewed for the predominantly Ger. immigrant population *Neaman & Silver*.

minces n. (rhyming sl.) mince pies = eyes *Normal:1*.

mind v. **1.** to protect, to act as a bodyguard *Payne*; **2.** (UK police use) to bribe regularly *Laurie*.

mind one's p's and q's v. to be careful, prudent, polite, cautious; poss. fr. 'please and thank-you'; basic manners taught to infants *Hotten*.

mind tripper n. (US campus/teen. use) anyone seen as eccentric, odd, abnormal; fr. mind + tripper (qv) *Underwood*.

mind-blowing a. astounding, amazing, remarkable; usu. stemming from hallucinogenic drug use *Wolfe:2*.

minder n. **1.** (journalistic use) a reporter, often large and aggressive, who doubles as the bodyguard of anyone a paper has persuaded to give them exclusive material and/or interviews on a major story *Thames TV 1983*; **2.** criminal's bodyguard; strong-arm man *Performance*.

mind-fuck n. an emotionally overwhelming experience, usu. through drugs *Shell*.

minge n. the vagina; fr. Romany.

minge bag n. derog. term for an unpleasant or disliked female; fr. minge (qv) *Bleasdale*.

mingy a. mean, tight-fisted, miserly *Sillitoe*.

mini n. (abbrev.) miniskirt; orig. created as *the* fashion (*pace* Courreges boots) of the 'swinging Sixties', more recently resurgent in the 1980s.

minimum n. (US prison use) the least amount of time one must serve of an indeterminate sentence (cf: maximum) *Klein*.

mink n. (Black use) pretty, sexy young woman (cf: fox) *Milner*.

minnow n. (US campus (spec. University of Arkansas) use) a 12 oz. bottle or can of beer *Underwood*.

MINS n. (US prison use) (acro.) *Minors In Need of Supervision* (cf: CHINS, PINS) *Neaman & Silver*.

misery n. a depressing person.

mishegaas n. (Yiddish) nonsense, absurdity *Goldman*.

Miss (homosexual use) a title prefixed

to a given name to imply that the subject's homosexuality is known or obvious *Legman*.

Miss Amy n. (US Black use) a young white girl *Folb*.

Miss Ann (US Black use) a white girl, usu. derog. *Major*.

Miss Fist n. the hand, in the context of masturbation (cf: corporal and four, five-finger Mary, five-fingered widow, four sisters on Thumb Street, Lady Five Fingers, Mother Fist and her five daughters, Mrs Palm and her five daughters, Rosy Palm and her five little sisters).

Miss Lillian n. (US Black use) white female of any age *Folb*.

miss the bus v. aka: *miss the boat*: to lose an opportunity, forfeit a chance, etc.

Miss Thing (homosexual use) greeting to a fellow homosexual male *White*.

Mr Average n. the average member of the public (cf: Joe Public) *Wham, 'Wham Rap', 1983*.

Mr Charlie (Black use) any white man (cf: Boss Charlie) *Greenlee*.

Mr Cracker n. (US Black use) a white person (cf: cracker) *Folb*.

Mr Do-You-Wrong n. (US Black use) a man who mistreats women *Folb*.

Mister Ed n. (US teen. use) 1. an unimpeachable inside source; 2. a trusted sidekick; fr. Ed McMahon, regular on US TV's 'Johnny Carson Show' *Sculatti*.

Mr Firstnighter n. a sophisticated, upper-class person, or one who poses as such; fr. US radio show 'Mr Firstnighter' of 1930s featuring a white-tie-and-tails star *Price: 2*.

Mr Gub (Aus. Aborigine use) the white man; fr. gub: diminutive of garbage. (cf: Mr Charlie) *Wilkes*.

Mr Nice Guy n. a pleasant, amenable person, although that status carries a certain conditionality, thus the phrase, 'no more Mr Nice Guy'.

Mr Peanut n. (US Black use) white male *Folb*.

Mr Right n. the ideal lover/husband for anyone so searching, male or

female; thus Miss Right *Jay & Young*.

Mr Ten Per Cent 1. spec. an agent, usu. in show business, who takes 10% (at least) of his/her client's earnings; 2. any form of middleman, esp. between interest groups and politicians, who arranges 'favours' and directs influence for some cut of the subsequent profits.

Mr Thomas n. (US Black use) see Uncle Tom *Folb*.

Mrs Palm and Her Five Daughters the hand, as used for masturbation *Humphries*.

mitt n. a hand *Humphries*.

mitt, hand one the v. to reject, to turn down, to dismiss (cf: give the glove).

mitt man n. (US Black use) a religious charlatan who use his flock's credulity to make himself a sumptuous income *Major*.

mittens n. boxing gloves *Heller*.

mix n. (US Black use) a difficult situation.

mix it v. to fight *Keyes*.

mixer n. a gossip, usu. deliberately malicious; one who 'stirs things up'.

mizzled a. drunk *Dickson*.

MO (criminal use) *modus operandi* = way of working = the distinguishing work methods of a given criminal or gang *Dunne*.

Mob n. the US Mafia *Price: 1*.

mob it v. (film use) for extras to break out of their specified places *Chandler: Notebk*.

mobbed out a. very full, crammed *Welsh:1*.

mob-handed accompanied by a large gang *Griffith*.

Moch n. derog. Jew, abbrev. of mockie (qv) *Bruce: 2*.

mockie (derog.) a Jew *Rosten*.

mod n. 1. (US use) fashionable, up to date, abbrev. of modern: 2. (UK use) member of a teenage cult orig. c.1961 who wore specifically distinguishing clothes, rode motor scooters and fought their main rivals, the motorbike riding, leather-clad rockers (qv).

mod squad n. plain clothes police, usu. young and dressed in the prevailing teenage and early 20s fashions, who look for crime in colleges and local youth centres.

mogadored a. (rhyming sl.) floored, thus beaten, defeated *Cole*.

mojo n. 1. any drug; 2. morphine *De Lannoy & Masterson*.

moll n. a woman, esp. a gangster's girl-friend *Farrell*.

moll buzzer n. pickpocket who specilizes in women as victims *Chandler: Notebk*.

Molly n. (rhyming sl.) Molly Malone (qv) = 'phone *Powis*.

Molly Malone n. (rhyming sl.) telephone *Jones: J*.

mollycoddle n.,v. weakling, mother's darling, milksop (qv); to indulge such a person in such weaknesses *Dickson*.

mollydooker (Aus. use) left-handed; poss. fr. duke = fist and moll = woman, with derog, sense that a woman, like a left-handed person, would be clumsy (?) *Wilkes*.

mollyfock n. (euph.) motherfuck *Wolfe: 2*.

Mom and Pop stores n. small, corner stores stocking just the bare essentials (cf: Ma and Pa store) *Price: 3*.

Mom-Dad-Buddy-and-Sis shorthand for the clichéd American nuclear family *Wolfe: 2*.

momma term of address to any female.

momma's game n. (US Black use) see the dirty dozens, a ritual that depends heavily on mutually abusing the participants' mothers *Folb*.

mo-mo n. aka: *momo*: a moron; fr. repetition of the abbrev. 'mo' *Price: 2*.

momser n. lit. bastard, fr. Yiddish, but catch-all term implying everything from great affection to deep dislike (cf: bastard) *Schulberg: 2*.

Monday morning quarterback n. an amateur critic of specialist activities; spec. a non-playing football fan who delivers his opinions on a Monday of the pro games the previous Sunday *P. Roth, 'Our Gang', 1971*.

Monday pills n. (US milit. use) anti-malaria pills taken once a week *Del Vecchio*.

mondo a. (Valley Girls (qv) use) completely, absolutely; fr. Ital. mondo: the world (cf: —city), like cowabunga!, dude (qqv) and other Californian teen slang, mondo gained a new lease of life with the Teenage Mutant Ninja Turtles craze *Pond*.

money n. (sex industry use) on a girl, the vagina; on a boy the anus.

money for jam anything, incl. money, that is gained for a minimal amount, if any, of effort, and available for purely pleasurable expenditure *Wodehouse: MOJ*.

money to burn n. spare cash, available for spontaneous excess (cf: money for jam).

moneymaker n. female genitals or buttocks *Rechy: 1*.

mong n. general term of opprobrium; presumably from mongol (cf: malco, spastic, spaz) *L Green*.

monged adv. stoned; esp. on ecstasy (qv) (cf: mong) *M Newell*.

monicker n. name; poss. fr. monogram *Burroughs: 1*.

monkey n. 1. (drug use) (abbrev.) monkey on one's back = narcotics addiction *Algren*; 2. (derog.) general insult *Higgins: 1*; 3. (UK criminal use) a padlock *Norman: 2*; 4. £500; $500 *LL*.

monkey v. to tamper, fiddle with, usu, in destructiove clumsy manner.

monkey on one's back to be addicted to narcotics, esp. heroin *Bruce: 2*.

monkey's cousin (bingo rhyming sl.) 12 (a dozen) *Wright*.

monkey's tails n. (rhyming sl.) nails *Jones: J*.

monkey-trap n. something decorative worn by women to make themselves attractive to men.

monotony n. (US campus use) one's single, steady girl-friend; pun on monogamy, and its tedium *Underwood*.

monster n. 1. (UK prison use) sexual offenders, child molesters, etc. (cf:

nonce, Rule 43) *Newman: 3*; **2.** (US milit. use) PRC-77 radio, used for secure transmissions; fr. the radio's weight and complexity *Del Vecchio*.

monte n. **1.** (criminal/gambling use) (abbrev.) three-card monte (qv), the three-card trick *Powis*; **2.** (Aus. use) an absolute certainty; fr. 'three-card monte' (qv) a card game played only by conmen *Wilkes*.

Montezuma's revenge n. diarrhoea or in worse cases, dysentery as suffered by tourists with tender stomachs; the specific monarch ruled Mexico c.1500 and the food-poisoning that some tourists suffer is laid at his posthumous feet (cf: Gyppy tummy) *Obs. 1983*.

monthlies n. the menstrual period *Bukowski: 1*.

moo n. a (foolish) woman; fr. 'moo-cow'; often as 'silly old moo' (cf: cow, mare, bitch) *BBC TV, 'Til Death Us Do Part', 1960s passim*.

moocah n. (drug use) marijuana (cf: mu) *Green: 1*.

mooch n. **1.** spec. beggar; **2.** general derog. term *Stone*.

moody a. illicit, stolen *Thames TV 1984*.

moody n. **1.** complaints, ill-temper, depression *Keyes*; **2.** deceit, lies, verbal trickery; fr. rhyming sl. *Moody & Sankey* = hanky-panky *Franklyn*.

mook n. see: mooch *Price: 2*.

moolah n. money *Sanders: 2*.

moon n. a month *Powis*.

moon n. (abbrev.) moonshine = illicit liquor *Higgins: 2*.

moon v. to drop one's trousers and underpants to present one's bare buttocks to onlookers; often performed through a car window (cf: drop trou) *Greaser Comics*.

moon (around) v. to wander around wretchedly lost in thought, often a victim of unrequited passion.

moon-ass n. an infatuated person who moons around for an unattainable love-object *Price: 3*.

mooner n. (US police use) a pathological lawbreaker; presumably fr. the effect of the moon on his mind *Neaman & Silver*.

moonlight v. to work at two jobs on each day in order to boost one's income; the second may well be unknown to the employer of the first and is usu. night work *Illustrated Fiction vol. 1, 1976*.

moonlighter n. (US Black use) a prostitute *Klein*.

Moor n. (UK police/criminal use) HMP Dartmoor.

moosh n. term pf address; fr. Romany mush = a man *LL*.

mootah n. aka: *mooter, muta* : marijuana *Green: 1*.

mop up v. to carry out conclusively; esp. of a gangland or military shooting *rr*.

moppet n. a pre-teen girl *Wodehouse: JO*.

moral n. a certainty; usu. in 'it's a moral . . .' *Humphries: 2*.

more ass than a toilet seat (cp) conspicuous sexual prowess, usu. in 'he gets . . .' *'The Deer Hunter', directed M. Cimino, 1979*.

more front than Brighton beach (cp) exceptionally cheeky, daring; pun on 'sea-front' and front: cheek, gall *'Only Fools and Horses', BBC-1 TV, 1983*.

more hide than Jessie (Aus. use) immensely cheeky; fr. a favourite elephant Jessie (1872–1939) who could be visited at the Taronga Park Zoo *Wilkes*.

more kicks than ha'pence (cp) of any situation which yields more trouble than it is worth.

more power to your elbow (cp) generally encouraging; the augmented elbow would doubtless be used for bending (cf: bend the elbow) *Capital Radio 1983*.

more pricks than a second-hand dartboard a description of a promiscuous female, usu. *She's had . . .*

morning after the night before the state of being hungover after an excess of alcohol.

morph n. (drug use) (abbrev.)
morphine *Green: 1*.

moshing n. a variety of slam-dancing
practised by heavy metal rock fans.
(cf: pogo) *Independent 9/1/92*.

Moss Bross n. Moss Brothers of
Covent Garden, the country's leading
hirers of dress clothes.

Motel Hell n. (US teen. use) any
situation or place that is considered
appalling or unacceptable – a job, a
bad place to stay, a relationship, etc.
Sculatti.

mother n. **1.** (abbrev. motherfucker
(qv) *Himes: 1*; **2.** (Black use)
effeminate male; **3.** homosexual who
introduces another into the gay world
(cf: daughter) *Stanley*.

**mother fist and her five
daughters** n. the human hand, as
used for masturbation *Jay & Young*.

mother ga-ga n. (homosexual use) a
fussy, gossipy, interfering older queen
(qv) *Legman*.

Mother Nature n. **1.** (drug use)
marijuana *Peter Townshend,
'Tommy', 1969*; **2.** menstruation.

Mother Nature's own tobacco n.
(drug use) marijuana (cf: God's own
medicine).

Mother Superior n. (homosexual use)
an older, experienced and open
homosexual *Legman*.

motherflunker n. (euph.)
motherfucker (qv) *Rawson*.

motherfouler n. (euph.)
motherfucker (qv) *Major*.

motherfucker n. **1.** (white use)
supreme insult/expletive based on the
incest taboo *Price: 2*; **2.** (black use) a
wide variety of meanings, fr. good to.
bad, often as a black-to-black term of
affection; also simply meaning 'thing';
frequently abbrev. to *mother Seale*.

mothergrabber n. (euph.)
motherfucker (qv) *Rawson*.

motherhugger n. aka:
mammyhugger: euph. motherfucker
Major.

motherjiver n. (euph.) motherfucker
(qv) *Major*.

motherjumper n. (euph.)

motherfucker (qv) *Farina*.

motherless a. (Aus. use) general
intensifier; thus a bastard *Wilkes*.

mother-love n. a homosexual male
having sex with a heterosexual woman
Legman.

motherlover n. (euph.) motherfucker
(qv) *Major*.

mother-raper n. (euph.)
motherfucker (qv) *Himes: 1*.

Mother's Day n. (US Black use) the
day when welfare cheques arrive from
the government *Klein*.

mother's ruin n. (rhyming sl.) gin
(though the 'rhyme' is not
immediately apparent) *Cole*.

motivate v. to force oneself to do
something which one dislikes *Milner*.

motor n. (abbrev.) motor car
Capital Radio 1983.

motorcycle n. (US Black use) a
woman (who can supposedly be
'ridden') (cf: bike).

motor-mouth n. an indiscreet person
who cannot stop talking *Higgins: 1*.

motorway n. (skiing use) a broad,
easy piste *Barr*.

motsa n. (Aus. use) a big gambling
win, a large sum of money; poss. fr.
Hebrew *motsa* = unleavened bread,
and which resembles an outsize round
biscuit, and thus an enormous coin (?)
Wilkes.

mount n. (US Black use) a
promiscuous female; who is 'ridden'
Folb.

mount v. to have sexual intercourse
Folb.

mountain wop n. derog. term of
abuse for an Italian *Selby: 1*.

mountains n. (US Black use) large,
noticeable female breasts *Klein*.

mouse n. a black eye *Morgan*.

mouse v. to blackmail *Maledicta 9*.

mouser n. **1.** moustache *Runyon*;
2. (US tramp sl.) a homosexual
Legman.

moustache Pete n. original Italian
immigrants to New York, typified by
their heavy moustaches; also original
members of the US Mafia *Price: 1*.

mouth like the inside of an Arab's

underpants (cp) referring to such ghastly physical feelings as are concomitant with a hangover.

mouth music n. the practice of cunnilingus *Powis*.

mouth off v. to boast, to brag.

mouth-breather n. a particularly stupid thug; such individuals are presumed to be breathing heavily.

mouthpiece n. a lawyer *rr*.

mouth-worker n. (homosexual use) a fellator *Legman*.

mouthy a. boastful, cocky *Robins:1*.

move on v. see: fire on *Folb*.

move one's ass v. to hurry up, to get a move on *Pynchon*.

mover n. an ambitious person; who moves both himself and others physically and emotionally *Caron*.

moves n. ideas, plans, ability to deal with various situations *Higgins: 1*.

moxie n. courage, guts, nerve; from the trade-name of a once-popular US soft drink *Rosten*.

MOY phr my place or yours? *AS 60.1 (1985)*.

mozzle n. phonetic pron. of mazel (qv).

MTF (UK 'society' use) *Must Touch Flesh*; of an overly amorous young man *Mortimer*.

mu n. (drug use) marijuana; fr. moocah (qv) *Green: 1*.

muck about v. to pretend, to act half-heartedly, to give less than total commitment, to tease *Mandelkau*.

muck in v. to join in. to lend a hand, esp. in a dirty or unpleasant task *Wright*.

mucker n. 1. a friend; 2. (euph.) fucker (qv).

muck-hole n. a filthy, unappetizing place or room *Performance*.

mud n. 1. opium; fr. colour and consistency *Burroughs:1*; 2. thick, strong coffee.

mud flap n. (derog.) a Black person.

mud flaps n. (US Black use) noticeably large feet *Klein*.

mudcrusher n. (US Black use) an extreme form of bully, whose aim is to crush everyone into the ground *Klein*.

muddy waters n. (US Black use) the loss of a man's erection prior to or during sex. *Folb*.

mud-kicker n. (pimp use) an unreliable, unprofessional prostitute (cf: flaky ho) *OUI 1975*.

mud-packer n. (derog.) a homosexual male (cf: fudge-packer).

muff n. the vagina; fr. supposed resemblance.

muff-diver n. cunnilinguist *Goldman*.

muffin n. the vagina *Higgins: 3*.

mug n. 1. the face *Wright*; 2. a fool *Gothic Blimp Works no. 2*; 3. derog. description of any given person *Norman: 2*; 4. the potential victim of a confidence trick or form of deception.

mug v. 1. (US campus use) to kiss *Underwood*; 2. (police use) to take identification pictures for prison/court use *Higgins: 2*; 3. to make funny faces; esp. show business/theatrical and film use; 4. to rob, usu. in the street and often with violence; orig. to garotte; thus *mugger* one who carries out such assaults.

mug book n. reference book used for casting purposes in theatre, TV and films; contains pictures of actual and aspirant stars, etc. *Chandler: LG*.

mug punter n. a sucker in any game of chance or at a racecourse (cf: punter).

mug up v. 1. to learn, to memorize; orig. theatrical use: 'paint one's mug' = face *Hotten*; 2. (US Black use) to put on one's hat; to leave *Klein*.

muggle n. (drug use) a cigarette with marijuana or hashish substituted for some of the tobacco and packed back inside it *Major*.

muggles n. (drug use) marijuana *Green: 1*.

mugs away! trad. excl. in darts matches when the winners of the previous game tell the losers to start the next contest.

mug's game n. a foolish endeavour, pointless effort *Sillitoe*.

mug's ticker n. (UK criminal use) a piece of worthless jewellery or a dud watch Powis.

mug-shot n. picture taken by police or in prison for identification of prisoner; fr. mug = face (qv).

mule n. 1. unattractive female *Price: 3*; 2. (smuggling use) an otherwise innocent person used to bring contraband goods, drugs, etc. through customs for a fee; fr. use of mules as beasts of burden. *Payne*.

mule mouth n. (US Black use) anyone who works regularly as a police informer *Klein*.

mulla n. money (cf: moolah) *N. Cassady, 'The First Third', 1971*.

mullahed (sp. unknown) (UK prison use) beaten severely *Cole*.

mulled up a. drunk *Runyon*.

Mulligan stew n. (tramp use) a stew made of whatever meats and vegetables are available *Waits*.

mulligrubs n. the blues (qv) *Major*.

mullyfogging (euph.) motherfucking (qv) *Wolfe: 2*.

mum a. silent, quiet.

mum n. (UK criminal use) one's mistress of many years or one's wife, but *not* one's actual mother *Powis*.

mumbo-jumbo a. meaningless nonsense *Thompson*.

mummy v. (US Black use) to beat a person to death, thus to make him/her into an Egyptian-style mummified corpse *Klein*.

mump v. to beg *Powis*.

mumper v. (US Black use) to travel around, to partner on someone's travels; prob. fr. UK 17th C. 'genteel beggar' who lived by nomadic begging along English roads *Klein*.

mumping n. (UK police use) for a policeman to accept cheap or free goods and services from friendly tradespeople (cf: mump) *Laurie*.

munchies n. the craving for food, often sweet or in an otherwise unlikely combination of flavours, that afflicts smokers of hashish or marijuana (cf: chucks) *Green: 1*.

munchkin n. a child, a small person; the term comes from the diminutive characters who featured in the film *The Wizard of Oz* (cf: muppet).

munger n. aka: *munga*: food; fr. Fr./Ital. root for 'eat', poss. since First World War *C. Clarke*.

munt n. (S. Afr. use) (derog.) Black person; fr. *muntu*: a person *Marcuson*.

muppet n. 1. a child, a small person; fr. the puppets created by Jim Henson and featured on the Muppet Show during the 1970s (cf: munchkin); 2. an unattractive person, possibly one who is mentally retarded.

murder ones n. (US Black use) dark glasses (cf: locs) (fr. legal j. murder one: first degree, or premeditated murder; the wearing of dark glasses is equated with a murderous image).

murphy n. a potato; fr. the common Irish surname and the assumption that potatoes are the supreme Irish staple.

murphy game n. (criminal use) for a prostitute to lure a client either to a room or a deserted alley, hallway, etc. and then, instead of having sex, the client is beaten and robbed by a male accomplice, who may just strike, but may also pose as an aggrieved father, lover, brother, etc. *Green, 'The Directory of Infamy', 1980*.

muscle n. strength; strong-arm thugs used by gangsters *Higgins: 1*.

muscle in v. to force an entrance; to use violence to gain something one desires *rr*.

musclehead n. a stupid, if brawny man *Price: 1*.

mush n. 1. the face; 2. greeting: similar to *mate*; orig. Romany *moosh*: a man *Powis*.

mush faker n. an umbrella repairer; fr. mush abbrev. mushroom: an umbrella *LL*.

musher n. (UK taxi-driver use) an owner driver; fr. mushroomer, one who has to get up early to earn a day's wages (cf: mushie) *Powis*.

mushie n. (taxi-driver use) a cabbie who owns his own cab *Powis*.

mushies n. (drug use) magic mushrooms, psilocybin.

music n. talking, esp. complaints or nagging *Higgins: 2*.

muski n. muscatel, cheap wine

Bukowski:1.

muso n. (abbrev.) musician, usu. in rock'n'roll bands *'The Boy Who Won The Pools', LWT, 1983.*

must have swallowed the dictionary (cp) referring to a person who habitually prefers longer to shorter words.

mustang n. **1.** (US Black use) an independant woman who is 'hard to ride' *Klein*; **2.** (US milit. use) an officer who has been commissioned from the ranks *Green: 2.*

mutie n. an adept, typically of skateboarding; the term comes from 'mutant'; the image is of a fan so involved that they have abandoned some of their human characteristics to their obsession *Skateboard magazine passim.*

mutt n. a dog *Runyon.*

Mutt and Jeff a. (rhyming sl.) deaf; fr. US cartoon characters, orig. by Bud Fischer in 1930s *Cole.*

Mutt and Jeff v. (police/criminal use) for police interrogators to take the parts of the 'good/sympathetic' and 'bad/potentially violent' officers when attempting to gain information from a suspect. Such 'roles' are assumed only for the situation in hand *Cole.*

mutton n. **1.** the penis (cf: mutton dagger) (cf: beef bayonet, pork sword) *Humphries*; **2.** the vagina *Norman: 2.*

mutton dagger n. the penis (cf: beet bayonet, pork sword) *Humphries.*

muzzle n. fr. Yiddish *mazel* (qv): luck *Norman: 1.*

muzzler n. a homosexual, spec. a fellator *Legman.*

muzzy a. **1.** vague, befuddled, confused; **2.** drunk *Dickson*; both meanings fr. SE bemused.

my ass! (excl.) don't try to fool me! you should be so lucky! I wasn't born yesterday!, etc. *Pynchon.*

my foot! (euph., excl.) see: my ass! (qv) *Chandler: LG.*

my gun n. (US Black use) a friend.

my man (US Black use) term of endearment and address between two Black men *'Hill Street Blues', Thames TV, passim.*

my old guv'ner n. my father *Powis.*

MYOB (acro.) *M*ind *Y*our *O*wn *B*usiness.

mystery n. an unknown young girl, often recently arrived in London from provinces *Norman: 2.*

mystery mad aka: *mystery punter*: any man who prefers his sex and/or relationships with mysteries (qv) *Neaman & Silver.*

N

nab n. (US Black use) a policeman, who nabs (qv) a villain *Major.*

nab v. to catch, esp. of a policeman's arrest *Wright.*

nabes n. (abbrev.) neighbourhoods, esp. local cinemas *Variety.*

naff a. in poor taste, unappealing, unfashionable; orig. prostitutes' use: nothing *'The Comic Strip Presents', Channel-4 TV, 1983.*

naff off! (excl.) go away! euph. fuck off (qv). *Waterhouse.*

nag n. (US pimp use) a woman who takes her time over making her daily money from her clients; fr. nag: lazy horse *Klein.*

nail v. **1.** to seduce, to pin down *Jenkins*; **2.** to charge with a debt *Higgins:3.*

nail 'em and jail 'em (US Black use) the police *Folb.*

nail one to the wall v. **1.** to punish severely; **2.** to beat up comprehensively.

nailed a. found out, thwarted, arrested *Higgins:1.*

nail-head n. (US Black use) an unattractive female, esp. one with short, nappy hair (cf: BB head) *Folb*.

naked a. **1.** (US Black use) without a gun, without possessions or money; generally at a disadvantage *Klein*; **2.** (US campus use) exactly, completely true, affirmative (often as a response to a previous statement) *Underwood*.

naked jazz n. basic, raunchy, lowdown (qv) jazz music *Major*.

nam n. (backsl.) man *Cole*.

name of the game n. the most important aspect of a given situation; whatever matters most.

nammo n. (backsl.) woman *Cole*.

nana n. fool, idiot, incompetent; esp in *a right nana*; fr. abbrev. for banana, soft (punning on soft = stupid) fruit.

nancy-boy n. aka: *nance*: derog. homosexual, effeminate male *Legman*.

nanny goat n. (rhyming sl.) coat, boat *Jones:J*.

nanny-goating (rhyming sl.) courting (imperfect rhyme) *Wright*.

Nap Town n. (US trucker use) Indianapolis, Ind. (cf: Circle City) *Klein*.

napper n. head *Wright*.

nappy a. **1.** (US Black use) crinkly, short black hair; disliked by those Blacks who aspire to the straight hair of whites *Klein*; **2.** Black, as in *nappy music*; fr. Black hair style *Price:3*.

narc n. **1.** spec. (abbrev.) narcotics agent; **2.** any informer *SF Comics*.

narc one over v. to betray a drug dealer or user to the narcotics police *Stone*.

narco n. (abbrev.) narcotics officer *Goldman*.

narco squad n. (abbrev.) narcotics squad *SF Comics*.

nark n. a police informer; fr. Romany *nak*: nose (cf: grass) *Hotten*.

nark v. **1.** to annoy, to irritate; **2.** to inform to the police (cf: grass) *Hotten*.

nark it! shut up!, stop it! '*Z Cars*', *BBC-TV, 1964*.

narked a. annoyed *Performance*.

narrow squeak n. a lucky and hairsbreadth escape *Wodehouse:MOJ*.

narrowback n. (derog.) Irish person *Higgins:5*.

Nashville n. (US Black use) any unsophisticated, suburban, middle-American town or person *Klein*.

nasty n. sexual intercourse *F. Zappa*, '*Brown Shoes Don't Make It,*' *1966*.

nasty a. (US Black use) exciting, particularly enjoyable; sexy (cf: bad) *Randy Newman*, '*Trouble in Paradise*', *1983*.

natch (abbrev.) naturally *Hoffman:a*.

natter v. to chat, to gossip. poss. fr. nag + chatter (?) *Humphries*.

natural n. **1.** an idiot, a fool; fr. a state of nature, thus untutored, unsophisticated, etc. *Obs. 6/2/83*; **2.** the ideal person for a given situation, often the potential victim for a confidence trick *Higgins:3*; **3.** see: Afro; **4.** (gambling use) in craps dice, a throw of 7 or 11.

natural woman n. (US Black use) female version of natural-born man (qv) *Folb*.

natural-born man n. (US Black use) a 'real' (heterosexual) man; a good lover, an honest, unpretentious person; the premise is that a 'natural' person is not hidebound by social conditioning, etc. *Folb*.

naughties n. sexual liaisons, intercourse *Humphries*.

Naughton and Gold (rhyming sl.) cold; fr. music hall duo *Wright*.

naughty a. (police/criminal use) criminal, violent, corrupt *Payne*.

naughty n. sexual intercourse.

naughty bits n. the genitals; this quite deliberate euph. coined c.1969 by the Monty Python's Flying Circus comedy team *BBC-2 TV, 1969 passim*.

naus n. pron. as abbrev. of nauseating and commonly used with a derog. inference, but in fact fr. rhyming sl. Noah's = Noah's Ark = nark = police informer *L. Brown, 20/4/83*.

nay-nay n. female breast (cf: ninnies) *Bruce:1*.

NB (UK 'society' use) (acro.) no

background; note appended to names of potential male escorts by debutantes or their mothers *T 18/7/83*.

NBG (acro.) *N*o *B*loody *G*ood.

near the mark somewhat corrupt, not wholly honest *Newman:1*.

near-sighted a. (homosexual use) an uncircumcised penis with its tip protruding slightly above the foreskin (cf: blind) *Legman*.

neat a. pleasant, satisfactory, attractive; term of general approval according to context *Jenkins*.

neatnik n. someone devoted to neatness and order *McFadden*.

nebbie n. (abbrev.) Nembutal, a barbiturate (cf: nembie) *Selby:1*.

nebbish n. fr. Yiddish *nebech*: a born loser *Norman:3*.

neck n. 1. audacity, daring; (abbrev.) brass neck; thus *stick one's neck out*: to chance one's luck *Howard*; 2. (US campus use) (abbrev.) redneck (qv) *Underwood*.

neck v. to pursue sexual pleasure that stops short of intercourse; usu. teen use and practice (cf: snog).

neckbreak v. (US Black use) to move swiftly *Major*.

necklaced (US Black use) extremely hip (qv): 'laced by the neck' *Klein*.

neck-oil n. alcohol *Tidy*.

necktie party n. a hanging, usu. an illicit, impromptu lynching.

Ned Kelly n. (Aus. rhyming sl.) belly *Humphries*.

need a foghorn v. (US preppie (qv) use) to be utterly confused, lost *Bernbach*.

needle n. resentment, bitterness, irritation *Powis*.

needle v. to annoy, to tease maliciously (cf: wind up) *Norman:2*.

needle and thread n. (rhyming sl.) thread *Wright*.

needle freak n. 1. (pimp use) a sadistic client who derives pleasure from hiring a woman with large breasts and paying her for every needle she permits him to stick into the flesh *OUI 8/75*; 2. (drug use) one who injects themself with narcotics

and other drugs and who is often as stimulated by the act of injection as by the action of the drug *Underwood*.

needle match n. (sporting use) any contest in which more than merely sporting rivalry divides the opponents; such a match will quite probably be violent, or at least ill-tempered.

needle-dick n. a particularly small penis; the man who has one *Porky's film 1983*.

Negro n. (US Black use) formerly the accepted name for the Black race, since 1960s radicalization, the preferred word is *black* and thus Negro implies the old-fashioned, subservient Uncle Tom (qv) style of Black person *Folb*.

nellie a. 1. overtly homosexual, effeminate man *Jay & Young;* 2. general term of disparagement *Capital Radio 1983*.

nelly n. (US campus use) a lesbian *Underwood*.

Nelson in cricket, the score of 111, spec. the English team (of any era) unlucky number; fr. the Admiral's attributes: one eye, one arm, one anus *BBC Radio 1983*.

nembie n. (abbrev.) Nembutal, a barbiturate (cf: nebbie) *Burroughs:1*.

nemmo n. (backsl.) woman *Powis*.

nerd n. an unpleasant person; anyone outside a given peer group and who thus fails to fit in with 'the gang' *SF Comics*.

nerd pack n. (factory use) a plastic, sectioned liner for the breast pocket that keeps pens from soiling the cloth (cf: nerd) *Kidder*.

nerf v. to bump another vehicle slightly with one's own car *Junker*.

nerk n. (UK public school use) fool, yob, generally unappetizing/ unacceptable person (cf: nerd) *Barr*.

nerts n. 1. the testicles (cf: nuts); excl. 2. a mild expletive (cf: nuts).

Nervo n. 1. (rhyming sl.) Nervo and Knox (former music hall comedy team) = pox = spec. syphilis *Powis*; 2. the box = television *Wright*.

nervy a. 1. nervous, scared, cowardly;

2. daring, audacious, pushing one's luck *I. J. Singer, 'The Brothers Ashkenazi', tr. J. Singer 1980*.

nest n. **1.** (US pimp use) the women who make up the pimp's stable (qv) of prostitutes *Klein*; **2.** the vagina *Klein*.

net (backsl.) ten *Cole*.

nettled a. annoyed, irritated *Sillitoe*.

never been kissed aka: *never had it* (bingo use) 17; fr. supposed sexual innocence of a 17-year-old girl.

never happen (cp) used to dismiss any idea that the speaker cannot support.

never-never n. the hire purchase system; one never finishes paying for one's purchase, also Peter Pan's 'Never-Never Land' (cf: on the drip).

neves n. **1.** (backsl.) seven; **2.** (UK prison use) a seven-year sentence *Norman:1*.

nevis (backsl.) seven *Cole*.

new jill a. see: new jack.

new fish n. (US prison use) a new inmate *Pearce*.

Newgate gaol (rhyming sl.) a tale, esp. of the 'hard-luck' variety *Cole*.

Newington Butts n. (rhyming sl.) guts = stomach *Dury*.

new jack a. (US Black use) superficial, flashy, meretricious *Ice T:2*.

News of the Screws n. nickname for the *News of the World* (UK Sunday paper) punning on its propensity for sex stories.

newsie n. newspaper seller, usu. US/Aus. use.

newted a. drunk, fr. pissed as a newt (qv) *May*.

NG (acro.) *No Good Caron*.

Niagara Falls n. (rhyming sl.) balls = testicles *Cole*.

nibhead n. a fool, a grotesque.

nice (US Black use) feeling well, happy, at one with the world *Major*.

nice bit n. (US prison use) see: long bit, big bit *Klein*.

nice one, Cyril! (cp) general term of approval; fr. Cyril Knowles, a Tottenham Hotspur footballer, 1960s.

nice work - if you can get it (cp) implying fairly open jealousy of the previous speaker.

nick n. **1.** prison; **2.** police station, esp. its cells *Laurie*.

nick v. **1.** to arrest; **2.** to steal; thus *on the nick*: going stealing *Dury*.

nick off v. to leave, to depart, to go from one place to another.

nicked a. (UK prison use) **1.** put on report to the governor for an infringement of prison rules *Obs. 1981*; **2.** arrested *'The Sweeney', Thames TV, 1974*.

nickel n. (general US use) the number five *Del Vecchio*; **2.** (US prison use) a five-year prison sentence *Klein*.

nickel-and-dime a. smalltime, second rate, insignificant *Stone*.

nicker n. pound sterling *Performance*.

niff n.,v. **1.** *n.* an unpleasant smell, a stink; **2.** *v.* to smell unpleasantly, to stink *Wodehouse:AAG*.

nifty a. neat, smart *Fiction Illus.3*.

nifty n. an attractive girl.

Nigerian n. (gay use) a black man.

Nigerian lager n. Guinness stout; fr. its colour *'Minder', Thames TV, 1982*.

nigette n. a black girl *Dre*.

nigger n. (derog.) Black person, by extension any non-white, but, in a reverse racism, taking pride in such epithets, used by radical Blacks of each other *Seale*.

nigger bait n. (derog.) an excessive display of chrome on one's automobile.

nigger box (US Black use) television (cf. wogbox) *Klein*.

nigger daytime n. (derog.) night-time.

nigger fronts n. (US Black use) extreme stylishness in dress *Folb*.

Nigger Hill / Nigger Town n. (derog.) the black community within an urban area.

nigger-driving n. (US Black use (fr. orig. in South)) the working of Blacks to exhaustion by white bosses *Klein*.

nigger-flicker n. (US Black use) a weapon, usu. a small knife or a razor blade with one side heavily taped to preserve the user's fingers *Folb*.

niggerish a. lazy, couldn't-care-less; fr, spurious stereotype of Blacks as lazy people *Heller*.

niggerlipping wetting the end of a cigarette while smoking it *Price:3*.

niggerlover n. (derog.) term of abuse, usu. aimed at a white lacking in the necessary loathing of Blacks *Selby:1*.

nigger-rich (Black use) deeply in debt but loaded down with glossy, flashy status symobls – car, jewellery, etc. *Milner*.

nigger's bankroll n. (US Black use) see California bankroll *Folb*.

niggly a. ill-tempered, obsessed with irrelevancies and petty problems.

night clothes n. (US criminal use) dark close-fitting clothes used when committing a breaking and entry at night *Klein*.

night fighter n. (derog.) a Black person.

night hawk n. (US criminal use) one who specializes in stealing at night *Klein*.

night stick n. (US Black use) anyone who lives their life in clubs and bars and generally indulges themself as a 'night person' *Klein*.

night watchman n. (cricket use) a poor batsman who is sent in in place of a superior player after a wicket has fallen near the end of a day's play and the team does not wish to chance that superior wicket *BBC Radio 3, 1983 Test Match commentaries passim*.

night-cap n. (US Black use) a small skull-cap worn by many black men *Klein*.

night-cap n. a final drink before bed, or before the bars shut *Goulart*.

night-club v. to go out at night for enjoyment at clubs, bars, parties, etc. *Grace Jones, LP title, 1980*.

nignog n. (derog.) Black person; fr. nigger (qv) *Le Carre*.

NIGYYSOB (acro.) Now I've Got You, You Son Of a Bitch: shorthand for a position reached between patient and therapist during an encounter session.

-nik general suffix; coined 1957 after launch of Russian Sputnik. First -nik word was *beatnik*, orig. by Herb Caen

in *San Francisco Chronicle Joyce Johnson, 'Minor Characters', 1983*.

Nina with her hair down (gambling use) the point of nine in craps dice *Chandler: Notebk*.

nine n. see: niner *Kurious: A Constipated Monkey (1994)*.

nine to five n. a regular, routine, uninspiring job; fr. the hours most usually worked.

niner n. a Tech Nine automatic pistol, one of the weapons of choice of those involved in drug-dealing wars.

nineteenth hole n. the bar at a golf club; spec. used by golfers but understood more widely *Neaman & Silver*.

ning-nong n. (Aus. use) stupid, foolish person *Humphries*.

ninnies n. female breasts; fr. sense of 'child' (cf: nay-nays) *Rawson*.

Nip n. (abbrev.) Nipponese: derog. Japanese *Sanchez*.

nip v. to scratch, to give a superficial wound *Klein*.

nipper n. a small child, who nips around *Performance*.

nisht aka: *nicht* fr. Yiddish: nothing *Norman:2*.

nit n. fool, idiot; fr. nitwit (qv) *May*.

nit-nit! shut up! *LL*.

nitty gritty n. basics, essentials, the grass roots *Seale*.

nitwit n. idiot, fool scatterbrain *Jenkins*.

nix v. to forbid, to veto, to say 'no'.

nix no *E. Presley, 'Jailhouse Rock', 1958*.

no account a. useless *Pearce*.

no better than he/she should be (cp) admitting that the person in question is simply human, warts and all; often used of a woman who is considered promiscuous.

no biggie (US teen. use) don't worry, it's all right, etc.; fr. no big deal (qv) *Pond*.

no cash, no Swiss phr. no help without payment in advance; fr. the traditional role of the Swiss as mercenary soldiers.

no chance no hope whatsoever;

general term of dismissal or negation.

no dice impossible, out of the question, on no account *Runyon*.

no fear! absolutely not, not a chance, etc. *Manser*.

no flies on (cp) as in 'no flies on me/her/etc.' implying the smartness and imperviousness to trickery of the speaker or subject.

no freak n. (pimp use) a client who wishes the prostitute to simulate the role of a rape victim, screaming 'No!' and 'struggling' before he overpowers her *OUI 8/75*.

no go impossible, pointless (cf: no chance).

no hoper n. a good-for-nothing, a loser, a derelict *Bickerton*.

no joy excl. of despair, disappointment, bad luck, etc.

no kidding?/! are you serious?/I'm absolutely serious.

no muss, no fuss (business use; cp) no problems, either practically or emotionally *Kidder*.

no rest for the wicked (cp) said of/by someone who, while in no way wicked, is kept very busy; said with pride rather than rancour.

no risk! (Aus. use) excl. of agreement, negating any other possibility than that just proposed *Ready*.

no shit! (excl.) you don't say! goodness me!; usu. ironic use *Higgins:5*.

no siree bob, no siree bobtail excl. (orig. US) phr. of absolute denial.

no skin off my ass (cp) no problem, no worries *Thompson:J*.

no skin off my nose! (cp) I don't care; it doesn't bother me *Dunne*.

no soap nothing doing, not a chance, no hope of that; poss. ex. US rhyming sl. bar of soap = dope, hence = no deal *Farrell*.

no stuff (US Black use) no fooling, no lies, absolutely honest and sincere *Major*.

no sweat (excl.) no problem; don't worry; it's all right *Higgins:1*.

no way! (excl.) absolutely not; you must be joking! you can't fool me! etc.

Powis.

noah's ark n. (rhyming sl.) **1.** park; **2.** nark (qv) = informer, when pron. naus (qv) *Jones:J*.

nob n. **1.** (abbrev.) nobility; the aristocracy, upper classes *Norman:3*; **2.** penis *Humphries*.

nob v. see: knob.

nobbing n. sexual intercourse *P. Marchbank*.

nobble v. **1.** (racing use) to interfere with a horse in order to spoil its chance of victory; **2.** *jury nobbling*: the interference with the impartiality of a jury – through threats or bribes – either by a defendant or his/her friends *Mortimer*; **3.** to ruin anything deliberately; esp. to impede a rival *Wodehouse:AAG*.

no-brand cigarette n. aka: *no-name cigarette*; a marijuana cigarette *Folb*.

nod v. to lapse into unconsciousness after an injection of heroin *Larner*.

nod out v. to fall asleep, esp. after an injection of heroin (cf: nod) *Burroughs:1*.

noddy n. (UK police use) (abbrev.) noddy bike; so-called from the fact that riders in motion could not salute their seniors who therefore ordered 'When you see me, nod your head!' *Laurie*.

noddy n. a wimp, a weakling; from the elf created by children's author Enid Blyton.

noffka n. aka: *nafka*: fr. Yiddish: a prostitute *Bruce:1*.

noggin n. the head *Price:2*.

no-knock n. a clause in US drug laws that permits police to enter premises without knocking first, and thus ensure surprise and probable arrests *Hoffman:a*.

nola n. (US criminal sl.) a homosexual male; fr. the female name *Legman*.

nommus! (London market use; back sl.) warning cry on sighting a policeman, lit. 'someone' *Powis*.

non n. (US Black use) a physically unco-ordinated person; a poor athlete; fr. non-performer (?) *Folb*.

non compos a. (abbrev.) *non compos*

mentis: (Lat.) 'not of sound mind', thus **1.** eccentric, crazy; **2.** drunk.

nonce n. (abbrev.) nonsense: sexual offender, spec. of young children; from the idea of a 'nothing', or 'non-person' (cf: beast) *Cole*.

nondescript n. an unmarked police car used for surveillance, etc. *Newman:1*.

nondy a. inferior, second-rate *Welsh:1* (fr. abbr. nondescript).

nong n. (Aus. use) an idiot, a fool, a general derog. description; fr. non compos (qv) *Ready*.

no-no n. an impossibility *Jay & Young*.

noodle n. **1.**head *Runyon*; **2.** (US Black) the penis.

noodle n. a fool, a dull person.

nookie n. sexual intercourse, by extn. anyone who seems likely to be easily seduced. poss fr. obs. *nug*: to fondle *Jay & Young*.

nooner n. (Aus. use) a lunchtime seduction, often of a secretary by a businessman. *C. Clarke*.

norks n. (Aus. use) breasts; fr. Norco Co-Operative Ltd, butter manufacturer of NSW *Humphries*.

north and south n. (rhyming sl.) mouth *Powis*.

North Pole n. (rhyming sl.) arsehole *Wright*.

NORWICH (acro.) (k)Nickers *O*ff *R*eady *W*hen *I* *C*ome *H*ome; used on the back of envelopes, orig. by British forces (cf: SWALK).

nose n. **1.** cocaine; which one inhales; **2.** (US prison use) a police spy. fr. orig meaning of nark (qv) *Chandler: Notebk*.

nose around v. to search, to look over, to survey *Fiction Illus.3*.

nose candy n. cocaine (cf: candy **1.**) *Schulberg*.

nosenheimer n. big shot cf: wisenheimer *PJ O'Rourke 'Parliament of Whores' (1991)*.

nosh n. food; thus The Nosh Bar, a long-lived delicatessen/cafe in Gt. Windmill Street, Soho.

nosh-up n. a feast.

nosper n. (backsl.) person *Powis*.

not a bean nothing at all, esp. of money *Chandler:LG*

not a brass razoo (Aus. use) absolutely penniless *Wilkes*.

not a hope in hell no chance whatsoever.

not a sausage absolutely nothing (cf: sausage and mash) *Laurie*.

not all there a. eccentric, insane, crazy *Hotten*.

not an earthly no chance at all, absolutely impossible *Manser*.

not backward in coming forward brash, direct and to the point (cf: accidentally on purpose).

not give a hoot v. not to care less about a given subject/person *Wodehouse:MOJ*.

not give a monkey's v. phr. to not care less; the missing word is 'fuck' or 'toss'.

not half! (excl.) certainly! really! absolutely! *Manser*.

not much chop (Aus. use) unimpressive, substandard, no good; fr. Hindi *Chhap*: a brand *Wilkes*.

not much you wouldn't (cp) rejecting the previous speaker's protestations: don't fool me, you certainly would.

not my cup of tea not to my taste *Green:2*.

not on your life! (cp) no way at all, totally impossible.

not on your Nellie! (cp) not a chance (qv), absolutely impossible; fr. not on your Nellie Duff, rhyming sl. = puff = breath (of life), thus not on your life (qv) *Norman:1*.

not playing with a full deck a. not completely sane or competent; fr. card use *Price:2*.

not ready for people a. (US Black use) one who acts stupidly, childishly, who calls attention to their own idiocies *Folb*.

not so dusty a. actually, rather good, not as bad as expected or advertised.

not taking any phr. unimpressed, disinclined, unconverted.

not the foggiest not the first idea, no

clue whatsoever; usu. as 'I haven't the foggiest', in answer to a query *Manser*.

not the full quid a. (Aus. use) mentally deficient, not all there (qv) *Wilkes*.

not to have both oars in the water (US campus use) anyone considered slightly insane, eccentric, odd *Bernbach*.

not tonight, Josephine (cp) general term of refusal; spec. of sex; allegedly first pleaded by the Emperor Napoleon to his wife.

not worth a bumper (Aus. use; cp) worthless, useless; fr. bumper (qv) *Wilkes*.

not worth a fart in a noisemaker (US cp) utterly useless *King*.

not worth a hill of beans absolutely useless *'Casablanca', 1941*.

not worth a light pointless, useless, worthless *Dury, 'Laughter', 1979*.

not worth a pisshole in the snow absolutely useless *Higgins:5*.

notch n. the vagina *Rawson*.

notes n. pounds sterling *Capital Radio 1983*.

nothing doing absolutely not, not a hope/chance (cf: no dice) *Manser*.

nothing to write home about insignificant, unexciting (despite rumours to the contrary).

nowhere n. an undesirable, tedious person, place, event or idea *Major*.

nowhere city n. irrelevant, pointless, of no use at all *Price:2*.

NQOCD (US preppie (qv) use) (acro.) *Not Quite Our Class, Dear Barr*.

NSIT (UK 'society' use) (acro.) *Not Suitable In Taxis*; note attached to the name of a prospective male escort by a debutante or her mother *T 18/7/83*.

nubian n. (US campus (spec. University of Arkansas) use) a socially unacceptable person; used for whites and blacks despite obvious racist base *Underwood*.

nuddy a. naked, undressed; usu. a coy euph. used by those who find any sexual reference embarrassing (cf: down there).

nudge, nudge, wink, wink, know

what I mean, say no more (cp) popularized by Eric Idle in 'Monty Python's Flying Circus' BBC-2 TV c.1969; Idle was dressed as a spiv and was making heavily sexual innuendos.

nudger n. (cant) pickpocket's assistant who nudges victims in a pre-selected direction, often into a crowded lift *Neaman & Silver*.

Nueva York n. New York; some reference to the large Puerto Rican population, but on the whole, merely an affectation *Pynchon*.

nuggety a. (Aus. use) chunky, squat, thickset; fr. shape of a gold nugget *Lawson*.

number n. 1. a marijuana or hashish cigarette *Green:1*; 2. (homosexual use) a casual partner picked up from the street, bar or baths *Stanley*; 3. a performance; a scene, a display of excessive emotion *Goldman*.

number one 1. (US criminal use) first degree (pre-meditated) murder *Folb*; 2. (milit. use) the best, fr. Korean and Vietnam wars (cf: number ten) *Webb*.

number ones n. (children's use) urination *May*.

number ten (milit. use) the worst, fr. Korean and Vietnamese Wars (cf: number one) *Webb*.

number twos n. (children's use) excretion *May*.

number-cruncher n. (computer use) a large, sometimes slow machine which is used to make its way through volumes of maths that would defeat, by quantity rather than complexity, mere human efforts. *Green:2*.

number-cruncher course n. (US campus use) any course that involves a large amount of maths *Underwood*.

numbers n. (gambling use) popular form of street gambling that involves predicting a combination of the winning numbers at a given racetrack; esp. widespread in US Black community.

numb-nuts n. an idiot, a fool *Price:3*.

numbskull n. a fool, an idiot, an incompetent.

numero uno a. fr. Sp: number one,

thus the best – of objects or persons *Price:1.*

nuremburgs n. haemorrhoids; fr. rhy. sl. Nuremburg trials = piles.

nut n. **1.** the head *Wright;* **2.** (entertainment use) the break-even sum in a theatre or cinema after which profit starts *Vidal;* **3.** an insane person; thus *nut doctor:* any form of mental health specialist; *nut house:* mental hospital *Price:2;* **4.** any required sum, extended from 2.

nut v. to butt one's opponent in the face, usu. the bridge of his nose, using one's own forehead.

nut house n. asylum, mental hospital *Thompson:J.*

nut on v. to attack physically.

nut up v. to lose one's temper completely, to go berserk *Underwood.*

nutcake n. a fool, an idiot, an eccentric *Higgins:5.*

nutcase n. an eccentric, an odd person.

nuts n. **1.** testicles *Price:2;* **2.** (US Black use) the clitoris (cf: cock) *Neaman & Silver.*

nuts a. insane *Price:2.*

nuts about obsessed with, usu. in the context of love *Baker.*

nuts and bolts the basics of a situation, the fundamental issues (cf: brass tacks).

nuts and sluts (US campus use) course in abnormal psychology *Bernbach.*

nutter n. a lunatic, an eccentric *Norman:2.*

nutting using the top of one's head to butt an opponent during a fight; such a blow can often end the fight instantly (cf: heading) *LL.*

nutty foolish, pleasantly eccentric; esp. in *nutty as a fruitcake SF Comics.*

nymph n. see: nympho *Bukowski:2.*

nympho n. (abbrev.) nymphomaniac, an allegedly sexually insatiable woman *Time Out, 3/84.*

O

O n. (drug use) opium *Green: 1.*

oat (backsl.) two *Cole.*

oats n. sexual satisfaction.

obbo n. (UK police use) (abbrev.) observation (on a criminal, illicit club, etc.) *Laurie.*

OBC n. (US prison use) (acro.) *o*ld, *b*rutal *c*onvict; who uses experience and power to take advantage of younger, newer inmates *Neaman & Silver.*

obo n. (police use) observation, *on obo:* on surveillance of a criminal or place where a crime might occur *Newman.*

ock it! (excl.) (US campus (spec. University of Arkansas use) stop it *Underwood.*

ocker n. (Aus. use) boorish, loutish, unsophisticated, ultra-nationalistic Australian; his rise, and celebration,

coincided with the Labour govt. of Gough Whitlam c.1974; a corruption of Oscar, and popularized in a character named 'Ocker' portrayed by Aus. actor Ron Frazer in a TV series c.1975.

OD v. (acro.) overdose (on drugs) *Jay & Young.*

oddball n. eccentric, odd, bizarre person *Uneeda Comix.*

odds v. to risk, to take a chance *Newman: 1.*

ofay a. white; fr. Yoruba *ofe* 'a charm that lets one jump so high as to disappear', thus trouble (the cause of such vanishing), thus a white man (the essence of trouble) *Southern.*

off n. (sporting use) the start of any race, esp. that of horses or dogs.

off v. **1.** to kill, esp. 1960s/70s radical use *Higgins: 2;* **2.** to have sexual intercourse (fr. male point of view) *Rawson*.

off like a bride's nightie (Aus. use) extremely fast, very speedy *Wilkes*.

off one's bean a. 1. insane, eccentric (cf: bean) 2. drunk *Dickson*.

off one's cake a. crazy, insane (cf: off one's nut) *Bleasdale*.

off one's chump a. see; off one's rocker, off one's onion, etc.

off one's feed a. depressed, miserable, nervous.

off one's gourd a. insane, crazy *McFadden*.

off one's nut a. mad. insane *Wright*.

off one's onion a. see: off one's rocker *Wodehouse: AAG*.

off one's rocker a. insane, crazy *Wodehouse: IJ*.

off (the) beam wrong, mistaken, misdirected; often as *way off beam* fr. RAF use, refers to radio beams that guide aircraft.

off the block n. local, a neighbour, a peer – always implying membership of the working class; someone who lives on the same street *Seale*.

off the cuff impromptu, spontaneous action or speech; fr. the practice of writing jokes or information on one's cuffs to aid a performer's memory.

off the hook 1. out of trouble, freed of a difficult situation; 2. phr. in ill health, in a bad temper, nervous.

off the top the first and poss. most attractive portion of any share-out, legal or otherwise *Klein*.

off the top of one's head spontaneously, extempore, ad lib *Bruce: 2*.

off the track behaving badly, making mistakes, out of order (qv) *Howard*.

off the wall a. 1. difficult, obstreperous, strange, peculiar; 2. bizarre, peculiar *Greenlee*; 3. spontaneously *McFadden*.

off-beat a. unconventional, out of the ordinary; fr. musical use *Bruce: 2*.

off-brand a. 1. (US Black use) odd, eccentric, peculiar, bizarre *Folb*; 2. (derog.) a Black person (cf: generic) *Snoop Doggy Dogg*

'Doggystyle' (1993).

off-brand cigarette n. (drug use) a marijuana cigarette *Folb*.

off-colour a. (US criminal use) homosexual *Legman*.

off-sider n. (Aus. use) assistant, helper *Bickerton*.

office n. 1. (US pimp use) wherever the pimp conducts his business, in this case, often the street or a neighbourhood bar; this borrowing of a trad. businessman's word, is common to such occupations as civil and military pilots: *office* = cockpit, and many others; 2. (US prison use) a signal *Chandler: Notebk*.

OG (abbrev.) (US Black use) original gangster, thus street-smart tough-guy *Ice T:3*.

oggin n. (nautical use) the sea: fr. hog-wash *Green: 2*.

oh, my dear n. (rhyming sl.) beer *Wright*.

-oholic widely used suffix based on the obsessive nature of an *alcoholic*: thus *chocoholic*: one who cannot stop consuming chocolate, *bookoholic*: an obsessive reader, etc.

oik n. an unpleasant youth, a yob (qv) *May*.

oil n. 1. (US Black use) alcohol, esp. wine *Folb*; 2. graft, bribery, and the money for paying it (cf: juice, grease) *Major*.

oil burner habit n. an extremely heavy level of heroin addiction *Grogan*.

oil it v. (US campus use) to stay up late studying; fr. 'burning the midnight oil' *Underwood*.

oil out v. to escape one's responsibility, to escape from an onerous duty or similar situation; to slide away as if well-lubricated.

oiled a. aka: *oiled up*; drunk *Dickson*.

oily n. 1.(rhyming sl.) oily rag = fag = cigarette; 2. (prison use) a solitor's clerk, sometimes a solicitor, both of whom visit their imprisoned clients to 'clean up' their pre-trial problems *Cole*.

OK corruption of *orl korrect* and thus

since at least 1839 a general term of agreement; despite the many conflicting claims as to the etymology of OK, this is that accepted by the *OED* Supplement (vol. III O–Scz, 1982 p.40).

oke-dokey see: OK *The People's Comic*.

okey-dokey (US Black use) **1.** white values and opinions; **2.** a swindle, a confidence trick *Major*.

old bastard n. a man.

old biddy n. old woman, fr. biddy = Bridget *Dunne*.

Old Bill n. the police *Newman: 1*.

old bill n. a police station *Robins:1*.

old boiler n. an old and unattractive woman (cf: boiler).

old cocker n. fr. Yiddish: *alte cacka*: old man, usu. disreputable *Price: 2*.

old coot n. foolish and/or cantankerous old person *Chandler: LG*.

old dog n. (US Black use) an expert in a given field *Klein*.

old Dutch n. the wife; fr. rhyming sl. Duchess of Fife (qv) *May*.

old Ear-ie see: on the Erie *Runyon*.

old enough to know better (cp) implying that someone who has just committed some blunder should not have done so.

old identity n. (Aus. use) anyone who has lived in the same place for a long time; a regular resident *Humphries: 2*.

old lady n. **1.** mother *Price: 2*; **2.** girlfriend; **3.** wife (actual or common law).

old man n. a woman's lover or husband.

old man n. (sex industry use) a pimp.

old moody n. a cunning trick, a fraud; thus *to pull the old moody Norman: 1*.

Old Nassau n. (US college use) Princeton University *Bernbach*.

Old Nick Satan, the devil *Farrell*.

old one-two n. a knock out blow, either in an actual fight or as a metaphor; fr. boxing use *Heller*.

old sport n. a man.

old sweat n. any veteran, orig. milit. use; fr. the sweating that resulted from

one's labours *Wodehouse: MOJ*.

old timer n. (pimp use) an experienced, older but not necessarily run down prostitute; such women are often used to train up their younger recruits to a pimp's stable (qv) *OUI 8/75*.

old-fashioned look n. a disapproving glance.

oldie n. (usu. teen. or youth use) the old, esp. those over 40, or at least those who fail to share or appreciate the nuances and delights of the current version of the rebellious youth culture (cf: dusty, geri, wrinklies).

oldie but goodie n. something no longer fashionable or chic but still beloved by its owner/wearer/user (cf: golden oldie) *McFadden*.

oliver n. (abbrev.) Oliver Twist: a deliberately incorrect entry in a ledger; usu. bookmaker use: fr. rhyming sl. Oliver Twist = fist, thus to write *Powis*.

olly n. (rhyming sl.) fr. Oliver Reed (UK actor, 1938–) = speed = amphetamine drugs *Cole*.

OMCD (homosexual use) (acro.) *O*ut of *M*y *C*lass, *D*arling *Jay & Young*.

omee n. (theatrical use) a man; fr. 19th C. theatrical sl. *parlyaree* and one of the few survivors still in use (cf: polone).

omee-polone n. (theatrical use) a homosexual, fr. *parlyaree* wds for man and woman (cf: omee, polone).

on (backsl.) no *Cole*.

on, to be v. to be in agreement, to offer one's commitment, one's support; usu. as 'are you on?', 'I'm on!', etc.

on a bat a. drunk, on a drinking binge *Dickson*.

on a bender on a drinking spree *Dickson*.

on a brannigan a. very drunk *Dickson*.

on a bust drinking heavily *Dickson*.

on a good wicket in a secure, rewarding position; fr. cricket use. Thus *on a sticky wicket*: in difficulties, or about to face them *Humphries: 2*.

on a hiding to nothing with absolutely no chance; esp. in a sporting contest *ES 8/2/83*.

on a pension (UK police/criminal use) anyone receiving regular bribes *Powis*.

on a promise (UK police/criminal use) awaiting a promised event, poss. money, a bribe, a tip-off, a material gift, etc. *Powis*.

on a rush (poker use) to be winning a succession of hands with unassailable ease *Alvarez*.

on a skate drinking heavily *Dickson*.

on a tight leash 1. deeply infatuated; 2. kept under extreme control.

on a tipple a. very drunk *Dickson*.

on a toot on a spree, usu. involving drink, drugs and/or degeneracy *Wodehouse: PGM*.

on appro (abbrev.) on approval *Wodehouse: PGM*.

on at critical of, nagging, telling off.

on contract (US police use) regularly accepting bribes *Neaman & Silver*.

on dab (UK police use) to be on a disciplinary charge *Laurie*.

on doog (backsl.) no good *Cole*.

on fire (US campus use) anyone who has just made a glaring social error (cf: flamer) *Bernbach*.

on flake (US Black use) passed out, unconscious (cf: flaked out) *Folb*.

on ice 1. in reserve; 2. out of the way *Price: 2*.

on it indulging (poss. to a noticeable excess) in a given drug, drugs or alcohol.

on jankers in prison; esp. in UK milit. use *Wodehouse passim*.

on my life! (excl.) an affirmation of absolute truth in the face of an audience's scepticism. one of those cliché phrases forced on every stage Jew *Payne*.

on offer liable to problems *Newman: 1*.

on one's ass, to be v.i. to pester, to harass, to annoy *Dunne*.

on one's case v. to harass, to persecute, to pursue *McFadden*.

on one's dick, to be v. phr. to be keen

on, to support. *Ice T:3*.

on one's high horse arrogant, acting superior, etc. *Neaman & Silver*.

on one's Jack (rhyming sl.) Jack Jones = alone *Norman: 4*.

on one's job (US Black use) well in control; successful at a given task *Folb*.

on one's last legs *in extremis*, 'at the end of one's tether', in great and seemingly irrefutable distress.

on one's Pat (Aus. use; rhyming sl.) Pat Malone = alone (cf: on one's Tod) *Wilkes*.

on (one's) puff adv. (rhy.sl.) on one's own *Welsh:1*.

on one's say-so on one's word of honour, on trust.

on one's Tod (rhyming sl.) Tod Sloan = alone; fr. the jockey *Norman: 2*.

on one's uppers in great poverty, without any money, broke (qv); fr. the uppers of one's shoes, the soles having long since worn away, unmended through lack of cash *Powis*.

on point adv. alert, sharp, aware *Wu Tang Clan: Enter the Wu Tang (1993)* (fr. milit j. point: the lead man of a patrol).

on speakers on speaking terms; usu. only found amongst devotees of Jessica Mitford's *Hons & Rebels* 1960.

on spec at a risk, without making a firm decision; fr. speculation.

on the ball sophisticated, aware, up to date; fr. sporting use *Junker*.

on the bash 1. working the streets as a prostitute (cf: bash) *Norman: 2*; 2. (Aus./NZ use) to go out on a heavy bout of drinking.

on the bat 1. out for a good, drunken, sexy, brawling time; 2. working as a prostitute *LL*.

on the batter see: on the bat *LL*.

on the battle (Aus. use) working as a prostitute (cf: on the bat, batter, etc.) *Neaman & Silver*.

on the beam (US Black use) right on course, heading in the right direction *Klein*.

on the bing adv. energetic,

enthusiastic (cf: on the ball).

on the blink malfunctioning, working badly *Dunne*.

on the block adv. phr. in business.

on the books adv. phr. good for credit.

on the booze drinking heavily *Dickson*.

on the bottle (UK cant) stealing by picking pockets in a crowd *Cole*.

on the bottle 1. drinking heavily; 2. (UK use) working as a male prostitute; fr. rhyming sl. bottle and glass (qv); 3. (US use) working in any form of prostitution; fr. rhyming sl. as 2 *Cole*.

on the bow see: on the elbow *Powis*.

on the bricks in the street, esp. of a prostitute's beat *Dunne*.

on the bum a. 1. travelling as a tramp; 2. feeling slightly unwell.

on the button 1. right on target, usu. of a blow *Runyon*; 2. up to the minute; fully aware *Higgins: 2*.

on the case (US pimp use) for a prostitute to be earning steadily and regularly from a given client *Klein*.

on the chopping block in a very disadvantageous position.

on the clock (taxi-driver use) the hiring of a cab by a freelance taxi-driver who then pays its owner a percentage of what is on the clock at the end of his working with the cab *Powis*.

on the coat (Aus. use) out of favour, 'getting the cold shoulder' *Wilkes*.

on the corn (Aus. prison use) to be serving time in goal; fr. hominy diet therein *Neaman & Silver*.

on the cuff on account; for free; fr. earlier practice of pencilling debts in shops or bars on a (celluloid) cuff *Higgins: 2*.

on the deck (milit. use) at ground level ; usu, air force term *Wolfe: 5*.

on the dot with perfect timing, absolutely promptly *Wodehouse: AAG*.

on the double fast, fr. milit. double-time *Capital Radio 1983*.

on the drip purchased on the hire

purchase scheme; one's cash just drips away (cf: on the never-never).

on the earhole (UK criminal use) on the scrounge *Powis*.

on the earie (criminal use) cf: on the earhole *Schulberg*.

on the edge a. (US campus use) nervous, neurotic *Underwood*.

on the elbow on the scrounge *Powis*.

on the Erie! (US prison use) aka: *on the Ear-ie*: (excl.) be quiet, someone is listening! *Chandler: Notebk*.

on the fence (homosexual use) turning to heterosexuality (cf: lose one's gender) *Legman*.

on the flip side on the other side, on the reverse, 'on the other hand'; fr. record industry use *McFadden*.

on the floor a. 1. (rhyming sl.) poor *Cole*; 2. drunk *Dickson*.

on the fritz a. 1. drunk *Dickson*; 2. of machinery: broken down, not working.

on the game involved in prostitution *Norman: 2*.

on the go active, lively.

on the grog a. aka: *on the sauce, on the juice*, etc.: very drunk.

on the hill a. pregnant *Selby: 1*.

on the hoof passing by; casual *White*.

on the hook playing truant *Pynchon*.

on the hop running away, escaping, on the run.

on the house free, a gift of the management, publican, etc. *'Minder', Thames TV, 1980 passim*.

on the hummer phr. 1. (of machinery) out of order; 2. (of a person) feeling unwell; 3. at a disadvantage.

on the hurry up at great speed, in a hurry *Powis*.

on the Jersey side on the wrong side, usu. jazz sl.; New York (esp. Manhattan) is the 'right side' *Goldman*.

on the job engaged in sexual activity *Capital Radio 1983*.

on the knocker 1. (UK criminal use) touring houses, ostensibly to buy or sell goods, but specifically to trick or bully people into selling heirlooms,

antiques, etc. for minimal prices
Powis; **2.** (Aus. use) at once, on
demand, esp. of cash payments
Wilkes.

on the lam on the run from prison
*A. Karpis, 'The AlvinKarpis Story',
1971.*

on the level honest; straightforward
Higgins: 2.

on the line at stake; fr. gambling use
Grogan.

on the make looking to benefit
oneself, ambitious, keen to do
whatever will be most useful for one's
own advancement; esp. sexually
Waits.

on the money excellent, perfect, just
right; fr. betting use *W. Allen,
'Manhattan', 1979.*

on the mooch phr. living as a
professional beggar *Welsh:1.*

on the Murray cod (Aus. use) in
gambling, rhyming sl. on the nod =
betting on credit *Wilkes*.

on the muscle 1. (US prison use)
quarrelsome, ready for trouble,
picking fights *Chandler: Notebk*;
2. working as protection for a top
gangster *Schulberg*.

on the needle (drug use) addicted to
narcotics.

on the nest (US use) pregnant
Neaman & Silver.

on the never-never bought by the
hire purchase credit system (cf: on the
drip).

on the nod under the influence of
heroin *Burroughs: 1.*

on the nose 1. (UK use) in betting, a
wager on the winning horse: '£5.00 on
the nose' . . .; **2.** (Aus. use)
unpleasant, lit. smelly, and thus
offensive morally/aesthetically as well
as in the nostrils *Wilkes*.

on the outer (Aus. use) to be
unpopular, to be out of favour *Wilkes*.

on the outs to be out of luck, money,
favour, popularity, etc. *D. McLintick,
'Indecent Exposure', 1983.*

on the pavement (UK police use) an
arrest carried out in the street *ST 3/4/
83.*

on the plastic (UK criminal/police
use) using stolen credit cards for a
variety of frauds and swindles *Powis*.

on the QT surreptitiously; on the quiet
Vidal.

on the rag 1. menstruating; thus, by
derivation; **2.** irritated, testy, bad-
tempered *Underwood*.

on the ran-dan on a spree *Howard*.

on the razzle indulging in a series of
parties, binges, and general self-
indulgent excesses.

on the rebound a relationship that is
initiated less through attraction than
to exorcise one that has recently
collapsed.

on the rocks (drinkers' use) with ice-
cubes or cracked ice.

on the Rory (rhyming sl.) Rory
O'More = on the floor = penniless
Powis.

on the sauce drinking heavily and
consistently *Neaman & Silver*.

on the shelf 1. put on one side for
unspecified future use; **2.** of a girl:
unmarried and, given the married
state of most of her contemporaries,
worried about it; feeling that as a
person she is becoming 1 *Hotten*.

on the short end (gambling use) at
the unfavourable end of the odds; thus
in a 20-1 bet the 1 is the short end
Heller.

on the side adv. in secret, clandestine
Shell.

on the skids on a social and economic
decline; fr. mixture of a slide
downwards and skid row (qv)
Humphries: 2.

on the slate on credit; fr. practice of
writing such debts on a slate *Payne*.

on the sleeve using narcotics; fr. the
rolling up of a sleeve prior to the
injection *Algren*.

on the spot (US police/criminal use)
marked for death, the subject of a
contract (qv) for assassination
Himes: 1.

on the square living an honest, law-
abiding (and tedious) life (cf: square)
Algren.

on the stem adv. (US tramp use)

walking the main street of a town, begging for subsistence.

on the stick efficient, aware, in control (cf: on the ball) *Price: 3*.

on the stones 1. homeless; 2. in the open air, usu. referring to a fight, often with sidebets and between local champions, arranged outside the normal boxing world *Robins:1*.

on the street out of gaol; in public life *Higgins: 1*.

on the take (criminal use) of a policeman – one who accepts bribes *Austin*.

on the tiles out all night having a riotous good time; fr. the nocturnal exploits of cats; usu. in a '*a night on . . .*' *Hotten*.

on the tin (US police use) free, gratis; fr. those gifts and favours – often free meals, drinks – obtained by showing one's official badge.

on the trot hiding away from the police to avoid an arrest; usu. by leaving one's home/town, etc. *Newman: 1*.

on the up and up in an increasingly favourable, lucky, pleasant situation.

on the wagon voluntarily stopping drinking alcohol. orig, abbrev. for 'on the water-wagon' *Norman: 3*.

on the whiz working as a pickpocket, one of the *whiz mob Powis*.

on the wire generally known, going the rounds of gossip and rumour (cf: bush telegraph) *X*.

on the wrist free, esp. in police (US) use for obtaining food, drink etc. on the strength of a badge *Greaser Comics*.

on tick on credit *Sillitoe*.

on time! excl. general expression of approval.

on top of having sexual intercourse with *Wilkinson*.

on top of one's head, to be phr. to be anxious, to be worried.

on velvet secure, cheerful, a life without problems *Schulberg*.

on your bike! excl. go away! *Welsh:1*.

on your Jack adv. on your own *Welsh:1* (abbr. on your Jack Jones

(qv)).

once a week n. (rhyming sl.) cheek *Powis*.

once in a blue moon extremely rarely.

once in a month of Sundays (cp) exceptionally rarely.

oncer n. 1. one pound note *J. le Carré, 'The Little Drummer Girl', 1983*;
2. (homosexual use) a homosexual who never repeats a sexual encounter with any one partner but continues to seek new people *Legman*.

ONE (acro.) *one night experience* (of sex) *AS 60.1 (1985)*.

one n. (US Black use) (abbrev.) one big lie *Klein*.

— one nothing, not a single one: usu. with qualifying negative, eg 'He won't get dime one out of me', etc. *'Hill Street Blues', Thames TV, 1983*.

one away! (UK prison use) the cry of alarm from prison officers, signifying an escape.

one bill n. $100 (cf: bill) *Major*.

one brick short of a load not all there, slightly insane, eccentric *Humphries: 2*.

187 n. homicide; fr. LAPD code. *Dre*.

one for the ditch n. a final drink; rather than the traditional 'one for the road', this variation acknowledges the perils of drunken driving. *Esquire 5/77*.

one for the road n. (cp) a final drink before parting; presumably coined prior to the invention of the internal combustion engine.

one good woman n. (US Black use) the ideal soulmate, helpful, considerate, sympathetic, prob, sexy too; hardly a feminist paradigm *Klein*.

one hundred per cent feeling very well, cheerful, high-spirited, etc.

one night stand n. 1. an affair that lasts only a single night *Higgins: 1*;
2. (rock business use) the giving of only one performance in a specific venue prior to moving on.

one of these morning's you'll wake

up and find yourself dead (cp) addressed to a very dozy, dull person.

one off the wrist the act of masturbation.

one over the eight a. drunk; the eight being pints, a supposed 'safe' amount of beer.

one percenter n. (Hells Angel use) an outlaw bike rider; that 1 per cent of motorcycle users who refuse to abide by the rules and the law *Thompson*.

one sandwich short of the picnic phr. crazy, eccentric; one of many similar phrases that mean 'not all there'.

one to meet n. an appointment *Newman*.

one-armed bandit n. a fruit machine, a coin-operated gaming machine, originally operated by a single lever, but now more likely to require one or more buttons.

one-eyed boy with his shirtsleeves rolled up phr. a circumcised penis.

one-eyed brother n. the penis *Caserta*.

one-eyed scribe n. (US Black use) a monumental liar; an insignificant person, poss. because they cannot be trusted to tell the truth *Klein*.

one-eyed trouser snake n. the penis *Humphries*.

one-hand magazine n. a pornographic magazine, used as an aid to masturbation (cf: stroke book) *Wolfe: 5*.

one-legged race n. masturbation *Dury, 'Laughter', 1979*.

one-lunger n. a single cylinder motorcycle *Selby: 1*.

one-on-one a. person-to-person, intimate *McFadden*.

one-pot screamer n. (Aus. use) aka: *two-pot screamer* one who cannot hold their liquor without becoming obstreperously drunk; they only need one or two drinks before they lose all control *Bickerton*.

one's number to be up v. to die; to lose one's opportunity or chance; to meet with one's unpleasant fate *rr*.

one-shot credit n. (drug dealer use) for the dealer to allow a client to default on a payment once only; any subsequent slip-ups will be met with violence *Thames TV, 1983*.

one-stick drum improvisation phr. masturbation (cf: beat the meat).

one-two-three at once, immediately, speedily *Larner*.

oogie n. (Southern US campus use) derog. reference to Black students; fr. boogie (qv) *Underwood*.

OP (Can. prison use) (acro.) *O*ff *P*rivilege, restricted *Caron*.

op n. (abbrev.) a surgical operation *Humphries: 2*.

open game n. (US pimp use) a prostitute with no specific affiliation to one stable (qv) *Klein*.

open slather n. (Aus. use) a situation with no restrictions or limits to one's wishes *Wilkes*.

open swinging n. (sex industry use) swapping parties in which all comers – married or single – are welcome and all end up in the same bed *SMD*.

operator n. **1.** the controller of a gambling game; **2.** a major criminal *Higgins: 1*.

OPM (acro.) *O*ther *P*eople's *M*oney: the ideal commodity in the eyes of any entrepreneur; if one's deals fail, one loses nothing of one's own; if they work out one is profiting without investment *NYT 2/82*.

OPP acro. other people's pussy: the wives and girlfriends of other men. Like the business world's OPM: other people's money, OPP is something one can enjoy, but need have no responsibility for.

oppo n. (abbrev.) opposite number: best friend *Minder, Thames TV, 1980*.

orangutan n. (derog.) a Black person (cf: ape, black ape).

orb v. (US teen. use) to stare at, to look over (cf: eyeball) *Sculatti*.

orbit v. to engage in fellatio/cunnilingus (cf: around the world); thus orbiter: one who does this. *AS 60.1 (1985)*.

orbital abbr. of orbital rave (qv); an acid house (qv) party.

orchestra stalls n. (rhyming sl.) balls (qv) = testicles *Jones: J*.

ordinary n. (US Black use) one's regular female companion *Klein*.

oreo n. (US Black use) derog. description of a fellow Black whose colour may be Black, but whose opinions, attitudes, lifestyle and goals are all taken from white society and standards; fr. 'oreo cookie' a popular US biscuit which is black on the outside and white within.

original (Black use) a fellow Black person; thus *all-originals party*: a party for Blacks only *Milner*.

originals n. (Hells Angel use) the Levi jeans and jacket (with sleeves cut off) which are worn at an Angel initiation ceremony liberally soiled and 'worn in' and which the rider wears every day until they fall to pieces *Thompson*.

Oscar n. (Aus. rhyming sl.) Oscar Asche = cash *Humphries*.

ossifer n. joking, slightly derog. ref to a police officer.

ossified a. extremely high (qv) on a given drug; a pun on stoned (qv) *Folb*.

OT & E (UK 'society' use) (acro) *O*ver-*T*ired and *E*motional; usu. describing a fractious child *Barr*.

OTT see: over the top.

Otto n. (derog.) German, with implication of lumpenprole stolidity *Price: 3*.

out (abbrev.) out of pocket, poor, in debt *Higgins: 1*.

out v. to expose someone as a homosexual against their will, a practice pioneered by the New York gay magazine *Outweek*. This is known as 'outing', and its converse is 'inning': the deliberate masking of homosexuality when a celebrity is known to be gay but the gay/lesbian community finds them (or more likely their politics) so reprehensible that it denies the fact.

out and out n. (US Black use) a totally unacceptable person; fr. 'an out and out villain/nightmare', etc. *Klein*.

out in the water adv. phr. in debt (cf: in the hole, on the nut).

out like a light collapsing – through a blow, drink, drugs, exhaustion – instantly.

out of it 1. unable to function adequately because of one's intoxication by drugs or alcohol; **2.** tired, exhausted *Underwood*.

out of left field a. peculiar, eccentric, in poor taste; fr. baseball use *Goldman*.

out of line breaking rules, unacceptable, out of the ordinary *J. Jackson, 'I'm the Man', 1980*.

out of (one's) box adv. unstable, mad, insane, *Welsh:1* (cf: off one's box, out of one's tree).

out of one's brain a. intoxicated with drugs *The Who, 'Quadrophenia', 1973*.

out of one's gourd a. extremely affected by a given drug, usu. cannabis or a hallucinogen; fr. gourd = head *Wolfe: 2*.

out of one's mind a. **1.** intoxicated, either through drink or drugs; **2.** crazy, insane *Higgins: 3*.

out of one's nut a. see: out of one's mind *Bruce: 2*.

out of one's skull a. see: out of one's mind *Bruce: 2*.

out of order unacceptable, excessive, in bad taste: of events, behaviour, people *Dury*.

out of pocket (Black use) unacceptable, tasteless behaviour; fr. pool use when an 'out of pocket' shot causes a player to miss a turn (cf: out of order) *Milner*.

out of sight a. excellent, first rate, exceptional (cf: outasite, far out) *Seale*.

out of state a. (US campus use) pun on out of sight (qv) *Underwood*.

out of the blue surprising, quite unsuspected; a 'bolt from the blue' (sky).

out of the box a. (Aus. use) exceptional, well above average *Wilkes*.

out of the picture a. irrelevant, unimportant; fr. cinema use.

out of this world a. fantastic,

amazing, wonderful, etc.

out of whack off centre, out of true, out of order *Bruce: 1*.

out of your tree a. out of your mind, insane *Price :2*.

out on a limb in a difficult situation, in trouble; the limb is one found on a tree.

out on one's ear ejected unceremoniously, thrown out.

out to lunch a. **1.** crazy, eccentric, weird; **2.** intoxicated by drink or drugs both imply a secretary announcing 'he's not here' of her boss (cf: not all there).

out with disenchanted with, opposed to *Seale*.

outasite a. excellent, wonderful, top quality (cf: out of sight) *The People's Comic*.

outers 1. unacceptable, distasteful; fr. out of order (qv) *Cole*; **2.** (UK criminal use) a means of escape *Powis*.

outfit n. **1.** (UK prison use) whatever is needed for attempting a given escape *LL*; **2.** the equipment – needle, spoon, cotton, etc. – used for narcotic injection (cf: works) *Grogan*; **3.** (US campus use) anyone seen as odd or eccentric, who fails to fit in *Underwood*.

outfront open, honest, uninhibited (cf: upfront) *Wolfe: 2*.

outhouse n. (US prison use) a 'half-way house' or hostel, in which newly released prisoners or parolees can learn to re-acclimatize themselves to the 'real' world *Klein*.

outlaw n. (Black pimp use) a prostitute without a regular pimp; any independent prostitute; thus outside the pimp 'laws' *Milner*.

outside a. (Can. prison use) out of prison; the world of free people *Caron*.

outfit n. **1.** (UK prison use) whatever is needed for attempting a given escape *LL*; **2.** the equipment – needle, spoon, cotton, etc. – used for narcotic injection (cf: works) *Grogan*; **3.** (US campus use) anyone seen as odd or

eccentric, who fails to fit in *Underwood*.

over a barrel in another's power, at a great disadvantage; thus *to have over a barrel*: to dominate, to control.

over the fence (Aus. use) extreme, beyond the bounds of taste (cf: beyond the rabbit-proof fence, over the top) *Wilkes*.

over the hill a. worn out, finished, useless, too old *Dury*, *'Laughter', 1979*.

over the hill n. a deserter from the armed forces *R. Stone, 'A Flag for Sunrise', 1981*.

over the hill ho n. see: fleabag *OUI 8/ 75*.

over the moon a. extremely cheerful, most delightful; cliché response attributed to sportsmen, esp. soccer players, when interviewed about a successful game or competition (cf: sick as a parrot).

over the side (UK police use) to be about one's private business, usu. sexual, when one should be on duty, fr. nautical use *Laurie*.

over the top beyond the usual bounds (of taste, of behaviour, etc.), esp. entertainment use where often cut to OTT (qv) *J. le Carré, 'The Little Drummer Girl', 1983*.

over the top a. very drunk *Wilkinson*.

over the wall, go v. to escape from prison.

over-amp v. (drug use) to overdose on cocaine or amphetamine.

overboard a. over-enthusiastic, very keen; thus *to go overboard Higgins: 1*.

overs n. (UK criminal use) proceeds of a theft that can, if not carefully disposed of, become vulnerable themselves to further theft, poss. by one of the gang *Powis*.

Oxford scholar n. (rhyming sl.) a dollar (qv) = 5s. = 25p *Jones: J*.

oyster n. a girl (cf: spear the bearded clam) *Schulberg*.

OZ n. (drug use) one ounce of marijuana (cf: LB) *Green: 1*.

P

P check n. (UK milit. use) (abbrev.) personality check: for establishing identification *A.F.N. Clarke, 'Contact', 1983.*

p.a. n. (acro.) *p*ublic *a*ddress system.

pace v. (US Black use) to live a fast, exciting and varied life *Klein.*

pachuco n. aka: *cholo*; a Mexican-American street gang youth *AS 50: 1–2 (1975).*

pack n. (US Black use) (derog.) a White person (cf: peckerwood).

pack v. to live as a female tramp, travelling the country; fr. the backpack she carries *Klein.*

pack 'em v. (Aus. use) to be frightened; fr. image of holding back fear-induced diarrhoea *Lambert.*

pack in v. to stop.

pack it in v. to stop doing something; usu. as a command *Dury, 'Do It Yourself'.*

pack peanut butter v. to engage in anal intercourse *Folb.*

packet n. 1. a large sum of money, esp. in win a packet *Wodehouse:MOJ*; 2. (UK gay use) the genitals, male or female (cf: box, basket) *Maledicta.*

pad n. a place, house or apartment. orig. an opium den, thence to beatnik use: where one could smoke cannabis, currently general use (if dated) *Grogan.*

pad a bill v. the fraudulent addition of items to a bill or to expense account statements in order to obtain money that one is not actually owed *Heller.*

padding crib n. (US criminal use) a place to hide or to rest; fr. 19th C. UK cant *Klein.*

paddy n. (US Black use) 1. white man, though not always Irish; 2. spec. policeman; fr. large numbers of Irish on the force *Seale*; 3. (UK prison use) (abbrev.) a padded cell for prisoners who have 'done their nut' (qv) in one way or another *LL.*

Paddy Irishman; fr. common Irish name: Patrick (cf: Mick) *Greenlee.*

paddy wagon n. (criminal/police use) the vehicle in which arrested people are transported to the local police station or gaol; either fr. paddy, abbrev. padlock, or Paddy, inference that most US police would be Irish *Seale.*

Paddy's funeral n. any boisterous occasion, not a wake.

Paddy's toothache n. pregnancy.

padre n. a (military) chaplain *Hotten.*

pads n. (UK prison use) (abbrev.) padded cell (cf: paddy) *LL.*

page three girl n. a pin-up; fr. the use by tabloid newspapers of under-dressed models in their pages as part of their ongoing rivalry; the *Sun* launched the battle and still has its girl on p.3; the *Daily Mirror* followed with p.5, but has recently excised such girls and the *Daily Star* offers p.7, but with colour to boot.

pain in the ass n. an annoying person *Higgins:1.*

pain in the neck n. an annoying person, a euph. for pain in the ass (qv) *Wodehouse:PGM.*

paint the town red v. to go on a spree.

paisan n. an Italian; usu. used by fellow-members of that race in an affectionate and congratulatory manner (cf: landsman) *Heller.*

Paki aka *Pakki* (derog. abbrev.) Pakistani.

Paki-basher n. a racist who specializes in beating up Pakis (qv) – Indians, Pakistanis and Bangladeshis (cf: queer-basher) *Green:3.*

Paki-bashing · racially motivated attacks on the UK Pakistani community, esp. by white skinhead (qv) youths (cf: queer-bashing).

pal n. a friend, an accomplice; fr. Romany.

paleface n. a white person *J. Pilger, 'The Last Day', Thames TV 1983.*

paleface nigger n. (US Black use) a
highly disliked white person; whose
skin does not save him from
opprobrium usu. heaped on Blacks
Klein.

pally a. friendly, affectionate fr. pal
(qv) (cf: chummy) *Wodehouse:AAG.*

palm v. to pass over money as a bribe
Higgins:5.

palm-presser n. a politician who
attemps to curry favour and win votes
by shaking hands with anyone he/she
meets (cf: flesh-presser).

palooka n. a boxer, usually one who is
both large and stupid; coined by Jack
Conway (d.1928) of *Variety* magazine,
and given wide currency by Ham
Fisher's comic strip 'Joe Palooka'
(launched 1930) *Schulberg.*

palsy-walsy a. overly friendly fr. pal
(qv) + reduplication
Wodehouse:AAG.

pamper pirate n. (US cant) a child
molestor (fr. Pampers: brandname of
a line of disposable diapers).

pan n. face *Runyon.*

pan v. to survey, to look around; fr.
film use *Price:3.*

pan out v. to work out, to result in; fr.
panning for gold '*Minder*',
Thames TV, 1983.

pancake n. attractive young girl; an
example of sex as food (cf: cookie,
etc.) *Runyon.*

panel v. to attack, to beat up, to hit
Welsh:1.

panel joint n. a brothel that features
mirrors on ceilings, two-way mirrors in
walls, etc.

panhandler n. one who begs in the
street; fr. a begging-bowl
Burroughs:1.

panic stations n. a crisis, a drama;
orig. naval use and punning on 'action
stations'.

pansy n. (derog.) effeminate
homosexual male (cf: nola) *Legman.*

panther piss n. homebrewed liquor
Bukowski:2.

panties n. (US prison use) the
underwear worn by a prison
homosexual *Klein.*

pants v. to remove someone's trousers
whether they like it or not mainly juv.
use (cf: debag) *Dickson.*

papa n. a masculine lesbian; fr. juv.
use: father *Legman.*

paper n. **1.** a measure of heroin,
contained in a folded square of paper
(cf: bindle) *Grogan*; **2.** any form of
money order, IOU, financial
documents others than actual cash
Higgins:3.

paper hanger n. (criminal use) one
who habitually passes bad cheques; fr.
pun on decorator *Breslin.*

paper pusher n. the lowliest rank of
bureaucrat/clerk; the implication
being that he never writes on, only
pushes, paper *PT.*

papers n. cigarette papers, esp. when
used for rolling marijuana joints (qv)
Folb.

par for the course (cp) as expected,
predictable, nothing special.

para adv. abbr. paranoid *Shell.*

paracki n. paraldehyde *Higgins:1.*

paraffin lamp (rhyming sl.) a tramp
Dury.

parallel parking n. (US preppie (qv)
use) sexual intercourse *Bernbach.*

paralytic a. extremely drunk, to the
point of passing out cold *Bernbach.*

paranoid a. frightened, worried,
disturbed; all non-clinical uses orig. in
1960s hippie era, often occasioned by
an excess of drug use; fr. 'Paranoia:
functional psychosis characterized by
delusions of grandeur and
persecution, but without intellectual
deterioration. . .' *C. Rycroft, 'A
Critical Dictionary of Psychoanalysis',
1968.*

pardon my French 'genteel' euph.:
excuse my swearing *Mortimer.*

Paris brothers n. (gay use)
homosexuals, esp. twins (cf: french).

park a custard v. (UK 'society' use) to
vomit *Barr.*

park your carcase an invitation to 'sit
down'; US radio comedian Harry
Einstein (1904–58) used the
pseudonym 'Parkyakarkus'.

parking n. (US teenage rite) couples

use the boy's car parked in a discreet spot for petting and poss. intercourse *Higgins:1.*

parking place n. the buttocks *Neaman & Silver.*

parlour pink n. a Socialist whose activism is limited by the confines of his dinner table and does not extend on to the streets, let alone the barricades.

parro a. paranoid *Time Radio FM.*

part brass rags v. to part on bad terms; fr. naval custom of two sailors when on good terms sharing their cleaning rags *Wodehouse:AAG.*

particulars n. (US prison use) any member of the authorities with immediate effect on a prisoner's life: a warder, the sentencing judge, the parole board, etc. *Klein.*

party n. any form of sex act, usu. provided by a prostitute *Legman.*

party v. 1. to enjoy oneself *Seale*; 2. (sex industry use) to have sex; often used in a prostitute's question, 'What kind of party would you like?; 3. to partake in an orgy.

party animal n. anyone notably devoted to going out and having a good time *PC World magazine 11/91.*

party girl n. a 'good-time girl'.

party hop v. to move from one party to the next and so on during the course of a single evening and night (cf: island hop) *Underwood.*

party pooper n. a spoilsport; one who sabotages the pleasures and enjoyments of their companions, whether at a party or other amusement *Whitcomb.*

pash n. a crush (qv); usu. between junior and senior pupils of girls' schools; fr. passionate *R. Boycott, 'A Nice Girl Like Me', 1984.*

pass v. 1. for a Jew to pretend to be a Christian *Bruce:2*; 2. for a homosexual to appear straight (qv) to those he/she encounters *Jay & Young.*

pass in one's dinner pail v. to die.

passion pit n. (lesbian use) the vagina *Maledicta.*

passion wagon any vehicle, often a van, in which teenage boys hope to seduce girls (cf: shagwagon).

passion-killers n. any female underwear deemed to reduce the chances of (male) exploration; orig. milit. use.

past it adv. over the hill, too old or worn out to be of use (cf: sell-by date).

past praying for utterly hopeless, usu. of a person, poss. of a broken down car.

paste n. semen.

paste v. to hit *Wright.*

pasting n. a violent assault, a beating up *Runyon:1.*

Pat Malone (rhyming sl.) alone (cf: Tod Sloan) *Humphries.*

pat one down v. to submit someone to a body search *Higgins:1.*

patacca n. fr. Ital.: worthless rubbish, spec. fake jewellery such as counterfeit Cartier watches, etc. *Powis.*

patch n. (orig. US) any form of insignia as worn by criminal or youth gangs, eg. the Hell's Angels or US prison gangs.

patch n. (UK police use) a policeman's area of operations (cf: manor) *'Parkin's Patch', TV series title, c.1975.*

patch v. (Can. prison use) to arrange for bribes to be paid, corrupt deals to be made, etc. (cf: fix) *Caron.*

patootie n. attractive young girl *Esq. 1977.*

patsy n. a fool, a sucker (qv); fr. the popular Irish name, Patrick and thus an example of racial cliché, in this case Irish stupidity *Variety 1983.*

Pattie n. a first-class degree; fr. rhy. sl. Pattie Hearst = first (cf: raging, richard).

pattin' leather (US Black use) a reference to being out of work *Folb.*

pavement princess n. (Citizens' Band radio use) prostitute *CB.*

paws n. hands *Hotten.*

pay one's dues v. to undergo (usually) undesirable experiences before one attains a given desirable

goal; the moral stance is unsaid
Bruce:1.

paybacks n. (US Black use) the
retaliation by one person for insults or
bad treatment from another; fr.
financial use *Klein*.

payday stakes n. (gambling use)
betting on credit, against the
guarantee of one's forthcoming wages
Seale.

pay-off n. **1.** a final payment for
services rendered; **2.** the denouement
of a book, film or play; **3.** one's
deserts.

pay-off queen n. (homosexual use)
anyone who regularly pays for his sex
Legman.

payola n. the practice (ostensibly
illegal and generally denied by its
practitioners) of bribing (with cash or
kind) those with access to the public to
tout a given product; esp. common in
the record business where disc jockeys
are offered massive inducements to
push a certain record or artist. Major
scandals in the US c.1959 supposedly
ended payola, but such optimism is
quite illusory and cosmetic at best (cf:
lurkola).

pc (UK 'society' use) (abbrev.)
postcard Barr; **2.** (medical use)
(abbrev.) Pinky Cheater = thin rubber
gloves used during gynaecological
examinations *Southern & Hoffenberg*;
3. (abbrev.) *politically correct*,
ideologically pure, etc. Esp. popular
among US Women's Movt, New Left,
etc. *Maledicta*.

PC (UK police/criminal use) (abbrev.)
Previous Conviction LL.

PDA (US preppie (qv) use) (acro.)
Public Display of Affection; kissing
and cuddling in public
Neaman & Silver.

pdq (abbrev.) *pretty damn quick*.

pea n. (Aus. use) the ideal, the perfect
choice, the favourite; fr. 19th C. UK
use *Wilkes*.

peace pills n. (US drug use) see: PCP.

peacemaker n. (US Black use) **1.** the
penis; **2.** a pistol or revolver (not only
Black use) *Klein*.

peach n. a pretty young girl *Klein*.

peachy a. wonderful, excellent,
delightful, etc. *Uris*.

peak v. **1.** to reach the limit of a
particular experience; **2.** (drug use)
the two hours or so in an LSD trip
when the hallucinogen is at its most
powerful.

peanut butter n. heroin; from the
brown treacly form that heroin takes
when heated preparatory to being
smoked.

peanut gallery n. **1.** spec. the top
gallery, the 'gods' in a theatre;
2. ignorant, vociferous spectators
Grogan; both meanings assume a large
consumption of peanuts by those so
defined.

peanuts n. anything insignificant,
petty; esp. money, wages *Schulberg:2*.

pearl diver n. a dish washer in a hotel
or restaurant *Chandler: Notebk*.

peas in the pot a. (rhyming sl.) hot
Cole.

peasouper n. a very dense fog; orig.
the pollution-based London fogs, but
since the Clean Air legislation of
1950s, any exceptionally impenetrable
fog.

peck n. **1.** (US Black use) food *Klein*;
2. see: peckerwood.

peck v. (US Black use) to eat *Klein*.

pecker n. penis *Selby:1*.

peckerwood n. (US Black use
(mainly)) white person (derog.) fr.
the red woodpecker, symbol of whites,
rather than the black crow, symbol of
blacks *Folb*.

peckham n. tie; fr. rhy. sl peckham
rye = tie.

pecking and necking n. (US Black
use) sexual foreplay, kissing and
cuddling *Klein*.

peckish a. hungry (cf: peck) *Hotten*.

pecks n. (drug and street gang use)
food *Salisbury*.

pedal one's dogs v. to leave, to go
away; esp. as an order 'pedal your
dogs!'; fr. dogs = feet (qv) *Goulart*.

peddle pussy v. to work as a
prostitute *Alvarez*.

pedigree chum n. a 'deb's delight', an

eligible young man; the pun is on the dog food of the same name.

pee v. to urinate; fr. abbrev./euph. for piss (qv) *Price:2*.

peek freak n. a homosexual voyeur who watches two other men during sex; fr. SE peek: to glance at, albeit briefly *Stanley*.

peel v. to strip off one's clothes *Klein*.

peel down v. see: peel.

peeler n. a policeman; this otherwise obsolete usage, which refers back to Sir Robert Peel, founder of the Metropolitan Police and used as such in Victorian England, is now found only in Northern Ireland.

peep n. a word; thus *not a peep*: saying nothing *Runyon:1*.

peep one's hole card v. (US Black use) to work out a person's hidden motives, ideas, opnions, etc. *Klein*.

pee-pee lover n. (homosexual use) one who prefers the youngest boys for sex; fr. childish *pee-pee*: penis *Legman*.

peeper n. **1.** a private investigator; with implications of voyeurism *Chandler:LG*. **2.** (abbrev.) Peeping Tom: a voyeur *Laurie*.

peepers n. eyes *Humphries*.

peer queer n. see: peek freak *Stanley*.

pee-wee n. nickname for any noticeably small person.

peg v. to recognize *Jay & Young*.

peg out v. to die *Wright*.

pegged off under surveillance: fr. peg (qv) *rr*.

pegged out dead; fr. cribbage use (cf: cash in one's chips, etc.) *Rawson*.

peg-house n. a male brothel; fr. East Indian equivalents where the boys allegedly sat on wooden pegs to maintain a well-distended anus *Legman*.

pelter n. a horse; esp. a fast one *Runyon:1*.

pen (abbrev.) penitentiary *Farrell*.

pen and ink v. (rhyming sl.) stink *Norman:2*.

pencil geek n. (US campus use) (derog.) anyone who works more devotedly than his/her peers see fit *Bernbach*.

pencil-pusher n. **1.** a clerk; a white-

collar worker *Selby:1*; **2.** a journalist 'Hill Street Blues', Thames TV, 1983.

pencil-squeezer n. masturbator *Dury*, 'Clever Bastards', 1978.

penitentiary agent n. (US cant) a lawyer who seems to be working more for the courts and police than for the defence of his client *Neaman & Silver*.

Penitentiary Despatcher n. (US criminal use) a Public Defender; fr. the supposed failing of these court-appointed lawyers whose caseload is often too heavy for them to put forward an adequate defence, and whose clients thus end up in the penitentiary. *Morgan*.

penman n. (UK criminal use) a forger *LL*.

penny-ante a. small-time, second-rate, insignificant; fr. poker use *Vidal*.

penocha n. (US Black/Sp. use) vagina *Folb*.

people n. (US Black use) narcotics agents *Major*.

pep-em-ups n. (drug use) amphetamine; thus *pep pills Folb*.

pepper and salt (US Black use) black and white people running together in the street *Klein*.

pepper 'em up v. (US Black use) **1.** to prepare for something; **2.** to get drunk or high (qv) on drugs; **3.** to work out in a gym; **4.** to fight and possibly injure one's assailant; all imply some preparatory seasoning *Klein*.

pepper gut n. (derog.) a Mexican-American. (fr. the chili pepper, a main constituent of Mexican cooking).

pepper-kissing a. negative intensifier, thus no good, useless, etc. *Folb*.

peppy a. cheerful, enthusiastic.

perch n. (US campus (spec. University of Arkansas) use) a pint of liquor *Underwood*.

percher n. (UK criminal/police use) **1.** a gullible victim for a swindle or con-game; **2.** a simple arrest *Powis*.

percy n. the penis *Humphries*.

perfecto! (excl.) wonderful, excellent, perfect 'Hill Street Blues', Thames TV, 1983.

perform v. (UK criminal use) to commit a given crime *LL*.

perishing a. general intensifier: *perishing cold*, *perishing hard*, etc. *Green:2*.

perk-up v. to improve, to cheer up.

perky a. jolly, cheerful.

perp n. (US police use) (abbrev.) perpetrator; the accused criminal *Neaman & Silver*.

persuader n. a weapon, usu. pistol or revolver, which persuades victims to its wielder's point of view *Klein*.

perv n. (abbrev.) pervert, spec. child-molester.

perv about v. to search for potential sexual conquests; the use of perv here is facetious rather than an actual reference to any sexual eccentricity.

pete-man n. (Can. prison use) safebreaker (Cf: peter 2) *Caron*.

peter n. **1.** the penis *Jay & Young*; **2.** safe; **3.** cell *Cole*.

peter eater n. fellator, fellatrix (cf: eat, peter l.).

peter puffer n. one who performs oral sex.

Peter-Jay n. (US Black use) the police *Folb*.

peter-man n. safecracker.

Petricelli n. (US Black use) a high fashion suit, fr. brand-name of tailors *Klein*.

petrified a. very drunk; fr. sense of being turned to stone rather than that of fear *Neaman & Silver*.

petrols n. (Aus. rhyming sl.) petrol bowsers = trousers *Humphries*.

pg (drug use) (abbrev.) paragoric; a cough medicine based on opium linctus which heroin addicts use when no stronger drugs are available *Burroughs:1*.

PH (drug use) (acro.) *P*urple *H*earts: amphetamine pills (cf: blues) *Keyes*.

pheasant plucker n. reverse of 'pleasant fucker', and always used ironically to attack the person so named *Dury*.

phiz n. face; fr. physiognomy *Algren*.

phlegm-cutter n. the first drink of the day, usu. that taken by an alcoholic soon after waking up (cf: eye-opener) *Higgins:5*.

Phoebe n. (gambling use) the point of five in craps dice *Algen*.

phone freak n. (pimp use) a client who arranges to phone up a prostitute and listen while she runs through a pornographic monologue and he masturbates *OUI 8/75*.

phoney n. (homosexual use) a mean or cheap client for a gay prostitute *Legman*.

phonus balonus a. rubbish, nonsense (cf: baloney) *Runyon:1*.

photo finish n. (rhyming sl.) (a pint of) Guinness (stout) *Cole*.

physics for poets (US campus use) course in basic physics for arts specialists *Birnbach*.

pi a. (abbrev.) pious, always in a derog. sense of self-righteous, unctuous, poss. hypocritical.

piano n. (US Black use) spare ribs; fr. resemblance to keys *Major*.

piccolo and flute n. (rhyming sl.) suit (cf: whistle and flute) *Jones:J*.

pick n. (cant) (abbrev.) pickpocket *Neaman & Silver*.

pick a bone with v. to argue with *Klein*.

pick man n. (Can. prison use) one who picks locks *Caron*.

pick up v. **1.** to accost for possible sex *Legman*; **2.** (drug use) to use narcotics *Burroughs:1*.

pick up fag-ends v. to listen in to other people's conversations and attempt to comment upon them or join in; often as in juv. admonition 'don't pick up fag-ends'.

pick up the soap for v. to permit oneself to be sodomized; from the posture necessarily adopted for both activities *Legman*.

pick up the tab v. **1.** to pay a bill, usu. in a restaurant; the implication is one of treating one's fellow eaters *Wodehouse: PGM*; thus **2.** to take responsibility, to accept the consequences.

pickaninny n.(derog.) Black, Negro; spec. a black child *Dunne*.

picking up the vibrations (homosexual use) watching other men perform a sex show; all-male voyeurism; fr. hippie use, when pleasures were more cerebral *Legman*.

pickled a. drunk (cf: stewed) *Dickson*.

pick-me-up n. any form of drink that relieves the physical and mental state of the imbiber; esp. used for those concoctions advertised as curing hangovers *Wodehouse:MOJ*.

pick-up n. a casual sex partner, met and seduced without previous introduction.

picnic n. 1. (UK use) any simple, pleasurable experience; 2. (Aus. use) an unpleasant, tricky experience, fr. ironic use of 1; 3. thus (both UK/Aus.) *no picnic*: an understated description of an unpleasant experience.

piddle v. to urinate.

piddle around v. to mess about, to waste time (cf: piss around) *Thompson:J*.

piddling a. small, insignificant, irrelevant *Bukowski:2*.

pie a. easy, simple; usu. in *easy as pie* *Wodehouse:PGM*.

pie n. (US campus use) an attractive, sexually desirable female (cf: cookie, pancake, etc.) *Underwood*.

pie in the sky n. fantasies, fond hopes and illusions; fr. Joe Hill (hero of the 'Wobblies'; the Industrial Workers of the World, prototype US union) song 'The Preacher and the Slave' with its ironical line 'There'll be pie in the sky when you die'.

piece n. (drug use) 1. a quantity of heroin, approx. 1 oz *Larner*; 2. a quantity of cocaine, approx. 1 oz. *Milner*; 3. (abbrev.) piece of ass (qv); 4. a gun, thus; 5. the penis.

piece of ass n. a woman, girl; not derog. but dismissive *Green, 'Book of Rock Quotes', 1977*.

piece of cake n. simple, easily achieved, no bother (cf: easy as pie) *McFadden*.

piece of piss supremely easy.

piece of the action n. share of proceeds, esp. of a robbery *Higgins:1*.

piece off v. to bribe, to pay off; to give out a 'piece' of cash *Goldman*.

pieces n. (US Black use) clothes (cf: leather piece) *Folb*.

pie-eater n. (Aus. prison use) small time criminal (cf: cruncher) *Neaman & Silver*.

pie-eyed a. drunk *Neaman & Silver*.

pig n. 1. (US horse-racing use) a slow or otherwise useless horse, not to be betted on *Bukowski:1*; 2. (US campus use) a female considered to be promiscuous and sexually available *Underwood*; 3. the police; despite 1960s radical obsession with this use, it existed at least as early as 1815; 4. any straight (qv) person, member of the Establishment or authorities *Tuff Shit Comics*.

pig brother n. (US Black use) (derog.) any Black who informs against his own people to the (white) police *Folb*.

pig hash n. see: pigswill.

pig heaven n. 1. (US Black use) a police station *Folb*; 2. a fantasy paradise that would delight the gross rather than the fastidious.

pig it v. to live in squalor, albeit unworried by that squalor.

pig out v. to overeat massively (cf: mac out) *Price:3*.

pig sty n. a police station (cf: pig heaven) *Cole*.

pig style (US Black use) living in filthy circumstances *Klein*.

pigeon n. 1. (abbrev.) stool pigeon (qv) *Burroughs:1*; 2. (criminal use) a sucker, a victim, a mark (qv) the opposite of rook (qv).

pigger n. (US Black use) a very fat female *Folb*.

pigging a. intensifier; euph. for fucking (qv) *Austin*.

pighead n. a stubborn, uncompromising person *Safire*.

pig-ignorant a. extremely stupid.

pig-mouth n. see: pigger *Folb*.

pigs! general excl. of disgust, contempt, negation, etc.

pig's ear n. 1. a mess, chaos, usu. *make a pig's ear of. . .*; 2. (rhyming sl.) beer *Powis*.

pigshit n. nonsense, rubbish; synonym for bullshit (qv).

pig-sticker n. any form of stabbing weapon (cf: toad-sticker).

pigswill n. 1. nonsense, rubbish; thus excl. 2. pigswill!: rubbish! (cf: hogwash, pig hash).

piker n. a mean, grasping person; one who will not take the least risk, esp. to help others *Chandler:LG*.

pikey a. vagrant; fr. orig. piker: a tramp who walked the turnpikes *Dury*.

pile n. a large sum of money, a fortune; esp. in 'I've made my pile. . .' etc. (cf: bundle, packet).

pile v. (US Black use) to have sexual intercourse *Folb*.

pile up some Zs v. (US teen. use) to get some sleep (cf: cop some Zs) *Sculatti*.

pile-up n. a car crash, esp. one involving a number of vehicles.

pill n. an unpleasant person, a weakling, a bore *rr*.

pill out (hot rod use) to accelerate sharply from a standing start and thus leave traces of rubber tyres on the tarmac *'American Graffitti', directed by G. Lucas*.

pill popper n. a regular user of any drugs in pill form – barbiturates, amphetamines, etc. *Jay & Young*.

pilled up a. under the influence of amphetamines or barbiturates *Mandelkau*.

pillhead n. a regular user of amphetamine or barbiturate drugs.

pills n. testicles; fr. pill = ball = testicle *Humphries*.

pimp a. (US Black use) stylish, expensive; fr. the enviable status of the pimp in Black street culture *Folb*.

pimp crazy a. (Black pimp use) a prostitute who goes from one sadistic, abusing pimp to another, apparently unable to break the habit *Milner*.

pimp dust n. (US Black use) cocaine; an expensive status symbol, to be used without regard to cost *Folb*.

pimp fronts n. (US Black use) particular style of dress associated with pimps) *Folb*.

pimp post n. aka: *pimp rest*: the armrest between driver and passenger in a car *Folb*.

pimp ride n. (US Black use) an expensive car, thus suitable for a pimp *Folb*.

pimp shades n. aka: *pimp tints*: style of dark glasses affected by pimps *Folb*.

pimp socks n. (US Black use) ultra-thin nylon socks, usu. with pattern of vertical stripes *Seale*.

pimp stick n. (Black pimp use) two wire coat hangers twisted together to make an improvised and vicious whip *Milner*.

pimp stride n. (US Black use) style of walking, associated with pimps, in which the subject rolls fr. side to side *Folb*.

pimped down a. (Black use) dressed in one's finest clothes, groomed to perfection *Milner*.

pimple n. the head *Runyon*.

pimple and blotch n. (rhyming sl.) Scotch (whisky) *Jones:J*.

pimpmobile n. a flashy, ostentatious car, potentially the choice of a pimp, but not restricted to such drivers (cf: spivmobile, pimp ride).

pimp's arrest n. when a pimp, who has to maintain a running bail bond for each prostitute he runs, has his girl arrested deliberately in order to retrieve that money; often occurs when the ho (qv) decides she wants a new pimp *Milner*.

pimpsy a. (UK 'society' use) far too easy, utterly simple *Barr*.

pin v. to mark down visually, to notice *Goldman*.

pin money n. small sums of money allotted to a woman for house-keeping; sometimes the money earnt by a woman at a part-time job.

pin on v. to accuse, to lay the blame on someone; fr. SE: to attach *rr*.

pin one's ears back v. to defeat, to punish – verbally or physically.

pin position n. (taxi-driver use) the first cab in a rank *Powis*.

pinch n. 1. an arrest *rr*; 2. (drug use) a

small amount of marijuana, enough
for perhaps two cigarettes *Folb*.

pinch v. to arrest; a police use that
took up the orig. meaning: to steal
Wodehouse: AAG; **2.** to steal; since
18th C.

pinch-hit v. to act as substitute, esp. in
an emergency; fr. baseball use
NYRB 29/9/83.

pineapple n. a bomb; a grenade; fr.
shape *Runyon*.

pineapple princess n. (gay use) an
Hawaiian person.

pineapple queen n. (gay use) an
Hawaiian person.

pinhead n. a stupid person *Safire*.

pin-jabber n. any drug user who
injects his preferred drug *Chandler:
Notebk*.

pink a. homosexual; used as such in
pre-Gay Liberation days (cf:
lavender).

pink n. (US Black use) a white person;
fr. real 'white' skin tone *Folb*.

pink elephants n. the supposed
fantasy creatures that traditionally
appear to those in the throes of
delirium tremens.

pink eye n. the vagina.

pink lady n. (drug use) Darvon
(propoxyphene); fr. colour of drug
Folb.

pink whoogie n. (derog.) a White
person (cf: pink).

pinkie n. a very light coloured Black
person *BvdB*.

pinko n. a Communist sympathizer
(cf: red) *Junker*.

pinktea n. (homosexual use) an
upper-class homosexual who stands
aloof from the pleasures and problems
of less insulated peers *Selby: 1*.

pinktoes n. (US Black use) a Black
man's white girl-friend *Major*.

pinky n. (lesbian use) a passive lesbian
(cf: femme) *Maledicta*.

pinned eyes in which the pupils are
reduced, irrespective of the light
available, to pinpricks; the basic sign
of a heroin addict *Grogan*.

pinner, pinroll n. (drug use) a very
small marijuana cigarette.

PINS (US prison use) (acro.) *Persons
In Need of Supervision* (cf: CHINS,
MINS) *Neaman & Silver*.

pins n. legs (rarely in singular) *Wright*.

pipe n. **1.** the penis (cf: lay some pipe);
2. a pipe used for smoking crack (qv).
Shell.

pipe down! (excl.) be quiet, shut up!
fr. nautical use *Gothic Blimp
Works no. 5*.

pipe (it) v. to smoke crack (qv)
cocaine.

pipe-man n. a crack (qv) seller *Shell*.

piping vbl. n. consuming crack (qv)
cocaine, which is smoked through a
pipe. *Shell*.

pipped a. beaten; (abbrev.) pipped to
the post *Wodehouse: Ukridge, 1924*.

-pipper n. (milit. use) *one-pipper*:
second lieutenant; *two-pipper*: first
lieut; fr. 'pips' that denote their rank
on uniforms.

pippin n. a perfect example of
whatever is under discussion; usu. *it's
a pippin*; fr. the name of an apple
Wodehouse: PGM.

pipsqueak n. an insignificant person
Wodehouse: JM.

pirates n. (UK police use) motorized
traffic police *Powis*.

piss v. to urinate; fr. Middle English
usage.

piss and vinegar energy, enthusiasm,
cheekiness *Uris*.

piss flaps n. the labia *Cole*.

piss around v. to waste time, to mess
about (cf: piddle around).

piss artist n. a regular drunk
Humphries.

piss away v. to waste *Bukowski: 7*.

piss blood v. to worry excessively, to
make a great fuss *Higgins: 1*.

piss broken glass v. to have venereal
disease, esp. gonorrhoea; one of the
first symptoms is pain during urination
Powis.

piss elegant a. pretentious,
ostentatious, self-obsessed male
homosexual *Stanley*.

piss in one's pocket v. to curry
favour, to be extremely close to
someone, to ingratiate oneself

Humphries: 2.

piss it v. to succeed with no difficulty whatsoever; to win very easily; often used of racehorses, greyhounds and similar sports *Barr*.

piss off v. **1.** to annoy; **2.** to leave *Newman: 1*.

piss on one's parade v. shatter illusions, ruin an otherwise satisfactory situation *Price: 2*.

piss one's pants v. to be utterly terrified *Higgins: 1*.

piss oneself v. to laugh uproariously.

piss or get off the pot see: shit or get off the pot *Uris*.

piss test n. (drug use) urine analysis, carried out to check for drug use.

piss-cutter n. generally obnoxious person *Uris*.

pissed a. **1.** (US use) annoyed; **2.** (UK use) drunk *Price: 2*.

pissed as a fart a. very drunk.

pissed as a newt a. very drunk.

pissed off a. furious, very annoyed *Seale*.

pissed to the ears a. extremely drunk *Bruce: 2*.

pissed up a. very drunk *Barr*.

pisser n. **1.** (US pro football use) a particularly rough tackler *Jenkins*; **2.** (general use) a tough, purposeful person *Schulberg*; **3.** hilariously funny (cf: piss oneself) *Selby: 1*.

pisshole n. **1.** spec. urinal, lavatory; **2.** any house, room or place that could be described as **1** *Performance*.

pisspoor very poor, both financially and qualitatively *Major*.

pisspot n. drunkard *Higgins: 4*.

piss-proud an early morning erection, more indicative of the need to urinate than of lust *'Minder', Thames TV, 1980*.

piss-take v. to tease.

piss-up n. a drunken party (cf: beer-up) *Keyes*.

pissy-ass n. insignificant, useless *Higgins: 3*.

pistol n. the penis (cf: gun, rod, piece, etc.).

pit n. **1.** a real mess, esp. a room that is so disordered *Underwood*; **2.** bed

Powis.

pit city n. a wretched, depressing situation (cf: —city; pits).

pit stop v. (skiing use) **1.** to stop drinking to visit the lavatory; **2.** to stop what one is doing to take a drink. *Barr*.

PITA n. (acro.) *Pain Iin The Arse* (qv).

pitch n. **1.** (US campus use) an unattractive, unpleasant, if promiscuous female; fr. pig + bitch *Underwood*; **2.** see: angle *Himes: 2*; **3.** prostitute's territory; **4.** area used by a three-card monte team; **5.** the line (qv) used by a swindler or a legitimate salesman *Powis*.

pitch a bitch v. (US Black use) to complain, to fight, to cause a disturbance *Major*.

pitch and toss n. (rhyming sl.) the boss *Jones: J*.

pitch fly n. someone who takes over another's street-selling position without permission *Powis*.

pitcher n. (US Black use) the male partner in heterosexual intercourse, the dominant partner in male homosexual intercourse; fr. baseball use *Klein*.

pitching and catching n. (sex industry use) the two opposed and complementary sides of any form of physical sex, esp. in S&M (qv) or coprophilia *Morgan*.

pits n. **1.** the depths of despair; a situation, object or person who is totally undesirable *Jay & Young*; **2.** (US campus use) body odour; fr. armpits *Underwood*.

Pitt Street farmer n. (Aus. use) aka *Collins Street farmer*: a businessman (Pitt Street, Sydney; Collins Street, Melbourne are the respective financial centres) who owns or shares a farm from which he takes annual profits but rarely visits *Wilkes*.

pitty a. (US campus use) messy, untidy, disgusting; fr. pit (qv) *Underwood*.

pixie n. a homosexual man; a synonym for fairy (qv) *Legman*.

pixillated a. drunk *Dickson*.

pizzazz n. style, glamour *Higgins: 5*.

pjs n. pyjamas.

placer n. middle-man who places stolen goods with safe purchaser (cf: fence) *Newman: 1*.

plain n. (Irish use) Guinness stout; the basic Irish drink *T 25/7/83*.

plain sailing simple, straightforward, easy *Wodehouse: GB*.

plank v. to have sexual intercourse; fr. 19th C.use: to lay down (cf: lay) *Wolfe: 3*.

plant n. (US police use) see: stakeout *McBain: 1*.

plant v. to bury a body *Dunne*.

plant v. 1. to hide *Burroughs: 1*; 2. (police/criminal use) for the police to hide evidence in the clothes, home or car of a suspected person in order to ensure they have something with which to charge their victim *PT*.

plaster v. 1. to hit (cf: paste); (US Black use) 2. to flatter; 3. to shoot someone *Klein*.

plastered a. drunk *Mandelkau*.

plastic a. synthetic, false, phoney *F. Zappa, LP, 1966*.

plastic job n. plastic surgery *Chandler: LG*.

plate v. to fellate; fr. rhyming sl. plate of ham = gam (qv) *J. Fabian & J. Byrne, 'Groupie', 1969*.

plates n. (rhyming sl.) plates of meat = feet *May*.

play n. (US Black use) any form of action *Klein*.

play v. to bet on; thus *play the horses*, *play the dogs Higgins: 1*.

play around v. to have a number of affairs, lovers, entanglements.

play ball v. to co-operate; fr. 'playing a game' with *Higgins: 2*.

play checkers v. (homosexual use) to move from seat to seat in a cinema in search of a receptive sex partner (US checkers = UK draughts) *Legman*.

play chicken v. 1. aka:*play chick*: to keep a lookout *Selby: 1*; 2. (US Black use) to intrude on another (man's) sexual advances *Folb*.

play chopsticks v. (homosexual use) mutual masturbation *Legman*.

play fathers and mothers v. to have sexual intercourse; the adult version of children's sex games, the main alternative one being *playing doctors and nurses*.

play footsie v. to nudge someone's foot with yours – out of sight of companions – as a possible prelude to further intimacy; thus to indulge in the cautious sounding out of any relationship – economic, political, etc. *Humphries*.

play funny buggers v. see: play silly buggers *Bleasdale*.

play gooseberry v. (teen. use) for an unwanted third party to hang around a couple who would prefer to be left alone; abbrev. of gooseberry fool *Waterhouse*.

play hard to get v. for a girl (usu.) to resist sexual advances, though not necessarily to reject them altogether.

play hardball v. to act ruthlessly and single-mindedly in pursuit of a goal; fr. baseball use *Vidal*.

play hookey n. to truant from school (cf: bunk off) *Larner*.

play hoop-snake with v. (homosexual use) mutual fellation; homosexual soixante-neuf *Legman*.

play it cool v. to act disinterestedly; to control every emotion.

play night baseball v. to have sexual intercourse *Neaman & Silver*.

play on Front Street v. to act openly, to abandon any pretences *Morgan*.

play one too close v. (US Black use) to involve oneself too intimately and without invitation, in another person's life *Klein*.

play one's cards right v. to behave sensibly: to act in one's best interests *Higgins: 3*.

play past v. (US black use) to circumvent obstacles. mental as well as physical *Milner*.

play pocket billiards v. to play with one's genitals through a trouser pocket.

play possum v. to pretend to be dead; fr. the animal.

play ring a rosie v. (US use) to fool

about, to make great effort with no result; fr. the children's game 'The Stone Killer', film, 1973.

play second fiddle v. to take a secondary, subsidiary role; fr. orchestra use.

play silly buggers v. to act uncooperatively; to mess around, to cause a deliberate nuisance.

play stuff v. (US Black use) to deceive by a smart line of verbal patter Klein.

play the chill v. to ignore, to avoid, to act coldly towards Runyon.

play the con v. pretend, attempt to swindle or deceive rr.

play the dozens v. (US Black use) to compete in ritualized mutual insults (cf: dirty dozens) Jones.

play the duck v. to avoid; fr. duck out (qv) Runyon.

play the field v. to enjoy a variety of lovers; fr. horserace betting: spreading one's money around several horses instead of concentrating on one Jay & Young.

play the heel v. to act unpleasantly, to be mean, cruel rr.

play the hop v. to play truant from school (cf: hop the wag) Cole.

play the nut role v. to pose as a shambling incompetent in order to swindle or otherwise trick a possible victim Klein.

play the sober Indian v. to resist joining in a drinking session.

play the Tom v. see: Tom, Uncle Tom Folb.

play the whale v. (Aus use) to vomit Humphries.

play with 44 cards to the deck v. to be mentally deficient, to be stupid; one of several phrases implying one is 'not all there' Higgins:4.

play with oneself v. to masturbate Joe Jackson, 'I'm the Man'.

play-away n. (UK 'society' use) a weekend staying in the country; poss. fr, sporting imagery Barr.

played out a. exhausted, finished, worn out; fr. gambling use: all one's chips/cash have been lost.

player n. (Black use) 1. a man who

uses his wits and charm to obtain money and other favours from wealthy white women Ice T:2; 2. a pimp Shulman; 3. anyone who uses intelligence, wit, brains to gain objectives, incl. businessmen, politicians, etc. as well as criminals Milner.

playing out of the pocket (US Black use) 1. to be cheated or tricked ; 2. to let something happen without noticing it Klein.

playing too close 1. (US prison use) becoming over-familiar and invading the privacy of a fellow inmate Klein; 2. to tease or intimidate.

plead v. (police/criminal use) to plead guilty; never innocent Laurie.

plead the fifth v. to avoid committing oneself, to refuse to take an action or make a statement; fr. criminal habit of using the Fifth Amendment to the US Constitution (no one is obliged to give testimony that will incriminate themself) to avoid prosecution.

pleasure and pain n. (rhyming sl.) rain Jones: J.

plex v. to show disrespect, to slander (cf: diss) T 8/4/91.

plonk n. cheap or second rate wine. the brand-name 'Plonque' was merchandized in the early 1970s; it lived up to its name Mortimer.

plonk v. 1. to copulate (cf: plank); 2. to put down.

plonker n. the penis, thus a general term of abuse (cf: dickhood, dork); the term gained enormous popularity with the BBC-TV series 'Only Fools and Horses'.

plot n. the place where three-card monte (qv) teams operate: the street, an alley or doorway, a deserted lot, etc. Powis.

plot up v. (UK police use) to study a criminal's personality, habits, technique and associates prior to making an arrest Laurie.

plot up v. (UK cant) for a gang or group to seek out and establish territory in a given place– soccer stadium, club, crowded place, etc; fr.

plot of land *Cole*.

plow v. (US use) to have sexual intercourse *Bruce: 2*. (cf: till)

plow the back forty v. (US use) to have sexual intercourse; fr. plow (qv) plus agricultural imagery *King*.

PLU (UK 'society' use) (acro.) *People Like U*s (cf: NQOCD).

pluck n. (US Black use) **1.** wine; fr. grapes that are plucked or pluck = courage; **2.** an attractive female *Folb*.

pluck v. (US Black use) to choose one's woman *Klein*.

plucked (US Black use) sexually satiated; euph. for fucked (?) *Folb*.

plug v. **1.** (homosexual use) to perform anal intercourse *Legman*; **2.** to shoot *Laugh in the Dark*; **3.** to hit, usu. with the fist *Wodehouse: AAG*; **4.** to perform sexual intercourse, usu. male use *Underwood*.

plugged in abreast of the times, fashionable, *au courant Safire*.

plugugly n. a thug, a hoodlum *Wodehouse: EBC*.

pluke n. a spot, pimple, boil *Welsh:1* (fr. Sc. dial: plook, pluke: a pimple, a spot).

plumb n. a very serious error *Major*.

plumber n. (US Black use) a man with a frequent and varied sex life *Folb*.

plums n. testicles.

plunk v. **1.** to pluck the strings of guitar; **2.** to place, usu. *plunk down* (cf: plonk).

po n. the lavatory; fr. chamber-pot, and Fr. pron. pf *pot de chambre*.

pocket pool n. playing with one's genitals through a trouser pocket *Junker*.

pocket roll n. (US Black use) a roll of paper money kept in the pocket *Klein*.

POed (US teen. use) pissed off (qv) *Pond*.

poet's day n. Friday; fr. acro: *p*iss *o*ff *e*arly, *t*omorrow's *S*aturday *Cole*.

po-faced a. arrogant, stand-offish, humourless.

poggler see: pogue **1**. *Powis*.

pogue n. **1.** (UK criminal use) purse, wallet *Powis*; **2.**(homosexual use) a

young boy; thus USMC use *poguey bait*: sweets *Legman*.

poindexter n. (Valley Girls (qv) us) an intellectual, bookish person; fr. pointy-head (qv) *Pond*.

point n. (drug use) a hypodermic syringe *Folb*.

point n. a bouncer or anyone standing guard; fr. the milit use, meaning the man walking at the head of a patrol.

point percy at the porcelain v. to urinate *Humphries*.

points n. single units of percentage *Higgins: 3*.

pointy-head a. (derog.) intellectual, cultured *Jones*.

poison n. an unpleasant person, best to be avoided *Klein*.

poisoned a. (US Black use) pregnant *Klein*.

poke n. a wallet; fr. Fr. *poche*: pocket *Burroughs: 1*.

poke v. to have sexual intercourse *R. Newman, 'Trouble in Paradise', 1983*.

poke along v. to walk slowly *Klein*.

poke one's mouth off v. (US Black use) to lose one's temper *Klein*.

poker n. (US criminal use) a single-barrelled shotgun *Klein*.

pokey n. gaol, usu. small, local; fr. pokey condition or fr. Fr. *poche*: pocket, and thus sense of 'putting away' (?) *Runyon*.

pol. n. **1.** (UK prison use) fr. Polly Parrot: a talkative person, a chatterer or gossip *LL*; **2.** (US use) (abbrev.) politician.

Polack n. **1.** (derog.) a Pole *Bruce: 2*; **2.** (Jewish use) a Jew whose family come from Poland (cf: Litvak).

Polack Town n. (US use) the Polish community within an urban area (cf: Jew town, nigger town, wop town).

pole n. the penis *Folb*.

pole v. to perform sexual intercourse; usu. male use *Underwood*.

pole hole n. the vagina *Folb*.

pole pleaser n. (derog.) a homosexual male.

polecat n. (US Black use) a dirty, untrustworthy woman *Klein*.

policy n. (US criminal use) the numbers (qv) racket.

Polish airlines n. (gay use) walking (cf: Italian airlines, Jewish airlines).

Polish handball n. (gay use) dried nasal mucus.

polish one's sword v. to masturbate (cf: polish the knob).

polish the apple v. (UK prison use) to curry favour, to act the sycophant; see apple-polisher *LL*.

polish the knob v. to perform oral sex.

polish the old German helmet v. to perform oral sex.

politician n. 1. a flatterer, a clever talker; 2. (US prison use) anyone who gains good jobs and maximum privileges *Neaman & Silver*; both uses take a dim view of the SE use.

politico n anyone involved in politics, both conventional and 'alternative' activists *Hoffman: a*.

polluted a. extremely drunk; fr. the state of one's bloodstream (?) *Bernbach*.

polone n. (theatrical use) female; one of the few surviving examples of *parlyaree*, the 19th C. showmans', costers' and actors' slang, based mainly on corruption of Italian (cf: omee).

poly bag n. (abbrev.) polythene bag, usu. the carrier bags available in shops and supermarkets *Wilkinson*.

pom (abbrev.) pommy, pommie (qv) *Humphries*.

pommy n. (Aus. use) aka: *pommie*: English person; fr. abbrev. of pomegranate, punning on immigrant *Humphries*.

Pompey n. (RN use) Portsmouth; also general use, as in Pompey Royal, a Hampshire-brewed beer (cf: Guz).

Pompey whore (bingo rhyming sl.) 24 *Franklyn*.

pom-pom n. (US criminal use) a pump-action shotgun; fr. the naval armament *Klein*.

ponce n. 1. spec. one who lives off the earnings of one or more prostitutes; 2. derog. epithet for any given male;

NB: many 'ponce' usages and combinations show the very different status of such a man in the UK compared with the US pimp (qv) *Norman: 2*.

ponce around v. to wander aimlessly, live as a good-for-nothing.

ponce off v. 1. to live off immoral earnings; 2. to scrounge (money) from someone *Norman: 2*.

ponce up v. to ornament (an object), to dress up (a person); both meanings implying some ostentation and flashiness.

poncy a. affected, ostentatiously 'artistic', poss. homosexual; there is no actual link in this use to a pimp or procurer *Barr*.

pong n. smell; usu. reserved for use in mass market children's comics or by 'society' speakers who retain much juvenile vocabulary from school (cf: bate, etc.) *Barr*.

pongo n. (New Zealand use) (derog.) British person: developed fr. 19th C. use: a monkey, thence a marine, a soldier.

pontoon n. (UK prison use) 21 month sentence; fr. card use *EN 12/11/57*.

pony n. 1. £25 *Payne*; 2. (rhyming sl.) pony and trap = crap = excretion *Newman: 3*.

pony in white n. (UK criminal use) £1.25 in silver coins *LL*.

pony up v. to pay one's debts, one's dues *Higgins: 4*.

poo n. 1. (US preppie (qv) use) (abbrev.) shampoo = champagne *Bernbach*; 2. exrement, usu. children's use only. fr. excl. announcing an unpleasant smell *Lucien Green*.

pooch n. 1. dog *Capital Radio 1983*; 2. (gambling use) a loser; fr. pooch = dog = abbrev. underdog *Alvarez*.

poodle n. (US Black use) a sexy or classy female (cf: fox) *Klein*.

poof n. homosexual (cf: poove) fr. 'camp' cries of 'pooh!' or 'poof!' *Performance*.

poof v. (US campus use) to kiss *Underwood*.

poof about v. to act in an

ostentatiously homosexual manner.

poofta n. see: poofter *Robins:1*.

poofter n. homosexual male (cf: poof)
Le Carré.

poon n. **1.** (Aus. use) simpleton, fool,
useless person (cf: nong) *Wilkes*;
2. (abbrev.) poontang (qv).

pooned up a. (Aus. use) flashily
dressed, usu. of youths looking to pick
up girls; poss. fr. US use of poon (qv)
Wilkes.

poontang n. vagina, thus a nubile girl;
fr. *putain* = whore (Fr.) *Junker*.

poop n. **1.** rubbish, tripe, nonsense
Uneeda Comix; **2.** news, information,
gossip, often as *hot poop*: fresh
information, etc.; **3.** excrement; **4.** the
buttocks; *Neaman & Silver*.

poop-butt n. (Black use) **1.** a lazy
person (cf: drag-ass); **2.** a young,
immature person *Milner*.

poop-chute n. the anus *Klein*.

pooped a. exhausted, tired out
Farrell.

pooper n. penis *May*.

pooper-scooper n. a small scoop used
by the cleanliness-minded for
removing traces of their dog's excreta
(poop, qv) from urban pavements
Capital Radio 1983.

poophead n. (US campus use) a fool,
a dullard *Underwood*.

poopie-plops n. (juv. use) excrement
Neaman & Silver.

poor-mouth v. to belittle *Price: 2*.

pootbutt n. see: poopbutt *Folb*.

poove n. homosexual (cf: poof)
Private Eye: passim.

poozle n. vagina *Big Ass Comics 1*.

pop n. **1.** (horseriding use) a horse's
jumping ability *Barr*; **2.** aka: *pops*;
father; fr. papa *LL*; **3.** (juv. use) a
fizzy drink; **4.** champagne; fr. the
uncorking process.

pop v. **1.** to feel elated, extremely
pleased, enthusiastic *Price: 2*; **2.** spec.
to inject a drug; thus *skin pop*: to
inject under the skin rather than into a
vein; **3.** to hit; **4.** to swallow pills
Selby: 1; **5.** (US campus use) to take
amphetamines specifically for staying
up and working all night *Underwood*;

6. to pawn; thus *popshop*:
pawnbrokers; **7.** to arrest *Guardian
6/6/87*.

pop corn n. anyone with a legitimate
job, rather than a criminal or a hustler
(qv) *Burroughs: 1*.

pop junk v. (US use) to gossip *T
8/4/91*.

pop off v. **1.** to exit, to vanish; **2.** to die
Runyon.

pop one's clogs v. to die; also pop
one's nuts, pop one's rocks.

pop one's cork v. **1.** to surrender
sexually; to come to orgasm *Shirley
Bassey, 'Big Spender', 1967*; **2.** to lose
one's temper, to lose patience.

pop one's nuts v. to achieve male
orgasm; also used transitively: to give
an orgasm *Morgan*.

pop shit v. to boast, to talk nonsense.

popcorn a. (Black use) lightweight,
second string, unintelligent (cf:
peanuts) *Milner*.

popcorn pimp n. (US Black use) a
small-time, ineffectual pimp; a man
who claims to be, but is not a pimp
Shulman.

popeyed a. drunk *Dickson*.

popped a. arrested *Larner*.

poppers n. (drug use) amyl nitrate (cf:
poppers); fr. the necessity to break
open the ampoule that contains the
drug.

poppy n. money *Powis*.

poppycock n. nonsense, rubbish;
orig. euph. for excreta *Rawson*.

popsy n. a female, usu. young and
attractive *Wodehouse: MOJ*.

porch monkey n. (derog.) a Black
person.

pork n. a fool *Price: 1*.

pork v. to have sexual intercourse, fr.
male point of view (cf: pork sword)
Higgins: 4.

pork sword n. the penis (cf: mutton
dagger, beef bayonet).

porker n. (derog.) a Jew. (fr. the
Jewish laws of *kashrut* which forbid
the consumption of pig's flesh).

porky n. (rhyming sl.) pork pie = a lie
D. Leitch.

porridge n. imprisonment: fr. the

staple morning diet of such establishments in the UK *Norman: 2*.

Porsche n. (US Black use) a female whose body, like the car, is small, rounded and compact *Folb*.

posh a. smart, pertaining to the upper classes; 'of obscure origin' (*OED Supp. O–Scz* 1982, which rejects traditional 'port out starboard home' derivation) *McBain: 1*.

posse n. v. a teenage gang; from the old Western term; also found as a verb, eg. 'posse down', meaning to move as a gang.

possesh n. possession: a homosexual boy who is used for sex by the tramp he accompanies *Legman*.

post a flyer v. (gay use) to advertise one's sexual availability *Maledicta 9*.

—pot sfx. a person; usu. found in combs. eg. barmpot, big pot, crankpot, fusspot, sexpot.

pot n. **1**. (abbrev.) pot belly: an enlarged stomach, usu. developed through excessive drinking; fr. pots of ale (cf: beer gut) *Humphries: 1*; **2**. marijunana, hashish. fr. Sp: *potaguaya Higgins: 2*.

pot and pan n. (rhyming sl.) old man *Wright*.

potato n. (Aus. rhyming sl.) potato peeler = sheila = woman, girl-friend *Humphries*.

potato jack n. illicit liquor, distilled in US prisons *Higgins: 1*.

potatoes n. money *Runyon*.

potatoes in the mould (rhyming sl.) cold (cf: taters) *Cole*.

pot-boiler n. a literary or similar work created purely for the money; to keep the creator's 'pot boiling'.

pot-lick v. see: arse-lick.

potsy n. (US police use) badge, identification card; fr. the tin (used for pots) that allegedly makes badges *McBain: 1*.

potted a. drunk; fr. pot = flagon.

potty a. crazy, eccentric *Humphries*.

pound (US prison use) a five-year sentence (cf: pound note) *J. Breslin, 'Forsaking All Others', 1982*.

pound note $5.00; fr. an exchange

rate of five dollars = £1 *Runyon*.

pound note geezer n. rich man (orig. Aus.) *Norman: 2*.

pound one's ear v. to sleep; fr. tramps attempting to sleep in the boxcars of US railroads as they bumped over the rails *Gruber*.

pound salt up one's ass v. usu. as a rebuke: go . . . : go to hell, stick it up your ass (qv) etc.

poundcake n. an attractive woman (cf: pancake, cookie, etc.) *Neaman & Silver*.

pour piss out of a boot, not enough sense to v. to be very stupid.

powder one's nose v. to use a toilet, rather than a 'powder-room' *Rawson*.

powder puff n. (derog.) effeminate male homosexual (cf: poof) *Legman*.

pow-wow v. chat, converse with, talk to; fr. US Indian use *Burroughs: Jr*.

pox n. venereal disease; fr. 16th C.

poxy a. unpleasant, dirty, disgusting (cf: pox) *Performance*.

P/P abbr. (contact ads use) photo/phone *SMD*.

prang v. to crash one's car; fr. Second World War RAF use (cf: shunt) *Humphries: 2*.

prannet n. a fool, an idiot *Dury*.

prat n. an idiot, a fool; fr. orig. use: buttocks, posterior *Dury, 'Laughter', 1981*.

pratt for v. (homosexual use) to indulge – actively or passively – in anal intercourse; fr. prat(t): buttocks *Legman*.

prawnhead n. (Aus. use) fool, simpleton, general derog. term *Ready*.

prayer, not have a phr. to have no chance whatsoever.

prayer-bones n. (US Black use) the knees.

preach one's funeral v. to tell off, to reprimand.

precheck n. (sex industry use) an inspection of a client's penis made by a prostitute prior to intercourse.

preggers a. pregnant.

preppie n. (US college use) anyone who attends one of the major US 'prep schools' (St Paul's, Choate, Groton,

Miss Porter's, Dana Hall, etc.), the equivalent of UK public (private) schools. The graduates of such schools – the children of the US establishment – share similar codes, styles, language and society *Bernbach*.

prescriptions n. (drug use) any drug that comes primarily in pill form: barbiturates, amphetamines, etc. *Folb*.

presents n. (US Black use) white spots on one's fingernails, supposedly auguring good luck *Klein*.

press flesh v. to shake hands, usu. of a politician on a campaign tour to meet the electors *Higgins:5*.

press ham v. (college use) to press a bare buttock against a window and hopefully shock passers by (cf: moon) *Junker*.

press one's hair v. (US Black use) to straighten one's hair (cf: conk) *Folb*.

press the bricks v. to stand around in the street, loafing and gossiping.

pressed a. (US Black use) very well dressed; fr. state of one's clothes *Folb*.

pressie n. aka *prezzie* (UK 'society' use) (abbrev.) present *Barr*.

pretties n. (sex industry use) new young sex objects, either male or female (cf: chicken 3.).

previous a. forward, cheeky; often as 'that's a bit previous' (cf: out of order).

previous n. (abbrev.) previous convictions (cf: form).

prick n. 1. the penis; 2. an idiot, a fool, an incompetent *O'Brien*.

pricktease v. to lead on sexually but stopping short of intercourse. The woman or man (in homosexual context) who so acts is a *prickteaser*.

priest n. a celibate; fr. status of such clerics *Higgins:1*.

priggling a. pregnant; mix of in pig and preggers (qqv).

prime cut n. the vagina *film title, 1972*.

prime one's pump v. to excite sexually *Dunne*.

primed a. 1. drunk; thus ready to 'explode into action' *Dickson*; 2. high on drugs *Shell*.

primo a. first rate, excellent; usually

referring to the quality of a given drug *Maupin:3*.

Princeton rub aka *Princeton-First-Year* n. (homosexual use) body to body rubbing (cf: collegiate fucking) *Jay & Young*.

print mittens n. (US criminal use) gloves worn to avoid leaving fingerprints *Morgan*.

priors n. (police/criminal use) prior convictions *Morgan*.

prison wolf n. (Can. prison use) a prisoner who prefers women when free, but turns to men when imprisoned *Caron*.

privy-queen n. (homosexual use) a homosexual who seeks sex in or around public lavatories *Legman*.

pro n. 1. (abbrev.) professional: an expert in a given field spec. *the pro*: the professional employed by a golf club; 2. (abbrev.) prostitute *Price:1*.

process n. (US Black use) straightened hair *Folb*.

prod n. the penis *Underwood*.

prod v. to engage in sexual intercourse; usu. male use *Underwood*.

professional woman n. (euph.) prostitute (cf: working girl) *Milner*.

promo n. (abbrev.) promotion: publicity, PR, etc. *Higgins:3*.

promoted pimp n. (US Black use) 1. a pimp who gives advice to other pimps or to their prostitutes; 2. a method of getting money *Klein*.

prong n. 1. penis; 2. an erection *Higgins:1*.

prong v. to seduce.

pronto immediately, at once; fr. Sp. *Humphries*.

prop up v. 1. (abbrev.) proposition, thus to make a proposition *Powis*; 2. to arrange, to suggest, to fabricate a story *Powis*.

prospect n. 1. (Hells Angels use) a recruit to an outlaw motorcycle gang prior to any initiation rites *Mandelkau*; 2. (homosexual use) a potential client for a street prostitute *Legman*.

prossie n. prostitute *'Minder'*,

Thames TV, 1980.

prosso n. (Aus. use) prostitute *Ready*.

provider n. (poker use) one who habitually loses when playing and thus provides his fellow-players with regular wins *Alvarez*.

prunes n. (derog.) a Black person.

pruno n. (US prison use) illegally distilled liquor *Morgan*.

pseud n. (abbrev.) pseudo-intellectual; derog. description, often of quite genuine, if pretentious intellectuals, who offend their perhaps less academic critics *Private Eye: passim*.

pseudie tudie n. an architectural style popular in the Home Counties; it features fake beams and the other appurtenances of (Hollywood-style) Elizabethan & Tudor England.

psych out v. 1. to astonish, to amaze *Underwood*; 2. to frighten or at least perturb someone else by playing on their inner fear; 3. to lose emotional control.

psych up v. to put oneself into a confident, aggressive, etc. frame of mind as preparation for adequate dealing with a given situation *Jay & Young*.

psyched to death a. (US teen. use) extremely excited (cf: psych up) *E. Beyer*.

psychedelic to the bone (US Black use) extremely intoxicated by a given drug, but not necessarily a hallucinogen *Folb*.

psycho n. (abbrev.) psychopath *McBain:1*.

PT (acro.) Prick *T*easer (qv).

pta (US Black use) (abbrev.) 1. *p*ussy, *t*itties and *a*rmpits; 2. a bad-smelling female *Folb*.

P-town n. Philadelphia *Jay & Young*.

pu the elop (backsl.) up the pole = pregnant *Cole*.

pubes n. pubic hair *Morgan*.

public n. (abbrev.) public bar *Robins:1*.

puck n. (US campus use) anyone deemed socially unacceptable *Underwood*.

pucky n. excrement.

pud a. (US campus use) soft, easy, esp. of course-work *Underwood*.

pud n. 1. (US teen./campus use) the penis *Underwood*; 2. fool, idiot *Price:3*.

puddlejumper n. a small car *Higgins:3*.

pudpuller n. a masturbator *Morgan*.

puff n. life *Welsh:1*.

puff n. see: poof.

pug n. (US Black use) a homosexual.

pug n. a prizefighter, a boxer; esp. one who relies more on savagery than skill; fr. pugilist *Fiction Illus.3*.

puggy n. a tough, a hoodlum; fr. pug (qv) *Wolfe:1*.

puke n., v. vomit; to vomit *Price:2*.

pukka a. genuine, correct, honest; fr. Hindi *pakka*: substantial.

pull n. 1. (horseracing use) a horse that is deliberately pulled up and stopped from winning so as to improve its odds in a subsequent, more important race *Bukowski:1*; 2. an arrest (cf: tug) *Norman:2*; 3. influence (cf: clout) *Hotten*.

pull v. 1. to arrest, to stop and search on the street *Capital Radio 1983*; 2. to seduce *Keyes*.

pull a coat v. to draw attention, to point out, to nag *Price:2*.

pull a fast one v. orig. in military use meaning to malinger; in contemporary general use it means to get away with something, usually a slightly nefarious scheme (cf: bit swift).

pull a jap v. to take by surprise, to ambush; fr. stereotype of the cunning Japanese.

pull a job v. carry out a robbery or other criminal act *Higgins:1*.

pull a quick park v. (US Black use) to make a snappy pick-up of a sexual partner *Folb*.

pull a stroke v. to attempt and/or get away with anything outrageous or daring *Dury*.

pull a train v. to be the subject of gang rape, esp. amongst Hells Angels; the female is the engine, her assailants the rolling-stock *Thompson*.

pull an act v. to put on a show with the intention of deceiving or defrauding someone *Neaman & Silver*.

pull down v. to earn money, usu. with a wage specified as object *Price:2*.

pull dude n. (US Black use) an informer.

pull one's card v. to attack, to beat up, to kill.

pull one's coat v. 1. to arrest (cf: feel one's collar); 2. to warn *Morgan*.

pull (one's) covers v. to reveal some hidden characteristic, either in another or in oneself.

pull one's finger out v. to get on with something; to stop malingering and commit oneself to positive action *'Minder', Thames TV, 1983*.

pull one's jacket v. to arrest (cf: feel one's collar).

pull one's joint 1. spec. masturbate; 2. to whine, complain (cf: jerk off) *Higgins:3*.

pull one's leg v. to tease.

pull one's pisser see: pull one's leg (qv) *Bleasdale*.

pull one's pud(ding) v. to masturbate *Junker*.

pull one's punches v. to restrain oneself, esp. in conversation/speech; fr. boxing use *Dickson*.

pull one's socks up v. to make greater efforts, to improve one's performance.

pull one's wire v. to masturbate.

pull the chain n. to masturbate.

pull the chain on n. to murder, to kill.

pull the plug v. to commit suicide.

pull the plug on v. to terminate, to bring to an end, usu. abruptly; fr. electrical use.

pull time v. (US prison use) to be sentenced to a term of imprisonment *Klein*.

pull to a set v. (US Black use) to attend a party *Folb*.

pull your head in! excl. of annoyance: mind your own business, don't interfere; fr. the action of the tortoise *Ready*.

pump n. 1. a gun, spec. a pump-action shotgun *Folb*; 2. a promiscuous female

Underwood; 3. the heart *Dunne*.

pump v. to ask questions, esp. to interrogate (in a police station) *Sillitoe*.

pump iron v. to work out with weights, to practise bodybuilding.

pump jockey n. petrol pump attendant *Thompson*.

pumped nuts n. temporary courage.

pumpernickel n. a Black prostitute, especially a mulatto.

pumpkin head n. a person with an abnormally large head *Klein*.

punch n. (US campus use) a promiscuous female; one who is always getting 'banged' (qv) (?) *Underwood*.

punch v. (US campus use) to engage in sexual intercourse *Underwood*.

punch house n (US Black use) a party frequented by pimps and their women; usu. an orgy *Klein*.

punch in the mouth n. cunnilingus *Simmons*.

punching bag n. (boxing use) a fighter who has no real abilities and is useful only as the recipient of a fortunate opponent's punches *Runyon:1*.

punch-out artist n. anyone who enjoys and is expert in beating up his opponents with his fists *Thompson*.

punch-up n. a fight, in the street, a pub, etc. *Norman:4*.

punchy a. 1. (boxing use) punch drunk, a boxer who has taken too many punches and is becoming eccentric; 2. disorientated, eccentric, out of control *Higgins:1*.

punishment n. (homosexual use) taking an extra-large penis either in the mouth or the anus *Legman*.

punk n. 1. nonsense, rubbish; 2. (US campus use) second-rate, inferior *Dickson*; 3. a youngster, a child *Runyon*; 4. (US prison use) a young inmate used for sex by older, stronger peers. 5. a young criminal or street gang member *Price:1*.

Punk n. mid-1970s youth cult, started in UK, spread to US by such apostles as the Sex Pistols, Malcolm McLaren, etc. Where the hippies (qv) had been bourgeois, punks were proletarian, complaining not against a consumer society but against their exclusion from its delights; they specialized in bizarre hair styles (mohican, multicoloured) ripped clothes, and safety pins, through flesh as well as fabric.

punk a. second-rate, inferior, distasteful *Humphries:2*.

punk v. to engage in anal intercourse *Folb*.

punk out v. to display cowardice *Price:3*.

punkette n. a female punk (qv).

punt v. to gamble, to wager.

punt v. i. (US campus use) to give up, esp. of one's work *Underwood*.

punt around v. 1. to try one's luck, esp. when looking for a given person *Newman:1*; 2. (UK police use) to go out on patrol, and gambling on an arrest *Laurie*.

punt off v. (US campus use) to forget, to put to the back of one's mind *Underwood*.

punter n. 1. spec: gambler (cards, dice, horses, dogs, etc.); 2. member of the general public, esp. when in role of customer; 3. the victim of a confidence trickster's schemes; 4. (skiing use) a guest at a chalet.

puppethead (US teen. use) any gullible, conventional person, esp. one who permits hearsay to 'pull their strings' in matters of current taste *Sculatti*.

puppies n. feet (cf: dogs) *Runyon*.

puppy n. (US Black use) 1. a small penis; 2. small bottle of wine; 3. love-sick young man; 4. sexually inexperienced male *Folb*.

puppy dog n. see: puppy (3, 4) *Klein*.

pure a., adv. simple, simply *Welsh:1*.

pure quill n. something excellent, flawless.

purler n. a crash, an accidental fall *Wodehouse: CW*.

push n. (Aus. use) 1. criminal gang (orig 1860s use); 2. a crowd *Humphries*.

push v. (abbrev.) push off (qv) *ES 21/4/83*.

push v. 1. to sell; 2. spec. to sell drugs *Higgins:3*.

push along v. to leave (cf: push off).

push iron v. see: pump iron *Klein*.

push off v. to leave *Humphries:2*.

push off! (excl.) go away.

push ponies v. for a pimp to promote his stable of whores.

push the boat out v. to spend heavily, usu. on pleasure, eating, drinking etc., often treating others also.

push up the daisies v. to die *Wright*.

pushed a. lacking, bereft; thus *pushed for cash*, *pushed for time Barr*.

pushed out of shape a. upset, angry *Underwood*.

pusher n. a seller of drugs *Burroughs:1*.

push-in job n. a mugging that takes place on the victim's doorstep.

pushover n. a person or situation that presents no difficulties or problems *Heller*.

puss n. 1. see: pussy *Southern & Hoffenberg*; 2. face; fr. Irish *pus*: mouth *Higgins:3*; 3. the 'female' of a lesbian couple (cf: pussy) *Powis*.

puss gentleman n. (US Black use) a weak male; fr. pussy (qv) *Klein*.

pussbucket n. (orig. US) general derog. term.

pussy n. 1. vagina; 2. coward, implications of homosexuality *O'Brien*; 3. women, poss. sexually available, in general; 4. (UK criminal/police use) a fur coat *Powis*.

pussy a. scared.

pussy in a can n. (US prison use) sardines sold in a can at a prison commissary; fr. derog. ref. to the vagina (cf: fish) *Klein*.

pussy posse n. (US police use) the Vice Squad, esp. those members who deal with prostitutes (cf: bunco squad) *Higgins:2*.

pussycat n. 1. (US Black use) the vagina *Folb*; 2. a weak or at least amiable and passive person *Stone*.

pussyfoot v. to compromise, to act in a cowardly or weakly manner; fr. the animal's cautious movements *Dickson*.

pussy-whipped a. any man who is dominated by a woman, esp. wife or girl-friend.

put a dent in one's hip (US Black use) to cost an appreciable amount of cash; one's wallet is carried on one's hip *Klein*.

put a hurting on v. (US Black use) to cause deliberate harm to someone *Klein*.

put a name up v. to inform against someone, often to save one's own skin (cf: body) *Newman:1*.

put a notice on v. (criminal use) arrange to have someone murdered (cf: contract) *Austin*.

put a sock in it v. to stop talking, to be quiet; the sock would gag a mouth *Wodehouse:MS*.

put away v. 1. imprison; 2. (show business use) for a comedian to score a big laugh from the audience *Goldman*; 3. (UK police/criminal use) to inform against and thus be instrumental in having imprisoned *Powis*; 4. to kill, to murder.

put beans up one's nose v. to do something stupid despite having been warned not to (cf: have beans up one's nose) (fr. the warning given to children: 'Don't put beans up your nose').

put down v. to deride, to slander, to attack verbally, to tease.

put down a routine v. to hoax or otherwise persuade someone with a clever story *Burroughs:1*.

put her on the block/corner v. (US Black use) to have a woman working for one as a prostitute *Folb*.

put in one's two cents v. to make a contribution, usu. gratuitous and/or malicious, to an argument or conversation *Algren:2*.

put in the acid v. (UK criminal use) to inform against *Powis*.

put in the poison v. to slander, to malign a person's character, esp. in court *Laurie*.

put it about v. to indulge in a wide-ranging sex life *Humphries*.

put it across v. to cheat or confuse someone.

put it all together v. to consolidate one's position, to work out one's life satisfactorily *McFadden*.

put it around v. to circulate information; esp. of police who attempt thus to use the criminal grapevine (qv) to glean specific facts *Powis*.

put it in the wind v. (US Black use) to leave *Folb*.

put it on the street v. to make available for general consumption; usu. of gossip, information, etc.

put it where the monkeys shove their nuts (euph.) shove it up your arse!

put lead in one's pencil v. to cheer up, to strengthen; esp. in sexual context *Humphries*.

put on v. 1. to tease, to joke with; to deceive for one's own gain *Goldman*; 2. to eat; fr. put on the feedbag; often specifying the food: *putting on the chicken pie* etc. *Runyon*.

put on a crosstown bus v. (US Black use) to mislead deliberately *Major*.

put on front street v. (US Black use) to reveal secrets about another person, esp. those they would prefer to be kept secret *Klein*.

put on hold v. to delay, to postpone, to defer; fr. telephone etiquette (cf: put on the back burner) *Price:3*.

put on ice v. 1. to put aside a project or idea for later development, or use; 2. (police use) to hide away a sensitive witness so as to stop their being killed by a wanted criminal; 3. to maintain a distant, minimally emotional relationship (cf: play the chill).

put on jam v. (Aus. use) to put on airs *Neaman & Silver*.

put on the back burner v. to consider for a later date; to reserve one's judgement; to postpone *Dickson*.

put on (the) dog v. 1. to assume airs and pretensions (but, cf: wear the dog)

Neaman & Silver; **2.** to do something energetically, noisily.

put on the feed bag v. to eat *Gruber*.

put on the front burner v. to make into a priority *AS LIV 1979*.

put on the guiver v. (UK criminal use) to affect an upper-class accent; fr. *guiver lad*: a working-class dandy (19th C.); itself fr. *guiver*: flattery, humbug, show fr. Hebrew word meaning pride *Powis*.

put on the high dick v. to dress in one's best clothes, to put on airs.

put one away v. to knock out, to win a fight *Bukowski:2*.

put one in v. (Aus. use) to inform against; 'one' = a report or the person thus 'put in gaol' (?) *Wilkes*.

put one on v. to hit; 'one' = a blow.

put one together v. to plan a crime *Newman:1*.

put one's ass in a sling v. to cause someone extreme trouble, whether actually physically damaging or not *Dunne*.

put one's back up v. to annoy, to irritate; fr. the risen hairs on a cat's back that denote, *inter alia*, aggression.

put one's business on front street v. (US Black use) to make indiscreet disclosures about another person *Klein*.

put one's checks in the rack v. to die; fr. gambling use *Runyon:1*.

put one's face on v. (female use) to put on make-up; however, gaining male currency among teenagers who enjoy make-up. *T 29/6/83*.

put one's flags out v. to have a menstrual period (cf: fly one's red flag, have the flag out).

put one's foot down v. to insist, to be adamant; fr. a pettish stamp of the foot *Wodehouse:VGJ*.

put one's foot in it v. to make an error; it = 'the shit'.

put one's foot in one's mouth v. to make an embarassing verbal mistake (discomfiting oneself as well as the hearer).

put one's foot up v. (US Black use) to make one's presence felt in an arrogant, threatening manner. (fr. the tradition among Black communities when two people were quarrelling for the injured party to appear at his or her enemy's home, put a foot up on the porch, or jam in it the front door, and curse out their family and forbears (cf: play the dozens)).

put one's hand up v. to confess; fr. classroom practice *Newman:1*.

put one's head on the block v. to declare oneself openly; to take a risk or a stand that may be dangerous; fr. the chopping-block *Teresa*.

put one's nose out of joint v. to discomfit, to embarrass, to irritate *Vidal*.

put one's papers in v. (US and UK police use) to submit one's resignation *Neaman & Silver*.

put one's shirt on v. (gambling use) to bet heavily *Wodehouse: MJ*.

put oneself about v. to lead an active social life *Powis*.

put out to offer oneself for sex *Price:2*.

put out one's hand v. to go through a drunk's pockets looking for cash, valuables *Burroughs:1*.

put out one's lights to knock unconscious; fr. *daylights*: eyes *Hotten*.

put some slobber on the knobber v. to perform oral sex.

put (someone's) pot on v. (Aus./NZ) to tell tales, to inform against.

put the arm on v. to pressurize with threats of violence; to extort 'protection' payments *Vidal*.

put the bag on v. to halt, to interfere with, to bring to a standstill *Humphries:2*.

put the bee on v. **1.** to air one's obsession, fr *a bee in one's bonnet*; **2.** see: put the bite on *Schulberg:2*.

put the bite on v. **1.** to extort, to blackmail *Wodehouse: CW*; **2.** to ask for a financial loan *Runyon:1*.

put the black on v. to blackmail

Dury.

put the blast on v. **1.** to attack verbally, to criticize severely *Runyon*;
2. to shoot dead *Chandler: LG*.

put the block on v. to interfere with, to stop.

put the blocks on v. (UK prison use) to tighten up regulations that have become temporarily lax *LL*.

put the boot in v. to kick someone as part of a fight *Humphries*.

put the bubble in v. (UK criminal use) to inform; fr. bubble (qv) *LL*.

put the bull on v. to pressurize, to act aggressively towards; fr. the animal *Breslin*.

put the cosh on v. to pressurize; to compel (cf: under the cosh) *Norman:2*.

put the cross on v. to mark for death *Chandler: Notebk*.

put the finger on v. to betray, to inform against *Algren*.

put the freeze on v.i., v.t. (US Black use) to stop *Folb*.

put the frighteners on v. (UK criminal use) to menace, blackmail, threaten with violence. *Performance*.

put the fritz on, put on the fritz v. to spoil, to render out of order, to put a stop to.

put the hammer down v. to drive fast, esp. used by truck drivers.

put the hammer on v. to attack verbally, to slander *Higgins:1*.

put the hard word on v. to make demands (esp. financial or sexual) of someone *Baker*.

put the kibosh on v. to spoil, to ruin; fr. kibosh: nonsense, rubbish *Hotten*.

put the leather in v. to kick someone during a fight *LL*.

put the lid on v. to cover up, to hide; esp. of a newspaper story that is offensive or embarrassing to a given Establishment *Chandler: LG*.

put the make on v. to make sexual advances.

put the mockers on v. to wish the worst of luck; to curse; poss. fr. Hebrew *maches*: a plague *Norman:2*.

put the mozz on v. (Aus. use) to jinx, to cause another person trouble, to inconvenience (cf: put the mockers on) *Wilkes*.

put the scream out v. (criminal use) to put out an alert for a given person *Austin*.

put the screws on v. to pressurize; fr. thumbscrews *Gruber*.

put the shoe on the left foot v. (US Black use) to put blame where it does not belong *Klein*.

put the shoe on the right foot v. (US Black use) to place blame where it duly belongs.

put the shuck on v. to trick to deceive, to fool (verbally); fr. shuck (qv) *Underwood*.

put the skids under v. **1.** to sack someone from a job; **2.** to make someone else hurry up, usu. in doing their work.

put the sleeve on v. to arrest *Runyon:1*.

put the smack down v. to hit, to assault.

put the squeeze on v. to pressurize, esp. for money *Humphries:2*.

put the touch on v. to attempt to borrow money *Goldman*.

put the whisper on v. to inform against *Austin*.

put the wind up v. to worry, to frighten *Norman:2*.

put the wood in the hole v. shut the door; usu. as a command.

put through changes v. to alter another person's mental or emotional state, opinions or attitudes (cf: go through changes) *Major*.

put up a black v. to make a mistake; poss. fr. two black balls hauled to the mast of RN ships when a ship was out of control.

put up job n. a pre-arranged, and usu. criminal or at least deceptive, plan.

put up or shut up! (cp) 'put your money where your mouth is!'; fr. gambling use.

puta n. (US Sp. use) a prostitute *Folb*.

put-down n. verbal attack, criticism, condemnation *Vizinczey*.

put-on n. a joke, a hoax *Thompson*.
putrid a. drunk (cf: stinking) *Dickson*.
putz n. **1.** fr. Yiddish: the penis; thus, by extension; **2.** an idiot, a fool, a simpleton *Price:2*.
PV n. (US prison use) Parole Violator *Klein*.

Q

Q n. (US criminal/police use) (abbrev.) San Quentin Prison, California *Dunne*.
Q boat n. (UK police use) unmarked police radio car for surveillance and similar uses; fr. First World War naval vessels that masqueraded as merchant ships *Powis*.
QE v. (UK prison use) to turn Queen's Evidence, thus to inform *Obs. 1981*.
quack n. **1.** (US Black use) a homosexual; who 'ducks down' for sex (?) *Klein*; **2.** doctor, irrespective of abilities *Humphries*.
quail n. a girl.
qualified a. (Black pimp use) experienced, of a prostitute *Milner*.
quandong n. (Aus. use) a girl who accepts any amount of gifts but still refuses to cede her sexual favours. fr. a fruit which is soft on the outside but hard inside *Wilkes*.
quarter to two n. (rhyming sl.) a Jew *Franklyn*.
quashie n. (Jamaican use) country bumpkin, peasant, stupid person *Thelwell*.
queeb n. (US teen. use) any small problem, esp. mechanical *Sculatti*.
queen n. effeminate (older) homosexual male *Performance*.
Queen's Park Ranger(s) n. (rhyming sl.) stranger(s); fr. the West London football club *Cole*.
Queen's Row (homosexual use) the Boston (Mass.) Public Gardens *Jay & Young*.
queer a. homosexual; (currently near-taboo in fashionable liberal circles, thus see gay).
queer as a nine bob note a. unusual,

particularly suspicious; the phrase survives the demise of the currency *Powis*.
queer basher n. one who specializes in beating up (and usually robbing) homosexuals (cf: paki-basher) *Green:3*.
queer detail n. (US police use) branch of the Vice Squad specializing in homosexual crime (cf: pussy posse) *White*.
Queer Street n. any difficult situation *Hotten*.
queerbait n. an effeminate young boy who attracts, or is supposed to attract older male homosexuals *Jay & Young*.
queer-bashing n. beating up (and robbing) male homosexuals; those who do this are unaffected by current rejection of queer as derog.
quick n. (US Black use) instantly available money *Klein*.
quick and dirty see: quick fix *Kidder*.
quick fix n. any kind of instant remedy, poss. not the best one for long-term dependance *Safire*.
quick on the draw a. bright, intelligent (cf: quick on the trigger, slow on the draw).
quick on the trigger a. bright, intelligent, alert *Dunne*.
quick starts n. (US campus use) rubber soled sneakers; popular for those who need to make a speedy exit *Underwood*.
quickie n. spontaneous and brief sexual intercourse *Price:2*.
quid n. pound sterling *Performance*.
quids in to be doing well; fr. image of making a successful bet and the money thus gained *LWT 1984*.

quiff n. 1. the vagina *Junker*; 2. females, esp. sexually available ones *Dunne*.

quill n. (drug use) a folded over matchbook cover which hides a narcotic drug *Major*.

quim n. vagina; poss. fr. Celtic *cwm*: a valley *Big Ass Comics 1*.

quit v. to die *Major*.

quitter n. (horseracing use) a horse that is leading the field but unaccountably fails to win the race *Bukowski:1*.

quod n. prison; fr. the quadrangle in which felons exercised *Wodehouse: passim*.

quoit n. (Aus. use) anus, buttocks; 'round with a hole in it' *Wilkes*.

R

R and R 1. (US milit. use) rest and recreation; temporary leave from active service *Del Vecchio*; 2. (US police use) rape and robbery *Neaman & Silver*.

raas n. (Jamaican use) abusive term, fr. English 'your ass'.

raasclat n. (Jamaican use) extreme derog. term; fr. English 'ass cloth'.

rabbit n. 1. a poor player, esp. in golf or tennis; 2. (US Black use) a white person *Folb*.

rabbit n. (sex industry use) a client who ejaculates quickly and thus leaves the prostitute free to carry on her trade.

rabbit v. (rhyming sl.) rabbit and pork = to talk *Norman:1*.

rabbit fever n. (US criminal use) 1. the compelling desire to run off whenever things get difficult; 2. the compulsion to attempt escapes from any form of imprisonment *Pearce*.

rabbit food n. vegetables or salad greens considered unfit for consumption, esp. by a carnivore (cf: hog feed).

rabbit skin n. (US college use) one college diploma or degree; fr. the fur tippet worn by graduating students.

rabbit's paw n. (rhyming sl.) jaw *Cole*.

race off v. (Aus. use) to seduce *Wilkes*.

rack n. bosom, breasts *Greaser Comics*.

rack v. 1. to sleep, fr. USMC rack: bed; 2. to seduce a woman, to make love *Price:2*; 3. (music business use) to categorize the varieties of rock music into their separate groups, and thus place them on separate racks within a store *Capital Radio 1983*.

rack attack n. (US campus use) a sudden onset of sleepiness *Underwood*.

rack monster n. (US campus use) sleepiness, exhaustion *Underwood*.

rack off! (Aus. use) go away! piss off! (qv) *Wilkes*.

rack out v. to fall asleep, to go to bed *Underwood*.

rack pick n. (US Black use) a comb designed specifically for use on a natural or Afro (qqv) hairstyle *Folb*.

racked a. tired out, exhausted; fr. rack = bed *Underwood*.

racket n. a noise *Dury, 'Laughter', 1979*.

rackets n. organized crime. fr. 19th C. UK cant racket: trick, plan *Tuff Shit Comics*.

rad a. extreme, excessive, very much; a general intensifier that comes from SE use of radical as 'basic, essential, from the roots' and eschewing political overtones (cf: mondo, safe) *Pond*.

Raddie n. an Italian living in London, orig. spec. in Clerkenwell *Powis*.

radge adv. mad, furious, insane *Welsh:1* (fr. North. dial, itself fr. SE rage).

radio adv. insane, mad; from rhy. sl. radio rental = mental (qv).

radishes! (US campus use) general excl. of disgust and annoyance *Underwood*.

rado n. (US Black use) (abbrev.)

Cadillac El Dorado (cf: LD) *Folb*.

Rafferty's Rules (Aus. use) no rules whatsoever, anything goes; not fr. an individual, but mispron. of 'refractory' *Bickerton*.

rag n. **1.** sanitary towel; abbrev. jam-rag (qv) *Price:1*; **2.** (derog.) newspaper *O'Brien*; **2.** (abbrev.) wet rag: a weak person *Price:1*; **3.** (Valley Girls (qv) use) an unpleasant person *Pond*.

rag baby n. (US Black use) a poor, ill-clothed girl who is nonetheless attractive *Klein*.

rag box n. (US Black use) the vagina *Klein*.

rag head n. (US Black use) **1.** anyone who is not absolutely up to date with current information, gossip, style, etc. *Klein*; **2.** Arab native of the Middle East (cf: towelhead).

rag top n. a soft-topped motor car; a convertible *Whitcomb*.

ragged down heavy (US Black use) exceptionally well-dressed (cf: rags) *Folb*.

ragged out a. (Valley Girls (qv) use) appalling, unattractive, etc. (cf: rag 3) *Pond*.

raggedy-ass a. poor, badly dressed, impoverished *Bruce:2*.

raging n. a first-class degree; fr. rhy. sl. raging thirst = first (cf:Pattie).

ragmop n. (US Black use) an unkempt, messy person *Major*.

rags n. (US Black use) clothes *Folb*.

rags and bones n. (US Black use) the corpse of a poor person *Klein*.

raid the ice box v. (necrophile use) to have intercourse with a corpse.

railbird n. (gambling use) a fan or spectator who crowds round the rails that surround a big game in a casino *Alvarez*.

railroad v. **1.** to arrest, try and convict without allowing the person concerned due process of law; to imprison on trumped up charges and faked evidence; to accelerate the legal process in order to ensure – through inadequate defence, legal knowledge, etc. – that a person will be found guilty and sentenced, even though their trial is ostensibly 'fair' *Seale*; **2.** (US campus use) to use influence in the pursuit of personal interests *Underwood*.

railroad whiskey n. (US Black use) cheap wine; fr. Santa Fe brand, the name of a US railroad *Folb*.

rain on v. to kill, to make suffer *Waits*.

rainbows n. (drug use) any form of pill in a coloured jacket *Bukowski:1*.

raincoat n. a contraceptive sheath.

rainmaker n. (sporting use) in Aus. Rules football, an exceptionally high kick that 'hits the clouds' *Channel-4 TV, 1983*.

rainy days n. (US Black use) hard times *Major*.

rainy-day money n. funds set aside to deal with unforseen difficulties *Performance*.

raise Cain v. to cause as much trouble as one can; fr. Adam's wicked son, Cain *Neaman & Silver*.

raise hell v. to cause a good deal of trouble deliberately (cf: raise Cain) *PT*.

raise sand v. (US Black use) to cause a stir; to cause commotion; to fight; fr. image of kicking sand in someone's face *Klein*.

raise up v. (US Black use) **1.** to leave a place; **2.** spec. to be given leave or parole to leave a prison *Klein*.

rake it in v. to make a great deal of money; poss. fr. the croupier's rake in a casino.

rake up the coals v. to snore.

rally v. (US campus use) to have a good time *Underwood*.

rally v. (US campus use) to act utterly madly, drunkenly, obstreperously *Birnbach*.

ralph n. vomit, fr. the noise made while vomiting (cf: buick, hughie) *Underwood*.

ram n. (Aus. use) **1.** a trickster's confederate who encourages the public to lose their money in a given con-game; fr. ramp (qv) and fr. the animal's horns, pushing at the victim *Baker*; **2.** a promiscuous male (cf: stud).

ramp n. any form of swindle or fraud *Newman:1*.

ram-raid n. v. a method of stealing from shops that have erected blinds, shutters, bars, etc. – popular c.1990/91 – whereby the thief steals a car, then drives at high speed into the shopfront, smashing his way through any defences; the car is filled with loot, then driven away.

ram-raider n. one who carries out ram-raids (qv).

ramrod n. the penis *Klein*.

randy a. sexually aroused, eager *Higgins:5*.

range n. (Can. prison use) open area outside cells *Caron*.

rank a. second rate, inferior, disgusting; fr. SE: rotten *Selby:1*.

rank v. (street gang use) to insult, often by ritual insults directed at the other person's mother (cf: dirty dozens) *Salisbury*.

rank one's style v. aka: *rank one's game/action/play*: deliberately to obstruct another's sexual advances (cf: cock block) *Folb*.

rank out v. (US Black use) to beg for help, to surrender to pressure, to behave badly or weakly.

rannygazoo n. nonsense, irrelevant, irritating activity *Wodehouse:AAG*.

rap n. 1. 1. slang term for speech or conversation; adoped during the 1960s by the hippies, drawing as they did so often on Black slang; 2. used in a variety of new therapies to mean conversations, typically in an encounter group, in a structured situation in which one's feelings are laid out, analysed, supported or criticized. Such therapy based conversations are also known as 'rap sessions', and the group as a 'rap group'. All the terms were used by a number of New Left political groups to describe meetings in which they planned their activities. 3. since the 1980s the term has gone back to its Black roots, and is used in hip-hop (qv) music to describe the singing or chanting of the lyrics of a rap song against the heavy bass line, usually produced by a drum machine or

synthesizer. 4. a blow, a hit. *Higgins:1*; 5. (Aus. use) congratulations, a word of praise, a boost *Wilkes*; 6. a criminal charge or allegation.

rap v. 1. to talk, to converse; thus rap session: an intense conversation; by extension, in new therapy use: an encounter group *Uneeda Comix*; 2. to hit *Selby:1*.

rap on the real v. (US Black use) to speak sincerely, honestly *Klein*.

rap parlor n. current euph. for massage parlour, itself a cover for a store-front organization behind which, while legitimate massage may be available, men pay for a variety of sexual service from 'relief massage' (masturbation) to full intercourse *Rawson*.

rap sheet n. criminal record (cf: form, previous) *Higgins:1*.

rape-o n. (US cant) a rapist.

rapt a. (Aus. use) overjoyed with, carried away, delighted: fr. irraptured + wrapped up in *Ready*.

rare a. all-purpose approval term (cf:rad, safe, etc).

rashing n. (US Black use) a mixture of thrashing and harassing *Klein*.

raspberry n. (rhyming sl.) raspberry ripple = cripple *Dury, interview, 1978*.

raspberry tart n. (rhyming sl.) 1. heart; 2. fart *Cole*.

raspy . 1. (US Black use) unattractive, unkempt *Folb*; 2. (Valley Girls (qv) use) excellent, wonderful (by bad = good syndrome) *Pond*.

Rastus n. (derog.) black man; fr. cliché Black name in slave era *Vidal*.

rat n. 1. an unpleasant person; 2. an informer.

rat v. to inform, to betray *Morgan*.

rat arsed a. drunk.

rat ass n. term of abuse *Southern & Hoffenberg*.

rat bastard n. general term of abuse *Southern & Hoffenberg*.

rat fink n. an unpleasant person, with overtones of working as an informer (cf: fink 2.).

rat fuck v. 1. orig. campus use: a prank, a practical joke; 2. devel. to electoral 'dirty tricks' à la Campaign to

Re-elect the President (CREEP) in 1972, sabotaging the opponent's campaign by illicit means.

rat fucker n. a home-made tool which approximates a car's starting-handle *Simmons*.

rat on v. to betray *Higgins:2*.

rat one out v. to betray, to inform against *Larner*.

rat one's hair v. to backcomb one's hair in order to create the once popular 'beehive' style, somewhat recreated by current teenage 'punk' fashions *Jan Harold Brunvand, 'The Vanishing Hitch-hiker', 1983*.

rat prick n. general term of abuse.

ratbag n. derog. description or address *Humphries*.

ratchet-mouth v. talking nonsense, talking for the sake of hearing oneself talk *Higgins:4*.

rat-hole v. to hide away, to save up money, to hoard *Thompson:J*.

ratshit a. unpleasant, disgusting, annoying.

ratshit! general excl. of annoyance or distaste *Farina*.

ratted a. (UK 'society' use) drunk *T 18/7/83*.

rattle v. 1. to unnerve, to frighten *Wodehouse:AAG;* 2. to have sexual intercourse.

rattle one's beads v. to complain; usu. homosexual use *Stanley*.

rattle one's dags v. (Aus. use) to hurry up, to get a move on (cf: dags) *Bickerton*.

rattler n. 1. (UK police use) the London underground railway *Powis;* 2. a promiscuous girl *Cole*.

ratty a. 1. rundown, ramshackle, unkempt *Price:3;* 2. irritated, annoyed, obstreperous *Sillitoe*.

raunchy a. sordid, degenerate, excessive, seedy *Wolfe:2*.

rave n. 1. in the early 1960s, a party, also 'rave-up'; those enjoying such parties were known as ravers; the terms were revived in the 1980s, with much the same meaning, although the parties concerned were often held in clubs or, in the case of the notorious

'acid parties', in disused warehouses, hangars and so on; 2. (theatre use) a highly congratulatory review *Norman:2*.

raver n. anyone devoted to having an energetically good time with variations of 'dope, sex and rock 'n' roll' as to individual taste and situation.

raw a. 1. naked *Runyon;* 2. inexperienced, a rookie, unsophisticated (cf: fish).

raw deal n. unfair, harsh treatment, particularly poor luck; usu. fr. point of view of victim.

raw sole n. (US Black use) a virgin Black girl (cf: fish, n., a.); pun on soul (qv) *Klein*.

rays n. sunshine.

razoo n. (Aus. use) a small amount of money; usu. in phrase 'not a brass razoo' (qv): absolutely penniless *Humphries:2*.

razor n. 1. a notably 'sharp' person *Klein;* 2. (rhyming sl.) razor blade = spade (qv) = Black person *Cole*.

razz v. to tease, to heckle, to barrack; fr. rhyming sl. raspberry tart = fart (qv) *Price: 2*.

razzle-dazzle v. (US Black use) 1. to hang around; to loiter; 2. to pretend something has happened/is happening when in fact nothing is *Klein*.

reach v. (US Black use) to help *Klein*.

read one's beads v. (homosexual use) chastise, berate, attack someone verbally *Stanley*.

read the riot act v. to tell off severely and threateningly; fr. 19th C. and earlier practice of reading Riot Act to unruly crowds prior to attacking with police or troops if they refused to calm or disperse *Farrell*.

read the Rocks and Shoals v. (USMC use) to tell off, to upbraid (cf: read the riot act) *Uris*.

read them and weep (cp) accept my superiority, like it or not; fr. poker use, a phr. used as the winner of a pot reveals his/her winning hand.

reader n. 1. (UK prison use) any form

of reading matter, books, magazines, comics, etc. *LL*; **2.** (US police use/ cant) warrant for arrest, 'wanted' poster; **3.** (cant) small-time thief who follows delivery men to their destination, having sneaked a look at the label, then claims to be the official recipient *Neaman & Silver*.

readers n. (gambling use) a crooked deck of cards which a cheat can read from the backs *Runyon:1*.

readies n. (abbrev.) ready money; cash, rather than cheques, etc. *Performance*.

ready a. (US Black use) aware, sophisticated, prepared to deal with the real world *Folb*.

ready n. (abbrev.) ready money (cf: readies) *Austin*.

ready for the fox farm phr. (of an animal or a human) old, broken-down, at death's door. (fr. practise of feeding horsemeat to foxes which are being raised for their fur).

ready-eyed fully aware of a given situation in all its ramifications, both obvious and hidden *Powis*.

readywash n. crack (qv); refers to the process of chemical purification that is used when making the drug (cf: wash).

real babe n. (US teen. use) an admirable, attractive person of the opposite (or preferred) sex *Pond*.

real deal n. **1.** (US Black use) see: bottom line *Klein*; **2.** genuine *Shell*.

real grit n. (US Black use) the absolute truth, the essential facts (cf: nitty-gritty) *Klein*.

real man n. (US prison use) a prisoner well-respected by his peers *Neaman & Silver*.

real McCoy n. the genuine article, fr. Norman Selby 'Kid McCoy' (1873–1940) a boxer in the US (cf: real McKay) *R. Boycott, 'Batty, Bloomers & Boycott', 1982*.

real McKay the genuine article, the real (and superior) thing; fr. the self-esteem of Scots in general and McKay's in particular (cf: real McCoy) *R. Boycott, 'Batty, Bloomers*

& Boycott', 1982.

real woman (US Black use) a heterosexual woman (cf: natural woman) *Folb*.

ream job to lick and suck the anus, usu. homosexual use *Klein*.

reaming n. see: rimming *Jay & Young*.

rear-ender an automobile accident in which one vehicle hits the back of another *McFadden*.

rebop n. nonsense (cf: all that jazz).

recce n. (abbrev.) reconnaissance; orig. milit. use, now a general term for making a preliminary exploration, assessment, etc.

recluse n. (US prison use) one who has been inside a prison for five years or more without hearing from anyone in the free world *Klein*.

recoup v. (US criminal/Black use) to start off fresh and determined on one's release from prison, undeterred by a few years' absence from the world; fr. recouping one's losses *Klein*.

red n. **1.** (UK criminal use) gold (cf: red stuff) *LL*; **2.** (US (Texas) use) chilli.

Red n. (abbrev.) Red Coat, a staff member of a Butlins Holiday Camp *Obs. 12/6/83*.

red a. **1.** communist (cf: pinko); **2.** (abbrev.) redneck (qv) *White*.

red ass n. bad temper, irritation *Underwood*.

red band n. (US prison use) a trusty; fr. the red band around his arm that denotes his privileged status *Norman:1*.

red biddy n. the cheapest red wine, beloved of down-and-outs.

red boys n. (Royal Agricultural Coll, Cirencester use) fire extingushers. *Barr*.

red dog on a white horse (US Black use) a woman having her menstrual period *Folb*.

red lane n. **1.** the throat *Hotten*; **2.** the vagina.

red Mary n. (US Black use) a menstrual period *Folb*.

red Ned n. (Aus. use) cheap red wine (cf: Dago red, red biddy, rotgut).

red pants n. irritation, bad temper *Underwood.*

red sails in the sunset adv. to be menstruating.

Red Sea pedestrian n. (Aus. derog. use) a Jew, fr. the exploits of the Hebrews during their Exodus from Egypt *Humphries:2.*

Red sea's out, the phr. (usu. male use) menstruation.

red snapper n. the vagina (cf: snapper, snapping turtle).

red stuff n. gold; esp. jewellery *Powis.*

red wings n. (Hells Angels use) cunnilingus with a menstruating woman *Mandelkau.*

redball n. (US milit. use) in Vietnam, an enemy trail or road *Del Vecchio.*

redeye n. the anus (cf: roundeye 1) *Morgan.*

redhot n. (US Black use) a highly aggressive, volatile person *Klein.*

red-light v. to throw someone out of a car or other vehicle and force them to walk home, often over a great distance; they watch the rear-lights recede into the distance (cf: shellroad) *Runyon.*

redloch n. (butchers' backsl.) shoulder, both human and as a cut of meat *Cole.*

redneck n. a peasant, esp. Southern US poor farmer who is stupid and racist *Jay & Young.*

redneck foreplay n. the complete absence of any preliminary physical contact (cf: redneck).

reds n. 1. barbiturates, fr. colour of pills. (cf: whites, yellows, purple hearts) *Dury*; 2. Communists, fr. predominant colour symbolizing world revolution.

redtape n. bureaucratic interference and obfuscation, inevitably leading to problems and delay for those which it entangles.

red-tapers n. bureaucrats, civil servants *Sanders:2.*

reeb n. (London backsl.) beer *Powis.*

reefer n. 1. marijuana; 2. a marijuana cigarette; both meanings fr. greefo (qv) *SF Comic.*

reeking a. drunk (cf: stinking) *Dickson.*

reel in the biscuit v. (US campus use) to seduce a girl successfully *Bernbach.*

reet a. ideal, perfect, excellent, quintessential; fr. mispron. of right.

reffo n. (Aus. use) (abbrev.) refugee, derog. term for any European (esp. Italian, Greek, Yugoslav) immigrants to Australia; the late 1930s influx of Jews to the US created 'refujew' *Humphries:2.*

regular guy n. a thoroughly good person – in the speaker's opinion his/her peer, intellectually, in sense of humour, opinions, politics, etc. *Farrell.*

regular Joe n. a conventional (conservative) person (cf: Joe Public) *Price:3.*

rehash n.,v. a recreation, a postmortem of an event; to discuss once more, to assess the past, either immediate or distant.

reimburse v. (US Black use) to lose one's life for the refusal or inability to pay off a debt or favour *Klein.*

reilo n. (Aus. use) a relative.

reload v. (conman use) to let a victim win at a game of three-card monte (qv) prior to having him bet a larger sum, which he will inevitably then lose *Powis.*

REMF n. (US milit. use) (acro., pron. 'rimph'): *Rear Echelon Mother-Fuckers*; used by combat troops *Del Vecchio.*

Renee n. girl-friend; fr. the popular name *G 28/3/83.*

rent party n. (US Black use) a party held in a private house to which a small admission fee is charged and used, if only in theory, for paying the rent (cf: house party).

rent-boy n. a youthful male prostitute.

renter n. see. rent-boy.

rep n. (abbrev.) reputation; spec. a member's standing and status in a street gang *rr.*

repap n. (backsl.) paper *Cole.*

repeat v. a genteel euph. for burping or farting; the food is 'repeating' itself.

repo man n. (abbrev.) repossession man: one who is employed by finance companies to repossess goods on which the owner is defaulting as to his payments.

reppock n. (backsl.) copper = policeman (cf: esclop) *Cole*.

reptiles n. (US Black use) shoes, fr. the skins used for many popular styles *Klein*.

rescue station n. (US Black use) liquor store; ironic corruption of rescue mission: a centre for alcoholics and other down-and-outs *Folb*.

resting a. (theatrical use) a euph. for unemployed; the US version is *at liberty Green:2*.

result n. a successful outcome to a given endeavour: a sporting victory; an arrest for policemen; a lucrative robbery for villains, etc. *Newman:1*.

retchtub n. (butchers' backsl.) a butcher *Cole*.

retread n. 1. anything old that has been trotted out for a new lease of life, specifically of anyone who has been retrained for a new job; from its original meaning of a tyre that has been reprocessed, with a new tread, to extend its practical life. 2. one who has recently been divorced.

rettes n. (US preppie (qv) use) (abbrev.) cigarettes *Bernbach*.

re-up v. to reenlist, to join up again; fr. milit. use *Price:3*.

rev. v. (UK 'society' use) to improve, to gee up; fr. motor car use *K. Clarke*.

revo n. the Revolution; that unspecified explosion that stands as a grail for radicals everywhere.

RF (acro.) Rat *F*uck (qv).

RFD queen n. a homosexual living in a rural area, outside the main gay world; fr. *R*ural *F*ree *D*elivery *Legman*.

rhino n. money *LL*.

rhubarb n. nonsense, rubbish, fr. actors' traditional muttering of 'Rhubarb' to provide background in crowd scenes *Austin*.

rib v. to tease, to make fun of *Goulart*.

ribby a. 1. fr. on the ribs: short of money, broke (qv); 2. second rate, poor quality *Powis*.

rib joint n. (sex industry use) any form of sex show which permits the customers to watch, but definitely not to touch.

rice man n. (US Black use) an Oriental (cf: ricer).

ricer n. (derog.) an Asian person; fr. the predominant Oriental staple *Folb*.

rich a. surprising, highly unlikely; usu. *that's rich*.

Richard n. (rhyming sl.) Richard the Third = bird = girl (friend) *LL*.

Richard the Third (rhyming sl.) 1. bird = girl (friend) (cf: Richard); 2. (theatrical use) the bird, ie booing from an audience *Franklyn*; 3. a turd *Cole*; 4. a third-class degree.

rick n. an error, a mistake; poss. abbrev. ricket: a mistake or fr. bookies' sl. *rick*: a spurious bet *Austin*.

ricket n. a mistake, a blunder *Norman: 2*.

ride n. 1. an automobile *Folb*; 2. sexual intercourse '*Not The Nine O'Clock News', BBC-2 TV, 1980*.

ride a blind piece v. (homosexual use) to fellate an uncircumcized penis *Legman*.

ride a cotton horse v. to be menstruating.

ride punk v. (US Black use) aka: *ride pussy, ride the bitch's seat*: for a woman to sit between two men in a car *Folb*.

ride shotgun v. to sit in the seat next to the driver in a car; fr. stagecoach era use of a shotgun-wielding assistant who sat next to the coachman and protected him against marauding Indians, bandits, etc.

ride the deck v. (US prison use) to perform anal intercourse *Legman*.

ride the planks v. (Aus. surf use) to go surfing *Humphries: 2*.

ride the porcelain Honda v. (US campus use) to have diarrhoea (cf: drive the porcelain bus) *Bernbach*.

ride the rag v. (US Black use) to have a menstrual period *Folb*.

ride the wagon v. (US Black use) to

enjoy a pleasant experience on a given drug *Klein*.

ride tough v. (US Black use) 1. to be intoxicated by a drug; 2. to be riding in a noteworthy car *Klein*.

ridgerunner n. derog. 1. a southern mountain farmer, a hill-billy; 2. (US Black) any white person (cf: cracker, honky, peckerwood, white trash).

ridgie-didgie a. (Aus. use) genuine, honest; fr. UK cant *ridge* = gold in 17th C. *Baker*.

riff n. (US Black use) familiar or habitual words; fr. jazz use *Folb*.

rig n. 1. (truck driver use) a truck; 2. (drug use) the needed used to inject narcotics *Underwood*; 3. the penis (cf: donkey-rigged).

rig a jig v. (US Black/pimp use) to set up a potential trick (qv) or victim for deception or for his paying one of the pimp's girls for sex *Klein*.

right a. extremely, very; thus, a *right bastard*, a *right good 'un*, etc.

right arm! (US campus use) see: right on! *Underwood*.

right from the giddyap phr. right from the start, the beginning; the image is of starting a horse with a cry of 'Giddyap!'.

right guy n. (US prison use) a popular prisoner, respected by his peers (cf: real man) *Neaman & Silver*.

right on! (excl.) excellent, perfect, exactly right; orig. Black use but taken up by white hippies, radicals, etc; fr. 'right on time' *Seale*.

right sort n. a promiscuous girl *Cole*.

right up one's alley absolutely as one wishes, specifically to one's taste *W. Allen, 'Manhattan', 1979*.

righteous a. 1. of people: honest, trustworthy, honourable; 2. of things, esp. drugs: excellent, first rate *SF Comics*; 3. ideologically pure *Seale*.

righteous moss n. (US Black use) white people's hair *Major*.

righto! (excl.) certainly! *Performance*.

rigid a. drunk, and passed out *Dickson*.

rim v. to stimulate the anus with the lips and tongue (cf: ream)

Jay & Young.

rim queen n. a homosexual who enjoys anilingus *Stanley*.

rim slide n. (US prison use) a silent but foul-smelling fart *Klein*.

rim-job n. see rim.

ring n. the anus, the buttocks.

ring v. to alter a car for the purposes of using it as a getaway vehicle, hold-up van, etc. *Newman: 1*.

ring a bell v. to remind one of something, to jog one's memory.

ring (her) bell v. to produce (female) orgasm during intercourse.

ring (his) bell v. to concuss, esp. in US football use when this may well follow a clash of helmets *Green: 2*.

ring it on v. to outwit, to fool *Powis*.

ring one's chimes v. to have or to give a partner an orgasm.

ring the changes v. (UK criminal use) to defraud, to deceive, esp. by passing counterfeit money *LL*.

ringburner n. (UK 'society' use) diarrhoea, the runs (qv) (cf: ring) *Barr*.

ring-ding n. fool, second-rate person, no-hoper; poss. fr. a punch-drunk boxer who has 'bells ringing' in his head *Farina*.

ringer n. 1. a fàke, someone posing as a person they are not; esp. a pool or bowling hustler (qv) who pretends not to be an expert; 2. a horse or dog substituted either for a better or a worse animal for the purposes of those betting either for or against it; 3. a second-hand car made up to look better than it is; 4. one who specializes in stealing then improving second-hand cars for sale in UK or Europe *Powis*.

ringside n. (show business use) in a nightclub or similar establishment, those tables nearest to the stage; fr. boxing use *Bruce: 2*.

rinky-dink a. cheap, second-rate *Underwood*.

rip and tear v. (rhyming sl.) to swear *Cole*.

rip her guts down v. (US Black use) to copulate aggressively, sadistically, but with implication that both partners achieve mutual satisfaction *Klein*.

rip into v. 1. to start a fight; 2. to criticize harshly (cf: tear into).

rip joint n. (US campus use) any store that charges exorbitant prices to students; fr. rip-off and joint (qqv) *Underwood*.

rip off n. a fraud, a cheat, a disappointment *Seale*.

rip off v. 1. to steal, to cheat *Tuff Shit Comics*; 2. to kill, to assassinate *Milner*.

rip off artist n. 1. a thief; 2. a prostitute who specializes in robbing her clients and as such is more thief than purveyor of commercial sex *OUI 8/75*; 3. any form of cheat, emotional as well as material *Price: 3*.

rip shit v. to have a party, to act energetically, to make a disturbance (cf: tear up).

ripcord n. the small loop attached to the back of some men's shirts (cf:fag tag, fruit loop).

ripe a. drunk *Dickson*.

ripped a. extremely intoxicated on drink, drugs or a mixture *Mandelkau*.

ripped to the tits a. an extreme version of ripped (qv).

ripper a. (Aus. use) excellent wonderful, perfect, etc.; has replaced the obs. *bonzer*; but cited in Hotten 1860 *Humphries: 2*.

rip-snorter n. anything exceptional or remarkable and of which the speaker approves.

rise and shine! jocular wake-up call; sometimes preceded by 'wakey-wakey!' (cf: hands off (your) cocks . . .).

ritz n. 1. glamour, elegance, wealth, sophistication, thus phr. 2. 'in the ritz': living well (cf: fat city); 3. put on the ritz: acting (justifiably or otherwise) as if one possessed these characteristics; 4. 'this ain't the Ritz': don't expect anything special (fr. the Ritz-Carlton Hotel, the New York City branch of the chain established by César Ritz (1850-1918); 3. was hugely popularized by Irving Berlin's song

'Putting On The Ritz' [1929]).

ritzy a. smart, chic, fashionable; fr. the Ritz Hotel, once the epitome of such attainments *Morgan*.

roach n. the unsmoked portion of a marijuana/hashish cigarette; fr. cockroach *Performance*.

roach clip n. a small spring clip or pair of tweezers used to hold the last fragments of a marijuana cigarette, which is otherwise too hot to hold in one's fingers.

roach killers n. extremely pointed shoes for men, popular in New York c.1960s; fr. idea of their stabbing cockroaches (cf: winkle-pickers) *Price: 1*.

road brew n. (US campus use) aka: *roadies, road sauce*: beer *Bernbach*.

road dog n. (US Black use) an extremely initimate friend (CF: running partner) *Klein*.

roadie n. (music use) road crew, member of rock band's support unit who sets up and dismantles stage, equipment, etc. *May*.

roaf (bacsksl.) four *Cole*.

roak v. (US Black use) to beat savagely about the head *Klein*.

Robert E. n. (rhyming sl.) Robert E. Lee = pee = urination *May*.

rock n. 1. diamond *Higgins: 1*; 2. a man who is sturdy and solid both emotionally, physically and in his character; 3. cocaine *Morgan*; 4. crack (qv).

rock and roll n. (rhy.sl.) the dole *Welsh:1*.

rock 'n' roll (US milit. use) firing a weapon on full automatic; the weapon tends to move violently around *Del Vecchio*.

rock of ages n. (rhyming sl.) wages *Cole*.

rock out v. (US Black use) to collapse, to be exhausted *Folb*.

rock spider n. (S. Afr. use) an Afrikaaner *Marcuson*.

rockers n. UK youth cult who wore leather, rode powerful motorbikes and fought their ritual rivals, the mods (qv); latterly the hard-core rockers developed into a UK version of the US Hells Angels.

rocket n. a severe reprimand or telling off.

rockets n. (US Black use) 1. bullets *Major*; 2. breasts.

rocks n. 1. the testicles; 2. courage, bravery *Higgins: 5*.

rocks for jocks (US campus use) undergraduate course in 'introductory geology' *Birnbach*.

rocky road n. the anus.

rod n. 1. penis *Gothic Blimp Works No. 4, 1969*; 2. a gun *Runyon*; 3. an overcoat *Powis*.

rod walloper n. masturbator; fr. rod 1. (qv) *Humphries*.

rodded a. carrying a gun.

rodge n. a fact, anything that's true; fr. airforce 'roger' = message received and understood *Underwood*.

Rods n. (UK 'society' use) Harrods (cf: Freds) *Barr*.

rofe n. (UK prison use) fr. backsl. four-year sentence *LL*.

roger v. to have sexual intercourse, to seduce; fr. the name often given to bulls in 18th C. *Keyes*.

roll n. (abbrev.) bankroll *Higgins: 3*.

roll v. 1. to rob. usu. *roll a drunk Burroughs:*1; 2. sexual intercourse, from 'roll in the hay'(qv); 3. (US Black use) to survive, to live, to conduct oneself.

roll a number v. to prepare a marijuana cigarette (cf: number).

roll in v. aka: *roll up*: arrive, come home *Higgins: 3*.

roll in the hay sexual intercourse, with implication of spontaneity, adultery, *al fresco Higgins: 5*.

roll out v. (US campus use) to leave, to depart *Underwood*.

roll them bones! (gambling use) throw those dice! used with consciousness of slight archaism and only in the context of a crap game.

roll with the punches v. to take events as they come and not to be unbalanced by problems; fr. boxing imagery *Higgins: 1*.

roll your own (US Black use) invitation to make yourself at home, do whatever you fancy; fr. rolling one's own cigarettes *Klein*.

Roller n. a Rolls Royce car *Dury*.

roller n. 1. a pickpocket who specializes in stealing from drunks (cf: lushworker) *Chandler: Notebk*; 2. (US criminal use) a policeman who specializes in stopping people on the street for an instant search in the hope of finding stolen goods or drugs *Klein*; 3. (US Black use) one who keeps moving continuously; 4. (drug use) a vein that rolls as one attempts to insert a needle *Klein*; 5. a police car *Ice T:1*.

rollick v. (rhyming sl) (euph.) bollick = tell off, reprimand; thus 'a good rollicking' and 'rollicks!' *Cole*.

rolling a. 1. (abbrev.) rolling with money: very well off *Schulberg*; 2. very drunk; fr. one's gait *Dickson*.

rolling in the aisles a. very much amused, reduced to near-hysterical laughter; fr. theatrical use referring to a comedian's success *Wodehouse: MOJ*.

roll-up n. a handmade cigarette of papers and tobacco *Cole*.

roman candle n. (RAF use) the failure of a parachute to open and the resultant plunge to his death of the parachutist.

Roman candle n. (gay use) 1. Italian-American penis; 2, any Italian.

Roman culture n. orgies, group sex; fr. popular fantasties of the 'decline and fall' of Rome *Rawson*.

Roman engagement n. (gay use) anal intercourse with a virgin girl.

Roman fountains n. (gay use) urinals.

Roman historian n. (gay use) an enthusiast of orgies.

Roman night n. (gay use) an orgy.

romp n. (horseracing use) an easy win, thus *to come home in a romp*: to saunter past the winning post, out-distancing all rivals.

romp it v. (US campus use) to accelerate in a car *Underwood*.

ronk n. (northern UK use) a stink; from the dial. ronk or rank, meaning over-ripe.

roof it v. to have sex on the roofs of New York apartment buildings *Sanders: 2*.

rook v. to cheat, to swindle, to steal; fr. allegedly larcenous character of the bird (cf: pigeon) *Hotten*.

rookie n. a novice, a beginner, a new recruit; esp. in milit., police, sports use; poss. fr. recruit *Runyon: 1*.

rooks n. see: rocks *Klein*.

room to rent n. (Valley Girls (qv) use) a stupid person, whose brain is 'vacant' *Harpers/Queen 1/83*.

rooster n. (US Black use) a sexually active male; fr. the farmyard bird *Folb*.

rooster time n. (US teen. use) the early morning, 'cock's crow' *Sculatti*.

root n. **1.** the penis; **2.** the person with whom one has intercourse; more usu. the female of the two.

root v. to have sexual intercourse.

root for v. to support, esp. a sports team *Grogan*.

rooted a. (Aus. use) exhausted, crippled, out of action *Humphries: 2*.

rooter n. **1.** a sports fan *P. Roth, 'The Great American Novel', 1973*; **2.** one who likes to root (qv) and thus anyone seen as being keen on sex.

root-faced a. humourless, sanctimonious, censorious; fr. a face carved into the hard twists of a tree root *Humphries: 2*.

rootiepoot n. (US Black use) see pootbutt *Folb*.

roots(y) a. (UK Black use) authentic, culturally sound.

rope n. (drug use) a vein *Goldman*.

rope in v. to involve, to include *Higgins: 4*.

ropeable a. (Aus. use) extremely angry; from the phrase 'fit to be tied'.

ropey a. second-rate, inadequate, mediocre, rundown, etc.; poss. fr. RAF use: an obsolete aircraft, overburdened with a variety of ropes.

rorty a. (Aus. use) rowdy, noisy, esp. of a party; fr. obs. SE (19th C.) *Humphries: 2*.

Rory n. **1.** (UK prison use; rhyming sl.) Rory O'Moore = door (of one's

cell *LL*; **2.** (rhyming sl.) floor *Wright*.

Roscoe n. a handgun *Chandler: Notebk*.

rose among the thorns n. (US pimp use) a good-looking prostitute in a stable (qv) of less attractive women *Klein*.

rosewood n. (US Black use) a policeman's nightstick; fr. wood from which it was made *Major*.

rosiner n. (Aus. use) any form of stiff drink, a pick-me-up *Wilkes*.

Rosy Lea (Lee) n. (rhyming sl.) tea.

Rosy Palm and her five little sisters n. the hand, as used in masturbation.

rot n. rubbish, nonsense; esp. in talk rot *Wodehouse: MOJ*.

rotgut n. cheap whisky; fr. its effects *X*.

rotten a. (Aus. use) very drunk *Wilkes*.

rough a. general pejorative *G Green* (1994).

rough end of the pineapple (Aus. use) hostile or unfair treatment *Wilkes*.

rough it v. to live deprived of life's material comforts; not simply to be poor, but to volunteer oneself – as in camping, the forces, etc. – for such hardy existence *Wodehouse: AAG*.

rough trade n. (homosexual use) a violent sexual partner; often a man who is or poses as a construction worker, serviceman, truck driver, motorcyclist, etc., with appropriate costumes, often of leather.

roughhouse v. to pursue rough trade (qv), to enjoy the sleazier aspects of sex *Morgan*.

rough-house v. to fight, to beat up *Goulart*.

roughneck a. see: rough *Snoop Doggy Dogg 'Doggystyle' (1993)*.

roughneck n. **1.** a thug, a hoodlum, a fighter *Heller*; **2.** a labourer on an oil rig *Green:2*.

round house v. (US pimp use) for a prostitute to go around the world (qv), licking, sucking and fucking (qv) every orifice and erogenous zone her client has to offer *Klein*.

round file n. (US campus use) wastepaper basket *Underwood*.

round pussy n. the anus (cf: roundeye).

round the houses n. (rhyming sl.) trousers *Cole*.

roundball n. (US Black use) basketball (as opp. to football, played with an oval ball) *Folb*.

rounder n. (Can. prison use) anyone who knows their way around the underworld *Caron*.

roundeye n. 1. the anus; 2. a white person, as opposed to an oriental (cf: slant).

roundhead n. 1. (drug use) any drug contained in a capsule with curved ends *Folb*; 2. a circumcised penis, the boy who has one (usu. school use) (cf: clipped).

rouser n. (drug use) any type of amphetamine or stimulant drug which 'gets one up' *Klein*.

rout v. (US campus use) to engage in sexual intercourse *Underwood*.

row in v. 1. (criminal use) to allow someone to join a scheme, a conspiracy *Norman: 2*; 2. (UK police use) to implicate a given suspect in a given crime *Laurie*.

row out v. (UK police use) to exonerate a given suspect from a given crime *Laurie*.

rower n. (UK prison use) an argument; fr. row *Obs. 1981*.

Roy n. (Aus. use) a chic, sophisticated 'trendy' Australian; the opposite of Alf (qv) *Wilkes*.

royal a. (Jamaican use) any Black person from a race other than West Indian *Thelwell*.

Royal Mail n. (rhyming sl.) bail, usu. criminal/prison use *Cole*.

rozzer n. 1. policeman; poss. fr. Romany *roozlo*: strong; or fr. *roast*, a villain *Humphries*; 2. (US Black use) a rubber contraceptive with small protrusions for extra stimulation of the vagina *Klein*.

R/S (contact ads use) (acro.) rough stuff; incl. sadomasochism,

urolagnia (cf: water sports, golden showers), infibulation (piercing of nipples), rubberwear, etc. *Neaman & Silver*.

rub v. (US Black use) to criticize *Klein*.

rub in v. to emphasise, often with malicious pleasure *Wodehouse: IJ*.

rub out v. murder, assassinate, kill *Fiction Illus. 3*.

rub up v. to stimulate the penis to erection using the hands *Higgins: 1*.

rub up the wrong way v. to annoy, to infuriate; fr. stroking a cat against the 'grain' of its fur.

rubadub m. sexual intercourse; esp. quick and spontaneous *Southern & Hoffenberg*.

rub-a-dub n. (rhyming sl.) pub *Norman: 2*.

rubbed a. murdered, killed; fr. rubbed out = erased.

rubber n. a contraceptive sheath.

rubber v. to look around, to gaze at; fr. rubberneck *Howard*.

rubber boot n. contraceptive sheath *Higgins: 3*.

rubber cheque n. a bouncing cheque (qv) that is not honoured by the writer's bank.

Rubber City n. (CB use) Akron, Ohio *CB*.

rubber heels 1. the Special Branch; 2. the internal investigations department of Scotland Yard, policing the police *Austin*.

rubber johnny n. contraceptive sheath.

rubberneck v. 1. (US Black use) masturbation, self-fellation (if one is acrobatically capable) *Klein*; 2. to act as an obvious tourist; fr. visitors to New York City craning their necks to view the high buildings *Wolfe: 2*.

rubbidy n. see: rub-a-dub *Humphries*.

rubbin' one's nubbin female masturbation *Maledicta*.

rubbish n. (UK police use) everyday, mundane and undemanding police duties *Laurie*.

rubbish v. 1. to attack verbally, to slander *Humphries*; 2. to treat badly, with disrespect *BBC Radio 3 1983*.

rubblehead n. fool, idiot, incompetent (cf: dickhead).

rube n. a fool, an unsophisticated person; fr. carnival use and 'yokel' name: Reuben *Norman: 1*.

rubyfruit n. the female genitals; fr. colour and supposed appearance; best known as title of Rita Mae Brown's 'Rubyfruit Jungle' *Maledicta*.

ruck n. a fight, an argument; abbrev. ruckus (qv) also fr. ruck: to disturb, orig. clothes and thence tempers *Norman: 2*.

rucker n. an arguer, a combative person *Norman: 2*.

rucking n. a severe reprimand *Norman: 1*.

ruckus n. a fight, a celebration, a noisy party or demonstration *Himes: 1*.

rude a. (euph.) sexual *Barr*.

rude parts n. (euph.) genitals, male or female (in the latter case extended to breasts also) *Barr*.

ruffle n. 1. (homosexual use) the passive partner in a lesbian relationship; poss. fr. 19th-C. *rufus*: the pudendum *Stanley*; 2. (US Black use) a fight *Klein*.

rug n. (derog.) a Black person.

rug n. toupee, hairpiece, usu. show business use; it lies on/covers one's bald patch (cf: syrup) *Price: 3*.

rug beat n. (US Black use) a noisy, festive party where the dancing 'beats the rug' *Klein*.

rug rat n. a small child who is still crawling on the carpet (cf: ankle-biter).

rugby team (bingo use) 15 *Wright*.

ruggsy a. aka: *warry* British milit. use (esp. paratroops), a consciously 'macho' image, featuring torn T-shirts, faded fatigues, large boots, and larger muscles *Green: 2*.

rugy n. (US Black use) unattractive; ill-tempered; elision of 'rude guy' (?) *Folb*.

ruin v. (homosexual use) deliberate exaggeration of one's effeminacy to shock fellow gays *Stanley*.

Rule 43 (UK prison use) voluntary solitary confinement for the sake of a prisoner's safety: child molesters, rapists, etc. choose this in preference to the natural justice of their peers *Newman: 3*.

rum a. odd, peculiar, strange *Wright*.

rumble n.v. 1. (US use) a street gang fight *Price: 1*; 2. (UK use) a fight *Payne*.

rumble v. 1. to discover, to find out *Powis*; 2. (drug use) to be searched by the police *Burroughs: 1*.

rum-dum n. a heavy drinker, a rummy (qv); fr. rum, the drink *Runyon*.

rummy a. odd, peculiar, bizarre; fr. rum (qv) *Wodehouse: YMS*.

rummy n. a drunkard.

rumour n. (teen. use) anything considered dead, finished or currently irrelevant *Sculatti*.

rump v. (US Black use) to copulate *Klein*.

rump ranger n. a male homosexual.

rumpo n. sexual intercourse.

rumpot n. a drunkard *Runyon: 1*.

rumpy-pumpy n. sexual intercourse; also 'humpy-pumpy'. *Green:3*.

run n. (Hells Angels use) 1. full scale club outing involving all the Hells Angels in a given chapter and devoted to maximum excess in all possible areas of activity *Wolfe: 2*; 2. the immediate and intense feeling that follows the injection of heroin into a vein (cf:rush).

run v. (drug use) to be an habitual drug user.

run a double train v. (US Black use) for two men to penetrate a woman simultaneously – by the vagina and the anus (cf: make a sandwich) *Folb*.

run a line v. see: shoot a line *Klein*.

run a tight ship v. to keep full control of a given situation; to be an efficient organizer or leader; fr. nautical use *Vidal*.

run down game v. (Black pimp use) to explain the principles of the pimping business, both from experienced pimps to novices and from the pimp to his girls, telling them the tricks of their tricks (qv).

run down one's best game v. (US Black use) to make one's best, cleverest and most skilful efforts *Shulman*.

run down some lines v. (US Black use) 1. to make conversation; 2. to attempt seduction by smooth talking *Folb*.

run game on v. (US black use) to bamboozle, deceive, confuse.

run in v. to arrest; run in to gaol *Southern & Hoffenberg*.

run into the ground v. to persist in an action or in speech to the extent that all meaning and importance is lost; fr. driving a car or riding a horse until it collapses.

run it down v. to explain, to point out facts *Seale*.

run off at the mouth aka: *run off at the jaw/jibs*: to talk to excess and to the irritation of one's audience *Folb*.

run one on v. to arrest.

run one way and look another v. (US Black use) to act in a duplicitous manner; to cheat deliberately *Klein*.

run one's hand up the flagpole v. to masturbate (cf: varnish one's pole).

run out of road v. for a motorcar (or its driver) to fail to negotiate a curve properly and to skid off the road rather than turn the corner.

run out on v. to abandon, to leave suddenly *Goulart*.

run over v. to victimize *Seale*.

run rings around v. to beat comprehensively; to make one to look foolish.

run sets on v. aka: *throw sets on, roll sets on:* to hit with combination left and right punches (cf: one-two) *Folb*.

run up side o' your head v. (Black use) to beat up *Milner*.

run with the ball v. to take on a problem and tackle it on one's own initiative, rather than passing the buck; fr. US football or UK rugby use *Dickson*.

runabout n. (US Black use) facts on a given situation *Klein*.

rundown n. explanation, the facts.

rung a. cars supplied with false plates,

documents, etc. for use in a robbery (cf: ringer) *Newman: 1*.

run-in n. an argument, a controversy, a fight *Wolfe: 2*.

runner n. (UK police/criminal use) one who is on the run from the police *Powis*.

runners (Aus. use) track shoes, training shoes.

running down assessing, going through *Price: 2*.

running out of one's head, running out of one's ears phr. referring to something that one posesses in full measure or to excess.

running partner n. (US Black use) a close friend with whom one pursues most of one's daily activities *Folb*.

running with allied to, in partnership with, on the same side as *Seale*.

runs n. diarrhoea (cf: trots) *Tidy*.

ruptured duck n. (US milit. use) the lapel pin or pocket insignia worn by an honourably discharged US serviceman; thus the honourable discharge itself *Chandler: LG*.

rush n. the immediate and intense feeling that follows the injection of heroin into a vein *Tuff Shit Comics*.

rush v. 1. to show intense interest in something or someone; 2. (US campus use) to pay court to a student with the hope of having them join a given fraternity.

Russian high n. (gay use) simultanous fellatio and anal intercourse.

Russian salad party n. (gay use) an orgy in which all participants are covered in baby oil.

Russki n. (derog.) a Russian *BvdB*.

rust-bucket n. (Aus. use) a car that is noticeably and dangerously rusty *Wilkes*.

rustle n. (US Black use) an orphan, esp. one whose parents are unknown (cf: drop) (fr. SE rustle: to act quickly, to hurry about; such a child is the product of a quick, brief relationship).

rusty a. exhausted; out of practice.

rusty dusty n. the buttocks, esp. with the inference that someone has been sitting around doing nothing – thus they are 'rusty' and 'dusty' from lack of movement *Burroughs: 1*.

rusty-gun a. veteran policeman *Grogan*.

Ruth Buzzy n. (US Black use) a plain-looking woman; fr. the actress best known for her work on 'Rowan & Martin's Laugh-In', c.1967. *Folb*.

RWV (UK police/prison use) Robbery With Violence *LL*.

ryache n. (backsl.) chair *Cole*.

S

sack n. **1.** a bed *Austin*; (US Black use) **2.** an uncoordinated, unathletic person who just lies dumpily around *Folb*; **3.** one's home; fr. its being where one sleeps (cf: rack) *Klein*.

sack v. to dismiss from a job.

sack it up v. (US Black use) to terminate, to bring to a conclusion *Klein*.

sack lunch n. see: box lunch *Folb*.

sack mouth n. (US Black use) one who talks too much; a gossip; thus a large, gaping mouth *Folb*.

sack o' nuts n. (US Black use) the scrotum; fr. nuts (qv) *Klein*.

sack out v. to fall asleep, to go to bed; fr. sack (qv) *Goldman*.

sack time n. time spent asleep, in bed *Fiction Illus.3*.

sacked out a. fast asleep *Bruce:2*.

sad a. second rate, inferior, unattractive; a general term of disparagement *L Green*.

sad sack n. a miserable, depressed (and depressing) individual, usu. thus singled out in an institution – prison, army, etc. *E. Presley, 'Jailhouse Rock', 1958*.

saddle up v. to engage in mutual fellatio / cunnilingus (cf:cannibal, sixty-nine) *AS 60.1 (1985)*.

safe! excl. all-purpose term of approval used by teenagers.

safe a. (contact ads use) the man advertising has had a vasectomy *SMD*.

safe n. (abbrev.) safety: a contraceptive sheath *Rawson*.

safe screw n. (UK prison use) aka: *safe twirl*: a prison officer who can be trusted to permit or even join in various illicit goings-on, transactions etc. *LL*.

sail close to the wind v. to take risks, esp. with a set of rules and regulations fr. naut. use.

sail into v. to attack, physically or verbally.

saint n. (US police use) a highly scrupulous, incorruptible officer; such virtues, within the Force, are presumably near-saintly *Neaman & Silver*.

St Grotlesex n. (US preppie (qv) use) a portmanteau description of St Marks, St Paul's, Groton and Middlesex *Bernbach*

Salisbury Crag n. heroin *Welsh:1* (rhy.sl. = skag (qv)).

Sally Ann aka: Salfy Army: (abbrev.) Salvation Army (cf: Salvo) *Powis*.

salmon n. (rhyming sl.) salmon and trout = snout = tobacco *Powis*.

salmon trout n. (rhyming sl.) snout = tobacco; esp. in prison use *Cole*.

saloon bar cowboy n. a man who specializes in picking up women who, like him, can be fround frequenting the saloon bars of public houses (cf: lounge lizard).

salt and pepper n. (US criminal use) black and white police car (cf: black and white) *Folb*.

salty a. irritated, annoyed; feeling sour *Selby:1*.

salty dog n. (US Black use) one who uses an excess of obscene language *Klein*.

Salvo n. (Aus. use) Salvation Army (cf: Sally Ann) *Baker*.

sam v. to cheat, to deceive; fr. 19th C.

sammy: a fool, thus to treat as a fool (?) *Powis*.

Sam and Dave n. the police; fr. well-known soul duo *Folb*.

Sam Hill n. (euph.) hell, usu. as in 'What in (the) Sam Hill. . .!' *Rawson*.

Sambo (derog.) Black man; first OED citation 1704, popular name in slavery era; also fr. children's bk 'Little Black Sambo' *BvdB*.

samfie n. (Jamaican use) confidence trickster *Thelwell*.

samfu (UK milit. use) *self-adjusting military fuck-up* (cf: snafu) *Rawson*.

same difference n. exactly the same thing, thus no difference at all.

same ol' same ol' (US Black use) usual routine or situation *Major*.

same shit, different day phr. see: same ol' same ol'.

SAN man n. (US prison use) (acro) *Stop At Nothing* man; dangerous and violent *Neaman & Silver*.

San Quentin briefcase n. see ghetto blaster *Morgan*.

San Quentin quail n. see jailbait.

Sancho n. (US prison use) the Mexican version of Jody (qv) *Morgan*.

sand n. (Can. prison use) sugar; since 19th C.

sandbag v. **1.** to ambush, to take by surprise fr. the silent, deadly weapon employed *PT;* **2.** (motor racing use) to drive very fast; **3.** (poker use) to resist raising the bet when immediately possible in the hope of making a larger raise later on.

sandnigger n. an Arab (cf:towelhead) *Morgan*.

sandwich man n. (US Black use) a man having sex with two women *Klein*.

sango n. (Aus. use) aka: *sanger* a sandwich (cf: sarnie) *Ready*.

sanno n. (Aus. use) sanitary carter or inspector *Ready*.

sanpaku a. out of touch, out of balance – physically and spiritually; fr. Zen use: visibility of the white of the eye below the iris as well as (as usual) on either side; fr. Jap. *san*: three + *haku*: white *Burroughs:Jr*.

Santa Claus n. (US Black use) a

vulgar, gaudy, flashy and tasteless dresser fr. the department store Santas (cf: caution sign) *Folb*.

sap n. **1.** a weighted blackjack made of leather and lead; **2.** a fool *Price:2*.

sapfu (milit. use) (acro.) surpassing all previous *fuck-ups* (cf: snafu) *Rawson*.

Sappho n. a lesbian; thus *sapphic*: code word for female homosexuality *Legman*.

sappy a. foolish, stupid; fr. sap (qv) *Higgins:5*.

sarky a. (abbrev.) sarcastic; usu. juv. use.

sarnie n. a sandwich *Payne*.

sass v. to answer back, to check.

sassy a. cheeky, spirited, back-talking *Folb*.

sassy box n. (US Black use) [the vagina of] a saucy young girl *Klein*.

satchel n. anus; into which things may be put *Higgins:1*.

satellite v. to hang around; fr. satellites circling a planet *Price:3*.

saturated a. very drunk; a lit. description of the bloodstream *Dickson*.

Saturday Night Special n. a small handgun, often used in the many fracas that occur over Saturday night in a big US city *Price:2*.

sauce n. drink *Higgins:1*.

sauce v. to have sex.

sauce hound n. drunkard, alcoholic *Schulberg*.

sauced a. drunk *Neaman & Silver*.

saucepan lid n. (rhyming sl.) Yid = Jew *Norman:3*.

sausage and mash n. (rhyming sl.) cash *Cole*.

sausage dog n. a dachshund; fr. its German origins (cf: dachsie).

save one's bacon v. to escape safely, from a place or situation; fr. 18th C. cant bacon = loot *Wright*.

savvy a. intelligent, aware; fr. Fr. *savoir*: to know *Higgins:1*.

saw n. (US Black use) the owner of a cheap rooming house *Major*.

saw wood v. to snore (cf: chop wood).

sawbones n. a doctor, a surgeon

Klein.

sawbuck a. $10; thus *double sawbuck*: $20 *Fiction Illus.3.*

sawed off a. see: sawn off.

sawn off n. (abbrev.) a sawn off shotgun *Higgins:1.*

sawn-off a. short; the presumption being that a short person was at one stage taller.

sawski n. see: sawbuck *Burroughs:1.*

say a mouthful v. 1. (homosexual use) to reprove a fellow homosexual in detail and at great length *Legman*; 2. to say something important (and true).

say something v. (US Black use) to make an important statement, to say something profound *Major.*

says you! aka: *sez you:* general excl. of contempt, dismissing as beneath argument the previous speaker's words.

SBD (teen. use) (acro) *S*ilent *B*ut *D*eadly/silent but dangerous: said by anyone smelling a hitherto unannounced fart *Neaman & Silver.*

scab n. 1. (US Black use) an exceptionally unattractive female *Folb*; 2. (industrial use) a strikebreaker, a blackleg (qv) fr. 16th C. scab: a scurvy rascal, thence to current use by 18th C.

scads n. large quantities.

scag n. see: skag *Grogan.*

scag hag n. (homosexual use) see: fag hag *Stanley.*

scale v. (Aus. use) to practise any form of fraud, deception, confidence trick *Wilkes.*

scally a. a hooligan youth, fr. scalliwag; the term originates in Liverpool, where it is tinged with a degree of admiration for the tearaway (qv) in question.

scalp v. 1. (theatre use) to tout tickets at above face value price; orig. Stock Exchange use: buy shares very cheap, then sell below the prevailing price; theatre scalpers (qv) look for greater profits *Variety: passim*; 2. (US Black use) to perform cunnilingus *Klein.*

scalper n. a ticket tout *Runyon.*

scam n. 1. a plan, a scheme *Goldman*; 2. spec. a large scale plan to smuggle and distribute illegal drugs *Grogan.*

scam v. to carry out any form of scam (qv); the verb can be used both transitively and intransitively.

scammered a. (US prison use) homosexual *Legman.*

scampi belt n. the middle-class commuter villages around London where, in the late 1950s/early 1960s, it was considered fashionable to eat scampi; of late scampi is reserved for the 'basket meal' trade and such areas should perhaps be renamed 'the fresh pasta belt'.

scandalous a. excellent, first-rate.

Scapa Flow v. (rhyming sl.) to go (cf: scarper) *Cole.*

scare the bejazus out of v. to terrify completely and utterly *Higgins:5.*

scare the pants off v. to terrify *Wodehouse:AAG.*

scare the shit out of v. to terrify (cf: scare the pants off).

scare up v. to obtain, usu. with some difficulty and poss. by threatening the supplier *Salisbury.*

scaredy-cat n. (juv. use) anyone who is, or appears frightened.

scarf v. 1. to eat, esp. to gobble up, to eat aggressively; fr. scoff (qv) *Price:2*; 2. (US campus use) to throw away, to abandon *Underwood.*

scarper v. to escape; to run off fr. Scapa Flow (qv) *Humphries.*

scat n. 1. an itinerant, a tramp *Wilkinson*; 2. (US Black use) the vagina *Folb*; 3. (abbrev.) scatology: defecation for sexual purposes *Jay & Young.*

scat v. to leave, to go away, fr. scatter *Sillitoe.*

scatter n. a bar, anywhere one can purchase drinks *Runyon.*

scene n. 1. choice, preference (cf: bag); 2. a place, esp. a party; 3. any situation *Greenlee.*

scene n. (gay use) a lengthy, paid-for sexual encounter; the antithesis of a quickie (qv) *Maledicta 9.*

scheme on v. (US bl.) to make

designs on *Kurious: A Constipated Monkey (1994)*.

scheme-on n. opening line used when chatting up a woman/man. *AS 60.1 (1985)*.

schemie n. a person working on a YTS or similar government-backed training scheme *Welsh:1*.

schicer n. aka:*sheister*: a cheat, spec. one who refuses to pay a debt (cf: welsh) *Powis*.

schitzi a. (abbrev.) schizophrenic, loosely used as crazy, insane *Bukowski:1*.

schizo a. see: schitzi.

schizzed a. very drunk, supposedly producing schizophrenia in the sufferer *Bernbach*.

schizzout to lose control mentally, to exhibit the signs of insanity; fr. abbrev. schizophrenic *McFadden*.

schlemiel n. fr. Yiddish; fool, useless person *Pynchon*.

schlep v. fr. Ger *shleppen*: to drag: to carry an inconvenient weight for an equally inconvenient distance; or just to travel further than one might prefer *Norman:3*.

schlepper n. second-rater, loser *Goldman*.

schlock n. cheap, inferior merchandise; anything defective; fr. Yiddish *schlock*: a curse.

schlock shop n. flashy but cheap clothes store *Goldman*.

schlong n. penis *P. Roth, 'Portnoy's Complaint', 1969*.

schlub n. a fool, a moron; fr. Yiddish *Goldman*.

schlubette n. a dumb, stupid, young girl, fr. schlub (qv) *Price:3*.

schmaltz n. fr. Yiddish 'fat': mawkish, over-emotional, esp. in show business use *Norman:3*.

schmeck n. heroin, fr. Yiddish 'to hit' (cf: smack) *Green:1*.

schmecker n. fr. Yiddish: heroin user *Grogan*.

schmeer n. fr. Yiddish: situation, circumstance, usu. 'the whole schmeer' *McFadden*.

schmo n. (euph.) schmuck (qv)

Rosten.

schmooze v. to flatter, to butter up; fr. Yiddish *Stone*.

schmoozefest n. any gathering devoted to mutual (if momentary and insincere) congratulation.

schmuck n. fr. Yiddish: 'penis'; a fool, an unpleasant person *Price:2*.

schmutter n. clothes; fr. Yiddish *shmatte*: rags *M. Jagger, K. Richard, 'Some Girls', 1981*.

schmutz n. filth, dirt; fr. Yiddish *Goldman*.

schnook n. fool, idiot; fr. Yiddish *McFadden*.

schnorrer n. fr. Yiddish: beggar *Gruce:2*.

schnozzle n. fr. Yiddish: the nose *Wright*.

schnozzola n. the nose *Vidal*.

school v. (US Black use) to explain a situation or a plan to someone else *Klein*.

school of hard knocks n. personal experience – as opposed, by those who attribute their education to this institution, to the soft option of actual academic life. (cf: university of life) *Whitcomb*.

school one v. to explain a situation *X*.

schoolbook chump n. (US Black use) 1. an overly studious person; 2. a naïve, innocent person, who has no knowledge beyond his/her books *Folb*.

schoolboy n. (US Black use) a neophyte in the street life; an apprentice criminal *Klein*.

schoolboy scotch n. (US Black use) wine *Folb*.

schoolie n. 1. (abbrev.) schoolgirl *Newman:2*; 2. (Aus. use) schoolteacher *Wilkes*.

schpritz v. to attack, to slander; fr. Yiddish 'to spray' *Bruce:2*.

schtick n. aka: *shtik, shtick* (qv): affair, event, happening *Price:2*.

schtup v. fr. Yiddish: to have sexual intercourse *Bruce:1*.

schvug n. fr. Yiddish: black *Price:2*.

schwartze n. fr. Yiddish 'black': a black person *Bruce:2*.

scoff n. food (cf: scarf) *Caron*.

scoff fishheads v. to have a difficult time, to encounter problems *Maledicta*.

scone n. (Aus. use) head *Ready*.

scone v. (Aus. use) to hit someone on the head *Ready*.

scoobied, skoobied adv. **1.** beaten up, defeated *Welsh:1*; **2.** under the influence of drink or drugs *Welsh:1*; **3.** confused *Welsh:1*.

scooby, skooby v. **1.** to defeat, to trounce, to outwit *Welsh:1* (cf: scupper); **2.** to confuse *Welsh:1*.

scoop n. (US teen./campus use) important, fresh information fr. journalist use (cf: poop) *Underwood*.

scoop v. to arrest (cf: lift) *Higgins:2*.

scoop the pool v. to make a major profit, fr. poker use *Sharpe:1*.

scoot off v. to run away.

scoots n. (US campus use) diarrhoea (cf: runs) *Underwood*.

scope n. the erect penis, fr. abbrev. telescope *Farina*.

scope v. (US campus use) to look for males, usu. female use; fr. telescope *Underwood*.

scope on v. (US Black use) to stare at intently, usu. with sexual interest *Folb*.

scope out v. to look over, to stare at, to investigate *Price:3*.

scorch n. (US Black use) best quality, top-rank goods; fr. *scorcher*: something exceptional *Klein*.

scorcher n. **1.** an attractive and sexually voracious female *May*; **2.** a very hot day; often found in tabloid press in cliché headline 'Phew! what a scorcher' *Sun passim*.

score n. the situation, the facts, what is going on; usu. as in *know the score*; **2.** £20; fr SE *Newman:1*; **3.** (criminal use) the profits from a robbery, fraud or similar criminal act *Teresa*.

score v. **1.** to buy drugs *M. Jagger, K. Richard, 'Sister Morphine', 1970*; **2.** to seduce *Jay & Young*.

score between the posts v. (Aus. use) to have sexual intercourse, to seduce a female; fr. sporting use *Wilkes*.

score yoks v. to make people laugh *Price:3*.

Scotch mist n. anything insubstantial, mythical.

scotch pegs n. (rhyming sl.) legs *Jones:J*.

Scotch screw n. a nocturnal emission.

scotial (US Black use) OK (qv), okey-doke, etc. *Klein*.

Scotland Yard n. (US Black use) plain clothes police; fr. films featuring UK detectives (?) *Klein*.

Scouse n. Liverpudlian; fr. popular local stew: lobscouse *Payne*.

scouser n. see scouse *Welsh:1*.

scrag v. to beat up, to harm, to kill; fr. orig use: to hang or garotte *Runyon*.

scram v. to escape, to run off; fr. scramble (?) *Wolfe:2*.

scramble n. **1.** (US Black use) money *Klein*; **2.** (US teen. use) any effort to stretch a thinning resource beyond realistic limits; fr. sl. for the effect achieved by a balding man who attempts to comb his hair to maximum effect *Sculatti*.

scrambled eggs n. (rhy. sl.) legs *Welsh:1* (cf: bacon and eggs).

scrambling for the gills v. to have a bad time, to meet problems *Maledicta*.

scran n. food *Powis*.

scrap n. a fight; fr. 18th C.: a blow, a punch *Farrell*.

scrape n. an abortion; fr. the operation on the uterus *White*.

scrape v. (Aus. use) to have sexual intercourse *Wilkes*.

scrape (bottom of) the barrel v. to make do with the most mediocre people, objects etc. simply because no others exist.

scrappy a. pugnacious, aggressive *Maupin:3*.

scratch n. money; a commodity for which most people must *scratch in the dirt Caron*.

scratch for work v. (UK police use) to look desperately for an arrest; pun on usual meaning *Laurie*.

scratch sheet n. the daily racing form; fr. scratch: a zero handicap; first pub.

1917 in New York *Selby:1*.

scratcher n. (UK prison use) a match *LL*.

scratchman n. (US cant) a forger; fr. the drawing and etching he performs *Neaman & Silver*.

scream n. **1.** a complaint, esp. against criminal activities, or to the police *Norman:2*; **2.** (US preppie (qv) use) ice cream *Bernbach*.

scream v. (US Black use) to inform to the police *Klein*.

scream sheet n. tabloid newspaper; fr. journ. use *screamer*: exclamation point, with which such papers' headlines are studded *Schulberg*.

scream some heavy lines v. (US Black use) **1.** to impress with one's smart talk; **2.** to debate or argue intensely and emotionally *Folb*.

screamer n. (US campus use) **1.** anything exceptionally challenging, difficult; esp. work *Underwood*; **2.** in gay use, a flagrant homosexual, ie a 'screaming queen'.

screaming a. (US Black use) fantastic, amazing, extreme *Klein*.

screaming abdabs n. the horrors, utter disgust, abhorrence; usu. as in 'gives me the screaming. . .'; spec. delirium tremens.

screaming blue murder in a state of hysteria; utterly and completely overwrought or terrified *Sillitoe*.

screw n. prison officer; orig. a skeleton key, thus (?) to prison meaning (cf: twirl) *Cole*.

screw v. **1.** to cheat, swindle, take advantage of *Jay & Young*; **2.** to copulate; poss. the most common eg. of sex = violence; **3.** to break into, to rob; orig. with a skeleton key, see: screw, n. *Powis*; **4.** to stare intently at someone *Powis*.

screw around v. **1.** to indulge a promiscuous sex life; **2.** aka: *screw off*: to waste time, take time off *Price:2*.

screw it! (excl.) the hell with it! forget it! etc.; euph. fuck it! (qv) *Underwood*.

screw it on v. to drive one's car or motorcycle very fast *Thompson*.

screw the arse off v. aggressive, vigorous copulation; a 'macho' man would always promise to make love in this way.

screw the pooch v. to waste time (cf: fuck the dog).

screw up v. to make a mess, to blunder badly; euph. fuck up (qv) *Underwood*.

screwball n. an eccentric, an out-of-the-ordinary person *S. Vizinczey, 'An Innocent Millionaire', 1983*.

screwdriver n. (UK prison use) Principal Officer who 'drives' his subordinate 'screws' (qv) *LL*.

screwed a. in trouble, in great difficulties; fr *screw*: to have intercourse (cf: fucked).

screwer n. burglary *Norman:1*.

screwsman n. a skilled housebreaker *Powis*.

screwy a. foolish, stupid, insane; fr. have a screw loose (qv) (?) *Laugh In The Dark*.

scribe n. newspaperman; fr. SE: a writer *Runyon*.

scrimshank v. to shirk one's work, to laze around; orig. milit. use; thus *scrimshanker*: one who acts thus.

scrub n. **1.** (US Black use) a fool; **2.** (derog.) a Black person.

scrub v. to cancel; to wipe out, to forget *Norman:1*.

scrub it v. to forget something, to ignore, to let it pass *LL*.

scrubber n. promiscuous girl, usu. young *Norman:2*.

Scrubs n. (UK police use/cant) HMP Wormwood Scrubs, London (cf: Ville) *Cole*.

scruff a. messy, unkempt; fr. scruffy *Pond*.

scrumptious a. delicious, extra-tasty; nearly always of food; usu. juv. use.

scrunge n. filth, mess, dirt *Underwood*.

scrungy a. filthy, messy, dirty, disgusting *Underwood*.

scuffer n. policeman, mainly Liverpool dial; fr. *scufter Keyes*.

scumbag n. **1.** spec. contraceptive

sheath; **2.** derog. term of general abuse *Price:2*.

scummy a. unpleasant, disgusting *Keyes*.

scumsucker n. derog. term of general abuse (cf: cocksucker).

scungy a. (Aus. use) see: scrungy.

scuttlebutt n. gossip, rumour; fr. USN use, orig. scuttlebutt was the ship's water barrel, around which sailors gathered and gossipped (cf: furphy) *Bruce:1*.

scuzz v. to make a mess of *Morgan*.

scuzzy a. unkempt, down at heel, ragged *Price:2*.

sea food n. (homosexual use) sailors *Legman*.

seat n. the buttocks.

secko (Aus. use) a sexual pervert, usu. prison use *Wilkes*.

second closet n. (homosexual/lesbian use) the hiding of one's specific sexual preferences and practices even if the basic fact of homosexuality can be admitted *Jay & Young*.

second hole from the back of the neck n. the vagina (cf: low Greek).

second-storey job n. a break-in, spec. one that involves climbing above ground level.

second-storey man n. a thief who climbs into buildings above the ground floor *Fiction Illus.3* (cf: high-wall job).

section eight n. **1.** spec. section eight discharge: discharge from the US army on grounds of mental instability; thus: **2.** insanity, instability *Price:1*.

seddity (US Black use) Blacks attempting to ape whites; fr. absurdity (?) *Folb*.

seducer n. (US Black use) one who supplies the means of making fast, poss. illegal, money *Klein*.

see (backsl.) yes *Cole*.

see a dog about a man v. to urinate (cf: see a man. . .) *Neaman & Silver*.

see a man about a dog v. to visit the lavatory *Rawson*.

see if it fucks phr. see if something works.

see off v. to deal with, to dismiss, to defeat.

see the King v. to have sexual intercourse; orig. to be sophisticated, knowing *Mortimer*.

see you in court general cp. used as synonym for 'goodbye'.

seedy (US Black use) common nickname for a dealer in pills *Klein*.

seeing-to n. **1.** of a woman: sexual intercourse; **2.** of a man: beating up, violence *A.F.N. Clarke, 'Contact', 1983*.

see-saw n. (US Black use) an up and down, uncertain relationship *Klein*.

seeyabye! (Valley Girls (qv) use) goodbye! fr. see ya plus goodbye *Pond*.

sef n. (US teen use) a street gang.

seg n. (US campus use) (acro) shit-eating grin *Simmons*.

sell a boy v. (homosexual use) for one man to obtain the services of a boy at a given price and then to offer him to a second man for the actual sex *Legman*.

sell a pup v. to deceive, esp. in business or financial transactions fr. stock market j. pup, a worthless investment *AS 41 (1966)*.

sell a wolf ticket v. (US Black use) **1.** boast, brag; **2.** talk nonsense, lie *Seale*.

sell one on v. to convince, to persuade, to convey enthusiasm.

sell-by date, past one's phr. out of date, over the hill, past it (qv). *Green:3*.

semen demon n. (derog.) a homosexual male.

semolia n. (US Black use) a fool *Major*.

send v. to excite emotionally; beatnik slang – particularly as used of music: near obsolete now, but central to the rhetoric c.1960.

send away with a flea in one's ear v. to dismiss sharply, to throw out after telling someone off severely *Wodehouse:MOJ*.

send down v. to imprison; fr. walking down the steps fr. the dock (at the Old Bailey) back to the cells.

send her down Hughie! (Aus. use)

general appeal to the gods for rain;
Hughie is also the mythical deity of
surfing and as such invoked by surfers
who want suitable waves *Baker*.

send on a humbug trip v. (US Black
use) to send on a wild goose chase, a
fool's errand *Folb*.

send to the cleaners v. aka: *take to
the cleaners*: to defraud, outwit and,
usu. thus deprive of one's every penny
Powis.

send up v. **1.** (US criminal/police use)
to imprison; poss. fr. 'send up the
river; (qv).

send up v. to mock, to tease, esp. to
paraody or imitate.

senior out v. (US teen. use) to give up
the teen. lifestyle, to act like an adult
(in the rejection of teen excess)
Sculatti.

septic n. (Aus. use; rhyming sl.) septic
tank = Yank = American *Wilkes*.

serious a. (UK 'society; use) all-
purpose intensifier, thus serious
drinking, seriously rich, etc. *Barr*.

serve n. (Aus. use) negative criticism,
a reprimand *Wilkes*.

serve v. (drug use) to sell narcotics
Burroughs:1.

sesh n. a session of drinking.

sess N (US black use) marijuana.

set n. (US gang use) a local gang, part
of the larger gang but working
autonomously in its own
neighbourhood or turf (qv); thus the
Crips are the larger gang, but sets
include Eight Trey Gangsters or
ETGs, West Side Crips, Compton
Santana Block Crips, etc.

set n. **1.** (Black use) wherever the
nightlife takes place; consciously using
the movie meaning with everyone
involved acting out their parts of the
drama *Milner*; **2.** (poker use) three of
a kind *Alvarez*; **3.** (US milit. use) a
party; fr. **1** *Del Vecchio*.

set mouth v. (US Black use) to
gossip, to malign *Folb*.

set one back v. cost a good deal, to be
expensive *Humphries:2*.

set the hair v. to surprise, to astonish,
to give pause (fr. farming j. 'to set the

hair' on end when one is butchering a
hog; the carcass is plunged into
scalding water which makes the hair
stand on end, thus rendering it simpler
to scrape it from the flesh).

set to rights v. to put straight, to set
right.

set tripping n. (US gang use)
attacking another gang.

set up v. to place a potential victim in
a position of weakness, esp. a target
for murder.

settle one's hash v. to deal with
someone who has wronged you; to
take revenge.

set-up n. **1.** a situation planned to put
a third party in a position of weakness,
poss. to be murdered; **2.** any situation,
experience *Burroughs:1*.

set-up man n. (criminal use) someone
who organizes and plans major
robberies, recruits those who carry
them out, disposes of the loot, etc.
Burroughs:1.

seven digits n. (US Black use)
telephone number (in the multiple
exchanges of the major cities) *Klein*.

sew v. (US Black use) to masturbate;
fr. the up-and-down motions of the
hand *Major*.

sew up v. to conclude, to possess
completely, to finalize *Hoffman:a*.

sew with a hot needle phr. to act
over-hastily, to work fast but poorly
(fr. phr. sew with a hot needle and
burning thread).

sewermouth n. (US campus use)
anyone who regularly use obscenities
or profanities *Underwood*.

sex v.t. to have sexual intercourse
Shell.

sexpot n. very attractive man or
woman *Jay & Young*.

Sexton Blake n. (rhyming sl.) **1.** cake;
2. fake; fr. fictional detective created
by 'Hal Meredith' (Harry Blyth) in
The Halfpenny Marvel magazine, 1893
Jones: J.

sexy a. (media use) anything that pulls
in audiences, readers, etc., thus usu.
violence, disaster, scandal, etc.; orig.
used by *Sunday Times* Insight team,

1960s *D. Leitch*.

shack v. (abbrev.) shack up (qv) *Bukowski: 6*.

shack job n. the person with whom one lives; a relationship *Bukowski: 5*.

shack up v. to live with; to have sex with *Goldman*.

shackle up v. (tramp use) to cook a midday meal *LL*.

shades n. dark glasses, sunglasses *Performance*.

shadow n. (US campus use) (derog.) Black (cf: shadow) *Underwood*.

shaft n. 1. woman's body, considered simply as a sexual object *Algren*; 2. unfair treatment *Underwood*.

shaft v. 1. to have sexual intercourse with a woman; 2. to defeat, defraud, harm *Wofe: 2*.

shafted a. 1. treated unfairly; 2. stood up by one's date; 3. suffering a broken relationship.

shag a. (US prison use) worthless *Chandler: Notebk*.

shag n. (drug use) heroin (cf: scag, skag).

shag v. to copulate; since 18th C. *Humphries*.

shag ass v. to work hard, to move fast, to expend effort and energy *Underwood*.

shag like a rattlesnake v. to make love very enthusiastically; usu. a term of recommendation used by one male to another of a female they both find attractive *K. Waterhouse, 'Billy Liar', 1959*.

shagbag n. a very promiscuous woman, usu. with implication of the physical deterioration that such promiscuity has supposedly brought (cf: bag).

shagged out a. exhausted *Keyes*.

shagger's back n. (Aus. use) a particularly painful backache *Ready*.

shagwagon n. a van or car used primarily for sex (cf: passion wagon).

shake n. (US campus use) a party; fr. the dancing therein *Underwood*.

shake a leg! get on with it! wake up! (both lit. and figuratively).

shake down v. 1. see: shakedown; 2.

(US Black use) to have sex with.

shake hands with an old friend v. to urinate *Rawson*.

shake hands with the baby v. to urinate.

shake hands with the fellow who stood up with me at my wedding v. phr. to urinate.

shake hands with the wife's best friend v. 1. to masturbate; 2. to urinate *Humphries*.

Shake 'n' Bake n. (US milit. use) a sergeant who attended NCO school and gained rank after only a short time in uniform; fr. brand name of popular US instant food; thus similar synonyms: *Ready Whip, Nestle's Quick Del Vecchio*.

shake the dew off the lily v. to urinate *Neaman & Silver*.

shakedown n. blackmail, extortion; fr. shaking the clothes until money falls out *Jay & Young*.

shakedown v. to blackmail, to extort *Morgan*.

shake-em-up n. (US Black use) white port and lemon juice *Folb*.

shakes n. delirium tremens, the shaking associated with an alcoholic who has been deprived of sufficient drink to achieve normality (cf: screaming abdabs) *Price: 2*.

Shaky City n. (US trucker use) Los Angeles, Calif.; fr. frequency of earthquakes along the San Andreas Fault *CB*.

shall I put a bit of hair on it? (cp) directed at a workman who is failing to put something into something else; the hair in question would be female and pubic.

sham on v. (US Black use) to cheat, to deceive *Folb*.

shame down v. to humiliate *L Green*.

shamus n. detective, esp. private operative; fr. Seamus, the common Irish name of many policemen *Fiction Illus. 3*.

shan adv. 1. unsteady *Welsh:1*; 2. bashful, confused (fr. Sc. dial.).

shandy (rhyming sl.) chandelier = queer.

shanghai v. to kidnap, to abduct; fr. alleged practice of pressing men into service at the port of Shanghai *Price: 2*.

shank n. (US prison use) a knife *Caron*.

shank v. (US prison use) to stab with a knife.

shape up v. (police use) to develop satisfactorily *Newman: 2*.

shape up v. to improve one's behaviour, activities, attitude, etc. *Newman: 1*.

share certificate n. (sex industry use) a pimp's favourite girl.

shark n. **1**. a sharp operator, a crooked businessman; **2**. (abbrev.) loan shark (qv).

sharking n. the practice of a private credit company taking high interest on loans *Higgins: 3*.

Sharon n. a derogatory description (used by the middle classes) of working-class girls whom they regard as overly flashy and socially unacceptable (cf: Kevin, Tracey).

sharp a. **1**. intelligent, perceptive; **2**. fashionable, ie *sharp dresser Higgins: 1*.

sharp end n. the challenging, demanding and sometimes unpleasant aspect of an experience; fr. the bow of a boat *T 18/7/83*.

sharpie n.**1**. a slick operator; one who lives and hopes to prosper by their wits *Goldman*; **2**. (Aus. use) member of a crop-haired teen cult, the equivalent of the British skinhead (qv) *Wilkes*.

sharpshooter n. (US Black use) a sexually adept and active person (cf: rod, gun, etc.) *Klein*.

shaver n. a person, often as *young shaver*; a child, or young person; fr. at least 1630 *Vidal*.

shazzam v. to flash dramatically, fr. comic strip excl. Shazam! *White*.

shebeen n. an unlicensed drinking place, an illegal late night drinking club *Powis*.

sheeny n. (derog.) a Jew; poss. fr. Ger, *schin*: a miser, a petty thief, a cheat; or fr. the 'sheen' of

Brylcreemed hair affected by early immigrants *Bruce ; 2*.

sheep n. a mild, weak, acquiescent person; fr. the animal's characteristics.

sheepish a. (US campus use) long-haired (of males) *Underwood*.

sheepskin n. a college diploma; fr. the fur that graduates wear for the graduation ceremony.

sheet n. **1**. newspaper, magazine *Gruber*; **2**. (US criminal use) an official police record *Major*.

sheet! (euph.) shit (qv) *Hoffman: a*.

sheila n. (Aus. use) a female; fr. Gaelic *sheela*: girl, opp. of Paddy (qv) *Humphries*.

shekels n. fr. Hebrew: money *Wright*.

shell out v. to hand over, usu. money; fr. the removal of a seed from a shell *Humphries: 2*.

shellacking n. a severe beating or defeat *Runyon*.

shell-back n. ultra-conservative, slow-witted person; fr. image of a turtle *Humphries*.

shell-road v. to throw a person, often a woman who refuses to have sex out of a vehicle and thus force them to walk home an inconvenient and possibly embarrassing distance (cf: redlight) *Runyon: 1*.

she-man (derog.) homosexual (cf: he-she, omee-polone).

shemozzle n. a fuss, a disturbance; fr. Yiddish.

Sherlock Holmes n. (US Black use) the police; fr. Conan Doyle's super-sleuth *Folb*.

sherm n. (US Black use) see: PCP (fr. smoking of Sherman cigarettes laced with the drug).

sherman n. masturbation; fr. rhy. sl. sherman tank = wank (qv).

Sherman Tank n. an American *Welsh:1* (rhy. sl. = yank (qv)).

shicker a. drunk, fr. Yiddish *Humphries*.

shicker n.v. alcohol, to drink (usu. to drunkenness) *Humphries*.

shift the weight v. to place the blame on someone else *Klein*.

shikse fr. Yiddish: **1**. a Gentile girl;

2. a char-woman.

shill n. (gambling use) a house player (in a casino); a member of the three-card monte (qv) team who appears to be another innocent gambler and who thus lures the actual punters (qv) into losing more money: fr. abbrev. *Shillaber*: one who publicizes a circus, carnival, etc. *Jenkins*.

shim-sham n. (US campus use) feelings of unease, of nervousness *Underwood*.

shin n. (US prison use) any contraband gun or knife *Chandler: Notebk*.

shin battle (street gang use) a fake, practice battle *Salisbury*.

shine a. (derog.) Black, Negro *Dunne*.

shine on v. (US Black use) to ignore *Milner*.

shiner n. a black eye *Farrell*.

shingle short a. (Aus. use) 'not all there', eccentric *Wilkes*.

shirtlifter n. (Aus. use) male homosexual *Humphries: 2*.

shit n. **1.** spec. excrement; **2.** (drug use) cannabis; heroin *Green: 1*; **3.** trouble, problems, difficulties *Jenkins*; **4.** an event, a thing, circumstance usu. as 'what is this shit?' etc. *Price: 2*; **5.** a notably unpleasant person; although shit is in general use, it is particularly associated with Conservative MPs where, meaning just the same thing, it has been raised through common understanding of the necessary qualities almost to a jargon term.

shit v. (abbrev.) bullshit (qv).

shit a brick! (excl.) extreme surprise, annoyance *Humphries*.

shit a brick aka: shit bricks v. to tremble with extreme fear *Price: 2*.

shit and derision! general excl. of annoyance.

shit and wish v. (US Black use) cp fr. phrase 'shit in one hand and wish in the other; see which fills up first' *Klein*.

shit detail n. any unpleasant/dirty task; fr. milit. use *Higgins: 3*.

shit, eh (Aus. use) expression of moderate astonishment or irony *Ready*.

shit for brains n. an all purpose insult.

shit hits the fan difficulties start to happen, usu. such problems have been expected to occur sooner or later *Higgins: 1*.

shit in high cotton phr. to live prosperously, to feel happy, to be important; euph. alternatives incl. 'fly in high cotton', 'live in high cotton', 'travel in high cotton'.

shit jacket n. (US Black use) outside lavatory *Klein*.

shit list n. a list pf people one considers distasteful, untrustworthy and otherwise unacceptable.

shit off v.t. **1.** to annoy, to irritate; v.i. **2.** to run away *Welsh:1*.

shit on a shingle n. (milit. use (mainly)) minced beef on toast.

shit on a stick n. (US Black use) a self-appointed tough guy, more words than action *Klein*.

shit on from a great height v. to be extremely unpleasant, to make a great deal of trouble for someone else.

shit oneself v. to be terrified, fr. physical effect of great fear *M. Mayer, 'Summer Days', 1983*.

shit or bust v. to make a last, absolute gamble (cf: go for broke).

shit, or get off the pot! (cp) either make a decision or let someone else do it; allegedly remarked by then Vice pres. Richard Nixon to Pres. Eisenhower when the latter was showing insufficient enthusiasm for his aide in 1952.

shit stompers n. (US campus use) **1.** cowboy boots; **2.** cowboys *Underwood*.

shit through one's teeth v. to lie blatantly *Klein*.

shit-bird n. **1.** (derog.) general term of abuse *Higgins: 1*; **2.** a narcotic drug abuser, a heroin addict.

shite n. derog. form of address; fr. shit (qv) *Bleasdale*.

shit-eating grin n. a smug, self-satisfied smile *Selby: 1*.

shitface a. (usually shitface drunk: extremely drunk.

shitface n. 1. an unpleasant, distasteful person *Underwood*; 2. a drunken party *Price: 2*.

shithead n. derog. term of general abuse *Price: 2*.

shitheap n. a dirty, unpleasant, disgusting place.

shitheel n. generally derog. term of abuse *Jenkins*.

shithook n. 1. (US campus use) a foolish, clumsy person *Underwood*; 2. (US milit. use) CH-47 'Chinook' helicopter; (cf: campus use) *Del Vecchio*.

shit-hot a. extremely, superlatively, especially.

shithouse n. 1. spec. lavatory; 2. any dirty, messy, disgusting place *Performance*.

shitkicker n. 1. spec. a farmer or other country person; 2. a fool, a person of meagre intelligence. *NYRB 17/2/83*.

shitkicking music n. music that makes the hearer want to get up and dance, shout, sing, generally have a good, boisterous time *Pynchon*.

shit-pit n. lavatory *Welsh:1*.

shit-scared a. terrified (cf: scare the shit . . .)

shit-skin n. (derog.) a black person *Welsh:2*.

shit-stab v. to practise sodomy *Welsh:1*.

shit-stick (US prison use) 1. a billy-club; 2. the penis, esp. when used for anal intercourse *Klein*.

shit-stirrer n. a malicious gossip, causing trouble for its own sake.

shitter n. 1. spec. a thief who likes to excrete inside the places he robs *Higgins: 3*; 2. lavatory *Dury, 'Do It Yourself', 1979*.

shitty a. unpleasant, disgusting *Higgins: 1*.

shitwork n. unpleasant, unwanted, probably dirty occupations *Robins:1*.

shiv n. a knife (cf: chiv) *Price: 2*.

shlemiel n. fr. Yiddish: a fool, a clumsy person, a misfit, a gullible person. etc. *Rosten*.

shlock n. fr. Yiddish:1. shoddy, cheap article; a phoney person; 2. spec. drugs, fr. *shlock* = junk, thus lit. drugs *Rosten*.

shmeer v. fr. Ger: grease: to flatter, to bribe *Rosten*.

shmegegge n. a fool, a loser, a useless person *Price: 3*.

shmooser n. a flatterer, a sycophant; fr. Yiddish.

shocks for jocks (US campus use) course in introductory engineering *Bernbach*.

shoe n. (US Black use) 1. a smartly dressed person; fr. Jazz use of 1950s *Major*. 2. (US campus use) highly acceptable person; fr. Black use of shoe (qv) *Bernbach*.

shonk n. (derog.) a Jew; prob. fr. shonnicker (qv) *LL*.

shonnicker n. (derog.) a Jew; fr. Yiddish = a small trader or pedlar *Farrell*.

shoo-fly n. (US cant) 1. a plain-clothes policeman on observation duty *Neaman & Silver*; 2. an undercover policeman who spies on his colleagues *ST 23/10/82*; both fr. song lyric 'Shoo fly! Don't bother me'.

shoo-in n. a dead certainty; usu. in political use *Vidal*.

shook on (Aus. use) infatuated with, obsessed with *Wilkes*.

shoomer n. a fan of acid house (qv); from London's Shoom club, which was at its most popular c. 1988.

shoot! (excl.) surprise, indignation, etc., poss. euph. for shit (qv) *Seale*.

shoot a cat v. (UK 'society' use) vomit (cf: cat) *Barr*.

shoot a line v. to concoct a smooth patter with the specific aim of seduction (cf: line).

shoot blanks v. (US Black use) to engage in idle conversation; words that have no 'target' *Folb*.

shoot down v. 1. to reject an invitation to dance, or go for a date (qv) *Price: 1*; 2. (US campus use) to humiliate, to ridicule *Simmons*; 3. to reject a line of argument; to overrule an opinion *Seale*.

shoot for the sky v. (gambling use) to bet one's entire funds against one's opponent's entire funds.

shoot from the hip v. (business use) to attack a problem head-on, to be a hard-nosed (qv) performer; fr. movie Westerns where gunfighters and cowboys 'shoot from the hip' *Kidder*.

shoot gravy v. (drug use) for a narcotics addict to reinject his own cooked (qv) blood *Major*.

shoot off v. 1. ejaculate *Jay & Young*; 2. to leave quickly.

shoot off at the mouth v. to boast, to brag *May*.

shoot on v. aka: *shoot jokes on*: to mock, to tease, to discredit *Folb*.

shoot one's best mack v. (US Black use) to make an all-out effort at seduction by one's persuasive conversation (cf: mack, macking) *Folb*.

shoot one's bolt v. to have given everything one has, to be incapable of further effort *Heller*.

shoot one's face v. to make a fuss (cf: shoot off one's mouth).

shoot one's load v. to ejaculate *Jay & Young*.

shoot one's mouth off v. to talk, esp. in loud or boastful way *Humphries*.

shoot one's star v. (US Black use) 1. to arrest a homosexual; 2. to perform anal intercourse *Klein*.

shoot one's wad v. to ejaculate.

shoot out one's marbles v. (US Black use) to go crazy (cf: lose one's marbles *Klein*.

shoot over v. to go quickly to a place *PT*.

shoot some hoop v. (US campus use) to play basketball *Underwood*.

shoot the breeze v. to gossip, to talk idly (cf: bat the breeze).

shoot the bull v. see: shoot the shit *Pearce*.

shoot the dozens v. see: play the dozens *Folb*.

shoot the moon v. to abscond from a house or flat, taking one's furniture and possessions, but avoiding payment of any outstanding rent, utility bills, etc.

shoot the regular v. (US Black use) to chatter on in the usual, predictable manner; 'shit' is unspoken *Klein*.

shoot the shit v. to banter, chatter, gossip *Price: 2*.

shoot the squirrel v. (US campus use) to catch a glimpse of a girl's panties or pubic hair *Underwood*.

shoot the thrill v. (US Black use) to lead a promiscuous and varied sex life *Klein*.

shoot through v. (Aus. use) to leave, to exit *Humphries*.

shoot to kill v. to aim ruthlessly for a goal without reservation or compromise *Klein*.

shoot up v. to take narcotic drugs by injection *Price: 2*.

shoot-'em-up n. (US Black use) a Hollywood Western movie; fr. the predominant activity *Major*.

shooter n. 1. (gambling use) the player currently throwing the dice in a game of craps; 2. (UK police/criminal use) a gun *Performance*.

shooting gallery n. a place, often an apartment or an abandoned building used by a number of heroin addicts to take the drug and nod out (qv) (cf: crack house) *Grogan*.

shoot-out n. 1. a gun battle; 2. a decisive confrontation *Seale*.

shop v. to inform; orig. 16th C. to imprison *Powis*.

shopping and fucking a. referring to a type of blockbusting novel, developed during the materialist 1980s, in which the normal ingredient of a certain type of best-seller – 'procrastinated rape' – is boosted by regular excursions into the world's upmarket shopping malls in search of lovingly delineated designer-labelled garments and other consumables. When bowdlerized the term is found as 'sex and shopping'. *Green:3*.

short a. 1. (US prison use) of a prisoner with only a few weeks or days of a sentence to be served out *Burroughs: Jr*; 2. (US milit. use) near

the end of a given term of duty, spec.
the twelve-month tours of Vietnam
(cf: wake-up) *Del Vecchio*;
3. insufficient, esp. of money, thus
short bread: not enough cash.

short n. an automobile *Price: 2*.

short n. (US Black use) a cigarette
butt *Klein*.

short arm n. the penis (cf: third leg).
Neaman & Silver.

short con n. (US criminal use) any
variety of confidence trick that can be
peformed spontaneously and on the
spot, with no elabrorate props,
preparation, etc. *Thompson: J*.

short dog n. (US Black use) a small
bottle of cheap wine *Folb*.

short end of the stick unfair
treatment; deliberately engineered
bad luck *Uris*.

short eyes n. (US prison use) a child
molester (cf: beast, nonce, shut eyes)
E Leonard Stick 1983.

short stuff n. (US criminal use) a
quick and spontaneous con trick,
thought up on the spur of the moment
and workable only while the target is
on hand (cf: short con) *Klein*.

short time n. **1.** (prison use) a short
sentence; or a short part of one's
sentence left to run; **2.** (milit. use) a
short-service commission or a short
period of enlistment; **3.** (prostitute
use) the time spent with one client
before taking on a new one; rather
than spending a whole night with the
same man *Norman: 2*.

short-arm inspection n. (milit. use)
medical inspection of the genitals; fr.
short arm (qv).

short-end money n. (gambling use)
money bet on the possibility of a given
team or individual (esp. in boxing)
losing a contest (cf: on the short end)
Schulberg.

shorts n. the last few puffs of a
discarded cigarette (cf: short) *Grogan*.

short-time girl n. basic, cheap
prostitute who satisfies her client's
immediate need and then looks for her
next customer *O'Brien*.

shorty n. (US Black use) a young
person.

shot a. exhausted, completely used up
Higgins: 3.

shot n. **1.** a measure of spirits; **2.** an
opportunity, a chance *Dunne*; **3.** an
injection of a narcotic drug *Price: 2*.

shot in the arm n. anything – verbal,
physical, stimulant – that cheers one
up, energizes one, etc.; fr. an
injection.

shot of crack, get a v. to have sexual
intercourse (cf: crack).

shotdown a. (US campus use)
miserable, useless, distasteful
Underwood.

shotgun n. (drug use) to blow
cannabis smoke into someone else's
mouth by reversing the cigarette inside
one's own mouth and blowing; the
other person places their open lips
near the stream of smoke and inhales
for as long as they can manage (cf:
give a blow).

shotgun seat n. the seat nest to that
of the driver in a car; fr. stagecoach
use 'riding shotgun' (qv) *Price: 3*.

shout n. **1.** turn to order a round of
drinks; thus *your shout, my shout*,
etc.; **2.** (UK police use) a call on the
car/personal radio indicating an
emergency, the scene of a crime, etc.;
also used by London Fire Brigade for
alarms coming over the teleprinter
Laurie.

shove it! excl. of dismissal and
rudeness; abbrev. of 'shove it up your
ass!' *Vidal*.

shove off v. to leave, to go away, usu,
in form of an order to someone else.

shove one's oar in v. to interfere
(where one is not wanted) *Wright*.

shovel and broom n. (US rhyming
sk.) room *Runyon*.

Shovel City n. (US teen. use)
anything one really digs, ie appreciates
and enjoys; a pun on the tool *Sculatti*.

shovel shit v. to talk nonsense, esp. in
an attempt to defraud or deceive
someone *Bukowski: 1*.

shovel shit against the tide v. (cp) to
make great effort without any
concomitant success *Higgins: 5*.

shovin' and pushin' (US Black use) trying as hard as possible to succeed *Klein*.

show a leg! wake-up call; orig. used to ensure that the leg (in an institution) was masculine and not, illicitly, female.

show it v. to become obviously drunk *Dickson*.

show one's cards v. to reveal oneself, usu. to a greater extent than desired; fr. poker use (cf: peep one's hole card) *Farrell*.

show out v. to lead on, to deceive *Norman: 3*.

show out n. (UK police use) a sign between a policeman and his informant who meet in a public place that means 'all clear' to speak *Laurie*.

show the flag v. (UK 'society' use) to attend (apparently reluctantly) any official function; with the image of white administrators displaying Imperial might to the natives, the inference is that the function will have been organized for less socially acceptable people *Barr*.

showboat n. a flashy car.

showboat v. to show off, esp. by parading oneself in front of an audience *Esq. 6/83*.

shower n. an unimpressive group of people; abbrev. of *shower of shit*.

showhouse n. (homosexual use) a brothel; a place where homosexuals can meet openly, sex is usually performed off the premises *Legman*.

shred the tube v. (Valley Girls (qv) use) to go surfing (cf: tube) *Pond*.

shrimp n. a small, weak, insignificant person; fr. the fish.

shrimper n. a foot fetishist; toes are supposed to resemble pink shrimps.

shrink n. **1.** fr. head-shrinker: a psychoanalyst, psychiatrist, etc. (cf: trick-cyclist) *Price: 2*; **2.** (US campus use) tight-fitting sweater (for girls) *Underwood*.

Shrinksville n. a state of mind in which it is advisable for the person so afflicted to consult a psychoanalyst (cf: shrink) *Safire*.

shtarka n. fr. Yiddish: **1.** a strong, brave man; a big shot (qv); used ironically *Rosten*; **2.** a thug, a hoodlum *Goldman*.

shtarker n. see: shtarka *Goldman*.

shtick n. (show business use) one's stage speciality, one's act, esp. of a comedian's monologue *Bruce: 2*.

shtum fr. Yiddish: quiet, silent, dumb *Performance*.

shuck n. a hoax, a lie, deceit; often in shuck and jive (qqv) *The People's Comic*.

shuck v. to defraud, to cheat, to fool *The People's Comic*.

shuck and jive see: shuck, jive *Seale*.

shuck down v. to strip off one's clothes, to undress; fr. shucking corn *Vidal*.

shucks mild excl. of surprise, regret, annoyance, etc. *Capital Radio 1983*.

shuffle n. (US Black use) a black man deliberately playing dumb and acting out the white man's stereotyped view of his race; the shuffling walk, along with shiny smiles and natural rhythm are major parts of this image *Klein*.

shuffle v. (street gang use) to have a fistfight *Salisbury*.

shuffled out of the deck a. dead, fr. card use (cf: go to the races, etc.) *Rawson*.

shufty n. a brief glance, a quick look; fr. Arabic orig. Second World War use.

shunt n. a car crash, esp. in professional drivers' use *'Minder', Thames TV, 1983*.

shut eyes n. (US police use) a sexual offender; fr. the pervert's suggestion to his youthful victim, 'Now just shut your eyes . . .' (cf: short eyes) *Neaman & Silver*.

shut one's trap v. to be quiet; usu. as demand: *shut your trap! Farrell*.

shut someone down v. **1.** spec. to beat a rival in a drag race; **2.** to gain a victory.

shut your face! shut up, be quiet, etc. *Manser*.

shuteye n. sleep, rest.

shuttle butt n. (US campus use) a fat

girl, esp. as to the buttocks
Underwood.

shy n. (abbrev.) shylock (qv)
Higgins: 3.

shylock n. one who supples private
loans fr. the villain of Shakespeare's
'Merchant of Venice' (cf: loan shark)
Runyon.

shyster n. a crooked lawyer; fr. shicer
(qv).

Siberia n. (US prison use) solitary
confinement cells *Chandler: Notebk*.

sic on v. to set on, to have someone
attack; fr. sicking a dog on to a given
victim *rr*.

sick a. **1.** annoyed; worried
Newman: 1; **2.** suffering from
withdrawal symptoms when addicted
to narcotics, esp. heroin *Lou Reed,
'Run, Run, Run', 1966*.

sick n. the illness that accompanies
withdrawal from drug addiction
Grogan.

sick as a parrot a. extremely
depressed; sick usually means
mentally rather than physically
distressed; the cliché response
attributed to many sportsmen, esp.
soccer players and managers, after a
loss or defeat (cf: over the moon).

sick-ass a. unpleasant, crazy.

sickener n. anything depressing,
disappointing, frustrating (cf: choker)
Payne.

sickie n. **1.** (Aus. use) a day's sick
leave *Wilkes*; **2.** anyone considered to
be 'sick in the head': insane, crazy
McFadden.

sicko n. a mentally unstable person,
with overtones of sexual perversion.

side n. (UK bl.) area, turf; often used
(in London) as West Side, South Side,
meaning Shepherds Bush or Brixton.
Somewhat romanticized analogies
with areas of US cities. *Time Radio
FM 1987*.

sides n. records.

sidies n. sideburns; popular in
Beatlemania era.

sidity aka: *saddity*: showing off,
arrogant, egotistical fr. early 20th C.
'side'; affectations, airs *Selby: 1*.

sight for sore eyes n. a welcome
appearance; often used as an
affectionate greeting: 'you're a sight
for sore eyes'.

sightseers n. (gambling use) see:
hedge *Powis*.

signify v. (Black use) **1.** to cause
trouble, to stir things up; often purely
for fun, whatever the actual results;
2. to pretend to a greater
sophistication than one actually
possesses *Milner*; **3.** (US Black use) to
recite one of a variety of purpose-
written 'tales', usu. recounting the
exploits of some mythical gangster-
cum-sexual athlete *Morgan*.

sil n. (abbrev.) silly about: a lesbian
involved in an affair *Legman*.

silent beef n. (US criminal use) a note
attached to an individual's police
record stating that they have been
suspected (but not charged due to lack
of proof) of committing a given crime;
the note requests that he/she be
punished to the maximum extent for
such lesser charges that can be brought
(cf: beef 2.) *Morgan*.

Silicon Valley n. Santa Clara County,
California: home of the USA's
microchip technology industry; the
'chips' are made from silicon *Esq. 6/83*.

silent city n. (US Black use) a
graveyard *Klein*.

silk n. **1.** a Queen's Counsel; fr. the
material of their gowns, rather than
the cotton of a junior barrister's
Newman: 1; **2.** (US Black use) a white
woman; fr. texture of her hair *Major*.

silk and satin n. (drug use) any
combination of amphetamines and
barbiturates or tranquilizers *Folb*.

silk stocking n. (US Black use) a rich
person; who might have worn them
Klein.

silks n. (US Black use) expensive
clothing, poss. actually silken *Klein*.

silly as a two-bob watch (Aus. use
cp) very silly indeed *Wilkes*.

silly-billy n. a fool, a simpleton; fr.
traditional clown's stooge in mid-
19th C. fairs/circuses, Silly Billy *Vidal*.

silvertail n. (Aus. use) a wealthy

person *Neaman & Silver*.

silvery spoon n. (rhyming sl.) coon (qv) = Black *Dury*.

simoleons n. money, usu, dollars *'Hart To Hart'*, *LWT*, *1983*.

simp n. (abbrev.) simpleton *Junker*.

simple pimp n. (Black use) one who barely manages as a pimp and has no hope of transcending that level of employment within the criminal hierarchy *Milner*.

Simple Simon n. (US rhyming sl.) diamond, usu. diamond ring *Runyon: 1*.

sin bin n. 1.(sports use) an enclosure where errant players, eg. in ice hockey, have to sit for a predetermined period of time; 2. (education) a school to which otherwise ineducable pupils, whose activities have disrupted their original school, are sent as a last resort.

Sin City n. (US trucker use) Las Vegas, Nevada; fr. its lurid reputation *CB*.

since the hog(s) ate grandma, since the hog(s) ate my brother, since the hog(s) ate my little sister phr. a very long time.

sing v. to make a confession to the police *Laugh in the Dark*.

sing like a canary v. (UK police/criminal use) to make a full confession to the police *Powis*.

singer n. an informer *Runyon*.

sink the sausage v. to have sexual intercourse (cf: hide the salami).

sinker n. a doughnut; fr. habit of dunking one's doughnut into one's coffee *Schulberg*.

sip at the fuzzy cup v. (US Black use) to engage in cunnilingus *Folb*.

sissy n. (derog.) effeminate homosexual male *Jay & Young*.

sister n. (homosexual use) fellow (male) homosexual; also used by lesbians for their peers *White*.

sister-act n. 1. a homosexual couple; 2. a homosexual man having sex with a heterosexual woman *Legman*.

sisters n. Black womanhood; dating esp. fr. use by Black radicals in 1960s

Seale.

sit a woman v. (US Black use) to entertain a woman *Klein*.

sit down v. (US teen. use) to make a telling, lasting impression; to have a major effect *Sculatti*.

sit eggs v. (US Black use) to overstay one's welcome; fr. a hen awaiting its chicks *Klein*.

sit on v. to suppress, to keep quiet *PT*.

sit on it and rotate! general term of abuse suggesting that a hard and painful object be thrust into the victim's anus *'Hill Street Blues,'* *Thames TV*, *1983*.

sit on one's face v. for a woman to position her vagina directly above a man's mouth, either literally sitting or squatting above his face, in order to facilitate cunnilingus *Green*, *'Book of Rock Quotes'*, *1977*.

sit on one's stuff v. (US Black use) to work as a prostitute *Folb*.

sit on the throne v. to use a lavatory *Rawson*.

sit tight v. to stay where one is, esp. to stand firm and unruffled in the face of adversity *rr*.

sit-com n. (media use) (abbrev.) situation comedy: 'Steptoe & Son', 'The Good Life', 'All in the Family', etc. (cf: soap opera).

sit-me-down n. the buttocks *Rawson*.

sitter n. 1. (cricket use) a very easy catch *BBC Radio 3 passim*; 2. an easy target, both in shooting and in metaphor.

sitters n. (sex industry use) see: B-girl (qv).

sitting pretty a. secure, safe, enjoying an easy life, esp. as to material things *Wodehouse: AAG*.

sit-upon n. (genteel euph.) buttocks.

six and four n. (drug use) heroin that has been adulterated and weakened by mixing one portion of pure heroin to six or four of sugar *Larner*.

six man n. (Can. prison use) a look-out *Caron*.

six-foot bungalow n. a coffin *Rawson*.

sixteen-year-old after shave n. (US

Black use) very cheap and nasty wine *Folb*.

sixty-eight fellatio: 'you suck me and I'll owe you one' (cf: 69) *Maledicta*.

sixty-nine fr. Fr. *soixante-neuf*: mutual oral-genital stimulation *Price: 1*.

size queen n. (homosexual use) one who is obsessed by the size of penis a potential partner can boast *Stanley*.

sizzle v. (US Black use) to be exceptionally prone to arrest, esp. when holding drugs and acting in an outrageous manner nonetheless (cf: hot) *Major*.

skag n. aka: *scag*: heroin *Tuff Shit Comics*.

skank n. unattractive, easily available girl *Price: 1*.

skank v. (West Indian use) to steal.

skanky a. (US Black) dirty, second-rate, unattractive.

skate a.v. (US campus use) easy, simple, esp. of work; a course one can skate through *Underwood*.

skedaddle v. to rush off, to scamper, to escape *Humphries*.

skeet v. (US Black use) to have sexual intercourse *Klein*.

sketch a. (US campus use) risky, dangerous; abbrev. sketchy *Underwood*.

skeeza, skeezer n. (US Black) (derog.) a girl who trades sex for status; her chosen partners are often drug dealers or performers.

skeeze v. (US Black) to have sexual intercourse (cf: skeeza)

skeggy a. unpleasant, disgusting, the implication is of rotting or fecal matter *G Green*.

skell n. a villain, a rogue, esp. a vagrant who lives in the streets.

skew-whiff a. crooked, cock-eyed (qv); thus drunk (cf: squiffy).

skezag n. (drug use) pig Latin -ez-insertion, fr. skag (qv) heroin; *Stone*.

skid artist n. (UK criminal use) an expert get-away car driver used on robberies; the speedily driven car skids around the corners *Powis*.

skid marks n. stains on one's

underwear *Humphries*.

skid row n. the centre, in any town or city, for down-and-outs, alcoholics, tramps, etc. *Bukowski:6*.

skidlid n. a crash helmet *T 8/6/83*.

skied a. (US campus use) pun on psyched up (qv): ready for anything *Bernbach*.

skillet .n. (US Black use) a Black person *Major*.

skimming n. stealing from the till, taking money 'off the top', esp. found at casinos, strip clubs and other places where a degree of criminality is already endemic.

skimmish n. beer, alcohol; usu. vagrant use *Powis*.

skin n. a dollar *Motor City Comics*.

skin and blister n. (rhyming sl.) sister *Dury*.

skin game n. 1. (US Black use) a card game, spec. tonk or coon can *Klein*; 2. the pornography trade (cf: skin flick, skin mag).

skin mag n. a pornographic magazine (cf: skin flick, skin game 2., one-hand magazine, stroke book).

skin me! (US Black use) invitation to give me some skin (qv) *X*.

skin the cat v. (US Black use) to have sexual intercourse *Folb*.

skin worker n. (US cant) a shoplifter *Neaman & Silver*.

skin-flicks n. pornographic films *Higgins:5*.

skinflint n. a mean person *BvdB*.

skinflute n. (US Black use) the penis *Klein*.

skinhead n. UK teenage youth cult whose main identifying features are bald heads, large 'bother' boots, turned up jeans and braces; they provide much of the 'heavy' element of the neo-Nazi National Front.

skinned a. deprived of one's money, esp. after gambling unsuccessfully.

skinner n. (Aus. use) in gambling, a betting coup *Wilkes*.

skinning see: skinpop *Larner*.

skinpop v. (drug use) to inject a narcotic beneath the skin rather than directly into a vein (cf: mainline)

Goldman.

skins n. cigarette papers, esp. those used for rolling cannabis joints (qv).

skint a. without money, out of funds corruption of *skinned* (cf: broke) *Griffiths.*

skip v. to leave, to escape, to run off *Sharpe:1.*

skip it! forget it, don't bother, etc. *Howard.*

skip tracer n. an investigator who tracks down those who default on hotel and other bills *Fiction Illus.3.*

skipper n. (UK police use) 1. a sergeant *Laurie* 2. shelter for tramps and other homeless people (cf: skippering).

skipper v. to sleep rough.

skippering sleeping in derelict, empty houses; orig. 16th C. *skipper*: a barn *Wilkinson.*

skippy n. (US Black use) an effeminate homosexual male *Major.*

skirt n. a woman, usu. an attractive woman *rr.*

skirt-chaser n. a Don Juan, a habitual and dedicated ladies man.

skite v. (Aus. use) to boast or brag; fr. Scot. blatherskite: a noisy person *Bickerton.*

skive (off) v. to neglect one's duties, one's work; orig. milit. use.

skiver n. a 'lazybones', a skirker; fr. skive (qv).

skivvies n. underwear *Pynchon.*

skoofer n. (drug use) aka: *skoofus, skroofus*: marijuana cigarette *Folb.*

skrungy a. unappealing, unappetizing, disgusting.

skulk v. (US campus use) to steal *Underwood.*

skull v. to fellate (cf: whip some skull on) *Morgan.*

skull n. (US Black use) cunnilingus (cf: head) *Klein.*

skull and crossbones n. (US Black use) 1. poison, thus; 2. anyone who is 'poison', esp. one who disrupts one's plans *Klein.*

skulldrag n. (US Black use) any activity that taxes the mind or emotions *Major.*

skulled a. intoxicated by a given drug or by an excess of alcohol; fr. out of one's skull (qv).

skullneck v. to decapitate *Wilkinson.*

skunk n. an exceptionally strong variety of marijuana with up to 30% tetrahydrocannibonol (THC) content; so high a THC rating – the element that actually gets the user high (qv) – pushes the effects from the merely stimulating to those of such hallucinogens as LSD. (fr. abbr. skunkweed: poss. fr. SE skunk, an animal with a particularly strong smell; but NB older drunk as a skunk (qv)).

skunked a. very drunk; from *drunk as a shunk Neaman & Silver.*

sky n. 1. (rhyming sl.) sky rocket = pocket *Norman:2*; 2. (US Black use) a policeman; fr. colour of uniform *Neaman & Silver.*

sky v. 1. (US milit. use) to leave (cf: sky off) *Del Vecchio*; 2. (drug use) to get high *Shell.*

sky off v. (US Black use) to depart, to exit *Klein.*

sky pilot n. a priest *Caron.*

slab n. (US Black use) $1 *Klein.*

slab boys n. (necrophile use) those who indulge in necrophilia.

slab city n. the morgue.

slabbed and slid a. (UK prison use) dead and gone, or certainly long since departed from the prison and thus the immediate knowledge or interest of those left behind *LL.*

slabbing pp. (necrophile use) having sexual intercourse with a corpse.

slabs n. (backsl.) balls = testicles *Cole.*

slack n. freedom, relief of pressure; *give some slack*: to let someone relax, to stop pressurizing *Price:2.*

slackman n. (US milit. use) the second man in a platoon or patrol when marching, immediately behind point (qv) (cf: drag) *Del Vecchio.*

slag n. 1. a promiscuous woman; 2. any unpleasant person; 3. general term for a group of unpleasant people: 'the slag' *Norman:2*; all derive fr.

18th C. *slag*: coward, fr. slack-mettled.

slag v. (abbrev.) slag off (qv) *T 11/2/83*.

slag off v. to critize, slander, attack verbally *Robins:1*.

slam v. **1.** to criticize particularly harshly *Klein*; **2.** to hit, to kill; **3.** (drug use) to use heroin regularly (cf: bang).

slam off v. to die *Chandler: Notebk*.

slambang a. rough, tough, aggressive *PT*.

slammer n. prison; fr. the slamming shut of cell doors *Higgins:1*.

slamming a. (US Black use) overwhelming, extraordinary, very big; fr. 19th C. UK use *Klein*.

slams n. (US prison use) cell doors, fr. the sound they make when shut (cf: slammer) *Klein*.

slant n. aka: *slant-eye*: derog. Oriental (cf: roundeye 2) *BvdB*.

slap n. make-up, esp. in theatre use; one 'slaps it on' *Norman:3*.

slap the pavement (US Black use) to walk around *Klein*.

slap five v. mutual hand-slapping ritual used by Blacks (and some whites) for greeting, emphasis, congratulation, etc. (cf: give me five, give me some skin) *Price:2*.

slap-bang a. exactly, completely, perfectly; usu. as *slap-bang in the middle*.

slap-dab directly, straight at, immediately *Runyon*.

slap-dash a. careless, enthusiastic if less than puntilious, happy-go-lucky.

slap-happy a. cheery, slightly eccentric; fr. boxing use: someone whose brain has suffered from an excess of fighting (cf: punchy) *Himes:2*.

slapper n. a whore.

slapping aka: *slip-slapping*: see slap five *Milner*.

slapping the plank see: slap five *Klein*.

slash n. **1.** urination *LL*; **2.** the vagina.

slash v. (US Black use) to demolish someone verbally; with a 'rapier-like' wit *Klein*.

slats n. the ribs; fr. resemblance *Runyon:1*.

slaughter n. (UK criminal use) an immediate dumping ground for recently stolen property, prior to sharing it out or hiding it more permanently and securely (cf: Aladdin's cave) *'Minder', Thames TV, 1983*.

slaughterhouse n. (US Black use) anywhere a couple can indulge in sexual intercourse (cf: killing floor) *Folb*.

slave n. (US Black use) work, any form of job *X*.

slay v. **1.** (homosexual use) to gossip maliciously behind a third party's back; **2.** to reduce to complete hysterical laughter; to amaze or shock.

sleaze n. an unappealing, seedy person; fr. sleazy (qv) *Higgins:4*.

sleazebag n. a distasteful person, with overtones of dirtiness and criminality (cf: sleaze).

sleazeball n. see: sleazebag.

sleazy a. of a person: unpleasant, poss. criminal, generally distasteful; of a thing: dirty, rundown, decayed.

sledge n. (criminal use) (abbrev.) sledgehammer, thus one who carries a sledgehammer for use in a bank-robbery, an assault or other violent crime *Mortimer*.

sledge v. (cricket use) the barracking and abusing of a batsman by fielders in order to disturb his concentration; fr. sledgehammer *ST 13/2/83*.

sleeper n. **1.** (US campus use) a lazy, useless person *Underwood*; **2.** (media use (publishing, films, records, etc.)) any product that gains acceptance and success only slowly; **3.** (drug use) any form of sleeping pill *Green:1*.

sleeping Jesus n. (US Black use) **1.** a dull, tedious person; **2.** a person who is nodding out (qv) under the influence of heroin; both senses punning on creeping Jesus (qv) *Klein*.

sleepy time girl n. a promiscuous female; a given man's mistress *Chandler:LG*.

slewed a. drunk; off-balance

Norman:3.

slice n. **1.** the vagina (cf: prime cut, etc.); **2.** (record business use) a 45 rpm record – a slice of an album (if seen as a circular cake) *Whitcomb*.

slice of life n. aka: *spice of life*: the vagina *Klein*.

slicer n. (US Black use) a knife *Folb*.

slick a. fashionable, smart, stylish, clever *Underwood*.

slick-'em-plenty n. (US Black use (derog.)) a Jew, implying the clichéd critique of Jews as sharp (dishonest) businessmen *Folb*.

slicker n. a dandy, a smart dresser *Farrell*.

slicks n. (US milit. use) see: Hueys *Del Vecchio*.

slickster n. (US Black use) a cheat, a smooth talker, a hustler (qv) *Folb*.

slide n. **1.** an establishment where transvestites can solicit normally dressed males *Legman;* **2.** (US three-card monte (qv) use) the member of the con-team who keeps an eye out for police and warns the rest so that all can 'slide off' in time *Shulman*; **3.** (drug use) a syringe, used for injecting narcotic drugs. (fr. the sliding plunger that is part of the syringe).

slide v. to be forgiven, pardoned, ignored *Underwood*.

slide by v. (US Black use) to drop in uninvited, without previous notice *Folb*.

slidewalk n. (US Black use) a specific style of walking: one foot takes normal paces, the other drags; one hand is tucked into the side, the other is positioned with the wrist pressed to the waist and the elbow sticking out (cf: diddy-bopping) *Klein*.

slim n. (US prison use) a police spy *Chandler: Notebk.*

sling v. (Aus. use) to pay a bribe or a commission, esp. on one's winnings at gambling (cf: bung) *Bickerton*.

sling off v. (Aus. use) to mock, to tease *Wilkes*.

sling one's hook v. to leave; poss. nautical, poss. mining origins *Dury*.

sling out v. to eject, to throw out

Griffith.

sling pussy v. to work as a prostitute; the image is that of the short-order cook who 'slings hash' in a diner or café *Morgan*.

sling shot n. (US Black use) a sanitary napkin *Folb*.

slinger n. (UK criminal use) one who passes forged notes *LL*.

slip v. (US Black use) to let one's attention waver, to become too casual, to abandon one's vigilance.

slip (her) a length v. to make love to a woman.

slip it to v. to have sexual intercourse with *Humphries*.

slit n. **1.** the vagina, thus; **2.** a female *P. Roth, 'The Great American Novel', 1973*; **3.** (derog.) an Asian or Oriental person; fr. shape of eyes *Folb*.

Sloane Rangers n. close-knit (essentially female) coterie representing the late teen/early twenties members of the UK aristocracy and such peers as they admit. Coined in *Harpers/Queen* magazine in 1978 by Peter York in an article that defines and explains the type. The specific name stems from the status of Sloane Square, London, SW1 as the centre of all SR life, style, etc. *Bernbach*.

slob n. fr. Slavic *zhlub*: coarse fellow: lazy, dirty, unkempt good-for-nothing man *Selby:1*.

slop chute n. (USMC use) any bar or restaurant on a Marine base *Uris*.

slop joint n. a cheap, unappetising restaurant (cf: slop chute).

slope n. (derog.) an Oriental, esp. Vietnamese, Korean; fr. shape of eyes *O'Brien*.

slopped a. drunk; fr. general sloppiness, of speech, mind, etc. *Dickson*.

sloppy seconds n. a girl who has just copulated with one man and about to take on a second *Carson*.

slosh v. to hit.

sloshed a. drunk; fr. 19th-C. *slosh*: drink *Dury*.

slot n. (Aus. use) a prison cell, usu.

criminal use; into which one is put
Wilkes.

slouch n. (pimp use) an eccentric,
lazy, unprofessional prostitute (cf:
flaky ho) *OUI 8/75*.

slow burn n. the gradual development
of an intense fury, slowly brought to a
peak, rather than simply exploding
with rage.

slow con n. a fraudulent scheme in
which the victim is nurtured slowly
and carefully towards his/her downfall
(cf: short con) *Pearce.*.

slow 'em ups n. (drug use)
barbiturates, tranquillizers, which act
as soporifics *Folb*.

slow on the draw a. not very
intelligent (cf: quick on the draw, slow
on the trigger).

slow on the trigger n. stupid, dull
Thompson:J.

slow one's row v. (US Black use)
to lower one's profile; to keep off
the streets, perhaps through fear of
police or rival criminal interest
Klein.

slow walk v. to stall, to put someone
off.

slow walker n. (US criminal use) one
who follows postmen on their rounds
with the intention of stealing the mail
they have just delivered
Breslin.

slug n. 1. a bullet; 2. a measure of a
drink *Selby:1*.

slug v. to hit.

slugger n. 1. a fighter, professional or
otherwise, who relies on brute force
rather than skill for his conquests fr.
slug = hit *Heller*; 2. (US campus use) a
sexual success, a seducer (cf: hitter)
Underwood.

slum n. fake, paste jewellery; fr.
19th-C. UK cant: trickery and skill; a
false document or begging letter
Runyon.

slummy n. an ill-dressed, unattractive
female *Klein*.

slums and bums n. (US campus use)
course in urban local government
fr. decayed housing, tramps
Dickson.

slush n. 1. (criminal use) forged,
counterfeit money *LL*; 2. (publishing
use) unsolicited, and thus almost
inevitably unpublished and rejected
manuscripts *Green:2*.

slush fund n. an emergency fund for
unforeseen expenditure, esp. that
which may be illegal or extra-legal;
such funds came into prominence
during the Watergate Affair of 1972–4
Pynchon.

slut-puppy n. (derog.) a lesbian (cf:
butt slut).

sly, slick and wicked n. (US Black
use) an individual who plans to be
caught out in a small act of deceit and
thus facilitate plans for a larger con
trick *Klein*.

slyboots n. cunning, deceptive
person, usu. with overtones of
affection rather than an expression
of outright disapproval
Vidal.

slygrog n. (Aus. use) liquor sold
without benefit of a licence
Bickerton.

S&M (acro.) sado-masochism
Jay & Young.

smack n. 1. fr. Yiddish *schmeck* = hit;
thus heroin (cf: hit) *Velvet
Underground, 'Heroin', 1966*; 2. (US
conman use) the use of a specially
doctored coin for heads-or-tails
gambling; the name comes from the
conman's smacking his hand on the
coin as he catches it *Thompson:J*.

smack freak n. heroin addict (cf:
smack) *Price:2*.

smack in the eye n. a rebuff, a
rejection, a severe and surprising
disappointment.

smacked out a. under the influence of
heroin; fr. smack (qv).

smacker n. a kiss; fr. the sound it
makes.

smackeroos n. pounds sterling *T 21/9/
83*.

smackers n. pounds sterling; orig. US
$1 *Humphries*.

smack-head n. heroin addict *Welsh:2*
(cf: acid-head, pill-head, pot-head,
etc.).

small change n. an insignificant, weak person; fr. monetary use *Waits*.

small potatoes a. insignificant; of little worth, irrelevant *Teresa*.

small time n.,a. mediocrity, failure, the second rate, unprofitable fr. theatre use: a vaudeville circuit for second-rate acts which offered three or even more programmes per day (cf: big time).

smart cookie n. a bright, opportunistic person *rr*.

smart guy n. see: wise guy.

smart money n. 1. spec. the way in which experienced gamblers bet; 2. good sense *Higgins:3*.

smart mouth n.,v. see: bad mouth *Folb*.

smart-ass n.,a. anyone who considers himself cleverer than his peers and than his own actual intelligence warrants *The People's Comic*.

smartiepants n. general term of light-hearted abuse *May*.

smarts n. wit, intelligence *Grogan*.

smash n. 1. small change; orig. counterfeit money, then rhyming sl., cash *Burroughs:1*; 2. (show business use) a great success, (abbrev.) smash hit *Performance*; 3. (US Black use) wine; back-formation fr. smashed (qv) (?) *Folb*.

smashed a. 1. very drunk *Junker*; 2. intoxicated with a given drug, esp, cannabis or LSD *Wolfe:2*.

smashing a. wonderful, delightful, excellent; mainly juv. use.

smear and smudge n. (rhyming sl.) judge *Wright*.

smeg n. dirty, unkempt person; from smegma.

smeggy a. dirty, unkempt.

smeghead n. general term of abuse.

smell a rat v. to be suspicious, of persons or situations *Sillitoe*.

smiling faces n. (US Black use) hypocrites, false friends *Klein*.

smogged a. (US prison use) executed in the gas chamber.

smoke n. 1. (derog.) a Black person (cf: shadow) *Dunne*; 2. any cheap, rotgut alcohol, spec. denatured alcohol shaken up with water and drunk by down and out alcoholic tramps *Himes:1*; 3. (drug use) marijuana; 4. (US campus use) one dollar; so small a sum 'goes up in smoke'.

smoke v. 1. to throw very fast, usu. of a ball *Underwood*; 2. to kill.

smoke out v. 1. (US Black use) to impress; to outdo *Folb*; 2. to entice into the open, to lure out; fr. hunting/rural use.

smoke stack n. (US Black use) a particularly Black person *Folb*.

Smoke, the n. London, as regarded from the provinces.

smoked haddock n. (racing use, rhyming sl.) the Paddock *Franklyn*.

Smokey n. traffic policeman, Highway Patrol; fr. US traditional country character 'Smokey the Bear' *Higgins:4*.

smoking a. first rate, excellent (cf: dope, fly) *T 8/4/91*.

smoking a. (US Black use) very urgent, very excited; esp. in sexual context *Klein*.

smooching n. kissing and cuddling, standing up and dressed *Price:1*.

smoodge v. (Aus. use) to ingratiate oneself, to cuddle up, to suck up (qv); fr. Yiddish *schmooze* or SE *smudge*: to caress *Dennis*.

smoothie n. a sophisticated, smart person – both mentally and physically *Thompson:J*.

smother n. a coat, a wrap; fr. smother: to hide, to cover up *Norman:2*.

smush n. the mouth; fr. mush (qv) *Runyon:1*.

smut n. pornography, obscenity; since such items are 'dirty'.

smut-butt n. (US campus use) (derog.) Black student *Underwood*.

smut-hound n. one who is obsessed by the tiniest trace of obscenity, esp. in the arts or media; thus a censor; coined by H. L. Mencken and one of the coinages of which he was 'vainest' *AS 41 (1966)*.

snafu (milit. use) (acro.) situation

normal: *all fucked-up* coined c.1940 by anon. member of British Army *Byrne*.

snag v. 1. to grab *Price:3*; 2. (street gang use) to attack an individual without warning *Salisbury*; 3. (US Black use) to have sexual intercourse *Folb*.

snags n. (Aus. use) sausages; rarely used in singular *Wilkes*.

snake n. (street gang use) a spy *Salisbury*.

snake v. (US campus use) to steal someone else's date *Underwood*.

snake in the grass n. (rhyming sl.) looking glass, mirror *Cole*.

snake-eyes (gambling use) the point of 2 (a pair of ones) in craps dice *Chandler: Notebk.*

snakes n. 1. urination; 2. abbrev. for snakes house (qv) and thus a lavatory.

snake's house n. (Aus. use) lavatory; fr. rhyming sl. snake's hiss: piss *Humphries*.

snaky a. devious, underhand, cunning; fr. the Eden myth.

snap n. anything easy, a simple task, achievement (cf: snip) *Selby:1*.

snap assholes v. see: lock assholes *Uris*.

snap it up v. to speed up, to hurry up; often as a command *Chandler:LG*.

snapper n. 1. (homosexual use) the foreskin *Legman*; 2. the vagina (cf: red snapper, snapping turtle).

snatch n. 1. spec. the vagina; 2. women, girls *Selby:1*.

snatch v. 1. to kidnap *Runyon*; 2. (US Black use) to threaten someone by grabbing their lapels and talking menacingly into their face *Klein*.

snazzy a. smart, fashionable, brightly coloured; fr. snappy + jazzy (?).

sneak job n. housebreaking *Runyon*.

sneak play n. a furtive entrance and exit from a brothel; from the baseball term.

sneaky a. underhand, crooked *Seale*.

sneaky Pete n. cheap, rotgut wine; its effects 'sneak up' on the drinker *Salisbury*.

sneaky-Pete v. to creep quietly, to move stealthily *Pynchon*.

sneeze v. to kidnap *Chandler: Notebk.*

sneeze in the cabbage v. to perform cunnilingus *Legman*.

sneeze it out v. to confess (cf: cough up) *Klein*.

sneezer n. prison *Runyon:1*.

snide a. 1. spec. counterfeit (money), thus; 2. fake, unpleasant, mean *Norman:2*.

sniff n. 1. narcotics; fr. the method of consuming them *Black Uhuru, 'Chill Out', 1982*; 2. rumour *Robins:1*; 3. glue, paint thinner and other chemicals used for intoxication.

sniffer n. 1. (pimp use) a client who enjoys sniffing a prostitute's dirty panties *OUI 8/75*; 2. (derog.) investigator from the DHSS who checks on the validity of unemployment benefit claims *Bleasdale*.

sniffy a. disdainful, arrogant; fr. sniffs of contempt.

snifter n. an alcoholic drink; fr. the brandy glass, shaped to be warmed by the hands and for the fumes, so intensified, to be sniffed *Wodehouse:GB*.

snip n. 1. a bargain; 2. anything simple, an easy task (cf: snap) *Capital Radio 1983*.

snipe n. 1. cigarette end (cf: fag-end, butt-end) *Algren*; 2. (USN use) a fireman or other member of a ship's engine-room gang *Pynchon*.

snipe v. (US Black use) to kill; fr. milit. use *Folb*.

snipe on v. (US Black use) to malign, to criticize, to gossip about someone; fr. milit. marksman *Folb*.

snippy a. hypercritical, complaining over petty problems; cutting down other people *Vidal*.

snit n. an outbreak of temper; generally a children's term.

snitch n. 1. an informer *Goldman*; 2. the nose *Wright*.

snitch v. 1. to inform; 2. to steal *Wodehouse:AAG*.

snitcher n. an informant, a tell-tale *Sanders:2*.

snockered a. drunk *Price:3.*

snog v. to enjoy sexual preliminaries, stopping short of intercourse, usu. of teenage experimentation (cf: necking) *May.*

snood n. see: crack.

snoop v. to pry, to interfere, to listen in.

snoot n. the nose *Runyon.*

snooter n. (drug use) anyone who inhales heroin or cocaine rather than injects it; fr. snoot (qv).

snootful n. an alcoholic drink; hence to *have a snootful*: to be drunk *Wodehouse:MOJ.*

snooty a. snobbish, stand-offish; one who looks down their nose (cf: snoot) *May.*

snooze job n. anything especially boring *Gene Hackman LWT, 1982.*

snore n. a bore; the image is of sending one's audience to sleep.

snorker n. (Aus. use) **1.** sausage, thus; **2.** penis *Humphries.*

snort v. to inhale narcotics, usu. cocaine or heroin, through the nostrils *Larner.*

snort n. a gulp of alcohol *Runyon.*

snot n. **1.** mucus; fr. 15th C. *Price:2*; **2.** (abbrev.) snotnose 2 (qv) *Thompson:J.*

snot box n. the nose.

snotnose n. **1.** a small child with a running nose; a grubby child; **2.** an arrogant, snobbish person (cf: snotty)

snotrag n. handkerchief; fr. snot 1 (qv) *Humphries.*

snotty a. superior, snobbish, stuck-up *Price:2.*

snout n. **1.** tobacco *Norman:1*; **2.** the nose *Higgins:2*; **3.** an informer (cf: snitch) *Newman:2.*

snow n. **1.** (Aus. school use) a blond-haired weakling, the butt of bullies who will call him 'snow!' *Humphries:2*; **2.** (Aus. use) derog. description of Italian or other Latin race; fr. snow: a white-coloured haircream à la Brylcreem and supposedly favoured by such men *Humphries:2*; **3.** cocaine; fr. colour and consistency *Vidal*; **4.** bluff,

bluster, lies; abbrev. snow job (qv) *Higgins:2*; **5.** (US Black use) a white girl *Klein.*

snow v. to fool, usu. by overwhelming with slick patter (cf: snow job).

snow bird n. (drug use) **1.** a cocaine user; fr. snow (qv); **2.** used in Florida to describe a winter tourist who comes south to avoid the chilly weather *Hiassen.*

snow bunny n. a girl who frequents the ski slopes as much for the sex as for the sport *Humphries:2.*

snow in one's game (US Black use) the introduction of a white person into a black person's life with the express intention of profiting financially by catering to their sexual wants *Klein.*

snow job n. an untrue but totally convincing story; a conman's patter *Caron.*

snow out v. to lose one's bearings; the image is of a blizzard.

snowball n. a brand of ecstasy (qv) *Welsh:2.*

snow-dropping n. (UK criminal use) stealing washing from unguarded clotheslines *LL.*

snowed over a. (US campus use) obsessively in love, infatuated *Underwood.*

snowed under a. over-burdened with work, commitments, responsibilities, etc.

snowfall n. see: snow job *'Taxi', Thames TV, 1983.*

snoz n. see: snozzle *Southern & Hoffenberg.*

snozzle n. the nose (cf: schnozzle) *Runyon:1.*

snuff v. to murder, to kill; abbrev. snuff out *Sanders.*

snuff it v. to die *Humphries.*

snuff movies n. films, usu. pornographic, which climax in the actual death of one of the participants, usu. an actress; snuff movies were allegedly common in California around the time of the psychotic Manson Family, c.1969, though no one seems to have seen or to possess a copy *Sanders.*

snuffer n. see: snuff movies *Morgan*.

snuggies n. (US campus use) female underwear; not particularly winter thickness *Underwood*.

so a. homosexual; 'Is he so?' (cf: that way) Q. Crisp, *'The Naked Civil Servant', 1975*.

so long goodbye, poss. fr. Hebrew *shalom*: the basic word of greeting and farewell, lit. 'peace' *rr*.

so what? widely used term of disinterest, a rejoinder to the previous speaker's announcement, revelation, or whatever.

soak n. a drunkard.

soak v. to extort money from *The People's Comic*.

so-and-so 1. euph. for any derog. name, esp. sonofabitch (qv); 2. unspecified object, thingamijig *Bruce:1*.

soap opera n. the daily radio and TV dramas – 'The Archers', 'Coronation Street', etc. – which tell the interminable tale of supposedly 'ordinary life'; fr. the original show 'The Goldbergs', used by US sponsor Proctor & Gamble to advertise their soap and similar products (cf: sitcom) *Green:2*.

SOB see: sonofabitch.

sob sister n. see: agony aunt.

sob story n. a pitiful tale, which may reduce the listener to tears, whether or not it has any basis in truth or is designed merely for felonious purposes.

sob stuff n. distressing facts, stories, etc.; often used to obtain sympathy and poss. money too.

sock v. to hit, to punch *Farrell*.

sock it to me! (excl.) amaze me, surprise me, etc.; fr. the catchphrase used in 'Rowan & Martin's Laugh-In', TV 1960s, *Uneeda Comix*.

sock the clock punch the time clock *Chandler: Notebk*.

socko a. wonderful, excellent, esp. in show business use and *Variety* magazine *Thompson*.

sod n. 1. an unpleasant person; fr. abbrev. sodomite, but sexual reference purely coincident; 2. (US campus use) a drunkard; pun on sot *Underwood*.

sod about v. to mess around, to waste time, etc.

sod widow n. an actual widow, whose husband has died, rather than a grass widow, whose husband is merely away; the corpse is 'under the sod' *Runyon*.

sodding a. adj. from sod (qv); derog. intensifier *Performance*.

soft a. fr. soft in the head: stupid, dull, foolish *Breslin*.

soft boy n. (UK Black use) a homosexual (cf: battiman).

soft money n. notes, bills, paper money *Klein*.

soft number n. an easy job.

soft one n. (necrophile use) a corpse before the hardening process of rigor mortis has set in.

soft soap n.,v. flattery, thus the act of flattering someone *Hotten*.

soft swing n. (sex industry use) a swinging (qv) party where the only intercourse is performed by couples who arrived together; non-penetrative sex, however, is enjoyed at random.

soft touch n. one who can easily be touched (qv), ie solicited for money.

soft-cop n. a sucker, esp. some form of community/social worker whose sympathies can be exploited *Robins:1*.

softie n. a weakling; a man whose external toughness hides a sentimental soul *Heller*.

soft-pedal v. to play down, to diminish, to keep a 'low profile'; fr. pedal on a piano.

soggies n. (UK 'society' use) breakfast cereal; a hangover from nursery talk *Barr*.

SOHF n. (UK 'society' use) (acro.) Sense Of Humour Failure; often discerned in someone who fails to appreciate the throwing of bread rolls, etc. *Barr*.

sold a. successfully persuaded (cf: sell) *Norman:2*.

sold on a. convinced, fascinated by (cf: sell).

soldier n. (US Mafia use) a lower echelon member of a Mafia family, the run-of-the-mill gangsters who fight the gangwars.

solid! excl. of approbation, implying a firm bond, honesty, excellence, etc.

solids hit the air conditioning phr. a euphemism for the more common shit hits the fan (qv).

solitary as a bastard on Father's Day (Aus. cp) extremely lonely *Humphries:2*.

sombitch n. see: sonofabitch *Vidal*.

some hope! (negative excl.) no hope whatsoever.

some mothers do have 'em (cp) describing a particularly foolish or absurd person *BBC-TV, situation comedy title, 1970s*.

some people! (cp) derisory or critical comment by the speaker on the opinions or more likely the activities of others; the details are unspoken but will be a condemnation of what 'some people; are doing.

someone blew out his/her pilot light (US campus use) cp referring to anyone considered somewhat odd, high on drugs, etc. and who thus has 'lost direction' *Bernbach*.

something else n. excl. or description of approval, or wonder *Bruce:2*.

something the cat brought in n. a distasteful, prob. dirty/unkempt, object or person *Wodehouse:MOJ*.

son of a bitch n. derog. general term of abuse *Higgins:1*.

sonofagun (euph.) sonofabitch (qv) *Bruce:2*.

sook n. (Aus. use) coward, crybaby *Humphries:2*.

sooner n. 1. (Aus. use) a lazy person; one who would 'sooner' loaf around than work or, in context, fight *Neaman & Silver*; 2. an illegitimate child (cf: come-too-soon).

sooty n. (derog.) black person (cf: chocolate).

SOP (police use) (acro.) *S*tandard *O*perating *P*rocedure *Vidal*.

sophisticated lady n. (US Black use) cocaine (cf: girl) *Folb*.

sopor n. (drug use) (abbrev.) soporific, any form of barbiturate drug *Stone*.

soppy a. (juv. use) vapid, naïve, esp. romantic; sometimes intensified as *soppy date*; fr. sopping wet (?).

sore a. angry, irritated *McBain:1*.

sorehead n. a grumpy, irritable person *Dunne*.

sorry and sad n. (rhyming sl.) dad = father *Wright*.

sort n. 1. (Aus. use) a companion of either sex; 2. (UK use) a girl *Humphries*.

sort out v. to deal with, esp. violently *Tidy*.

sorted adv. worked out, happy, content.

soul n. the essential quality of Black being, unavailable, however much aped and pirated, to anyone who is not Black (and American).

soul a. Black; fr. soul n. (qv); thus *soul food, soul sister etc. Price:2*.

soul child n. (US campus use (Black students)) anyone with conspicuous Black pride and identity *Underwood*.

soul kiss n. a deep kiss, involving putting one's tongue into one's partner's mouth (cf: french kiss) *Jay & Young*.

soul shake n. see: slap five *Folb*.

sound n. (street gang use) conversation; talk *Salisbury*.

sound v. (street gang use) to tease, to joke with *Salisbury*.

sound off v. to boast, brag.

sounds n. music, spec. records.

sounds and tunes n. (US campus use) songs *Underwood*.

soup and fish n. a dinner jacket; fr. the food one eats when wearing it *Wodehouse passim*.

souped-up a. intensified, accelerated; usu. of a car that has been modified by its owner to exceed the basic factory-created performance; fr. soup = engine fuel (?) *Humphries:2*.

souse n. a drunkard (cf: soak).

soused a. drunk; fr. souse (qv) *Schulberg*.

sov n. (abbrev.) sovereign: a pound

sterling *Newman:1*.

sozzled a. drunk *Wright*.

SP (racing use) (abbrev.) Starting Price, thus: basic information, facts *Griffith*.

space v. **1.** (US teen. use) to daydream, to drift off; fr. spaced out (qv) *Pond*; **2.** (US Black use) to leave, to depart.

space base n. (drug use) a mixture of PCP and rock cocaine or crack (qv).

space cadet n. (drug use) any heavy user of drugs, esp. cannabis or hallucinogens who is, thus, continually 'flying' *Sanders*.

space case n. a crazy person. (cf: space cadet) *Maupin:3*.

space-cake n. see hash-cake *Welsh:1*.

spaced see: spaced out *Goldman*.

spaced out 1. intoxicated by a drug; esp. the hallucinogens; fr. the image of flying through space; **2.** generally disorientated, with or without drugs *Tuff Shit Comics*.

spacey a. **1.** anything that simulates the intoxication of LSD or other hallucinogens **2.** see: spaced out *McFadden*.

spade n. a Black person, esp. West Indian or African; fr. 'black as the ace of spades' *Price:2*.

spag n. (Aus. use) (abbrev.) spaghetti: derog. term for Italian *Wilkes*.

spag bol n. (UK 'society' use) aka: *spag bog*: spaghetti bolognese (most likely in some adulterated British version); a retained juv. use *Barr*.

spaghetti n. (hi-fi use) the collection of wires usually found behind the linking amplifiers, record decks, etc. *Sony Corp., ad., 1983*.

spaghetti bender n. (derog.) Italian; fr. popular Ital. foodstuff *BvdB*.

Spaghetti Corner n. (US use) an Italian community within an urban area.

spaghetti head n. an Italian (cf: spaghetti bender).

Spanish archer n. dismissal, rejection; a pun on 'El Bow' = the elbow (qv) *A Payne*.

Spanish cure n. treatment of drug addiction by forced, total abstinence.

Spanish rice n. (gay use) lumpy semen.

spank v. to beat up *Austin*.

spank one's monkey v. to masturbate (cf; beat one's meat, etc) *Morgan*.

spar n. (UK Black use) friend (cf: spee) *Robins*.

spare a. overwrought, distraught '*Minder*', Thames TV, 1983.

spare prick at a wedding absolutely useless; usu. a cp: *as much use as a . . .*

spare tyre n. the roll of flesh that surrounds an overweight stomach (cf: bagel, love handle).

spark out v. fall fast asleep *Norman:2*.

sparkers see: spark out *Powis*.

sparkler n. **1.** jewellery, spec. diamonds *Powis*; **2.** a lie.

sparko adv. exhausted, sparked out (qv).

sparks n. an electrician, usu. theatrical and film use.

sparrow fart n. dawn *Humphries*.

sparrowhawk v. (sex industry use) to pick up homeless youngsters (of either sex) for sexual exploitation, esp. runaways who have just arrived at rail or bus stations; fr. the predatory bird of the same name (cf: chicken hawk) *Morgan*.

spas n. (student/school use) useless, clumsy, incompetent and thus socially unacceptable person; abbrev. spastic *Underwood*.

spastic a. **1.** convulsed with laughter and thus incapable of coherent mental or physical activity; **2.** see: spas.

spawny a. lucky *Welsh:1* (origin unknown, but poss. link to Sc. game spawnie, played with buttons. One player throws his button, the others attempt to throw theirs nearest to it; the button that comes within a spawn (SE span) is the winner).

spaz n. a fool, an idiot, an unappealing person; fr. spastic (qv) *Harpers/Queen 1/83*.

spaz pads n. orthopaedic shoes

Morgan.

speaker n. (US Black use) a gun *Major*.

spear v. 1. (ice hockey use) to stab at another player with the shaft of one's stick; an illegal foul *D. Atyeo, 'Blood & Guts', 1979*; 2. (US prison use) to arrest *Chandler: Notebk*.

spear the bearded clam v. (Aus. use) to have sexual intercourse *Humphries*.

spearchucker n. a Black; fr. tribal/ African origins *Price:1*.

special n. (pimp use) a client who has any particular tastes: costumes, bondage, foot-fetishes, etc. *OUI 8/75*.

special K n. (drug use) ketamine, a mildly hallucinogenic drug, developed as a battlefield anaesthetic, associated chemically with PCP and often used as a legal substitute for ecstasy (qv) (fr. the breakfast cereal Special K, supposedly a source of extra energy).

speck n. (US Black use) a Black person *Folb*.

specky a. wearing spectacles *Welsh:1*.

spee n. English pronunciation of spar (qv) = friend, and used as such by white youngsters.

speeching n. (UK Black use) 1. to chat up; 2. to talk fluently and well; 3. to defeat in an argument *Robins*.

speed n. any amphetamine-based stimulant drug *Price:2*.

speed freak n. 1. (drug use) a user of amphetamines; 2. (US Black use) one who enjoys driving or being driven at high speed.

speed limit (bingo use) 30; fr. urban speed limit in UK, 30 mph.

speedball n. a mixture of cocaine and heroin, either injected or sniffed by the user *ES 24/3/83*.

spell v. to fill in for, to substitute *Morgan*.

spend a penny v. (euph.) to urinate; fr. the penny (pre-decimalization) charge in public lavatories, now risen with inflation to 10p *James Tucker, 'The Novels of Anthony Powell', 1976*.

spew v. to vomit *Norman:3*.

spew one's guts v. to vomit violently, thus, figuratively, to make a full

confession of crimes. (cf: spill one's guts).

spic n. 1. (derog.) Puerto Rican, Mexican (but cf: wetback); orig. used for Italian, mispron. of 'spaghetti' or 'no speaka da English' *Price:2*; 2. (US campus use) course in Spanish; fr. 1 *Underwood*.

spick n. see: spic 1 *Jenkins*.

spider n. (US campus use) a hard worker; fr. the industrious arachnid *Bernbach*.

spiel n. patter, speech, line (qv); esp. of salesman or market stallholder.

spiel v. 1. to gamble; fr. Yiddish: to play; 2. to patter, to talk glibly, to 'shoot a line'.

spieler n. (illegal) gambling club; fr. Yiddish 'to play' *Norman:2*.

spiff n. a dandy; fr. spiffy (qv) *Dunne*.

spiffed up a. dressed particularly well; fr. spiffy (qv) *Price:3*.

spiffy a. excellent, wonderful, neatly dressed; fr. mid-19th C. *Price:3*.

spifflicated a. drunk *Chandler: LG*.

spiffing a. excellent, wonderful, first rate (cf: spiffy).

spike n. 1. hypodermic syringe *Caron*; 2. a lodging house, orig. local authority workhouse or lodging house *G. Orwell, 'Down and Out in Paris and London', 1933*.

spike v. to inject with a hypodermic syringe *Welsh:1*.

spill v. 1. (drug use) to miss the vein when making an injection and thus waste the heroin/water mixture *Goldman*; 2. see; spill the beans *rr*.

spill one's breakfast v. to vomit *Dunne*.

spill one's guts v. (UK cant) to confess one's crimes in full.

spill one's nut v. to confess, to make an admission *Gruber*.

spill the beans v. to confess, to let out a secret, to talk unguardedly *Waterhouse*.

spill the works v. see: spill the beans *rr*.

spillin' n. (US Black use) a gunfight in which quantities of bullets are fired and wounds inflicted *Klein*.

spin n. (taxi use) an authorized cab rank *LL*.

spin v. (UK police use) to search, usu. in *spin a drum*: to search a house *Powis*.

spin a drum v. (UK police use) to search a suspect's premises *Neaman & Silver*.

spin one's own propellor v. to masturbate.

spinach n. money (cf: cabbage, green, kale).

spirit n. (US Black use) jazz or blues music *Klein*.

spit out of the window v. (homosexual use) to spit out one's partner's semen after fellatio; on to a towel, a tissue, etc. *Legman*.

spit-bit n. (US Black use) smooth, persuasive talk *Klein*.

spitter n. (baseball use) a spitball, now outlawed as a foul pitch *Sanchez*.

spiv n. obs. and for historical use only: a flashy, sharp individual who exists on the fringes of real criminality, living by his wits rather than a regular job; poss. origins: fr. reverse of *VIPs*; fr. police abbrev. 'suspected persons and itinerant vagrants'; most likely from Romany for 'sparrow', used by gypsies as derog. ref. to those who existed by picking up the leavings of their betters, criminal or legitimate.

spivmobile n. an exceptionally ostentatious and flashy car, such as might be driven by a spiv (qv) or his successors (cf: pimpmobile) *T 5/10/83*.

splang n. (US Black use) sharp words *Klein*.

splash n. a woman who is the object of gang-rape or a voluntary participant in multiple intercourse *NWA Niggaz4Life 1991*.

splash the boots v. to urinate *Humphries*.

splatter movie n. a genre of ultra-violent films, coined as a name by director George Romero; typical are such as the 'Texas Chainsaw Massacre' in which the main action/appeal is the covering of the screen in blood.

splendiferous a. intensifier of 'splendid' *Hotten*.

splib n. (abbrev.) slip-de-wib: a fellow black person *Milner*.

splice the mainbrace v. to drink; fr. nautical use *Hotten*.

spliff n. a marijuana cigarette; esp. West Indian and Rastafari use *Thelwell*.

splish and splash v. (US Black use) to debate a topic; to ponder without coming to a decision *Klein*.

split v. to leave. fr. the subsequent division in the group that such a departure makes (?); also fr. 18th-C. UK use: to move, run, gallop, etc. *Price:2*.

split beaver n. see: wide-open beaver.

split the cup v. (US Black use) to deflower a virgin *Klein*.

splitsville n. the end of a relationship, a divorce, etc.

splosh n. tea *Norman:2*.

splosh it on v. to bet heavily, esp. at racetracks.

splurge v. to spend freely, generously and foolishly.

spod n. a school child who has been rejected by its fellows, (cf: goggy, gunk, Wendy, zoid) *Maledicta 9*.

spoiler n. (journalistic use) a reporter who uses any methods, ethical or otherwise, to steal or otherwise ruin a rival paper's supposed scoop *'World In Action', Granada TV, 1983*.

sponditious a. excellent *L Henry passim*.

spondulicks n. money *Waterhouse*.

spook n. 1. a Black person *Norman:2*; 2. (US use) an intelligence agent, esp. CIA; derived fr. the Yale University secret society 'Skull & Bones' from amongst whose members were recruited the personnel of the OSS, the Second World War predecessor of the CIA *Esq. 1976*.

spook v. to scare, to unnerve *Grogan*.

spooked a. (gambling use) a crooked, marked deck of cards; under the influence of a malign spirit *Austin*.

spoon n. (drug use) two grams or one sixteenth of an ounce of heroin *Grogan*.

spoon v. (US campus use) to eat together *Underwood*.

sport n. 1. a playboy, a man about town, with accent on gambling, womanizing and other areas of the fast life *Heller*; 2. general term of address to a man, esp. Aus. use.

sporting goods n. a male homosexual prostitute (cf: sporting life).

sporting life n. the 'good' life: money, liquor, women, all the desired pleasures of the flesh; the term is particularly popular as a description of the lifestyle of a US pimp (cf: sport) *Schulberg*.

spot v. to advance on credit *Tuff Shit Comics*.

spot on perfect, exactly right, accurate.

spot one out v. (US Black use) to ascertain the characteristics, hidden or otherwise, of a given person (cf: peep one's hole card) *Klein*.

spout off v. gabble on.

spout on v. see: spout off.

spray one's tonsils v. (homosexual use) to ejaculate in one's fellator's mouth *Legman*.

spread a technicolour rainbow v. (US campus use) to vomit (cf: technicolour yawn) *Neaman & Silver*.

spread eagle n. a position of heterosexual intercourse.

spread the broads v. to play cards, esp. to cheat or to play a swindling game such as 'find the lady' (qv) (cf: broads) *Powis*.

spread the bull v. to talk boastfully, if inaccurately, of one's prowess (cf: bull, bullshit) *Farrell*.

spring v. to get a person out of prison; to have someone released *Humphries*.

spring for v. to pay for.

spring it v. to reveal (a plan), with some element of surprise *Wodehouse: PGM*.

springer n. (US criminal use) bail bondsman.

spritz v. fr. Yiddish: 'spray': in show business use: to perform a stage monologue with much impromptu ad libbing, free-associating, etc. à la

Lenny Bruce *Goldman*.

sprog n. a child; orig. milit. use: recruit *Obs. 20/3/83*.

spruik v. (Aus. use) to speak in a way that resembles a spruiker (qv) *Dennis*.

spruiker n. (Aus. use) 1. a loud and continual talker; 2. spec. a barker for a fairground/carnival sideshow or a cinema, theatre or similar entertainment, who stands on the street to ballyhoo (qv) the show and attract an audience *Humphries:2*.

spud n. a potato *Wodehouse: COJ*.

spud-bashing n. peeling potatoes; orig. milit. use, when the job was compulsory and part of kitchen fatigues.

spunk n. 1. semen, thus; 2. courage, bravery, guts *Schulberg*.

spunk rat n. (Aus. use) a sexually attractive person.

spunk-gullet n. general term of abuse, spec. a fellator *Welsh:1*.

spunko a. (UK teen. 'society' use) an attractive, intelligent and fashionable male.

spunky a. courageous, brave, plucky.

Spurs n. Tottenham Hotspur Football Club.

SQPQ (UK 'society' use) (acro.) *Suspiciously Quiet, Probably Queer*; note appended to the name of a possible male escort by a debutante or her mother *T 18/7/83*.

Squad n. (abbrev.) the Flying Squad (cf: Sweeney) *Newman:1*.

squaddy n. regular private soldier *A. F. N. Clarke, 'Contact', 1983*.

square n. 1. a traditional, conservative person; fr. jazz use *Grogan*; 2. (Black pimp use) a naive person, a sucker (qv), anyone who believes in white America's promises; one who has little sexual sophistication *Milner*; 3. a cigarette (cf: joint, straight) *Morgan*.

square v. to put right, spec. to deal with problems, often by using influence, bribes, threats, etc. *Wodehouse: PGM*.

square away v. to deal with, to settle; fr. milit. use *Higgins:3*.

square broad n. (Black pimp use) any

woman not a prostitute *Milner*.

Square John n. a respectable member of society (cf: John Q. Public) *Pearce*.

square one off v. to pay; can be used quite legitimately, but often carries a sense of corruption/bribery etc. *Humphries:2*.

square shake n. a fair deal, honest treatment *Algren*.

square shooter n. honest, trustworthy person *Farrell*.

square to the wood (US Black use) intensifier of square (qv) *Folb*.

square with v. to make amends, to make up for, to even up *rr*.

squarebrain n. (US Black use) a fool, a dullard, with overtones of conservatism *Folb*.

squaredom the world of the unsophisticated, the unwordly, the unhip (qv) *Greenlee*.

square-eyes n. one who watches an excess of TV and thus, supposedly, develops eyes the same shape as the screen.

square-go n. a fair fight *Welsh:1*.

squarehead n. (derog.) German; fr. the severe 'Prussian' haircuts (?) *BvdB*.

squarejohn a. respectable, upright.

squashed a. very drunk *Bernbach*.

squat see: diddley-squat (qv) *Higgins:1*.

squatter n. the buttocks *Rawson*.

squawk n. (UK prison use) any form of petition, to the Governor or to the Home Secretary *LL*.

squawk v. to complain; like some raucous bird *Runyon*.

squeak n. a precociously trendy youngster, so termed by his/her (slightly) elders; fr. abbr. of 'pipsqueak'.

squeaky-clean a. as clean as one could imagine; so shiny and taut that it almost squeaks with its own perfection *Whitcomb*.

squeal n. (US police use) the report of a crime by a member of the public *McBain:1*.

squeal v. (US police use) **1.** to report

a crime to the police *McBain:1*; **2.** to inform against one's partners in crime *rr*.

squealer n. an informer *Edgar Wallace, bk. title, 1927*.

Squeedunk n. a generic name for a small town (cf: Podunk).

squeeze n. **1.** (UK criminal use) silk; fr. the quality of the fabric which will squeeze into a minuscule space *Powis*; **2.** a close friend; fr. physical affection (cf: main squeeze) *Folb*.

squeeze off (on) v. to fire a gun (at).

squibbed off a. shot, murdered. fr. 19th C. UK cant *squib*: to fire a gun *Chandler: Notebk.*

squid n. (US campus use) a particularly hard worker *Bernbach*.

squiff out v. to collapse through drunkenness; fr. squiffy (qv) *Chandler: LG*.

squiffy a. drunk; fr. skew-whiff (qv) *Dickson*.

squillion a hypothetical and enormous number, a multiple of many millions *Obs. 26/6/83*.

squire general term of address, no particular rank or intimacy indicated *Newman:2*.

squirrel n. (US campus use) **1.** an eccentric person; **2.** the female pubic hair; **3.** a female *Underwood*.

squirrelly a. (US campus use) eccentric, odd *Underwood*.

squirrel-shooter n. (derog.) a farmer, a rustic. [fr. SE].

squirt n. a small, insignificant person, often of a child *Runyon*.

squirt game n. drinking the cheapest forms of alcohol for intoxication's sake alone; fr. squirt: very cheap beer *Norman:2*.

squizz n. a glance, a brief look; fr. quiz, quizzical, etc. *Humphries:2*.

SRO (acro.) *S*tanding *R*oom *O*nly; orig. entertainment use, by extn. anything that sells out, a full house *Green:2*.

SS n. (acro.) *S*uspended *S*entence *Higgins:3*.

S/S abbr. (contact ads use) safe sex; either condoms used or the sex is *non-penetrative SMD*.

stab n. a try, an attempt; thus *make a stab at*: to try; fr. a lunge with a knife.

stable n. (Black pimp use) those women currently working for a given pimp *Milner*.

stache n. (US campus use) (abbrev.) moustache *Underwood*.

stack up v. to emerge, to develop; to maintain (or fall beneath: 'don't stack up') a given standard *Thompson: J*.

stacked a. well-built, of a woman *Algren*.

stag n., a. an unaccompanied man at a dance or similar gathering *Price:1*.

stag film n. a pornographic film; enjoyed by stags (qv) *Bruce:1*.

stag party n. the traditional eve-of-wedding all-male party given for a bridegroom and featuring an excess of drink, probably a stripper and possibly a prostitute.

stage fright n. (rhyming sl.) light = light ale *Powis*.

stage-door johnny n. a man, poss. rich, who hangs around theatre stage doors hoping to meet his female idols *NYRB 29/9/83*.

stains n. a nerd (qv); the stains are of semen, produced not by intercourse but masturbation.

staked long and deep (US Black use) the investment of large sums of cash *Klein*.

stake-out n. the surveillance of a suspect by police stationed in clandestine hiding places *Fiction Illus. 3*.

stalk n. 1. cheek (cf: neck) 2. the (erect) penis *Powis*.

stalking n. (taxi-driver use) London cabbies' illegal practice whereby one keeps the meter on 'hired', although one has no actual fare, while cruising the streets looking for what may be a very lucrative fare, for whom one *will* stop *Powis*.

stall n. (US cant) a pickpocket's assistant who blocks the passage of the intended victim *Neaman & Silver*.

stall v. to play for time, to make excuses, to delay *Hotten*.

stallion n. 1. (US Black use) a tall, good looking woman, poss. highly sexed *Milner*; 2. a man with greater than average sexual powers (cf: steed, stud).

stammer and stutter n. (rhyming sl.) butter *Jones: J*.

stamping ground n. one's home territory, one's area of operations (cf: manor; turf).

stand n. an erection.

stand at ease n. (rhyming sl.) cheese *Jones: J*.

stand on me! (excl.) believe me! *Performance*.

stand over v. (Aus. use) to demand (money) with menaces; thus *stand over man*: a thug, a heavy (qv); fr. menacing position the demander adopts *Wilkes*.

stand pat v. to stay as one is; fr. poker use: a player who does not wish to change his hand.

stand point v. (Can. prison use) to be on the alert; fr. milit. point: the lead man of a patrol *Caron*.

stand still for v. tolerate, permit, accept *Stone*.

stand to n. (rhyming sl.) stand to attention = pension *Powis*.

stand up v.t. to fail to arrive for a scheduled meeting, to break a date *Junker*.

stand up v. 1. to confess (cf: put one's hand up); 2. to withstand pressure, esp. police questioning *Higgins:1*.

stand up guy n. an honest, dependable person, one who 'stands up to be counted' *Higgins:1*.

standing on the top step (UK criminal use) of a man on trial who is facing the likely prospect of a maximum sentence *LL*.

stank n. 1. (US Black use) the anus; fr. possible malodorousness *Klein*; 2. (US Black use) the vagina (cf: stank = anus) *Folb*.

star n. 1. (UK prison use) a first offender; abbrev. star prisoner *Cole*;

2. (US Black use) a man's favourite woman; a very attractive woman; fr. show business use *Folb*.

star fucker n. see: celebrity fucker D. McLintick, 'Indecent Exposure', 1983.

star of the line n. (US Black use) a pimp's favourite whore within a stable (qv) (cf: star) *Klein*.

stark, staring bonkers a. absolutely crazy *Denis Healey, 1983 election campaign*.

starkers a. nude; fr. stark naked *Humphries*.

stars for studs (US campus use) course in basic astronomy *Birnbach*.

starters n. initial actions, plans, etc. *Powis*.

starve the lizards! (Aus. use) see stiffen the lizards *Wilkes*.

stash v. to hide. fr. 18th C. cant *stash*: put a stop to, or fr. Fr. *cacher*: to hide *Higgins:1*.

stash n. **1.** a hiding place, usu. for drugs *Goldman*; **2.** (US campus use) any drug, esp. cannabis; fr. stash: hiding place for that drug *Underwood*.

stat (medical use) immediately, emergency; used to summon medical staff over the public address system fr. Lat *statim Breslin*.

state raised a. of one who has been brought up in institutions.

static n. difficulties, aggravation; fr. radio use *Higgins:1*.

stay loose the equivalent of 'goodbye' in communities influenced by California's post-hippie era 'new therapies' (cf: hang loose) *Mcfadden*.

stay on one's case v. to attack, to harass continually and consistently *Folb*.

steady n. a regular girl/boy-friend *Howard*.

steady the Buffs! (cp) keep calm, don't lose control, etc.; poss. milit. origin fr. Buffs: the East Kent regiment.

steam n. (drug use) PCP (phencyclidine); (cf: angel dust, hog) *Sanders*.

steam v. to be annoyed, to talk aggressively *Heller*.

steam in v. to commit oneself completely, esp. in a fight (cr: wade in).

steamboats a. drunk *Welsh:1*.

steamed up a. **1.** tense, annoyed; **2.** fighting drunk *Wilkinson*.

steamer n. (rhyming sl.) steam tug = mug = fool, sucker (qv) *Powis*.

steaming a. intensifier, euphemistic overtones, since usu. in negative use, ie *steaming great prawn*: absolute, utter fool *Capital Radio 1983*.

steaming n. the act of mugging, especially when performed *en masse* against a 'captive audience' by a gang on a bus or, more likely, underground train.

steed n. sexual expert although he does the 'riding' (cf: stallion, stud).

steel pot n. (US milit. use) a GI helmet *Del Vecchio*.

steerer n. (gambling use) one who tempts players into a poker game or similar opportunity for them to lose their money *Algren*.

stem-wheeler n. (derog.) a homosexual male.

stench trench the vagina *Cole*.

stencil n. (drug use) a long, thin marijuana cigarette *Folb*.

step v. (US Black use) to work as a prostitute; poss. fr. *stepney*: a white-slaver's temporary best girl (?) or more simply fr. her 'street-walking' *Folb*.

step fast v. (US Black use) do whatever is necessary to survive in a harsh world *Folb*.

step off (on) v. (US Black use) (of a husband) to leave, to desert one's family.

step off the curb v. to die, to fail.

step on v. to adulterate narcotics for more profitable sales *Goldman*.

step on one's dick v. see: step on one's prick *Bruce:2*.

step on one's prick v. to make a fool of oneself *Thompson*.

step out on the green v. (US Black use) to challenge to a fight; fr. 'going outside' to some supposed turf *Folb*

step to v. (US Black use) **1.** to challenge; **2.** to make sexual advances towards. (fr. SE step towards or step up to).

stepper n. (US Black use) a prostitute *Folb*.

steppin' n. (US Black use) the street-walking that a prostitute must carry out to meet her customers *Klein*.

stew n. (abbrev.) stewardess, air hostess *Higgins:2*.

stewed a. drunk *Runyon:1*.

stewed as a prune a. extremely drunk *Wodehouse: GB*.

stewed to the eyebrows a. very drunk (cf: stewed to the gills) *Wodehouse: MOJ*.

stewed to the gills a. extremely drunk *Algren*.

stick n. **1.** a marijuana cigarette *Selby:1*; **2.** (Black pimp use) a prostitute *Milner*; **3.** the penis (cf: creamstick) *Folb*; **4.** a reprimand, a criticism.

stick v. to stab with a knife *Sillitoe*.

stick around v. to stay close-by *White*.

stick him on! (UK police use) charge him (with a crime)! what he is 'stuck on' is the police station charge sheet *Powis*.

stick in the mud n. an old-fashioned, conservative person.

stick it! (excl.) (abbrev.) stick it up your ass; thus a derog. reply to a given question, ie 'What shall I do with this?' or in response to an opinion with which one disagrees *Uneeda Comix*.

stick it to v. **1.** to copulate; **2.** to tease, to malign, to attack *Price:3*.

stick it up v. to take advantage of, esp. financially *Humphries:2*.

stick it up your jumper! (derog. cp) (usu. children's use) rejecting the previous speaker's idea, opinion, insult, etc. *John Lennon & Paul McCartney, 'I Am The Walrus', 1967*.

stick one on v. to hit *Keyes*.

stick one's bib in v. (Aus. use) to interfere, to intrude *Wilkes*.

stick one's neck out v. exceed one's brief, to interfere in affairs in which one is not directly concerned and often, having stuck out one's neck, to figuratively have one's head cut off *Schulberg*.

stick out like a sore thumb v. to be very conspicuous or obvious.

stick up n. an armed robbery; thus *to stick up*.

stickman n. **1.** the member of a pickpocket gang who is handed the stolen goods by the actual pickpocket who does the physical stealing; the stickman must also try to hinder any attempts to capture his confederate by police or public *Powis*; **2.** a good lover, a potent, experienced male; fr. stick = penis (qv) *Price:2*.

sticks n. **1.** articles of household furniture; fr. their wooden construction *Hotten*; **2.** anywhere other than the big cities; fr. sticks = trees *Newman:2*.

sticksing (West Indian use) picking pockets *Powis*.

stick-up artist n. armed robber *Grogan*.

sticky a. (Aus. use) (abbrev.) stickybeak (qv): inquisitive, curious *Baker*.

sticky-beak n. (Aus. use) an inquisitive person; one who 'sticks their nose in' *Humphries:2*.

sticky-fingered a. habitually larcenous, one to whose fingers things are always sticking.

stiff a. **1.** very drunk; and passed out cold *Higgins:1*; **2.** depending on context, harsh ('a stiff penalty') or expensive ('a stiff fine') *Wodehouse: PG*.

stiff n. **1.** a corpse; fr. rigor mortis *Price:2*; **2.** a note; usu. between prisoners in a gaol, or passed illicitly into a gaol by a relation, etc. *Norman:3*; **3.** an average person; often with description: working stiff (qv) etc.; poss. fr. stiff = corpse, ie one so dull as to be 'half-dead' anyway; or as one who can be stiffed (qv) due to their rectitude *Higgins:3*;
4. (horseracing use) a useless, losing horse and thus an erroneous, losing wager *Bukowski:1*.

stiff v. to cheat, to rob.

stiff as a crutch (Aus. cp) completely penniless, totally broke (qv) *Baker*.

stiff 'un n. (horseracing use) a horse that appears, for whatever reason, not to have been ridden to its full competitive capacity (cf: stiff = dead).

stiffen v. to bribe, to corrupt *Runyon*.

stiffen the lizards! (Aus. use) exclamation of surprise, shock, etc. *Humphries*.

stiffie n. 1. an invitation; fr. the card on which it was printed *T 18/7/83*; 2. an erection.

stiffin' and jivin' n. (US Black use) unreal, phoney conversation (cf: stiff = cheat, jive) *Klein*.

sting n. a reasonably large sum of money – $500 average – obtained by some form of deception or hustle (qv) *Milner*.

sting v. to steal, both in fact and as merely overcharging *Goldman*.

stinger n. (US Black use) a hotplate which is run from two wires attached to a light socket *Klein*.

stink n. 1. a fuss, a furore *Farrell*; 2. (US Black use) the vagina (cf: stank) *Klein*.

stink finger manual stimulation of the female genitals *Folb*.

stinker n. 1. a promiscuous woman (cf: scrubber) *Cole*; 2. anything or person considered particularly unpleasant *Wodehouse: AAG*.

stinking a. 1. aka: *stinko*: very drunk *Junker*; 2. (abbrev.) stinking rich: very well-off.

stinko a. very drunk *Goulart*.

stinkpot n. (US Black use) the vagina (cf: fish) *Folb*.

stinky finger n. see: stink-finger *Pearce*.

stir n. prison; fr. Romany *sturiben*, to confine, or fr. stir = porridge (qv) *Cole*.

stir v. to gossip maliciously, to cause trouble deliberately by so doing.

stir bugs a. (Can prison use) insane from too long a confinement in gaol (cf: stir crazy) *Caron*.

stir crazy a. deranged from an excess of prison *Caron*.

stir the possum v. (Aus. use) to create a disturbance, to start things moving, to jolt the general apathy; fr. animal's habit of keeping quite still for long periods (cf: play possum) *Wilkes*.

stirrer n. an unpleasant, malicious gossip.

stitch n. (US preppie (qv) use) anything or anyone seen as amusing. Thus intensified as *stitch and a half* fr. physical 'stitch' that can accompany laughter *Bernbach*.

stitch up v. for the police to ensure a conviction by planting evidence, faking confessions, etc.; fr. sewing up a garment neatly and conclusively *Newman: 1*.

stockbroker Tudor n. fake Tudor architecture, with emphasis on exposed beams, to be found in the wealthy commuter villages of the Home Counties wherein live many brokers (cf: pseudie Tudie).

stogie n. 1. cigar, abbrev. Conestoga *SF Comic*; 2. (drug use) an over-sized marijuana cigarette, fr. 1 *Folb*.

stoked a. 1. drunk *Dickson*; 2. (US teen. use (esp. California) elated, delighted, very pleased, thrilled, etc. *Pond*.

stoked out a. exhausted *Wolfe: 5*.

STOL (acro.) short time of love; euphemism for a one-night (or evening) stand; possibly analogous with military acro. meaning short take-off and landing. *AS 60.1 (1985)*.

stomp n. (US Black use) a shoe; fr. its potential use *Klein*.

stomp v. to beat up *Price: 2*.

stompers n. (US campus use) boots, esp. cowboy boots *Underwood*.

stone a. absolutely, purely, completely *Price: 2*.

stone me! excl. of surprise.

stone the crows! excl. of surprise, wonder, alarm *Dennis*.

stoned a. 1. intoxicated with some form of drug *Caserta*; 2. drunk.

stoneface n. a totally unemotional person; Buster Keaton (1898–1966) the unsmiling silent era comedian was

'The Great Stone Face' *Dunne*.

stoneginger a. absolutely certain; fr. a phenomenally successful racehorse *Newman: 1*.

stones n. testicles; thus courage, bravery, etc. (cf: balls) *Price: 2*.

stones and bones (US campus use) course in prehistory *Dickson*.

stonewall v. to put up barriers; to obfuscate, to prevaricate *Price: 3*.

stonicky n. (UK criminal use) a cosh; original naval use: a rope's end, used for punishment *Powis*.

stonkered a. drunk; orig. milit. use: out of action *Humphries*.

stonking a. enormous, excellent, etc; a general term of approval highly popular among pop music DJs in the late 1980s; often as 'stonking great...'.

stony a. (abbrev.) stony broke: absolutely penniless.

stooge n. 1. (show business use) a comedian's assistant or 'straight man' who feeds lines for his jokes; 2. any underling (cf: gofer) *Higgins: 1*.

stooge v. to work for as an assistant or underling.

stool n. see stoolie *Guardian 6/6/87*.

stoolie n. (abbrev.) stool-pigeon (qv) *Vidal*.

stool-pigeon n. an informer, one who makes a confession implicating others.

stoop v. (US Black use) to indulge in sexual intercourse (cf: get down) *Klein*.

stop moing me! (US preppie (qv) use) a demand made of one prep school boy to another who he feels is pushing or jostling him unnecessarily *Bernbach*.

stop work (bingo use) 65; fr. male retirement age *Wright*.

stoppo driver n. a getaway driver. fr. *take stoppo*: to be forced to run away *G. F. Newman, 'Law & Order', BBC-2 TV 1977*.

stork v. (US campus use) to make pregnant; fr. myth of storks bringing babies *Underwood*.

stotious / stoshious a. tight-lipped, discreet.

stoush n.,v. (Aus. use) a fight; to have a fight *Lawson*.

stove lid n. (derog.) a Black person; fr. blackening of the utensil *Runyon*.

straight a. 1. (drug use) cured of one's sickness (qv) by an injection of heroin *Larner*; 2. general intensifier *Dre*.

straight n. 1. a conventional person; 2. a cigarette (cf: joint); 3. in outlaw terminology: someone one can trust, and thus, usually not at all straight 1 *Wolfe: 2*; 4. (homosexual use) a heterosexual person *Stanley*.

straight arrow n. an honest, clean-living, clean-cut, upright, if naive and unsophisticated person *Junker*.

straight goods n. the absolute truth *Wodehouse: MJ*.

straight shit 1. the truth *Higgins: 1*; 2. utter lies.

straight shooter n. an honest, dependable, trustworthy person *Vidal*.

straight shot n. (US Black use) sexual intercourse without any means of contraception (cf: bareback) *Klein*.

straight trick n. (sex industry use) a client who requires no 'extras' beyond normal intercourse.

straight up (excl.) honestly, really *Performance*.

straighten v. 1. to bribe successfully *Newman: 1*; 2. to settle an argument or a grudge by fighting *Cole*.

straightener n. a bribe *Powis*.

strain the potatoes v. aka: *strain the spuds*; to urinate *Humphries*.

strange n. an unknown girl or woman, usu. in a sexual context; thus a bit of strange, a piece of strange.

strap n. (US Black use) a gun; thus strapped: carrrying a gun.

strap v. (UK police use) to interrogate intensely but, in theory, without force *Powis*.

strap on v. 1. to have sexual intercourse; n. 2. a dildo.

strapped adv. carrying a gun *Ice T:2*.

strapped for cash a. impoverished, poor *Sanders: 2*.

straps it to his ankle description of a man with a supposedly extra-large penis; often used ironically of a sexual braggart.

Strat n. (abbrev.) Stratocaster guitar *Dury*.

streak n. (US campus use) an exciting time, esp. at a party *Underwood*.

streak v. see streaker.

streaker n. one who runs naked through a public place; the practice of 'streaking' originated on US campuses, where it amounted to the traditional mooning (qv) writ much larger; it then transferred itself into a variety of larger arenas, notably the venues of major sporting events.

streaking n. see streaker.

street n. a. the mythical world of 'real life' which exists on the streets, rather than in the protected environments of home, office, family, etc. Often used adjectivally: 'X is truly street...'.

street cred n. adj. from street credible / credibility: acceptable on a street (qv) level; used originally in the rock business and now popular in any of the industries that cater for the young consumer; based in the belief that the 'artist' must relate genuinely to the 'people', i.e. the working-class youth of the streets and housing estates.

street people n. the derelict remainder of the hippies and similar 'beautiful' people of the 1960s, now reduced to begging, living rough and often addicted to narcotics.

street smart a. able to survive in the inner city or the ghetto streets despite a lack of material, bourgeois advantages (cf: streetified) *Morgan*.

street wise a. see: street smart.

streetcleaner n. (US Black use) a promiscuous woman, a prostitute.

streetified a. (US Black use) well-versed with the ways of the urban lifestyle as seen on the inner-city streets (cf: street smart) *Klein*.

strength n. the facts, the details of a situation *Griffiths*.

stress v. to panic, to loss control.

stretch n. (UK criminal/prison use) 12 months sentence *Norman: 1*.

stretched a. very drunk *Neaman & Silver*.

strewth! (euph.) God's truth *Payne*.

strictly! (US campus use) excl. really, honestly, absolutely, etc. *Underwood*.

strictly from in the style of, derivative of, exactly like fr. beatnik/jazz use, thus *strictly from Dante Burroughs: Jr*.

stride v. (US Black use) to perform with great skill *Folb*.

strides n. (Aus. use) trousers *Humphries*.

strike a light! general excl. of surprise, shock, amazement, etc. (cf: strike me blind, strike me pink).

strike it rich v. to gain sudden wealth *Wright*.

strike me blind! general excl. of surprise, amazement; implies calling on God/the gods to make some concomitant gesture (cf: strike me pink!).

strike me pink! see: strike me blind! *Wodehouse: AAG*.

strike out v. 1. attempt to make sexual contact and fail through the other party's lack of interest; fr. baseball use *Jay & Young*; 2. to die; fr. baseball use *Neaman & Silver*.

strike paydirt v. to gain one's objective, often but not invariably financial; for a journalist, for instance, the 'dirt' could be a given revelation; fr. mining use, esp. for gold.

striker n. a match *Norman: 2*.

string n. the penis *Bukowski: 1*.

string along v. to deceive someone over a period of time; fr. the image of dragging a toy along on the end of a string *Farrell*.

string and nuggets n. the penis and testicles *Bukowski: 1*.

string bean n. 1. a skinny person; 2. (US Black use) a very thin penis *Folb*.

stringer n. (newspaper use) a local correspondent, often with his own job, who works on a regular but freelance basis for a national newspaper *Sanders: 2*.

stripe n. a scar, usu. the result of being slashed with an open razor *Norman: 2*.

stripe v. to slash with a cut-throat razor *Norman: 2*.

stripped to the buff a. naked, without

one's clothes (cf: in the buff) *Hotten*.

stroke v. (US Black use) to have sexual intercourse *Folb*.

stroke book n. pornographic book or magazine; fr. its use in masturbation *Goldman*. (cf: tit mag)

stroke one's beef v. to masturbate.

stroked out a. exhausted *Wolfe: 2*.

stroll n. (US pimp use) those streets or blocks on which prostitutes ply their trade *Shulman*.

stroll on! (excl.) 'you must be joking!' *Newman: 1*.

strong a. (euph.) pornographic; use restricted to advertisements in such magazines.

strong arm v. (criminal use) to rob someone through threats and potential, rather than actual violence.

strong arm man n. a thug, a hoodlum, a gangster (cf: standover man) *Larner*.

strong box n. (prison use) a punishment cell.

strong it v. to act in an aggressive manner (cf: come it).

stroppy a. bad-tempered, irritable; fr. obstreperous *Keyes*.

strung out a. 1. addicted to, usually, but by no means invariably to narcotics; 2. unhappy, depressed *SF Comics*.

strunz n. fr. Ital: rubbish, shit *R. Stone, 'A Flag For Sunrise', 1981*.

stub one's toe v. (euph.) to menstruate (cf: sprain one's ankle) *Rawson*.

stuck on a. 1. obsessed with, devoted to *Seale*; 2. in love with.

stuck-up a. (school use) arrogant, snobbish, reserved; from the sticking of one's nose in the air.

stud n. 1. (white use) a sexually active male *Wolfe: 5*; 2. (Black use) a sophisticated male, but no sexual connotation *Major*; 3. (sex industry use) a male prostitute catering to either sex.

stud v. to pursue sexually (cf: horse around).

stud broad n. (derog.) a masculine lesbian.

study v. (homosexual use) to appraise

a potential sexual conquest/partner *Stanley*.

stuff n. 1. (US Black use) things or activities in general, varying as to context; 2. drugs, spec. heroin *Higgins: 1*.

stuff v. 1. to defeat, to outwit *Higgins: 5* ; 2. to copulate.

stuffed a. put down, mocked, denigrated *Higgins: 5*.

stuffed shirt n. pompous, aristocratic but ineffectual person; a bore *Schulberg*.

stuffer n. a drug addict; fr. stuff (qv) *R. Stone, 'Dog Soldiers', 1975*.

stuffing (US Black use) tricking, conning a victim *Klein*.

stuffy a. 1. wealthy, rich *Powis*; 2. pompous, snobbish *Wodehouse: GB*.

stumblebum n. shambling, useless, foolish person *X*.

stumer n. a dud cheque or other fraudulent monetary draft *LL*.

stumm and crum a. extremely quiet, 'silent as the grave' (cf: shtum) *Powis*.

stump n. the penis *Klein*.

stump v. (US Black use) to rob or mug a person; fr. stomp (?) *Klein*.

stung a. (Aus. use) drunk *Humphries: 2*.

stunt v. (US pro football use) to produce particularly baffling plays *Jenkins*.

stupe n. (abbrev.) stupid; a fool, an idiot *Heller*.

style v. to show off, to strut around *Milner*.

stymied a. in difficulties; frustrated; fr. golfing use.

sub v. to give an advance on wages, a loan; fr. subsistence (money) *Payne*.

sub up v. to hand over money, whether owing or not; fr. sub (qv).

subway dealer n. (US cant) a crooked card sharp who deals from the bottom of the pack; fr. subway = underground *Neaman & Silver*.

suck n. the act of fellatio. *L Reed New York 1989*.

suck v. 1. (US campus use) cf: suck wind *Underwood*; 2. to make someone

into a victim of one's plans, tricks, etc;
(?) back formation fr. sucker (qv)
Klein; **3.** to be worthless, pointless
Higgins: 1; **4.** to perform fellatio.

**suck a hoe handle, suckle a hoe
handle** v. to work lazily.

suck ass v. to curry favour; to attempt
to win over someone *Klein*.

suck face v. (US campus use) to kiss
(cf: chew face) *Bernbach*.

suck hind tit v. to curry favour (cf:
suck ass) *Higgins: 4*.

suck it and see! (cp) aimed derisively
at someone who has asked what is
considered a stupid or impudent
question.

suck off v. to fellate *Bukowski: 7*.

suck up n. one who curries favour
with others; a creep (qv).

suck up to v. to curry favour, to be
obsequious, to grovel shamelessly in
return for favours, esteem, etc. (cf:
bootlick) *Hotten*.

suck wind v. to be on one's last legs,
to be struggling; fr. image of gasping
for breath *Price: 2*.

suck-ass a. useless, pointless,
unpleasant – all deriving from the
need to be obsequious *Price: 3*.

sucker n. **1.** (euph.) fucker; generally
derog. description *Price: 2*; **2.** the
victim of any kind of crooked plan;
the bettors at casinos
Wodehouse: PGM.

sucker-bait n. young girls hired by
casinos to appear available and thus
lure and distract gamblers *Sharpe: 1*.

sucker-punch v. **1.** to hit when the
victim is not looking or otherwise
unprepared; n. **2.** a surprise punch.

sucker-weed n. (drug use) inferior or
even bogus marijuana; for the
consumption of the gullible only *Folb*.

sucks to you! disdainful, dismissive
cp; usu. school use *Wodehouse: AAG*.

suds n. (US teen. use) beer; fr. the
product's intense soap-suds-like
fizziness and (to UK palates) taste
Underwood.

Sue City n. (US teen. use) involved in
a court case or similar legal situation
(cf: — City) *Sculatti*.

suede n. (Black use) a Black person
Milner.

suedehead n. a form of skinhead (qv)
whose hair was grown slightly longer
than the usual absolute bald look and
thus presents a slight fuzz, slightly
reminiscent of suede.

suffering cats! aka:*suffering Christ!*:
mild excl.

sugar n. **1.** money; fr. rhyming sl.
sugar and honey *Runyon*; **2.** (US
Black use) semen; thus Bessie Smith:
'Want Some Sugar in My Bowl'
Neaman & Silver; **3.** general term of
endearment, can be used of and to
either sex *L. Reed, 'Take a Walk on
the Wild Side', 1972*.

sugar! (euph.) shit! (cf: fudge!)
Rawson.

sugar daddy n. an older man who is
willing to provide the various material
wants of his younger mistress *Waits*.

sugar pimp n. a pimp who prefers
charm and persuasion to threats and
violence when dealing with his girls
(cf: sweet mack) *Milner*.

suitcase n. the anus (cf: keister).

suited down a. (US Black use) well
dress *Folb*.

sumbitch n. see: sonofabitch *Jenkins*.

summertime ho n. (pimp use)
occasional prostitute who works, not
necessarily in summer, but only when
she needs the money or the mood
takes her; often incl. high school girls
who turn to whoring in summer
holidays *OUI 1975*.

sunbeam n. (Aus. use) an item of
crockery or cutlery laid out on the
table but still unused and as such as
bright and clean as a sunbeam
Humphries: 2.

sunburned Irishman n. a black
person.

Sunday punch n. one's best effort; fr.
boxing use *P. Pringle & W. Arkin,
'SIOP', 1983*.

sunk a. hopeless, finished, no chance;
fr. nautical use *Big Ass Comics 1*.

sunny side (abbrev.) sunny side of the
street: the good, easy, materially
satisfying life.

sunshine n. **1.** a variety of LSD, fr. the orange colour of the pills containing the drug: **2.** generally affectionate term of address *Payne*.

super honkie n. (US Black use) an exceptionally authoritarian white person (cf: honkie) *Klein*.

superbad a. see superfly.

supercharge n. see: crack.

superfly a. (US Black use) excellent, first rate; of people, situations, drugs, etc. *film title 1969*.

supergrass n. (police/criminal use) an informer who betrays a large number of important fellow-criminals, thus helping with the solution of a number of hitherto unresolved crimes (cf: grass) *Mortimer*.

supermario n. a brand of LSD *Welsh:2* (fr. the Nintendo computer game character).

supernotch n. (UK Black use) style leader, charismatic male (cf: superfly) *D Robins*.

supersoul n. (US campus use (Black students)) an exceptionally sophisticated, hip (qv) Black (cf: soul) *Underwood*.

sus a. (abbrev.) suspicious; thus the 'sus laws': controversial powers that permitted the police to stop and search persons allegedly suspected of a crime and which were considered as racist by the Black and Asian communities *Norman*.

susfu (milit. use) (acro.) *s*ituation *u*nchanged, *s*till *f*ucked *u*p (cf: snafu) *Byrne*.

suss n. street smarts (qv), natural intelligence.

suss out v. to understand, to work out, to discover; fr. suspicious *Robins:1*.

sussed out a. aware, perceptive *Welsh:1*.

sussy a. (abbrev.) suspicious (cf: sus) *Newman: 1*.

Susy n. (rhyming sl.) Susy Anna = tanner (qv) = 6d. (old pence) = 2½p. *Wright*.

swab jockey n. **1.** (USN use) a sailor who mops down the ship's decks;

2. (USMC use) derog. for sailors in general *Uris*.

swack n. (US Black use) the penis *Klein*.

swacked a. drunk *Dickson*.

swaddy n. a soldier; fr. 18th C. *swad*: soldier *Hotten*.

swag n. **1.** (US Black use) liquor *Folb*; **2.** (cant.) loot; almost obs; a part of traditional villain with mask, striped jersey and bag marked 'swag'.

swag v. to take forcibly, to arrest *Norman: 2*.

swagging (US prison use) stealing, spec. stealing state-owned property *Rawson*.

swags n. (butchers' backsl.) sausages *Cole*.

swailer n. (UK criminal use) a cosh *Powis*.

SWALK (acro.) *S*ealed *W*ith *A* *L*oving *K*iss; usually found on the back of envelopes; other versions include SWAK: *s*ealed *w*ith *a* *k*iss; SWANK: *s*ealed *w*ith *a* *n*ice *k*iss, and SWALCAKWS: *s*ealed *w*ith *a* *l*ick '*c*os *a* *k*iss *w*on't *s*tick (cf: NORWICH).

swallow (it) v. to accept, esp. a lying story that one is told; fr. swallowing a bait.

swamp v. (US prison use) to arrest *Chandler: Notebk.*

swan about v. to wander blithely and carelessly without a care in the world; like a swan gliding over water.

swank v. **1.** to boast, to show off; **2.** to pretend *Powis*.

swanky a. smart, sophisticated, chic *Goulart*.

swap cans v. (US prison sl.) to take alternate active/passive roles in anal intercourse fr. can (qv) *Legman*.

swap spit v. (US campus use) to kiss, usu. a French kiss (qv) *Bernbach*.

swartzer n. fr. Yiddish *schwartz*: black, thus any Black person *Newman: 1*.

swear and curse (cuss) v. (rhyming sl.) bus *Wright*.

sweat n. a problem, a worry, a struggle, a challenge; anything that works up real or figurative sweat

Wodehouse: PF.

sweat v. 1. to worry about, to take trouble over; 2. to put someone under pressure.

sweat hog n. (US campus use) exceptionally unattractive female *Underwood.*

sweat it out v. to endure hardships and difficulties in the hope of achieving solutions/successes in the end.

sweats n. the sweating that is one of a heroin addict's withdrawal symptoms *Price: 2.*

swede n. 1. (US use) a blunderer; fr. the sterotype of Swedish immigrants as strong but stupid; 2. ignorant country person; fr. urban conception of the country's main product, foodstuff, etc; thus *Swedey*; Metropolitan Police nickname (punning on Sweeney, qv) for Operation Countryman, an investigation into alleged corruption carried out by officers of rural/provincial forces *Norman: 1.*

swedge n. (Sc. use) a fight *Welsh:1.*

Swedish n. (sexual use) the use of rubber garments in sex; refers to the sweating one experiences in a Swedish sauna bath *Maledicta.*

Swedish n. mutual masturbation.

Swedish culture n. (sex industry use) the use of rubber, PVC, etc. in sex.

Swedish headache n. intense sexual frustration (cf: blue balls).

Sweeney n. (rhyming sl.) Sweeney Todd = Flying Squad *Ian Kennedy Martin, Euston Films, TV series, 1977.*

sweep one's own doorstep v. to mind one's own business.

sweet n. (US Black use) a male homosexual *Folb.*

sweet a. excellent, perfect, simple (cf: handsome) *Linda Brown.*

sweet as a nut (UK criminal use) easy, simple, no problems, delightful, esp. of a robbery or other 'job' *Powis.*

sweet daddy n. aka: *sweet poppa, sweet sugar*; a male lover *Folb.*

sweet FA (abbrev.) sweet Fanny Adams (qv) = (euph.) sweet fuck all

= nothing at all.

sweet Fanny Adams (euph.) sweet fuck all = nothing (cf: sweet FA).

sweet kid n. (Can. prison use) a younger prisoner who joins up with an older man (cf: punk) *Caron.*

sweet pea n. girl-friend *Runyon.*

sweet potato pie n. (US Black use) 1. an attractive girl or boy; 2. male or female genitals; example of sex = food *Folb.*

sweet talk v. 1. to persuade, to charm, to lull into (false) confidence; 2. spec. to seduce *Thompson: J.*

sweetheart contract n. a union-employer contract that favours the company over its employees *Selby: 1.*

sweetman n. (UK criminal use) a ponce who runs only one prostitute and lives off her earnings alone *Powis.*

swell a. excellent, wonderful, delightful.

swell n. an aristocrat, a sophisticated, rich person, a toff (qv) *rr.*

swellhead n. (US Black use)1. a braggart, a boaster; 2. one who has passed out through drug use *Klein.*

swift a. smart, clever, cunning; of a policeman: any illegal activities, esp. during an arrest *Underwood.*

swift 'un n. corrupt police procedure when arresting a suspect (cf: stitch up, fit up, bit swift) *Newman: 1.*

swig v. to drink, to gulp down; since 17th C.*Runyon.*

swill v. to drink heavily; in New South Wales fr. 1916–55 pubs took 'last orders' at 6 pm and the resultant rush of the all-male drinkers was termed 'the six o'clock swill'; fr. the desperate, animal-like gulpings of the drink.

swindle sheet n. 1. (boxing use) the accounts made up by a manager and shown to his fighter; bitter fighters felt that these rarely had much relevance to the actual money involved; 2. expense accounts in general *Heller.*

swing v. 1. (homosexual use) to fellate *Legman*; 2. (US teen. use) to achieve the supreme level of well-being and satisfaction *Sculatti*; 3. to arrange husband/wife swapping parties; **4.** to carry on an affair with someone; **5.** to enjoy an active and varied sex life *Bruce: 2*.

swing both ways v. to practise bisexuality.

swing daddy n. (US Black use) an attractive, well-dressed male; a male lover *Folb*.

swing either way v. see: swing both ways *McFadden*.

swing it v. to cope, to deal with a situation *Price: 2*.

swing like sixty v. (US teen. use) to perform at one's peak, to achieve ultimate success/pleasure *Sculatti*.

swing shift n. a work shift that bridges late afternoon and early evening or early morning and early afternoon *Waits*.

swing the lamp v. (UK milit. use) to tell exaggerated stories; fr. the lamp that swung inside a tent as the tales were told *Neaman & Silver*.

swing the lead v. to malinger, to avoid one's duties; orig. milit. use *Wright*.

swing with v. to ally oneself to a group; to agree with a concept *McFadden*.

swing with v. to enjoy, to appreciate *Southern*.

swinger n. **1.** one who leads an active and varied sex-life; **2.** (contact magazine use) one who participates in wife-swapping parties *Stone*.

swipe n. (US Black use) the penis; fr.

swipe = hit, or kidney-wiper (qv) (?) *Klein*.

swipe v. to steal *Wodehouse: AAG*.

swish n. a homosexual male; fr. his effeminate style *Burroughs: Jr*.

swish v. to accentuate one's homosexuality.

Swish Alps n. (US homosexual use) gay area in the Hollywood Hills (cf: Boystown, swish) *White*.

Swiss a. (US teen. use) neutral, of no specific opinion; fr. trad. role of Swiss in international relations *Sculatti*.

switched on see: turned on *Powis*.

switcheroo n. the opposite, the reverse *Stone*.

switch-hitter n. a bisexual. fr. baseball use: an ambidextrous batter *Jay & Young*.

Swone one (UK 'society' use) Battersea, London SW11 (sw-one-one) *Barr*.

swoop n. (police use) a raid; a sudden arrest *Folb*.

swordsman n. male sexual athlete *S. Alexander, 'Very Much a Lady', 1983*.

swuft a. (US campus use) pun on swift (qv) *Underwood*.

syph n. aka: *siff*: (abbrev.) syphilis *Bukowski: 2*.

sypho n. (Aus. use) syphilis.

syphon the python v. to urinate *Humphries*.

syrup n. (rhyming sl.) syrup of figs = wig (cf: rug) *Powis*.

T

T n. (drug use) PCP (cf: tac, tic).

T and A (abbrev.) *T*its and *A*ss (qv) *Bruce:1*.

tab n. abbr. tablet; spec. a pill containing an hallucinogenic drug, typically LSD or ecstasy (qv) *Kurious: A Constipated Monkey (1994)*.

tab n. **1.** the bill, account, credit

Price:1; **2.** (abbrev.) tabloid newspaper *Schulberg*.

tabbed a. (US Black use) well dressed *Folb*.

table hopper n. (necrophile use) a necrophile.

table topper n. (necrophile use) a necrophile.

tac n. (drug use) PCP (cf: T, tic).

tack n. **1.** food orig. naut use: ship's biscuit *Farren;* **2.** money *Howard;* **3.** bad taste; thus 'tack attack': a rush of bad taste.

tackle n. the genitals (cf: wedding tackle).

tacky a. unattractive, second-rate, off-putting, poor taste *Variety 19/1/83.*

tackyhead see: BB head *Folb.*

taco bender n. (derog.) Chicano; fr. popular Mexican food (cf: bagel bender) *Folb.*

taco head n. (derog.) Mexican, Chicano (cf: taco bender) *Dunne.*

Taco Town n. (US use) San Jose.

Tad n. Irish Catholic, fr. Thaddeus, popular Irish name *Higgins:5.*

tadger n. the penis.

taff a. (backsl.) fat *Cole.*

Taffy n. Welshman; fr. Dafydd, Welsh version of David *BvdB.*

tag n. the 'signature' used by a graffito artist, spraying his/her name on walls, subway trains, etc. *Indep. 24/10/91.*

Taig n. (derog.) Roman Catholic, spec. used by Protestants in N. Ireland.

tail n. **1.** young boys suitable for homosexual relation *Legman;* **2.** a woman, women; **3.** sexual intercourse *Higgins:1;* **4.** the posterior, the buttocks; **5.** the vagina; 'a piece of tail'.

tail v. to follow, to keep under police surveillance *Higgins:2.*

tailgate v. to drive a car closely (too closely) behind the one in front *Higgins:2.*

tailormade n. (UK prison use) a factory-produced cigarette (cf: roll-up) *Cole.*

take n. **1.** bribery, thus *on the take:* receiving regular bribes *Bruce:2;* **2.** (Aus. use) a thief, a villain *Ready.*

take v. **1.** to accept bribery *Higgins:2;* **2.** to arrest; abbrev. thief-take *Higgins:2;* **3.** to break in.

take a back seat v. to accept a secondary role voluntarily (cf: play second fiddle) *Neaman & Silver.*

take a bath v. to lose badly, in

business, sport, gambling *Higgins:3.*

take a Brody v. to commit suicide by leaping from a bridge; in fact the original Stephen Brody only promised, amid much publicity to leap from the Brooklyn Bridge in New York; his eventual reneging on this promise led to the theatrical use of the phrase to denote a (much touted) flop *Pynchon.*

take a dive v. (boxing use) for a fighter deliberately to lose a fight (cf: go in the tank, etc.) *Bukowski:6.*

take a dump v. to excrete, usu. in sense of incontinence *Price:2.*

take a fall v. to be arrested; to be imprisoned (cf: fall money) *Higgins:2.*

take a flying fuck! derisory, dismissive exclamation *Dunne.*

take a gander v. to look at, to glance at; fr. the bird's long neck *Chandler:LG.*

take a hike v. to leave; esp. as a command to someone the speaker wishes to go away *'Hill Street Blues', Thames TV, 1983.*

take a hinge at v. to look at; fr. the turning of one's head *Schulberg.*

take a leak v. urinate *Waits.*

take a nose-dive v. to collapse, to fail utterly; fr. flying use *Gruber.*

take a pop (at) v. **1.** to make an attempt; **2.** to hit someone.

take a powder v. to escape, to run away; the 'powder' is supposedly a laxative *Himes:1.*

take a rain check v. to defer until a later, and unspecified, time; fr. sporting use: a check (ticket) issued for future use if a baseball game was cancelled due to rain *Uris.*

take a running-jump! excl. of dismissal or dislike.

take a run-out powder v. see: take a powder *Runyon.*

take a screw at v. to stare at in aggressive manner; thus 'who you screwin'?' as ritual challenge to a fight (cf: screw) *Robins:1.*

take a shine to v. to find attractive, appealing, of an object or more likely, a person; fr. shiner: sweetheart.

take a shot v. to try, to make an attempt *Higgins:4*.

take a squat v. to defecate.

take a turn on shooter's hill (US Black use) to have sexual intercourse *Klein*.

take an application v. (Black pimp use) to interview a woman as a prospective prostitute *Milner*.

take away n. a cafe or restaurant that supplies food that can be taken out and eaten elsewhere (cf: take-out).

take care of v. 1. to kill; 2. to bribe *Runyon*.

take care of business v. (Black use (though increasingly widespread)) to deal efficiently with matters in hand *Milner*.

take care of number one v. aka: *look after number one*: to put oneself first, no matter what the situation.

take down v. to challenge, to overcome; fr. 'take down a peg (or two)' *Morgan*.

take for a ride v. 1. (criminal use) to assassinate, usu. by taking the victim out in a car and killing him/her at some stage, then dumping the body far from one's base; 2. to deceive, to fool, to trick (usu. for financial gain) *Runyon*.

take for an airing v. see: take for a ride *Runyon*.

take in v. to arrest.

take it! (homosexual use) excl. demanding fellatio *Legman*.

take it any way v. (homosexual use) to enjoy pedication or fellatio *Legman*.

take it on the chin v. to suffer hardship and adversity without complaint; fr. boxing use.

take it on the lam v. to run away, to escape (cf: lam) *Runyon*.

take it up the ass v. to submit to anal intercourse *Legman*.

take no shit v. brook no arguments, accept no diversions, irritations *Higgins:1*.

take off v. 1. to leave; also an excl. go away!; 2. to use heroin; fr. getting high (qv) *Larner*.

take on some backs v. (US Black use) to have anal intercourse *Folb*.

take one down a peg v. to reduce a person, usu. in their own excessive esteem *Hotten*.

take one to the cleaners v. to remove all of a victim's assets, either in a wager or by extortion or similar legal or illegal means *Vidal*.

take one's best hold v. to prepare oneself emotionally for dealing with a problem *Klein*.

take one's best shot v. do the best one can; try one's hardest.

take one's lumps v. to accept and deal with one's problems and setbacks *Schulberg*.

take one's meat out of the basket v. (homosexual use) to reveal one's genitals to another man *Legman*.

take out v. to kill, to destroy a specific target; fr. its complete removal *Higgins:1*.

take tea with v. (UK criminal use) to outsmart a clever person or to defeat someone in authority *Powis*.

take the air v. to leave, to escape *Runyon*.

take the big jump v. (US western use) to die *Adams*.

take the biscuit v. to beat all rivals, esp. with implication that the person, announcement, even, etc. is even more startling, appalling than might have been expected.

take the bus v. (US teen. use) to go on the cheap, to bargain-hunt; fr. bus, as opposed to airfares *Sculatti*.

take the cake v. to be the best, to carry off a prize; fr. the awarding of a cake as prize, but not always congratulatory.

take the dairy off v. to divert suspicion *Norman:2*.

take the easy way out v. to commit suicide *Neaman & Silver*.

take the fall v. to volunteer oneself as a victim, usu. as the alleged perpetrator of a crime, in the place of the real villain *Dunne*.

take the fatal step v. to get married; thus also take the leap, take the plunge.

take the gas v. to endure punishment, esp. in a boxing ring *Heller*.

take the knock v. **1.** to accept the blame (cf: take the fall); **2.** to suffer an unpleasant surprise *Wodehouse:AAG*.

take the mickey v. to tease *T 12/9/83*.

take the piss v. to tease.

take the rap v. **1.** (criminal use) to take a punishment, often a prison sentence, that is actually due to someone else (cf: take the fall), thus; **2.** to take the blame when one is not the guilty party *Wodehouse:AAG*.

take the scenic route v. (US teen. use) to concentrate on pleasure at the expense of efficiency or speed; fr. touring in car or train *Sculatti*.

take the wind v. to leave *Runyon*.

take to v. (Aus./NZ) to attack, usu. with the fists.

taken short forced to make an emergency visit to the lavatory *Newman:3*.

take-off artist n. (US criminal use) a successful robber, rapist or killer; anyone who does the job then 'takes off' *Stone*.

take-out n. **1.** food that can be consumed off the premises where it is purchased (cf: take away); **2.** (US conman use) a convenient 'phone message' that arrives for the conman when it appears that his marks (qv) are becoming suspicious and permits him to vanish before problems start cropping up; usu. arranged, for a price, with a friendly barman or similar *Thompson:J*.

take-out guy n. the man in a crooked card game who always wins and as such attracts attention away from the real cheat who is manipulating all winning and losing cards (cf: mechanic) *Breslin*.

talent n. attractive young women, esp. those standing around at a party, in a club or dancehall, etc. *Powis*.

talk a blue streak v. to talk both fast and at great length *Runyon*.

talk business v. (US Black use) to seduce; to shoot a line (qv) *Folb*.

talk fuck v. to murmur or shout obscenities during sexual intercourse for the gratification of one or both partners *Klein*.

talk game v. (Black pimp use) to chatter about pimping, whoring and those involved, thus talk a good game: to be persuasive *Shulman*.

talk like a book v. to appear well-educated and literate.

talk out of school v. to tell tales, to talk unguardedly.

talk talk and walk walk v. (US Black use) to do whatever is natural and comfortable *Folb*.

talk that talk v. (US Black use) to chatter inconsequentially *Klein*.

talk the hind leg off a donkey v. to talk continually and obsessively, seemingly with no sign of ever stopping.

talk through one's ass v. to talk nonsense; thus coarse cp: be quiet/ shut your mouth and give your ass a rest *Bleasdale*.

talk through one's hat v. to talk nonsense, talk rubbish *Heller*.

talk through the back of one's neck v. to talk nonsense, rubbish.

talk to one's plate v. to say grace before a meal (cf: brag the potatoes).

talk to the engineer, not the oily rag (cp) deal with the boss, not an assistant *ad for Olympus cameras, 1982*.

talk turkey v. to talk honestly, about the facts; to talk business fr. the bird's central role in traditional Christmas dinner (cf: get down to brass tacks) *PT*.

talker n. (pimp use) a client who wishes only to talk, either of sex or merely of his (wretched) life *OUI 8/75*.

talking n. (lesbian use) having a relationship with another woman while in prison *Maledicta*.

talking out of the side of one's neck (US Black use) talking surreptitiously to ensure that one's conversation remains unheard by eavesdroppers *Klein*.

talking shit 1. talking nonsense; **2.**

(Black use) any verbal byplay, banter between men, flirtation between man and woman, etc. *Milner*.

talking trash (euph.) talking shit (qv) *Milner*.

tall a. (US Black use) a large quantity, esp. of money *Klein*.

tall poppies n. (Aus. use) conspicuously high earners or other VIPs *Wilkes*.

tallawah a. (West Indian use) honest, honourable, decent *Powis*.

tamale n. (gay use) see: Mexican nightmare.

tan v. to attack, to hit; also used fig. 'tan the bevvy': drinking heavily *Welsh:1*.

tan one's hide v. aka: *tan one's arse*: to beat severely; of a child, to spank severely; fr. tannery (leather-making) use.

tan track n. the anus (cf: dirt road, hershey highway).

tangle assholes v. see: lock assholes *Higgins:1*.

tank n. (Can/US prison use) a holding cell *Caron*.

tank v. (US campus use) to drink heavily *Underwood*.

tank fight n. (boxing use) a contest in which one fighter has been bribed to lose; *tanking* has been extended to other sports, ie tennis, as cited in *Obs*. 26/6/83 'the deliberate throwing of a match'.

tank town n. a small, insignificant town; fr. the positioning of water tanks at such railway stops, thus providing the only reason why a train might need to stop there (cf: jerkwater town) *Price:3*.

tanked (up) a. drunk *Wodehouse passim*.

tanker n. a prizefighter who has agreed to accept cash in return for losing a given fight; ie to 'take a dive' into the tank (swimming pool) *'On The Waterfront', directed E. Kazan, 1954*.

tanner n. sixpence, thus post-metrication, 2½ pence.

tan-tracker n. (Aus. use) homosexual

male (cf: brown, Brown Family, etc.).

tap v. to borrow, or attempt to borrow money; fr. tapping their arm to attract attention (cf: put the arm, bite on).

tap a keg v. (US use) to urinate; fr. brewery use *Neaman & Silver*.

tap city n. the state of being unable to raise a stake for further betting (cf: tap) *Higgins:4*.

tap dance v. to wriggle out of trouble, to evade cleverly.

taped up a. (US Black use) a girl already with a boy-friend; thus secured from other admirers *Klein*.

tapioca a. (US campus use) absolutely broke (cf: tap city, tapped out) *Bernbach*.

tapped out a. out of money, nothing to use for further betting.

tar n.(drug use) heroin (fr. the colour and consistency of Mexican heroin).

tard a fool; abbr. of retard.

tarfu (milit. use) (acro.) *t*hings *a*re *r*eally *f*ucked-*u*p *Rawson*.

tarnation! euph. excl. that substitutes for damnation! *Rawson*.

tarp n. (abbrev.) tarpaulin *rr*.

tart n. **1.** spec. promiscuous woman, prostitute; **2.** any girl, not esp. derog; girl-friend *Humphries*.

tart about v. for a girl or woman to act like a tart 1 (qv).

tart up v. to decorate, to ornament *Austin*.

tash n. (abbrev.) moustache *Sillitoe*.

taste n. **1.** (criminal use) a share, of a bribe, of the proceeds of a robbery, etc. *Newman:1*; **2.** a sample of drugs *Grogan*.

taste bud n. the clitoris *Klein*.

tasty a. **1.** of a person: smart, sharp, prob. criminal; **2.** of a thing; valuable, worthwhile, usu. some form of criminal plan *Newman:1*.

tat n. (US conman use) **1.** con tricks performed with dice; fr. tatts (qv) *Thompson:J*; **2.** (US prison use) abbrev. of tattoo.

ta-ta goodbye! *Performance*.

taters aka: *taties*: fr. rhyming sl. taters in the mould = cold *Norman:2*.

tatts n. dice; orig. *tats*: crooked dice,

fr. 16th C. *Powis*.

taxi-cabs n. (rhyming sl.) crabs = body lice *Norman:2*.

TB (UK teen 'society' use) *Très B*rill.: absolutely wonderful (cf: brill) *P. Wickham*.

TBA abbr. (US use) a young man who is '*to be a*voided' (cf: NSIT).

T-bird n. **1.** Ford Thunderbird; **2.** Thunderbird wine, a cheap wine drunk primarily by alcoholics.

T-bone (US Black use) common Black nickname *Klein*.

TCB see: take care of business.

tea n. **1.** alcohol *Higgins:3;* **2.** marijuana *Goldman*.

teahouse n. a house or apartment where people gather specifically to buy and enjoy marijuana (cf: tea 2) *Klein*.

tealeaf n. (rhyming sl.) thief *Norman:1*.

team n. **1.** a posse of police; **2.** a gang of criminals.

team cream n. (homosexual use) an orgy *Stanley*.

team-handed working in a group; thus spec. two-handed, five-handed, etc. *Farren*.

tear ass v. to move extremely quickly, to drive very fast *Price:2*.

tear into v. see: rip into.

tear loose v. (US Black use) to escape, fr. person or situation *Klein*.

tear off v. to rush away, to leave at speed *Barr*.

tear off a piece v. (orig. Aus.) (usu. fr. male point of view) to have sexual intercourse.

tear off a strip v. to criticise severely, to reprimand; orig. milit. use.

tear one a new asshole v. to attack savagely, either physically or verbally.

tear one's ass v. to criticise severely *Himes:1*.

tear up v. (US Black use) to enjoy oneself; to do something with relish *Folb*.

tearaway n. a minor gangster, a small-time villain *Norman:2*.

tear-jerker n. (film use) a heavily romantic film, with either a sad or happy conclusion, either of which should guarantee a weeping audience; similarly used to describe mawkish ballads/love-songs *Whitcomb*.

tearoom n. (US homosexual use) a public toilet popular for casual sex and assignations (cf: cottage) *Jay & Young*.

tearoom queen n. a homosexual who hangs around public lavatories for sex *Stanley*.

teaspoon n. (drug use) half a spoon (qv) of narcotic drugs *Klein*.

technicolour yawn n. (orig; Aus. use; now general) the act of vomiting; fr. the multicoloured effluvia so produced *Humphries*.

Ted Frazer n. (rhyming sl.) razor, always a cut-throat open model *Powis*.

Teddy Bear n. (Aus. use) a show-off, esp. a cricketer who jokes around on the field and plays to the crowd; fr. rhyming sl. lair (qv) *Wilkes*.

teddybear n. (US Black use) a plump but none the less sexy woman *Klein*.

tee kay n. (butchers' use) (abbrev.) town killed, ie English meat (cf: cold) *Cole*.

teed off a. annoyed, irritated, upset *Seale*.

teed up a. drunk *Dickson*.

teensie-weensie a. (juv. use) very small, minuscule *Thompson:J*.

teenybopper n. young girl, usu. in early teens, with a predeliction for rock music and the boys who play it.

tee-tee a. (US milit. use) in Vietnam, very small *Del Vecchio*.

tekram n. (backsl.) market, spec. Covent Garden *Powis*.

Tel almost invariable nickname for Londoners called Terry '*Minder*', *Thames TV, passim*.

telephone J/O (homosexual use) telephone jerk off; masturbation while using the telephone, not necessarily while exchanging a specifically erotic conversation *Jay & Young*.

telephone numbers extremely large sums of money; fr. the digits used in big city exchanges.

tell it like it is v. (Black, hippie, now general use) to be absolutely honest;

to reject dissembling.

tell it to the marines! (excl.) dismissive statement of disbelief in a previous, far-fetched statement; fr. naut. use: sailors had a low opinion of Marine intelligence *Price:1*.

tell me another! (cp) indicating disbelief and implying that the previous speaker is telling not facts but a string of jokes.

tells n. (poker use) nervous tics, mannerisms, idiosyncrasies – all of which help to inform rival players of a players state of mind and of cards *Alvarez*.

Ten n. (US criminal use) (abbrev.) the Ten Most Wanted Criminals List, est. 1930s by J. Edgar Hoover, head of the FBI *Dunne*.

ten n. the ideal woman or man; fr. the film *10* directed by Blake Edwards (1979); ten is also used for sexual intercourse in schoolboys/girls petting scale of 1 to 10 *White*.

ten cent bag n. (drug use) $10 bag of marijuana (cf: dime bag) *Folb*.

ten miles of bad road n. (US Black) bad luck, esp. if it persists.

ten pounds of shit in a five pound bag phr. anything considered ugly, esp. obese, over-weight.

tender box n. (homosexual use) a young boy with alluring buttocks *Klein*.

ten-four message received and understood; fr. the US police 'ten codes', 10:4, thus *10:15* civil disturbance, *10:31* crime in progress, etc. *Jenkins*.

tenspot n. a $10 bill; similarly 'fivespot' *Morgan*.

ten-two traditional payment for sex in US: $10 for the girl, $2 for the room.

texan rude (backsl.) next door *Cole*.

texan rude nam n. (backsl.) lit. next door man, thus neighbour *Cole*.

Texas steel n. (US prison use) a prison *Klein*.

TGIF (acro.) *T*hank *G*od *I*t's *F*riday (cf: poet's day).

TH (backsl.) eight *Cole*.

thanks a bunch thank you very much,

poss. ironic use; bunch synonymous with many, thus 'many thanks' *Griffith*.

thanks for nothing (cp) exclamation of annoyance and contempt.

that way a. **1.** homosexual (cf: so) *Jay & Young*; **2.** in love.

that'll pin your ears back (cp) that will surprise you (and poss. cause you trouble).

that's news to acknowledge one's interest in whatever one has just been told *Klein*.

that's so ill! (Valley Girls (qv) use) all-purpose denunciation of an object or activity; ie I want to be sick! *Pond*.

that's the ball game (cp) that's it; no arguments accepted; forget it; fr. sporting use *'T.J. Hooker'*, *Thames TV, 1983*.

that's the shot! (Aus. use) excl. of general approval *Wilkes*.

that's the ticket just what is wanted, the ideal thing *Hotten*.

that's the way the cookie crumbles one must accept the facts, like it or not *Junker*.

that's torn it that has ruined it, spoiled it *Wodehouse:MOJ*.

THC (abbrev.) *t*etra*h*ydro*c*annabinnol, the active chemical substance in cannabis, which gets users 'high' (cf: tincture).

the gun n. (US milit. use) an M-60 light machine-gun, thus termed by troops in Vietnam *Del Vecchio*.

the rabbit died (cp) I am pregnant; fr. the test used to determine pregnancy *Dunne*.

the works n. (sex industry use) a complete range of sexual services, perhaps including around the world (qv) and anilingus.

there'll be blue murder if. . . (cp) warning against performing any action with inevitably disastrous consequences.

there'll be hell to pay see: there'll be blue murder.

there's one born every minute (cp) refers to an event or a person that has exhibited great foolishness; fr. a dictum of master-showman P.T. Barnum (1810–91) to whom 'one' was a sucker (qv).

thespian n. a lesbian, pun on that word, plus alleged prevalence of *male* homosexuals in theatre (?) *Maledicta*.

thick a. 1. (US campus use) emotionally involved, romantically attached; abbrev. thick with *Underwood*; 2. (US Black use) something intellectually demanding, a deep topic *Klein*; 3. stupid, dull, foolish *Barr*.

thick as fiddlers in hell phr. very plentiful.

thickie n. a fool; fr. thick (qv) *Dury*.

thigh opener n. see: leg opener.

thin on the ground sparse, well spread-out.

thing n. 1. use. as *one's own thing*: one's lifestyle, one's opinion etc.; 2. (euph) the penis *Dunne*.

thingmummijig n. see: thingummibob (cf: whatchamacallit).

thingummibob n. anything, often small, to which one cannot put a name.

thingummy n. indefinite noun for any nameless object *Wodehouse:PGM*.

think-box, think-thank n. the brain.

thinker n. the mind *R. Chandler, 'The Little Sister', 1949*.

thinks it's just to pee through (cp) denigrating an unsophisticated, inexperienced youth who supposedly has yet to appreciate the alternative function of his penis.

third degree n. (police/criminal use) the beating up and similar physical abusing of suspects by policemen in order to extract confessions; allegedly outlawed in last couple of decades, but reality proves otherwise.

third eye n. the anus (cf: round eye).

third leg n. the penis (cf: short arm) *Neaman & Silver*.

Third World briefcase n. a large, portable stereophonic tape-deck/ radio, particularly popular among Black youths in US and UK (cf: ghettoblaster, boofer-box, etc.) *Green:2*.

thirty-eight n. .38 pistol *Higgins:1*.

this is where we came in (cp) we've come full circle, we're back where we started; refers to conversation or discussion rather than physical movement; fr. the cinema's non-stop 'continuous performances'.

thoroughbred n. (pimp use) a prostitute with style, sophistication, knowledge; younger than an old-timer (qv) and generally considered among the elite of her profession; fr. horseracing use *OUI 8/75*.

thoroughbred black(US Black use) the ideal black girl *Klein*.

thousand eyes n. (US Black use) a particular style of man's shoe with many perforations in the leather *Folb*.

thousand yard stare n. (milit. use) the look in the eyes of a soldier who has been shattered by his experience of combat but who must continue fighting; orig. during the Vietnam War; looking into the middle distance.

thrash v. (Aus. use) to drive at great speeds (usu. teen. use) *Ready*.

thrasher n. a show-off; from surfing jargon.

threads n. clothes; fr. jazz/beatnik use, 1950s *Price:2*.

three balls n. (US Black use) a Jew; fr. traditional three brass balls that hang outside a pawnshop *Folb*.

three sheets to the wind drunk; also: six sheets, four sheets, etc.

three squares n. (abbrev.) three square meals; regular eating *SF Comic*.

three tears and a bucket (US Black use) cp. meaning 'I should care less' (qv) *Klein*.

three-bullet Joey (US Black use) the police *Folb*.

three-card monte n. the three-card trick (cf: find the lady) *Powis*.

three-dollar bill n. eccentric, odd; no such currency exists (cf: nine-bob note).

three-hour tour n. (US teen. use) anything too tedious to be tolerated *Sculatti*.

three-letter man n. (euph.)

homosexual; orig. the letters were
f-a-g, now g-a-y *Rawson*.

three-piece set n. aka: *three-piece suite*
the male genitals *Neaman & Silver*.

three-sheet v. to advertise, thus to
boast, to brag. fr. carnival/theatre use:
a three-sheet poster is larger than
usual *Green:2*.

threesome n. group sex involving
three people of same or mixed sexes
Jay & Young.

three-time loser (US cant) n. a
prisoner who has been convicted of
two crimes worthy of prison sentence
and faces life sentence or execution if
convicted a third time *Fiction Illus.3*.

three-way deal n. sex involving three
partners at once; thus *four-way deal*,
etc. (cf: threesome) *Price:2*.

three-way girl n. a prostitute who will
offer any orifice in her body to clients.

thrill and chill n. (US Black use) a
sexual experience so wonderful it
sends chills up one's spine *Klein*.

throat n. (US campus use) anyone
who works harder than the average –
and enjoys it *Bernbach*.

throne n. the lavatory.

through and through n. (US Black
use) a wholly admirable (Black)
person *Klein*.

through the gate (cricket use) for a
batsman to be bowled by a ball that
slips through the space between his bat
and his pads *BBC Radio, 1983*.

through the nose a. very expensive
Sharpe:1.

throw v. to have sexual intercourse
Folb.

throw a buttonhole on v. (US Black
use) to have anal intercourse *Folb*.

throw a moody v. to become sulky,
truculent, ill-tempered *Bleasdale*.

throw a punch v. to defend oneself,
verbally as well as physically; fr.
boxing use *Klein*.

throw a seven v. (Aus. use) to faint,
to collapse; fr. seven as the losing
throw in a game of craps dice *Wilkes*.

throw a wobbly v. to exhibit signs of
mental stress, to have a (minor)
breakdown *Blacker*.

throw down on v. to blame someone;
fr. cant use: hold a gun on
Burroughs:Jr.

throw hands v. (US Black use) to
punch, to hit *Seale*.

throw in v. to add, to include
Capital Radio 1983.

throw in one's hand v. to give in, to
surrender; fr. card use.

throw in the sponge v. 1. see throw
in the towel; 2. to die; fr. boxing use
Rawson.

throw in the towel v. to give in, to
capitulate; fr. boxing use, whereby the
seconds of a losing fighter toss his
towel into the ring to save him from
any further punishment.

throw iron v. see: pump iron *Seale*.

throw one for a loop v. to disturb; to
worry considerably, to put off one's
stride *Thompson:J*.

throw one's cookies v. to vomit
Higgins:1.

throw one's hat in the ring v. to join
a contest, to register one's candidacy
or opinion *T 16/6/83*.

throw one's voice v. (Aus. use) to
vomit (cf: yell 2) *Humphries:2*.

throw one's weight about v. to act
in an arrogant, aggressive manner
Thompson:J.

throw some dirt on v. (US Black use)
to malign, to slander *Klein*.

**throw the baby out with the
bathwater** v. to be so keen on
eliminating the large-scale errors that
one simultaneously tosses out the less
visible but highly valuable entities
hidden amongst them.

throw the book at v. to discipline
heavily, to reprimand severely; the
'book; is the 'book of rules' that one
has contravened.

throw up v. to vomit *Price:1*.

throw up one's boots v. to vomit
intensely.

throw up one's heels v. to vomit
copiously.

thrower n. (UK criminal use) in three-
card monte (qv) gangs, the member
who actually deals the three cards and
exercises the fraudulent sleight-of-

hand *Powis*.

thumb n. (US Black use) a fight *Folb*.

thumper n. (US milit use) M-79 grenade launcher *Del Vecchio*.

thunder chicken n. (US Black use) an unattractive or unpleasant female *Folb*.

thunderbags n. (Aus. use) male underwear.

thunder-box n. 1. a lavatory *Humphries*; 2. a portable commode *E. Waugh, 'Officers & Gentlemen', 1955*; 3. the buttocks.

thunderthighs n. an overweight girl.

tic n. (drug use) PCP (cf: T, tac).

tick n. 1. unpleasant, insignificant person; fr. the vermin *Wodehouse: VGJ*; (US campus use) 2. overweight person; 3. a greedy or selfish person; *Underwood*; 4. credit; fr. abbrev. ticket, since 17th C. *Hotten*.

tick one off v. (US campus use) to prompt thoughts in the hearer *Underwood*.

ticked off a. irritated, annoyed.

ticker n. 1. a watch; fr. its mechanism *Wright*; 2. the human heart; fr. the regular beat *Runyon:1*; 3. accountant; who ticks off sums of money *Payne*.

ticket n. 1. (UK police use) a warrant to search or to arrest *Powis*; 2. a person, esp. used by 'mods' of early 1960s *The Who, 'Quadrophenia', 1973*.

ticketty-boo a. fine, wonderful, all in order, etc. fr. that's the ticket (?); orig. naval use.

tickle n. 1. (UK police use) a piece of information; it 'tickles one's fancy'; 2. (UK criminal use) a successful and lucrative crime fr. tickling trout (?) *Powis*.

tickle one's pickle v. to masturbate *Maledicta*.

tickle the ivories n. to play the piano, fr. the ivory keys.

tickled a. amused, pleased; tickled pink (qv): extremely amused *Runyon:1*.

tickled pink a. extremely pleased or amused *Wodehouse:MOJ*.

tickled to death delighted, very

happy, amused *Heller*.

tickler n. a junior official or assistant who is used by his superior(s) to disseminate to still lower ranks such policies that the leaders wish adopted, without making face-to-face contact themselves *PT*.

ticky-tacky a. vulgar and banal, tasteless, unsophisticated, corny (cf: tacky) *Whitcomb*.

tiddler's bait (rhyming sl.) late *Cole*.

tiddly a. slightly drunk; fr. rhyming sl. *tiddly wink* = drink *Cole*.

tiddly wink n. (rhyming sl.) Chink = Chinese *Dury*.

tidy a. 1. competent *Welsh:1*; 2. many, several, as in 'a tidy few'; interj. 3. general statement of agreement, admiration *Welsh:1*.

tie off v. (drug use) to tie up a vein and isolate it prior to injecting narcotic drugs *Caserta*.

tie one on v. 1. (UK and US use) to be drunk *Schulberg*; 2. (Aus. use) to provoke a fight *Baker*.

tied up a. busy *Higgins:1*.

tie-up n. (drug use) the rubber tube, handkerchief, string or other object used for tying off a vein prior to injecting narcotics *Burroughs:1*.

tiger for n. (Aus. use) an enthusiast for a given task: fr. the aggression of the animal *Wilkes*.

tight a. 1. mean, avaricious, ungenerous; fr. tight-fisted and tightwad (qv) *Higgins:2*; 2. very close, friendly, intimate *Dunne*; 3. reasonably, but not excessively drunk *Bernbach*.

tight with a. very friendly with someone; fr. physical/mental intimacy.

tight-assed a. repressed, self-denying, puritan *Higgins:5*.

tightbuck n. (homosexual use) the foetal position, popular for tying up participants in sado-masochistic sex *Jay & Young*.

tighten up one's game v. (US Black use) to take control of one's life, of a given situation in which one is interested *Folb*.

tightwad n. an ungenerous, mean person *BvdB*.

tight-weak a. (poker use) a weakness in one's play that develops when a player is too frightened about losing his money *Alvarez*.

Tijuana bible small, illustrated pornographic book; named for the era when US citizens saw Tijuana, Mexico, as the Port Said of Central America (cf: eight-pager).

Tijuana racetrack n. stains on the underwear that result from an attack of diarrhoea (cf: Montezuma's revenge).

tile loose a. eccentric, foolish, 'not all there'.

till v. (US Black use) to have sexual intercourse. (cf: plow)

till hell freezes over see: till the cows come home.

till the cows come home for an indefinite time; for ever.

Tilly n. (homosexual use) the police *Stanley*.

time and a half n. payment of the basic wage plus 50% extra – for overtime or similar bonus payment; thus, *double time*: double the basic rate, *two and a half-time*, etc.

tin n. (US police use) the official police badge (cf: potsy) *Neaman & Silver*.

tin can n. (USN use) destroyer *Pynchon*.

tin flute n. (rhy.sl) suit *Welsh:1*.

tin soldier n. (prostitute use) a man who wishes no actual sex but only to act as a servant or 'slave' to the prostitute; usu. fr. middle or upper-class background *Paul Bailey, An English Madam, 1982*.

tin-arsed a. (Aus. use) thick-skinned, impervious to pain, lucky *Wilkes*.

tincture n. (drug use) tincture of cannabis (cf: THC) *Green:1*.

tincture n. a drink; fr. 'Dear Bill' column, lampooning Denis Thatcher, husband of Prime Minister Margaret, in *Private Eye* passim.

tinhorn a. second rate, inferior, superficially flashy *rr*.

tinkle n. a ring on the telephone; usu:

give one a tinkle *Performance*.

tinkle v. to urinate; often children's use *Vidal*.

tinnie n. (Aus. use) a can of beer; now general, orig. surfer use *Humphries: 2*.

Tinsel Town n. Hollywood, Calif. fr. its glittering, fantasy image *CB*.

tin-tack n. (rhyming sl.) the sack = dismissal from a job *Franklyn*.

Tio Taco n. a Mexican who is considered insufficiently nationalistic by his peers (cf: taco bender, taco head, taco town, uncle Tom) (fr. Mex. *tio*: uncle + *taco*: the foodstuff).

tip n. (US Black use) aspect, point of view, angle. e.g. 'on the art tip': from the artistic point of view, 'on the sales tip': from the aspect of sales.

tip n. (abbrev.) tip off, but used as any reason for an arrest, not simply information given to the police *Seale*.

tip v. (US Black use) 1. to cheat on one's lover or mate; 2. to perform an illicit act; 3. to be in a place where one should not be *Folb*; 4. (US campus use) to drink heavily; fr. tipple *Underwood*; 5. see tip off.

tip in v.t. to inform against *Higgins: 1*.

tip off v. to warn.

tip out v. (US Black use) to have sex with anyone other than one's spouse or regular lover (cf: tip, v. 1) *Major*.

tip the wink v. to warn, to signal, usu. with an actual wink, but also figuratively *Hotten*.

tippin' a. (US Black use) in full control; on top of one's game; fr. 'tip-top' *Klein*.

tipsy a. slightly drunk *Bruce: 1*.

tired a. (homosexual use) to describe an exceptionally dull and boring person *Stanley*.

tired and emotional (euph.) extremely drunk; coined in *Private Eye* fr. the popular euph. to mask the activities of the famous.

tired people n. (US Black use) weak or displeasing people *Klein*.

tired woman n. (US Black use) a female who lacks sophistication, who is not streetwise (qv) *Klein*.

tit n. 1. something extremely simple

and usu. rewarding, esp. a criminal scheme. fr. the simplicity of a child's finding its mother's breast; **2.** a breast *Price:1* thus; **3.** anything considered to resemble a breast, or, more often, the nipple; a button or small switch, etc. *Price: 1*.

tit for n. (pron. titfer) rhyming sl. tit for tat = hat *Powis*.

tit mag a magazine, à la *Playboy*, *Penthouse*, *Hustler*, etc. which features scantily clad girls, interspersed with varying amounts of prose, reviews, etc. but in effect, for all other pretensions, an aid to masturbation. (cf: stroke book)

tit man a man who finds a woman's breasts her most attractive feature (cf: ass man, leg man).

tits and ass burlesque show; cheap sex-orientated entertainment which features strippers, etc. (cf: T&A) *White*.

tits on a bull a. (cp) utterly useless; usu. 'no more use than tits on a bull'.

tits, the n. perfection, excellence, an ideal situation (cf: hind tit).

tits-up a. (Can. prison use) dead; thus laid out on one's back *Caron*.

titty n. the female breast (cf: tit); orig. the nipple, as diminutive of tit *Vidal*.

tizzy n. a panic, a 'state', of flap.

TJ (abbrev.) *Ti*juana, Mexico.

TKO v. (boxing use) (acro.) to achieve *T*echnical *K*nock-*O*ut *Higgins: 1*.

TLC (abbrev.) *T*ender *L*oving *C*are.

TNT **1.** (abbrev.) *T*wo *N*ifty *T*its: the female breasts *Rawson*; **2.** (US Black use) a popular name for dynamite, thus describing anyone or anything that is metaphorically 'dynamite', wonderful, exceptional, etc. *Klein*.

to die a. (US campus use) excellent, wonderful, perfect, ie that boy is to die pretty, etc. *Bernbach*.

to kill for a. perfect, wonderful, incomparable (cf: drop dead, to die).

to the bad in debt, 'in the red'.

to the bone phr. (US Black) to the extreme, to the ultimate extent; thus funky to the bone, laid to the bone, tabbed to the bone, etc.

to the max phr. the best, the most extreme; the term originated in the California youth cultures, but has gained wider use; thus there is a computer program 'VP To The Max'.

toad n. (derog.) a Black person.

toast n. (US criminal use) a long and epic poem, often trad. in prisons *Goldman*.

toast v. (West Indian use) for a disk jockey to perform his own lyrics to the background of a reggae song, usu. in a dub (no lyrics, only bass and rhythm lines) version.

toasted a. (drug use) very high (qv) *Folb*.

toby n. (UK police use) an area, a police division fr. 19th C. *toby*: highway, the road; thus those roads the division supervises (cf: manor) *Powis*.

toch eno! (backsl.) hot one!, ie look out, take care, etc. *Cole*.

toches n. fr. Yiddish: posterior, buttocks *Rosten*.

Tod Sloan (rhyming sl.) alone; thus on one's Tod (qv) *Cole*.

toddle off v. to leave *Wodehouse passim*.

todger n. see tadger.

to-do n. an argument, a set-to, a lively situation *Parade 7/83*.

toe popper n. (US milit. use) in Vietnam, the M-14 anti-personnel mine which maims the foot *O'Brien*.

toe queen n. foot fetishist (cf: queen) *Stanley*.

toe-rag n. orig. a tramp (from the foot-bindings they wear); currently any unappetizing (old) person; UK prison use: any highly unpopular person, young or old *Dury*.

toes lively a. very fast *Cole*.

toey a. (Aus. use) nervous, touchy *Wilkes*.

toff n. aristocrat; anyone considered either to be or to be posing as a superior person; also *you're a toff*: you're very kind/generous; thank you very much *Dury*, *'Laughter'*, *1981*.

toffee n. nonsense; flattery; fr. the 'sweetness' of its content (?) *Powis*.

toffee-nosed a. snobbish, arrogant; fr. toff (qv) *Keyes*.

together a. aware, in control, united, happy, *au fait*, sophisticated.

togged to the bricks a. (US Black use) dressed in absolute chic and style *Major*.

togs n. clothes *Vidal*.

toilet n. anywhere considered disgusting, esp. show business use for a third-rate venue *Goldman*.

toilet talk n. obscenities, coarse language *Humphries*.

toke n. (US Black campus use) a marijuana cigarette; fr. toke, v. (qv) *Folb*.

toke v. to puff on a marijuana cigarette (cf: toke, n.) *Wolfe: 2*.

Tom (abbrev.) Uncle Tom (qv) *Greenlee*.

tom n. 1. a prostitute working in Mayfair (cf: Edie) *Austin*; 2. (rhyming sl.) tomfoolery = jewellery *Norman: 2*; both meanings date prior to 1959 Street Offences Act, but with new upsurge of street prostitution during the current economic depression they may revive; 3. (abbrev.) Tommy, a British soldier *A. F. N. Clarke, 'Contact', 1983*.

tom v. for a Black person to act in an inferior and obsequious manner to whites; to act as a Black stereotype; fr. Uncle Tom (qv).

Tom and Dick v. (rhyming sl.) to be sick *Dury*.

Tom, Dick & Harry n. any men, young or old, irrespective of given names.

Tom Mix n. (rhyming sl.) fix = problem, predicament; fr. film cowboy (1880–1940) *Powis*.

tom out v. (US Black use) for one Black to inform against another; fr. Uncle Tom (qv) *Folb*.

Tom Pepper n. a liar; fr. nautical use: TP was a mythical sailor who was ejected fr. Hell for lying *Newman: 3*.

Tom Slick (US Black use) a Black police informer (cf: Uncle Tom) *Folb*.

tom thumb n. (rhyming sl.) rum *Jones: J*.

tomato n. girl, woman; fr. the luscious ripeness of the fruit *Runyon*.

tomb n. the anus.

tom-cat v. to strut around looking for sexual conquests; fr. the animal.

tomfoolery n. (rhyming sl.) jewellery *Cole*.

tommy rollocks n. (rhyming sl.) bollocks = testicles.

tommy tucker n. (rhyming sl.) supper *Jones: J*.

toms n. (Aus. use; rhyming sl.) tomtits = shits = diarrhoea, food poisoning *Humphries: 2*.

tomtit n. (rhyming sl.) shit = excretion *Powis*.

ton n. one hundred, esp. of money; orig. gambling use, but spread elsewhere, esp. to sport.

tongue v. 1. (homosexual use) to perform cunnilingus *Legman*; 2. to kiss with each partner's tongue in the other's mouth *Price: 2*.

tongue bath n. see: around the world *Legman*.

tongue job n. fellatio.

tongue lash v. to perform fellatio or anilingus *Klein*.

tongue sushi n. (US preppie (qv) use) French kissing (qv); fr. sushi: Japanese raw fish, a popular dish (cf: swap spit) *Bernbach*.

tonight's the night! (cp) underlining the speaker's expectation of something exciting/important, esp. of a possible seduction.

tonk n. (Aus. use) a male homosexual, or an effeminate, if heterosexual male *Wilkes*.

tons a. (US campus use) very, extremely, really, etc. *Underwood*.

tonsil polish n. alcohol *P J O'Rourke 'Give War a Chance' (1992)*.

Tonto n. a Native American who is considered insufficiently nationalistic and overly subservient to the white man by his peers (cf: Uncle Tomahawk) (fr. the character Tonto, the obsequious 'Red Indian' sidekick who rode with TV's Lone Ranger).

ton-up boy n. aka: *Rocker*: member of a motorcycle gang; fr. ton: 100 mph *Mandelkau*.

tony a. classy, sophisticated, chic; fr. Fr. *ton*: tone *Higgins: 3*.

too Irish stew! (rhyming sl.) too true! *Cole*.

too much! excl. of surprise, shock *Stanley*.

too right! excl. of agreement *Ready*.

too slow to catch cold, to be v. to be extremely slow.

tool n. 1. (US campus derog. use) a very hard worker *Bernbach*; 2. penis *Vidal*; 3. weapon, usu. gun or knife *Norman: 2*; 4. burglar's implement, spec. jemmy (qv) *Powis*; 5. (US campus use) a stupid, useless person *Underwood*.

tool around v. (US campus use) to drive around at random in a car *Underwood*.

tool in v. (US campus use) to arrive, usu. at speed *Underwood*.

toolbox n. the vagina; fr. tool 2 *Maledicta*.

tooled up a. carrying a weapon (cf: tool 3) *Mandelkau*.

toolhead n. (US campus use) a fool, an idiot; fr. tool = penis (cf: prick, etc.) *Underwood*.

toon n. abbr. of cartoon, thus an animated cartoon; the word was coined for the film *Who Killed Roger Rabbit?* (1987), which mixed animation and normal live action. *Green:3*.

tooshie n. buttocks, fr. Yiddish *tuchus Goldman*.

toot n. (drug use) 1. cocaine *Price: 3*; 2. a device for inhaling cocaine; 3. a measure of cocaine, usu. one line (qv).

toot v. to inhale cocaine.

toot one's horn v. to experience the immediate post-inhalation high from cocaine; the top of one's head is 'lifted' like that of a boat whistle (cf: toot) *Safire*.

toothpick n. (US Black use) 1. a thin marijuana cigarette; 2. a pocket knife *Folb*.

tooti-frooti n. (US Black use) (derog.) homosexual male.

tootle v. to ring cheerily, of a telephone or horn *Wodehouse: MOJ*.

toots n. 1. a girl; 2. general form of address, usu. to a female.

tootsie n. see: toots (1, 2) *Bruce: 2*.

tootsie roll n. (US Black use) 1. an attractive female; fr. US sweet of that name; plus ref. to jellyroll (qv) (?) *Klein*; 2. dark brown, Mexican heroin; the original Tootsie Roll was a form of chocolate cake.

top v. 1. to surpass *Higgins: 3*; 2. to kill, esp. to execute by hanging; thus *top oneself*: to commit suicide *Caron*.

top bollocks n. female breasts.

top cat n. (US Black use) the leader of a group, esp. of a clique of down-and-outs *Klein*.

top dog n. the boss, the senior member of an organization, a leader.

top drawer a. socially elite, aristocratic, upper class *Chandler: LG*.

top hole! excellent, wonderful, perfect, etc.

top man n. the dominant partner in a homosexual sado-masochist couple (cf: bottom man) *Jay & Young*.

top notch a. excellent, first class *Payne*.

top of the house (bingo use) 1. 99; 2. 100.

top out v. to reach a limit.

top sergeant n. (homosexual use) a masculine lesbian; fr. milit. use *Legman*.

top shelf a. (US Black use) excellent, first class, the best *Klein*.

top up v. to end up, to conclude *Newman*.

topkick n. (US Army) first sergeant *Grogan*.

top-off n.,v. (Aus. use) informer, to inform; to 'finish' a person off *Wilkes*.

topped up a. drunk *Powis*.

tops n. 1. (gambling use) doctored dice used for cheating purposes *Runyon*; 2. the best, the winner *Vidal*; 3. at the most, at the top estimate *Dunne*.

torch v. to commit arson; fr. tool employed *Breslin*.

torch for v. see: carry a torch.

torch song n. a love song that takes as

a theme unrequited love or a dead affair (cf: carry a torch) *Runyon*.

torn down (US Black use) most distressed, miserable; (cf: bring down) *Major*.

torpedo n. a thug, a hoodlum; the 'weapon' used by a gang boss and sent out to destroy enemies *Fiction Illus. 3*.

TOS n. (US pimp use) (acro.) *T*ricks *O*ff the *S*treet; usu. used by hotel clerks in those hotels which let out rooms to working prostitutes: men picked up in the street (cf: trick) *Shulman*.

tosh n. **1.** nonsense, rubbish *H. L. Mencken*, '*A Carnival of Buncombe*', *1947*; **2.** form of address (cf: mush, moosh); poss. fr. Scot. dial *tosh*: smart, neat, thus a smart, neat person *LL*.

tosheroon n. half a crown (obs.) *Norman: 3*.

toss n. see tosser *Welsh:2*.

toss in the bucket v. to imprison (cf: can) *Algren*.

toss off v. **1.** to masturbate; **2.** to throw away, to discard.

toss one's cookies v. (US campus use) to vomit *Bernbach*.

toss one's tacos v. (US campus use) to vomit; spec. when eating Mexican food (?) *Bernbach*.

toss the squares v. (US Black use) to pass a pack of cigarettes; fr. the packet's shape *Klein*.

toss-bags n. see tosser.

tosser n. a useless person, spec. a masturbator, fr. toss off (qv).

tosspot n. a drunkard.

total v. **1.** to crash one's car so badly as to render it beyond repair – a total disaster; **2.** to destroy or maim anything or any one.

total blowchoice (Valley Girls (qv) use) 'well, kinda cool (qv), but really, who cares?'; appealing but irrelevant *Pond*.

total wreck n. (rhyming sl.) a cheque *Wright*.

totally a. (Valley Girls (qv) use) intensifier to mean utterly, absolutely, completely, etc. *Harpers/Queen 1983*.

totty n. young girl, usu. sexually available; fr. 19th C.a high-class prostitute *Keyes*.

touch v. to borrow money from (cf: tap) *Wodehouse: GB*.

touch base v. to communicate with, to check in; fr. baseball use.

touch of the seconds second thoughts, last minute hesitation *Powis*.

touch of the tar brush n. derog. phr. implying, often erroneously, that someone has a degree of non-white blood *Sharpe*, '*Indecent Exposure*', *1973*.

touch up v. to molest sexually *Tidy*.

touch-on n. an erection *Newman: 2*.

tough a. (US campus use) admirable; on bad = good analogy *Underwood*.

tough shit! (excl.) so what! see if I care! response indicating little or no sympathy with the speaker *Jay & Young*.

tough stuff (US Black use) (on good/ bad reversal) anything appealing, pleasing in the realms of sex or drugs *Klein*.

tough titties bad luck *Price: 2*.

touristas n. any form of stomach upset contracted on a foreign holiday; fr. Sp. (cf: Montezuma's revenge, etc.) *Neaman & Silver*.

tout n. (IRA use) informer '*Harry's Game*', *LWT, 1983*.

towelhead n. (derog.) Arab native of the Middle East; the term became particularly popular during the Gulf War of 1991 (cf: hankie-head, raghead).

town bicycle n. highly promiscuous girl or woman, who is constantly 'ridden' (cf: town pump).

town pump n. highly promiscuous girl or woman (cf: town bicycle).

town punch n. see: town pump, town bicycle *Underwood*.

toy-boy n. a young attractive boy popular among older, richer women (cf: bimbo).

toys n. appliances designed to increase sexual pleasure or fantasies: dildoes, vibrators, whips, chains, etc.

Jay & Young.

Tracey n. see: Sharon.

track n. (Black use) the world of pimping, hustling, confidence tricks, etc., the Eastern cities are the *fast track*, California and the West are the *slow track*, *soft track Milner*.

track v. to maintain emotional/verbal stability, to keep on the right track *McFadden*.

tracks n.punctures and scar tissue that accumulate on the veins of a regular drug addict who injects himself with a given drug *Burroughs: 1*.

trade n. (homosexual use) a man with whom one has (commercial) sex *Jay & Young*.

train n. multiple orgasms; thus 'toot one's train': to achieve multiple orgasms.

tram line n. a scar (cf: stripe) *Norman: 1*.

tramp n. a promiscuous woman *Price: 2*.

tramps's lagging n. (UK prison use) a sentence of 90 days in jail; commonly that meted out for vagrancy *LL*.

tranks n. (abbrev.) tranquillizers: barbiturates, Librium, Valium, etc.

tranny n. transistor radio.

trap n. 1. mouth (cf: keep one's trap shut) *Higgins: 3*; 2. a place, spec. a nightclub; fr. the extortionate prices charged those lured within (?) *Runyon*; 3. (US prostitute use) the number of customers a ho (qv) is assigned as a daily tally by her pimp to reach a given financial target *Shulman*.

trapeze artist n. a woman who enjoys cunnilingus, esp. as part of sex exhibitions *Legman*.

traps n. drums *Algren*.

trash n. (abbrev.) white trash: poor (Southern US) whites *Wolfe: 2*.

trash . 1. to break windows, destroy appliances, etc. as part of a demonstration; coined by the radical Weathermen movement, c.1969. fr. trash: rubbish, garbage *White*; 2. to malign someone else (cf: rubbish, v.).

trash around v. to slum; acting poorer

than one is *White*.

trashed a. very drunk *Bernbach*.

trashmouth n. (US campus use) anyone who regularly uses profanity or obscenity *Underwood*.

treach a. (teen use) very good, excellent; from abbr. of treacherous which, like bad (qv) = good, is reversed by its young users (cf: wicked).

tremblers n. female breasts, usu. large, thus able to tremble *Whitcomb*.

triangle n. an three-way relationship: two men, one woman, or two women, one man both heterosexual and male and female homosexual *Legman*.

trick a. fancy, technologically hip; fr. SE tricky, tricksy.

trick n. 1. the client of a prostitute, whether hetero- or homosexual; the implication is of conning any such client into parting with money *Higgins: 1*; 2. (homosexual use) any casual sex partner *White*: 3. a period of work, usu. physically demanding or unpleasant; fr. nautical use *trick*: turn at the wheel *Powis*.

trick v. 1. to work as a prostitute *Dre*; 2. (homosexual use) to pick up a partner for casual, unpaid sex *Jay & Young*.

trick baby n. (US Black use) the illegitimate child born to a prostitute; given no positive evidence to the contrary, she assumed the father to have been one of the paying customers *Iceberg Slim, book title*.

trick bag n. (US Black use) an unpleasant and disadvantaged position *Klein*.

trick cyclist n. pun on psychiatrist (cf: shrink).

trick flick n. (homosexual use) a pornographic film (cf: stag film) *Stanley*.

trick suit n. (sex industry use) a dress that can be removed easily and is thus suitable for business.

trick towel n. (homosexual use) a towel for wiping oneself after intercourse *Stanley*.

Trick Willy n. (US Black use) a

gullible black man *Klein*.

trick-ass a. general derog. (cf: wack-ass) *Dre*.

triff a. (abbrev.) terrific, wonderful *Capital Radio 1984*.

trigger (man) n. a gunman working for organized crime (cf: soldier).

triflin' (US Black use) acting irresponsibly; as a parasite fr. SE trifling *Klein*.

trim n. (US Black use) the female genitalia; thus, a woman *Folb*.

trim v. to cheat.

trimmer n. (Aus. use) anything excellent, wonderful, approved of; fr. 19th C. *trimming*: excellent, first-rate, etc.

trip n. 1. spec. the experience that follows the taking of LSD; 2. any form of experience, event *Hoffman: a*.

trip v. 1. (drug use) to take an hallucinogenic drug, esp. LSD (qv); 2. (US Black use) to lose control, to go mad, to act under a misapprehension.

trip out v. to lose control, to leave normality; fr. the LSD trip (qv) *Price: 2*.

trip to the moon n. (homosexual use) anal intercourse (cf: moon) *Legman*.

triple clutcher n. (euph.) motherfucker; coined by Black truck-drivers in US Army fighting in Korean War *Rawson*.

triple hip a. (US Black use) extra-smart, very wise *Major*.

tripper n. (drug use) one who takes LSD or similar hallucinogens.

-tripping general suffix denoting a style of action or opinion: *power-tripping*: asserting oneself over others; *head-tripping*: thinking, etc. *McFadden*.

trippy a. 1. bizarre, strange, disturbing; fr. LSD trips (qv) *ES 23/9/83*; 2. (Valley Girls (qv) use) excellent, first-rate, etc. *Pond*.

trog n. general term of disdain; abbrev. of troglodyte.

Trojan horse n. (gay use) manly façade; from the Homeric myth of deception.

trolleys n. trousers; fr. Lancashire dial. meaning a woman's drawers, and prob. troll / trolly, meaning anything that drags along the ground.

trolling see: cruising; fr. SE: saunter along *Junker*.

tromp v. to tramp around *Higgins: 4*.

trophy n. (US campus (spec. U. of Arkansas) half a gallon of alcohol *Underwood*.

troppo a. (Aus. use) mad, insane, fr. effects of the tropical heat (cf:Doolally) *Humphries*.

Trot n. (abbrev.) Trotskyite; used indiscriminately for any hard-left group in the UK; thus media use of *trot-slot*: a programme that concerns itself with or apparently propagandizes for such groups.

trots n. diarrhoea (cf: runs) *Higgins: 4*.

trotter n. (UK criminal use) a deserter from the British armed forces; one who is 'on the trot', running *Powis*.

trotters n. 1. feet *Wright*; 2. racehorses.

trouble and strife n. (rhyming sl.) the wife *Cole*.

trouser v. to pocket.

trouser bandit n. male homosexual (cf: arse bandit).

trouser chuff n. a fart *Viz comic passim*.

trouser trout n. the penis.

trout n. (US Black use) 1. the vagina; 2. a female *Folb*.

truck v. to move, to travel; esp. in hippy rallying cry of 1960s: 'Keep on trucking!' *Underwood*.

truck driver n. (US Black use) an ostentatiously 'masculine' homosexual, poss. dressed in trucker, or similar macho clothes (cf: butch, rough trade) *Major*.

trucking moving, struggling along; esp. as *keep on trucking*: exhortation to continue with one's life *Trashman, Berkeley, Calif. 1969*.

trumpet n. 1. the telephone *Powis*; 2. a fart.

try it on v. to attempt to get away with anything, usu. that which one is not entitled to have.

try-on n. an attempt to try it on (qv).

ts (abbrev.) *t*ough *s*hit, often used ironically or mockingly as well as sympathetically *Uris*.

TS n. (abbrev.) *T*rans-*S*exual (cf: TV) *Maledicta*.

T/T abbr. (contact ads use) tit torture *SMD*.

TTFN (cp) (abbrev.) *Ta-Ta For Now* = goodbye; orig. created and popularized on comedian Tommy Handley's BBC Radio show 'ITMA' (It's That Man Again); Dorothy Summers, as 'Mrs Mopp' (the comic charlady) actually used the cp; currently featured by BBC Radio-2 disc jockey Jimmy Young *Whitcomb*.

tub n. a boat, spec. the tubs (qv) *Runyon*.

tub of lard n. a fat person (cf: bucket of blubber, bucket of lard, lard-bucket).

tub thumper n. a vehement preacher, either clerical or secular *Hotten*.

tube n. **1.** (UK prison use) a prison officer who makes a habit of listening for information from prison informers (cf: bubble) *LL*; **2.** television, fr. cathode ray tube, a basic component of the TV; **3.** (Aus. use) a can of beer *Humphries*; **4.** (Sc. use) a person *Welsh*.

tube v. (US campus use) to do badly at work; fr. 'go down the tubes' *Underwood*.

tube it v. to watch television *Underwood*.

tubed a. very drunk; thus vanishing 'down the tubes' *Dickson*.

tubesteak n. (US Black use) the penis *Folb*.

tubs n. **1.** (obs.) transatlantic liners; **2.** drums *Algren*.

tubular a. (Valley Girls (qv) use) even better than awesome or massive (qqv), prob. fr. surfers' use of *tube*: the inside curve of a good wave *Harpers/Queen 1983*.

tuches n. see: toches.

tuck v. to tape the penis to the groin; used by transvestites.

tuck up v. to defraud, to steal from *Newman: 1*.

tucked up a. (UK police use) captured without any chance of escape fr. 17th C. cant *tuck (up)* : to hang.

tucker n. (Aus. use) food; devel fr. use at 19th C. gold diggings: rations *Humphries: 2*.

tuckered out a. exhausted, worn out *Runyon: 1*.

tug n. an arrest (cf: pull) *'The Sweeney', Thames TV, passim*.

tumble v. **1.** to seduce, to have intercourse *Thompson: J*; **2.** to realize, to notice *Newman: 1*.

tummler n. **1.** fr. Yiddish: noise, disorder; 'the life and soul of the party'; a person who talks a great deal but accomplishes little; **2.** (show business use) the MC of a (Jewish) hotel in Catskill Mts, NY (cf: Borscht belt) *Rosten*.

tummy banana n. the penis.

tump over v. (US campus use) to knock over; fr. SE tumble *Underwood*.

tuna n. **1.** (US campus use) a girl-friend, a female *Bernbach*; **2.** (US Black use) a female and by extension, the vagina (cf: fish) *Folb*.

tune off v. to calm someone down; esp. when this will stop them from 'broadcasting' facts detrimental to one's own interest; fr. radio use *PT*.

tuned in a. aware of what is going on, at one with the nuances and niceties of a situation or conversation; fr. radio use (cf: hip).

turd n. **1.** piece of excrement; since 11th C. *Price: 1* thus; **2.** an unappealing person.

turd-burglar n. (Aus. use) homosexual male; fr. anal intercourse.

turd-packer n. homosexual *Legman*.

turf n. **1.** spec. the area controlled by a given US urban street gang; **2.** the area with which one is familiar and which in turn recognizes one as a regular figure *Greenlee*.

turf out v. to eject, to throw out; supposedly on to some grass.

Turk n. (homosexual use) one who enjoys anal intercourse; fr. racial cliché *Legman*.

turkey n. 1. a failure, an incompetent *Price: 1*; 2. a dull, incompetent, unappealing person *Junker*; 3. an appalling, unquestionable disaster; esp. in show business.

turkey on a string n. (US Black use) one who is infatuated and thus easily led and controlled *Folb*.

turkey shoot n. (milit. use) a combat in which one's own side wins without any difficulty, killing and destroying on a large scale *Esq. 6/83*.

turkey-neck n. the penis; fr. supposed resemblance *Bukowski: 6*.

turking n. sexual intercourse *Powis*.

Turkish delight n. (gay use) pederasty; from the supposed Turkish propensity for such pleasures.

turn n. (Aus. use) a party (usu. teen. use) *Ready*.

turn a trick v. (sex industry use) to service a client (cf: trick).

turn around v. (police use) to persuade a criminal to turn informer *Higgins: 2*.

turn it up! stop doing that; since 17th C.*Dury*, *'Do It Yourself'*.

turn off v. repel sexually *Jay & Young*.

turn on n. a thrill, sexual or otherwise *McFadden*.

turn on v. 1. to take drugs; as in Dr Timothy Leary's exhortation: 'turn on, tune in and drop out' *Goldman*; 2. to stimulate sexually, to appeal to someone *Jay & Young*.

turn on the fan v. to hurry, to move quickly.

turn on the waterworks v. to start crying *Neaman & Silver*.

turn one's crank v. to give pleasure *Underwood*.

turn one's face to the wall v. to die *Algren: 2*.

turn out v. 1. (pimp use) to run a prostitute on the streets *OUI 8/75*; 2. (Hells Angel use) to use a woman for multiple sex *Mandelkau*; 3. to beat up; poss fr. turn over (qv) *Maledicta 9*.

turn over v. 1. (police/criminal use) to search a house or apartment, usu. with the maximum of damage, mess, etc.

'Minder', Thames TV, 1983; 2. (homosexual use) to allow anal intercourse; fr. the physical act that may precede it *Legman*.

turn the set out v. (US Black use) to disrupt (permanently) a given situation or occasion *Folb*.

turn the tables v. (homosexual use) for a male homosexual prostitute to blackmail a client *Legman*.

turn tricks v. to engage in prostitution (cf: trick) *Price: 2*.

turn up n. surprise *Lynda La Plante*, 'Widows', Thames TV, 1983.

turn up one's toes v. to die *Barr*.

turned on a. aware, sophisticated, up to the minute; fr. image of the awareness gained through drug use *SF Comics*.

turnip greens n. (US Black use) marijuana; fr. popular 'soul food' *Folb*.

turnkey job n. a commission in which one major contractor delivers the finished product to the client and deals with all sub-contractors and affiliates himself; thus on completion all the client need do is 'turn a key' and his machine, factory, new house, etc. is all ready to start operations *Thompson: J*.

turps n. (Aus. use) any form of alcohol; thus *on the turps*: drinking (heavily) (cf: metho) *Ready*.

turtles n. (rhyming sl.) turtle doves = gloves, spec. those worn by housebreakers to hide fingerprints *Powis*.

tushie n. fr. Yiddish: *tuchus* = buttocks *Price: 1*.

tushroon n. (US Black use) money (cf: tosheroon) *Major*.

tuskie n. (US Black use) a large marijuana cigarette; resembling an elephant's tusk (?) *Folb*.

TV n. (acro.) TransVestite (cf: TS) *Jay & Young*.

twang v. to engage in spontaneous sexual intercourse; since 17th C. *Klein*.

twang one's wire v. to masturbate *Humphries*.

twank n. (prostitute use) an older man who enjoys watching girls at work but has no personal interest in sex.

twat n. vagina; thus a term of abuse; since 17th C.*Powis*.

tweak v. to suffer heroin withdrawal.

tweedler n. (UK police/criminal use) a stolen vehicle which is passed off as perfectly legitimate for sale to a sucker (qv). *Powis*.

tweedling (UK police/criminal use) selling stolen property or even non-existent property to innocent purchasers who assume the goods are legitimate *Powis*.

tweeked a. (Valley Girls (qv) use) very drunk or drugged *Pond*.

twenties n. (US conman use) one asks the store clerk for change for $20 rather than give the right, small amount of money; then, after pocketing that, you find the right money, say 20 cents, and offer that, simultaneously asking for or just snatching back the $20 bill *Thompson: J*.

twenty-four/seven adv. every day, all the time; lit. twenty four hours a day, seven days a week; alternatively as 'seven / twenty-four' *Morgan*.

twenty-nine and wake-up (US prison use) the period between receiving a notice of parole and one's actual release, ie a month (cf: wake-up) *Klein*.

twerp n. idiot, nincompoop *Waterhouse*.

twig v. to understand *Payne*.

twink n. (gay use) any available attractive young boy, whether a rent boy (qv) or not. (cf: twinky).

twinky n. (sex industry use) a child seen as suitable for sexual exploitation (cf: chicken, pretties).

twirl n. 1. (UK prison use) a prison officer – from the keys he carries and twirls *Norman: 1*; 2. (UK criminal use) a key, spec. a skeleton or duplicate key *Powis*.

twist n. 1. a girl, woman; fr. rhyming sl. twist and twirl = girl; 2. the passive

member of a lesbian relationship *Stanley*.

twisted a. 1. extremely intoxicated by a specific drugs, esp. the hallucinogens or cannabis; 2. annoyed, out of emotional control *Stone*; 3. very drunk *Bernbach*.

twister n. 1. (US Black use) a front-door key *Major*; 2. an untrustworthy person, a crook *Wodehouse: PGM*.

twit n. fool, idiot; fr. twerp + twat (qqv) (?) *L. Deighton, 'Close-Up', 1974*.

two n. (criminal use) a two-year sentence *Mortimer*.

two and eight n. (rhyming sl.) a state, a panic *Norman: 2*.

two bricks short of the load someone who is 'not all there', a dunce *Obs. 6/2/83*.

two cents worth n. one's personal opinion, a remark about a given topic *Larner*.

two ducks (bingo use) 22 (from the shape) *Wright*.

two fat ladies (bingo use) 88; fr. the shape *Dury, 'Laughter', 1979*.

two little crutches (bingo use) 77, fr. alleged shape *Wright*.

two pence short of a bob eccentric, slightly crazy; fr. bob = 1s. *Humphries: 2*.

two sandwiches short of a picnic phr. crazy, eccentric; one of many similar phrases that mean 'not all there'.

two shakes of a lamb's tail immediately, at once; usu. *In . . .*

two-bit second-rate; inferior; lit. worth 25 cents *R. Newman, 'Almost Made It To The Top', 1979*.

two-bit hustler n. 1. a low-priced whore; 2. any promiscuous woman.

two-bob a. (Aus. use) inferior, useless, second-rate; lit. worth 2s. (10p) (cf: two-bit) *Wilkes*.

twocker n. from 'Taking Without Owners Consent' – youths who steal cars for ram-raids (qv) and hotting (qv).

two-dollar words n. any language considered 'difficult' or 'intellectual' by its user, most likely a speaker who claims to despise/avoid such locutions; usu. derog. *Dickson*.

twoed-up (UK prison use) two men in the same cell; thus **threed-up**, etc. *Cole*.

twoer n. £200 *Newman: 1*.

twot n. see: twat *Griffith*.

two-time v. to cheat, esp. to double-cross.

two-timer n. a cheat, a double-crosser *rr*.

two-timing a. duplicitous *Himes: 1*.

two-way man n. a male prostitute who is willing to act as passive or active partner in pedication or fellatio *Legman*.

typer n. typewriter *Bukowski: 2*.

T-zone a. (US teen. use) lost in one's own world, spaced out (qv), in a state of transcendental bliss *Sculatti*.

tzuris n. bad luck, endless problems; fr. Yiddish: troubles *Rosten*.

U

UBs n. (US campus use) (abbrev.) underbodies = underwear, usu. female use *Underwood*.

U/C abbr. (contact ads use) uncircumcised, fr. abbr. uncut *SMD*.

Ugandan discussions n. (euph.) sexual intercourse; popularly thought to have derived from the alleged discovery, *in flagrante delicto* of Uganda's Minister of Foreign Affairs (female) in an airport lavatory, and so underwritten by *Private Eye*, which magazine coined the phrase, aka *talking about Uganda*; latterly repudiated by Corinna Adam, whose letter to *The Times* (Sept 1983) claims that in 1971 a passionate literary critic was the first to offer this excuse.

U-ie aka: *U-ey*, *youee* a U-turn.

ultimate a. (contact ads use) swinging in which all those present have intercourse; the opposite of couples-only soft swinging. *Nocturnal Emissions 12/91*.

umbrella n. (boxing use) an incompetent boxer who 'folds up' when hit by his opponent *Runyon:1*.

umbrella brigade n. (UK police use) the Special Branch; who may dress in the Whitehall uniform of bowler hat and rolled umbrella *Powis*.

umpteen unspecified large number or amount; orig. milit. use, deliberately

replacing a specific number with a noncommittal 'um' for communications secrecy.

unbuttoned a. unprepared, caught by surprise, taken unawares (cf: naked, a.).

uncle n. a pawnbroker.

Uncle n. (abbrev.) Uncle Sam (qv) = the USA, spec. the US military forces or other authorities (FBI, CIA, etc.) *Higgins:1*.

Uncle Bert n. (rhyming sl.) shirt *Jones: J*.

Uncle Dick see: Tom and Dick *Powis*.

Uncle Fred n. (rhyming sl.) bread (food) *Jones: j*.

uncle nabs n. (US Black use) the police; fr. nab, v. (qv) *Folb*.

Uncle Ned n. (rhyming sl.) bed *Wright*.

Uncle Sam the USA, esp. the armed forces of the USA; Uncle Sam (the equivalent of the UK's Britannia or John Bull) is always pictured as a bewhiskered, high-hatted old gentleman, garbed in red, white and blue.

Uncle Tom n. a subservient Black person, fitting willingly into the stereotyped and inferior image refined by generations of white supremacy *Seale*.

Uncle Tom v. (US Black use) to act in

a subservient, obsequious manner to
whites (cf: tom v.) *X*.

Uncle Tomahawk n. see: apple (cf:
Uncle Tom).

uncool a. unpleasant, square (qv),
emotional, rude; various negative
meanings as to given context (cf: cool)
Wolfe:2.

under glass a. imprisoned, arrested;
as in a museum *Chandler: Notebk.*

under house a. (US teen. use) in an
uncontrollable state, emotionally
unstable, furious; fr. under house
arrest *Sculatti*.

under one's own steam alone and
unaided; fr. railway use.

under the cosh see: under the gun.

under the gun under great pressure,
stress *Price:3*.

under the influence a. drunk; 'of
alcohol' is assumed *Neaman & Silver*.

under the odds a. easy, better than
expected; fr. betting use *Mortimer*.

under the table a. 1. clandestine,
secret, corrupt *Larner*; 2. drunk; one
has fallen there.

under the weather a. 1. drunk; 2. not
feeling perfectly well, miserable
Rawson.

under wraps a. secret, hidden away;
as in a new design, esp. milit.

underlay n. (horseracing use) a horse
that starts a race at odds lower than
those listed in the 'morning line' that
preceeds each day's racing
Bukowski:1.

undertaker job n. 1. a hopeless
proposition, thus 'dead'; 2. (gambling
use) a horse or greyhound which is
deliberately – for the odds sake – not
meant to win, whatever legitimate
bettors may presume *Runyon:1*.

underwear n. (pimp use) a client who
enjoys buying or otherwise employing
the prostitute's used underwear *OUI
8/75*.

undie a. clandestine, secret.

unglued a. unstable, emotional,
lacking control *McFadden*.

uni n. (abbrev.) university
Humphries:2.

uniform n. (homosexual use) any

member of the armed forces: less freq.
policemen, firemen, etc. (cf: rough
trade) *Legman*.

union card n. (US campus use) a
university degree certificate
Underwood.

union wage n. (US Black use) the
police; the sole motivation for their
activities (?) *Folb*.

university of life n. that college
attended by those who claim personal
experience as infinitely superior to
academic knowledge (cf: school of
hard knocks) *Whitcomb*.

unkjay n. (Pig Latin) junkie (qv)
Algren.

unload v. to get rid of; spec. to break
off an affair *Dury*.

unlucky for some (bingo use) 13; the
number most prone to superstitious
interpretation *Wright*.

unreal a. 1. (Aus. surfer use)
unbelievable, unacceptable,
unpleasant; an all-purpose negative
that depends for precise meaning on
context; 2. (Aus. use) term of all-
encompassing approbation as used by
upper-middle class Aus. teenage girls
Humphries; 3. (US campus use) as 2.

unsus a. (abbrev.) unsuspicious:
plausible. (cf: sus, sussy) *Norman:2*.

untogether a. anyone not in full
possession of their faculties; a
situation that is less than satisfactorily
under control (cf: uncool).

untold a. immeasurable, a vast
number, extreme; like the SE, but
used with slight different, and often
ungrammatical emphasis.

up a gumtree a. (orig. Aus. use, now
general) in trouble, facing a problem;
fr. the chasing of an animal into such a
tree.

up a tree a. (US campus use)
annoyed, emotionally unstable; fr. out
of one's tree (qv); or fr. a cat perched,
spitting down at an adversary, high in
a tree *Underwood*.

up against the wall a. (US campus
use) dumb, foolish, stupid; fr. 1960's
radical slogan: 'Up against the wall,
motherfucker', and its root, the

putting of prisoners against a wall to face a firing squad *Underwood*.

up and dust v. (US Black use) to leave in a hurry; to run away *Klein*.

up and up a. fair, honest, straightforward *Schulberg*.

up each other phr. (Aus. use) indulging in mutual flattery; the image is of buggery (cf: jerking each other off).

up for grabs a. 1. available, on the market; 2. vulnerable *Bruce:2*.

up her like a rat up a drain (cp) the assumption that a given woman will be freely, easily and speedily sexually available to the speaker.

up in the bucks a. phr. wealthy, prospering.

up in the paints a. depending on context: old, high, superior; all meanings infer something more extreme; fr. gambling use: *paints* = high (royal) cards *Runyon:1*.

up shit creek without a paddle a. in deep trouble *Humphries*.

up the chute anal intercourse (cf: poopchute) *Price:2*.

up the creek a. 1. (Aus. use) pregnant (cf: up the flue, etc.); 2. in trouble, facing problems (cf: up shit creek) *Ready*.

up the duff a. pregnant (cf: up the spout).

up the gazoo 2. up the anus; 2. to excess *Higgins:5*.

up the river a. in gaol, fr. the penitentiary at Ossining ('Sing-Sing') which is sited up the river from New York City.

up the spout a. 1. pregnant (cf: up the duff, knocked up); 2. in the pawnshop *Baker*.

up the stairs on trial; fr. the steps that lead from the cells beneath the Old Bailey up into the dock.

up the steps see: up the stairs *Powis*.

up the flue a. (Aus. use) pregnant (cf: up the spout, duff, etc.) *Ready*.

up there Cazaly! (Aus. use) cry of encouragement; fr. Australian Rules player Roy Cazaly (1893–1963), star of the South Melbourne team, and especially noted for his athletic leaps into the air for a 'mark' *Ready*.

up to here a. bored, disgusted, utterly intolerant of an event, someone's statements, actions, etc.

up to snuff a. efficient, capable, aware *D. McLintick, 'Indecent Exposure', 1983*.

up West the West End of London, as seen either from the East End or from the Western or suburban areas *Dury*.

up your ass! to hell with you! 'stick it . . .' is taken as read.

up your jacksie! alternative version of up your ass! (qv).

up yours! excl. of contempt; abbrev. of up your ass! (qv).

up-and-downer n. a fight, a tussle *Mortimer, 'Rumpole and the Golden Thread', 1983*.

upchuck v. to vomit (cf: throw up) *Farina*.

upfront a. open, honest, outspoken, outgoing *McFadden*.

upper crust a. conceited, snobbish; fr. the 'crust' that sits on the great 'pie' of society *Underwood*.

uppers n. amphetamines (cf: speed).

uppity a. cheeky, arrogant, one who refuses to 'know their place' (cf: hincty) often as *uppity nigger*: a Black person who refuses to fall into a second-class line *Neaman & Silver*.

ups see: uppers.

upsadaisy! soothing excl. offered a fallen child as one picks it up again.

upside a. (US Black use) next to, up against *Folb*.

upstairs n. (US Black use) the mind *Klein*.

upstate n. (New York criminal use) prison; the main New York state prisons being in upstate New York *Selby:1*.

upta a. (Aus. use) aka: *upter* useless, no use whatsoever; fr. *up to shit Lambert*.

uptight a. 1. tense, annoyed; 2. close, friendly; 3. OK, satisfactory, good *SF Comics*.

uptown a. sophisticated, worldly, rich; fr. that area of US cities considered residential, rather than *downtown*, where business is carried on *Capital Radio 1983*.

upways n. (US Black use) a snobbish, stand-offish person *Klein*.

urban surfing n. riding on the outside of moving vehicles.

US a. abbr. useless *Welsh:1*.

use v. to be taking or addicted to narcotics *Higgins:1*.

use one's loaf v. to think, to work things out; fr. rhyming sl. loaf of bread = head (qv).

use the chump v. to act intelligently.

use the English v. (rare) to wriggle one's buttocks while being penetrated anally; fr. snooker use *Legman*.

useless as a slice of bacon at a Jewish wedding phr. totally useless.

useless as a spare prick at a (lesbian) wedding phr. totally useless.

user n. a drug addict.

ute n. (Aus. use) (abbrev.) utility vehicle, small truck *Ready*.

UVs n. (US teen. use) (abbrev.) ultraviolet rays, thus sunshine; *soak up UVs*: to get a tan *Pond*.

V

v a. (UK 'society' use) (abbrev.) very *Barr*.

vag n. (US police use) a charge of vagrancy.

Valley Girls n. teenage Californian girls, spec. the daughters of the affluent middle-classes in the Los Angeles area; the description, and the core vocabulary was coined by Moon Unit, daughter of rock star Frank Zappa, c.1980; slang etymologists will note that the bulk of the vocabulary descends directly from surfing, US college, drug user, and general US teen terminology.

Vallie n. (drug use) (abbrev.) Valium *Humphries:2*.

vamoose! go away! fr. Sp. *vamos!* *Schulberg*.

vamp on v. (US Black (radical) use) to make an unjust attack; to arrest; also used, when aimed at the oppressor to correct, to upbraid, to force him to mend his ways *Seale*.

vanilla a. plain, simple, no frills (fr. the plainest ice-cream flavour; while the term has come into general use since the 1980s, it was allegedly coined by the saxophonist Lester Young c.1935).

Vaseline Heights n. (US homosexual

use) gay centre of Portland, Ore. fr. the lubricant uses of Vaseline *White*.

VAT (acro.) vodka and tonic *Minder passim*.

Vatican roulette n. the notoriously unpredictable rhythm method of contraception; the only form permitted by the Catholic Church. *D Lodge The British Museum Is Falling Down (1965)*.

vato n. a member of a Mexican teen gang *Morgan*.

veg n. (abbrev.) vegetable = moron, madman.

veg out v. (US campus use) to let oneself slip into a totally apathetic and passive state; to vegetate *Neaman & Silver*.

vegetable a. (US campus use) very drunk *Underwood*.

vegetarian n. (US cant) prostitute who refuses to offer fellatio to her clients, who 'won't eat meat' *Neaman & Silver*.

veggie n. a vegetarian.

velcro head n. (derog.) a black person.

Vera Lynn n. (rhyming sl.) gin; fr. the 'forces' sweetheart' of the Second World War *Wright*.

Vera Vice n. (homosexual use) the

police vice squad *Stanley*.

verbal v. (UK criminal/police use) for
the police to fake a confession by
claiming that one's statement under
interrogation – the verbal – admitted
to all the crimes for which in court one
is pleading not guilty *Powis*.

verbals n. (UK police/criminal use) a
statement to the police either
voluntarily or during and after
interrogation *Powis*.

verboten a. fr. Ger.: forbidden
Price:2.

very swift (UK criminal use) the
taking of grossly unfair advantage by
the police *Powis*.

vet prostitute n. a senior member of
the stable, responsible for teaching
and disciplining her younger sisters; fr.
abbrev. veteran *Klein*.

Vette n. (abbrev.) Corvette *Higgins:5*.

vg (UK 'society' use) (abbrev.) *very
good Barr*.

vibe v. to experience, enjoy, fr. vibes/
vibrations *Shell*.

vibes n. (abbrev.) vibrations:
atmosphere, feelings; thus *good vibes*
or *bad vibes*; fr. 1960s hippie use
Uneeda Comix.

vicious a. (Valley Girls (qv) use)
wonderful, excellent, etc. (on bad =
good premise) *Pond*.

vig n. (abbrev.) vigorish (qv)
Higgins:3.

vigorish n. (US bookmaker use)
interest on a loan, or debt; fr. SE
vigorous (?), since it 'intensifies' the
payments, by increasing them.

Viking queen n. (gay use) **1.** blond; **2.**
blond male homosexual slang.

-ville general suffix, fr. abbrev. for

'village', and esp. popular in jazz and
beatnik eras.

Ville n. HMP Pentonville (cf: the
Scrubs).

vine n. **1.** (US Black and teen. use) a
suit *Goldman*; **2.** (UK criminal use)
(abbrev.) the grapevine, the unofficial
underground network of information
LL.

vineyard n. (US Black use) ironic ref.
to anywhere that alcoholics
congregate (cf: shooting gallery)
Klein.

vino n. wine *SF Comics*.

virgin n. a criminal with no convictions
Higgins:2.

vitamin A n. acid, ie LSD or, more
recently, ecstasy (qv).

vitamin C n. cocaine.

vitamin E n. ecstasy (qv).

vitamin K n. **1.** a synthetic
hallucinogen, allegedly 5,000 times
stronger than LSD (qv). According to
researchers it takes the user to
'subatomic reality…(one feels) the
consciousness of inanimate objects.' *J
Stevens Storming Heaven (1987)*; **2.**
Ketamine, a synthetic substitute for
Ecstasy (qv) and normally used as an
emergency anaesthetic, popular
among ravers (qv) in 1992. *Ind 3/4/92*.

vitamin T n. tea (qv), ie marijuana.

vitamin X n. ecstasy (qv).

vitamin XXX n. alcohol *P J O'Rourke
'Give War a Chance' (1992)*.

vitamins n. (drug use) any drugs
available in pill or capsule form *Folb*.

voddy n. vodka *Welsh:1*.

VPL abbrev. *visible pantie line. GQ
magazine 10/91*.

W

W n. (UK police use) a warrant –
arrest, search, etc. *Norman:2*.

wack n. aka: *wacker*: Merseyside term
of address to a male *Payne*; a. **1.** angel

dust (qv); **2.** (US black use) second-
rate, phoney, unsatisfactory – a
general term of opprobium.
Ice T:1.

wack attack n. (US Black use) the onset of apparent insanity, usu. through the use of drugs.

wack-ass a general negative intensifier (cf. trick-ass) *Dre*.

wacky a. amusing, jolly, funny; one of the many words popularized during the Beatlemania craze of the mid-1960s.

wacky baccy n. (drug use) marijuana.

wade in v. to commit oneself whole-heartedly, esp. to a fight.

waffle n. (US criminal use) a male homosexual *Legman*.

waffle stompers n. (US campus use) heavy boots with thick cleated soles that resemble a waffle iron *Underwood*.

wag n. (US police use) a vagrant *Chandler: LG*.

wag v. (US Black use) to procrastinate, to find it hard to make any decisions; fr. wag = vagrant (qv) *Klein*.

wag it v. play truant (cf: bunk off, hop the wag).

wag off v. see: wag it.

wail v. to abandon one's inhibitions, to lose oneself in a given activity; esp. used of musicians during an improvised solo, or of sexual pleasure *Bruce:2*.

wake it up! (Aus. use) hurry up, get on with it *Ready*.

wake up v. see: wise up.

wake-up n. (drug use) 1. a heroin user's first injection of the day *Grogan*; 2. any form of stimulant and amphetamine *Folb*; 3. (US milit. use) in Vietnam, the last day of a tour in Vietnam; thus days left calculated as 'X and a wake-up'; similarly used in US prisons; one 'wakes up' in an institution, but goes to bed in freedom *Del Vecchio*.

walk on! (US campus use) term of dismissal, disbelief, contempt (cf: stroll on!) *Bernbach*.

walk on one's cap-badge to be very drunk; orig. milit. use *Dickson*.

walk on rocky socks v. (US use) to walk unsteadily owing to an excess of drink *Neaman & Silver*.

walk the bricks v. (US police use) to patrol a foot beat rather than work from a patrol car *Dunne*.

walk the check v. (US campus use) to walk deliberately out of a restaurant without paying the check (bill) *Underwood*.

walkabout n. the public mingling with attendant crowds of any celebrity, esp. a member of the UK Royal Family.

walk-about money n. daily expenses, petty cash rather than a large amount that needs investing or depositing somewhere *Runyon*.

walker n. a man, often rich, invariably personable and socially acceptable, who accompanies the wives of very prominent men – presidents, chairmen, etc. – to parties, on shopping expeditions, to the theatre, etc. *Green:2*.

walking papers n. (US prison use) official notice to inform a prisoner that he/she has finished a given sentence *Klein*.

Wall Street didn't jump (US teen. use, cp) anything that fails to produce the anticipated/desired excitement from bystanders, let alone produce an effect on the US economy *Sculatti*.

wallah n. a person, a man; fr. Anglo-Indian (milit.) use, thus through to UK general use *Dury*.

wallbanging n. (US gang use) painting graffiti, esp. gang slogans or gang nicknames on walls (cf: gangbanging).

wallflower n. (UK prison use) a prisoner obsessed with the possibility of escape; fr. dance/party use: one who doesn't want to join in *LL*.

wallflower week those days during which a woman is menstruating and thus, traditionally, sexually inactive *Rawson*.

wallop n. beer, alcohol in general; Second World War milit. use for beer only *A. Green 1983*.

walloper n. (Aus. use) a policeman; fr. his activities *Baker*.

wallopies n. (US campus use) female

breasts, esp. large ones *Underwood*.

wall-to-wall a. everywhere, all over; like carpet *Higgins:1*.

wally n. **1.** an unfashionable, unintelligent, 'suburban' person, lacking in taste and sophistication; **2.** a trainee policeman *Newman passim*; **3.** a pickled cucumber.

waltz v. to achieve something easily, esp. in sporting use *'Minder', Thames TV, 1983*.

wamba n. see wonga.

wampum n. money; fr. American Indian word for money *Vidal*.

'wana n. (abbrev. and corruption) marijuana *Folb*.

wang n. penis *Bruce:1*.

wangle v. to obtain what one wants, often through a degree of manipulation or cunning.

wang-tang n. (US Black use) anything, esp. on a sexual level, that is especially desirable *Klein*.

wank v. to masturbate. this sp. has generally superseded *whank*.

wanker n. **1.** spec. a masturbator; **2.** derog. general description: lazy, incompetent person *Farren*.

wanna do a thing? (US Black use) (cp) asking a passing woman if she fancies intercourse *Klein*.

wanna go out? (prostitute use) ritual come-on from a prostitute to a passing male *Rawson*.

wannabe n. orig. from US Black use, where the term simply meant a fantasist, and from surfing jargon, where it meant a learner, it became more specific with the rise of the rock star Madonna, whose legions of fans declared, either verbally, or in the way they dressed, aping their heroine, 'I wanna be . . . like Madonna'. Wannabes are not exclusively Madonna clones - film stars, sports stars and other icons are all eligible – but she remains the primary reference.

want to make something of it? (cp) ritual request that may well herald a fight, but still gives the other person the chance to back down.

warehouse v. to go to warehouse

parties, a popular teenage amusement in the mid-1980s.

warm a. (US teen. use) a very attractive, sexy girl; deliberate understatement of hot (qv) *Pond*.

warm beer n. (sex industry use) urine.

warm up n. either sexual foreplay or merely a wash prior to intercourse.

warpaint n. cosmetics, make-up.

was she worth it? (bingo use) 76; fr. former price of UK marriage licence, 7/6d *Wright*.

wash n. crack (qv); refers to the process of chemical purification that is used when making the drug (cf: readywash).

wash n. (West Indian use) the mash of cheap grain and sugar that is distilled to produce the home-made spirit that are sold in shebeens (qv) *Powis*.

wash v. see: launder *PT*.

wash out v. to remove, to cancel, to dismiss *Jay & Young*.

washed up a. useless, exhausted, a failure *Heller*.

wash-out n. a failure *Jay & Young*.

WASP n. (acro.) White Anglo-Saxon Protestant, the predominant racial group in the USA.

waste v. to kill, esp. milit. use *O'Brien*.

wasted a. **1.** utterly overcome by a given drug *Price:2*; **2.** killed, esp. in a battle *O'Brien*; **3.** very drunk *Bernbach*.

watch one's ass v. to take care, to take note, to be warned *Bruce:2*.

watch one's lip v. to mind one's manners, to talk politely *Chandler: LG*.

watch queen n. a male homosexual voyeur fr. queen (qv) *Stanley*.

watch the ant races v. to be excessively drunk, probably face down on the bar or the floor *Neaman & Silver*.

watch the dickey-bird! (cp) photographers' (both professional and amateur) exhortation to their subjects to ensure smiling and alert faces for the picture; smiles are also encouraged by *say cheese*.

watch the submarines v. (US use) to indulge in sexual by-play *Neaman & Silver*.

Water n. the River Thames; thus *over the Water*: South of the Thames *Newman:1*.

water of life n. (US Black use) semen.

water sports urinating on a partner for sexual stimulation (cf: golden shower) *Jay & Young*.

waterboy n. (boxing use) a useless boxer who accepts money to lose fights (cf: tanker, take a dive, etc.) *Runyon*.

watering hole n. 1. a restaurant, a bar, anywhere where alcoholic refreshment is available; 2. (UK gay use) a neighbourhood cruising locale, usually a park grounds or a bar.

watermelon man n. (US Black use) a drug seller *Klein*.

wax v. see: wax one's tail *Underwood*.

wax one's tail v. to beat up; also used by milit. fliers for taking the advantage in an aerial dog-fight, getting on the enemy's tail *Wolfe:6*.

wax up v. (US Black use) 1. to propitiate someone whom one has insulted or annoyed (cf: apple-polish); 2. to hide evidence *Klein*.

waxed a. (US Black use) of anyone whose personality and characteristics are known well (cf: peep one's hole card) *Klein*.

way a. (Valley Girls (qv) use) very, extremely, etc.; fr. way-out (qv) (cf: total) *Pond*.

way out a. bizarre, fantastic, exceptional; fr. hippie use in 1960s *Thompson*.

way to go! excl. of approval, ie. 'that's the right way to go . . .'.

ways n. the style and standards of the US Mafia *Higgins:3*.

wazz n. urination.

wazzocked a. drunk *Obs. 13/3/83*.

w/e abbr. (contact ads use) well endowed (cf: donkey-rigged, hung); also VW/E: very well endowed *Nocturnal Emissions 12/91*.

weak a. poor, disappointing *Salisbury*.

weakheart n. (West Indian use) policeman *Powis*.

wear a cut glass veil v. to attempt unsuccessfully to hide one's homosexual preferences *Legman*.

wear a mourning veil v. attempt to hide one's homosexual proclivities *Legman*.

wear it v. (US cant/police use) to take the blame for a crime even when not actually guilty '*The Stone Killer*', film 1973.

wear one's badge v. to wear an outward sign of being a homosexual; formerly this was a red tie, now obs. *Legman*.

wear the bells v. to act the fool.

wear the dog v. (US Black use) to go around looking deeply depressed (but, cf: put on (the) dog) *Klein*.

wear the trousers v. to dominate; usu. implying that the female half of a relationship is the one who dictates the rules (formerly 'wear the breeches' *Hotten*).

wearing one's medals phr. walking around with one's fly open.

wearing the ring a. (US Black use) infatuated with someone, thus sexually exclusive as if, in theory, married *Folb*.

weasel n. (rhyming sl.) weasel and stoat = overcoat *Powis*.

wedding tackle n. the male genitals.

wedge n. a thick, chunky roll of banknotes, usu. folded in half *Powis*.

wedgeass n. general derog. term of abuse *Uris*.

Wee Georgie Wood a. (rhyming sl.) good; fr. music hall star *Wright*.

weed n. 1. (commercial use) the practice of pocketing a certain amount of the cash that should be placed untouched into one's employer's tills *Green:2*; 2. marijuana *White*; 3. a cigarette, spec. the tobacco it contains *Uris*.

weedhead n. (drug use) marijuana smoker *De Lannoy & Masterson*.

weedy a. weak, cowardly, spineless; either juv. or upper-class UK use; fr. gardening use *Barr*.

weekend n. (UK prison use) a very short period of imprisonment *LL*.

weekend ho n. (pimp use) part-time prostitute, often without a pimp but poss. helping out her boyfriend with cash *OUI 8/75*.

weekend man n. (US Black use) a family man who can only manage the street life at weekends *Klein*.

weekend warriors n. 1. part-time prostitutes, amateurs who work weekends only *Neaman & Silver*; 2. (US use) a member of the National Guard *Morgan*.

weenie n. the penis, usu. children's use; fr. supposed resemblance to a wiener or other sausage *Vidal*.

weenie waver n. an exhibitionist *Morgan*.

weepie n. (film use) a film whose main effect is to reduce its audience to tears, usu. consciously romantic; thus – on model of *three alarm fire*, etc. – *three-handkerchief weepie*: a very emotional film (cf: tearjerker).

weeping willow n. (rhyming sl.) pillow *Jones: J*.

weigh in v. to join in, esp. in an argument; fr. racing use.

weigh into v. to attack verbally, to criticize *Capital Radio 1983*.

weigh off v. (UK criminal/police use) to sentence a convicted prisoner *Norman:1*.

weight n. 1. one pound of marijuana, cannabis; 2. one ounce of heroin *Larner*.

weird out v. to horrify, to play mental games *Price:3*.

weirdo n. an eccentric, a peculiar · person *Bruce:2*.

welch v. aka *Welsh*: to refuse to pay a gambling debt or other bill; fr. the ethnic slur.

welcher n. aka *Welsher*: anyone who refuses to pay their debts, gambling or otherwise *Performance*.

welfare mother n. (US Black use) any woman, irrespective of status *vis-à-vis* welfare, who is poorly dressed and unkempt *Folb*.

well a. very; thus *well tasty*, *well sus* (qqv) etc. *Newman:1*.

well away a. 1. drunk; 2. making headway in a given seduction.

well heeled a. rich; fr. quality of shoes, *inter alia*.

well hung a. a well-endowed male.

well in a. 1. (UK use) popular, secure, entrenched; 2. (Aus. use) wealthy, affluent *Wilkes*.

wellie, give it some v. to apply some force.

wellies n. (abbrev.) wellington boots *May*.

Wellies n. (Exeter University (UK) use) the public-school educated, upper-middle and upper-class students who are seen as playing, rather than working their way through college; fr. wealthy, and fr. green wellingtons such students wear for various rural pleasures *T 3/10/83*.

wellington n. (Aus. rhyming sl.) wellington boot = root = sexual intercourse *Humphries*.

well-lined a. rich, prosperous; fr. 'lining one's pockets' *Humphries:2*.

well-oiled a. very drunk (cf: neck oil).

Welsh v. see: welch.

wen n. (backsl.) new, thus: *teg a wen eno* get a new one *Cole*.

Wendy n. a school child (of either sex) who has been rejected by its fellows, (cf: goggy, gunk, spod, zoid) *Maledicta 9*.

went down like a pork chop at a Jewish wedding (cp) extremely unpopular; fr. the Jewish religious prohibition of pork *A. F. N. Clarke*, '*Contact*', 1983.

were you born in a barn? (cp) aimed at anyone who has failed to shut a door.

were you born in a tent? (Aus. use) see: were you born in a barn? *Wilkes*.

West Hams n. (rhyming sl.) West Ham reserves = nerves *Powis*.

wet a. (US Black use) suspicious (cf: fishy) *Klein*; 2. weak, spineless, usu. an upper-class word, spec. of members of Tory party who do not back Mrs Thatcher's hard line monetarist economics.

wet n. a drink *Hotten*.

wet behind the ears a. naïve,

inexperienced, gauche *Gruber*.

wet blanket n. a dreary person, a spoilsport; fr. a wet blanket being used to quench fires.

wet foot n. a naïve, inexperienced, innocent person *Powis*.

wet goose n. a foolish, naive person.

wet leg n. a self-pitying person.

wet one's pants v. to panic, to lose control. fr. the involuntary urination that may follow great fear *Thompson: J*.

wet one's whistle v. to take a drink; fr. *whistle* throat; dates fr. 14th C. *Neaman & Silver*.

wet smack n. a weakling, an ineffectual person.

wet the baby's head v. to drink in celebration of a baby's birth.

wetback n. 1. an illegal Mexican immigrant to the USA; fr. the condition of the immigrants who traditionally swim the Rio Grande as the best means of beating border checks, thus; 2. (derog.) Mexicans in general *Vidal*.

wethead n. (US Black use) a simpleton, an innocent, a novice (cf: wet behind the ears) *Folb*.

WGF abbr. (sex industry use) used by transexuals to mean whole girl fantasy *Maledicta 9*.

whack n. share, usu. of money *Griffith*.

whack v. 1. to charge money, usu. *whack for . . . Higgins:1*; 2. to hit.

whack off v. to masturbate *Price:1*.

whack out v. to kill, to murder; fr. whack 2 *Bruce:2*.

whack-a-doo n. lunatic, eccentric *Price:3*.

whacked out a. 1. crazy, insane, eccentric *Price:3*; 2. under the influence of a given drug or of alcohol *Goldman*.

whacking a. general intensifier usu. in *whacking big*, *whacking horrible*, etc. *Wodehouse: PGM*.

whacko a. crazy, insane, eccentric.

whacko n. an unstable or mentally ill person *Price:2*.

whacko the diddle-oh (Aus. use) a

remark offered on seeing an attractive girl *Humphries*.

whacky a. see: whacked out.

whale the piss out of v. see: whale the shit out of *Higgins:3*.

whale the shit out of v. to beat viciously *Higgins:1*.

wham n. (US Black use) a large, aggressive man who finds few rivals on the street *Klein*.

wham bam thank you ma'am (cp) epitomizing brief sexual intercourse intended on the whole for male satisfaction only (cf: bip bam . . .).

whammer n. the penis *Morgan*.

whammy n. a punchline; anything devastating and beyond a similarly powerful response.

whang n. the penis (cf: wang) *Vidal*.

whangee n. a cane *Wodehouse: JO*.

whap v. to hit; fr. onomatopoeia (?) *Higgins:2*.

whap that thing! (US Black use) congratulatory remark to a passing woman, implying her supreme sexiness *Klein*.

wharfie n. (Aus. use) docker; fr. wharf *Bickerton*.

what a turn-up! what a surprise; fr. turn up for the book, racing use 'Widows', Thames TV, 1983.

what are you pushing? (US Black use) what sort of car do you drive? *Klein*.

what can I do you for? (cp) facetious reversal of usual 'what can I do for you?' *BBC-1 TV 1983*.

what else is new? deprecating comment on anything the previous speaker has said, esp. if that speaker had intended to make a big impression *Price:3*.

what gives? fr. Yiddish: *vi geht's*: how goes it? what's happening (qv), what's new, etc. *Rosten*.

what in blue blazes? excl. of extreme surprise, absolute confusion, etc.

what it takes n. (orig. US) money (cf: actual, needful).

what the dickens? (excl.) euph: what the devil? *Hotten*.

what the hell! general excl. of

surprise, shock, alarm, etc.
Wodehouse: MOJ.

whatchamacallit n. anything to which
one cannot give a name when required
(cf: thingummibob).

what-d'you-call-it n. see:
whatchamacallit *Wodehouse: MOJ.*

what's biting you? what's the
matter? what's the problem? *Manser.*

what's cooking? what's going on?
(qv) *Hoffman.*

what's going on? common greeting
(cf: what's happening?).

what's happening? a greeting: hello
and how are you; what are you/have
you been doing? (cf: what's shaking?)
Seale.

what's in it for me? (cp) an honest
statement of selfishness.

what's it in aid of? what exactly is the
reason for all this?

what's it to you? aggressive reply to a
questioner implying that whatever it
may be, it is none of his/her business.

what's new? see: what's happening?

what's shaking? a greeting: hello and
how are you (cf: what's happening?)
Price:2.

what's that when it's at home? (cp)
deliberate misunderstanding of a word
or statement which the speaker is
implying to be too 'clever' for his/her
understanding.

what's the big idea? (excl.) more a
threat than a question; usu. asked
when someone is doing or saying
something of which the speaker
disapproves *Manser.*

what's the percentage? what's the
point? what's the intention? fr.
gambling use *McFadden.*

what's your poison? aka: *name your
poison*: jocular invitation to a fellow
drinker to make a choice of drink at a
party or in a bar.

whatshisface n. a reference to
anyone whose name one has
(temporarily) forgotten *Dickson.*

whazood a. (US campus use) drunk
(cf: wazzocked) *Underwood.*

wheel n. (abbrev.) big wheel (qv)
Selby:1.

wheel, wheels n. the record turntable
or turntables as used by hip-hop and
rap DJs (qv) (fr. the circular shape of
the turntable; usu. used in pl.: the DJ
manipulates two turntables, some
even use three, simultaneously,
selecting the portions of given records
and mixing them together).

wheeler-dealer n. entrepreneur,
operator (qv) *Higgins:4.*

wheelie n. trick riding on the back
wheel only of a motorcycle *Higgins:1.*

wheelman n. expert car driver, either
for police or for criminals *Powis.*

wheels n. a car *Shulman.*

when the chips are down (cp) in the
final event, at the denouement, when
one has no option; fr. poker use.

when the crow shits (Aus. use) aka:
when the eagle shits: payday *Wilkes.*

when the morning comes (US Black
use) when hard times finally disappear
Klein.

where it's at the right place, the ideal
situation, opinion, experience; an
expression of approval/affirmation
Bruce:2.

where one is coming from see:
where you're at *McFadden.*

where the Queen goes on foot n.
the lavatory, also as where the Queen
sends nobody.

where you're at what your stance is
on a particular topic, your attitude and
opinion, the way you live: esp.
popular in the new therapies of
California (cf: where you're coming
from) *McFadden.*

where you're coming from how you
are feeling, what your opinions are;
esp. used in new therapies of
California *Price:2.*

where's the fire? (cp) where are you
running to? what's the hurry? *Farrell.*

whiff n. an odour, a smell.

whiff v. to smell *Wilkinson.*

whip around n. a collection, usu. of
money – for a round of drinks, a
present to a third party, etc.

whip it on me 1. to explain and
inform one of facts and events;
2. (drug use) to inject one with

narcotics *L. Reed, 'Sister Ray', 1967*;
3. to give, to hand over *Morgan*.

whip off v. (US campus use)
masturbate *Underwood*.

whip one's ass v. to beat completely
and comprehensively, whether or not
with violence *Price:1*.

whip one's wire v. (US campus use)
to masturbate *Underwood*.

whip shack n. (US Black use)
anywhere one can have sexual
intercourse (cf: killing floor) *Folb*.

whip some skull on v. to fellate (cf:
give head).

whip up v. to create or make
something quickly, at short notice
Dunne.

whipped a. (US campus use)
dominated, subservient, meek
Underwood.

whipped cream n. (US Black use)
semen *Folb*.

whips n. (US Black use) 1. the white
establishment; 2. the police *Folb*.

whiskyhead n. delirium tremens.

whisper n. a rumour, usu. of
impending crimes *Newman:2*.

whistle n. (rhyming sl.) whistle and
flute = suit *Dury*.

whistle and toot n. (rhyming sl.) loot
= money *Cole*.

whistle Dixie v. to boast, to brag
without substance *Dave Anderson,
'Count-Down to Superbowl', 1969*.

whistle in the dark v. to hazard a
guess, to speculate wildly.

whistle up v. to send for; fr. naut.
'whistling up the wind'.

whistle-blower n. a scandalmonger,
an investigator who reveals facts that
disturb an hitherto satisfactory – if
corrupt – status quo. *Newman:2*.

white a. honest, upright, fair-dealing;
fr. the characteristics the white
(Anglo-Saxon) races like to assume
they have, as opposed to 'lesser'
(coloured) breeds; usu. as 'you're a
white man . . .', 'that's white of you'
Wodehouse: MOJ.

white bread (US preppie (qv) use)
anything pertaining to WASP (qv)
styles; bland, unexciting (cf: yankee

white) *Bernbach*.

white cross n. (drug use)
amphetamine pills with a white cross
cut into one surface *Underwood*.

white dove n. a variety of ecstasy (qv)
Welsh:1.

white hat n. (USN use) an officer; fr.
his uniform cap *Pynchon*.

white lady n. (Aus. use) methylated
spirits *Wilkes*.

white lightning n. illicit homebrewed
whisky or poteen *Wolfe:1*.

white line fever n. 1. the obsessive
use of cocaine; fr. the lines of the
powdered drug that are snorted (qv)
by users; 2. an obsessive driver; fr.
white lines that divide traffic lanes.

white liver n. a homosexual who has
no interest whatsoever in women
Legman.

white meat n. (Black use) a white
girl, regarded in a sexual context
punning on the genteel euph. for the
'breast' of a chicken (cf: dark meat).

white meat n. 1. a white person (cf:
dark meat); 2. a white penis.

white owl n. a white penis.

white Russian n. (gay use) the oral
exchange of semen.

white shirt n. (UK prison use) a
senior prison officer, who wears a
white rather than blue (for junior
ranks) shirt *Cole*.

white shit n. heroin *Higgins:1*.

white space n. free time; the space in
question is in the speaker's Filofax.

whitecoat n. (taxi-driver use) the
senior examiner at the Police Public
Carriage Office, in charge of the
testing of London taxi drivers *Powis*.

white-haired boy n. especial
favourite, one who can, in the right
eyes, do no wrong.

white-man's disease n. the relative
inability of Caucasians to jump; a
black term of derision usually used in a
basketball context.

whites n. (drug use) amphetamines
(cf: reds) *Green:1*.

whitewash n. 1. in sport, the
complete defeat of one team by
another; 2. (political use) a cover-up,

the official denial or burying of facts detrimental to their own power, no matter how important such facts are to the public *PT*.

Whitey n. (Black use) the white race in general *Greenlee*.

whiz n. 1. a pickpocket *Powis*; 2. amphetamine (cf: speed) *Cole*.

whiz-pop n. (US campus use) a stupid person *Underwood*.

whizz off v. to leave quickly, to go somewhere fast *Barr*.

whizzing the jizzum phr. masturbating.

who cut the cheese? popular cp (usu. college, school use): who farted? (qv).

who you screwin'? aggressive question aimed at someone who is staring, or perhaps is not, but with whom the speaker wishes to start a ritual that might lead to a fight *Robins:1*.

whodunnit n. (UK prison use) meat pie; the 'murder victim' is the prison cat *LL*.

whole bag of tricks n. everything necessary to deal with a given situation.

whole ball of wax n. see: whole kit and caboodle *'T. J. Hooker'*, *Thames TV, 1983*.

whole bang shoot n. everything relevant and involved.

whole boiling lot absolutely everything.

whole kit and caboodle n. the lot; everything there is *Runyon*.

whole nine yards n. everything, the complete package.

whole shebang n. absolutely everything; orig. US milit. use *shebang*: a soldier's tent, where his possessions were kept.

whoogie n. (derog.) a White person (cf: pink whoogie).

whoop and a holler n. a short distance, also two whoops and a holler.

whoop it up v. to have a noisy, ostentatious good time *NYRB 29/9/83*.

whopper n. a particularly gross lie; fr. whopper = a big one *Hotten*.

whopping a. enormous, very large; usu. school use only *Hotten*.

whore n. 1. a promiscuous woman, but not necessarily (not even usually) an actual prostitute *Underwood*; 2. (poker use) the queen *Uris*.

whore scars n. (US Black use) the scars left from continuous injections of narcotics (cf: tracks) *Major*.

whore splash n. a brief, cursory shower; as taken by a prostitute between clients *Morgan*.

whup v. (US Black use) to attack, to beat up; fr. whip *Folb*.

whup the game v. (US Black use) to succeed in life (cf: have it knocked) *Folb*.

why keep a dog and bark yourself? (cp) urging one to use all available facilities if one is fortunate enough to have access to them.

wicked a. excellent, wonderful (cf: bad).

wicked lady n. (UK prison use) cat o' nine tails *EN 12/11/57*.

wicked thing n. (US Black use) an extraordinary event or situation *Klein*.

widdle v. to urinate *Dury*, *'Spasticus Autisticus', 1981*.

wide a. (police use) corrupt; since 16th C. *Newman:2*.

wide boy n. a minor villain dabbling in various schemes to get rich quick (cf: spiv) *LL*.

wide place in the road n. (derog.) a small town or hamlet (cf: greasy spot on the road).

wide-o n. see wide-boy *Welsh:1* (cf: rape-o).

wide-open a. vulnerable, undefended; fr. boxing use *Schulberg:2*.

wide-open beaver n. a photograph or film shot of the inner labia (cf: split beaver).

widgie n. (Aus. use) the female counterpart of a bodgie (qv) *Ready*.

Widow n. nickname for Veuve Cliquot champagne; fr. Fr. *veuve* = widow.

widow n. (drug use) black widow (qv) *Underwood*.

-widow n. suffix to denote a woman who is left behind while her husband devotes himself to a given obsession, usu. sport or a hobby; thus *golf-widow*, *bicycle-widow*, etc. *McFadden*.

widow maker n. (US milit. use) see MA *Del Vecchio*.

wienie n. **1.** the penis; **2.** a fool, an incompetent (both fr. wienie, lit. wienerwurst or frankfurter) *Underwood*.

wife n. the supposedly subservient, 'female' partner in a homosexual couple *Legman*.

wig n. the head, the brain or its functions.

wig bust (US Black use) the altering of a natural crinkly black head of hair into a straight 'process' (qv) style *Klein*.

Wig City a. (US teen. use) eccentric, unbalanced, nearly insane (cf: wiggy) *Sculatti*.

wig out v. **1.** to lose control, to have a breakdown; fr. wig (qv) *Price:2*; **2.** enjoy oneself, lose one's inhibitions *Seale*; both fr. wig = head (qv).

wigged out see: wiggy.

wigging n. a reprimand, a telling off; fr. ear-wigging *Hotten*.

wiggy a. odd. bizarre, unpleasant, disturbing; fr. wig = head (qv) *Wolfe:1*.

wild a. **1.** eccentric, bizarre, weird, odd *Bruce:2*; **2.** (US prison use) consecutive, referring to a sentence (cf:bowlegged) *Morgan*.

wild v. (US Black use) to go out looking for victims to mug and attack; the term became widespread in the press reports of the savage rape and beating of New York's 'Central Park jogger' in 1989; according to the accused, 'wild' like its noun form 'wilding' was a nonce word, used by them alone and meaning the usual thing – going wild, before it was elevated to a slang term after a report in the New York *Times* on 22/4/89; however the term is used, in the criminal sense, by the rapper (qv) Ice

T on his album *Rhyme Pays*, released in 1987.

wild about very keen on, excited by; often in negative 'I'm not exactly wild about . . .' *T 12/9/83*.

wild prints n. (police use) fingerprints that as yet have not been identified *McBain:1*.

wild-ass a. crazy, insane, unbalanced *Higgins:1*.

wildcat n. (US Black use) someone who participates intensely and also to his own advantage in the street life *Klein*.

wilding n. see: wild.

Wilkie Bard n. (rhyming sl.) **1.** (theatre use) a professional card, used to get free admission to the theatre by an actor; **2.** (plural): playing cards; fr. the comedian *Wright*.

willie peter n. (US milit. use) white phosphorus, usu. in form of incendiary artillery round or grenade *Del Vecchio*.

willies n. nerves, worries, tension *Bruce:2*.

willy n. the penis, usu. children's use only.

wimmin n. women, preferred sp. among some radical gay women who thus censor even the written 'men' *Jay & Young*.

wimp n. weakling *Payne*.

wimp out v. to act in a cowardly manner, to act like a wimp (qv).

wind jammer n. (Aus. use) homosexual male.

wind up v. **1.** to bring to a conclusion, to end up, to find oneself somewhere, to result *Larner*; **2.** to tease, usu. maliciously; fr. winding up clockwork to 'make it go' *Payne*.

wind up merchant n. someone who specializes in teasing, possibly to the point of at least verbal retaliation *Robins:1*.

windbag n. a boastful, loud-mouthed (qv) person.

window dressing n. any form of illusion, cosmetic adornment, etc. which is used to hide the facts of an unpleasant and thus publicly or personally unpalatable reality.

windy a. cowardly (generally used by schoolchildren); from 'get the wind up'.

Windy City n. Chicago; fr. its weather *title of musical, 1983*.

wing it v. to improvise, to ad lib, to play a situation by ear without practice or rehearsal; fr. a bird's flying *Price:3*.

wing-ding n. a boisterous, noisy party *Major*.

wingman n. (Aus.) a drug dealer (cf: bagman).

winker-stinker n. (US prison use) the anus (cf: roundeye) *Klein*.

winkle n. penis *Dury, 'Do It Yourself', 1979*.

winkle-pickers n. highly pointed boots or shoes, orig. favoured by Teddy Boys in 1950s but latterly absorbed into the wide variety of 1980s teen. fashions. (cf: roach-killers).

winks n. (US campus use) sleep; fr. *forty winks* = a nap *Underwood*.

wino n. an alcoholic, usu. living in poverty; fr. the cheap wine that he/she drinks *Gothic Blimp Works No.4*.

wipe v. (Aus. use) to forget, to dismiss from one's mind *Wilkes*.

wipe out n. 1. a failure; 2. (ski/surf use) a spectacular fall from skis or surfboard.

wipe out v. to beat up *Larner*.

wiped out a. exhausted *Price:1*.

wire n. the pickpocket who actively steals from his victim, rather than the various accomplices on his team (cf: hook) *Chandler: Notebk*.

wire up v. (US Black use) to explain the current situation, to tell what has been/is happening; fr. electrical use *Klein*.

wired 1. spec. using some form of amphetamines; 2. tense, nervous, irritable; full of 'electricity' *Higgins:2*.

wired for sound a. (drug use) experiencing the most extreme effects of cocaine or amphetamine (cf: wired).

wired up a. see: wired *Wilkinson*.

wise a. 1. stupid, foolish; in ironic use (cf: wise guy) *Thompson*; 2. homosexually experienced *Legman*.

wise guy n. anyone who thinks they are particularly knowing or clever; thus a person too clever for their own good *Price:2*.

wise guys n. the Mafia; both positive and negative meanings of the phrase *Higgins:2*.

wise up v. to act sensibly, to cease from being stupid *Ice T:2*.

wise-ass a. see: *smart ass* (qv) *Motor City Comics*.

wisenheimer n. a know-it-all, a self-appointed smart fellow.

wish (up)on v. to foist something – an article, a task, etc. – on someone who in no way had requested the burden.

with it a. sophisticated, chic, aware of current fashions, styles, language, etc., fr. 1960s 'Swinging London' era.

with knobs on! the same to you, and more so! usu. children's use.

with the program a. phr. in tune with the prevailing situation in a positive manner. (fr. Alcoholics Anonymous/ Narcotics Anonymous and other groups that offer their variously habituated members a 12 point program of self-help).

wizard a. (UK 'society' use) excellent, wonderful; general term of approval used only by prep school boys when both young and adult *Barr*.

wodge n. thick, chunky, dense lump.

wog n. 1. (derog.) any non-white, esp. Indian or Pakistani, and latterly, in UK, Bangladeshi; [ety. unknown; suggestions include that of F. C. Bowen in *Sea Slang* (1929) who includes 'Wogs, lower class Babu shipping clerks on the Indian coast', but provides no detail; popular belief has always chosen the acronym WOG: 'westernized oriental gentleman' or 'wily oriental gentleman', while EP opts for what he sees as the simplest and most obvious root: an abbreviation of SE golliwog. Certainly this once-popular doll, with its caricatured 'black' features, has long since been

marginalised as politically incorrect);
2. (Aus., N.Z.) illness, esp. influenza.

wog-box n. a large, portable stereo
tape-recorder-cum-radio, particularly
beloved of ghetto youths (cf:
ghettoblaster, Third World briefcase)
Cole.

Woler n. (UK 'society' use) Rolls
Royce motor car (cf: Roller) *Barr*.

wolf n. **1.** predatory male pursuing
women for sex; **2.** (homosexual use)
the active partner in anal intercourse
Legman.

wolfing it v. (US Black use) to talk big
but fail to back up such boasts with
actual performance *Klein*.

wolf-pussy n. (US Black use)
unpleasant vaginal odours *Klein*.

wollied a. drunk.

wolly n. **1.** a uniformed (junior)
policeman; criminal and detective
branch use *Newman:1*; **2.** a fool, a
stupid, boring person poss. fr. *wall-
eyed*: squinting, short-sighted *Obs. 13/
3/83*.

wollyhumper n. (rock music use) a
bouncer (qv) employed by a rock band
to make sure no fans manage to climb
on stage while they play or, if they
have climbed up, to throw them down
again; fr. wolly = tedious person
P. Marchbank.

womba n. see wonga.

womble n. a fool, a nerd (qv) (cf:
gonk, muppet).

womon n. woman, preferred sp. by
some radical gay women (cf: wimmin)
Jay & Young.

wonelly a. (Valley Girls (qv) use)
admirable, very good, etc; fr. *one hell
of a . . . Pond*.

wonga n. money *Cole*.

wonk n. (US campus use) anyone who
works harder than the rest of the
students see fit *Bernbach*.

wonk one's conker v. to masturbate
(cf: wank).

wonky a. unsteady, unstable, out of
kilter.

wood n. (US Black use) (derog.) a
White person (cf: peckerwood).

wooden v. (Aus. use) to knock down,

knock out; fr. the use of a blunt
instrument (?) *Wilkes*.

wooden kimono n. see: wooden
overcoat *Rawson*.

wooden nickel n. (orig. US)
something worthless.

wooden overcoat n. a coffin, often
used in fictional versions of organized
crime *Rawson*.

wooden spoon n. (UK sports use) a
metaphorical prize for the competitor
or team who comes last in a sporting
contest (cf: leather medal) *ST 6/3/83*.

woodener n. (UK prison use (rare)) a
one-month sentence; fr. the wooden
spoon once issued and rhyming sl.
wooden spoon = moon = month =
short sentence *LL*.

woodentop n a uniformed policeman.

woodie n. (surfer use) a wood-
panelled station wagon, beloved of
surfers in US and Australia
Beach Boys, passim.

woof v. **1.** (US Black use) to speak
continually and forcefully, often
requiring no replies, only an audience;
fr. canine barking (cf: yap) *Klein*;
2. (US Campus use) to vomit; fr.
'barking' noise that accompanies
intense vomiting *Bernbach*.

woofer n. a joint (qv) Beastie Boys.

wool n. **1.** spec. female pubic hair,
thus; **2.** a girl or woman *Jenkins*.

Woolies n. nickname for Woolworth
department stores (cf:M&S).

Wooloomooloo Yank (Aus. use) a
relatively unsophisticated person who
attempts to ape the supposedly hip
style of an American.

wooly-back n. an unsophisticated,
country person; who thus resembles
his sheep *Bleasdale*.

Woop Woop n. (Aus. use) an
imaginary place which is a byword for
backwardness and remoteness; its
inhabitants are *woops* Wilkes.

woozy a. **1.** vague *J. Tucker, 'The
Novels of A. Powell', 1976*; **2.** under
the influence of drugs or drink, poss.
of a blow on the head.

wop n. Italian (derog.); fr. Sp.
guapo:a dandy, which was taken up in

Sicily during an occupation and thus taken to US by 19th C. immigrants *Price: 2*.

Wop Town n. (US use) an Italian community within an an urban area.

word! (US teen. use) excl. of approval, admiration, agreement, etc. fr. my word! *E. Beyer*.

word freak n. (pimp use) a client who wishes the prostitute to speak in obscenities for his sexual gratification *OUI 8/75*.

word up! see: word!

work n. (US cant/police use) the written records held by illegal bookmakers *Neaman & Silver*.

work a crowd v. to ply one's trade to an audience – begging, preaching, etc.

work a ginger v. (Aus. use) for a prostitute and her accomplice to rob her customer (cf: murphy game) *Baker*.

work both sides of the street v. to work exceptionally hard.

work one's ass off v. to work extremely hard.

work one's butt off v. see: work one's ass off *Higgins: 5*.

work one's ticket v. to malinger, to escape onerous duties by shamming illness or similar unsuitability; fr. Br. Army use, obtaining a discharge through faking illness.

work out v. to exercise *Higgins: 1*.

work over v. to beat up (qv); to hurt to any extent short of murder *Higgins: 1*.

work the hole v. (US cant) to rob drunks who have passed out in the subway *Burroughs: 1*.

work the room v. to chatter to people at a party or meeting; fr. show business use in which a entertainer will move through the audience at a nightclub, chatting to people and using them in his/her act *D. McLintick, 'Indecent Exposure', 1983*.

work the well v. (US cant) for a pickpocket to use the crush getting on and off buses for stealing from travellers *Neaman & Silver*.

working from a book (Black pimp use) a pimp who conducts his business through his book of addresses and telephone numbers for his girls' clients; this method of work cuts down on many of the problems – esp. the police – that are met in street prostitution *Milner*.

working girl n. 1. a prostitute *Farren: passim*; 2. (gay use) a male prostitute (cf: rent boy).

working stiff n. an average, unexceptional working man *Whitcomb*.

working the cuts phr. (sex industry use) of a prostitute who works on the street rather than out of a brothel.

workoholic n. anyone who is obsessed by working and thus very rarely stops (cf: -oholic).

works n. the equipment used by a heroin addict for injecting him/herself (cf: outfit) *Grogan*.

worky n. an employed person *Welsh: 1*.

World n. (US milit. use) in Vietnam, the USA *Del Vecchio*.

worm farm n. an eccentric, one whose mind is 'full of worms' *McFadden*.

worse things happen at sea (cp) somewhat empty words of consolation when nothing deeper seems available to the speaker.

wotcher Cockney greeting, fr. 'what cheer', which dates back at least to 16th C.

would I shit you . . . you're my favourite turd (US cp) in answer to the previous speaker's 'Don't (bull)shit me . . .' *Price: 1*.

wouldn't tell one the time of day (cp) said by one who ignores a given person completely, spurning any and all advances *McFadden*.

wouldn't touch it with a ten foot barge pole see: don't fancy yours!

wouldn't touch it with yours (cp) popular phrase betw. two men observing a woman when the speaker finds her unattractive; 'yours' is the penis.

wow v. to delight, to enthrall, to please very much; esp. show business use. fr. excl. of approval and acclaim.

wowser n. (Aus. NZ use) a puritan, a self-appointed censor, a 'Mrs Grundy' (or Mrs Whitehouse).

WPLJ (abbrev.) White Port and Lemon Juice.

wrap n. end, conclusion; fr. film use: a wrap: the end of a day's shooting *Jenkins*.

wrap up v. to stop talking, esp. as a command: *wrap up!*

wrapped (Aus. use) see rapt *Wilkes*.

wrapped tight (US teen. use) feeling fine, happy *Safire*.

wrapping n. (US teen. use) clothes, esp. female *Sculatti*.

wreck v. (homosexual use) 1. to degrade a fellow homosexual when he is not expecting it; 2. see: ruin *Stanley*.

wrecked a. 1. heavily affected by a given drug; 2. very drunk *Bernbach*.

wrinklies n. the old; mainly UK upper/upper-middle class youth use (cf: crumblies, dusties) *ES 11/5/83*.

write off n. anything that is

completely destroyed, beyond all hope of repair and thus, in orig, service use, must be written off the inventory.

write scrip(t) v. to give out prescriptions for narcotics *Grogan*.

writer n. a graffitti artist.

writer n. see: writing doctor.

writing doctor n. (drug use) a doctor who will write prescriptions for narcotics and ask no questions about the user (cf: write scrip(t), hungry croaker) *Stone*.

wrong guy n. an incompetent, an untrustworthy person; spec. an informer *Higgins: 1*.

wrong side of the tracks the poor, undesirable area of a town; fr. the building of many US towns athwart the railway tracks.

wrong 'un n. 1. (cricket use) a googly; 2. an untrustworthy, incompetent person.

W/S abbr. (contact ads use) urolagnia; fr. abbr. water sports (qv) *SMD*.

X

x n. a ten dollar bill, ten dollars.

X ray n. (film use) a still photo *Chandler: Notebk*.

xed out (US Black use) tricked, fooled *Klein*.

XTC n. (drug use) see: ecstasy.

Y

Y n. (abbrev.) Young Men's Christian Association (YMCA).

yacoo n. (US Black use) 1. a white person; 2. a racist; both fr. *Yacub*: the devil-figure white man in Black Muslim mythology *Folb*.

yak v. to talk, usu. garrulously; like a raucous bird *Price:1*.

yakka n. (Aus. use) work; fr. Aborigine *Humphries*.

yakkety-yak n. meaningless, if enthusiastic and earnest, chatter *Sanders:2*.

yang n. the penis.

yank v. to drag, to pull *Selby:1*.

yank one's chain v. to irritate, to annoy, to remind forcibly or distract (cf: jerk one's chain).

yank one's crank n. to masturbate.

Yankee n. (gay use) masturbation;

from yank off meaning 'to masturbate'.

Yankee v. to cheat, to drive a hard bargain.

Yankee dime n. a kiss (cf: dutch kiss) (used in US South where Yankee is generic for thief, such a kiss has therefore been 'stolen').

Yankee's yawn n. (gay use) the open mouth of a climaxing male.

yanta n. (derog.) a Black person.

yap n. the mouth; usu. in derog. sense: 'shut your yap!' etc. *Price:2*.

yap v. to talk, esp. to shout at, like a dog *Higgins:1*.

yard n. one hundred, usu. money *Morgan*.

yard Negro n. see: house nigger *X*.

yard on v. (US Black use) to be unfaithful sexually.

yardbird n. 1. (US milit. use) a recruit, a rookie (qv) *Uris*; 2. civilian dock workers in US naval dockyards *Pynchon*; 3. (US Black use) anyone confined to a restricted area – home, a prison, etc. – by the authority of an unassailable superior *Klein*.

yardie n. a member of a gang of organized Jamaican criminals who specialize in purveying drugs and violence on an international level; from 'yard', Jamaican for 'home'.

yarra a. (Aus. use) insane; fr. mental hospital at Yarra Bend, Victoria *Wilkes*.

yawp v. to talk loudly, foolishly; to nag (cf: yap) *Algren*.

ye gods! mild. oath; abbrev. ye gods and little fishes! *Wodehouse:AAG*.

yea a. use. as *yea big, yea high*: this big, this high.

year dot n. a very long time ago; usu. *from the year dot*: for ever.

yeasting (US Black use) exaggerating, boasting; fr. the way in which yeast makes otherwise flat dough rise up *Major*.

yegg n. (US criminal use) a thief, spec. a safecracker; poss. from John Yegg, a well-known practitioner *Morgan*.

yell n. 1. a good time; 2. a vomit (cf:

throw the voice).

yellib n. (butchers' backsl.) belly; both human and as a cut of meat *Cole*.

yellow a. cowardly *Selby:1*; in this defintion yellow has a number of synonyms: yellowback, yellow-belly, yellow-guts, yellow-heel.

yellow ass n. a light-coloured Black girl *Jones*.

yellow girl n. a Mulatto *Himes:1*.

yellow peril n. (derog.) any oriental person, the Communist Chinese *BvdB*.

yellow sheet n. (US police use) a criminal's record of arrests (cf: rap sheet, form) *Neaman & Silver*.

yellow-bellied a. cowardly *Gruber*.

yellowjackets n. barbiturates; fr. colour of pills *Higgins:1*.

yellows n. pills, usu. tranquillizers *Dury*.

yenep n. (butchers' backsl.) penny *Cole*.

yennom n. (butchers' backsl.) money *Cole*.

yenshee baby n. hard impacted faeces produced (often painfully) by a heroin addict during a period of withdrawal; one of the effects of addiction is long-term constipation; the term comes from the opium addicts' 'yenshee', a Chinese word meaning the residue left in a pipe after the opium has been smoked *Morgan*.

yenta n. a nagging, whining person, usu. of a woman; fr. the character Yenta Telebende, created at the Lennox Theatre in Harlem, 1920s, and Yiddish: 'shrew, gossip (cf: kvetch) *Neaman & Silver*.

yes-man n. an obsequious, subservient person, esp. in business, who always says 'yes' to his superiors, in the belief that is what they like to hear.

yid a Jew; both derog. and general use, depending on context *Big Ass Comics 1*.

Yiddish highway n. US30 – the route from New York City to Miami.

Yiddish Renaissance n. over-elaborate furniture in doubtful taste (cf: Jewy Louis).

Yiddle n. a Jew (cf: yid) *Schulberg*.

Yidney n. (UK 'society' use (derog)) Sidney, Australia; fr. Jewish population of the city (cf: Jew York).

yikes n. 1. worries, nervousness; 2. excl. of surprise, shock *Higgins:1*.

yinyang n. the anus.

yob n. 1. (backsl.) boy, no spec. pejorative connotations *Cole*; 2. an uncouth, vulgar youth, prob. fr. backsl. boy *Powis*.

yobbo n. extension of yob (qv) and as such poss. even more pejorative.

yodel v. aka: *yodel in the canyon of love*: to perform cunnilingus *Legman*.

yodel in the canyon v. aka: *dive/grin/ sneeze. . .*: perform cunnilingus *Folb*.

yodel up the valley v. to perform cunnilingus *Humphries*.

yok n. 1. (theatrical use) a belly laugh *Rosten*; 2. (Jewish use) a Gentile (cf: goy).

yom n. black street kid, from common excl. 'Yo' mother!' *R Price Clockers 1992* (cf: yo-yo).

yomo n. (derog.) a Black youth.

yonks n. a long time, often found as 'for yonks'; the word originated among the upper-middle classes, but has gradually permeated through society.

yoof a. an all-purpose adjective to describe a variety of television programmes – high on pop gossip and fashion, low (in critical eyes) on intelligence – that are aimed at the young. Yoof, meaning 'youth', is a deliberate mimickry of the 'street-cred' London accents of presenters of such programmes. *Green:3*.

yoo-hoo boy n. an effeminate homosexual; allegedly given to shouting 'yoo-hoo!' at all and sundry *Legman*.

you ain't just whistling 'Dixie' (US cp) you really mean what you're saying, you're not just being flippant.

you and me (bingo rhyming sl.) 3 *Wright*.

you and me n. (rhyming sl.) tea *Powis*.

you and who's army? (children's (usu.) cp) addressed to anyone who is threatening violence *Manser*.

you bet! excl. of absolute aggrement, confidence.

you can say that again! (cp) underlining the speaker's agreement with the previous statement.

you can't take it with you (cp) urging someone to spend their money, enjoy their possessions, etc.; the un-named journey is beyond the grave.

you can't win 'em all (cp) self-explanatory; offering some slight comfort.

you could have knocked me down with a feather (cp) indicating maximum surprise and shock.

you don't know the half of it! (cp) self-explanatory, with the assumption that the speaker *does G. Vidal, 'Myron', 1974.*

you don't look at the mantelpiece when you're poking the fire (cp) a woman's looks are irrelevant if she's sexually available.

you got it! (excl.) general affirmative reply, usu. to a yes/no question and often Black use *Underwood*.

you know the great interjection of the illiterate; it means nothing more than its parallel: *er*.

you know it is! (US Black/teen. use) yes indeed, you're right, etc.; any form of emphatic agreement *Malcolm McLaren, LP, 1983.*

you know what n. sexual intercourse *Rawson*.

you know where n. (euph.) depending on context: if sexual: the vagina or penis; if hostile, the anus.

you pays your money and you takes your choice (cp) self-explanatory.

you reckon? semi-rhetorical response: is what what you really believe?

you scratch my back and I'll scratch yours (cp) promising mutual aid in a given situation; 'one good turn deserves another'.

you wouldn't read about it! (cp) describing anything amazing, unbelievable, and proving that nature is infinitely more bizarre than mere art.

you wrote the book! (cp) used when
offering what is appreciated as
gratuitous advice to one whose ideas
are the same as, if not an improved
version of, one's own *Humphries:2*.

you'll be a long time dead (cp)
addressed to anyone the speaker feels
is wasting time, not putting his life to
its best advantage, etc.

you'll be sorry! semi-jocular cry of
warning fr. those who have
experienced a situation to those who
are about to encounter it; orig. use
amongst Second World War troops.

young blood n. (US Black use) the up
and coming youth who are learning
the mores of the street life *Folb*.

young blood n. junior members of an
organization, firm, team, etc.,
recruited in the hope of their
providing a degree of vital
rejuvenation.

young fogey n. a young(ish) middle-
class man of the 1980s who posed in
dress, attitude and mannerisms as his
middle-aged predecessor of the 1950s.
Evelyn Waugh at his crustiest is
supposedly the supreme avatar, the
author A. N. Wilson its most perfect
embodiment.

young in the head (US Black use)
childish, immature *Folb*.

young kipper n. an inadequate meal;
the term puns on the Jewish festival of
'Yom Kippur', the Day of Atonement,
at which time it is customary to spend
the day fasting.

your business is open phr. (US use)
your fly is open, a statement which
elicits the reply: 'Is my salesman in or
out?'.

your guess is as good as mine (cp)
don't ask me, I don't know either.

your mother n. (homosexual use)
oneself, thus 'your mother needs a
drink', etc. *Maledicta*.

your mother! (US teen. use) rejoinder
to an insult, implying that whatever
that insult is, it applies most to the
speaker's own mother (cf: dozens).

your (yer) actual an emphatic
intensifier of a person or object: 'your
actual Rolls Royce', etc.; supposedly
coined by Peter Cook for sketches in
BBC-TV's 'Not Only . . . But Also',
1960s.

you're darn tootin' you're absolutely
right *Whitcomb*.

you're singing my song! you and I
agree in every way; you're my kind of
person *Thompson:J*.

yours truly jocular reference by a
speaker to him/herself *Wolfe:5*.

youthquake n. the upsurge of
(radical) youth in 1960s, early 1970s;
not only potentially revolutionary, this
essentially disaffected young
bourgeoisie also offered a huge
purchasing base to those who wished
to exploit it *Hoffman:a*.

you've got a nerve! (cp) how dare
you!

yo-yo n. a fool, an unpredictable
person whose moods and actions go up
and down *Price:2*.

yo-yo, yo-yo boy n. black US street
kid (fr. excl./greeting. Yo!) *Shell*.

yuck! all-purpose juv. excl. of distaste.

yucky a. unpleasant, disgusting; with
overtones of stickiness or smelliness;
usu. juv. use.

Yug n. (abbrev.) Yugoslav.

yuks n. see: yoks *Bruce:2*.

yummy a. tasty, delicious,
flavoursome *Vidal*.

yummy n. attractive teenage girl,
'good enough to eat' *Farren*.

yum-yums n. (drug use) any drugs in
pill or capsule form *Folb*.

yuppie n. (US use) young, upwardly
mobile professional (cf: preppie)
ST 29/4/84.

yuppie puppie n. a child born to a
member of the yuppie (qv)
generation, seen as something of a
fashion accessory in the early 1990s.
Ind. on Sun. 5/1/92.

yutz n. penis; fr. Yiddish *Price:3*.

Z

Z v. (US teen. use) to sleep; fr. the noise of one's breathing; sleep is often indicated in cartoons by 'Z-z-z-z-' issuing fr. sleeper's mouth *Pond*.

za n. (US campus use) (abbrev.) pizza *Bernbach*.

zaftig a. fr. Yiddish: juicy: a plump. buxom woman *Rosten*.

zap n. energy, enthusiasm *Bukowski:1*.

zap v. 1. to shock, to alarm *Jay & Young*; 2. to kill, esp. milit. use *A.F.N. Clarke, 'Contact', 1983*; 3. to engage in sexual relations.

zazzle n. (US Black use) sexual desire or sensuality *Major*.

Z-bird n. (US teen. use) a failure, a loser; fr. position of Z at end of alphabet *Sculatti*.

Z'd out (US teen. use) unable to wake up properly, still sleepy (cf: Z) *Pond*.

zeek out v. (Valley Girls (qv) use) to act outrageously, to lose control, esp. through drugs/drink *Pond*.

zero n. a nobody, a totally useless and insignificant person *R. Crumb, 'Shuman the Human', c.1967*.

zero in v. to concentrate on, to focus on *Wolfe:2*.

zero minus (US campus use) utterly, completely impossible, unacceptable; less than nothing *Underwood*.

zero out v. to run out of cash.

zilch zero, nothing *Underwood*.

zillion n. an undefined, but enormous sum (cf: squillion).

zimmer n. (US teen use) a girl *T 8/4/91*.

zing n. energy, enthusiasm *Runyon*.

zinger n. a witty line, a one-line joke or repartee *Goldman*.

zip zero, nothing.

zip n. 1. a speedy, energetic, mobile person *Price:1*; 2. speed, enthusiasm, fervour, energy; 3. a home made firearm capable of firing single bullets. (fr. SE zip: the noise of a fired bullet. One takes a short length of pipe, 4–10 ins. long with an inside diameter that of a bullet. A bullet is placed at one end and detonated by a sharp tap from a pointed steel rod which in turn is hit by the heel of one's hand or by a small object).

zip v. 1. to run around energetically, to be highly energetic *Price:3*; 2. to kill (cf: zap) *Morgan*.

zip it up! be quiet, shut up! (cf: zip one's lip) *Klein*.

zip one's lip v. to stop talking *Klein*.

zipalid n. a complete moron; fr. *zipperlid*: one whose head has been 'unzipped' and the brain removed *E. Barker*.

zip-five (US prison use) a maximum of five years sentence *Larner*.

zip-gun n. homemade gun, favoured by US street gangs.

zippered adv. drunk *Shell*.

zipperhead see: zipalid *Morgan*.

zippy a. fast, speedy.

zits n. acne spots *Junker*.

zizz n. a nap, a snooze, a brief sleep (cf: Z) *Dickson*.

zod n. (Valley Girls (qv) use) an eccentric, a strange person; fr. 'he's odd' *Pond*.

zoid n. a school child who has been rejected by its fellows, (cf: goggy, gunk, spod, Wendy) *Maledicta 9*.

zol n. (S. Afr. use) a dagga (cannabis) joint (qv) (cf: aap).

zombie n. 1. (US Black use) a very African looking person short of stature, with a dark complexion and broad features *Klein*; 2. (UK prison use) any prison officer who looks permanently miserable and humourless *LL*.

zone out v. to lose consciousness or concentration.

zoned a. (US preppie (qv) use) utterly exhausted, burned out; in the twilight zone (?) *Bernbach*.

zonked a. see: stoned *Wolfe:2*.

zonker n. anyone who takes drugs to

excess *Wolfe:2*.

zonko n. (US campus use) boring, dull person and thus socially unacceptable *Underwood*.

zoom off v. to exit at speed, to leave quickly.

zoom one out v. to amaze, to fascinate, to surprise (cf: blow one's mind).

zoon out v. (Valley Girls (qv) use) see: *zeek out Pond*.

zot (US campus use) zero (in an examination) *AS 50 (1965)*.

zotz v. to kill, to murder; fr. Yid. *zetz*:

a strong blow or a punch *Morgan*.

zowie n. keenness, enthusiasm, energy.

Zs n. sleep; (pron. with US Z = zee, not zed) *O'Brien*.

zubber n. (film use) a man dressed in top hat, white tie, tails, spats and a cane *Chandler: Notebk*.

zulu n. (derog.) a Black person.

Zulu princess n. (gay use) a young, handsome black man.

zuuzuus and whamwhams n. (US prison use) confectionery sold to the prisoners *Morgan*.

Bibliography

NB: All editions cited were published in London unless otherwise specified.

Adams   Ramon F. Adams, *Western Words*, 2nd revised edn, U. of Oklahoma
Press, Norman, Okla., 1968.
Algren   Nelson Algren, *The Man with the Golden Arm*, Doubleday, NY, 1949.
Algren:2   Nelson Algren, *A Walk on the Wild Side*, Corgi Books, 1964.
Alvarez   A. Alvarez, *The Biggest Game in Town*, André Deutsch, 1983.
AS   *American Speech* magazine, U. of Alabama Press, 1925–.
Austin   Max Austin, *Out*, Arthur Barker, 1978.
Baker   Sidney J. Baker, *The Australian Language*, 2nd edn, Currawong
Publishing, Sydney, 1966.
Baker:2   Mark Baker, *Nam*, Sphere Books, 1982.
Barr   Ann Barr & Peter York, *The Official Sloane Ranger Handbook*, Ebury
Press, 1982.
Bernbach   Lisa Bernbach, *The Official Preppy Handbook*, Eyre Methuen, 1981.
Bickerton   Anthea Bickerton, *Australian/English, English/Australian*, Abson
Books, Bristol, 1976.
Big Ass Comics   *Big Ass Comics 1*, Rip Off Press, San Francisco, 1969.
Blacker   Terence Blacker, *Fixx*, Bloomsbury 1989.
Bleasdale   Alan Bleasdale, *Boys from the Blackstuff: Five Plays for Television*,
Granada Publishing, 1983.
Breslin   Jimmy Breslin, *The World of Jimmy Breslin*, Hutchinson, 1968.
Bruce:1   Lenny Bruce, *How to Talk Dirty and Influence People*, Peter Owen,
1966.
Bruce:2   *The Essential Lenny Bruce*, ed. John Cohen, Ballantine Books, NY,
1967.
Bukowski:1   Charles Bukowski, *Erections, Ejaculations, Exhibitions and General
Tales of Ordinary Madness*, City Lights Books, San Francisco, 1972.
Bukowski:2   Charles Bukowski, *Notes of a Dirty Old Man*, City Lights Books, San
Francisco, 1973.
Bukowski:3   Charles Bukowski, *Post Office*, Black Sparrow Press, Santa Barbara,
1971.
Bukowski:4   Charles Bukowski, *Factotum*, Black Sparrow Press, Santa Barbara,
1975.
Bukowski:5   Charles Bukowski, *Women*, Black Sparrow Press, Santa Barbara,
1978.
Bukowski:6   Charles Bukowski, *South of No North*, Black Sparrow Press, Santa
Barbara, 1973.
Bukowski:7   Charles Bukowski, *Ham on Rye*, Black Sparrow Press, Santa
Barbara, 1982.
Burroughs:1   William Burroughs ('William Lee'), *Junkie*, Ace Books, NY, 1953.
Burroughs: Jr.   William Burroughs Jr, *Kentucky Ham*, Pan Books, 1975.
BvdB   Lester V. Berrey & Melvin Van Den Bark, *The American Thesaurus of*

Slang, 2nd edn, George G. Harrap, 1954.

Byrne Josefa Heifetz Byrne, *Mrs Byrne's Dictionary of Unusual, Obscure & Preposterous Words*, Granada Publishing, 1979.

Caron Roger Caron, *Go-Boy!*, Hamlyn Paperbacks, 1979.

Carson Tom Carson, *Twisted Kicks*, Arrow Books, 1983.

Caserta Peggy Caserta, *Going Down With Janis*, Futura, 1975.

Cassidy F. Cassidy (ed.), *Dictionary of American Regional English*, vol. I, Belknap/Harvard, 1985.

Cassidy F. Cassidy and J. Hall (eds.), *Dictionary of American Regional English*, vol. II, Belknap/Harvard, 1991.

CB *The Complete CB Slang Dictionary*, Merit Publications, N. Miami, 1980.

Chandler:FML Raymond Chandler, *Farewell, My Lovely*, Hamish Hamilton, 1940.

Chandler:LG Raymond Chandler, *The Long Good-bye*, Hamish Hamilton, 1953.

Chandler: Notebk *The Notebooks of Raymond Chandler*, ed. Frank MacShane, Weidenfeld & Nicolson, 1977.

Cole Nicholas Cole, private lists 1982/1983.

De Lannoy & Masterson William C. De Lannoy & Elizabeth Masterson, 'Teen-age Hophead Jargon', American Speech xxvii:1, 1954.

Del Vecchio John M. Del Vecchio, *The Thirteenth Valley*, Sphere Books, 1983.

Dennis C. J. Dennis, *The Sentimental Bloke*, Angus & Robertson, Sydney, 1957.

Dickson Paul Dickson, *Words*, Arena Books, 1983.

dl *Dreams of Love*, comics, IW Enterprises, NY, n.d.

Dre Dr Dre, *The Chronic*, 1993.

Dunne John Gregory Dunne, *True Confessions*, Circus Books, 1979.

Dury Ian Dury, *The Ian Dury Songbook*, Blackhill Music, 1979.

Ellroy:1 James Ellroy, *The Big Nowhere*, Mysterious Press, 1989.

Ellroy:2 James Ellroy, *LA Confidential*, Mysterious Press, 1990.

Farina Richard Farina, *Been Down So Long It Seems Like Up To Me*, NEL, 1968.

Farrell James T. Farrell, *Studs Lonigan*, Constable, 1936.

Farren Mick Farren, *The Tale of Willy's Rats*, Granada Publishing, 1974.

Fiction Illus. *Fiction Illustrated*, vols. 1 & 3, Pyramid Publications, NY, 1976.

Folb Edith A. Folb, *Runnin' Down Some Lines*, Harvard University Press, 1980.

Franklyn Julian Franklyn, *A Dictionary of Rhyming Slang*, 2nd edn, Routledge & Kegan Paul, 1981.

Goldman Albert Goldman (from the journalism of Lawrence Schiller), *Ladies and Gentlemen, Lenny Bruce!*, W. H. Allen, 1975.

Goulart Ron Goulart, *The Hard-Boiled Dicks*, T. V. Boardman, 1967.

Greaser *Greaser Comics*, Rip Off Press, San Francisco, 1972.

Green:1 Jonathon Green, *The Book of Drugs*, unpub. ms., 1974.

Green:2 Jonathon Green, *Newspeak: A Dictionary of Jargon*, Routledge & Kegan Paul, 1983.

Green:3 Jonathon Green, *Neologisms*, Bloomsbury, 1991.

Greenlee Sam Greenlee, *The Spook Who Sat by the Door*, Allison & Busby, 1969.

Griffiths Leon Griffiths, The Bengal Tiger, TV script, Euston Films, 1979.

Grogan Emmett Grogan, *Ringolevio*, Little, Brown, Boston, 1972.

Gruber Frank Gruber, *The Last Doorbell*, Sydney Pemberton, Manchester, 1951.

Heller Peter Heller, *In This Corner*, Dell Publishing, NY, 1973.

Hiaasen Carl Hiaasen, *Native Tongue*, Knopf, NY, 1991.

Higgins:1 George V. Higgins, *Cogan's Trade*, Secker & Warburg, 1981.

Higgins:2 George V. Higgins, *The Friends of Eddie Coyle*, Secker & Warburg, 1972.
Higgins:3 George V. Higgins, *The Digger's Game*, Secker & Warburg/Ballantine Books, NY, 1973.
Higgins:4 George V. Higgins, *The Rat on Fire*, Secker & Warburg, 1981.
Higgins:5 George V. Higgins, *A City on a Hill*, Secker & Warburg, 1975.
Higgins:6 George V. Higgins, *Requiem for Jerry Kennedy*, 1985.
Himes:1 Chester Himes, *Cotton Comes to Harlem*, Frederick Muller, 1966.
Himes:2 Chester Himes, *The Big Gold Dream*, Panther Books, 1968.
Hoffman Alice Hoffman, *Property Of*, Hutchinson, 1978.
Hoffman:a Abbie Hoffman, *Woodstock Nation*, Vintage Books, NY, 1969.
Hotten John Camden Hotten, *A Dictionary of Modern Slang, Cant, and Vulgar Words ... by a London Antiquary*, 2nd edn, Hotten, 1860.
Howard Kent Howard, *Small Time Crooks*, Cooperbooks, n.d.
Humphries Barry Humphries, *Barry McKenzie*, strip cartoon, *Private Eye* passim.
Humphries:2 Barry Humphries, *A Nice Night's Entertainment: Sketches & Monologues 1956–1981*, Granada Publishing, 1981.
Ice T:1 *Rhyme Pays*, Sire Records, 1987.
Ice T:2 *Power*, Sire Records, 1988.
Ice T:3 *OG: Original Gangster*, Sire Records, 1991.
Jay & Young Karla Jay & Allen Young (eds.), *The Gay Report*, Summit Books, NY, 1979.
Jenkins Dan Jenkins, *Semi-Tough*, Star Books, 1978.
Jones LeRoi Jones (Imamu Amiri Baraka), *Tales*, McGibbon & Kee, 1969.
Jones:J Jack Jones, *Rhyming Cockney Slang*, Abson Books, Bristol, 1971.
Junker Howard Junker, *The Fifties*, *Esquire* magazine, 1969.
Keyes Thom Keyes, *All Night Stand*, W. H. Allen, 1966.
Kidder Tracy Kidder, *The Soul of a New Machine*, Allen Lane, 1982.
King Stephen King, *The Raft*, *Twilite Zone* magazine, June, 1983.
Klein Ronald Klein, PhD, *Jailhouse Jargon & Street Slang*, unpub. ms., 1983.
Lambert Eric Lambert, *Twenty Thousand Thieves*, Corgi Books, 1955.
Landy Eugene S. Landy, *The Underground Dictionary*, Simon & Schuster, NY, 1967.
Larner Jeremy Larner & Ralph Tefferteller, *The Addict in the Street*, Grove Press, NY, 1964.
Laugh in the Dark *Laugh in the Dark*, comics, Last Gasp Eco-Funnies, Berkeley, 1971.
Laurie Peter Laurie, *Scotland Yard*, The Bodley Head, 1970.
Lawson Henry Lawson, *Complete Prose Works*, Angus & Robertson, Sydney, 1948.
le Carré John le Carré, *The Little Drummer Girl*, Hodder & Stoughton, 1983.
Legman G. Legman, 'The Language of Homosexuality: A Glossary'; as Appendix VII in Henry, G. W. *Sex Variants: A Study of Homosexual Patterns*, NY, 1941.
LL Paul Tempest, *The Lag's Lexicon*, Routledge & Kegan Paul, 1950.
Maupin:1 Armistead Maupin, *Tales of the City*, Corgi, 1984.
Maupin:2 Armistead Maupin, *More Tales of the City*, Corgi, 1984.
Maupin:3 Armistead Maupin, *Further Tales of the City*, Corgi, 1984.
McBain Ed McBain, *Shotgun*, Hamish Hamilton, 1969.
McFadden Cyra McFadden, *The Serial: A Year in the Life of Marin County*, Picador, 1978.

MacInnes:1 Colin MacInnes, *Absolute Beginners*, MacGibbon & Kee, 1959.

MacInnes:2 Colin MacInnes, *City of Spades*, MacGibbon & Kee, 1957.

MacInnes:3 Colin MacInnes, *Mr Love & Justice*, MacGibbon & Kee, 1960.

Major Clarence Major, *Black Slang*, Routledge & Kegan Paul, 1971.

Maledicta *Maledicta: The International Journal of Verbal Aggression*, VI: 1–2, 1982.

Mandelkau Jamie Mandelkau, *Buttons: The Making of a President*, Open Gate, 1971.

Manser Martin H. Manser, *A Dictionary of Contemporary Idioms*, Pan Books, 1983.

Maurer David W. Maurer, *Language of the Underworld*, U. of Kentucky Press, Lexington, Ky, 1981.

May Jonathan May, *Confessions of a Gas-Man*, Sphere Books, 1977.

Michaels Leonard Michaels & Christopher Ricks (eds.), *The State of the Language*, U. of California Press, Berkeley/Los Angeles, 1980.

Milner Christine & Richard Milner, *Black Players: The World of Black Pimps*, Michael Joseph, 1972.

Morgan Seth Morgan, *Homeboy*, Chatto & Windus, 1990.

Moore Charles Moore, *CB Language in Great Britain*, Star Books, 1981.

Mortimer John Mortimer, *Rumpole & the Golden Thread*, Penguin Books, Harmondsworth, 1983.

Motor City *Motor City Comics*, Rip-Off Press, San Francisco, 1969.

Neaman & Silver Judith S. Neaman & Carole G. Silver, *A Dictionary of Euphemisms*, Hamish Hamilton, 1983.

Newman:1 G. F. Newman, *A Villain's Tale*, Sphere Books, 1977.

Newman:2 G. F. Newman, *A Detective's Tale*, Sphere Books, 1977.

Newman:3 G. F. Newman, *A Prisoner's Tale*, Sphere Books, 1977.

Newspapers: *The Times* (T), *Guardian* (G), *Daily Telegraph* (DT), *Financial Times* (FT), *Daily Mail* (DMa), *Daily Express* (DE), *Daily Mirror* (DM), *Sun* (Su), *Daily Star* (DS), *(Evening) Standard* (ES), *Sunday Times* (ST), *Observer* (Obs), *Mail on Sunday* (MoS), *Sunday Telegraph* (STe), *Sunday Express* (SE), *News of the World* (NoW), *Sunday Mirror* (SMi), *Sunday People* (SP).

Norman:1 Frank Norman, *Bang To Rights*, Secker & Warburg, 1958.

Norman:2 Frank Norman, *Stand On Me*, Secker & Warburg, 1960.

Norman:3 Frank Norman, *The Guntz*, Secker & Warburg, 1962.

Norman:4 Frank Norman, *Banana Boy*, Secker & Warburg, 1969.

O'Brien Tim O'Brien, *If I Die in a Combat Zone*, Calder & Boyars, 1973.

OED *The Oxford English Dictionary*, 12 vols. plus Supplement, Oxford University Press, 1933; Supplements A–G (1972), H–N (1976), O–Scz (1982), OUP.

Partridge:1 Eric Partridge, *Slang Yesterday and Today*, 4th edn, Routledge & Kegan Paul, 1970.

Partridge:2 Eric Partridge, *Dictionary of Slang & Unconventional English*, 2 vols, 7th edn, Routledge & Kegan Paul, 1970.

Partridge:3 Eric Partridge, *A Dictionary of the Underworld*, 3rd edn, Routledge & Kegan Paul, 1968.

Partridge:4 Eric Partridge, *A Dictionary of Catch Phrases*, Routledge & Kegan Paul, 1977.

Partridge:5 Eric Partridge *Dictionary of Slang and Unconventional English*, 8th edn.ed. Paul Beale, Routledge and Kegan Paul, 1984.

Payne Andrew Payne, *You Need Hands*, TV script, Euston Films, 1981.

Payne:2 Andrew Payne, *Dream House*, TV script, Euston Films, 1981.

Pearce Donn Pearce, *Cool Hand Luke*, Secker & Warburg, 1966.
People's Comic *The People's Comic*, Golden Gate Publishing, San Francisco, 1972.
Performance Film, directed Nicholas Roeg, produced Donald Cammell, 1970.
Pond Mimi Pond, *The Valley Girl's Guide to Life*, Dell Publishing, NY, 1982.
Poston Lawrence Poston III & Francis J. Stillman, 'Notes on Campus Vocabulary', *American Speech* magazine xlix, 1964.
Powis David Powis, *The Signs of Crime*, McGraw Hill (UK), 1977.
PT *The Presidential Transcripts: The Complete Transcripts of the Nixon Tapes*, Dell Publishing, NY, 1974.
Price:1 Richard Price, *The Wanderers*, Chatto & Windus, 1975.
Price:2 Richard Price. *Bloodbrothers*, Houghton, Mifflin, Boston, 1976.
Price:3 Richard Price, *The Breaks*, Simon & Schuster, NY, 1983.
Pynchon Thomas Pynchon, *V*, Jonathan Cape, 1963.
Rawson Hugh Rawson, *A Dictionary of Euphemisms and Other Doubletalk*, Macdonald, 1983.
Ready Susan Ready, private lists, 1983.
Rechy:1 John Rechy, *City of Night*, McGibbon & Kee, 1964.
Rechy:2 John Rechy, *The Sexual Outlaw*, W. H. Allen, 1978.
rr *Realistic Romances*, I. W. Enterprises, NY, n.d.
Robins:1 David Robins & Philip Cohen, *Knuckle Sandwich*, Penguin Books, Harmondsworth, 1978.
Robins:2 David Robins, *Personal Communication*.
Rodgers Bruce Rodgers, *The Queens' Vernacular*, Straight Arrow, San Francisco, 1972.
Rosten Leo Rosten, *Hooray for Yiddish!*, Elm Tree Books, 1983.
Runyon Damon Runyon, *Runyon On Broadway*, Constable, 1950.
Safire William Safire, *On Language*, Avon Books, NY, 1980.
Sanchez Thomas Sanchez, *Hollywoodland*, Magnum Books, 1981.
Sanders Ed Sanders, *The Family: The Story of Charles Manson's Dune Buggy Attack Battalion*, Avon Books, NY, 1972.
Sanders:2 Ed Sanders, *Tales of Beatnik Glory*, Stonehill Publishing, NY, 1975.
SF Comics *San Francisco Comic Book 2 & 3*, Rip Off Press, San Francisco, 1970.
Salisbury Harrison E. Salisbury, *The Shook-Up Generation*, Ace Books, NY, 1961.
Schulberg Budd Schulberg, *On The Waterfront*, The Bodley Head, 1956.
Schulberg:2 Budd Schulberg, *What Makes Sammy Run?*, The Bodley Head, 1941.
Sculatti Gene Sculatti, *Cool: A Hipster's Dictionary*, Vermilion, 1983.
Seale Bobby Seale, *Seize the Time*, Arrow Books, 1970.
Selby Hubert Selby, Jr, *Last Exit to Brooklyn*, Calder & Boyars, 1966.
Sharpe:1 Tom Sharpe, *Vintage Stuff*, Secker & Warburg, 1982.
Sharpe:2 Tom Sharpe, *Wilt*, Secker & Warburg, 1976.
Shell Ray Shell, *Iced*, Flamingo, 1993.
Shulman Alix Kates Shulman, *On The Stroll*, Virago Press, 1983.
Sillitoe Alan Sillitoe, *The Loneliness of the Long-Distance Runner*, W. H. Allen, 1959.
Simmons Donald C. Simmons, 'Some Special Terms Used in a U. of Connecticut Men's Dormitory', *American Speech* magazine xlix, 1969.
Skeat W. W. Skeat, *Etymological Dictionary of the English Language*, Oxford University Press, 1879–82.
SMD *The Sex Maniacs' Diary 1991*, ed. Tuppy Owens.

Southern Terry Southern, *Red Dirt Marijuana & Other Tastes*, Jonathan Cape, 1971.

Southern & Hoffenberg Terry Southern & Mason Hoffenberg, *Candy*, New English Library, 1968.

Stanley Julia P. Stanley, 'Homosexual Slang', *American Speech* magazine xlv, 1970.

Stone Robert Stone, *Dog Soldiers*, Secker & Warburg, 1975.

Teresa Vincent Teresa, 'A Mafioso Cases the Mafia Craze', in *The Crime Society*, ed. Francis Ianni & Elizabeth Rheuss-Ianni, NAL, NY, 1976.

Thelwell Michael Thelwell, *The Harder They Come*, Pluto Press, 1980.

Thompson Hunter S. Thompson, *Hells Angels*, Penguin, 1966.

Thompson:J Jim Thompson, *Four Novels*, Zomba Books, 1983.

Tidy Bill Tidy, *The Cloggies*, cartoon strip, *Private Eye* passim.

Tuff Shit *Tuff Shit Comics*, Print Mint, Berkeley, 1972.

TZ *Twilite Zone* magazine, Twilite Zone Publications, NY, 1980.

Underwood Gary Underwood, 'Razorback Slang', *American Speech* magazine li, 1976.

Uneeda *Uneeda Comix*, Print Mint, San Francisco, 1969.

Uris Leon Uris, *Battle Cry*, Alan Wingate, 1953.

Usborne Richard Usborne, *Wodehouse at Work to the End*, Barrie & Jenkins, 1977.

Vidal Gore Vidal, *Duluth*, Heinemann, 1983.

Vizinczey Stephen Vizinczey, *An Innocent Millionaire*, Hamish Hamilton, 1983.

Waits Tom Waits, *Small Change*, Warner Bros. Records, 1976.

Waterhouse Keith Waterhouse, *In the Mood*, Michael Joseph, 1983.

Webb James Webb, *Fields of Fire*, Granada Publishing, 1981.

Webster *Webster's Third New International Dictionary*, G & C Merriam, NY, 1966.

Welsh:1 Irvine Welsh, *Trainspotting*, Secker & Warburg, 1993.

Welsh:2 Irvine Welsh, *The Acid House*, Jonathan Cape, 1994.

Wentworth Harold Wentworth & Stuart Berg Flexner, *Dictionary of American Slang*, 2nd Supplemented edn, Thomas Crowell, NY, 1975.

Whitcomb Ian Whitcomb, *Rock Odyssey: A Musician's Chronicle of the Sixties*, Doubleday, NY, 1983.

White Edmund White, *States of Desire*, André Deutsch, 1980.

Wilkes G. A. Wilkes, *A Dictionary of Australian Colloquialisms*, Routledge & Kegan Paul, 1978.

Wilkinson Tony Wilkinson, *Down & Out*, Quartet Books, 1981.

Wodehouse:P P. G. Wodehouse, *The Pothunters*, A & C Black, 1902.

Wodehouse:MJ P. G. Wodehouse, *My Man Jeeves*, Newnes, 1919.

Wodehouse:IJ P. G. Wodehouse, *The Inimitable Jeeves*, Herbert Jenkins, 1923.

Wodehouse:COJ P. G. Wodehouse, *Carry On, Jeeves*, Herbert Jenkins, 1925.

Wodehouse:VGJ P. G. Wodehouse, *Very Good, Jeeves*, Herbert Jenkins, 1930.

Wodehouse:TJ P. G. Wodehouse, *Thank You, Jeeves*, Herbert Jenkins, 1934.

Wodehouse:RHJ P. G. Wodehouse, *Right Ho, Jeeves*, Herbert Jenkins, 1934.

Wodehouse:YMS P. G. Wodehouse, *Young Men in Spats*, Herbert Jenkins, 1936.

Wodehouse:CW P. G. Wodehouse, *The Code of the Woosters*, Herbert Jenkins, 1938.

Wodehouse:EBC P. G. Wodehouse, *Eggs, Beans & Crumpets*, Herbert Jenkins, 1940.

Wodehouse:JM P. G. Wodehouse, *Joy in the Morning*, Herbert Jenkins, 1947.

Wodehouse:MS P. G. Wodehouse, *The Mating Season*, Herbert Jenkins, 1949.

Wodehouse:JO   P. G. Wodehouse, *Jeeves in the Offing*, Herbert Jenkins, 1960.
Wodehouse:PF   P. G. Wodehouse, *Performing Flea*, Herbert Jenkins, 1961.
Wodehouse:PB   P. G. Wodehouse, *A Pelican at Blandings*, Herbert Jenkins, 1969.
Wodehouse:GB   P. G. Wodehouse, *The Girl in Blue*, Barrie & Jenkins, 1970.
Wodehouse:MOJ   P. G. Wodehouse, *Much Obliged, Jeeves*, Barrie & Jenkins, 1971.
Wodehouse:PGM   P. G. Wodehouse, *Pearls, Girls & Monty Bodkin*, Barrie & Jenkins, 1972.
Wodehouse:AAG   P. G. Wodehouse, *Aunts Aren't Gentlemen*, Barrie & Jenkins, 1974.
Wolfe:1   Tom Wolfe, *The Kandy-Kolored Tangerine Flake Streamline Baby*, Jonathan Cape, 1966.
Wolfe:2   Tom Wolfe, *The Electric Kool-Aid Acid Test*, Weidenfeld & Nicolson, 1969.
Wolfe:3   Tom Wolfe, *The Pump House Gang*, Weidenfeld & Nicolson, 1969.
Wolfe:4   Tom Wolfe, *Radical Chic & Mau-Mauing the Flak-Catchers*, Farrar, Straus & Giroux, NY, 1970.
Wolfe:5   Tom Wolfe, *Mauve Gloves & Madmen, Clutter & Vine*, Farrar, Straus & Giroux, NY, 1976.
Wolfe:6   Tom Wolfe, *The Right Stuff*, Farrar, Straus & Giroux, NY, 1979.
Wolfe:7   Tom Wolfe, *From Bauhaus to Our House*, Jonathan Cape, 1982.
Wolfe:8   Tom Wolfe, *In Our Time*, Pan Books, 1980.
Wright   Peter Wright, *Cockney Dialect & Slang*, Batsford, 1981.
X   *The Autobiography of Malcolm X*, with the assistance of Alex Haley, Hutchinson, 1966.

OTHER MACMILLAN SUBJECT DICTIONARIES

The Macmillan Dictionary of American Slang
Robert L. Chapman

'American slang at its rip-roaring, zany, zappy best.' So said Dr Robert
Birchfield, Editor of the *Oxford English Dictionary* – and with words such
as *zass up*, *zoid*, *schlubbo* and *schtoonk*, *rube*, *rug ape* and *tube steak*, who
could disagree?

ISBN: 0-333-63405-5

The Macmillan Book of Proverbs from Around the World
Norma Gleason

A delightful collection of 1500 proverbs from the far corners of the world,
arranged according to subject, from advice to wishful thinking. As the
Chinese say, 'You cannot open a book without learning something.'

ISBN: 0-333-63191-9

The Macmillan Dictionary of English Proverbs Explained
Ronald Ridout and Clifford Witting

This collection of hundreds of current English proverbs, with origins and
explanations, will prove invaluable to both teachers and students of
English, and also to crossword solvers and anyone interested in our
language. 'A useful reference book,' commented *The Times Literary
Supplement*.

ISBN: 0-333-63406-4

The Macmillan Dictionary of Current English Usage
Frederick T. Wood, R. H. Flavell & L. M. Flavell

This accessible A–Z guide to the intricacies of punctuation and idiom,
style, spelling and syntax, has, through its various editions, proved to be a
great friend to generations of students learning English, as well as to
native English speakers.

ISBN: 0-333-63410-1

The Macmillan Dictionary of English Colloquial Idioms
Frederick T. Wood & R. J. Hill
Another invaluable companion for learners of English as a foreign
language, with some 3000 headwords – from *ace* to *zombie* – arranged
alphabetically, and with numerous examples of usage.

ISBN: 0-333-63409-8

The Macmillan Dictionary of Synonyms and Antonyms
Lawrence Urdang

With its single A–Z listing of some 5000 words for which alternatives are
most often needed, this dictionary is quicker and easier to use than a
conventional thematic thesaurus. In addition, antonyms – words that
mean the opposite of the headword – are also included.

ISBN: 0-333-63408-X